No Permanent Waves

No Permanent Waves

Recasting Histories of U.S. Feminism

EDITED BY
NANCY A. HEWITT

RUTGERS UNIVERSITY PRESS

NEW BRUNSWICK, NEW JERSEY, AND LONDON

LIBRARY OF CONGRESS CATALOGING-IN-PUBLICATION DATA

No permanent waves : recasting histories of U.S. feminism / edited by
Nancy A. Hewitt.
    p. cm.
Includes bibliographical references and index.
ISBN 978–0–8135–4724–4 (hbk. : alk. paper)—
ISBN 978–0–8135–4725–1 (pbk. : alk. paper)
   1. Feminism—United States—History.   2. First-wave feminism—United States.
3. Second-wave feminism—United States.   4. Third-wave feminism—United States.
I. Hewitt, Nancy A., 1951–
HQ1410.N57   2010
305.420973—dc22   2009020401

A British Cataloging-in-Publication record for this book is available
from the British Library.

Visit our Web site: http://rutgerspress.rutgers.edu

Manufactured in the United States of America

To my feminist friends

CONTENTS

PART TWO
Coming Together/Pulling Apart

PART THREE
Rethinking Agendas/Relocating Activism

ACKNOWLEDGMENTS

The idea for this volume originated in two sites of feminist praxis: the *Feminist Studies* editorial collective, on which I served from 1997 to 2003, and the Institute for Research on Women (IRW), which I directed from 2004 to 2007. I especially want to thank Claire Moses, the founding editor of *Feminist Studies*, for her efforts to sustain and transform feminist practices while continuing to turn out a wonderful journal three times a year. I owe special appreciation as well to Sharon Groves, who inspired me to move forward on this volume when I had almost given up on it, and to my other colleagues on the *Feminist Studies* editorial collective who offered intellectual and political insight and inspiration. My constant colleagues at the IRW—Associate Director Beth Hutchison and Administrative Assistant Marlene Importico—provided support, encouragement, and wisdom throughout my term as director. More immediately for this volume, they helped organize the No Permanent Waves Symposium in spring 2005, bringing together scholars, activists, and scholar-activists to address the issues that form the core of this book. They also reminded me regularly of the intimate links among friendship, work, intellectual exchange, and good food. Several participants in the IRW symposium contributed to this book—either allowing me to reprint articles published in *Feminist Studies* or writing original essays—and I thank them for their continued commitment to this project. All those who participated and attended provided ideas and energy that refueled my interest in this project despite numerous delays. I especially want to thank Lori Ginzberg, Leslie Brown, and Temma Kaplan for their contributions to the symposium and to my thinking about histories of feminism and women's activism over many years.

This project was supported by a fellowship from the John Simon Guggenheim Foundation in 2000–2001, which allowed me the freedom to reimagine narratives of women's history, woman's rights, and feminism.

During that year, I wrote the first versions of what turned out to be the introduction to this volume. I also revised my ideas about the Seneca Falls–to-suffrage story, which I had originally conceived while a fellow at the Stanford Center for Advanced Study in the Social and Behavioral Sciences in 1996–1997. The essay that appears here, "From Seneca Falls to Suffrage?" benefited from questions and critiques provided by audiences at numerous invited lectures, especially at California Polytechnic State University—San Luis Obispo, the Southern Association of Women Historians Conference, DePauw University, SUNY–Brockport, Canisius College, the University of Rochester, and the University of Florida.

I also want to thank the friends who ensured that *No Permanent Waves* made it into print. Nancy Cott allowed me to test out the ideas that frame this book at the Schlesinger Library's 2008 Summer Institute on "Sequels to the Sixties." Anne Valk and Dorothy Sue Cobble provided generous advice at critical moments and often on short notice, reminding me that sisterhood, however flawed as a concept, can still be critical in practice. I also owe a special thanks as well to Allison Xantha Miller, whose editorial skills, technological expertise, and good humor saved me on more than one occasion. And Thomas Dublin and Kathryn Kish Sklar generously agreed to allow me to reprint an expanded version of an article by Dorothy Sue Cobble originally published online as "The Labor Feminist Origins of the U.S. Commissions on the Status of Women" on the Scholar's Edition of *Women and Social Movements in the United States, 1600–2000,* 13, no. 1 (March 2009), at http://asp6new.alexanderstreet.com/was2.

I could not have found a better home for this book than Rutgers University Press. Marlie Wasserman and Leslie Mitchner are marvels in many ways. They and their staff provided support, guidance, and enthusiasm throughout this project. A special thanks to Beth Kressel, Marilyn Campbell, and Pamela Fischer for seeing this book through production and offering such expert and gentle counsel. Rutgers University offered support as well by making research funds available to help offset the ever-rising costs of publication. And finally to Steven Lawson, who rightly considered this one project too many, I thank you once again for your love and forbearance.

No Permanent Waves

Introduction

NANCY A. HEWITT

*N*o *Permanent Waves* engages the ongoing debates over the adequacy of the "wave" metaphor for capturing the complex history of women's rights and feminism in the United States. But it also moves beyond these debates to offer fresh perspectives on the diverse movements that constitute U.S. feminism, past and present. The volume brings together seventeen essays—both original and reprinted—to address the connections among movements for women's rights and gender justice over time as well as the conflicts and divisions within such movements at any one time. The contributors, from different generations and backgrounds, argue for new chronologies, more inclusive conceptualizations of feminist agendas and participants, and fuller engagements with contestations around particular issues and practices than has been possible when using dominant analytical frameworks. They address issues of race, class, and sexuality within histories of women's rights and feminism as well as the cultural and intellectual currents and social and political priorities that marked movements for women's advancement and liberation. The concept of waves surging and receding cannot fully capture these multiple and overlapping movements, chronologies, issues, and sites.

It is impossible to pinpoint the exact moment when feminists in the 1960s first identified themselves as part of a "second wave." The rubric gained popular currency, however, with Martha Weinman Lears's article "The Second Feminist Wave," published in the *New York Times Magazine* in March 1968.[1] But the wave metaphor had been wielded much earlier. Irish activist Frances Power Cobbe, writing of social movements more generally in 1884, claimed that some "resemble the tides of the Ocean, where each wave obeys one uniform impetus, and carries the waters onward and upward along the shore." Women's movements, she argued, were the best example of such waves: "Like the incoming tide . . . it [sic] has rolled in separate waves . . . and has done its part in carrying forward all the rest."[2] The metaphor's origin is less important, however, than the fact that by 1968 feminists in the United States had collectively lumped all their foremothers into a "first wave" that stretched back to the 1840s. Widely embraced by activists, this version of feminist waves also shaped understandings of the movement in the media and among scholars. In the 1990s, younger activists constituted themselves a "third wave," accepting the metaphor if not the modus operandi of their foremothers.

The propagation of new waves was not simply a means to recognize distinct eruptions of activism across time. Rather, feminists in each wave viewed themselves as both building on and improving the wave(s) that preceded them. Thus even as advocates of women's liberation in the 1960s and 1970s eagerly sought out foremothers in the nineteenth and early-twentieth centuries—Susan B. Anthony, Elizabeth Cady Stanton, Sojourner Truth, Emma Goldman—they also insisted that they were broader in their vision, more international in their concerns, and more progressive in their sensitivities to race, class and sexual politics than early feminists. Indeed, despite the diversity among celebrated foremothers, many feminists and scholars of feminism identified the first wave as comprising largely white, middle-class women focused on achieving narrowly defined political goals, most notably suffrage. In contrast, they claimed the second wave as more inclusive and more transformative. When a third wave emerged, its advocates, too, recognized the advances made by their (more immediate) foremothers but insisted on the limits of the goals and assumptions of second wave feminists. Spokeswomen for the third wave considered themselves broader in their vision, more global in their concerns, and more progressive in their sensitivities to transnational, multiracial, and sexual politics than earlier feminists. In most third wave writings, the second wave appeared as largely white and middle-class and focused narrowly on economic, educational, and political access. In contrast, the third wave viewed itself as championing greater inclusiveness and more transformative strategies.

These battles over feminist legacies have influenced popular as well as scholarly understandings. Feminist claims about previous generations have been incorporated into books and articles in many disciplines as well as into newspaper and magazine stories, museum exhibits, political rhetoric, and documentary films. In the process, images of the various waves have become circumscribed. Although scholars who work on particular time periods or issues offer compelling stories filled with diverse characters and contentious struggles, these rich histories get lost in the more synthetic versions, whether offered by scholars, journalists, or activists.

Even in positive portrayals, the first wave is almost always limited to the period between the Seneca Falls Woman's Rights Convention of 1848 and the ratification of the Nineteenth Amendment in 1920 with the battle for women's suffrage considered its primary (sometimes its sole) focus. This version echoes the portrait drawn by two of its most historically minded advocates: Anthony and Stanton. As they had hoped, the six-volume *History of Woman Suffrage* they launched in the 1880s ensured the centrality of the campaign for voting rights in future renditions of the feminist past. Although scholars now recognize Stanton and Anthony's work as politically inspired, their version remains dominant in textbooks, synthetic works, and documentary films.[3] Yet the *History of Woman Suffrage*, along with Stanton's autobiography and speeches, has also fueled a critical portrait of the first wave that focuses on leaders' efforts to limit suffrage and other rights to white, educated women. This view has led to claims that the movement as a whole was narrow in its goals and racist and elitist in its vision. In this version, the few women of color who advocated woman's rights, most notably Sojourner Truth, are presented as heroic but unable to overcome the prejudices of their white counterparts.[4] Still, whether positive or negative, the first wave in most renditions remains fixed to suffrage and its white, middle-class advocates.

Recent synthetic studies of second wave feminism reinforce this attenuated legacy, using representations of the first wave to clarify what was distinct, and distinctly radical, about the second. Sara Evans, for example, begins *Tidal Wave* by noting, "The 'first wave' of women's rights activism in the United States built slowly from its beginnings in the middle of the nineteenth century, finally cresting in 1920 with the passage of the nineteenth Amendment to the U.S. Constitution guaranteeing women the most fundamental right of citizenship, the vote. It swelled, slowly and steadily, riding this single symbolic issue. By contrast, a 'second wave' . . . in the last half century arose almost instantly in a fast-moving and unruly storm, massive from the very outset." In *The World Split Open*, Ruth Rosen claims that "each generation of women activists leaves an unfinished agenda for the next generation. First Wave suffragists fought for women's citizenship [and] created international organizations dedicated to universal disarmament, but left many customs and beliefs unchallenged.... Second Wave feminists questioned nearly everything, transformed much of American culture, expanded ideas of democracy ... , and catapulted women's issues onto a global stage."[5] She admits that her generation left unfinished business as well, but far less than their foremothers. Both of these widely hailed works on late-twentieth-century feminism thus present the first wave as narrowly focused and reformist compared with the transformative, even revolutionary, character of their own wave.

Feminist activists who came of age in the 1980s and 1990s learned too well from the preceding generation how to circumscribe the efforts of their foremothers. This practice is particularly visible in the introductions to third wave anthologies, which often focus on setting young feminists apart from their predecessors. *The Fire This Time* offers a typical example. Editors Vivien Labaton and Dawn Lundy Martin, founders of the Third Wave Foundation, begin hopefully, "One of the luxuries that our generation has enjoyed is that we've reaped the benefits of all the social justice movements that have come before us," and note, "Our feminism has *roots* in past feminist work."[6] Yet when they turn to detailed discussions of the second wave, the roots hardly seem worth watering. The second wave "placed a select few issues at the center of what is thought of as feminist activism, neglecting the full range of experiences that inform women's lives." That movement's "inattentiveness to racial, cultural, sexual, and national differences" made clear "that a feminist movement cannot succeed if it does not challenge power structures of wealth and race." Thus, Labaton and Martin conclude, "unlike second wave feminism, which operated from a monolithic center, [the] multiplicity [of the third wave] offers the power of existing insidiously and simultaneously everywhere."[7] Rosen's revolutionary transformation and Evans's "massive," "unruly storm" have disappeared.

These authors do not intentionally denigrate their foremothers nor are they especially egregious in their critiques. Rather they remind us how ubiquitous such characterizations of previous waves have become. The script of feminist history—that each wave overwhelms and exceeds its predecessor—lends itself all too easily to whiggish interpretations of ever more radical, all-encompassing, and ideologically sophisticated movements. Activists thus highlight their distinctiveness from—and often superiority to—previous feminist movements in the process of constituting themselves as the next wave.

Several important dimensions of feminist activism are lost in the standard narratives. First, the chronology of woman's rights and feminist activism in the United States is contained in discrete and separate waves, while in reality such movements overlapped and intertwined across U.S. history. The decades excluded from the waves—before 1848 or from 1920 to 1960—are assumed to be feminist-free zones, an assumption belied by recent scholarship. Second, the issues that define the feminist agenda are often foreshortened as well. Racial justice, labor rights, divorce, religious authority, domestic abuse, the plight of prostitutes, and sexual freedom all attracted the attention of women activists in the nineteenth century and early-twentieth century, yet suffrage remains the centerpiece of most references to the first wave. Similarly, in the 1960s and 1970s, campaigns for welfare rights and other economic-justice issues occurred alongside and in collaboration with the more familiar feminist movements; working-class women and women of color played central roles in defining and challenging sexual harassment and other forms of workplace discrimination; and battles over pornography, prostitution, and lesbian rights erupted locally and nationally. In addition, across the nineteenth and twentieth centuries, U.S. feminists were influenced by and worked with activists in other parts of the world—Great Britain, Europe, and the Caribbean in the nineteenth century, and Canada, Mexico, Latin America, Europe, Africa, and Asia in the twentieth.

Third, common struggles facing feminists in the United States—the way sex discrimination is always complicated by race and class, for instance, or the relations between U.S. feminism and global campaigns for social justice, or the role of sexuality in women's rights campaigns—are lost in narratives that assume that each wave improves on the last. The feminist learning curve is thus foreshortened. Campaigns to nurture connections with female abolitionists and radical women in Europe in the 1830s and 1840s, for example, resonate—in their successes and their shortcomings—with attempts to build international alliances with suffragists and pacifists at the turn of the twentieth century or to create bonds with "sisters" in Third World liberation movements in China, Cuba, Ghana, Vietnam, and other nations in the 1970s. Feminists involved more recently in global campaigns against sweatshops, the traffic in women, and the World Trade Association echo these movements even as participants develop their own distinct strategies, agendas, and technologies. Yet the failure to recognize previous efforts narrows the ground on which new programs, strategies, and coalitions are built. Alternately, it nurtures, in Joan Scott's apt phrase, a "fantasy echo" that allows current activists to create a version of past movements rooted more in imagination and desire than in historical evidence.[8]

Still, it is easy to see how younger generations of activists come to their perspectives on older movements. For example, despite the wide range of women who participated in feminist movements during the 1960s and 1970s, most studies of the so-called second wave are organized around competing factions of liberal, socialist, and radical feminists, which are presented as largely white and either middle-class or classless. Although more studies now incorporate the activities of African American, Chicana, Asian American, American Indian, working-class, and lesbian feminists, too many present these women's efforts as reactions to or critiques of a straight, white, middle-class movement. At the same time, studies that focus on black or Chicana feminism often treat these movements as isolated from or parallel to rather than in conversation with predominantly white, or "mainstream," feminism. One simple indication of the continued hegemony of white, middle-class understandings of feminism is the constant use of descriptors—black, Chicana, Red, labor, or lesbian—to describe other participants, organizations, or theoretical interventions. Despite desires to move beyond the confines and conflicts of previous movements, third wave activists confront many of the same difficulties in mobilizing diverse constituencies around common goals. Thus third wave scholars, too, often write about, even as they lament, racially distinct segments of contemporary feminist movements.

Despite the continued prominence of popular and synthetic narratives that circumscribe U.S. feminist movements on the basis of chronology, agendas, participation, and ideology, many scholars have challenged such histories. In recent years, critiques of the wave model have multiplied alongside a flurry of studies on the complex trajectories of feminist activism. Scholarly panels, review essays, forums, and special issues of *Feminist Studies* and the *NWSA Journal* have focused on complicating specific waves or contesting the wave model itself. The on-line journal *Third Space* has also included discussions and critiques of waves; and a number of anthologies, led by Jo Reger's *Different Wavelengths*, have addressed these issues as well.[9] Stephanie

Gilmore's edited collection, *Feminist Coalitions*, and community studies of women's movements in Washington, D.C., and the Midwest by Anne Valk and Anne Enke are among works that challenge common assumptions about the origins, scope, and priorities of feminist movements of the 1960s and 1970s.[10]

Other scholars have recast early movements for woman's rights, highlighting both their distinctiveness and their complexity. In *Untidy Origins*, for instance, Lori Ginzberg shows that even before the Seneca Falls Woman's Rights Convention of 1848 some women demanded civil and political rights. Studying the decades after Seneca Falls, Joanne Passet highlights debates over sexuality; Martha Jones focuses on African American women's battles for rights in churches, fraternal orders, and other public arenas; Allison Sneider examines suffrage campaigns in the context of U.S. imperialism; and Lara Vapnek explores struggles for economic justice among working women.[11] At the same time, scholars like Nancy Cott, Joanne Meyerowitz, Dorothy Sue Cobble, Barbara Ransby, and Kate Weigand have demonstrated that the decades between 1920 and 1960 were filled with efforts—some explicitly and others implicitly feminist—to claim women's equality, sexual rights, and social justice on a wide range of fronts.[12] And, finally, studies by Whitney Peoples, Elizabeth Allen, and others have sought to link contemporary feminist activism to previous generations and agendas.[13]

Despite this burgeoning body of scholarship, the wave model continues to thrive in academic and popular media. The contributors to *No Permanent Waves* address the persistence of wave imagery and rhetoric in a variety of ways. Of particular importance, they insist on the messy multiplicity of feminist activism across U.S. history and beyond its borders. The essays included here destabilize standard chronologies; incorporate a diverse array of actors; emphasize both coalition building and contestation; expand the range of feminist locations, techniques, and technologies; highlight economic and cultural as well as political agendas; and locate feminist activism in a multiracial and global setting. Moreover, many of the movements explored here radiate out across place and time, although their development is uneven and often contested. These studies make clear that efforts to advance women's interests and gender justice never disappear completely but continue in local areas or in muted form until changed circumstances allow them to ignite broad mobilizations and new contestations over priorities, strategies, and alliances.

It may be impossible to jettison the concept of feminist waves. Indeed, the Library of Congress is now introducing *first wave* and *second wave* as topical categories.[14] Thus, it is especially important to think about other types of waves, such as radio waves, that can help us conceptualize the feminist past.[15] Radio waves allow us to think about movements of different lengths and frequencies; movements that grow louder or fade out, that reach vast audiences across oceans or only a few listeners in a local area; movements that are marked by static interruptions or frequent changes of channels; and movements that are temporarily drowned out by another frequency but then suddenly come in loud and clear. Rather than being members of the first, second, or third wave, we can be the National Public Radio of feminism, the Corporate Broadcasting System, or the community radio station; and we can switch stations periodically as well. Radio waves echo Elsa Barkley Brown's description of gumbo ya-ya—everyone talking at once—and remind us that feminist ideas are "in the air" even when people are not actively listening.[16] Best of all, radio waves do not supersede each other. Rather signals coexist, overlap, and intersect.

No Permanent Waves is organized into three parts, each of which addresses a central concern that is muted by the traditional wave metaphor. But there are also dimensions of feminist activism that radiate across these sections: struggles for economic justice; interracial, multiracial, and intergenerational organizing; the possibilities and problems of coalition work; the complicated chronologies of feminist mobilizations; and the multiple sites and modes of feminist activism.

Part I, Reframing Narratives/Reclaiming Histories, contains articles that challenge dominant conceptualizations of woman's rights and feminist movements in the United States. The first essay challenges a familiar narrative—the Seneca Falls–to–suffrage story of the first wave. Others by Ula Taylor, Marisela Chávez, and Becky Thompson recast dominant histories by centering on the experiences of black and Chicana feminists and on women involved in multiracial feminism. A final essay by Leela Fernandes engages common (mis)understandings of contemporary feminism by addressing intersectionality and identity politics in third wave scholarship that was produced, chronologically, during the second wave. These authors are not seeking to establish a new singular narrative of U.S. feminism but rather to offer new possibilities and pathways. For instance, although Thompson extends the chronology of post–World War II feminism into the 1980s in order to capture the contributions of women of color, Fernandes highlights the ways that work by scholars of color initiated a new intellectual wave during the 1980s that was in dynamic tension with the ongoing political and theoretical work of second wave scholars and activists. Such simultaneous and contested eruptions of feminist thought and action cannot be captured by a generational concept of waves. These two efforts to reimagine the relationships between intersectional or multiracial identities and feminism in the late twentieth century offer important challenges to current interpretations and also to each other.

Part II—Coming Together/Pulling Apart—explores conflicts and coalitions between and among feminist activists. The authors analyze understandings of politics and priorities among feminists from different racial, class, generational, and ideological backgrounds; explore claims of sisterhood and efforts at coalition building; interrogate the role of sexuality in theory and practice; and illuminate issues and tropes that define political and cultural agendas. Martha Jones and Premilla Nadasen analyze the efforts of African American activists to shape autonomous campaigns in the nineteenth-century church and around twentieth-century welfare rights, respectively. They make clear that white women addressed some of the same issues but not always in collaboration with their African American counterparts. Like Nadasen, Dorothy Sue Cobble highlights issues of economic justice, revealing the labor origins of feminist agendas in the post–World War II era. She and Judy Tzu-Chun Wu both illuminate the international contexts in which and with which U.S. feminists struggled. At the same time, Wu, along with Anne Valk, Stephanie Gilmore, and Leandra Zarnow, engages issues of sisterhood. These authors explore bonds forged and broken among peace activists, lesbian separatists, sex workers, and various circles of feminists from the 1970s to the early twenty-first century. Analyzing generational, racial/national, sexual, and ideological conflicts as well as unlikely coalitions, these contributors make clear the multiple agendas and disparate conceptualizations that mark particular moments of feminist activism.

In Part III—Rethinking Agendas/Relocating Activism—the authors push conventional boundaries of feminist activism by highlighting movements focused on economic rights or cultural expression. Ranging from Lara Vapnek's analysis of the Working Women's League in late-nineteenth-century Boston to Whitney Peoples's hip-hop feminism in the early twenty-first century, the articles expand feminist agendas while recognizing continued struggles over basic rights of property and personhood. Roberta Gold and

Nancy MacLean focus on the late twentieth century but follow Vapnek in tracing the centrality of economic justice to feminist organizing. Gold addresses the ways that tenant organizing by Old Left women in New York City provided a training ground for younger feminists in the 1970s and 1980s, while MacLean highlights the centrality of working women to campaigns for affirmative action that challenged traditional patterns of gender, class, and racial inequality in the job market and the workplace. In both cases, women of color joined white women and men of color in demanding access to basic rights of housing and decent jobs. Turning to the 1990s and early 2000s, Ednie Kaeh Garrison and Peoples focus on the refashioning of cultural agendas among young feminists who wield music, computer technology, and performance to claim public space and a public voice. Garrison analyzes Riot Grrrls and other young feminists of the 1990s, highlighting predominantly white subcultures that used the internet to spread their political message; Peoples highlights a range of hip-hop feminists and their ties to black women activists of the 1970s and 1980s. Although these final two articles suggest the ways that racial difference continues to divide feminists, they also demonstrate the links (or perhaps hyperlinks) between earlier and more recent campaigns for women's equality and female empowerment. They also bring us back to radio waves and other modes of communication that allow previous struggles to resonate across time and place.

No single volume can explore the full range of feminist activism across the history of the United States. Instead, *No Permanent Waves* introduces a broad array of actors, organizations, and movements that challenge scholars, activists, and students to rethink easy generalizations about historical and contemporary feminist movements. By recasting U.S. feminism in a way that integrates women from diverse racial, ethnic, and class backgrounds; recognizes the centrality of economics, sexuality, culture, and politics; and highlights the shared and contested character of women's rights, gender equality, and sexual liberation across time, these articles inspire us to rethink our visions of feminisms past and present and thereby to reimagine possibilities for the future.

NOTES

1. Lears describes the reemergence of feminism and then writes, "Proponents call it the Second Feminist Wave, the first having ebbed after the glorious victory of suffrage and disappeared, finally, into the great sandbar of Togetherness." Clearly,

she did not coin the term herself. Martha Weinman Lears, "The Second Feminist Wave," *New York Times Magazine*, March 10, 1968, 24.

2. Frances Power Cobbe, introduction to *The Woman Question in Europe*, by Theodore Stanton (1884). Thanks to Karen Offen for this reference.

3. See, especially, Susan B. Anthony, Elizabeth Cady Stanton, and Matilda Joslyn Gage, *History of Woman Suffrage*, vols. 1 and 2 (New York: Fowler and Wells, 1881 and 1882). For a discussion of the political character of this history, see Julie Des Jardins, *Women and the Historical Enterprise: Gender, Race and the Politics of Memory, 1880–1945* (Chapel Hill: University of North Carolina Press, 2003), 179–191.

4. For more nuanced analyses of Sojourner Truth and other black woman's rights advocates, see Nell Painter, *Sojourner Truth: A Life, a Symbol* (New York: Norton, 1996); Rosalyn Terborg-Penn, *African American Women in the Struggle for the Vote, 1850–1920* (Bloomington: Indiana University Press, 1998); and Martha S. Jones, *"All Bound Up Together": The Woman Question in African American Public Culture, 1830–1900* (Chapel Hill: University of North Carolina Press, 2007).

5. Sara M. Evans, *Tidal Wave: How Women Changed America at Century's End* (New York: Free Press, 2003), 1, and Ruth Rosen, *The World Split Open: How the Modern Women's Movement Changed America* (New York: Viking Penguin, 2000), 344.

6. Vivien Labaton and Dawn Lundy Martin, eds., *The Fire This Time: Young Activists and the New Feminism* (New York: Anchor Books, 2004), xxv, xxvii.

7. Ibid., xxviii, xxix, xxxi.

8. Joan W. Scott, "Fantasy Echo: History and the Construction of Identity," *Critical Inquiry* 27(Winter 2001): 284–304.

9. See, for example, *Feminist Studies* 28 (Summer 2002) issue on second wave feminism in the United States and *Feminist Studies* 34 (Fall 2008) on the 1970s; *NWSA Journal* (August 2009) debate on the wave metaphor; *Third Space: A Journal of Feminist Theory & Culture* 8 (Summer 2008) at http://www.thirdspace.ca/journal.htm, accessed February 23, 2008; and Jo Reger, ed., *Different Wavelengths: Studies of the Contemporary Women's Movement* (New York: Routledge, 2005).

10. Stephanie Gilmore, ed., *Feminist Coalitions: Historical Perspectives on Second-Wave Feminism in the United States* (Urbana: University of Illinois Press, 2008); Anne M. Valk, *Radical Sisters: Second-Wave Feminism and Black Liberation in Washington, D.C.* (Urbana: University of Illinois Press, 2008); and Anne Enke, *Finding the Movement: Sexuality, Contested Space and Feminist Activism* (Durham, NC: Duke University Press, 2007).

11. Lori D. Ginzberg, *Untidy Origins: A Story of Woman's Rights in Antebellum New York* (Chapel Hill: University of North Carolina Press, 2005); Joanne E. Passet, *Sex Radicals and the Quest for Women's Equality* (Urbana: University of Illinois Press, 2003); Jones, *"All Bound Up Together"*; Allison L. Sneider, *Suffragists in an Imperial Age: U.S. Expansion and the Woman Question, 1870–1929* (New York: Oxford University Press, 2008); and Lara Vapnek, *Breadwinners: Working Women and Economic Independence, 1865–1920* (Urbana: University of Illinois Press, 2009).

12. Nancy F. Cott, *The Grounding of Modern Feminism* (New Haven. CT: Yale University Press, 1987); Joanne Meyerowitz, ed., *Not June Cleaver: Women and Gender in Postwar America, 1945–1960* (Philadelphia: Temple University Press, 1994); Dorothy Sue Cobble, *The Other Women's Movement: Workplace Justice and Social Rights in Modern America* (Princeton, NJ: Princeton University Press, 2004); Barbara Ransby, *Ella Baker and the Black Freedom Movement: A Radical Democratic Vision* (Chapel Hill: University of North Carolina Press, 2002); and Kate Weigand, *Red Feminism: American Communism and the Making of Women's Liberation* (Baltimore: Johns Hopkins University Press, 2001).

13. See Whitney Peoples, ch. 17, this volume, and Elizabeth Allen, "First Wave Wisdom for a Third Wave World," *Third Space* 8 (Summer 2008).

14. Thanks to Nancy Cott for alerting me to this fact.

15. In her Spring 2000 *Feminist Studies* article, ch. 16, this volume, Ednieh Kaeh Garrison mentions radio waves in passing. The image must have resonated with me because two years later I gave a talk at the Organization of American Historians elaborating on radio waves as offering a better analogy for feminist movements than ocean waves. Much like feminism itself, the image has popped up in various conversations, presentations, articles, and books, and it is impossible to trace a specific lineage. I thus make no claim for originating the idea, only for developing it along with others on the same wavelength.

16. Elsa Barkley Brown, "'What Has Happened Here': The Politics of Difference in Women's History and Feminist Politics," *Feminist Studies* 18 (Summer 1992), 297, quoting Luisah Teish in *Jambalaya: The Natural Woman's Book of Personal Charms and Practical Rituals* (New York: HarperCollins, 1985).

PART ONE

Reframing Narratives/ Reclaiming Histories

1

From Seneca Falls to Suffrage?

Reimagining a "Master" Narrative in U.S. Women's History

NANCY A. HEWITT

In recent years, historical studies have revealed the multifaceted movements that constituted woman's rights campaigns in the nineteenth and early twentieth century. Yet one narrative continues to dominate understandings of the period. First crafted in the late 1800s by advocates of women's suffrage and embraced in the late 1960s by feminists who created themselves as the "second wave," this narrative highlights voting rights as the singular goal and purpose of the "first wave." Women's seemingly universal exclusion from the right to vote before 1920 served as the linchpin of this tale, and the Seneca Falls Woman's Rights Convention of 1848—where women first collectively demanded the right to vote—and the ratification of the Nineteenth Amendment to the U.S. Constitution in 1920—granting woman suffrage—were its touchstones. Despite vibrant scholarship since the turn of this century, the Seneca Falls–to-suffrage story continues to frame popular histories, political discourse, documentary films, and synthetic studies of U.S. feminism and women's history.

Reimagining the story is no simple task. Woman's rights pioneers first identified 1848 and 1920 as the critical turning points in women's struggle to achieve sex equality. Elizabeth Cady Stanton and Susan B. Anthony, coauthors of the multi-volume *History of Woman Suffrage*, were brilliant strategists who recognized the importance of documenting their version of events—including the Seneca Falls–to–suffrage story—and did so in compelling fashion. In the 1960s and 1970s, the story of a seventy-two-year battle that succeeded in advancing women's rights through federal intervention resonated with feminists seeking a favorable Supreme Court ruling on abortion and a constitutional amendment guaranteeing equal rights for women. Journalists covering the movement reinforced activists' assumptions, distinguishing this "Second Feminist Wave" from "the first," which "ebbed after the glorious victory of suffrage."[1] Women's historians, beginning with Eleanor Flexner in her 1959 classic *Century of Struggle*, also highlighted the centrality of suffrage to the early woman's rights movement.[2] The establishment of the Seneca Falls Woman's Rights National Historical Park in 1982 and Ken Burns's 1999 PBS documentary, *Not for Ourselves Alone*, brought the Seneca Falls–to-suffrage narrative to even larger audiences.

This version of the woman's rights movement has not been immune to critique. Scholars of African American, immigrant, and working-class women have detailed the racist, nativist, and elitist tendencies of many white women suffragists. They have highlighted the exclusion of poor, black, and immigrant women from the political organizations and the agendas of more well-to-do activists and their inclusion in community-based efforts, often alongside men, to advance their own economic, social, and political interests.[3] These challenges have tarnished the images of several pioneer figures and have added a few women of color to the pantheon of feminist foremothers. But they have generally left intact the standard chronology and the focus on suffrage as the primary goal of the early women's movement.

We can recast this narrative in several ways: by broadening our focus to include the emergence and meaning of women's rights for African American, American Indian, Mexican American, immigrant, and white working-class women; by highlighting the entire range of issues addressed by early woman's rights advocates, whatever their background; by recognizing the ways that international events—the Mexican-American War, revolutions in Europe, the abolition of slavery in the West Indies, and the Wars of 1898— shaped the early U.S. women's movement; and by reframing the suffrage movement through the lens of racial, ethnic, class, regional, and ideological differences at the local and state as well as national level. This article will focus on the first and last approach in an effort to widen our view of woman's rights and suggest the multiple stories yet to be told.

As origin stories go, the Seneca Falls Woman's Rights Convention of 1848 is compelling.[4] Although both participants and scholars recognized earlier influences—particularly abolitionism and battles for married women's property rights—Seneca Falls stands as the moment when disparate forces came together to provide the impetus, leadership, and program for a distinct woman's rights movement in the United States.[5] Stanton told and retold the story of Seneca Falls, inscribing her version of events in the *History of Woman Suffrage*, her autobiography, and a variety of speeches and articles.[6] In her version, she and Lucretia Mott first discussed the idea for a woman's rights convention during the World Anti-Slavery Convention in London in 1840. But soon after her return to the United States, Stanton became immersed in domestic responsibilities in the small town of Seneca Falls, New York, and had little time to engage the wider world of activism. In part, it was her domestic isolation and frustration that finally spurred Stanton to organize the convention when she next met Mott in 1848. Mott was visiting friends in neighboring Waterloo, New York, and Elizabeth was invited for tea. Stanton recalls, "I poured out, that day, the torrent of my long accumulating discontent with such vehemence and indignation that I stirred myself, as well as the rest of the party, to do and dare anything."[7] Within days, Stanton, Mott, Mott's sister Martha Wright, and her hostess Jane Hunt along with Waterloo neighbors Mary Ann and Elizabeth McClintock drafted a call for a woman's rights convention, prepared a list of grievances and resolutions, found a site, and organized a slate of speakers.

Although, for Stanton, the Seneca Falls Woman's Rights Convention disrupted years of isolation, her co-organizers spent much of the time between 1840 and 1848 debating women's roles in religion, education, the family, and the antislavery movement. To them, the Seneca Falls gathering was a logical extension of this ongoing work. Indeed, the period before and after the convention was so hectic that by the mid-1850s, Mott could not remember whether the convention met in 1847 or 1848 and recalled that she and Stanton first discussed the possibility of such a gathering in Boston in 1841 rather than in London the year before. But Mott deferred to Elizabeth's version of events because she considered Stanton, along with the McClintocks, as the "moving spirits" of the convention.[8]

The McClintocks were old friends of James and Lucretia Mott, joining them along with Hunt and Wright as members of the Society of Friends, or Quakers. They were all active in antislavery efforts as well.[9] They belonged to religious and reform societies that encouraged women to participate fully: speaking and preaching, organizing meetings, circulating petitions, writing testimonies and resolutions, raising funds, and serving as recorders and officers. In both arenas, moreover, women asserted their rights to equal treatment, challenging abolitionist and Quaker men to uphold the egalitarian principles on which their movement and their religion were founded.[10] The Hunts and McClintocks were active in the Western New York Anti-Slavery Society, a mixed-race, mixed-sex organization in which women were regularly elected to office and spoke at conventions. Some, like Mott, had participated in the annual meetings of the American Anti-Slavery Society in the late 1830s, when debates first erupted over women's right to serve as lecturers and officers in the organization. In the Society of Friends as well, the McClintocks and Motts joined with like-minded women and men to argue that working with "worldly," that is non-Quaker, anti-slavery societies did not challenge the Friends' Discipline. And, by the mid-1840s, some women and men in the Genesee Yearly Meeting, which included Waterloo, Seneca Falls, and Rochester, were disowned by or withdrew from fellowship when the meeting refused to accept either worldly antislavery activity or women's equal rights. A number of members and former members of the Genesee Yearly Meeting, including the McClintocks and Hunts as well as Amy Post, Mary Post Hallowell, Sarah Fish, and Catherine Fish Stebbins, attended the Seneca Falls Convention in July 1848.[11] There they expanded arguments first crafted in Quaker meetings and antislavery conventions.

The ideas about woman's rights that engaged radical Quakers and abolitionists in the 1840s were influenced by the even earlier activities of Frances Wright, Maria Stewart, Angelina and Sarah Grimké, and the members of the Philadelphia Female Anti-Slavery Society. During the 1820s and 1830s, these individuals and groups regularly linked women's exploitation to issues of race and labor. During the 1820s, for instance, Frances (Fanny) Wright, a Scottish émigré, spoke before "promiscuous" audiences of women and men on labor, land reform, abolition, divorce, and working woman's rights. In 1825, she established a utopian community based on principles of racial equality and free love at Nashoba, near Memphis, Tennessee. Within five years, the experiment failed, but only after being widely publicized, mainly through reports denigrating its alleged promotion of interracial sex. The publicity may help account for the fifteen hundred men and women who turned out to hear Wright speak in New York City in January 1829. Typical of her lectures throughout the United States, this one condemned religion as oppressive to women, claimed that sexual passion was "the strongest and . . . the noblest of passions" in women as well as men, and declared U.S. education, religion and laws to be "narrow, prejudiced, [and] ignorant." She also urged women to learn about their bodies and advocated health reform and women's medical education.[12]

As the controversy over Nashoba reached a crescendo in the northern press, Maria Stewart, a free-born black widow, declaimed against racial and gender injustice in Boston. Sponsored by the Afric-American Female Intelligence Society, Stewart spoke at Franklin Hall in October 1832 before an audience of women and men. She recognized the economic and personal hardships faced by African Americans and embraced many of the tenets of nineteenth-century womanhood, including the importance of housewifery and motherhood. Yet she also criticized white women who conspired to keep black women from "rising above the condition of servants," and she then demanded of her sisters: "Possess the spirit of men, bold and enterprising, fearless and undaunted. Sue for your rights and privileges."[13] A collection of her speeches was published by William Lloyd Garrison and was circulated among antislavery advocates, but Stewart was hounded by controversy in her native Boston for her outspoken (that is, unwomanly) critiques of the free black community. She settled in New York City in 1833, where she lived for more than a decade before moving on to Baltimore and finally Washington, D.C.

In the mid-1830s, Angelina and Sarah Grimké reversed Stewart's course, moving to Philadelphia from Charleston, South Carolina. They left their plantation family behind to plead the cause of the slave among northern audiences. Lecturing throughout New England in the late 1830s under the auspices of the American Anti-Slavery Society, the Grimké sisters faced condemnation from the press and pulpit. They were criticized as well by some of their fellow abolitionists for explicitly linking the status of slaves to that of women and thereby drawing attention away from the principal issue of slavery. Whatever the political costs, the Grimkés articulated the fundamental rationale for women's participation in both antislavery and women's rights campaigns.[14]

A broad spectrum of antebellum activists were influenced by Wright, Stewart, and the Grimkés—attending their lectures; reading their speeches; responding to the tirades they provoked in press and pulpit; discussing their ideas with family, friends, coworkers and coworshippers; and sharing their experiences as utopian communalists, free blacks, or Quakers. The Philadelphia Female Anti-Slavery Society was especially tied to this trio of activists. An interracial organization established in 1833, the society was

founded by Lucretia Mott, the Grimkés, and other Quakers along with local
free black women active in the abolition cause, including Sarah Douglass and
Charlotte Forten. White and black women shared leadership in the society
and attempted, although not always successfully, to overcome the prejudices
that divided the two communities.[15] Their efforts flowed directly into the
formation of the Anti-Slavery Convention of American Women in 1837, which
met annually for three years, crafting resolutions in opposition to slavery but
also in support of women's equality in many arenas. A resolution offered by
Angelina Grimké in 1837 included the claim that "the time has come for
woman to move in that sphere which Providence has assigned her, and no
longer remained satisfied in the circumscribed limits with which corrupt
custom and a perverted application of Scripture have encircled her." These
words would be repeated nearly verbatim in the Seneca Falls Declaration of
Sentiments of 1848.[16]

Participants at the Anti-Slavery Convention of American Women
launched a massive antislavery petition campaign in 1837 that engaged
thousands of women in dozens of communities throughout the Northeast.
It served as a seedbed for many who combined interests in racial justice and
woman's rights. By 1845, Jeremiah Burke Sanderson reported from the annual
meeting of the American Anti-Slavery Society that "the progress manifest at
the present of the idea of Woman's Rights in the public mind is an earnest
[indication] of what a few years[,] comparatively, may effect."[17] About the
same time, the term *woman's rights* appeared with increasing regularity in
state legislative debates, especially over women's property rights. At the New
York State Constitutional Convention of 1846, where women's property
rights were avidly debated, a small circle of women from the rural hinter-
lands of northern New York petitioned delegates for the right to vote.
Perhaps they were inspired in part by the Reverend Samuel May's "Sermon
on the Rights of Women," preached and published in Syracuse in 1845 and
sold at Western New York Anti-Slavery fundraising fairs in 1846 and 1847.[18]

The developments just described, increasingly noted by historians of
woman's rights, transform the chronology of the movement.[19] Although
some of the activists noted above, such as Frances Wright and Maria Stewart,
labored independently to advance racial and gender justice, most early
woman's rights advocates worked within broad religious, social, and political
movements, in which at least some of their colleagues supported their
efforts. In the *History of Woman Suffrage*, Stanton and Anthony recognized the

importance of some of these pioneer activists. They placed an image of Wright on the flyleaf of the first volume, noted the outrage over the Grimké sisters' lecture tour, and claimed Mott as the inspiration for the Seneca Falls Convention. Yet while granting Wright, Mott, and the Grimkés the status of foremothers of the woman's rights movement, they effectively removed them as active participants by claiming 1848 as *the* moment of its conception and relegating all that came before to prehistory. If instead we incorporate the whole range of early claims for woman's rights into the movement, the Seneca Falls Convention appears as a critical moment when *certain* strains of woman's rights ideology and activism crystallized. But it is not the birthplace for the movement as a whole.

The focus on the Seneca Falls Convention not only obscures the full range of individual woman's rights advocates but also circumscribes the geographical scope of the early movement. By widening our lens, we can highlight the political claims that women from diverse racial, national, class, and regional backgrounds brought to the U.S. woman's rights movement.

In the early to mid nineteenth century African American women were especially important in defining the scope of woman's rights. As orators, writers, members of black literary and reform associations, and advocates in interracial women's antislavery societies, they engaged in debates over women's roles in both the black community and the larger society. Many of these women defined rights in immediate, material ways, seeking access to education and jobs and aid to fugitive slaves.[20] Forten, a member of an affluent, free black family of Philadelphia, pursued her work for education, fugitive slaves, abolition, and woman's rights with the support of friends, relatives, and the Philadelphia Female Anti-Slavery Society. Other free black women in the North, many from working-class backgrounds, organized fundraising fairs, challenged segregated schools, and boycotted slave-produced goods. In several cases, they also armed themselves to protect fugitive slaves. In Cincinnati, for instance, in the summer of 1848, freedwomen used washboards and shovels to fend off slave catchers harassing blacks in the city.[21] Although not all articulated an explicit claim to woman's rights, some demanded equal treatment in fraternal societies, churches, and voluntary associations in the free black community.[22]

Among enslaved women, more drastic measures were required than those taken by free blacks. Ellen Craft, an enslaved woman in Macon, Georgia, planned a daring escape in fall 1848. Married to William Craft, a free

black cabinetmaker, the light-skinned Ellen dressed herself as a young gen-
tleman, swathed her jaw in bandages to make it appear she was ill, and
boarded a train and then a steamer to Philadelphia, with the dark-skinned
William posing as her/his manservant. They arrived safely in port on
Christmas morning 1848 and became noted abolitionist speakers in the
United States and England.[23] Although not specifically claiming woman's
rights, Ellen Craft embodied the concept of property rights for enslaved
women—the ownership of one's person and the integrity of one's family.
These rights were just of a different sort than those envisioned by most white
activists.

As slavery spread westward, property rights also became a concern of
women in northern Mexico. Between 1846 and 1848, the plight of Mexican
women intersected with the path of conquest as the Mexican-American War
brought vast new territories under U.S. authority. According to Spanish law,
and, after 1821, Mexican law, women retained rights to property after marriage; they could inherit, loan, convey, or pawn property whether single or
married; they shared custody of children; and they could sue in court without a male relative's approval.[24] These rights were almost uniformly denied
under Anglo-American law. The number and range of cases Mexican women
brought to court—involving abusive husbands, adultery, assault, property
disputes, and debts—make it clear that Mexico was no feminist utopia.
Nonetheless, joint and community property statutes did offer important
protections for women in the region as did their distance from federal
authorities in Mexico City. After U.S. officials, Protestant missionaries, and
white settlers took control of the "New" Mexico territory in 1848, they tried to
remove such protections.[25] Thus, just at the time that Anglo-American
women demanded legal and political rights at the Seneca Falls Convention,
Mexican women were threatened with the loss of precisely those rights in the
newly acquired Southwest territories.

Another issue became deeply intertwined with these contests over
rights. "New" Mexican women were losing claims to respectability, accused
by U.S. whites of being sexually promiscuous and culturally inferior. And not
only Protestant ministers and federal agents voiced these concerns.
Mrs. Susan Magoffin, the first U.S.-born white woman to travel in the "New"
Mexico territory, was shocked at the clothes worn by Mexican women,
including loose blouses, flowing skirts, and no corsets. She interpreted these
women's freedom of movement as tied to loose sexual mores, although she

recognized as well that they had greater legal rights than women in the United States.[26] Increasingly marked as "foreigners," Mexican women in the West shared much with racially marked groups back east, including not only African Americans but also Irish immigrants.

During the very week of the Seneca Falls Woman's Rights Convention, 812 Irish men, women, and children disembarked in New York City, part of the million fugitives from famine who settled in the United States between 1846 and 1851.[27] Unlike other immigrant groups in this period, the Irish sent more daughters than sons to the United States. For these women, the "rights" of employment, domestic authority, and community leadership were thrust on them. More than 40 percent of Irish women over twelve were gainfully employed at mid-century, their wages—like Mexican women's domestic labor—critical to family survival.[28] Many Irish families moved to New England or New York City, where textile mills and garment factories provided extensive employment for women and children. There, they came in contact with native-born working women whose claims for rights focused on hours, pay, and working conditions. In 1825, New York seamstresses staged the first all-women strike in U.S. history. Three years later, Fanny Wright arrived in the city, introducing women workers to a European brand of class-conscious feminism. By 1831, striking tailoress Sarah Monroe asked, "If it is unfashionable for the men to bear oppression in silence, why should it not also become unfashionable with the women? or do they deem us more able to endure hardships than they themselves?"[29] Throughout the 1830s and early 1840s, Monroe's counterparts in New England textile towns like Lowell, Massachusetts, raised their voices in protest, forming tight-knit coalitions forged in lodging houses as well as factories.

New York City workers, who were more widely dispersed and ethnically diverse than their laboring sisters in New England, formed a Ladies Industrial Association in the early 1840s. During a strike in 1845, the association's leader, Elizabeth Gray, declared of the walkout that "we know it be our duty, and that of every female who wishes to earn an honest livelihood." Her striking sisters concurred: "The boon we ask is founded upon RIGHT alone." They vowed "to take upon themselves the task of asserting their rights against the unjust and mercenary conduct of their employers."[30] Similar concerns led at least one Irish daughter, Susan Quinn, to the 1848 Woman's Rights Convention. Living in Seneca Falls with her father, an illiterate but successful gardener, she signed the Declaration of Sentiments, the youngest participant to do so.[31] Quinn and her sisters in the Ladies Industrial Association sought better education, better jobs, and better wages for working-class immigrant as well as middle-class native-born women.

While the flood of Irish immigrants was fueled by famine, the surge in German immigration in the 1840s was motivated as well by the failed revolution of 1848. Radical Quakers, free blacks, and their abolitionist coworkers were deeply engaged by the revolutions that spread across Europe that year.[32] They followed events closely in Garrison's *Liberator*, Frederick Douglass's *North Star*, and other reform newspapers. When the victory of the republicans in France led to the abolition of slavery in the French West Indies, U.S. abolitionists took note. Indeed, in its July 14 edition, the *North Star* announced an August 1 celebration to mark the emancipation of slaves in the French Caribbean alongside the call for the July 19 Seneca Falls Woman's Rights Convention. And Lucretia Mott urged her coworkers to "take courage" from such advances. "We cannot separate our freedom from that of the slave," she proclaimed. They are "inseparably connected in France . . . and are beginning to be so in other countries."[33]

Just before the Seneca Falls convention, Mott carried the message of revolutionary change to the Seneca Indians and reported, "They, too, are learning somewhat from the political agitations abroad[,] . . . are imitating the movements of France and all Europe, in seeking a larger liberty—more independence."[34] The Seneca were embroiled in their own debates over women's rights and tribal government. Prior to and for more than a century after contact with Europeans, the Seneca—like other Iroquois groups— passed names and property through the mother's line, husbands moved into their wives' households upon marriage, and women controlled agricultural production. Women also held positions of religious and political authority, although chiefs and sachems were almost always men. Over the course of two centuries of trade, warfare, disease, missionary efforts, and U.S. governmental pressure, the Seneca had lost most of their tribal lands, moved to reservations (like Cattaraugus south of Buffalo), and converted to patrilineal descent and men's control of agriculture.[35]

During the 1830s and 1840s, Seneca women in New York State petitioned federal officials, demanding recognition of their property rights and protection of individual allotments that had been fraudulently acquired by the Ogden Land Company in treaties with male chiefs.[36] In spring 1848, the tribe was on the verge of adopting a new "republican" form of government and its first written constitution. Traditionally, women could veto a range of tribal decisions—from the appointment of chiefs to the signing of treaties—but, with the new constitution, they lost these powers. Yet they did retain the right to vote. Under the new constitution, Seneca men and women elected judges and legislators by majority vote, and three quarters of all voters and three quarters of all *mothers* had to ratify legislative decisions.[37] Like their Mexican counterparts, then, Seneca women were battling to maintain precisely those rights demanded by participants at the Seneca Falls Convention.

Clearly, woman's rights were born in multiple arenas, defined in myriad ways, and advocated by diverse groups of "American" women in the early to mid nineteenth century. The Seneca Falls Convention occurred in a period when the concept of woman's rights was widely debated, when no one could say with any certainty where it had first been conceived and where it might lead. Many of those who attended the Seneca Falls Convention were aware of these alternate versions of woman's rights. Indeed, one of the largest contingents at the meeting—Quaker abolitionists from Rochester, Waterloo, Seneca Falls, and Philadelphia—had been enmeshed in several of the movements described above. Four of the five organizers of the convention and at least one-quarter of those signing the Seneca Falls Declaration of Sentiments were part of this network of radical Friends. Several were in correspondence with Seneca Indians, and the Motts had visited one of their reservations just before traveling to Seneca Falls. Other Quaker participants had demonstrated against the U.S. war with Mexico in 1846, and several had begun to explore working conditions among native-born and Irish seamstresses and domestic servants.[38] In the months surrounding the Woman's Rights Convention, they organized a half-dozen antislavery conventions, broke with the Society of Friends over their stance on women and abolition, founded a new interracial and sex-integrated reform organization called the Friends of Human Progress, established the Working Women's Protective Union in Rochester, New York, and followed the efforts of their radical counterparts in France and Hungary.[39]

At the same time, women revolutionaries in Europe looked to U.S. women for support, especially after the tide of revolution turned against them. French radicals Jeanne Deroin and Pauline Roland wrote a letter from their prison cell to U.S. woman's rights advocates in 1851, reminding them that the chains of the throne and the scaffold, the church and the patriarch, the slave, the worker, and the woman must all be broken simultaneously

if "the kingdom of Equality and Justice shall be realized on Earth." Other
activists, like German revolutionary Mathilde Anneke, carried on their campaigns for workers' and women's rights in the United States after fleeing persecution in their homeland.[40]

For these globally focused activists, the campaign for woman's rights not
only was born in many places but embraced a multifaceted agenda. They
refused to define woman's rights primarily as suffrage and were concerned
instead with increased access to opportunities in the church, the family, the
society, and the economy. Here it is critical to remember that among radical
Quakers both men and women opposed participation in a government that
used violence to achieve its aims. Most believed that women should have the
same right to vote as men, but, given their active campaigns against slavery
and U.S. military intervention in Mexico, it was unlikely that they would see
suffrage as the key to women's emancipation. Instead they thought that
women's advancement must be tied to broad claims for racial and economic
justice, individual autonomy, and human rights.

We could follow many threads from the woman's rights activities of the
early and mid nineteenth century into the following decades. But even if
we focus on the traditional concern with suffrage, the wider lens used to capture the earlier movement offers important new perspectives. As scholars
have amply demonstrated, despite the popular notion that American women
were granted suffrage by the Nineteenth Amendment, when it was ratified,
women were already voting in a dozen states and hundreds of towns, cities,
and school districts. In addition, thousands attempted to vote and dozens
succeeded in the late 1860s and early 1870s as they sought to prove that the
Fourteenth and Fifteenth Amendments granting citizenship and suffrage to
newly emancipated African Americans applied to women as well. These
efforts, known as the New Departure, ended in 1875, when the U.S. Supreme
Court decided against women's claims to suffrage as a benefit of national citizenship. But by that time women had gained voting rights in Wyoming and
were seeking it in many other states and territories. Tracing these campaigns
from the 1860s to 1920 reveals that women's suffrage, too, is a tale of uneven
developments marked by both place and race.

Virginia-born suffragists and lawyers Francis and Virginia Minor developed a plan, known as the New Departure, to test the Fourteenth and
Fifteenth Amendments through coordinated excursions of women to the
polls. The Minors argued that the Fourteenth Amendment made all persons

born or naturalized in the United States citizens, including women. The Fifteenth Amendment then guaranteed voting as a right of citizenship, even if it did not explicitly mention sex in the same way it did "race, color and previous condition of servitude." The Minors urged suffragists to attempt to register and vote, thereby creating test cases that would force judicial recognition of their position. The New Departure was presented to a meeting of the newly formed National Woman Suffrage Association and was launched in October 1869.[41]

A few women tested this strategy—without necessarily having worked out the legal logic—as early as 1868; many more embraced the New Departure from 1869 to 1873. In 1872, Anthony was arrested by federal marshals in Rochester, New York, for casting a ballot; that same year, the Minors instituted a test case against a St. Louis registrar—a Mr. Happersett—who denied Virginia the right to register. In the meantime, women in cities and towns across the country attempted to claim voting rights. In the North and Midwest, many supporters of the New Departure were long-time abolitionists, woman's rights advocates, and temperance reformers. Some supported the Fourteenth and Fifteenth Amendments, and others—like Stanton and Anthony—opposed them. But all embraced efforts to expand their reach to include women. Southern women, too, confronted election officials in Baltimore, Memphis, Richmond, Charleston, Washington, D.C., and Johnson County, North Carolina.

In a few communities a similar strategy was developed independently. In South Carolina, for instance, African Americans asserted women's right to register and vote under the federal Enforcement Act of 1870.[42] Seven of South Carolina's eight black Reconstruction-era congressmen supported woman suffrage; and three sisters from a free black family in Charleston—Louisa, Charlotte, and Frances Rollin—organized on behalf of woman's rights immediately following the war. In 1869, Louisa Rollin spoke on behalf of universal rights before the South Carolina House of Representatives. A year later, Charlotte chaired the founding meeting of the South Carolina Woman's Rights Association in Columbia.[43] Encouraged by African American election officials, at least five black women registered and voted in October 1870. In this case, election officials were arrested and punished for accepting "fraudulent" ballots. Nonetheless, in early 1871 two more African American women attempted to vote in Charleston and were arrested and fined ten dollars and court costs for their trouble. The largest number of southern women to turn out for a single election, however, appeared at the polls in Johnson County, North Carolina, in July 1871. There two hundred women successfully registered and cast ballots. All were African American, and they were reported to have been dressed in men's clothing.[44] It is not clear whether they were trying to pass themselves off as men or simply claiming male status symbolically as well as politically. Whether following the New Departure or the Rollin sisters or their own consciences, these women's presence at the polls makes clear that individuals from a wide range of backgrounds considered voting rights crucial by the 1860s and 1870s.

In towns and cities across the country, women joined the New Departure campaign. From Rochester, New York, to Richmond, Virginia; Baltimore, Maryland, to Vineland, New Jersey; Topeka, Kansas, to Battle Creek, Michigan; Memphis, Tennessee, to Worcester, Massachusetts; Olympia, Washington, to Taylor County, Iowa; Philadelphia to Santa Cruz, California, they demanded the right to register and vote.[45] In some cases only white women voted, in others only black, and a few mixed-race groups cast ballots together. Local records provide a glimpse of the array of women who participated in this campaign. In Rochester, Vineland, and Battle Creek, for instance, most women voters were long-time abolitionists and woman's rights advocates. It is likely that participants voted as much to protest the larger disabilities of sex and race as to gain the singular right of suffrage. In these communities, women wore bloomers to the poll, refused to pay taxes, and protested other forms of economic and occupational discrimination. Aging abolitionist-feminists like Amy Post and Rhoda DeGarmo were joined by younger activists who came of age politically during the Civil War and linked suffrage more closely to temperance and economic advancement than to racial justice.[46]

In Washington, D.C., a border city as well as the nation's capital, black women with roots in northern antislavery struggles, such as journalist Mary Ann Shadd Cary, law student Charlotte Ray, and activist Mrs. Frederick Douglass Jr., attempted to register and vote in 1871 in D.C.'s first "territorial" elections. Frederick Douglass Sr. accompanied them to the Board of Registrars that April, demonstrating his continued support for women's voting rights even after the acrimonious battles over the Fifteenth Amendment. They were joined by some sixty other women, some of whom had first attempted to register and vote two years earlier. At that point, most of the activists emerged from the interracial ranks of women working in the post–Civil War "contraband camps" near the nation's capital. But in 1871 a significant new contingent joined the campaign: female civil servants who worked as clerks in the Internal Revenue Service, the Treasury Department, and other federal offices. These were white women, most single or widowed, who sought not only the right to political participation but also increased leverage to improve their wages and working conditions.[47]

After the Supreme Court ruled against the New Departure strategy in *Minor v. Happersett* in 1873, some women refocused their energies elsewhere, agitating for working women's rights, racial equality, or sexual freedom.[48] Others continued to demand the vote. Wyoming had granted women's suffrage in its first constitution in 1869, suggesting that a new strategy rather than a new goal was needed. Many suffragists came to believe that their greatest chance for victories lay in the West, where more and more territories, states, and cities granted women the right to vote in the late nineteenth and early twentieth centuries. By 1911, six states—all in the West—extended statewide suffrage to women, and twenty-two more granted women school or municipal suffrage or both.[49] Seven years later, the number of full-suffrage states had doubled and now included two outside the West—Illinois and New York. In addition, tens of thousands of women battled for the right to vote for deacons, elders, and other church officials, or for union delegates and third-party political candidates, or for officers of fraternal societies and mixed-sex community organizations.[50] Women battled for the ballot, then, in diverse arenas and institutions throughout the half-century following the Civil War.

Race

Historians, like suffragists, have hailed the West as the vanguard of the movement. Yet the story becomes complicated if we focus on the racial dimensions of these campaigns.[51] Asian American, Mexican American, and American Indian women were often denied the rights accorded native-born white women in western states and territories. Idaho, for instance, supposedly granted women full suffrage in 1896 but specifically excluded the insane, felons and convicts, bribe takers, polygamists, persons of Chinese descent, and Indians.[52] In the Southwest, Mexican American women were denied the vote, alternately, as Mexicans and as women. Arizona granted the vote to women in 1912 but denied it to most people of Mexican descent, women or men. In neighboring New Mexico, Mexican Americans could vote, but not women, whatever their race.[53] For Indians, federal laws created a confusing array of possibilities—the most blatant division being that between "civilized" and "uncivilized" Indians. Native Americans could be endowed with citizenship (and thereby civilization) through individual allotment or congressional tribal grants. The 1887 Dawes Act, which broke reservations into individual landholdings, increased the number of Indian citizens dramatically; and by 1905 more than half of all resident Indians had become U.S. citizens. But granting citizenship did not necessarily alter the status of reservation Indians when it came to voting rights. In an Arizona case that followed the passage of the Nineteenth Amendment—*Porter v. Hall*—"disfranchisement of the state's Indians was upheld on the grounds that natives were federal wards."[54]

Western states also erected barriers to voting at the state level—residency requirements, poll taxes, and literacy tests—that denied many women and men from racial and ethnic communities the right to vote. These laws echoed those passed in the South, where methods for disfranchising African American men were honed in the late nineteenth and early twentieth centuries. Although restrictions on voting were employed in many states, the South gained the reputation as the region most hostile to women's suffrage, a stance paralleling its virulent and long-standing resistance to African American voting rights.

Yet even the narrative of women's suffrage in the South appears less uniformly reactionary if we focus on shifting opportunities rather than on universal exclusion. Virginia offers a case in point. In the immediate post–Civil War years, African American women voted alongside men in Richmond, Virginia. Black delegates to the 1867 state constitutional convention, for instance, were selected at a mass meeting held at the four thousand–seat African Baptist Church. A standing vote allowed all those present, including women, to participate. When African American men were enfranchised under the new state constitution, their wives and sisters lobbied male voters, accompanied them to the voting booth, and continued to vote themselves in communitywide meetings. As Elsa Barkley Brown has argued, African Americans viewed the vote as a collective or familial, rather than an individual, possession.[55] Moreover, African American women also demanded the vote in other arenas, including black Baptist and Methodist churches, local voluntary associations, and labor unions.[56] Meanwhile white women in Virginia founded an array of civic associations, including suffrage organizations. Excluded from these groups, most black women remained silent during Virginia's campaign to ratify the Nineteenth Amendment for fear of reinforcing antisuffragists' attempts to equate women's suffrage and black enfranchisement. But, with ratification, black as well as white women mobilized to vote. In Richmond, more than twenty-four hundred black women registered, more than 10 percent of the black female population of the city.[57]

Richmond was by no means unique. Large numbers of African American women voted in 1920 across the South—in Salisbury, Greensboro, Charlotte, Asheville, and Raleigh, North Carolina; Nashville and Memphis, Tennessee; Clifton Springs, Norfolk, and Hampton, Virginia; Tampa and Jacksonville, Florida; Tuskegee, Alabama; Houston, Texas; and elsewhere.[58] State and local authorities quickly recovered from the shock of the Nineteenth Amendment—ratified on August 26, 1920—and closed whatever loopholes it had opened. Nonetheless the ability of black women to mobilize in such vast numbers between August and November provides a glimpse of what must have been a well-established political infrastructure within African American communities.

After the disfranchisement of African American women in the early 1920s, most would have to wait until passage of the 1965 Voting Rights Act before returning to the polls. Yet the infrastructures women built through churches, fraternal societies, women's clubs, and voluntary associations did not disappear. They were mobilized once again in the civil rights struggles of the 1950s and 1960s. Indeed, historians Darlene Clark Hine and Christine Anne Farnham have argued that for black women in the South the answer to the question "When did women get the vote?" is not 1920 but 1965; and many struggled throughout the intervening decades to secure that right for black men as well as women.[59]

Southern black women were the largest contingent of female voters barred from the polls after passage of the Nineteenth Amendment, but they were not alone. Millions of Asian and Mexican Americans in the West and American Indians across the country were denied suffrage until the 1940s, and some waited until the Voting Rights Act and its extension in 1970 addressed the bilingual needs of Spanish-speaking citizens. Puerto Rican and Filipina women, too, were denied voting rights when a judge advocate in the War Department, relying on precedents from the New Departure era, ruled that the Nineteenth Amendment did not apply in the nation's colonial possessions. Not until 1929 did Puerto Rican women gain the right to vote, and even then literacy tests and property requirements significantly limited their participation. Filipinas struggled throughout the 1930s, alternately seeking enfranchisement as a U.S. territory or voting rights in an independent Philippines.[60] Other groups of women (and men) suffered disfranchisement as a result of laws the primary intent of which was to bar racial minorities from the polls—for instance, Cuban and Italian immigrants in Florida and Louisiana and poor whites in many states with literacy tests. In addition, Chinese women, like men, were barred from citizenship and thus voting until the federal government repealed the Chinese Exclusion Act in 1943.

Although battles for enfranchisement, especially the civil rights movement, have been recognized as seedbeds of feminism in the 1960s, they must also be acknowledged as outgrowths of suffrage campaigns that reach back deep into the nineteenth century. In this story, the Nineteenth Amendment, like the Seneca Falls Woman's Rights Convention before it, sits at the midpoint rather than the endpoint of the tale.

To create a narrative of woman's rights and suffrage movements that does justice to the diversity of their origins and the complexity of their development requires an expanded chronology, a wider geographical focus, and a broader definition of politics than is allowed by the conventional Seneca Falls–to–suffrage framing. The Seneca Falls convention and the Nineteenth Amendment are important parts of this story, but they form only a single thread in a variegated tapestry. From the 1820s through the 1850s, many women who did not attend formal woman's rights conventions fought for sex equality in their own communities and participated in politics in innovative ways. African Americans, American Indians, Mexicans and Mexican Americans, revolutionary refugees, and native-born and immigrant working women joined these struggles, defining rights in ways that spoke to their material, social, and political needs. Similarly, in the late nineteenth century and across the twentieth century, women wielded ballots as weapons of protest, fought for access to electoral politics, won victories for women suffrage based on excluding other women, claimed the right to vote in community, church, and union forums, and found ways to influence those in power despite disfranchisement. No single trajectory or chronology, such as that from Seneca Falls to suffrage, can capture these multifaceted developments.

Those participants in woman's rights and suffrage movements who envisioned themselves as part of broad campaigns for racial, economic, and gender justice provide a critical bridge between feminism and other initiatives for progressive social change. The largest contingent of nineteenth-century "bridge women" were radical Quakers and African Americans with deep roots in abolitionism and passionate commitments to racial equality, utopian communalism, Indian rights, health reform, land reform, and religious freedom. Less concerned with suffrage than with more general questions of political, economic, educational, and occupational access, these pioneer feminists created the foundation on which later generations of women could build antiracist, global, and multicultural coalitions. African American women, Mexican American women, labor-union women, and radical immigrant women played similar roles across the twentieth century, whether or not they embraced the term *feminism*. Until we recognize the breadth and depth of woman's rights activism in previous eras, many contemporary feminists will continue to teeter atop the fragile legacy of a nineteenth-century movement dominated by white, middle-class women focused on the single issue of enfranchisement. Far broader landscapes and richer legacies are available to support and to caution us.

NOTES

1. Martha Weinman Lears, "The Second Feminist Wave," *New York Times Magazine*, March 10, 1968, 24.

2. Eleanor Flexner, *Century of Struggle: The Woman's Rights Movement in the United States* (Cambridge, MA: Harvard University Press, 1959), remains one of the most important studies of this movement.

3. See, for two oft-cited examples, Rosalyn Terborg-Penn, *African American Women in the Struggle for the Vote, 1850–1920* (Bloomington: Indiana University Press, 1998), and Louise Newman, *White Women's Rights: The Racial Origins of Feminism in the United States* (New York: Oxford University Press, 1999). Newman does extend the chronology beyond 1920, exploring feminist activism and especially intellectual debates in the following decades.

4. Previous versions of this part of my analysis appear in Nancy A. Hewitt, "Rerooting American Women's Activism: Global Perspectives on 1848," *Oesterreichische Zeitschrift fur Geschichtswissenschaften* (Spring 1999), reprinted in Patricia Grimshaw, Katie Holmes, and Marilyn Lake, eds., *Women's Rights and Human Rights: International Historical Perspectives* (New York: Palgrave, 2001).

5. On the Seneca Falls Convention providing impetus, leadership, and program, see Eleanor Flexner, *Century of Struggle* (repr., New York: Atheneum, 1973), 71.

6. Susan B. Anthony, Elizabeth Cady Stanton, and Matilda Joslyn Gage, *History of Woman Suffrage* (New York: Fowler and Wells, 1881), 1:79–81, and Elizabeth Cady Stanton, *Eighty Years and More: Reminiscences, 1815–1897* (1898; repr., New York: Schocken Books, 1971), 147–150.

7. Stanton, *Eighty Years and More*, 148.

8. Lucretia Mott to Elizabeth Cady Stanton, 16 March 1855, Philadelphia, in *Selected Letters of Lucretia Coffin Mott*, ed. Beverly Wilson Palmer (Urbana: University of Illinois Press, 2002), 236.

9. On the McClintock and Hunt families and Wright, see Judith Wellman, *The Road to Seneca Falls: Elizabeth Cady Stanton and the First Woman's Rights Convention* (Urbana: University of Illinois Press, 2004), esp. ch. 4.

10. On Quakers, abolition, and woman's rights, see Nancy A. Hewitt, "Feminist Friends: Agrarian Quakers and the Emergence of Woman's Rights," *Feminist Studies* 12 (Spring 1986): 27–49.

11. Ibid.

12. On Wright's 1829 speech, see Lori D. Ginzberg, *Women in Antebellum Reform* (Wheeling, IL: Harlan Davidson, 2000), 91–92; on her broader views on woman's rights, see Lori D. Ginzberg, "'The Hearts of Your Readers Will Flutter': Fanny Wright, Infidelity, and American Freethought," *American Quarterly* 46 (1994): 195–226. See also Celia Morris, *Fanny Wright: Rebel in America*, rev. ed. (Urbana: University of Illinois Press, 1992).

13. Paula J. Giddings, *When and Where I Enter: The Impact of Black Women on Race and Sex in America* (New York: Bantam Books, 1985), 49–54, quotes 51, 52. See also Carla L. Peterson, *"Doers of the Word": African-American Women Speakers and Writers in the North, 1830–1880* (New Brunswick, NJ: Rutgers University Press, 1995), ch. 3, and Marilyn Richardson, *Maria W. Stewart: America's First Black Woman Political Writer: Essays and Speeches* (Bloomington: Indiana University Press, 1987).

14. See Gerda Lerner, *The Grimke Sisters from South Carolina* (New York: Schocken Books, 1977; rev. ed., Chapel Hill: University of North Carolina Press, 2004), and Kathryn Kish Sklar, *Women's Rights Emerges within the Antislavery Movement, 1830–1870: A Brief History with Documents* (Boston: Bedford/St. Martin's, 2000).

15. See Jean R. Soderlund, "Priorities and Power: The Philadelphia Female Anti-Slavery Society," and Carolyn Williams, "The Female Antislavery Movement: Fighting against Racial Prejudice and Promoting Women's Rights in Antebellum America," both in *The Abolitionist Sisterhood: Women's Political Culture in Antebellum America*, ed. Jean Fagan Yellin and John C. Van Horne (Ithaca, NY: Cornell University Press, 1994), 67–88, 159–177.

16. Resolutions from 1837 Anti-Slavery Convention of American Women, quoted in Sklar, *Women's Rights Emerges*, 105.

17. Jeremiah Burke Sanderson to Amy Post, 8 May 1845, Isaac and Amy Post Family Papers, Rare Books and Manuscripts Room, University of Rochester, Rochester, NY (cited hereafter as Post Family Papers).

18. On the 1846 petition, see Lori D. Ginzberg, *Untidy Origins: A Story of Woman's Rights in Antebellum New York* (Chapel Hill: University of North Carolina Press, 2005). See also Nancy Isenberg, *Sex and Citizenship in Antebellum America* (Chapel Hill: University of North Carolina Press, 1998). On the Reverend Samuel J. May's

"Sermon on the Rights of Women," see Samuel J. May to Isaac Post, 20 December 1846, Post Family Papers.

19. See, especially, Isenberg, *Sex and Citizenship*; Ginzberg, *Untidy Origins*; and Peterson, *"Doers of the Word."*

20. On black women's antislavery and woman's rights activism, see Martha S. Jones, *"All Bound Up Together": The Woman Question in African American Public Culture, 1830–1900* (Chapel Hill: University of North Carolina Press, 2007), and Dorothy Sterling, ed., *We Are Your Sisters: Black Women in the Nineteenth Century* (New York: Norton, 1984), pt. 2.

21. Sterling, *We Are Your Sisters*, pt. 2.

22. See Jones, *"All Bound Up Together,"* and Martha Jones, ch. 6, this volume.

23. William Craft and Ellen Craft, *Running a Thousand Miles for Freedom* (1860), with an introduction by Barbara McCaskill (Athens: University of Georgia Press, 1999), pt. 1.

24. Janet Lecompte, "The Independent Women of Hispanic New Mexico," *Western Historical Quarterly* 22, no. 1 (1981): 17–35.

25. On the influence of Spanish law on women's property rights in former Spanish colonies, see Mark M. Carroll, *Homesteads Ungovernable: Families, Sex, Race, and the Law in Frontier Texas, 1823–1860* (Austin: University of Texas Press, 2001); Sara L. Zeigler, "Uniformity and Conformity: Regionalism and the Adjudication of the Married Women's Property Acts," *Polity* 28, no. 4 (1996): 472–477; and Patricia Seed, "American Law, Hispanic Traces: Some Contemporary Entanglements of Community Property," *William and Mary Quarterly* 52, no. 1 (January 1995): 157–162.

26. Magoffin, quoted in Lecompte, "The Independent Women of Hispanic New Mexico," 25, and Jane Dysart, "Mexican Women in San Antonio, 1830–1860: The Assimilation Process," in *History of Women in the United States*, ed. Nancy F. Cott, vol. 14, *Intercultural and Interracial Relations* (New York: Saur, 1992), 167–177.

27. *The Irish Immigrants* (Baltimore: Baltimore Genealogical Publishing Co., 1984), vol. 3, lists the ships and the names, sex, and occupation of immigrants arriving in New York City between July 14 and 20, 1848.

28. See Hasia R. Diner, *Erin's Daughters in America: Irish Immigrant Women in the Nineteenth Century* (Baltimore: Johns Hopkins University Press, 1983).

29. Quoted in Christine Stansell, *City of Women: Sex and Class in New York City, 1789–1860* (New York: Knopf, 1986), 133.

30. Quoted in ibid., 146.

31. On Susan Quinn, see Wellman, *Road to Seneca Falls*, 5, 205, 206, 223, 237.

32. A detailed discussion of these European influences appears in Nancy A. Hewitt, "'Seeking a Larger Liberty': Remapping Nineteenth-Century Woman's Rights," in *Sisterhood and Slavery: Transatlantic Perspectives on Abolition and Woman's Rights*, ed. Kathryn Kish Sklar and James Stewart (Yale University Press, 2007), 266–278.

33. *North Star*, July 14, 1848, and Lucretia Mott, "Law of Progress," in *Lucretia Mott: Her Complete Speeches and Sermons*, ed. Dana Greene (New York: Edwin Mellen Press, 1980), 75.

34. Lucrtia Mott to Edmund Quincy, 24 August 1848, in *The Liberator*, 6 October 1848, p. 1.

35. For an overview of Seneca women's status, see Joan M. Jensen, "Native American Women and Agriculture," in *Women and Power in American History*, ed. Kathryn Kish Sklar and Thomas Dublin (Englewood Cliffs, NJ: Prentice-Hall, 1991), 1:8–23.

36. See, for example, Women of the Tonawanda Reservation, petition to President John Tyler, 14 March 1842, Post Family Papers. The presence of this petition in the Post Family Papers attests, like Mott's visit to the Cattaraugus Reservation, to the interplay of woman's rights and Indian rights in this period. On this issue, see also Sally Roesch Wagner, *Sisters in Spirit: The Haudenosaunee (Iroquois) Influence on Woman's Rights* (Summertown, TN: Native Voices Press, 2001).

37. For a detailed account by a Quaker missionary of Seneca Indian life, see Harriet S. Clarke Caswell, *Our Life among the Iroquois Indians* (Boston and Chicago: Congregational Sunday School and Publishing Society, 1892), esp. 79–80, on the new 1848 constitution.

38. On protests against the U.S. war with Mexico, see Isenberg, *Sex and Citizenship*, 139–147. See also Joseph and Mary Robbins Post to Isaac and Amy Post, 29 May 1846 and [May] 1847, Post Family Papers. See *Anti-Slavery Bugle*, September 17, 1847, for one of many examples from the antislavery press. On working women's rights, see Nancy A. Hewitt, *Women's Activism and Social Change: Rochester, New York, 1822–1872* (Ithaca, N.Y.: Cornell University Press, 1984), 131–135, 136, 237.

39. See Hewitt, "Feminist Friends" and "'Seeking a Larger Liberty.'"

40. Jeanne Deroin and Pauline Roland, "Letter to the Convention of American Women" (June 15, 1851), in Anthony, Stanton, and Gage, *History of Woman Suffrage*, 1:234–237, quote 237; and Bonnie Anderson, *Joyous Greetings: The First International Women's Movement, 1830–1860* (New York: Oxford University Press, 1999), esp. ch. 7.

41. See Ellen Carol DuBois, "Taking the Law into Our Own Hands: Bradwell, *Mimor*, and Suffrage Militance in the 1870s," in *Visible Women: New Essays on American Activism*, ed. Nancy A. Hewitt and Suzanne Lebsock (Urbana: University of Illinois Press, 1993), 19–40.

42. Benjamin Quarles, "Frederick Douglass and the Woman's Rights Movement," *Journal of Negro History* 25 (June 1940): 35.

43. See Terborg-Penn, *African American Women in the Struggle for the Vote*, 42–45.

44. See Ann D. Gordon, ed., *The Selected Letters of Elizabeth Cady Stanton and Susan B. Anthony*, vol. 2, *Against an Aristocracy of Sex* (New Brunswick, NJ: Rutgers University Press, 2000), Appendix C, 648, 650.

45. See DuBois, "Taking the Law into Our Own Hands," 19–40, and Gordon, *The Selected Letters of Elizabeth Cady Stanton and Susan B. Anthony*, 2:Appendix C.

46. On this pattern in Rochester, see Hewitt, *Women's Activism and Social Change*, ch. 6; on Vineland, New Jersey, see Delight Dodyk, "Education and Agitation: Women Suffrage of New Jersey" (PhD diss., Rutgers University, 1997).

47. The profiles described here are based on checking the lists of names in Appendix C of Gordon, *The Selected Letters of Elizabeth Cady Stanton and Susan B. Anthony, vol. 2,*

with city directories and historical studies of the cities noted. On Washington, D.C., see also Terborg-Penn, *African American Women in the Struggle for the Vote*, 46–47, and Allison L. Sneider, *Suffragists in an Imperial Age: U.S. Expansion and the Woman Question, 1870–1929* (New York: Oxford University Press, 2008), ch. 2.

48. On these other paths to woman's rights, see, for example, Lara Vapnek, *Breadwinners: Working Women and Economic Independence, 1865–1920* (Urbana: University of Illinois Press, 2009); Michele Mitchell, *Righteous Propagation: African Americans and the Politics of Racial Destiny after Reconstruction* (Chapel Hill: University of North Carolina Press, 2004); and Joanne E. Passet, *Sex Radicals and the Quest for Women's Equality* (Urbana: University of Illinois Press, 2003).

49. Bertha Rembaugh, comp., *The Political Status of Women in the United States: A Digest of Laws Concerning Women in the Various States and Territories* (New York: Putnam, 1911).

50. For an analysis of church-based suffrage battles, see Martha Jones, ch. 6, this volume.

51. For important work on western women's suffrage and woman's rights more broadly, see Sarah Barringer Gordon, *The Mormon Question: Polygamy and Constitutional Conflict in Nineteenth-Century America* (Chapel Hill: University of North Carolina Press, 2001), and Sneider, *Suffragists in an Imperial Age*.

52. Rembaugh, *Political Status of Women*, 28–29.

53. Joan M. Jensen, "'Disfranchisement Is a Disgrace': Women and Politics in New Mexico, 1900–1940," *New Mexico Historical Review* 56, no. 1 (1981): 5–35.

54. Fred Hoxie, *A Final Promise: The Campaign to Assimilate the Indians, 1880–1920* (Lincoln: University of Nebraska Press, 1984), 236. See also Wendy Wall, "Gender and the 'Citizen Indian,'" in *Writing the Range: Race, Class and Culture in the Women's West*, ed. Elizabeth Jameson and Susan Armitage (Norman: University of Oklahoma Press, 1997), 202–229, and Sneider, *Suffragists in an Imperial Age*, ch. 3.

55. On black women's political activism in Richmond, see Elsa Barkley Brown, "Negotiating and Transforming the Public Sphere: American Political Life in the Transition from Slavery to Freedom," *Public Culture* 7 (1994): 107–146.

56. On Baptists, see Evelyn Brooks Higginbotham, *Righteous Discontent: The Women's Movement in the Black Baptist Church, 1880–1920* (Cambridge, MA: Harvard University Press, 1993); on Methodists, see Martha Jones, ch. 6, this volume.

57. Suzanne Lebsock, "Woman Suffrage and White Supremacy: A Virginia Case Study," in *Visible Women: New Essays on American Activism*, ed. Nancy A. Hewitt and Suzanne Lebsock (Urbana: University of Illinois Press, 1993), esp. 82–90.

58. For examples, see ibid.; Adele Logan Alexander, "Adella Hunt Logan, the Tuskegee Women's Club, and African Americans in the Suffrage Movement," in *Votes for Women! The Woman Suffrage Movement in Tennessee, the South, and the Nation*, ed. Marjorie Spruill Wheeler (Knoxville: University of Tennessee Press, 1995); Glenda Gilmore, *Gender and Jim Crow: Women and the Politics of White Supremacy in North Carolina, 1896–1920* (Chapel Hill: University of North Carolina Press, 1996); Elna Green, *Southern Strategies: Southern Women and the Woman Suffrage Question*

(Chapel Hill: University of North Carolina Press, 1997); and Nancy A. Hewitt, "In Pursuit of Power: The Political Economy of Women's Activism in Twentieth-Century Tampa," in *Visible Women: New Essays on American Activism*, ed. Nancy A. Hewitt and Suzanne Lebsock (Urbana: University of Illinois Press, 1993), 199–222.

59. Darlene Clark Hine and Christine Anne Farnham, "Black Women's Culture of Resistance and the Right to Vote," in *Women of the South: A Multicultural Reader*, ed. Christine Anne Farnham (New York: New York University Press, 1997), 204–219.

60. Sneider, *Suffragists in an Imperial Age*, ch. 5, Epilogue, and Yamila Azize-Vargas, "The Emergence of Feminism in Puerto Rico, 1870–1930," in *Unequal Sisters: A Multi-cultural Reader in U.S. Women's History*, 2nd ed., ed. Vicki L. Ruiz and Ellen Carol DuBois (New York: Routledge, 1994), 260–267.

2

Multiracial Feminism

Recasting the Chronology of Second Wave Feminism

BECKY THOMPSON

In the last [decade of the twentieth century], a number of histories [were] published that chronicle[d] the emergence and contributions of second wave feminism.[1] Although initially eager to read and teach from these histories, I have found myself increasingly concerned about the extent to which they provide a version of second wave history that Chela Sandoval refers to as "hegemonic feminism."[2] This feminism is white-led, marginalizes the activism and worldviews of women of color, focuses mainly on the United States, and treats sexism as the ultimate oppression. Hegemonic feminism deemphasizes or ignores a class and race analysis, generally sees equality with men as the goal of feminism, and has an individual rights–based rather than justice-based vision for social change.

Although rarely named as hegemonic feminism, this history typically resorts to an old litany of the women's movement that includes three or four branches of feminism: liberal, socialist, radical, and sometimes cultural feminism.[3] The most significant problem with this litany is that it does not recognize the centrality of the feminism of women of color in second wave history. Missing too from normative accounts is the story of white antiracist feminism, which, from its emergence, has been intertwined with, and fueled by the development of, feminism among women of color.[4]

Telling the history of second wave feminism from the point of view of women of color and white antiracist women illuminates the rise of multiracial feminism—the liberation movement spearheaded by women of color in the United States in the 1970s that was characterized by its international perspective, its attention to interlocking oppressions, and its support of

coalition politics.[5] Bernice Johnson Reagon's naming of "coalition politics";
Patricia Hill Collins's understanding of women of color as "outsiders within";
Barbara Smith's concept of "the simultaneity of oppressions"; Cherríe Moraga
and Gloria Anzaldúa's "theory in the flesh"; Chandra Talpade Mohanty's
critique of "imperialist feminism"; Paula Gunn Allen's "red roots of white feminism"; Adrienne Rich's "politics of location"; and Patricia Williams's analysis
of "spirit murder" are all theoretical guideposts for multiracial feminism.[6]
Tracing the rise of multiracial feminism raises many questions about common
assumptions made in normative versions of second wave history. Constructing
a multiracial feminist movement timeline and juxtaposing it with the normative timeline reveals competing visions of what constitutes liberation and
illuminates schisms in feminist consciousness that are still with us today.

The Rise of Multiracial Feminism

Normative accounts of the second wave feminist movement often reach back
to the publication of Betty Friedan's *The Feminine Mystique* in 1963, the founding of the National Organization for Women in 1966, and the emergence of
women's consciousness-raising (CR) groups in the late 1960s. All signaled a
rising number of white, middle-class women unwilling to be treated like
second-class citizens in the boardroom, in education, or in bed. Many of the
early protests waged by this sector of the feminist movement picked up on
the courage and forthrightness of 1960s' struggles—a willingness to stop traffic, break existing laws to provide safe and accessible abortions, and contra-
dict the older generation. For younger women, the leadership women had
demonstrated in 1960s' activism belied the sex roles that had traditionally
defined domestic, economic, and political relations and opened new possibilities for action.

This version of the origins of second wave history is not sufficient in
telling the story of multiracial feminism. Although there were Black women
involved with NOW from the outset and Black and Latina women who participated in CR groups, the feminist work of women of color also extended
beyond women-only spaces. In fact, during the 1970s, women of color were
involved on three fronts—working with white-dominated feminist groups;
forming women's caucuses in existing mixed-gender organizations; and
developing autonomous Black, Latina, Native American, and Asian feminist
organizations.[7]

This three-pronged approach contrasts sharply with the common notion that women of color feminists emerged in reaction to (and therefore later than) white feminism. In her critique of "model making" in second wave historiography, which has "all but ignored the feminist activism of women of color," Benita Roth "challenges the idea that Black feminist organizing was a later variant of so-called mainstream white feminism."[8] Roth's assertion—that the timing of Black feminist organizing is roughly equivalent to the timing of white feminist activism—is true about feminist activism by Latinas, Native Americans, and Asian Americans as well.

One of the earliest feminist organizations of the second wave was a Chicana group—Hijas de Cuauhtemoc (1971)—named after a Mexican women's underground newspaper that was published during the 1910 Mexican Revolution. Chicanas who formed this *femenista* group and published a newspaper named after the early-twentieth-century Mexican women's revolutionary group were initially involved in the United Mexican American Student Organization, which was part of the Chicano/a student movement.[9] Many of the founders of Hijas de Cuauhtemoc were later involved in launching the first national Chicana studies journal, *Encuentro Feminil.*

An early Asian American women's group, Asian Sisters, focused on drug abuse intervention for young women in Los Angeles. It emerged in 1971 out of the Asian American Political Alliance, a broad-based, grassroots organization largely fueled by the consciousness of first-generation Asian American college students. Networking between Asian American and other women during this period also included participation by a contingent of 150 Third World and white women from North America at the historic Vancouver Indochinese Women's Conference (1971) to work with Indochinese women against U.S. imperialism.[10] Asian American women provided services for battered women, worked as advocates for refugees and recent immigrants, produced events spotlighting Asian women's cultural and political diversity, and organized with other women of color.[11]

The best-known Native American women's organization of the 1970s was Women of All Red Nations (WARN). WARN was initiated in 1974 by women, many of whom were also members of the American Indian Movement, which was founded in 1968 by Dennis Banks, George Mitchell, and Mary Jane Wilson, an Anishinabe activist.[12] WARN's activism included fighting sterilization in public health service hospitals, suing the U.S. government for attempts to sell Pine Ridge water in South Dakota to corporations, and networking with indigenous people in Guatemala and Nicaragua.[13] WARN reflected a whole generation of Native American women activists who had been leaders in the takeover of Wounded Knee in South Dakota in 1973, on the Pine Ridge reservation (1973–1976), and elsewhere. WARN, like Asian Sisters and Hijas de Cuauhtemoc, grew out of—and often worked with—mixed-gender nationalist organizations.

The autonomous feminist organizations that Black, Latina, Asian, and Native American women were forming during the early 1970s drew on nationalist traditions through their recognition of the need for people-of-color–led, independent organizations.[14] At the same time, unlike earlier nationalist organizations that included women and men, these were organizations specifically for women.

Among Black women, one early Black feminist organization was the Third World Women's Alliance, which emerged in 1968 out of the Student Nonviolent Coordinating Committee (SNCC) chapters on the East Coast and focused on racism, sexism, and imperialism.[15] The foremost autonomous feminist organization of the early 1970s was the National Black Feminist Organization (NBFO). Founded in 1973 by Florynce Kennedy, Margaret Sloan, and Doris Wright, it included many other well-known Black women including Faith Ringgold, Michelle Wallace, Alice Walker, and Barbara Smith. According to Deborah Gray White, NBFO, "more than any organization in the century [,]. . . launched a frontal assault on sexism and racism."[16] Its first conference in New York was attended by 400 women from a range of class backgrounds.

Although the NBFO was a short-lived organization nationally (1973–1975), chapters in major cities remained together for years, including one in Chicago that survived until 1981. The contents of the CR sessions were decidedly Black women's issues—stereotypes of Black women in the media, discrimination in the workplace, myths about Black women as matriarchs, Black women's beauty, and self-esteem.[17] The NBFO also helped to inspire the founding of the Combahee River Collective in 1974, a Boston-based organization named after a river in South Carolina where Harriet Tubman led an insurgent action that freed 750 slaves. The Combahee River Collective not only led the way for crucial antiracist activism in Boston through the decade, but it also provided a blueprint for Black feminism that still stands a quarter of a century later.[18] From Combahee member Barbara Smith came a definition of feminism so expansive that it remains a model today. Smith writes that "feminism is the political theory and practice to free *all* women: women of color, working-class women, poor women, physically challenged women, lesbians, old women, as well as white economically privileged heterosexual women. Anything less than this is not feminism, but merely female self-aggrandizement."[19]

These and other groups in the early and mid-1970s provided the foundation for the most far-reaching and expansive organizing by women of color in U.S. history. These organizations also fueled a veritable explosion of writing by women of color, including Toni Cade's pioneering *The Black Woman: An Anthology* in 1970, Maxine Hong Kingston's *The Woman Warrior* in 1977, and in 1981 and 1983, respectively, the foundational *This Bridge Called My Back: Writings by Radical Women of Color* and *Home Girls: A Black Feminist Anthology*.[20] While chronicling the dynamism and complexity of a multidimensional vision for women of color, these books also traced for white women what is required to be allies to women of color.

By the late 1970s, the progress made possible by autonomous and independent Asian, Latina, and Black feminist organizations opened a space for women of color to work in coalition across organizations with each other. During this period, two cohorts of white women became involved in multiracial feminism. One group had, in the late 1960s and early 1970s, chosen to work in anti-imperialist, antiracist militant organizations in connection with Black Power groups—the Black Panther Party, the Black Liberation Army—and other solidarity and nationalist organizations associated with the American Indian, Puerto Rican Independence, and Chicano movements of the late 1960s and early 1970s. These women chose to work with these solidarity organizations rather than work in overwhelmingly white feminist contexts. None of the white antiracist feminists I interviewed (for a social history of antiracism in the United States) who were politically active during the civil rights and Black power movements had an interest in organizations that had a single focus on gender or that did not have antiracism at the center of their agendas.

Militant women of color and white women took stands against white supremacy and imperialism (both internal and external colonialism); envisioned revolution as a necessary outcome of political struggle; and saw armed propaganda (armed attacks against corporate and military targets along with public education about state crime) as a possible tactic in revolutionary struggle. Although some of these women avoided or rejected the term "feminist" because of its association with hegemonic feminism, these women still confronted sexism both within solidarity and nationalist organizations and within their own communities. In her autobiographical account of her late-1960s' politics, Black liberation movement leader Assata Shakur writes: "To me, the revolutionary struggle of Black people had to be against racism, classism, imperialism and sexism for real freedom under a socialist government."[21] During this period, Angela Davis was also linking anticapitalist struggle with the fight against race and gender oppression.[22] Similarly, white militant activist Marilyn Buck, who was among the first women to confront Students for a Democratic Society (SDS) around issues of sexism, also spoke up for women's rights as an ally of the Black Liberation Army.

Rarely, however, have their stories—and those of other militant antiracist women—been considered part of second wave history. In her critique of this dominant narrative, historian Nancy MacLean writes: "Recent accounts of the rise of modern feminism depart little from the story line first advanced two decades ago and since enshrined as orthodoxy. That story stars white middle-class women triangulated between the pulls of liberal, radical/cultural, and socialist feminism. Working-class women and women of color assume walk-on parts late in the plot, after tendencies and allegiances are already in place. The problem with this script is not simply that it has grown stale from repeated retelling. It is not accurate."[23]

The omission of militant white women and women of color from second wave history partly reflects a common notion that the women's movement followed and drew upon the early civil rights movement and the New Left, a trajectory that skips entirely the profound impact that the Black Power movement had on many women's activism. Omitting militant women activists from historical reference also reflects a number of ideological assumptions made during the late 1960s and early 1970s—that "real" feminists were those who worked primarily or exclusively with other women; that "women's ways of knowing" were more collaborative, less hierarchical, and more peace loving than men's; and that women's liberation would come from women's deepening understanding that "sisterhood is powerful."

These politics were upheld both by liberal and radical white feminists. These politics did not, however, sit well with many militant women of color and white women who refused to consider sexism the primary, or most destructive, oppression and recognized the limits of gaining equality in a system that, as Malcolm X had explained, was already on fire. The women of color and white militant women who supported a race, class, and gender analysis in the late 1960s and 1970s often found themselves trying to explain their politics in mixed-gender settings (at home, at work, and in their activism), sometimes alienated from the men (and some women) who did not get it, while simultaneously alienated from white feminists whose politics they considered narrow at best and frivolous at worst.

By the late 1970s, the militant women who wanted little to do with white feminism of the late 1960s and 1970s became deeply involved in multiracial feminism. By that point, the decade of organizing among women of color in autonomous Black, Latina, and Asian feminist organizations led militant antiracist white women to immerse themselves in multiracial feminism. Meanwhile, a younger cohort of white women, who were first politicized in the late 1970s, saw feminism from a whole different vantage point than did the older, white antiracist women. For the younger group, exposure to multiracial feminism led by women of color meant an early lesson that race, class, and gender were inextricably linked. They also gained vital experience in multiple organizations—battered women's shelters, conferences, and health organizations—where women were, with much struggle, attempting to uphold this politic.[24]

From this organizing came the emergence of a small but important group of white women determined to understand how white privilege had historically blocked cross-race alliances among women, and what they, as white women, needed to do to work closely with women of color. Not surprisingly, Jewish women and lesbians often led the way among white women in articulating a politic that accounted for white women's position as both oppressed and oppressor—as both women and white.[25] Both groups knew what it meant to be marginalized from a women's movement that was, nevertheless, still homophobic and Christian biased. Both groups knew that "there is no place like home"—among other Jews and/or lesbians—and the limits of that home if for Jews it was male dominated or if for lesbians it was exclusively white. The paradoxes of "home" for these groups paralleled many of the situations experienced by women of color who, over and over again, found themselves to be the bridges that everyone assumed would be on their backs.

As the straight Black women interacted with the Black lesbians, the first-generation Chinese women talked with the Native American activists, and the Latina women talked with the Black and white women about the walls that go up when people cannot speak Spanish, white women attempting to understand race knew they had a lot of listening to do. They also had a lot of truth telling to reckon with, and a lot of networking to do, among other white women and with women of color as well.

Radicals, Heydays, and Hot Spots

The story of second wave feminism, if told from the vantage point of multiracial feminism, also encourages us to rethink key assumptions about periodization. Among these assumptions is the notion that the 1960s and early 1970s were the height of the radical feminist movement. For example, in her foreword to Alice Echols's *Daring to Be Bad: Radical Feminism in America, 1967–1975*, Ellen Willis asserts that by the mid-1970s, the best of feminism had already occurred.[26] In her history of the women's liberation movement, Barbara Ryan writes that the unity among women evident in the early 1970s declined dramatically by the late 1970s as a consequence of divisions within the movement.[27]

Looking at the history of feminism from the point of view of women of color and antiracist white women suggests quite a different picture. The fact that white women connected with the Black power movement could rarely find workable space in the early feminist movement crystallized for many of them with the 1971 rebellion at Attica Prison in New York State in response to human rights abuses.[28] For antiracist activist Naomi Jaffe, who was a member of SDS, the Weather Underground, and WITCH (Women's International Terrorist Conspiracy from Hell), attempts to be part of both early second wave feminism and an antiracist struggle were untenable. The Attica rebellion, which resulted in the massacre by state officials of thirty-one prisoners and nine guards, pushed Jaffe to decide between the two. She vividly remembers white feminists arguing that there was no room for remorse for the "male chauvinists" who had died at Attica. Jaffe disagreed vehemently, arguing that if white feminists could not understand Attica as a feminist issue, then she was not a feminist. At the time, Black activist and lawyer Florynce Kennedy had said: "We do not support Attica. We ARE Attica. We are Attica or we are nothing." Jaffe claimed: "That about summed up my feelings on the subject."[29] With this consciousness, and her increasing awareness of the violence of the state against the Black Panthers, antiwar protesters, and liberation struggles around the world, Jaffe continued to work with the Weather Underground. She went underground from 1970 to 1978.

Naomi Jaffe, like other white women working with the Black power movement, was turned off by a feminism that she considered both bourgeois and reductionist. They stepped out of what antiracist historian Sherna Berger Gluck has termed "the master historical narrative,"[30] and they have been written out of it by historians who have relied upon a telling of second wave feminism that focused solely on gender oppression. Although the late 1960s and early 1970s might have been the "heyday" for white "radical" feminists in CR groups, from the perspective of white antiracists, the early 1970s were a low point of feminism—a time when many women who were committed to an antiracist analysis had to put their feminism on the back burner in order to work with women and men of color and against racism.

Coinciding with the frequent assumption that 1969 to 1974 was the height of "radical feminism," many feminist historians consider 1972 to 1982 as the period of mass mobilization and 1983 to 1991 as a period of feminist abeyance.[31] Ironically, the years that sociologists Verta Taylor and Nancy Whittier consider the period of mass mobilization for feminists (1972–1982) are the years that Chela Sandoval identifies as the period when "ideological differences divided and helped to dissipate the movement from within."[32] For antiracist women (both white and of color), the best days of feminism were yet to come when, as Barbara Smith explains, "Those issues that had divided many of the movement's constituencies— such as racism, anti-Semitism, ableism, ageism, and classism—were put out on the table."[33]

Ironically, the very period that white feminist historians typically treat as a period of decline within the movement is the period of mass mobilization among antiracist women—both straight and lesbian. The very year that Taylor and Whittier consider the end of mass mobilization because the ERA failed to be ratified, 1982, is the year that Gluck rightfully cites as the beginning of a feminism far more expansive than had previously existed. She writes: "By 1982, on the heels of difficult political struggle waged by activist scholars of color, groundbreaking essays and anthologies by and about women of color opened a new chapter in U.S. feminism. The future of the women's movement in the U.S. was reshaped irrevocably by the introduction of the expansive notion of feminisms."[34] Angela Davis concurs, citing 1981, with the publication of *This Bridge Called My Back*, as the year when women of color had developed as a "new political subject," due to substantial work done in multiple arenas.[35]

In fact, periodization of the women's movement from the point of view of multiracial feminism would treat the late 1960s and early 1970s as its origin and the mid-1970s, 1980s, and 1990s as a height. A time line of that period shows a flourishing multiracial feminist movement. In 1977, the Combahee River Collective Statement was first published; in 1979, *Conditions: Five*, the Black women's issue, was published, the First National Third World Lesbian Conference was held, and Assata Shakur escaped from prison in New Jersey with the help of prison activists.[36] In 1981, Byllye Avery founded the National Black Women's Health Project in Atlanta; Bernice Johnson Reagon gave her now-classic speech on coalition politics at the West Coast Women's Music Festival in Yosemite; and the National Women's Studies Association held its first conference to deal with racism as a central theme, in Storrs, Connecticut, where there were multiple animated interventions against racism and anti-Semitism in the women's movement and from which emerged Adrienne Rich's exquisite essay "Disobedience and Women's Studies."[37] Then, 1984 was the year of the New York Women against Rape Conference, a multiracial, multiethnic conference that confronted multiple challenges facing women organizing against violence against women—by partners, police, social service agencies, and poverty. In 1985, the United Nations Decade for Women conference in Nairobi, Kenya, took place; that same year, Wilma Mankiller was named the first principal chief of the Cherokee Nation. In 1986, the National Women's Studies Association conference was held at Spelman College. The next year, 1987, the Supreme Court ruled that the Immigration and Naturalization Service must interpret the 1980s' Refugee Act more broadly to recognize refugees from Central America, a ruling that reflected the work on the part of thousands of activists, many of whom were feminists, to end U.S. intervention in Central America.

In 1991, Elsa Barkely Brown, Barbara Ransby, and Deborah King launched the campaign called African American Women in Defense of Ourselves, within minutes of Anita Hill's testimony regarding the nomination of Clarence Thomas to the Supreme Court. Their organizing included an advertisement in the *New York Times* and six Black newspapers which included the names of 1,603 Black women. The 1982 defeat of the ERA did not signal a period of abeyance for multiracial feminism. In fact, multiracial feminism flourished in the 1980s, despite the country's turn to the Right.

Understanding second wave feminism from the vantage point of the Black power movement and multiracial feminism also shows the limit of the frequent assignment of the term "radical" only to the white antipatriarchal feminists of late 1960s and early 1970s. Many feminist historians link the development of radical feminism to the creation of several antipatriarchy organizations—the Redstockings, Radicalesbians, WITCH, and other CR groups. How the term "radical" is used by feminist historians does not square, however, with how women of color and white antiracists used that term from the 1960s through the 1980s. What does it mean when feminist historians apply the term "radical" to white, antipatriarchy women but not to antiracist white women and women of color (including Angela Davis, Kathleen Cleaver, Marilyn Buck, Anna Mae Aquash, Susan Saxe, Vicki Gabriner, and Laura Whitehorn) of the same era whose "radicalism" included attention to race, gender, and imperialism and a belief that revolution might require literally laying their lives on the line? These radical women include political prisoners—Black, Puerto Rican, and white—some of whom are still in prison for their antiracist activism in the 1960s and 1970s. Many of these women openly identify as feminists and/or lesbians but are rarely included in histories of second wave feminism.

What does it mean when the term "radical" is only assigned to white, antipatriarchy women when the subtitle to Cherríe Moraga and Gloria Anzaldúa's foundational book, *This Bridge Called My Back*, was *Writings by Radical Women of Color*?[38] To my mind, a nuanced and accurate telling of second wave feminism is one that shows why and how the term "radical" was itself contested. Recognizing that there were different groups who used the term "radical" does not mean that we then need an overarching definition of "radical feminism" that includes all these approaches. It does mean understanding that white feminists of the "daring to be bad period" (from 1967 to 1975) do not have exclusive rights to the term.[39] An expansive history would emphasize that second wave feminism drew on the civil rights movement, the New Left, *and* the Black power movement, which, together, helped to produce three groups of "radical" women.

Principles of a Movement

Although analysis of the feminist movement that accounts for competing views of what it means to be "radical" is a step forward in developing a complex understanding of second wave history, what most interests me about comparing normative feminist history with multiracial feminism are the contestations in philosophy embedded in these coexisting frameworks. Both popular and scholarly interpretations of second wave feminism typically link two well-known principles to the movement—"Sisterhood Is Powerful" and "The Personal Is Political." From the point of view of multiracial feminism, both principles are a good start but, in themselves, are not enough.

Conversations and struggles between women of color and white women encouraged white women to think about the limits of the popular feminist slogan "Sisterhood Is Powerful." There were many reasons why the editors of *This Bridge Called My Back* titled one of the sections of the book "And When You Leave, Take Your Pictures with You: Racism in the Women's Movement." Lorraine Bethel's poem "What Chou Mean *We*, White Girl? or the Cullud Lesbian Feminist Declaration of Independence" ("Dedicated to the proposition that all women are not equal, i.e., identical/ly oppressed") clarifies that a "we" between white and Black is provisional, at best.[40] Anthropologist Wendy Rose's critique of "white shamanism"—white people's attempt to become native in order to grow spiritually—applies as well to white feminists who treat Native American women as innately spiritual, as automatically their spiritual mothers.[41]

Cross-racial struggle made clear the work that white women needed to do in order for cross-racial sisterhood to *really* be powerful. Among the directives were the following: Don't expect women of color to be your educators, to do all the bridge work. White women need to be the bridge—a lot of the time. Do not lump African American, Latina, Asian American, and Native American women into one category. History, culture, imperialism, language, class, region, and sexuality make the concept of a monolithic "women of color" indefensible. Listen to women of color's anger. It is informed by centuries of struggle, erasure, and experience. White women, look to your own history for signs of heresy and rebellion. Do not take on the histories of Black, Latina, or American Indian women as your own. They are not and never were yours.

A second principle associated with liberal and radical feminism is captured in the slogan "The Personal Is Political," first used by civil rights and New Left activists and then articulated with more depth and consistency by feminist activists. The idea behind the slogan is that many issues that historically have been deemed "personal"—abortion, battery, unemployment, birth, death, and illness—are actually deeply political issues.

Multiracial feminism requires women to add another level of awareness—to stretch the adage from "The Personal Is Political" to, in the words of antiracist activist Anne Braden, "The Personal Is Political and The Political Is Personal."[42] Many issues that have been relegated to the private sphere are, in fact, deeply political. At the same time, many political issues need to be personally committed to—whether you have been victimized by those issues or not. In other words, you don't have to be part of a subordinated group to know an injustice is wrong and to stand against it. White women need not be victims of racism to recognize it is wrong and stand up against it. Unless that is done, white women will never understand how they support racism. If the only issues that feminists deem political are those they have experienced personally, their frame of reference is destined to be narrowly defined by their own lived experience.

The increasing number of antiracist white women who moved into mixed-gender, multi-issue organizations in the 1980s and 1990s after having helped to build women's cultural institutions in the 1970s and 1980s may be one of the best examples of an attempt to uphold this politic. Mab Segrest, perhaps the most prolific writer among lesbian antiracist organizers, provides the quintessential example of this transition in her move from working on the lesbian feminist journal *Feminary* in the late 1970s and early 1980s, to becoming the director of North Carolinians against Racist and Religious Violence in the 1980s. A self-reflective writer, Segrest herself notes this transition in the preface to her first book, *My Mama's Dead Squirrel: Lesbian Essays on Southern Culture*. Segrest writes: "In the first [essay] I wrote, 'I believe that the oppression of women is the first oppression.' Now I am not so sure. Later I wrote, 'Relationships between women matter to me more than anything else in my life.' Now what matters most is more abstract and totally specific: the closest word to it, justice. . . . During the early years the writing comes primarily out of work with other lesbians; later on, from work where I am the only lesbian."[43] The book opens with autobiographical essays about her family and women's writing, but the last essays chronicle the beginning of her organizing against the Klan—essays that became the backdrop to her second book, *Memoir of a Race Traitor*. In Segrest's view, by 1983, her work in building lesbian culture—through editing *Feminary* and her own writing—"no longer seemed enough, it seemed too literary." Segrest found herself both "inspired

by and frustrated with the lesbian feminist movement." Segrest recalls
that she

> had sat in many rooms and participated in many conversations
> between lesbians about painful differences in race and class, about
> anti-Semitism and ageism and ablebodiedism. They had been hard
> discussions, but they had given me some glimpse of the possibility of
> spinning a wider lesbian movement, a women's movement that truly
> incorporates diversity as its strength. But in all those discussions,
> difficult as they were, we had never been out to kill each other. In the
> faces of Klan and Nazi men—and women—in North Carolina I saw
> people who would kill us all. I felt I needed to shift from perfecting
> consciousness to putting consciousness to the continual test of action.
> I wanted to answer a question that had resonated through the lesbian
> writing I had taken most to heart: "What will you undertake?"[44]

This, I believe, remains a dogged and crucial question before us and one
that requires us to move beyond litanies ultimately based on only a narrow
group's survival.

The tremendous strength of autonomous feminist institutions—the
festivals, conferences, bookstores, women's studies departments, women's
health centers—were the artistic, political, and social contributions activists
helped to generate. All of these cultural institutions required women to ask
of themselves and others a pivotal question Audre Lorde had posited: Are
you doing your work? And yet, by the mid-1980s, the resurgence of the radical Right in the United States, [which] fueled a monumental backlash against
gays and lesbians, people of color, and women across the races, led multiracial feminists to ask again: Where and with whom are you doing your work?
Many antiracist feminists who had helped to build the largely women-led
cultural institutions that left a paper trail of multiracial feminism moved on,
into mixed-gender, multiracial grassroots organizations, working against the
Klan, in support of affirmative action and immigrant rights, and against
police brutality and the prison industry. It is in these institutions that much
of the hard work continues—in recognizing that "sisterhood is powerful"
only when it is worked for and not assumed and that the "personal is
political" only to the extent that one's politics go way beyond the confines of
one's own individual experience.

Blueprints for Feminist Activism

There are multiple strategies for social justice embedded in multiracial feminism: a belief in building coalitions that are based on a respect for identity-based groups; attention to both process and product but little tolerance for "all-talk" groups; racial parity at every level of an organization (not added on later but initiated from the start); a recognition that race can not be seen in binary terms; a recognition that racism exists in your backyard as well as in the countries the United States is bombing or inhabiting economically; and a recognition of the limits to pacifism when people in struggle are up against the most powerful state in the world. Multiracial feminism is not just another brand of feminism that can be taught alongside liberal, radical, and socialist feminism. Multiracial feminism is the heart of an inclusive women's liberation struggle. The race-class-gender-sexuality-nationality framework through which multiracial feminism operates encompasses and goes way beyond liberal, radical, and socialist feminist priorities—and it always has. Teaching second wave feminist history requires chronicling how hegemonic feminism came to be written about as "the" feminism and the limits of that model. Teaching second wave history by chronicling the rise of multiracial feminism challenges limited categories because it puts social justice and antiracism at the center of attention. This does not mean that the work done within hegemonic feminism did not exist or was not useful. It does mean that it was limited in its goals and effectiveness.

Although the strategies for multiracial feminism were firmly established in the 1970s and 1980s, I contend that these principles remain a blueprint for progressive, feminist, antiracist struggle in this millennium. These are principles we will need in order to build on the momentum begun in Seattle (as activist energy shocked the World Trade Organization out of its complacency) while we refuse to reproduce the overwhelmingly white composition of most of the groups involved in that protest. We will need the principles introduced by multiracial feminism to sustain a critique of the punishment industry that accounts for the increasing number of women caught in the penal system. These are principles we will need to nurture what critical race theorist Mari Matsuda has named a "jurisprudence of antisubordination." Matsuda writes: "A jurisprudence of antisubordination is an attempt to bring home the lost ones, to make them part of the center, to end the soul-killing tyranny of inside/outside thinking. Accountability revisited. I want to

bring home the women who hate their own bodies so much that they would
let a surgeon's hand cut fat from it, or a man's batter and bruise it. I want to
bring home the hungry ones eating from the trashbins; the angry ones who
call me names; the little ones in foster care."[45] The principles of antisubordination embedded in multiracial feminism, in antiracism feminism, are a
crucial piece of this agenda.

Because written histories of social movements are typically one generation behind the movements themselves, it makes sense that histories of the
feminist movement are just now emerging. That timing means that now is
the time to interrupt normative accounts before they begin to repeat themselves, each time sounding more like "the truth" simply because of the repetition of the retelling. This interruption is necessary with regard to second
wave feminism as well as earlier movements.

In her retrospective account of Black nationalism of the late 1960s and
early 1970s, Angela Davis describes how broad-based nationalism has dropped
almost completely out of the frame of reference in popular representations of
the Black power movement. This nationalism included alliances between Black
and Chicano studies, in which students in San Diego were demanding the creation of a college called Lumumba-Zapata, and Huey Newton was calling for an
end to "verbal gay bashing, urging an examination of black male sexuality, and
calling for an alliance with the developing gay liberation movement." Davis
writes: "I resent that the legacy I consider my own—one I also helped to construct—has been rendered invisible. Young people with 'nationalist' proclivi-
ties ought, at least, to have the opportunity to choose which tradition of
nationalism they will embrace. How will they position themselves en masse in
defense of women's rights, in defense of gay rights, if they are not aware of the
historical precedents for such positionings?"[46]

In a parallel way, I want young women to know the rich, complicated,
contentious, and visionary history of multiracial feminism and to know the
nuanced controversies within second wave feminism. I want them to know
that Shirley Chisholm ran for president in 1972; that Celestine Ware wrote a
Black radical feminist text in the 1970s which offered an inspiring conception of revolution with a deep sense of humanity; that before Mab Segrest
went to work for an organization against the Klan in North Carolina, she and
others published an independent lesbian journal in the 1970s that included
some of the most important and compelling race-conscious writing by white
women and women of color to date.[47] I want people to know that there are

antiracist feminist women currently in prison for their antiracist activism in the 1960s and since.[48] Among them is Marilyn Buck, a poet, political prisoner, and, in her words, "a feminist with a small 'f,'" who is serving an eighty-year sentence in California.[49] Her poems, including "To the Woman Standing behind Me in Line Who Asks Me How Long This Black History Month Is Going to Last," eloquently capture why Buck must be included in tellings of multiracial feminism.[50] She writes:

> *the whole month*
> *even if it is the shortest month*
> *a good time in this prison life*
>
> you stare at me
> and ask why I think February is so damned fine
>
> I take a breath
> *prisoners fight for February*
> *African voices cross razor wire*
> *cut through the flim-flam*
> *of Amerikkan history*
> *call its cruelties out*
> *confirm the genius of survival*
> *creation and*
> *plain ole enduring*
>
> a celebration!
>
> The woman drops her gaze
> looks away and wishes
> she had not asked
> confused that white skin did not guarantee
> a conversation she wanted to have
>
> she hasn't spoken to me since
> I think I'll try to stand
> in line with her
> again

Marilyn Buck's poems and the work of other multiracial feminist activists help show that the struggle against racism is hardly linear, that the consolidation of white-biased feminism was clearly costly to early second wave feminism, and that we must dig deep to represent the feminist movement that does justice to an antiracist vision.

NOTES

The original version of this essay appeared in *Feminist Studies* 28, no. 2 (Summer 2002). The author would like to thank several people for their generous help on this article, especially Monisha Das Gupta, Diane Harriford, and two *Feminist Studies* anonymous reviewers.

1. For examples of histories that focus on white feminism, see Sheila Tobias, *Faces of Feminism: An Activist's Reflections on the Women's Movement* (Boulder, CO: Westview Press, 1997); Barbara Ryan, *Feminism and the Women's Movement: Dynamics of Change in Social Movement Ideology and Activism* (New York: Routledge, 1992); and Alice Echols, *Daring to Be Bad: Radical Feminism in America, 1967–1975* (Minneapolis: University of Minnesota Press, 1989).

2. Chela Sandoval, *Methodology of the Oppressed* (Minneapolis: University of Minnesota Press, 2000), 41–42.

3. Of these branches of feminism (liberal, socialist, and radical), socialist feminism, which treats sexism and classism as interrelated forms of oppression, may have made the most concerted effort to develop an antiracist agenda in the 1970s. For example, "The Combahee River Collective Statement" was first published in Zillah Eisenstein's *Capitalist Patriarchy and the Case for Socialist Feminism* (New York: Monthly Review Press, 1979), 362–372, before it was published in Barbara Smith's (ed.), *Home Girls: A Black Feminist Anthology* (New York: Kitchen Table, Women of Color Press, 1983). *Radical America*, a journal founded in 1967 and whose contributors and editors include[d] many socialist feminists, consistently published articles that examined the relationship between race, class, and gender. The 1970s' socialist feminist organization the Chicago Women's Liberation Union, which considered quality public education, redistribution of wealth, and accessible childcare key to a feminist agenda, also made room for a race analysis by not privileging sexism over other forms of oppression. However, the fact that socialist feminist organizations were typically white-dominated and were largely confined to academic and/or middle-class circles limited their effectiveness and visibility as an antiracist presence in early second wave feminism. For early socialist feminist documents, see Rosalyn Baxandall and Linda Gordon, eds., *Dear Sisters: Dispatches from the Women's Liberation Movement* (New York: Basic Books, 2000).

4. For an expanded discussion of the contributions and limitations of white antiracism from the 1950s to the present, see Becky Thompson, *A Promise and a Way of Life: White Antiracist Activism* (Minneapolis: University of Minnesota Press, 2001).

5. For a discussion of the term *multiracial feminism*, see Maxine Baca Zinn and Bonnie Thornton Dill, "Theorizing Difference from Multiracial Feminism," *Feminist Studies* 22 (Summer 1996): 321–331.

6. Bernice Johnson Reagon, "Coalition Politics: Turning the Century," in *Home Girls: A Black Feminist Anthology,* ed. Barbara Smith (New York: Kitchen Table, Women of Color Press, 1983), 356–369; Patricia Hill Collins, *Black Feminist Thought: Knowledge, Consciousness, and the Politics of Empowerment* (Boston: Unwin Hyman, 1990), 11; Smith, introduction to *Home Girls,* xxxii; Cherríe Moraga and Gloria Anzaldúa, eds., *This Bridge Called My Back: Writings by Radical Women of Color* (Watertown, MA: Persephone Press, 1981); Chandra Talpade Mohanty, "Under Western Eyes: Feminist Scholarship and Colonial Discourses," in *Third World Women and the Politics of Feminism,* ed. Chandra Talpade Mohanty, Ann Russo, and Lourdes Torres (Bloomington: Indiana University Press, 1991), 51–80; Paula Gunn Allen, "Who Is Your Mother? Red Roots of White Feminism," in *The Sacred Hoop: Recovering the Feminine in American Indian Traditions* (Boston: Beacon Press, 1986), 209–221; Adrienne Rich, *Blood, Bread, and Poetry* (New York: Norton, 1986); and Patricia Williams, *The Alchemy of Race and Rights* (Cambridge, MA: Harvard University Press, 1991).

7. Here I am using the term "feminist" to describe collective action designed to confront interlocking race, class, gender, and sexual oppressions (and other systematic discrimination). Although many women in these organizations explicitly referred to themselves as "feminist" from their earliest political work, others have used such terms as "womanist," "radical women of color," "revolutionary," and "social activist." Hesitation among women of color about the use of the term "feminist" often signaled an unwillingness to be associated with white-led feminism, but this wariness did not mean they were not doing gender-conscious justice work. The tendency not to include gender-conscious activism by women of color in dominant versions of second wave history unless the women used the term "feminist" fails to account for the multiple terms women of color have historically used to designate activism that keeps women at the center of analysis and attends to interlocking oppressions. Although the formation of a women's group—an Asian women's friendship group, a Black women's church group, or a Native American women's arts council—is not inherently a feminist group, those organizations that confront gender, race, sexual, and class oppression, whether named as "feminist" or not, need to be considered as integral to multiracial feminism.

8. Benita Roth, "The Making of the Vanguard Center: Black Feminist Emergence in the 1960s and 1970s," in *Still Lifting, Still Climbing: African American Women's Contemporary Activism,* ed. Kimberly Springer (New York: New York University Press, 1999), 71.

9. Sherna Berger Gluck, "Whose Feminism, Whose History? Reflections on Excavating the History of (the) U.S. Women's Movement(s)," in *Community Activism and Feminist Politics: Organizing across Race, Class, and Gender,* ed. Nancy A. Naples (New York: Routledge, 1998), 38–39.

10. Miya Iwataki, "The Asian Women's Movement: A Retrospective," *East Wind* (Spring/Summer 1983): 35–41; Gluck, "Whose Feminism, Whose History?" 39–41.

11. Sonia Shah, "Presenting the Blue Goddess: Toward a National Pan-Asian Feminist Agenda," in *The State of Asian America: Activism and Resistance in the 1990s,* ed. Karin Aguilar-San Juan (Boston: South End Press, 1994), 147–158.

12. M. Annette Jaimes with Theresa Halsey, "American Indian Women: At the Center of Indigenous Resistance in Contemporary North America," in *The State of Native America: Genocide, Colonization, and Resistance*, ed. M. Annette Jaimes (Boston: South End Press, 1992), 329.

13. Stephanie Autumn, ". . . This Air, This Land, This Water—If We Don't Start Organizing Now, We'll Lose It," *Big Mama Rag* 11 (April 1983): 4, 5.

14. For an insightful analysis of the multidimensionality of Black nationalism of the late 1960s and early 1970s, see Angela Davis, "Black Nationalism: The Sixties and the Nineties," in *The Angela Davis Reader*, ed. Joy James (Malden, MA: Blackwell, 1998), 289–296.

15. Ibid., 15, 314.

16. Deborah Gray White, *Too Heavy a Load: Black Women in Defense of Themselves, 1894–1994* (New York: Norton, 1999), 242.

17. Ibid., 242–253.

18. Combahee River Collective, "The Combahee River Collective Statement," in *Home Girls: A Black Feminist Anthology,* ed. Barbara Smith (New York: Kitchen Table, Women of Color Press, 1983), 272–282.

19. See Barbara Smith, "Racism and Women's Studies," in *All the Women Are White, All the Blacks Are Men, But Some of Us Are Brave: Black Women's Studies*, ed. Gloria T. Hull, Patricia Bell Scott, and Barbara Smith (Old Westbury, NY: Feminist Press, 1982), 49.

20. Toni Cade, ed., *The Black Woman: An Anthology* (New York: New American Library, 1970); Maxine Hong Kingston, *The Woman Warrior* (New York: Vintage Books, 1977); Moraga and Anzaldúa, *This Bridge Called My Back*; Smith, *Home Girls*.

21. Assata Shakur, *Assata: An Autobiography* (Chicago: Lawrence Hill Books, 1987), 197.

22. Angela Davis, *Angela Davis: An Autobiography* (New York: Random House, 1974).

23. Nancy MacLean, "The Hidden History of Affirmative Action: Working Women's Struggles in the 1970s and the Gender of Class," *Feminist Studies* 25 (Spring 1999): 47.

24. As a woman who was introduced to antiracist work through the feminist movement of the late 1970s—a movement shaped in large part by women of color who called themselves "womanists," "feminists," and "radical women of color"—I came to my interest in recasting the chronology of second wave feminism especially hoping to learn how white antiracist women positioned themselves vis-à-vis second wave feminism. I wanted to learn how sexism played itself out in the 1960s and how antiracist white women responded to second wave feminism. And I wanted to find out whether the antiracist baton carried in the 1960s was passed on or dropped by feminist activists.

One of the most compelling lessons I learned from white women who came of age politically before or during the civil rights and Black power movements was how difficult it was for many of them to relate to or embrace feminism of the late 1960s and early 1970s. White antiracist women resisted sexism in SDS and in militant organizations. As they talked about the exclusions they faced in the 1960s' organizations and criticized early feminist organizing that considered gender oppression its main target, I realized how much different the feminist movement they saw in the early 1970s was from what I was introduced to in the late 1970s. By then, there was a critical mass of seasoned feminists who were keeping race at the center of the agenda. They were teaching younger feminists that race, class, gender, and sexuality are inextricably connected and that it is not possible to call oneself a feminist without dealing with race.

25. Several key Jewish feminist texts that addressed how to take racism and anti-Semitism seriously in feminist activism were published during this period and included Evelyn Torton Beck, ed., *Nice Jewish Girls: A Lesbian Anthology* (Trumansburg, NY: Crossing Press, 1982); Melanie Kaye/Kantrowitz and Irena Klepfisz, eds., *The Tribe of Dina: A Jewish Women's Anthology* (Boston: Beacon Press, 1989), first published as a special issue of *Sinister Wisdom*, nos. 29/30 (1986); Melanie Kaye/Kantrowitz, *The Issue Is Power: Essays on Women, Jews, Violence, and Resistance* (San Francisco: Aunt Lute Books, 1992); Irena Klepfisz, *Periods of Stress* (Brooklyn, NY: Out & Out Books, 1977); and Irena Klepfisz, *Keeper of Accounts* (Watertown, MA: Persephone Press, 1982).

   For key antiracist lesbian texts, see Adrienne Rich, *On Lies, Secrets, and Silence: Selected Prose, 1966–1978* (New York: Norton, 1979); Joan Gibbs and Sara Bennett, *Top Ranking: A Collection of Articles on Racism and Classism in the Lesbian Community* (New York: Come! Unity Press, 1980); Mab Segrest, *My Mama's Dead Squirrel: Lesbian Essays on Southern Culture* (Ithaca, NY: Firebrand Books, 1985); Elly Bulkin, Minnie Bruce Pratt, and Barbara Smith, *Yours in Struggle: Three Feminist Perspectives on Anti-Semitism and Racism* (Brooklyn, NY: Long Haul Press, 1984).

26. Ellen Willis, foreword to Echols, *Daring to Be Bad*, vii.

27. Ryan, *Feminism and the Women's Movement.*

28. Howard Zinn, *A People's History of the United States* (New York: HarperPerennial, 1990), 504–513.

29. For a published version of Florynce Kennedy's position on Attica and Naomi Jaffe's perspective, see Barbara Smith, "'Feisty Characters' and 'Other People's Causes,'" in *The Feminist Memoir Project: Voices from Women's Liberation*, ed. Rachel Blau DuPlessis and Ann Snitow (New York: Three Rivers Press), 479–481.

30. Verta Taylor and Nancy Whittier, "The New Feminist Movement," in *Feminist Frontiers IV*, ed. Laurel Richardson, Verta Taylor, and Nancy Whittier (New York: McGraw-Hill, 1997), 544–545.

31. Gluck, "Whose Feminism, Whose History?" 34.

32. Chela Sandoval, "Feminism and Racism: A Report on the 1981 National Women's Studies Association Conference," in *Making Face, Making Soul: Haciendo Caras: Creative and Critical Perspectives by Women of Color*, ed. Gloria Anzaldúa (San Francisco: Aunt Lute Books, 1990), 55.

33. Smith, "'Feisty Characters,'" 479–480.

34. Gluck, "Whose Feminism, Whose History?" 32.

35. Davis, *Angela Davis*, 313.

36. Activists who helped Assata Shakur escape include[d] political prisoners Marilyn Buck, Sylvia Baraldini, Susan Rosenberg, and Black male revolutionaries.

37. Rich, "Disobedience and Women's Studies," in *Blood, Bread, and Poetry*, 76–84.

38. Moraga and Anzaldúa, *This Bridge Called My Back*.

39. I am borrowing that phrase from Echols's chronicling of white radical feminist history.

40. Lorraine Bethel, "What Chou Mean *We*, White Girl? or the Cullud Lesbian Feminist Declaration of Independence," in *Conditions: Five* (1979): 86.

41. Wendy Rose, "The Great Pretenders: Further Reflections on Whiteshamanism," in *The State of Native America: Genocide, Colonization, and Resistance*, ed. M. Annette Jaimes (Boston: South End Press, 1992), 403–493.

42. Thompson, *A Promise and a Way of Life*. See also Anne Braden, *The Wall Between* (Knoxville: University of Tennessee Press, 1999), and Anne Braden, "A Second Open Letter to Southern White Women," *Southern Exposure* 6 (Winter 1977): 50.

43. Segrest, *My Mama's Dead Squirrel*, 12.

44. Mab Segrest, "Fear to Joy: Fighting the Klan," *Sojourner: The Women's Forum* 13 (November 1987): 20.

45. Mari Matsuda, "Voices of America: Accent, Antidiscrimination Law, and a Jurisprudence for the Last Reconstruction," *Yale Law Journal* 100 (March 1991): 1405.

46. Davis, "Black Nationalism," 292.

47. See *Feminary: A Feminist Journal for the South Emphasizing Lesbian Visions*. Schlesinger Library, Radcliffe Institute for Advanced Study, Harvard University, has scattered issues of *Feminary*. Duke University Rare Book, Manuscript, and Special Collection Library has vols. 5–15 from 1974 to 1985. For analysis of the import of working on this journal on Mab Segrest's consciousness and activism, see Jean Hardisty, "Writer/Activist Mab Segrest Confronts Racism," *Sojourner: The Women's Forum* 19 (August 1994): 1–2; Segrest, *My Mama's Dead Squirrel*.

48. Marilyn Buck, Linda Evans, Laura Whitehorn, and Kathy Boudin are among the white political prisoners who are either currently in prison or, in the case of Laura Whitehorn and Linda Evans, recently released, serving sentences whose length and severity can only be understood as retaliation for their principled, antiracist politics.

49. Marilyn Buck is in a federal prison in Dublin, California, for alleged conspiracies to free political prisoners, to protest government policies through the use of violence, and to raise funds for Black liberation organizations.

50. Marilyn Buck's poem, "To the Woman Standing behind Me in Line Who Asks Me How Long This Black History Month Is Going to Last," is reprinted with written permission from the author.

3

Black Feminisms and Human Agency

ULA Y. TAYLOR

As both an analytical tool and a political paradigm, black feminisms—referred to here in the plural because there is no one feminism—are fluid and diverse, focusing in various ways on the convergence of race, gender, sexuality, class, spirituality, and culture. This diversity is often oversimplified in an effort to provide a single, coherent picture of black women activists. As human agents against domination, black women's feminist practices and theories "teach us about the complex interworkings of changing structures of power."[1]

The primary expressions of black feminisms in the United States are marked by three distinct periods that are directly connected to, and are outgrowths of, key movements in African American history: the abolitionist movement, which culminated with the suffragists' securing passage of the Nineteenth Amendment in 1920; the modern civil rights and black power movements, which peaked with the enforcement during the 1970s of Title VII and Title IX of the Civil Rights Act of 1964; and the post–civil rights era, which helped to usher in the professionalization and institutionalization of feminisms. Although these periods overlap in part with traditional conceptualizations of feminist waves, they also challenge—in both their theory and practice—any linear narrative of a singular feminist history. In order to fully comprehend the development and the transformative nature of black feminisms, via the political, personal, and moral autonomy of women's agency, this essay identifies central voices assessing problems (theory) as well as turning points where women acted to secure their goals (practice).

Abolitionists and the Roots of Black Feminisms

The development of a distinctly feminist consciousness began during the enslavement period. Slave codes and laws defined black folks as chattel and thereby allowed "owners" of their bodies to deny them rights and privileges of citizenship, to physically exploit their labor, and to abuse them for their perverse pleasure. As legal "property," enslaved women were constantly confronted with sexual abuse and lacked even the limited legal recourse used by their "free" counterparts. Primarily because of the mythical, stereotypical images surrounding black womanhood—a dichotomy, as Deborah Gray White has pointed out, that included the Jezebel to excuse the sexual exploitation of black women on the one hand and the Mammy to codify the domestic role of black women in households on the other—both "free" and enslaved women were blamed for their own victimization.[2] Like their enslaved sisters, "free" women could not escape the harmful consequences of these myths; and, as abolitionists, they organized simultaneously against slavery as a legal institution and against racially gendered sexual oppression.

To argue for racial and sexual equality in an environment that was hostile to both required courage and a passion for righteousness. The abolitionist and liberal reformer Sojourner Truth is celebrated as the fountainhead of black feminist thinking in the nineteenth century. Born into slavery in New York State around 1799, Truth became an itinerant preacher (the meaning of her name) in 1843 and went on to argue for the black feminist cause in evangelical language. Slave status, she preached, denied black women the "God given rights" of motherhood, protection from exploitation, and their innate feminine qualities.[3] Truth's Bible-based feminism, charged by her riveting personal testimony, called attention to the way slavery stranded black women on the periphery of "becoming a woman." Although Truth was not the only black woman of her era—others include Jarena Lee and Maria Stewart—to advocate for women's rights through an appeal to the Bible, she was often the lone black voice among a chorus of prominent white feminists.[4] By challenging the dominant ways of thinking in her time, Truth disrupted a political movement that sought to keep black women on the outskirts.

As a pioneering black feminist, Truth is particularly influential among contemporary feminists who, as Nell Painter observes, often combine the 1851 "ar'n't I a woman?" speech long attributed to Truth with her 1858 gesture of proving her sexual identity by publicly baring her breast to a heckling white audience. Although the merging of these events created an image of defiance that many modern feminists also appreciate, Painter points out that it does not offer an accurate portrayal of the evangelical preacher herself.[5] Hoisting a revolutionary banner on the liberal Truth speaks to the unwillingness of many feminist scholars to decouple religion from patriarchy and the automatic mapping of passivity and repression onto religiously inspired goals.

The other most noted black woman in the nineteenth century, Harriet Tubman, was no doubt, as Joy James and Denean Sharpley-Whiting aptly point out, the genuine embodiment of a revolutionary abolitionist's black feminist spirit.[6] Challenging the exploitative system of slavery from the inside, Tubman worked over the course of her life to free herself and many others. Called "Moses" by all who loved and respected her, Tubman's refusal to be complacent in her own subjection demonstrates a core feature of black feminisms. Born to enslaved parents about 1821, Tubman fled Maryland in 1849 on learning that she would be sold into the horrific cotton belt. Resisting slavery with flight and thereby repudiating the idea that running away was exclusively a masculine form of resistance, Tubman not only produced dramatic change in her own life but also served as an example to others. As a celebrated conductor on the Underground Railroad, Tubman used discursive tactics and imaginative disguises to lead out of bondage more than two hundred enslaved persons, creating an important political marker for black feminisms. As a zealous abolitionist, Tubman's resignification was a law-breaking endeavor in that her agency pushed resistance to include the revolutionary destruction of unjust laws.[7] Her mode of action was linked to a political movement and culture that were in opposition to the violent world and racist discourses that elite plantation owners had created to rationalize the institution of slavery.

As a spy, scout, and military leader for the Union Army, Tubman piloted black troops up the Combahee River in South Carolina, securing the additional freedom of close to eight hundred enslaved persons.[8] Once again behaving in a way that brazenly defied the social expectations of a woman, "General Tubman" used warrior activism to add a thread of militancy to the future tapestry of revolutionary black feminisms. After the Civil War, Tubman was active in women's organizations and was a popular speaker at suffrage meetings. An advocate of increased attention to the needs of poor and aged persons, Tubman was also in the vanguard of the human rights struggle.

The Growth of Black Feminisms

With the passage of the Fifteenth Amendment, which secured the right of black men to vote, a distinct woman's suffrage movement emerged that culminated in the years 1890–1920. Rosalyn Terborg-Penn chronicles the organized efforts of African American women to earn the right to vote. She places the activism of black women in the historical context of racist Jim Crow laws, pointing out the courage and vision it took for black women to pursue the right to vote when white men and women alike sought to exclude them from it.[9] At this time legal segregation and the theater of violence that surrounded public lynching kept African Americans under siege and in "their place."

Despite the fact that many white suffragists willingly discussed how the vote could seal white supremacy, black feminists pressed for alliances with them. Refusing to desert the suffrage cause, black women organized in voters' leagues and clubs. Noted black club women such as Ida Wells-Barnett and Mary Church Terrell rallied with fervency for the vote. They believed that black women needed the vote even more than their white counterparts because it would enable them to protect their inalienable rights and improve their schools and their conditions as wage laborers. Wells-Barnett's lifelong commitment to justice illustrates how a black woman's political activities could fluctuate between liberal and radical black feminisms.[10] Scaffolding her radical liberatory projects, Wells-Barnett was a vocal suffragist and a leader in the international antilynching campaign. She challenged the myth that all white women were chaste, all black women were without virtue, and all black men were rapists. As a radical, black, feminist journalist, Wells-Barnett documented the economic realities of lynching victims, the possibility—considered blasphemous—that a white woman could be attracted to a black man, and, finally, the fact that black women were violated and abused at alarming rates. She also wielded economic boycotts against racist institutions and businesses and was not above advocating armed resistance.

As a prominent leader in the black woman's club movement, however, Wells-Barnett also promoted nonpolitical self-help activities, supported largely by liberal black feminists who were personally invested in what Evelyn Brooks Higginbotham has called the "politics of respectability."[11] Moving beyond Truth's theological feminism but refusing to completely rid feminism of Christian moralism, club women believed that to display "proper" manners and to participate in bourgeois racial "uplift" organizations was the duty of a dignified "race woman." Terrell consistently argued that the advancement of the black race depended on "uplifting" the masses of black women, especially because society judged the race by the "womanhood of our people." Overly concerned with the white gaze, liberal black feminists at the turn of the century struggled to craft a political agenda that would allow them to be included as voters acceptable to whites even as they resisted the harmful stereotypes that had become ubiquitous among white racists.

Radical black feminists considered middle-class club women's attempts to "elevate" the black masses by attacking their "morals" and regulating their behavior condescending and patronizing.[12] Blues women of the era, by contrast, simply refused to let themselves be stifled by bourgeois proscriptions for black womanhood. Performers such as "Ma" Rainey and Bessie Smith generated their own black feminist consciousness, including what Daphne Harrison has identified as an assertive, independent, and sexually aware model for black women.[13] In both their live performances and their recordings, they critiqued male chauvinism, patriarchy, and domestic violence. Determined to embrace their autonomous will, blues women genuinely resisted norms and modalities that thwarted exploration and happiness. As women who freely expressed sexual desire, including lesbianism, during a period when heterosexual norms reigned supreme, blues singers pushed beyond middle-class black feminist restraint by asserting their sexual equality with men in both public and private spheres.

The Women's Liberation Movement

Reaching beyond the limits of conventional notions of respectability and honor, black feminists during the period from 1965 to 1975, often labeled the second wave, tackled an array of issues as they chipped away at legalized Jim Crow and demanded empowerment on their own terms. Following the tradition of their foremothers by developing feminist critiques in and alongside a movement to rid the country of racial injustices, black women struggled to sculpt organizational agendas to address their concerns and needs. Although the civil rights movement nurtured feminists across the color line, its organic relationship to black feminisms was unique.

Despite the fact that the most celebrated leaders of the modern civil rights movement were men, African American women were leaders and foot soldiers at every stage and in every arena of the liberation struggle. In 1955, JoAnn Gibson Robinson and the Women's Political Council organized the Montgomery bus boycott, which catapulted Martin Luther King Jr. into the leadership of the "nonviolent" movement.[14] Ella Baker, former field secretary for the NAACP and interim director of the Southern Christian Leadership Conference (SCLC), organized college students in 1960 into the Student Nonviolent Coordinating Committee (SNCC). Under Baker's guidance, SNCC activists ushered in the "nonviolent," direct-action phase of the movement during the 1960s. Students initiated sit-ins and freedom rides to expose racial segregation and the violence used by whites to maintain separate and unequal facilities. As "the movement" grew in numbers and expanded regionally, it served as a political training ground for many women who would later participate in the women's liberation movement.

Initially, the most common response by African American women to sexism in "the movement" was to hold individuals who engaged in it personally accountable. Baker struggled to maintain her self-expression with Baptist ministers and their patriarchal practices in the SCLC, whereas Ruby Doris Smith Robinson and other SNCC women personally asserted themselves and refused to be manipulated by male coworkers under the guise of promoting "the struggle." Thus, it is not surprising that historical documentation of a collective response by African American women to chauvinism during the "nonviolent," direct-action stage of the movement is scarce.

In a departure from previous black feminists, however, black women at the end of the 1960s began to embrace collective action against the complex attitudes of many black movement men. Toni Cade Bambara eloquently articulates a point that many African American women understood: "Racism and chauvinism are anti-people. And a man cannot be politically correct and a chauvinist too."[15] Black women who shared a longing to be free from regnant masculine notions created optimal conditions for achieving their feminist goals by separating into women's organizations and meeting in "consciousness raising" groups to address the problems of sexism. Clayborne Carson documents that the only successful SNCC project after 1968 was the Black

Women's Liberation Committee, renamed in 1970 the Third World Women's Alliance, under the principled leadership of Frances Beal.[16]

With Beal as its New York City coordinator, the alliance of about two hundred members expanded beyond SNCC activists, successfully organizing political education programs and study groups. Beal's influential 1970 essay, "Double Jeopardy: To Be Black and Female," exemplified the status of the alliance as both a think tank and an action group against counterrevolutionary institutions. Beal wrote, "Those who consider themselves to be revolutionary must begin to deal with other revolutionaries as equals. And, so far as I know, revolutionaries are not determined by sex."[17] The alliance was marked by radicalism in both its understanding of relations between black women and men and its advocacy of armed struggle to bring about a socialist society.

Another departure from previous black feminisms involved the issue of welfare. Although black women activists in other periods had worked to advance economic autonomy for African Americans, welfare as a federal program emerged only with the passage of New Deal legislation in the 1930s. By the 1960s, African American women had joined local welfare groups throughout the country, demanding that the federal government treat welfare recipients as rights-bearing citizens and advocating programs to end (rather than simply alleviate) poverty. In 1967 George Wiley, an African American antipoverty activist, believed that black women needed a national organization to end poverty and helped found the National Welfare Rights Organization (NWRO). NWRO members pushed the civil rights movement to advocate economic entitlement and challenged feminists by linking the welfare issue to women's work and women's rights.

NWRO comprised primarily black single mothers with little formal education who believed that the government had a responsibility to them and that they had the right to protest to change conditions. These black feminists courageously challenged a welfare system that dehumanized women and children. Johnnie Tillmon organized the first welfare rights group in Watts, Los Angeles, in 1963 and served as the first chairwoman of the NWRO. A brilliant political theorist, Tillmon eloquently detailed how women on welfare were devalued, especially those who received Aid to Families with Dependent Children (AFDC). She ably refuted the belief that "AFDC mothers keep on having kids just to get a bigger welfare check. . . . Having babies for profit is a lie that only men could make up, and only men could believe."

She concluded, "If people are willing to believe these lies, its partly because they're just special versions of all the lies that society tells about all women." Human agency, for Tillmon, required a determined spirit. She explains the political transformation of self in the following way: "You have to learn to fight, to be aggressive, or you just don't make it. If you can survive being on welfare, you can survive anything. It gives you a kind of freedom, a sense of your own power and togetherness with other women."[18]

Although most liberal black feminists did not view the expansion of welfare as a victory and preferred to concentrate on white-collar employment, Tillmon and her fellow activists were justified in their focus, given that the majority of black women were struggling to make ends meet. As radical black feminists, NWRO leaders refused to accept being stigmatized for exercising the right of motherhood. This was no easy feat considering the bipartisan call to "restore" black families by cementing the role of men as patriarchal heads. This placement of single, poor mothers on the margins of respectability produced what Ange-Marie Hancock terms the "politics of disgust."[19] The distorted public identity of single black mothers as "welfare queens," Hancock argues, is rooted in two traceable terms linked to slavery: their alleged "laziness" (drain national resources, refuse to work, commit crime, abuse the system) and "hyperfertility" (highlighting overly fertile teen mothers, cross-generational dependency, and single-parent families).[20] These racially coded markers of welfare recipients produced a pathological portrait of a "bad mother." Determined not to internalize a racist public identity, NWRO members pressured both state agencies and the federal government to reform AFDC by demanding increased welfare benefits and an end to humiliating service. The members of the NWRO saw clearly that empowerment under capitalism required the ability to earn a living above the poverty line. It was a matter not just of eliminating sex discrimination in white-collar employment but of eliminating poverty.

By 1970 explicit discussions of sexuality had taken center stage in the women's movement, while black feminists' efforts to sculpt organizational agendas to address their concerns were often marginalized or interpreted as divisive. Such racism in the women's liberation movement pushed black feminists to organize independently. Yet as E. Frances White points out, the paucity of scholarship critiquing sexism in the black liberation struggle compared with that describing racism in the women's liberation movement also demands our attention. She cites evidence of how "Afrocentric ideology can be radical and progressive in relation to white racism and conservative and repressive in relations to the internal organization of the black community."[21]

As black feminists experienced tensions with both black men and white society, a cadre formed the National Black Feminist Organization (NBFO). It began modestly, with thirty or so members. But, after a single press conference, the NBFO received hundreds of calls and letters from all over the country inquiring about how to join and form local chapters.[22] When its first conference was held in November 1973, more than 250 women attended. These women envisioned a multipurpose organization that would address an array of issues, ranging from employment and childcare concerns to sexuality, addiction, and black women's relations to each other and to the women's movement. White women who attended the conference later wrote that they now saw that "the coalitions we, as white women, need and want with black women will be hard coming unless we prove we're not racist."[23] During the nineteenth and early twentieth centuries, black suffragists struggled with the racism of white women, but feminists in the 1960s and 1970s required nonracist entry tickets that proved difficult for white women to produce. Although white women and all men could attend the plenary assembly at the conference, they were not admitted into the workshops.[24]

Unfortunately, after this conference the NBFO did not achieve far-reaching political influence. First, African American women had to deal with many issues in their own lives, and they were not able to generate a powerful political movement around a few issues, the way the National Organization of Women (NOW) could. Second, the most commonly held notion of who these "women's libbers" were, combined with their selective agenda, confirmed to many African American women that anything associated with "feminism" was bourgeois and advantageous only to white women. Toni Morrison wrote in 1971: "It is a source of amusement even now to black women to listen to feminists talk of liberation while somebody's nice grandmother shoulders the daily responsibility of child rearing and floor mopping and the liberated one comes home to examine the housekeeping, correct it, and be entertained by the children. If Women's Lib needs those grandmothers to thrive, it has a serious flaw."[25] The majority of African American women did not have the choice to be liberated from the "kitchen." The economic realities of most African American women dictated that they work outside the home. Indeed, their underpaid labor as domestic workers often provided the means to "liberate" white women from household responsibilities in the first place.

Although the NBFO did not survive long as an active organization, it motivated small clusters of black women to continue to put pressure on NOW leaders to include on their agenda issues important to all women, regardless of class and status. Even with this added pressure, the overall participation of black women in the mainstream women's liberation movement drastically declined by 1975. As organized activism in NBFO, NWRO, and NOW waned, many black feminists continued to struggle collectively in radical groups, especially those identified as lesbian or socialist or both. Their identity as lesbians made some black feminists aware of heterosexuality as an institution and of the need to challenge patriarchy, while socialists carried on traditions of seeking economic empowerment. In 1974, the Combahee River Collective was formed by a small group of black socialist feminists who were disappointed by what they saw as the NBFO's "bourgeois" stance and lack of a clear political focus. They chose to identify with Tubman's militancy. Three years later, the group issued a widely quoted statement defining its political commitment to dismantling "interlocking" racial, sexual, and economic oppression.[26] These women, along with black lesbian groups, such as the Salsa Soul Sisters, envisioned organizing other black feminists and lesbians through writing and publishing.

Many historians of second wave feminism trace its decline to the early to mid-1970s. But by the early 1980s feminist writers' collectives and black feminists who had taken advantage of civil rights and black power victories by hunkering down in the academy were generating a profound discourse about black women, expressed in both theory and fiction. This work was indebted to Toni Cade Bambara's foundational work, *The Black Woman: An Anthology* (1970), which featured writers such as Audre Lorde, Alice Walker, and Nikki Giovanni and thoughtful essays on the experiences of African American women. Gloria Hull recalls that, "among early readings, the most precious of all for me was *The Black Woman: An Anthology*. . . . It gave me theory, analyses of current issues and cultural works, poetry, and fiction. It was uncompromisingly radical female perspectives; *The Black Woman* taught me how our position could be both thoroughly feminist and for-real Black."[27] Other groundbreaking literary and political essays and historical and fictional works appeared by writers as varied as Jeanne Nobel, Darlene Clark Hine, Terborg-Penn, Sharon Harley, Beal, Angela Davis, Barbara Smith,

Barbara Christian, Mary Helen Washington, and Morrison, signaling the coming of age of contemporary black feminist studies.

Contemporary Feminisms

During the decade of the 1980s a growing number of black women writers and literary critics rigorously theorized about sex, gender, and black women as subjects in historical and contemporary contexts. bell hooks's vanguard scholarship in particular represented a shift in black feminisms. She charged that stories of personal experience, while valuable, could not do the work of theory. hooks recognized the significance of black feminists like Truth, whose personal testimonies "validated" the need for a movement. Yet she encouraged black women to develop a theoretical framework to evaluate strategies and to challenge and change structures of domination in order to create a "liberatory feminist theory and praxis."[28]

Although they recognized theory as a means of stimulating a particular mode of action, and vice versa, many black feminists nevertheless resisted the theory-practice dichotomy, which they saw as privileging Western knowledge over other forms of analysis. Barbara Christian, in her seminal essay "The Race for Theory," explains how "theory has become a commodity which helps determine whether we are hired or promoted in academic institutions—worse, whether we are heard at all."[29] In addition, by exalting theory as the sacred mark of brilliance, we too often undermine the narrative forms, such as creative writing, that are central to black women thinkers. Many noted black women poets and fiction writers—such as Walker, Morrison, Gloria Naylor, Cade Bambara, June Jordan, and Lorde—were political activists in "the movement" and participated in feminist consciousness-raising groups. Sketching out new ways of thinking about capitalism, sexism, identity formation, and black cultures, their work has transformed the "individual" and has given black women multiple voices of inspiration as well as multiple visions of how things ought to be. In essence, black feminists truncated the academic binary of theory and practice by making use of all the methods—speeches, songs, written text, and activisms—previously employed by black women to reread and reinterpret the intellectual, social, political, economic, legal, and emotional worlds of black people.

Nowhere is this fusion of theory and practice more evident than in the area of black feminist jurisprudence. Black feminist legal scholars such as

Paulette Caldwell, Patricia Williams, Angela Harris, Kimberlé Crenshaw, Cheryl Harris, and Regina Austin are committed to demystifying legal issues that are unique to black women. For example, Caldwell argues that the law does not adequately recognize how so many cases concerning "black women's issues slip through the cracks of legal protection" because Title VII did not create a subcategory for "black women."[30] As a result, it is extremely difficult for black women to win cases in which white women or black men have been hired in their stead or have received promotions over them. Collectively, the work of these legal scholars has galvanized black feminist scholarship by carving out an important niche in advocating feminism that directly affects the lives of black women. With an approach that combines personal histories and a focus on legal cases, their writings have exposed the interconnectedness of laws, race, gender, and class in a way that challenges the traditional, technical forms of legal discourse. Allegorical and case-contextual, their language is accessible (an important prerequisite for empowerment) to legal scholars, policy makers, and grassroots activists alike.

Overall, these and other academic black feminists have asserted the significance of black women's experiences while developing new ways to debate and dissect the master narrative of Western knowledge and cultural practices. Anchoring in practice their analysis that racism, patriarchy, and material location drastically affect options and choices for black women, many academicians have been mindful that theory must be rooted in practice if it is to remain inclusive and nonelitist. Unfortunately, it has often proven difficult for many of these black feminists to find intellectual homes in either women's studies or black studies programs. Too often branded as "troublemakers," black feminists have struggled in departments that are hostile to their analytical projects and scholarly imaginations.

The professionalization of feminism also occurred outside the academy. Contemporary feminist projects such as the National Black Women's Health Project (NBWHP), under the leadership of Byllye Avery, and women's refuge shelters created to deal with violent crimes against women offer institutional examples of critical feminist practice. These projects also indicate how institution building in the "real world" can make use of the insights that theory has given us. For instance, in 1983 NBWHP members organized a conference to break the "conspiracy of silence" around health issues. Avery points out that to talk about abortion first requires being able to talk about birth control, which in turns requires being able to talk about sex. Understanding that black women's health issues must be addressed within a cultural context, Avery asserts, "We have participated in this silence that has been passed down through generations. A sister will tell you, 'I've got to have surgery.' And you say, 'What kind of surgery?' 'Well, female surgery.' 'Well, you're female from head to toe, what is the problem?'"[31] More than two thousand women attended the 1983 NBWHP conference and later formed self-help groups focused on the problems that make them sick—obesity, domestic violence, sexual abuse, and drugs. As black feminists, these women sought empowerment through wellness of the body and spirit.

Moving in the direction of allowing a number of characteristics to be considered indicators of feminist thought, black feminists' interventions both inside and outside the academy have framed problems of women within a larger discourse of rethinking "woman" and hegemonic power. Contemporary feminists have theorized the cultural meaning of "woman," going beyond a fixed, unified subject and separating gendered behavior from the biological body. Ironically, the diversity of women's experiences has been used by some to obliterate the progressive political essence of feminism, and the result is the apolitical concept of a "lifestyle feminist." hooks claims that "the notion that there could be as many versions of feminism as there were women" suggests that "any women could be a feminist no matter her political beliefs."[32] In her essay "Must We Call All Women 'Sister'?" she critiques the black feminists who campaigned in support of Anita Hill, despite Hill's conservative, antifeminist political history.[33] In short, the spread of lifestyle feminism explains why conservative and reactionary political voices or even female hip-hop artists who promulgate sexual stereotypes—as opposed to attacking the culture of violence and misogyny within the male-dominated industry—see no contradiction in claiming black feminist identities. Lifestyle feminists are a good example of how a woman's agency does not always resist hegemonic norms or domination. In fact, attributing human agency exclusively within a feminist consciousness is an intellectual blunder because all forms of resistance are not politically progressive.

Conclusion

Given the discursive power of race, black feminists have not had the privilege of abandoning the construction of a singular racial identity, although they recognize the plurality of identities within their own existence.

As theoreticians who draw on a range of frameworks—Marxist, Afrocentric, psychoanalytic, religious, socialist, postmodern, poststructuralist, pan-African, nationalist—black feminists have used their utterances, writings, and activism to grapple systematically with the institutionalized oppression of black women. Black feminists' interventions not only have changed over time but have also varied within the same material location, thereby uprooting the notion of a singular black experience and a unitary feminist thought. With their unique perspectives on the intersection of race, sexuality, and class within particular historical moments, the varieties of black feminism attest to the many ways black women have found to take a stand against sexism while remaining in critical solidarity with other political discourses.

Clearly, there are many black feminist traditions. Despite the intellectual demand for coherence within feminist theory, it is important to go beyond a one-dimensional view of the concept. Indeed, coming to grips with the diversity of black feminisms is one way of coming to grips with the diversity of black women's experiences and of feminist theories and practices.

NOTES

A previous version of this essay was published in Darlene Clark Hine, ed., *Black Women in America, an Historical Encyclopedia* (New York: Oxford, 2002), 435–443.

1. Saba Mahmood, *Politics of Piety: The Islamic Revival and the Feminist Subject* (Princeton, NJ: Princeton University Press, 2005), 9.

2. Deborah Gray White, *Ar'n't I a Woman?: Female Slaves in the Plantation South* (New York: Norton, 1999), 27–62.

3. K. Campbell, "Style and Content in the Rhetoric of Early Afro-American Feminists," *Quarterly Journals of Speech* (1986), 72.

4. Evelyn Brooks Higginbotham, *Righteous Discontent: The Women's Movement in the Black Baptist Church, 1880–1920* (Cambridge, MA: Harvard University Press, 1993), 123.

5. Nell Painter, "Sojourner Truth," in *Black Women in White America: A Documentary History* (New York: Vintage Books, 1992), 1176, and Nell Painter, *Sojourner Truth: A Life, a Symbol* (New York: Norton, 1996), 271–272.

6. Joy James and T. Denean Sharpley-Whiting, eds., *The Black Feminist Reader* (Malden, MA: Blackwell, 2000).

7. I want to thank gaidi faraj for pointing out to me this aspect of Tubman's revolutionary behavior.

8. Gerder Lerner, "Nurse, Spy and Scout: Harriet Tubman," in *Black Women in White America: A Documentary History* (New York: Vintage Books, 1992), 326.

9. Rosalyn Terborg-Penn, *African American Women in the Struggle for the Vote, 1850–1920* (Bloomington: Indiana University Press, 1998).

10. Paula J. Giddings, *Ida: A Sword among Lions* (New York: HarperCollins, 2008).

11. Higginbotham, *Righteous Discontent*, 185–229.

12. Ula Y. Taylor, *The Veiled Garvey: The Life and Times of Amy Jacques Garvey* (Chapel Hill: University of North Carolina Press, 2002).

13. Daphne Duval Harrison, *Black Pearls: Blues Queens of the 1920s* (New Brunswick, NJ: Rutgers University Press, 1988).

14. I am using quotes around the word "nonviolent" because during this phase of the movement numerous activists defended themselves. See Christopher B. Strain, *Pure Fire: Self-Defense as Activism in the Civil Rights Era* (Athens: University of Georgia Press, 2005).

15. Toni Cade, ed., *The Black Woman: An Anthology* (New York: New American Library, 1970), 107.

16. Clayborne Carson, *In Struggle: SNCC and the Black Awakening of the 1960s* (Cambridge, MA: Harvard University Press, 1981), 296.

17. Frances M. Beale [*sic*], "Double Jeopardy: To Be Black and Female," in *Sisterhood Is Powerful: An Anthology of Writings from the Women's Liberation Movement*, ed. Robin Morgan (New York: Random House, 1970), 352.

18. Johnnie Tillmon, "Welfare Is a Women's Issue," *Liberation News Service* 415 (1972): 151–156.

19. Ange-Marie Hancock, *The Politics of Disgust: The Public Identity of the Welfare Queen* (New York: New York University Press, 2004), 43.

20. Ibid., 64.

21. E. Frances White, "Africa on My Mind: Gender, Counter Discourse, and African American Nationalism," *Journal of Women's History* 2, no. 1 (Spring 1990), 76–77.

22. *off our backs* (Washington, DC), December-January 1974, 2.

23. Ibid.

24. Ibid.

25. Toni Morrison, "What the Black Woman Thinks about Women's Lib," *New York Times Magazine*, August 22, 1971, 64.

26. Combahee River Collective, "A Black Feminist Statement," in *Words of Fire: An Anthology of African American Feminist Thought*, ed. Beverly Guy-Sheftall (New York: New Press, 1995), 231–240.

27. Gloria Hull, "History/My History," in *Changing Subjects: The Making of Feminist Literary Criticism*, ed. Gayle Greene and Coppelia Kahn (New York: Routledge, 1993), 58.

28. bell hooks, *Feminist Theory: From Margin to Center* (Boston: South End Press, 1984), 30.

29. Barbara Christian, "The Race for Theory," *Contemporary Postcolonial Theory: A Reader*, ed. Padmini Mongia (London: Arnold, 1996), 148.

30. Paulette M. Caldwell, "A Hair Piece: Perspectives on the Interaction of Race and Gender," *Duke Law Journal* 365, no. 2 (April 1991), 367.

31. Byllye Avery, "Empowerment through Wellness," *Yale Journal of Law and Feminism* 4, no. 1 (Fall 1991), 150–151.

32. bell hooks, *Feminism Is for Everybody: Passionate Politics* (Boston: South End Press, 2000), 5–6.

33. bell hooks, "Must We Call All Women 'Sister'?" *Z Magazine*, February 1992.

4

"We Have a Long, Beautiful History"

Chicana Feminist Trajectories and Legacies

MARISELA R. CHÁVEZ

In early 1970, Francisca Flores, a seasoned activist in Mexican American politics, was asked by Manuel Banda, the organizer of the upcoming Mexican American National Issues Conference, to organize a women's workshop. She readily agreed. Whatever Banda's reasons for requesting such a workshop, for Flores, the request came at a most fortuitous time. In 1966, in response to the lack of recognition shown women by Mexican American organizations of the time, she cofounded the League of Mexican-American Women (LMAW) in Los Angeles, one of the first Mexican American feminist organizations of the post–World War II era in the nation.[1] By 1970, however, Flores believed that only a national Chicana women's organization would be able to significantly improve the economic and political condition of Mexican women in the United States. The Mexican American National Issues Conference in Sacramento provided the means by which Flores would reach her goal.

So, in mid-1970, Flores began to organize for the conference. She started by using her own network of sisters in the struggle. These women included Lilia Aceves, Connie Pardo, Dolores Sánchez, and Grace Montañez Davis, all of whom she had met during the 1950s and early 1960s in organizations like the Mexican American Political Association and the Community Service Organization. She asked each one, "If I have a women's workshop, will you attend?" They all agreed to participate. Having secured an initial cadre, she then sent out flyers about the women's workshop to mailing lists culled from her decades of political activism. Flores envisioned a workshop that would address topics such as women's rights, public office, family, childcare, abortion, equal pay for equal work, maternity leave, protective labor legislation, feminism, the draft, higher education, and the future of "Mexican/Chicana women."[2] She succeeded in recruiting approximately forty women to the meeting in Sacramento, including Aceves and Pardo. And there these women founded the Comisión Femenil Mexicana Nacional, the first national Chicana feminist organization in the nation.

Because of its successful community programs, the Comisión stands as one of the most important Chicana organizations of the twentieth century. By the late 1970s, the Comisión had opened the Chicana Service Action Center (CSAC), a job-training center in Los Angeles; two bilingual childcare centers (Centro de Niños); and a shelter for survivors of domestic violence. Members also organized a national Chicana conference in Goleta, California; organized against forced sterilization; helped formulate a Hispanic women's plank for the 1977 National Women's Conference in Houston; and established over twenty local chapters nationwide. By the mid 1980s, the Comisión claimed approximately three hundred members nationwide and thirty members in the Los Angeles chapter, a seemingly small number of women given their ambitious range of activities and their accomplishments.

The foundation of the LMAW and the Comisión Femenil tells a larger story about how and why modern Chicana feminisms developed. Various factors contributed to the emergence of the practical feminism that Flores and her allies practiced. First, contrary to most scholarly and popular claims, the Comisión Femenil and Chicana feminism in general have longer and deeper roots than the Chicano and women's liberation movements that emerged in the 1960s and 1970s. Second, the experiences of exclusion within both Chicano and women's liberation movements acted as catalysts for Chicanas to form their own feminist organizations. And, third, the political experiences of Flores and women of her generation engendered an astute use of governmental programs to achieve their goals.

The Emergence of Chicana Feminisms

For Chicanas and Chicanos, the tumult of what we consider sixties activism began in 1966, exploded in 1968, and continued throughout the 1970s. But the advent of the Comisión and the Chicano movement more generally also speaks to a historical timeline that is not bound by the decade of the 1960s. This history forces us to extend the Chicano movement back into the 1950s and 1940s. The Comisión Femenil Mexicana Nacional challenges us to reconsider the history of Chicana activism because it reveals a link to pre-Chicano movement politics, a link that has not been clearly identified before. This important connection provided the Comisión Femenil with important lessons in political strategy learned by women who had engaged in politics from World War II on. These women had founded organizations, networked, built alliances, learned how to run electoral campaigns, and coordinated voter-registration drives. The lessons learned would prove useful as the Comisión put their ideas into practice. In addition, in attempting to create and sustain a Chicana sisterhood, both personal and political, the Comisión Femenil practiced consciousness raising and provided concrete solutions to the problems many Chicanas faced as workers and as political activists.

When Flores and those of her generation founded the LMAW and the Comisión Femenil, they signaled a profound change in the political actions of Mexican American women. Ethnic Mexican and Latina women had long been active in, and, indeed, had often provided the backbone of, mutual-aid societies, social committees, healthcare organizations, unions, and other organizations, including the American G.I. Forum, the Congress of Spanish-Speaking Peoples, the Mexican American Political Association, and the Community Service Organization.[3] In the pre–World War II period, and under a maternalist aegis, ethnic Mexican women in Texas had founded specific women's organizations, including the Liga Femenil Mexicanista (Feminine Mexicanist League) and the Círculo Cultural Isabel la Católica (Cultural Circle of the Isabel Catholic). But, until the founding of the LMAW and the Comisión Femenil, ethnic Mexican women had not organized under the ideology of equal rights for gender-specific political, economic, and social goals in separate, same-sex organizations. This major shift in Mexican American women's organizing occurred because of changing economic, political, and social circumstances in their communities before and during the 1960s.

Conditions for Mexican Americans had advanced since the 1940s and 1950s, but there was still much room for improvement. In California in the 1960s and 1970s, most ethnic Mexicans remained concentrated in low-wage and low-skill occupations categorized as "operative or kindred workers," "clerical and kindred workers," and "service workers, except private household." As a group, their annual income stood far below that of Euro-Americans and nonwhites. Nineteen percent of Spanish-surnamed families in California earned an annual income of less than $3,000 in 1960, when the state average stood at above $6,000.[4] In addition, 16 percent of Mexican American families received public assistance, at least double the rate of all families in the nation.[5] When the Chicano movement exploded on the scene in the late 1960s, Mexican Americans in California were largely unrepresented in national, state, and local politics. The Golden State, for example, had only one Mexican American congressional representative, Edward R. Roybal, who served in the U.S. House of Representatives from 1962 to 1992. In comparison, Colorado had one Mexican American representative, Arizona had four, and Texas had ten; the great exception was New Mexico, with thirty-three.[6] Locally, the situation was equally bad. Julian Nava was the sole representative in local politics; he served on the Los Angeles school board in the late 1960s. Moreover, the few individuals who represented the community politically were all male. In 1976, Martha Cotera, an archivist and librarian wrote, "There are no Chicana state legislators, no Chicana federal judges, no Chicana U.S. Congresswomen, and no governors."[7]

In the educational realm, too, Chicanos and Chicanas fared worse than their Euro-American and minority counterparts up to 1960. They experienced some advancement, however, in the following two decades, especially those under twenty-five. For example, in 1960, Spanish-surnamed women and men over twenty-five years old finished high school at a rate approximately half that of their Euro-American peers. The gap in the college-attendance rate in this age group—the percentage of Spanish-surnamed men and women who attended some college—was also severe: the attendance rate for Spanish-surnamed people was less than half that of their Euro-American counterparts. In addition, the educational attainment of Spanish-surnamed people was below that of nonwhites in California. In younger groups, however, those aged twenty to twenty-four had a higher percentage of men (60 percent) and women (58 percent) who had finished high school than those in the older group, a statistic that reflects new social programs in effect during this period.[8] Although the gap in wages and educational achievement between Mexican Americans and the larger population persisted, demographic changes during this period facilitated an increase in educational attainment, citizenship, and English-language acquisition. At the same time, Mexican Americans became increasingly concentrated in urban areas.[9] Taking a national perspective, however, and focusing on Mexican American women over twenty-five years of age, the picture had changed little by 1970.

Only 34 percent of Mexican American women completed high school and only 2 percent went on to college. In addition, on average Mexican American women completed four fewer years of school than white women.[10]

The Chicano movement of the period, with its militant approach, provided the inadvertent impetus for women to strike out on their own. Initially, ethnic unity trumped most issues—like feminism—that could seemingly divide the movement. Women's experiences within early Chicano organizations ranged from complete and equal partnership with men to marginalization and ostracism because they espoused women's issues. Many of the women who ended up in feminist organizations were motivated in large part by their negative experiences within male-dominated organizations. The issues they brought to the table were seen as secondary to the goals of the *movimiento*. The women themselves thus became secondary as well. Ostracism was often coupled with harsh backlash in the form of ridicule and denigration: feminists were accused of being co-opted into what most Chicanos and Chicanas saw as "white" women's liberation and of espousing feminist ideas that put the goals of the entire *movimiento* in jeopardy. In 1973, Cotera noted, "Suddenly, mujeres involved in the struggle for social justice, who have always advocated more and stronger woman[,] . . . are suspect. They are suspected of assimilating into the feminist ideology of an alien culture, that actively seeks our continued domination."[11] Accusations such as these led many Chicana activists to begin to search for feminism within Mexican and Mexican American history in order to validate their conviction that race, ethnicity, class, and gender affected their lives in mutually constitutive ways, ways distinctive to women. In Chicana feminists' search for a usable past, they needed to look no further than Flores and the women of her generation.

Francisca Flores, an activist with more than thirty years experience in politics, stood at the helm of one strand of a burgeoning Chicana feminism; and her organizational experience, practical political strategy, and economic and political vision provided a solid foundation for the establishment of one of the longest-lasting Chicana feminist organizations in the nation. She helped establish Chicana feminist institutions that remain active to this day. Based on their experiences in politics at both the grassroots and the institutional level, Flores and her cadre sought a Chicana feminist praxis that was based not solely on rhetoric or ideology but also on practicality. They advocated the use of governmental institutions and resources for the benefit of Mexican American women as they pursued the two core goals of political representation and economic stability.[12]

The experiences of Aceves, Flores, Montañez Davis, Pardo, and Sánchez manifest a trajectory of Chicana feminism rooted in premovement politics, buoyed by extensive knowledge of political processes on local, state, and national levels, and guided by decades of network building in both Mexican American and other communities. In addition, although these women had been born into the working class, most achieved middle-class status by the 1960s and used this status for the benefit of the institutions they established, financially, practically, and ideologically. They had also already come to believe that, as Mexicans in the United States, they held inalienable rights, and they pursued these rights regardless of the obstacles. In addition, they had already experienced the repercussions of political activity and recognized disparate treatment based on gender in various organizations.

Born between 1913 and 1936, Flores and her cadre constituted part of a political generation shaped and influenced by World War II and the Cold War. These women's experiences allowed them to call on a common historical memory of both repression and activism once they entered the decades of the 1960s and 1970s. Flores and her cohort did not represent all ethnic Mexican women; others of their generation followed alternative routes through the political arena. But the Comisión Femenil and Flores brought together women of like experiences and like minds to craft a new platform that paved the way for Chicana feminism in the late 1960s and early 1970s.[13]

Collectively, these women had worked with the Congress of Spanish-Speaking Peoples, which was founded in 1939, and the Sleepy Lagoon Defense Committee in the early 1940s, and they had founded or had been members of various local Democratic clubs. During the 1950s, they had organized underground screenings of the then-controversial film *Salt of the Earth*, when they knew such activities could be detrimental to their livelihoods, and they became active members of the Asociación Nacional Mexico Americana (National Mexican American Association), an organization Red-baited during the McCarthy era. They had worked in voter-registration and electoral campaigns for city, school board, state, and national offices. They had also been involved in the Democratic party, and most had worked with the Community Service Organization, founded in 1947. In addition, they all were cofounders of the Mexican American Political Association (MAPA) in 1959.[14] Sánchez recalled why she joined MAPA and other political efforts at the time: "I think I also had a more militant view of things after what happened with the House Un-American Activities Committee coming to town and the kind of pressure that people like Connie and Frank Muñoz, Delfino Varela, and a lot of people that I knew had been put under. . . . So that made me a lot more militant than I had ever been. I was upset that we were spied upon. I was upset by the fact that we were called communists and that our political activities were looked at as something dangerous."[15]

In addition to their collective historical memory and organizational experience, each of these woman brought unique skills to the table when they joined both the LMAW and the Comisión Femenil. Flores was an experienced writer and had a wealth of knowledge about Mexican American history. When she moved to Los Angeles from San Diego in 1939, she supported herself by working for various Mexican American and Latino and Latina periodicals. Through her experience as a writer, Flores learned the newspaper business, and in 1963 she began editing and publishing *Carta Editorial* (Editorial Letter), a newsletter "for the informed-interested in Mexican-American affairs." It was dedicated to local, state, and national legislative issues. For Flores and other Mexican American activists of the era, *Carta Editorial*, which had been established as a "Democratic voice fighting for Democratic rights," provided a sustained response to the McCarthy era's Red baiting.[16] In 1970, Flores revamped *Carta Editorial* and named the publication *Regeneración* (Regeneration), which became one of the most significant periodicals of the Chicano movement.

In renaming the publication, Flores connected the issues that she articulated in the Chicano movement to a history of activism on the part of Mexicans in the United States. *Regeneración* had been the title of the newspaper of the Partido Liberal Mexicano (PLM), an anarchosyndicalist organization headed by Ricardo and Enrique Flores Magón during the Mexican Revolution of the early twentieth century.[17] Flores had no relationship to the Flores Magón brothers, but, as a teenager, she had been diagnosed with tuberculosis and sent to live in a sanitarium in her hometown of San Diego, California. There, she and other women founded the Hermanas de la Revolución Mexicana (Sisters of the Mexican Revolution), a political discussion group and an auxiliary committee of La Sociedad de la Revolución (the Revolution Society). As a member of these organizations, Flores would have learned about the Flores Magón brothers, their politics, and their newspaper. Given that veterans of the Mexican Revolution were also members of

these groups, Flores also would have learned about women's participation in
the revolution and the PLM. This knowledge, coupled with her own experience within a women's political discussion group became the foundation of
her beliefs about the rights of ethnic Mexicans in the United States, both
men and women.[18]

In the first issue of *Regeneración*, Flores announced that the publication
sought the "elimination of inequality, poverty and war" as well as "an end to
discrimination of all minorities." In addition, her editorial addressed the
desire for improved education and healthcare, "respect from law enforcement agencies and 'justice' in the courts," as well as "more and better
employment opportunities" and "higher annual income." Flores's first
editorial also spoke subtly to gender issues and espoused support for men
and women in the movement: "REGENERACIÓN will also serve all men
and women of goodwill as a resource for understanding and cooperation."[19]
Addressing gender more forcefully one year later, Flores insisted that
Chicana liberation was central to the liberation of the entire Chicano community: "The issues of equality, freedom and self-determination of the
Chicana—like the right of self-determination, equality and liberation of the
Mexican community—*[are] not negotiable* . . . FREEDOM IS FOR EVERYONE."[20]
Flores's insistence on Chicanas' rights to the goals of the *movimiento*
resonated strongly with the women of her generation who helped found the
Comisión Femenil.

The experiences of Flores's generation of activists coalesced between
1966 and 1970 when their personal experiences with discrimination, police
brutality, federal harassment and scrutiny, and community organizing
merged with issues of differential treatment based on gender. For Montañez
Davis, consciousness of gender disparity arose in higher education and in
community organizations. After earning a B.S. in chemistry from Immaculate
Heart College in Los Angeles in 1948, she received a master's degree in
biochemistry from the University of California at Los Angeles in 1955.
At UCLA, Montañez Davis experienced both ethnic and gender discrimination in her field of study. There had never been any Mexicans in the biochemistry department at UCLA before she was accepted, very few women,
and certainly no Mexican American women. At the same time, her experiences in the Community Service Organization in the 1950s reflected an era
when men assumed public leadership roles. She remembered that although
women were actively involved in the organization, "we didn't . . . [in] the

early beginnings, have ever [women] committee chairpersons or anything like that."[21] Montañez Davis was keen to challenge such gender disparities in educational institutions and community organizations.

Others formulated their politics at the nexus of the workplace, community organizations, and women's liberation. Pardo, for example, worked in the garment and laundry industries as a teenager and young woman, and also read political and feminist theory by authors such as Karl Marx and Simone de Beauvoir. Through her involvement with the MAPA, she (like Montañez Davis) struggled on behalf of African American civil rights. Pardo joined the National Association for the Advancement of Colored People and the Student Nonviolent Coordinating Committee. In 1965, with MAPA paying her way, Pardo traveled to Selma, Alabama, to participate in the historic Selma-to-Montgomery march in support of voting rights. Yet it was Pardo's experiences with the National Organization for Women (NOW), founded in 1966—the same year as the LMAW—that cemented her belief in a separate struggle for ethnic Mexican women. In the late 1960s, Pardo attended some of the first NOW meetings in the Los Angeles area. She recalled, "When I went to the first meeting . . . I was the only woman of color—the only one. . . . I was . . . sort of invisible . . . but I still kept going." For Pardo, the most obvious difference in her experiences and beliefs appeared in class terms. She remembered, "They [the women in NOW] were just going towards feminism without really having a political ideology in mind or any ideology with reference to the class struggle."[22] These vignettes underscore how race, class, and gender affected the lives of ethnic Mexican women and how these issues acted as catalysts to inform the emergence of a specifically Chicana feminism.

The Legacy of Chicana Feminisms

A strong cohort of Comisión members entered that movement from a trajectory rooted in the Mexican American politics of the World War II and Cold War periods or through Democratic politics. When they all joined MAPA, most of them as founding members in 1959, they began to analyze their experiences in politics through a gendered lens. And so these women followed the well-worn tradition of feminist groups emerging in response to negative experiences in various social-movement organizations. Although MAPA became the springboard from which these women launched their feminist activities, the founding of the LMAW and the Comisión Femenil Mexicana

Nacional depended on the vision of Flores, who had long seen women as having worth equal to that of men. Experiences in MAPA led these women to strike out on their own through the LMAW in 1966, the year that most historians point to as the birth of the Chicano movement. Although these women experienced marginalization within or exclusion from mainstream feminist organizations, specifically NOW, they nonetheless saw the potential for a larger and stronger Chicana organization and a more inclusive women's movement.

The League of Mexican-American Women

Flores helped found LMAW to provide avenues for women's leadership in politics during a period when opportunities had been closed off to them because of gender. Her cofounder was Ramona Morín. In the tradition of MAPA, which was founded in 1959 in Los Angeles to increase Mexican American political representation, Flores and Morín formed LMAW for two main reasons. First, they wanted to increase the presence of Mexican American women in politics, especially political appointments to city, state, and national commissions. Second, they wanted to recognize the achievements and contributions of Mexican American women in politics.[23] As former LMAW member Sánchez remembers, "Yes, [gender] became an issue. . . . The women in MAPA got kind of fed up—Grace Davis, Francisca [Flores], Connie [Muñoz], can't remember who the other women [were]—we became fed up with always doing the work and never [being] called on to give a speech. We were never given an award, and so we formed an organization."[24]

LMAW, therefore, unlike previous organizations, explicitly placed Mexican American women in the forefront of political advocacy. LMAW's goal of political representation for Mexican Americans did not differ much from MAPA's, except that LMAW focused solely on women. As the preamble to the LMAW constitution stated: "In order to stimulate and promote the interest of the Mexican-American women in fields of social and legislative action, this organization is formed. It will also give special recognition to women for outstanding work in these fields" because, "unfortunately, for many reasons the Mexican-American woman's work, contribution and/or activity has not been properly recognized."[25] LMAW saw itself as an organization that would unite Mexican American women of similar consciousness in an effort to facilitate dialogue among women and effect social change through its leadership training. The roots of these efforts could be traced to

Flores's experiences in the Hermanas de la Revolución and her participation in the organization El Congreso. But LMAW went beyond these groups as it sought to broaden the "socio-economic, political and cultural horizons" of Mexican American women with the ultimate goal of "undertaking responsibility and giving leadership to the community it serve[d]."[26]

Active in Los Angeles from 1966 through 1970, and with an average membership of twenty women, LMAW campaigned for consumer education in East Los Angeles, supported Mexican American women for political office, and recognized women for their political achievements. In East Los Angeles, LMAW waged a lengthy consumer-education campaign, focusing on local supermarkets. In this project, women from LMAW joined with members of the Mexican American community in East Los Angeles to disseminate information, meet with grocery-store management, and start a boycott leading to the successful clean-up of a local store.[27] LMAW also participated with the Consumer Action Council of Los Angeles in writing a proposal to establish a comprehensive consumer-protection project.[28] In addition to this campaign, LMAW sought positions for Mexican American women in a variety of public institutions and recognized their achievements. For example, in 1969, LMAW supported Soledad García for principal of Roosevelt High School and supported Irene Tovar in her campaign for the Junior College Board, holding fundraisers on her behalf.[29] To recognize Mexican American women in politics, LMAW sponsored several dinners at various East Los Angeles restaurants.

For many of its members, LMAW was their first woman-centered activity. Their entrance into politics began with the Mexican American community, but, after recognizing gender disparities, they joined LMAW and received training and a sense of empowerment. As Sánchez recalls, "Well, one of the things that it [LMAW] did, I think, was allow us to learn to work together. I don't think that as women we had ever really worked just [as] women together. And you begin to kind of learn to organize within ourselves and for ourselves and to be able to go into an organization and demand a say on what went on more so than we had ever done. And I think it was a shock to the males who didn't ever experience that and it was kind of a shock to us, too, to find out we can, we could really get a say into how things were done."[30]

During the four years of its existence, LMAW established a precedent for Mexican American women in politics. Through the efforts of Flores and

Morín and continuing the legacy of activists of the 1930s and 1940s, LMAW became the first Mexican American women's political organization focused on developing and recognizing women's political leadership. LMAW also became a training ground by providing Mexican American women with a sense of empowerment. Although a small organization, it became the fore-mother of the Comisión Femenil Mexicana Nacional, founded by Flores in 1970. From her experiences with LMAW, Flores knew that only a large organization could affect the political and economic changes that she envisioned for Mexican American women.

The Comisión Femenil Mexicana Nacional

The cohort of women who heeded Flores's call to attend the National Issues Conference in 1970 represented a variety of organizations and age groups, including members of LMAW and MAPA and the more radical and younger Movimiento Estudiantil Chicano de Aztlán (Chicano Student Movement of Aztlán, a college student organization). At the conference, they merged the topics that Flores had proposed into five main resolutions. These resolutions represented broad goals that addressed issues of the invisibility of Mexican American women on local, state, and national levels as well as practical concerns such as childcare and abortion. They also resolved that the outcome of the workshop would be a Mexican American women's organization, to be called the Comisión Femenil Mexicana Nacional (National Mexican Women's Commission).[31] Although the Comisión was formed as part of the Chicano movement, it is noteworthy that the organization's name was in Spanish but did not include the term *Chicana*. Aceves recalled that the rationale for the name was based on history. She stated, "This used to be Mexico. And it's not only Mexicana because of Mexican women. It's not only named Comision Mexicana Nacional because we're Mexicans. It's named that way because of . . . the history of the Southwest."[32]

Given this history and the situation of Mexican American women at the time, the workshop participants focused their resolutions on national and state as well as local levels. They demanded "that proportionate and representative appointments of the Mexican-American women be made to the Commission on the Status of Women at the State and Federal levels." They resolved to form networks with other women's organizations. Another resolution supported "free and legalized abortions for all women who want or need them." They resolved that "every Chicano community" should "promote and set up 24-hour day care facilities . . . to service our people." Echoing ideologies prominent in the Chicano movement, they stated that the childcare centers should "reflect the concept of La Raza as the united family. . . . Men and women, young and old, must assume the responsibility for the love, care, education, and orientation of all the children of azlan [sic]."[33]

Although all the resolutions addressed issues specifically related to women, those regarding abortion and childcare were demands usually regarded as feminist issues by Chicano movement advocates and society at large. Yet the women at the workshop couched these two resolutions in rhetoric familiar to the Chicano movement. They related the right to abortion to the issue of "self-determination," a consistent rallying cry of the movement, and they demanded childcare centers that would instill ethnic pride in the children they served.

After the 1970 conference, the Comisión established its base of operations in Los Angeles, building on work already begun by LMAW. The organization existed on two levels—the local chapter and the national. Local chapters developed their own directions, but with oversight from the national governing body, which also sponsored projects. For example, in 1971, Frances Bojórquez, the student-body president at California State University, Los Angeles (CSULA), and a member of the Movimiento Estudiantil Chicano de Aztlán, established the first chapter of the Comisión Femenil at CSULA. During the same period, the Comisión Femenil governing-body members held meetings at the International Institute in Boyle Heights to discuss their vision for Chicanas in the community. These women agreed that job training and childcare were essential needs for women in their community.

The Chicana Service Action Center

In September 1972, the Comisión Femenil accomplished one of its goals: it opened the CSAC in East Los Angeles. A job-training and employment center specifically for Chicanas and Latinas in the community, the center came about through careful strategizing and the effective use of federal resources. In 1972, Flores, along with one hundred other Latinas and Chicanas from across the country, attended the Consultation for Spanish-Speaking Women in Phoenix, Arizona, sponsored by the Women's Bureau, a division of the U.S. Department of Labor.[34] This was the Bureau's first meeting with Spanish-speaking women, although it had been established in 1920. Richard Nixon had been elected president in 1968, but the programs that his predecessor, Lyndon B. Johnson, had put into place as part of his War on Poverty were still in existence. In 1964, Congress passed the Economic Opportunity Act and established the Office of Economic Opportunity to coordinate efforts. One of the Office of Economic Opportunity's aims was to lift citizens out of poverty by involving them in self-help through educational, job-training, and community-development programs.

Once again, Flores saw an opportunity, and the Comisión was able to use this meeting to secure funding for a job-training center. At the conference, Flores and other Comisión Femenil members, according to an observer, "cornered a Department of Labor official (a Chicano) regarding the implementation of a work program for Chicanas." The official told Flores, "I happen to have $50,000 of discretionary funds. And if you . . . write a proposal, I will . . . give you those $50,000."[35] At that point, "Francisca responded by opening her purse and presented him with the proposal!"[36] With the $50,000 grant from the Department of Labor, Flores and the other women established the CSAC, with Aceves as its first director.[37]

After receiving the start-up funds in 1972, CSAC developed into a full-fledged job-training and employment center for Mexican American women in the Los Angeles area. Continued financial support from 1973 through 1977 came from the Department of Labor, the Comprehensive Employment and Training Act, the governor of California's discretionary funds, and a Los Angeles city grant. Flores, founder of both the organization and the center, worked as executive director of CSAC until 1982.[38]

The CSAC is still functioning today. The center has various satellite locations and serves women in the counties of Los Angeles, Orange, Riverside, and San Bernadino. Beginning with its $50,000 start-up grant in 1972, it now operates with a budget of over $500,000 annually. The CSAC continues to receive federal funding as a contractor with the Department of Labor, serves as a WorkSource center, a program put in place through the Workforce Investment Act of 1998, and contracts yearly with the County of Los Angeles. The CSAC provides business courses, training programs to place women in nontraditional jobs, and youth employment services.[39]

When Flores and the women of the Comisión Femenil opened the CSAC, they put into practice what they hoped to teach those who utilized the center: to use "the system" to their advantage. They also hoped that the women they served would develop into a new generation of leaders to help resolve the social and economic problems faced by Mexican American women. The opening of the CSAC also reflected the experiences of Flores and her generation of women: they knew when and how to obtain federal funds to achieve their goals. The founding of the Comisión Femenil began as an effort to achieve Chicana sisterhood, but its founders also hoped it would establish fully functioning institutions. The CSAC was its first tangible outcome.

El Centro de Niños and Other Projects

In 1973, the Comisión Femenil also made itself visible to the state government. In February of that year, Aceves and other members of the Comisión Femenil testified before the California Commission on the Status of Women about the state of Chicanas and employment.[40] As sociologist Elena Gutiérrez argues, the women of the Comisión Femenil used the opportunity to begin to dispel some of the myths prevalent in society about women such as themselves by focusing on Chicanas as workers.[41] And because one of the Comisión Femenil's goals was to increase the number of Chicanas on local, state, and national commissions, the organization lobbied the Commission on the Status of Women to appoint a Chicana to its board. Partly because of the Comisión Femenil's efforts, that same year Governor Ronald Reagan appointed Carolyn Orona, a Chicana Republican, to the commission.[42] Despite her political affiliation, the Comisión Femenil regarded Orona's appointment as a victory. There would be a Chicana voice on the Commission.

The Comisión Femenil's institution-building remained strong throughout the 1970s and reached into the early 1980s. In 1973, the Comisión fulfilled one of its major goals: it established the Centro de Niños, a childcare program with affordable rates so that mothers, such as those whom the CSAC served, could gain employment. In March 2008, the Centro de Niños celebrated its thirty-fifth anniversary. From humble beginnings as what its current director, Sandra Serrano Sewell, says was a "nice babysitting situation," the center is now a model childcare program according to Los Angeles County officials. It has served over fourteen hundred children in its thirty-five years.[43] In 1982, the organization established Casa Victoria, which still exists, for adolescent girls who were in the juvenile-justice system. The center maintains six beds for young women ages twelve to seventeen and provides bilingual services to the young women and their parents.[44]

Beyond the institutions it built and sustained in Los Angeles, the Comisión Femenil also extended its influence nationally and internationally.

In 1975, many of its members traveled to the International Women's Year Conference in Mexico City to voice Chicana concerns and ideas to a global audience. And, in 1977, the Comisión Femenil's members played a major role in the formulation of the Minority Women's Plank at the National Women's Conference. Members also attended the Equal Rights Amendment March in Washington, D.C., in 1978. Additionally, in 1980, the Comisión Femenil gained nongovernmental-organization status and attended the International Women's Conference in Copenhagen. Through these events, the Comisión Femenil acted as national and international representatives of Chicana feminism and in doing so subverted a male-identified Chicano movement and a Euro-American dominated women's movement.[45]

Conclusion

The Comisión Femenil Mexicana Nacional succeeded in establishing social-service institutions for Mexican American and Latina women because of the experiences of and long-term goals set forth by its founders, especially Flores. According to the Ford Foundation, the CSAC has served over thirty thousand women since its inception.[46] Of the various Chicana feminist groups that arose and then folded throughout the 1970s, 1980s, and 1990s, I could find no other that built the kind of lasting institutions that the Comisión Femenil built. Flores and her contemporaries, with their years of political experience, brought knowledge of how politics worked, and they knew what the stakes were in their endeavors. Unlike the generation of women who came of political age during and because of the Chicano movement of the late 1960s and early 1970s, Flores and her generation had already identified gender disparities in organizations, had experienced the backlash to their political activities during the 1950s, and were confident in their identities as Mexican American women, indeed Chicanas.

The story of the Comisión Femenil, the CSAC, and the Centro de Niños is a tale of both reaction and pro-action. The male-centered culture of Mexican American politics and the middle-class nature of the mainstream feminist movement propelled women of older and younger generations to create a space for themselves where they could address the issues they believed were ignored by others. But the Comisión Femenil's history is also a story of a political generation of Mexican American women activists who brought a wealth of knowledge and experience to organizations formed during the

Chicano movement. In this manner, they defy the historiographical legacy of a dramatic split between Mexican American and Chicano and Chicana activists. Indeed, these women adapted to the times and used their expertise to bolster and strengthen the institutions that they founded. Instead of feeling challenged by the strident militancy of a younger generation, Flores and her cadre joined the struggle, became agents of lasting change, and exemplified what Texas Chicana feminist Cotera called the "long, beautiful history" of Chicana activism.[47]

NOTES

1. Mexican American women had organized politically prior to 1966, but they had not organized for political representation for themselves as women. See Cynthia Orozco, "Beyond Machismo, La Familia, and Ladies Auxiliaries: A Historiography of Mexican-Origin Women's Participation in Voluntary Associations and Politics in the United States, 1870–1990," *Perspectives in Mexican American Studies* 5 (1995): 1–34; Emma Pérez, *The Decolonial Imaginary: Writing Chicanas into History* (Bloomington: Indiana University Press, 1999); and Gabriela González, "Carolina Munguía and Emma Tenayuca: The Politics of Benevolence and Radical Reform," *Frontiers: A Journal of Women Studies* 24 (2003): 200–229.

2. Comisión Femenil, "Women's Workshop Outline [Mexican American Issues Conference]," Comisión Femenil Mexicana Nacional Records, Conference Series, Box 1, Folder 2, California Ethnic and Multicultural Archives, University of California, Santa Barbara, hereafter cited as CFMN Records; emphasis in original.

3. For a general overview of Mexican women's organizational efforts, see Orozco, "Beyond Machismo, La Familia, and Ladies Auxiliaries." For women in mutual-aid societies, social clubs, healthcare organizations, and auxiliaries to larger organizations in Texas, see Pérez, *The Decolonial Imaginary*, especially ch. 4, and Teresa Palomo Acosta and Ruthe Weingarten, eds., *Las Tejanas: 300 Years of History* (Austin: University of Texas Press, 2003). For women in unions, see Vicki L. Ruiz, *Cannery Women, Cannery Lives: Mexican Women, Unionization, and the California Food Processing Industry, 1930–1950* (Albuquerque: University of New Mexico Press, 1987); Patricia Zavella, *Women's Work and Chicano Families: Cannery Workers of the Santa Clara Valley* (Ithaca, NY: Cornell University Press, 1987); and Margaret Rose, "Women in the United Farm Workers: A Study of Chicana and Mexicana Participation in a Labor Union, 1950–1980" (PhD diss., University of California, Los Angeles, 1988). On women in the El Congreso and the Mexican American Political Association, see George J. Sánchez, *Becoming Mexican American: Ethnicity, Culture and Identity in Chicano Los Angeles, 1900–1945* (New York: Oxford University Press, 1995); David G. Gutiérrez, *Walls and Mirrors: Mexican Americans, Mexican Immigrants, and the Politics of Ethnicity* (Berkeley: University of California Press, 1995); and Mario T. García, *Mexican Americans: Leadership, Ideology, and Identity, 1930–1960* (New Haven, CT: Yale University Press, 1991). On women in the Community Service Organization, see Margaret Rose, "Gender and Civic Activism

in Mexican American Barrios: The Community Service Organization, 1947–1962,"
in *Not June Cleaver: Women and Gender in Postwar America, 1945–1960*, ed. Joanne
Meyerowitz (Philadelphia: Temple University Press, 1994), 177–199.

4. State of California, Fair Employment Practices Division, *Californians of Spanish
Surname: Population, Education, Income, Employment* (San Francisco: Fair
Employment Practices Commission, Division of Fair Employment Practices, State
of California, 1964, repr., 1966), 16, 17, 40, 48. In 1960, the employed Spanish-surnamed population in California totaled 622,397, with 410,023 men and 212,374
women.

5. Martha P. Cotera, *Diosa y Hembra: This History and Heritage of Chicanas in the U.S.*
(Austin: Information Systems Development, 1976), 145. Material cited from U.S.
Department of Health, Education, and Welfare, *A Study of Selected Socio-Economic
Characteristics of Ethnic Minorities Based on the 1970* Census, vol. I, *Americans of
Spanish Origin* (Washington, DC: Government Printing Office, 1974), 35.

6. Mexican-American Study Project, "California Mexican-Americans Score Zero in
State Legislature," *Mexican-American Study Project Progress Report*, no. 9 (Los
Angeles: University of California, Los Angeles, May 1967), 3.

7. Cotera, *Diosa y Hembra*, 168.

8. State of California, Fair Employment Practices Division, *Californians of Spanish
Surname: Population, Education, Income, Employment: A Summary of Changes between
1960 and 1970—Based on U.S. Census of Population* (San Francisco: Fair Employment
Practice Commission, Agriculture and Services Agency, Department of Industrial
Relations, State of California, June 1976), II.

9. Juan Gómez-Quiñones, *Chicano Politics: Reality and Promise, 1940–1990*
(Albuquerque: University of New Mexico Press, 1994), 31.

10. Ursula Vils, "Chicanas Stand Up and Speak Out," *Los Angeles Times*, June 26, 1980.

11. Martha P. Cotera, "Mexicano Feminism," *Magazín* I, no. 9 (1973): 30. For an analy-
sis of other women targeted with the same accusations, see Maylei Blackwell,
"Contested Histories: Las Hijas de Cuauhtémoc, Chicana Feminisms, and Print
Culture in the Chicano Movement, 1968–1973," in *Chicana Feminisms: A Critical
Reader*, ed. Gabriela Arredondo, Aída Hurtado, Norma Klahn, and Olga Nájera-
Ramírez (Durham, NC: Duke University Press, 2003), 59–89, and Dionne Espinoza,
"Revolutionary Sisters: Women's Solidarity and Collective Identification among
Chicana Brown Berets," *Aztlán* 26, no. I (Spring 2001): 17–58.

12. Although there have not been many links between pre-Chicano movement politics and Chicano movement politics, one figure emerges in Bert Corona, who, like
Flores, had been active in many of the same organizations. Corona was involved in
labor issues as well as community politics; Flores tied herself to community issues
and politics. See Mario T. García, *Memories of Chicano History: The Life and Narrative
of Bert Corona* (Berkeley: University of California Press, 1994).

13. On political generations, see García, *Mexican Americans*. See Rodolfo Alvarez,
"The Psycho-historical and Socioeconomic Development of the Chicano
Community in the United States," *Social Science Quarterly* (March 1973): 920–942,

for the original use of the idea of political generations among ethnic Mexicans, which focused on biological generations rather than political generations. Also see Ernesto Chávez, *"¡Mi Raza Primero!": Nation, Identity, and Insurgency in the Chicano Movement in Los Angeles, 1966–1978* (Berkeley: University of California Press, 2002), 10–11. For a critique of the generational argument, see Gutiérrez, *Walls and Mirrors*, 117–119.

14. Bill Flores, "Francisca Flores, 1913–1996," *Tonatiuh Quinto Sol* (June 1996): 2–4; Marcie Miranda-Arrizón, "Building Herman(a)dad: Chicana Feminism and Comisión Femenil Mexicana Nacional" (master's thesis, University of California, Santa Barbara, 1998)," 58–60. The Sleepy Lagoon Defense Committee, a grassroots legal-defense committee, was organized in 1942, after the arrest of seventeen Mexican American youths in Los Angeles on charges of murder. In 1943, the seventeen youths were convicted by an all-white jury on a variety of charges, including first-degree murder, on the basis of highly circumstantial evidence. Because of the work of the Defense Committee, all seventeen men were eventually released from jail and acquitted. See Sánchez, *Becoming Mexican American*, 246; Gutiérrez, *Walls and Mirrors*, 124, 126–130; Rodolfo Acuña, *Occupied America: A History of Chicanos*, 3rd ed. (New York: Harper & Row, 1988), 254–255; Mauricio Mazón, *Zoot-Suit Riots: The Psychology of Symbolic Annihilation* (Austin: University of Texas Press, 1989), 19–23; and Eduardo Pagán, *Murder at the Sleepy Lagoon* (Chapel Hill: University of North Carolina Press, 2003).

15. Dolores Sánchez, interview by Marisela R. Chávez, May 9, 2002, City of Commerce, CA, tape recording.

16. William (Bill) V. Flores, interview by Marisela R. Chávez, December 17, 2003, Los Angeles, tape recording.

17. See Juan Gómez-Quiñones, *Sembradores: Ricardo Flores Magon y el PLM: A Eulogy and Critique* (Los Angeles: Aztlan Publications, Chicano Studies Center, University of California, Los Angeles, 1973), and Pérez, *The Decolonial Imaginary*, 55–76.

18. Flores, "Francisca Flores, 1913–1996." Also see Miranda-Arrizón, "Building Herman(a)dad," 57–58, and Naomi H. Quiñones, "Francisca Flores," in *Latinas in the United States: A Historical Encyclopedia*, ed. Vicki L. Ruiz and Virginia Sánchez-Korrol (Bloomington: University of Indiana Press, 2006), 264.

19. Francisca Flores, "Editorial," *Regeneración* 1, no. 1 (January 1970): n.p., all capitals in original.

20. Francisca Flores, "Editorial," *Regeneración* 1, no. 10 (1971): n.p.; emphasis and capitals in original.

21. Grace Montañez Davis, interview by Phillip C. Castruita, July–September 1994, Grace Montañez Davis Personal Collection, Los Angeles, transcript.

22. Connie Pardo, interview by Marisela R. Chávez, March 29, 2002, Los Angeles, tape recording.

23. Lilia Aceves, interview by Marisela R. Chávez, April 15, 2002, Alhambra, CA, tape recording.

24. Sánchez interview. Also see Juan Gómez-Quiñones, *Chicano Politics*, 68.

25. League of Mexican-American Women, "Aims and Purposes," (n.d.), 1, Personal Papers of Lilia Aceves, Alhambra, CA, and League of Mexican-American Women, "Achievement Awards," 7 May 1966, CFMN Records, Conference Series, Box 1, Folder 1.

26. League of Mexican-American Women, "Aims and Purposes," 1.

27. Consumer Action Council, "Proposal for the Establishment of a Comprehensive Consumer Protection Project," 14–15, Personal Papers of Lilia Aceves, Alhambra, CA.

28. League of Mexican-American Women to MACPF, n.d., Personal Papers of Lilia Aceves, Alhambra, CA.

29. League of Mexican-American Women, meeting minutes, 12 April 1969, Personal Papers of Lilia Aceves, Alhambra, CA.

30. Sánchez interview.

31. Miranda-Arrizón, "Building Herman(a)dad," 55. Because women established the organization at a national Mexican American conference, the founding of the Comisión Femenil echoes the circumstances under which women founded NOW in 1966 at the National Conference of State Commissions on the Status of Women. But while NOW founders envisioned an organization for all American women, the Comisión Femenil saw itself as an organ only for Mexican American women because, during the first four years of NOW's existence, Mexican American women believed that NOW did not represent their interests.

32. Aceves interview.

33. Women's Workshop (National Mexican American Issues Conference), "Resolutions—Women's Workshop," 11 October 1970, Conference Series, Box, 1, Folder 2, CFMN Records.

34. U.S. Department of Labor Employment Standards Division, Women's Bureau, "Consultation for Spanish-Surnamed Women List of Participants," 25–26 March 1972, CFMN Records, Box 1, Folder 4. In addition to Flores, other Comisión Femenil members in attendance included Gracia Molina de Pick and Corinne Sánchez.

35. Aceves interview.

36. Gloria Moreno-Wycoff, ["Tribute to Francisca Flores"], 10 February 1982, Administrative Records Series, Box 5, Folder 2, 1, CFMN Records.

37. Also see Miranda-Arrizón, "Building Hermana(a)dad," 66.

38. Chicana Service Action Center, "CSAC Fact Sheet," n.d. [1976], CFMN Records, Box 2.

39. National Council of La Raza, "NCLR Affiliates," http://www.nclr.org/content/affiliates/detail/1008/, accessed June 21, 2008.

40. The first Commission on the Status of Women was established as a presidential commission by President John F. Kennedy in 1961 and was headed by Eleanor Roosevelt. Individual states established their own women's commissions.

41. Elena R. Gutiérrez, *Fertile Matters: The Politics of Mexican-Origin Women's Reproduction* (Austin: University of Texas Press, 2008), 94–95.

42. Miranda-Arrizón, "Building Herman(a)dad," 67.

43. Adolfo Guzmán-López, "East L.A. Daycare Center Celebrates 35th Anniversary," February 14, 2008, Southern California Public Radio, http://www.scpr.org/news/stories/2008/02/14/08_east_la_daycare_0214.html, accessed June 21, 2008.

44. "Comisión Femenil Mexicana Nacional," http://www.fordfound.org/archives/item/0138/text/027, accessed July 8, 2008.

45. Marisela R. Chávez, "Pilgrimage to the Homeland: California Chicanas and International Women's Year, Mexico City, 1975," in *Memories and Migrations: Mapping Boricua and Chicana Histories*, ed. Vicki L. Ruiz and John Chávez (Urbana and Chicago: University of Illinois Press, 2008), 170–195.

46. "Comisión Femenil Mexicana Nacional."

47. Martha P. Cotera, *The Chicana Feminist* (Austin, TX: Information Systems Development, 1976), 9.

5

Unsettling "Third Wave Feminism"

Feminist Waves, Intersectionality, and Identity Politics in Retrospect

LEELA FERNANDES

The body of scholarship associated with "third wave" feminism has had a transformative impact on contemporary feminist intellectual agendas. Such work spans a vast set of writings that have addressed the ways in which multiple forms of inequality have shaped women's subjectivities, lives, and modes of resistance. One of the distinctive features of third wave feminism was the systematic challenge that such work explicitly posed to previous conceptions of feminist thought and practice. In the language of one of the classic texts that marked the emergence of this challenge, *This Bridge Called My Back*,[1] U.S. feminists of color sought both to decenter conceptions of feminism based narrowly on the experience of white, middle-class women and to call attention to inequalities that have historically shaped relationships between women in the United States.[2] The forceful political and intellectual challenges of such writing had far-reaching implications as feminist and women's studies programs sought to redefine intellectual agendas and curricula in order to address systematically and to integrate questions of difference.

Although the call for feminists to address questions of difference such as race, sexuality, and class was not new, the impact and breadth of this new surge of writing and activism by feminists of color led to the characterization of this work as a new wave of feminism that had moved past the exclusions of past (and in particular second wave) feminist approaches. This classification sought to capture the significance and distinctiveness of this new flourishing field within feminist scholarship. However, the application of the conventional form of the historical periodization of feminism as distinctive waves also has inadvertently led to misreadings and misrepresentations of the substantive contributions of emerging paradigms within this scholarship. Dominant narratives of third wave feminism tend to focus on three central paradigms—multicultural inclusion, identity politics, and intersectionality. Although these have certainly been key paradigms within feminist scholarship, third wave feminism represents a more complex and various set of debates and interventions than these paradigms suggest.

This essay seeks to interrogate and move beyond the dominant narratives that currently depict third wave feminism within the field of interdisciplinary women's studies. As Chela Sandoval has argued, the term *third wave* casts this field of knowledge into a teleological historical narrative that misses the ways in which such work has simultaneously occupied intellectual spaces in past feminist intellectual traditions even as it has often argued against or sought to move beyond dominant paradigms within women's studies.[3] Drawing on Sandoval's theory of differential consciousness, the essay interrogates the institutionalization of third wave feminism through narratives of multiculturalism, intersectionality, and identity politics. The essay then moves beyond these dominant narratives and elaborates on both the points of connection between recent third wave feminist theory and other waves of feminist scholarship and the substantive theoretical contributions of third wave feminist theory that have often been rendered invisible by the three-wave approach to multiculturalism, identity, and intersectionality. I engage in this effort through a series of theoretical reflections that draw in part on my own observations of the ways in which third wave feminism is often deployed within and institutionalized by interdisciplinary feminist practices. My arguments are not intended to represent a comprehensive survey of third wave feminist theorists but instead draw on engagements with the intellectual work of various feminist scholars including Gloria Anzaldúa, Sandoval, Patricia Hill Collins, Jacqui Alexander, and Norma Alarcon.

Third Wave Feminism: Narratives of Multiculturalism, Identity Politics, and Intersectionality

The emergence of third wave feminism within the academy is conventionally associated with the trend within women's studies and feminist scholarship to focus on questions of differences, with a particular emphasis on the integration of studies of race, class, and gender within the United States.[4] One of the underlying effects of the three-wave model of feminism is the inadvertent representation of feminist thought as a teleological historical narrative of progressive inclusion. By framing new challenges to the existing terms of feminist thought and practice as a new "wave," such work is defined primarily as a move toward the increasing inclusion of women of color within feminism. In other words, according to this historical narrative, if second wave feminism was the preserve of white, middle-class women, third wave feminism marked a new phase in which feminists of color and questions of race and gender were now included. The feminist wave model thus implicitly rests on a narrative of multicultural inclusion.

Aspects of third wave challenges to the existing feminist terrain certainly included political and intellectual claims for inclusion within institutional and intellectual feminist sites.[5] However, the substantive challenges of these writings also represented a theoretical challenge to narratives of multicultural inclusion. Norma Alarcon, for instance, argued that writings by feminists of color in *This Bridge Called My Back* represented a theoretical challenge to the "logic of identification" that had characterized the subject of feminism as "an autonomous, self-making, self-determining subject."[6] This project called for a rethinking of feminist languages of inclusion that sought to integrate "difference" within existing models of subjectivity. At one level, this challenge sought to create a feminism that did not presume gender as its foundational category or "common denominator."[7] As Alarcon put it, "The female subject of *This Bridge* is highly complex. She is and has been constructed in a crisis of meaning situation which includes racial and cultural divisions and conflicts. The psychic and material violence that gives shape to that subjectivity cannot be underestimated nor passed over lightly. The fact that not all of this violence comes from men in general but also from women renders the notion of 'common denominator' problematic."[8]

Such criticisms have now become well institutionalized as part of a broad series of debates on the category of "woman."[9] However, at a second level, Alarcon's argument points to a deeper challenge, or what Alarcon called "a process of disidentification" with the existing subject of feminism that was inherent in writings characterized as third wave feminism.[10] Although Alarcon does not elaborate at length on the meaning of disidentification, her argument gets at the heart of some of the substantive theoretical challenges of this phase of feminism. Yet it is precisely this politics of disidentification (a point I turn to later in the essay) that has been rendered invisible by the wave model of feminism. Instead, the three-wave model of feminism has largely tended to highlight paradigms that fit within or represent a logical expansion of the narrative of inclusion.

Consider two of the central paradigms that dominate feminist intellectual narratives now associated with third wave feminism—identity politics and intersectionality. In the first case, hegemonic feminist narratives have often sought to depict the impact of third wave feminism through the frame of identity-based claims. At one level, this framing has often shaped attempts at integrating work associated with third wave feminism within existing curricula and feminist research agendas. In this narrative second wave feminism is (erroneously) associated purely with the essentialized figure of "middle-class, white woman." Third wave feminism then becomes an expansion of this subject to include the voices and experiences of women marked by a diverse set of identities. The politics of inclusion rests on the marking of identities that can subsequently be integrated within the subject of feminism. This project of inclusion in effect rests on the logic of identification that Alarcon describes.

Given that the wave model of feminism lends itself to a misclassification of the substantive contributions of this period of feminist thought through the politics of identification, it is perhaps unsurprising that critical responses to third wave feminism have often been founded on this depiction. Thus in both everyday discourses in academic settings and intellectual writings, such critiques have generally rested on dominant narratives of the limits of "identity politics." At one level, this critique tends to cast the challenges of third wave writing in terms of a set of static, discrete identity frames. This tendency is perhaps best captured in Judith Butler's early critique of this serial approach to identity in which she calls attention to "an embarrassed 'etc.'" which concludes the list of identities ("race, class, gender, sexuality etc.") when feminists attempt to address diversity.[11] Butler was pointing to the theoretical limits of multicultural models of identity politics that provide a surface understanding of subjectivity. However, this narrative of identity politics has often been mistakenly used to classify and then criticize third wave feminist writing. The underlying assumption in this conflation of multiculturalism and third wave feminism is that the contributions of U.S. feminists of color is reducible to a series of political-intellectual claims for inclusion within the discursive and institutional sites associated with feminism. In this narrative, the varied intellectual contributions of U.S. feminists of color become reducible to the creation of "women of color" as a singular identity category.[12]

The model of women of color feminism as third wave has thus proved problematic in a number of ways. I have been suggesting that this evolutionary model of feminist progression has served to reinforce an identity-based framing of feminist thought that reproduces hegemonic models of multiculturalism. Feminist thought is presented as a series of expanding identities that need to be included within contemporary feminism. This approach has little to do with the substantive contributions and challenges of writing classified as third wave. However, the impact of this framework is not just a question of rhetoric about identity politics. At a deeper level, the use of feminist waves as an epistemological device has produced gaps in our understandings of feminist scholarship. On the one hand, the discrete periodization of feminist waves has tended to miss both intellectual continuities and discontinuities between work that has been classified within second and third wave feminisms. On the other hand, the idea of feminist waves tends to present an image of homogeneous waves of knowledge that underestimates the differences and divergences among writers located within specific waves. Let us consider this problem further through a central model that is now conventionally identified with third wave feminism—the paradigm of intersectionality.

Intersectionality has become one of the most recognized paradigms associated with third wave feminism. The concept of intersectionality refers to a series of cross-disciplinary interventions that analyzed the ways in which the intersection between inequalities such as race, gender, and class shaped women's lives and structured the social location of specific groups of women of color in distinctive ways. For instance, Kimberlé Crenshaw's groundbreaking work analyzed the relationships among gender, race, and the law in the United States. In one of her seminal essays on violence against women, she analyzed the ways in which both the experiences of such violence and the effects of institutional and political responses were structured in distinctive ways by the intersections of race and gender.[13] Or, to take another example, Evelyn Nakano Glenn's classic essay on the stratification of reproduction illustrated the ways in which systemic historical inequalities of race and gender structured the labor market in ways that tracked specific groups of women of color into paid domestic work in different historical periods.[14]

A defining element of such contributions was the reconceptualization of our understandings of the structural reproduction of inequalities and the move away from unitary understandings of social structure to what Patricia Hill Collins called "interlocking systems." As she argued, "Viewing relations of domination for Black women for any given socio-historical context as being structured via a system of interlocking race, class, and gender oppression expands the focus of analysis from merely describing the similarities and differences distinguishing these systems of oppression and focuses greater attention on how they interconnect. Assuming that each system needs the others in order to function creates a distinct theoretical stance that stimulates the rethinking of basic social science concepts."[15] As these scholars illustrated, conventional understandings of structural inequality as a series of discrete, singular, and homogenized categories failed to capture the unique structural location of women of color in the United States. However, as Collins noted, the need for an analysis of intersecting inequalities was not purely a descriptive project for women of color but a theoretical analysis of the broader "matrix of domination" that has shaped contemporary U.S. society.[16] The paradigm of intersectionality provided a broad theoretical reconceptualization of the systemic nature of domination and inequality in order to redress the erasure of women of color by existing concepts.

Given the focus of these approaches on structural and systemic inequality, the paradigm of intersectionality has proved particularly fruitful in shaping research agendas in the social sciences. The modular nature of the paradigm has allowed social scientists to use it in a range of methodologically diverse empirical studies.[17] Meanwhile, within interdisciplinary feminist writing and teaching, intersectionality has now become the central paradigm associated with third wave feminist scholarship. Although such developments have produced a rich intellectual agenda, the institutionalization of intersectionality also forecloses a richer and broader understanding of the field. Intersectionality has increasingly become the paradigm that both stands in for third wave feminism and signifies a break from second wave feminism. This use of the paradigm overlooks some of the intellectual continuities between second and third wave feminisms. At one level, for instance, Collins's rethinking of systemic inequality drew heavily on standpoint theory even as it challenged and sought to rethink the concept of "standpoint." Or, to take another example, Glenn's work represented a critical engagement with existing strands of materialist feminist research on

labor and pushed that analysis in new directions. At another level, the transformation of intersectionality as a signifier of third wave feminism has led to
homogenized understandings of both intersectionality and third wave feminism.[18] In its institutionalized forms within women's studies curricula and
intellectual agendas in the academy, intersectionality is increasingly becoming a marker of multicultural inclusion in many of the same ways that previous narratives of identity politics were.[19] Intersectionality in this context has
been transformed into a heuristic device that is used to signify a politics of
inclusion.[20] This incorporation of the paradigm has the unintentional effect
of disciplining existing intellectual histories of feminism in ways that produce silences and erasures. Despite the richness of much of the writing on
intersectionality and the growing complexity of research in this field, the
mainstreaming of this paradigm has entrenched the three-wave approach to
contemporary U.S. feminism in ways that marginalize alternative political
and intellectual visions of subjectivity and resistance.

In Between the Waves of Feminism:
Shifting Fields of Consciousness

In *Methodology of the Oppressed*, Chela Sandoval uses a reading of works by
feminists of color to challenge conventional historical accounts of feminist
intellectual history that emerged in the 1980s.[21] Sandoval argues that these
accounts presented the evolution of feminism through four phases of intellectual development—liberal, Marxist, radical/cultural, and socialist feminism. Drawing on a reading of typologies by leading feminist scholars writing
during this period, Sandoval argues that this historical narrative corre-
sponded to four conceptions of feminist consciousness.[22] Liberal feminism
rested on the notion of women's equality with men, Marxist feminism sought
to focus on the primacy of class, and radical/cultural feminism focused on
differences between men and women and the superiority of such feminized
differences. The last phase, socialist feminism, according to Sandoval, sought
to confront racial and class divisions between women. Sandoval argues that
this feminist typology both subsumed critiques by U.S. feminists of color and
erased the specific theoretical alternatives produced by these critiques.

Sandoval argues that writings by feminists of color in the 1970s and
1980s—when second wave feminism occupied a central role among feminists
in the academy—provided the groundwork for an alternative theory and

method of oppositional consciousness. "U.S. Third World Feminism," as Sandoval identifies this approach, represented a distinctive form, the "differential mode of oppositional consciousness."[23]

> I think of this activity of consciousness as the "differential," insofar as it enables movement "between and among" ideological positionings (the equal rights, revolutionary, supremacist, and separatist modes of oppositional consciousness) considered as variables, in order to disclose the distinctions among them. In this sense, the differential mode of consciousness functions like the clutch of an automobile, the mechanism that permits the driver to select, engage, and disengage gears in a system for the transmission of power. The differential represents the variant; its presence emerges out of correlations, intensities, junctures, crises.[24]

According to Sandoval's theory/method, the writings and challenges that feminists of color produced did not represent a simplistic rejection of or progression beyond previous modes of feminist consciousness or practice. Rather these writings produced a distinctive form of consciousness that simultaneously occupied, moved between, and produced new spaces and sites of thought and practice.

Although Sandoval's theoretical formulation does not explicitly address the current three-wave model of feminism, it provides critical insights that can be used to think through and move beyond some of the limits of that model. The idea of third wave feminism took us beyond the four-phase model, which Sandoval criticizes. Third wave feminism is meant to represent the body of thought that Sandoval argues was rendered invisible by previous feminist typologies, which subsumed scholarship on race and ethnicity. In that vein, the delineation of a third wave of feminism has represented an advance over past histories of feminist thought. However, the wave approach to feminism reproduces the underlying epistemological framework of these previous typologies in ways that miss the dynamic movement of differential consciousness that Sandoval presents. What remains unchanged is a teleological approach that divides feminist thought into a series of discrete and progressive stages of evolution.

Consider the ways in which Sandoval's theory/method of differential consciousness enables a rethinking of the concept of intersectionality. Within the wave model of feminism, intersectionality often has the appearance of a somewhat static model of identity. Karen Barad, for instance, has criticized the use of this metaphor, arguing that it reproduces a limited Euclidean geometric imaginary. Thus, Barad argues, "The view of space as container or context for matter in motion—spatial coordinates mapped via projections along axes that set up a metric for tracking the locations of the Inhabitants of the container, and time divided into evenly spaced increments marking a progression of events—pervades much of Western epistemology."[25]

This depiction captures some of the dangers by which dominant narratives now depict intersectionality as a mechanistic tool that stands in for difference and inclusion. However, drawing on an understanding of differential consciousness, intersectionality is a theory that is both located within Western epistemological foundations associated with past waves of feminism (such as standpoint theory and materialist feminism) and a move to represent social locations, subjectivities, and forms of consciousness that cannot be captured by previous conceptions.

From this perspective, intersectionality is neither a static formulation nor a signifier of a homogeneous field of third wave feminism; intersectionality is a method/theory that expresses one aspect of the mode of differential consciousness of which Sandoval speaks. This conceptualization moves us far away from mechanistic formulations that take intersectionality as an all-inclusive paradigm that can then be applied in diverse disciplinary or interdisciplinary fields. This mechanistic approach misses both the rich diversity and the deep political implications of the writings that are now in danger of becoming homogenized by the narrative "third wave feminism as intersectionality." Sandoval's discussion of differential consciousness, for instance, foregrounds the way that the mobile and fluid nature of this form of consciousness stems precisely from the intersectional nature of the social location of women of color. As I noted before, a key focus of this theory has been on the workings of intersectional structures that shape social locations of social groups. The mobility of this form of consciousness is thus tactical because of the complex material/discursive "intersectional" nature of this location. This tactical mobility is not reducible to poststructuralist understandings of the fluidity of identity and difference. This subject simultaneously occupies the contained space of a structured social group even as it moves beyond the limits of these contexts and forms of consciousness.[26] Sandoval's concept of differential consciousness is thus not a rejection or critique of intersectionality; rather the subject of differential consciousness provides us with a broad understanding of the theoretical, political, and historical context of third wave feminism that is not reducible to a singular paradigm such as intersectionality.

Anzaldúa's *Borderlands* and the Disidentified Subject

Consider further how this theory/method of differential consciousness necessitates a break with the three-wave model of feminism. One of the classic works often associated with third wave feminism is Gloria Anzaldúa's *Borderlands*.[27] Anzaldúa's articulation of a "new mestiza" consciousness provides an important example of a text that disrupts the discrete periodization between second and third wave feminism. The new mestiza subject that Anzaldúa creates occupies spaces of opposition associated with second wave feminist conceptions of patriarchy and feminized spaces even as it moves and is transformed into the liminal spaces of the "borderlands" that are the well-known identifiers of her work. Consider Anzaldúa's analysis of the gendering of culture and religion: "Culture is made by those in power—men. Males make the rules and laws; women transmit them. . . . The culture expects women to show greater acceptance of, and commitment to, the value system than men. The culture and the Church insist that women are subservient to males."[28] Anzaldúa presents a critique of the reproduction of patriarchal culture that has long been associated with previous feminist thought. As she further notes, echoing Simone de Beauvoir, "Woman is the stranger, the other. She is man's recognized nightmarish pieces, his Shadow-Beast."[29] Anzaldúa moves in and out of this intellectual/political narrative of woman as a foundational source of otherness throughout the text. Consider, for instance, the remaking of subjectivity that is considered one of the distinctive markers of her work. The liminal identities associated with the borderlands (in-between cultures, U.S.-Mexico territorial borders, racial-ethnic-gender identities, and psychic-material spaces) have meant that Anzaldúa is often classified along with theorists of diaspora and hybridity.[30]

However, Anzaldúa's new mestiza consciousness also rests on the writing of a matrilineal history. The new mestiza subjectivity is inextricably linked to Anzaldúa's reworking of embodiments of a conception of a "divine feminine." She reclaims the goddess Cihuacoatl from early Aztec society, and this figure provides the material-psychic passageway into new mestiza subjectivity. Anzaldúa describes this formation of subjectivity as a complex process that is simultaneously an engagement with a primordial sense of selfhood and bodily knowledge and an engagement with the liminal political-discursive spaces produced by intersecting identities. This "Coatlique state" of transformation is, for Anzaldúa, "the consuming internal whirlwind, the symbol of the underground aspects of the psyche. *Coatlique* is the mountain, the Earth Mother who conceived all celestial beings out of her cavernous womb. Goddess of birth and death, *Coatlique* gives and takes away life; she is the incarnation of cosmic processes."[31] This process of engaging with her inner self (which Anzaldúa also depicts materially as a process that "pulsates in my body")[32] embodies concepts of the self that are clearly at odds with later "third wave" feminist writings, which claim a sharp break with any form of essentialism. One of the discursive effects of the wave model of feminism has been the erasure of such dimensions of Anzaldúa's thought. Scholars writing from a third wave perspective have sought to secularize Anzaldúa's work in order to fit it within conventional narratives that seek to represent third wave feminism purely through concepts such as intersectionality, diaspora, and hybridity. In dominant representations of third wave feminism, Anzaldúa's concept of borderlands is usually invoked and disciplined by such concepts.[33]

Anzaldúa's work in fact exceeds the binary opposition between second and third wave feminism. If Anzaldúa's new mestiza cannot be disciplined by the concept of intersectionality, neither can she be reduced either to previous conceptions that identified patriarchy as the foundational concept of feminism or to essentialist ideas of feminine culture. As Sandoval's theory/method of differential consciousness indicates, the new mestiza tactically occupies and moves between fields that have been territorialized as second wave or intersectional locations. However, the nature of differential consciousness is such that the new mestiza is marked by a process of disidentification from such spaces. Anzaldúa argues:

> But it is not enough to stand on the opposite river bank, shouting questions, challenging patriarchal, white conventions. A counter-stance locks one into a duel of oppressor and oppressed; locked in mortal combat, like the cop and criminal, both are reduced to a common denominator of violence. . . . At some point, on our way to a new consciousness, we will have to leave the opposite bank, the split between the two mortal combatants somehow healed so that we are

on both shores at once, and at once, see through the serpent and eagle eyes. Or perhaps we will decide to disengage from the dominant culture, write it off altogether as a lost cause, and cross the border into a wholly new and separate territory.[34]

Her phrase "separate territory" does not denote a cultural nationalist narrative of separatism. Rather she is speaking of a politics of disidentification that moves beyond conventional oppositional modes of thought that demarcate oppositions such as those between subject and object, male and female, and the psychic/spiritual and rational/material.[35] This disidentified subject occupies the material space defined by intersectional structures of inequality and recognizes the reality of identity categories, yet it moves us far from dominant narratives of identity politics and static understandings of intersectionality. Such a form of subjectivity cannot be contained within homogenized waves of feminism even as it is represents the heart of the distinctive intellectual and political challenges associated with third wave feminism.

Unsettling Epistemologies: Memory, Time, and Knowledge

These reflections on Anzaldúa's work point to the ways in which the wave model of feminism rests on a flawed form of historical periodization. The intellectual and political challenges that provide the foundation for what is now classified as third wave feminism unfolded in and were in effect temporally part of (or at the very least overlapped with) second wave feminism. Leading feminist thinkers such as Anzaldúa, bell hooks, Cherríe Moraga, and Audre Lorde were clearly located within the historical period associated with the second wave. A critical reconsideration of the wave framework of feminism thus asks us to pause and consider some of the deep implications of the conception of time that is now commonly used to periodize the history of feminist thought. I argue that two key issues produce this (mis)framing of feminist history. The first rests on the ways in which this periodization stems from misunderstandings of the substantive contributions of feminists of color that I have been discussing. The second issue stems from links between race and conceptions of temporality.

One of the distinctive features commonly associated with third wave feminism is the challenge to the category of "woman." It is now unremarkable in feminist discussions to speak of differences among women and the varied and complex construction of gender. However, this intellectual shift was marked by the convergence of two distinct (though sometimes overlapping) streams—the thinking of U.S. feminists of color and poststructuralist feminism. The 1980s and 1990s witnessed the growing dominance of poststructuralist challenges to conventional categories and forms of feminist thought. Joan Scott's seminal book on gender as a central category of historical analysis was emblematic of the use of gender to denote the process of historical and cultural construction (as opposed to essentialist understandings of "woman").[36]

The assumption that such critiques occurred in a distinctive temporal phase after the explosion of feminist writings and activism in the 1960s and 1970s stems partly from a misunderstanding and erasure of the writings of U.S. feminists of color during this period of second wave feminism. Many poststructuralist feminists writing in the 1980s and 1990s constructed the previous writings and political claims of feminists of color as lodged within static identity claims. These claims were then depicted as another version of essentialism. For instance, feminist poststructuralist critiques of the use of "experience" as a basis for feminist knowledge were targeted as much at U.S. feminists writing about racism as they were at second wave, middle-class, liberal feminists.[37] The theoretical contributions of these writings (and the complexity of simultaneously making identity-based claims while providing alternative theories of subjectivity) were not recognized by most poststructuralist feminists as an existing theoretical approach to the construction and interrogation of categories such as difference, experience, and identity (rather than simply as an expression of difference).[38] Thus, ironically, the shift from an emphasis on equality, associated with second wave feminism, to an emphasis on differences among women, associated with third wave feminism, was temporally conflated with the rise of the poststructuralist feminist emphasis on difference. This conflation was also unintentionally facilitated by the ways in which new feminist discussions of race and postcoloniality began to draw on poststructuralism as a tool for decentering Eurocentric conceptions of feminism.[39]

The disciplinary impetus to classify discrete waves of feminism in effect ended up drawing boundaries that displaced the substantive interventions of second wave feminists writing about race into a different temporal space. As Becky Thompson has argued, this chronology has suppressed the centrality of both feminist women of color and white antiracism feminism in second wave feminism.[40] This displacement has had two key effects. First, it has produced a construction of second wave feminism as a white, middle-class movement rather than a complex and conflicted social and intellectual movement that struggled with defining the terms of feminism. Second, it has produced a historical narrative that constructed feminists of color as a kind of temporal other. This practice stems from a broad connection between race and the construction of narrative that has permeated epistemological practices in the Western academy. Johannes Fabian, for instance, has argued that the discipline of anthropology was marked by a set of practices in which Western anthropologists constructed the subjects of non-Western cultures as being located within a different temporal space. Drawing on an evolutionary conception of time, this form of narrative thus constructed the Western subject as the marker of progress and development through making the non-Western object the other.[41] The process is intrinsic to the hegemonic form of temporality produced by these disciplinary practices. The wave model of feminism, I suggest, inadvertently engages in a similar kind of process by transforming feminists of color writing within the historical period of the second wave into a subject dislocated from their historical context. The construction of such a narrative ends up removing a sense of dynamism and contestation from the historical periods associated with second and third wave feminism.

This question of time and historical narrative points to the political and intellectual significance of historical memory. In an essay reflecting on her memories of *This Bridge Called My Back*, Alexander writes:

What brings us back to re-membrance is both individual and collective; both intentional and an act of surrender; both remembering desire and remembering *how* it works ([Toni] Morrison, *Beloved*, 20). Daring to recognize each other again and again in a context that seems bent on making strangers of us all. Can we *intentionally* remember, all the time, as a way of never forgetting, all of us, building an archaeology of living memory which has less to do with living in the past, invoking a past, or excising it, and more to do with our relationship to time and its purpose. There is a difference between remember *when*—the nostalgic yearning for some return—and a living memory that enables us to re-member what was contained in *Bridge* and what could not be contained within it or by it.[42]

It is precisely this living memory—which embodies the original insights of works such as *This Bridge Called My Back*—that is lost within a three-wave model of feminism. Alexander's eloquent discussion of the transformative power of memory provides us with a deeper possibility for producing a richer and more transformative narrative than we now have to capture the complexities of feminist intellectual and social history.

What would such a living memory of the histories of U.S. feminism look like? It would potentially be more powerful but also more challenging than the current alternative. In one sense, such a living memory would enable successive generations of feminists to realize that nonlinear understandings of history (breaking from evolutionary conceptions of temporality) in fact necessitate periodic and tactical returns to earlier political/intellectual strategies and visions. This is in effect one of the central implications of Sandoval's method of differential consciousness. A move from the wave model of feminism to a history rooted in living memory is not simply a symbolic strategy for honoring the contributions of previous generations of feminists. Rather it is a question of remembering that successive generations of feminism can never move beyond past histories through a simplistic attempt at creating a clear temporal break from the past.

Consider the example of *This Bridge We Call Home*, a text published both as a commemoration of and a continuation of the intellectual work of *This Bridge Called My Back*.[43] The volume provides an important example of Alexander's discussion of an alternative approach to memory and history. *This Bridge We Call Home* presents both substantive continuities and critical engagements with the first *Bridge*. Like the first *Bridge*, the volume presents a series of essays that speak to the persistence of discrimination—in particular, forms of racism and homophobia—both within contemporary society and as persistent elements within feminist spaces. Yet several of the contributors also speak to some of the discrepancies with the first book. AnaLouise Keating, co-editor of the volume, introduces the collection with a cautionary note, "If you've opened this book expecting to find a carbon copy of *This Bridge Called My Back*, don't bother. Stop now."[44] In contrast to the first *Bridge*, this volume includes contributions by both men and white women (a decision that, Keating writes, produced some significant criticism as a violation of the spirit of the first *Bridge*). This question of inclusion reflects a critique of identity in the volume as several of the contributors provide critical theoretical and substantive alternatives to concepts such as "identity" and "authenticity."[45] Taken together the two *Bridges* provide a rich illustration of an alternative to the history of feminism understood as a series of discrete waves. The second *Bridge* embodies the continued intellectual and political relevance of the first volume even as it produces new visions for social change. Helen Shulman Lorenz calls this a theory of "reframing and restoration," which was embedded in *This Bridge Called My Back.*[46] Such an approach, Lorenz argues, both continually ruptures naturalized borders and inclusions and looks for restoration in the resources of prior histories—"with one foot in older discourses and another at a growing opening edge."[47]

This alternative to a teleological approach to feminist waves requires a challenge to some of the dominant models of interdisciplinary feminist scholarship that have become mainstreamed within the academy. Such models are implicitly defined by ideologies of newness that presuppose that intellectual innovation rests on critical ruptures from past ways of knowing. This ideology is not unique to feminist scholarship as the commercial organization of intellectual life commodifies knowledge so that the substantive nature of intellectual contributions is increasingly measured by the newness (and therefore the marketability) of the product. However, within interdisciplinary fields such as feminist scholarship this ideology of newness has been accentuated by the teleological conception of time embodied in postmodernist approaches. The suffix *post* in itself suggests the moving beyond and past older forms of thought (somewhat paradoxically as postmodernist thought has itself interrogated teleological approaches to history). The result is a strong impetus within interdisciplinary feminist scholarship to emphasize the creation of concepts or linguistic expressions that can capture this sense of newness and rupture. What is lost in such an approach is both that sense of living memory that Alexander describes and an understanding of the historical continuities and resources that are vital for feminism and feminist thought.[48]

Conclusion

The three-wave model of feminism has in many ways shortchanged our understandings of the substantive contributions of scholarly writings classified as "third wave feminism." The static nature of this model has leant itself to a reduction of the rich and varied contributions of this work through modular and reductive representations of paradigms such as intersectionality and identity politics. In this discussion I have drawn on a number of scholars who in practice bridge and simultaneously occupy feminist locations associated with second, third, and fourth wave feminism. The method of oppositional consciousness that Sandoval delineates speaks precisely to this form of simultaneity. The movement between these temporal/political spaces of feminist thought represents the spirit of much of this writing. As third wave feminist writings become mainstreamed through these singular devices, deep understandings of time, politics, and subjectivity risk being written out of history. The movement inherent in the conceptions of temporality and memory contained in the writings discussed here exceed the metaphor of a series of waves crashing onto land and then receding. Feminist thought, in retrospect, requires a conception of history that can contain both the insights of the past and the potential breakthroughs of the future within the messy, unresolved contestations of political and intellectual practice in the present.

NOTES

1. Cherríe Moraga and Gloria Anzaldúa, eds., *This Bridge Called My Back: Writings by Radical Women of Color* (New York: Kitchen Table, Women of Color Press, 1984).

2. See, for example, Evelyn Nakano Glenn, "From Servitude to Service Work: Historical Continuities in the Racial Division of Paid Reproductive Work," *Signs* 18, no. 1 (1992): 1–43.

3. Chela Sandoval, *Methodology of the Oppressed* (Minneapolis: University of Minnesota Press, 2000).

4. Third wave feminism also has included work on international issues; early seminal interventions by scholars such as Chandra Mohanty and M. Jacqui Alexander explicitly connected such questions to U.S.-based debates on race and gender. See, for example, Chandra Talpade Mohanty, "Under Western Eyes: Feminist Scholarship and Colonial Discourses," in *Third World Women and the Politics of Feminism*, ed. Chandra Talpade Mohanty, Ann Russo, and Lourdes Torres (Bloomington: Indiana University Press, 1991), and M. Jacqui Alexander, "Not Just Any(Body) Can Be a Citizen: The Politics of Law, Sexuality and Postcoloniality in Trinidad and Tobago and the Bahamas," *Feminist Review* 48 (Autumn 1994): 5–23. Given the focus of this volume on U.S. feminism and constraints of space, I will not address such scholarship on Third World feminism and transnationalism in depth. There are also differing conceptions of what work is considered third wave. See, for example, Leandra Zarnow, ch. 12, this volume.

5. See, for example, Barbara Smith, "Racism and Women's Studies," and Maxine Baca Zinn, Lynn Weber Cannon, Elizabeth Higginbotham, and Bonnie Thornton Dill, "The Costs of Exclusionary Practices in Women's Studies," both in *Making Face,*

Making Soul: Haciendo Caras: Creative and Critical Perspectives by Feminists of Color, ed. Gloria Anzaldúa (San Francisco: Aunt Lute Books, 1990).

6. Norma Alarcon, "The Theoretical Subject of *This Bridge Called My Back* and Anglo-American Feminism," in *Making Face, Making Soul: Haciendo Caras: Creative and Critical Perspectives by Feminists of Color,* ed. Gloria Anzaldúa (San Francisco: Aunt Lute Books, 1990), 357.

7. Ibid., 359.

8. Ibid.

9. These challenges to the category of woman were not limited to feminists of color but also included poststructuralist critiques of essentialism and queer-theorist critiques of heteronormative constructions of gender. See, for example, Judith Butler's now classic *Gender Trouble: Feminism and the Subversion of Identity* (New York: Routledge, 1990).

10. Alarcon, "The Theoretical Subject," 366.

11. Butler, *Gender Trouble*, 143.

12. This characterization has led to a feminist variant of the backlash against identity politics in the U.S. academy that periodically resurfaces in the everyday practices and discourses of universities. My point is not that there are no streams of thought in third wave feminism that focus on identity-based claims but that that is only one aspect of a much more diverse intellectual field.

13. Kimberlé Crenshaw, "Mapping the Margins: Intersectionality, Identity Politics, and Violence against Women of Color," *Stanford Law Review* 43, no. 6 (1991): 1241–1299.

14. Glenn, "From Servitude to Service Work." See also Evelyn Nakano Glenn, "Racial Ethnic Women's Labor: The Intersection of Race, Gender and Class Oppression," *Review of Radical Political Economy* 18, no. 1 (1985): 1–43, and Evelyn Nakano Glenn, *Unequal Freedom* (Cambridge, MA: Harvard University Press, 2002).

15. Patricia Hill Collins, *Black Feminist Thought: Knowledge, Consciousness, and the Politics of Empowerment* (New York: Routledge, 1990), 222.

16. Ibid.

17. See Leslie McCall, "The Complexity of Intersectionality," *Signs* 30, no. 3 (2005): 1771–1800.

18. Most recently, the 2008 Democratic primary election provided the terrain for this distorted wave model of feminism. In an online article Linda Hirshman presented women's support for Barack Obama over Hillary Clinton as an effect of a generational shift toward a focus on intersectionality rather than gender. Hirshman reproduces the teleological approach to feminism, where she conflates differences between second and third wave feminism with a generational shift from gender to intersectional analyses (conflating third wave feminism with intersectionality). In this endeavor she essentializes and misrepresents both second and third wave feminism, implicitly coding second wave feminism as a gender-based struggle for issues raised by middle-class, white women and third wave feminism

as shifting feminism away from women's issues. Linda Hirshman, "Looking to the Future: Feminism Has to Focus," Washingtonpost.com, June 8, 2008, B01.

19. In this discussion I am distinguishing between the substantive contributions of writers associated with the paradigm and the dominant intellectual discourses and institutional sites in which the paradigm has become institutionalized. On the need to retain a focus on intersectionality, see Avtar Brah and Ann Phoenix, "Ain't I a Woman? Revisiting Intersectionality," *Journal of International Women's Studies* 5, no. 3 (2004): 75–86.

20. For instance, in my own discipline, political science, intersectionality has just now emerged as a central paradigm of interest. Yet the paradigm as it is debated and deployed is usually decontextualized from the richer and more varied field of third wave feminist writing. The result is a mainstreaming of the paradigm in ways that have produced important research agendas but also silences and erasures as the paradigm has been "disciplined" to meet the dominant norms of political science. See Patricia Hill Collins, *Fighting Words: Black Women and the Search for Justice* (Minneapolis: University of Minnesota Press, 1998), for a discussion of some of the dangers in the ways in which the concept of intersectionality has been misappropriated.

21. Sandoval, *Methodology of the Oppressed*, 43. Note that Sandoval uses the term *U.S. Third World Feminism* rather than *third wave feminism* in her classification of the writings by feminists of color that emerged in the 1970s and 1980s.

22. Sandoval argues that this historical narrative was shared by a diverse group of scholars including Julia Kristeva, Toril Moi, Hester Eisenstein, and Allison Jaggar. Ibid., 47.

23. Ibid., 54.

24. Ibid., 57. Note that the phrase "the equal rights, revolutionary, supremacist, and separatist modes of oppositional consciousness" is Sandoval's classification of paradigms inherent within the four phases of liberal, Marxist, radical/cultural, and socialist feminism.

25. Karen Barad, *Meeting the Universe Halfway: Quantum Physics and the Entanglement of Matter and Meaning* (Durham, NC: Duke University Press, 2007), 223. Barad's critique of intersectionality is fully elaborated in "Re(con)figuring Space, Time, and Matter," in *Feminist Locations: Global and Local, Theory and Practice*, ed. Marianne DeKoven (New Brunswick, NJ: Rutgers University Press, 2001), 75–109.

26. For an interesting contemporary example of similar new forms of consciousness and practice that unsettle the wave chronology, see Whitney Peoples's discussion of hip-hop feminism in ch. 17, this volume.

27. Gloria Anzaldúa, *Borderlands: The New Mestiza* (San Francisco: Aunt Lute Books, 1987).

28. Ibid., 16.

29. Ibid., 17.

30. See Brah and Phoenix, "Ain't I a Woman?"

31. Anzaldúa, *Borderlands*, 46.

32. Ibid., 51.

33. On this point, see AnaLouise Keating, *Entre Mundos / Among Worlds: New Perspectives on Gloria Anzaldúa* (New York: Palgrave Macmillan, 2005).

34. Anzaldúa, *Borderlands*, 78.

35. I elaborate on the question of disidentification at length in Leela Fernandes, *Transforming Feminist Practice: Non-violence, Social Justice and the Politics of a Spiritualized Feminism* (San Francisco: Aunt Lute Books, 2003).

36. Joan W. Scott, *Gender and the Politics of History* (New York: Columbia University Press, 1988).

37. See, for example, Joan W. Scott's well known essay "Experience" in *Feminists Theorize the Political*, ed. Judith Butler and Joan W. Scott (New York: Routledge, 1992), 22–40.

38. Such theories by feminists of color either were not viewed as theoretically relevant or were used as empirical, embodied references. Thus, for example, Haraway's "A Theory of Cyborgs" did draw on Anzaldúa's conception of hybridity as an example of cyborg identity but did not include an extensive theoretical discussion of Anzaldúa's work on identity and experience; Donna Haraway, "A Manifesto for Cyborgs: Science, Technology and Socialist Feminism in the 1980s," in *Feminism/Postmodernism*, ed. Linda Nicholson (New York: Routledge, 1990).

39. Classic theorists writing at the time from different perspectives but drawing on critical engagements with poststructuralist theory include Gayatri Spivak and Mohanty. Scholars such as Sandoval and Alarcon, writing about race and gender within the United States, have also drawn on and critically engaged with poststructuralist theory.

40. Becky Thompson, "Multicultural Feminism: Recasting the Chronology of Second Wave Feminism," *Feminist Studies* 28, no. 2 (Summer 2002): 337–360; ch. 2, this volume.

41. Johannes Fabian, *Time and the Other: How Anthropology Makes Its Object* (New York: Columbia University Press, 1983).

42. M. Jacqui Alexander, "Remembering This Bridge, Remembering Ourselves: Yearning, Memory and Desire," in *This Bridge We Call Home: Radical Visions for Transformation*, ed. Gloria Anzaldúa and AnaLouise Keating (New York: Routledge, 2002), 96.

43. Ibid.

44. AnaLouise Keating, "Charting Pathways, Marking Thresholds . . . A Warning, an Introduction," in *This Bridge We Call Home: Radical Visions for Transformation*, ed. Gloria Anzaldúa and AnaLouise Keating (New York: Routledge, 2002), 17.

45. See, for example, AnaLouise Keating, "Forging El Mundo Zurdo: Changing Ourselves, Changing the World," 519–529, and Sarah Cervenak, Karina Cespedes, Caridad Souza, and Andrea Straub, "Imagining Differently: The Politics of Listening in a Feminist Classroom," 341–356, both in *This Bridge We Call Home: Radical Visions for Transformation*, ed. Gloria Anzaldúa and AnaLouise Keating (New York: Routledge, 2002).

46. Helen Shulman Lorenz, "Thawing Hearts, Opening a Path in the Woods, Founding a New Lineage," in AnaLouise Keating, *Entre Mundos / Among Worlds: New Perspectives on Gloria Anzaldúa* (New York: Palgrave Macmillan, 2005), 497.

47. Ibid., 503.

48. Thus, in the wave model that persists, it is now a common assumption that we can move past third wave feminism and thus no longer need to address issues such as racial exclusion. The issue of racism is thus increasingly viewed in women's studies as dated, as an issue characteristic of third wave feminism. The "postracial" assumptions are a somewhat ironic reflection of the "postfeminist" rhetoric in public discourses.

PART TWO

Coming Together/
Pulling Apart

6

Overthrowing the "Monopoly of the Pulpit"

Race and the Rights of Church Women in the Nineteenth-Century United States

MARTHA S. JONES

Waves have long served as an evocative metaphor for the history of women's movements in the United States. This notion brings to mind a vivid image of the sea cresting and then crashing to the shore. As this volume's title suggests, little is permanent about waves. On closer scrutiny, what appears to be synchronized choreography is actually a momentary coming together. At the water's edge, currents are as likely to pull us under as to carry us along. Still, the metaphor of waves is apt. The history of women in the United States and of their strivings for rights has crested and crashed. At rare moments it has appeared to be a seamless surfer's curl, tempting us to imagine an endless ride toward sisterhood. More often it has been a history of cross-currents, clashing, churning, and cutting to produce sea foam and spray. Few women in U.S. history have managed to remain completely dry.

In the nineteenth-century United States, church women were among those standing at the water's edge. Some dove into battles over women's religious authority. Others found themselves unavoidably dampened by the spray of the debates. Still others did a sort of back step so as to avoid the advancing surf. There were many such beaches on which women gathered—Quaker, Methodist, Congregationalist, Universalist, Baptist, and Presbyterian. Often race further delineated this metaphorical space, with black and white women assembled at separate waterfronts. Still, they often navigated shared seas, including debates over the right to be licensed to preach, to vote and hold office in church assemblies, to control fund-raising societies, and to be ordained as ministers. This essay explores two sets of such gathering places—African American church conferences and woman's rights conventions—and the debates over church women's rights generated there. In these settings women shared a common ground born of a critique that religious institutions reserved formal authority largely for men. But social distance left women to work in separate circles of interest. Many currents flowed through debates over rights of church women in the nineteenth-century. It is often difficult to discern, however, whether these currents produced a wave.

Benjamin Tanner, a minister and editor of the *Christian Recorder*, well knew how to generate waves. His purpose appeared to be just that when, in 1874, Tanner inquired about the prospects of the "woman movement" in the African Methodist Episcopal (AME) Church. His apt phrasing pointed to the complex cross-currents of nineteenth-century women's rights, of which church women's missionary work was one part.[1] Tanner noted the efforts of his denomination's recently founded Female Mite Missionary Society and queried whether women would be adept at raising support for "laborers in Haiti and Africa." He chided female church activists working through the newly constituted, women-led society to "prove" their abilities in a tone that was easy and optimistic. After all, women had been raising much of the money for the denomination for more than half a century. Intriguing was Tanner's characterization of these efforts as a "woman movement." It was true that this female-headed religious society was more than a revenue-generating scheme for the church. Although the women's immediate challenge was that of raising funds, their missionary society was also a proving ground in the broad campaign for church women's rights. And although the primary interest in the women's missionary work was in black Methodist circles, their accomplishments resonated with other of the era's movements for the rights of women.

Tanner continued, further complicating the notion of a church-based woman movement. The fundraising work of white women might serve as a model for the AME Church's female activists, he suggested. Tanner related how women in white-led Methodist, Baptist, and Presbyterian churches had raised tens of thousands of dollars in missionary funds to further the "spread of Christianity." Would not the women of the AME Church "determine that what others have done, they may, and can, and will do," he asked?[2] Implicit were provocative questions: Should the work of white women serve as a touchstone or frame of reference for black church women? Were AME women's struggles for rights tied to the rights white women also sought? Race constructed a social distance between black and white Protestant women that was broad and often insurmountable. They generally claimed membership in separate denominations, worshipped in separate sanctuaries, and raised funds in separate missionary societies. But race never wholly disrupted the exchange of ideas. Nor did it obscure the gaze of watchful eyes. Black and white church women were aware of one another's activism and often operated, at least in part, by way of shared critiques. In Tanner's formulation there were multiple, overlapping church women's movements at work in the post–Civil War United States: that of "our [AME] church" and that of the "grand movement . . . for the spread of Christianity," which encompassed Baptists, Methodists, and Presbyterians of all colors. To invoke a church women's movement in 1874 was to call up a complex array of ideas and types of activism that both reified and transcended the social distance produced through race and religion.

This essay explores the dynamics of church, women's rights, and race that animated Tanner's commentary by focusing on two key chapters in the history of women's rights in the nineteenth century. The first is the end of the 1840s, a moment frequently associated with the inaugural women's conventions held in Seneca Falls and Rochester, New York. This essay reframes those conventions by examining a contemporaneous campaign for church women's rights being waged in black Methodist churches. The second is the 1870s, a period often understood as shaped by disagreements over the terms of the Fifteenth Amendment and a resulting rupture of an antebellum woman's rights–abolitionist coalition. Here, this moment is recast through consideration of how African American church women injected the question of women's rights into debates over black Methodist law and polity in the wake of the Amendment's ratification. In both cases, black and white women generally worked apart from one another, with lines of denomination and of race dividing their movements. They did share, however, a critical vantage point that centered on churches as contested terrain and church women as among the activists in a women's movement. There is little question that these activist women were mindful of one another, even as social distance led to diluted or distorted understandings. All these women were covered in the spray of women's rights. Standing at separate places along the seashore, they waded into confrontations that gave their discrete campaigns broadreaching significance. Whether all women who called for the rights of church women were part of one wave is difficult to say until we recall that any wave is the by-product of many cross-currents.

Church Women's Rights in 1848

By the spring of 1848, black Methodist church women were well into a campaign for rights. Their forum was the denomination's quadrennial General
Conference, a national gathering of the church's ministerial and lay leadership. Their objective was to secure a change in church law such that women
would be granted licenses to preach in the denomination's pulpits. It was a
long-standing campaign. Female preachers had achieved noteworthy success
in converting new church members since the late eighteenth century.[3] Such
women had labored for the church without formal approval or privilege,
with their ability to occupy public venues subject to the capriciousness of
male ministers. It was not until the 1830s that a small number of women
began to seek formal approval for their work in black Methodist churches.
Individual applications for permission to preach were at some moments
sidestepped and at others silently denied by male leaders.[4] If church women
were to achieve formal standing and authority in their denominations, more
sophisticated tactics than individual appeals for approval appeared to be
called for. When the major church conferences of the 1840s convened,
women were armed with a two-pronged strategy. They enlisted male allies
with access to conference podiums, thus overcoming their exclusion from
tightly regulated church deliberations. At the same time, church women
reframed their petitions as collective demands, demonstrating that female
preachers were supported by a visible and organized constituency that
endorsed their right to preach.

By the time of the General Conference of 1844, this strategy was in place.
The Reverend Nathan Ward, a missionary delegate and founding member of
the church's Indiana Conference, had been recruited to act as spokesperson
for the women.[5] Confronting the sixty-eight ministerial delegates in attendance, Ward spoke on behalf of forty "others," all signatories to a petition.
His proposal called for the amendment of church law to permit the licensing
of female preachers. Julia Foote, who had been refused a preaching license a
few years before, described the controversy that Ward's petition engendered:
"This caused quite a sensation, bringing many members to their feet at once.
They all talked and screamed to the bishop, who could scarcely keep order.
The Conference was so incensed at the brother who offered the petition that
they threatened to take action against him."[6] The women's petition ultimately met with defeat. But women's isolated requests for exceptions to

church law had grown into a collective campaign that sought rights for all church women.

By the spring of 1848, a call for the rights of church women was both an anticipated and an unwelcome event at the year's AME General Conference. Female activists, organized as the Daughters of Zion, resurrected the 1844 proposal, again demanding the licensing of women to preach. They confronted an imposing gathering of 175 ministers and 375 male lay leaders from fourteen states and competed for a place on an ambitious "official agenda" that included the election of a second bishop, the structure of the church missionary society, the establishment of a book depository, a plan for common schools, and sanctions for divorce and remarriage.[7] To overcome their exclusion from the proceedings, female activists turned to Dr. J. J. Gould Bias of Philadelphia, who agreed to place their petition on the conference agenda. Bias was an apt ally. His commitment to women's equality in antislavery politics had been proven by way of his work as a Garrisonian abolitionist activist and member of the American Moral Reform Society in the 1830s.[8] Bias's words on the subject of church women's rights have not survived, but the "dissenting report" that followed gives a sense of how they provoked a debate about gender and power in the church.

A shrewdly crafted argument defeated the women's petition.[9] Speaking against the licensing of female preachers, Daniel Payne, a Baltimore-based minister and later the denomination's senior bishop, deployed a complex construction of black womanhood in his effort to defeat the Daughters of Zion.[10] Payne argued that female preaching ran counter to ideals of respectability and domesticity. The licensing of female preachers was "calculated to break up the sacred relations which women bear to their husbands and children," he warned. It would lead to the "utter neglect of their household duties and obligations."[11] This view incorporated well-understood arguments made by antislavery and temperance advocates of the period. Like slavery, women's rights threatened the sanctity of African American family life. And, just as the consumption of alcohol led men to neglect their families, so too would women become irresponsible if they bore the burdens that being licensed to preach imposed. Payne's reasoning likely appeared flawed to the Daughters of Zion. They had long managed whatever tensions existed between their public responsibilities and their domestic obligations. Yet Payne understood that in 1848 defeating a demand for church women's rights required the mobilization of heavy ideological artillery.

The following summer's western New York women's conventions at Seneca Falls and Rochester attracted the attention of many black Methodists. Among the participants were some of abolitionism's most admired activists, including Frederick Douglass. The women's meetings received coverage in the African American and the antislavery press, as well as in newspapers nationwide.[12] Because these conventions occurred just months after their latest debate over the rights of church women, black Methodists may have made particular note of how the issues were situated within the proceedings. Indeed, the nascent, nominally secular, and largely white women's movement gave considered attention to the very issues that had been debated in the AME Church for much of the preceding decade. At Seneca Falls and Rochester, a woman's right to preach was set forth as one dimension of church women's rights and was further incorporated into a broad spectrum of entitlements that extended from churches into the realms of law and politics.

The proceedings of the women's conventions are perhaps best remembered for their sheer ambition—the rights called for encompassed a wide range of women's interests, most remarkably the largely unprecedented demand for women's political enfranchisement. But activists at Seneca Falls and Rochester espoused rights that dovetailed with the ambitions of AME women. The Seneca Falls Declaration of Sentiments criticized the sort of thinking that deprived women of preaching licenses: "He allows her in Church, as well as State, but in a subordinate position, claiming Apostolic authority for her exclusion from the ministry, and, with some exceptions, from any public participation in the affairs of the Church."[13] That meeting's final resolutions included two demands that endorsed the right to preach from the pulpit: "*Resolved*, . . . it is pre-eminently his duty to encourage her to speak and teach, as she has an opportunity, in all religious assemblies," and "*Resolved*, That the speedy success of our cause depends upon the zealous and untiring efforts of both men and women, for the overthrow of the monopoly of the pulpit."[14]

When the matter of church women's rights arose weeks later in Rochester, a debate erupted. The men present are recorded as having split over the question, with some advocating the emancipation of women from "all the artificial disabilities, imposed by false customs, creeds, and codes," and others arguing that "woman's sphere was home[,] . . . seriously deprecat[ing] her occupying the pulpit."[15] Lucretia Mott, the Philadelphia-based Quaker and antislavery activist, is remembered for having spoken forcefully on this point. Mott was not surprised to find some men opposed to church woman's rights. Education had indoctrinated them in this view. Still, she rejected clerical authority and turned directly to the Bible. Mott explained that the text included "none of the prohibitions in regard to women" promoted by clerical leaders and challenged those who opposed women's preaching to point out "anything there to prohibit woman from being a religious teacher."[16] The result was that among Rochester's final resolutions were calls for women's equality and authority in churches. The delegates objected to "restricting her to an inferior position in social, religious, and political life" and insisted instead "that it is the duty of woman, whatever her complexion, to assume, as soon as possible, her true position of equality in the social circle, the church, and the state."[17] Religious life and churches were expressly cast as sites of power and contestation in these early women's meetings, a point of view that was mirrored in the era's contests within black Methodist circles.

The obvious touchstone for claims of church women's rights at Seneca Falls and Rochester was the era's challenges of gender and religious authority within the Society of Friends. Quaker activists had provided leadership and intellectual force for the earliest women's conventions. There is no evidence of direct black Methodist influence on the proceedings.[18] Still, the wording of one of the Rochester resolutions is intriguing: "It is the duty of woman, whatever her *complexion*, to assume . . . her true position of equality in the social circle, the church, and the state" [emphasis added]. Was the resolution's reference to women of all complexions a phrasing intended to encompass black as well as white church women? Perhaps. In common usage the term *complexion* referred to the color or appearance of the skin; it was frequently used in antislavery circles to refer to differences in skin color and, by inference, race. But in mid-nineteenth-century usage the term might refer generally to an individual's quality, character, condition, or "style of mind."[19] In this sense, the phrase *whatever her complexion* might have signaled that the women's convention intended to speak on behalf of women across religious denominations or political-party affiliations. Or perhaps these were not mutually exclusive uses of the term. The ambitions of Seneca Falls and Rochester allowed room for ideals that extended across fissures of race, religion, and politics.

In 1848, black and white women were thinking along similar lines. Churches had become a battleground for rights claims that demanded women's formal authority in religious bodies. But can we say that the petitions of AME women and the declarations of western New York women's rights activists were of one current in the history of nineteenth-century women's rights?[20] Such connections are difficult to discern. There is no hint that white women were in attendance at the year's AME General Conference. Had they read the related press reports they would have found only summary notices that did not report on the Daughters of Zion petition.[21] Nor were black women reported to have participated in the Seneca Falls and Rochester women's meetings, although historians have suggested that they were likely in attendance as spectators.[22] We can glimpse, however, some of the avenues by which the ideas and experiences of these two communities of female activists may have been exchanged. AME women read news of the Seneca Falls and Rochester proceedings in the African American and antislavery press.[23] Participants in the Seneca Falls and Rochester meetings brought news of those proceedings, as well as women's rights ideas, into African American political circles. Such was the case at the fall 1848 meeting of the National Convention of Colored Freedmen in Cleveland. There, when Douglass demanded that women take "equal" part in the proceedings, he was endorsed by a white woman, Rebecca Sanford, who had herself just come from taking part in the Rochester women's convention.[24]

Antislavery gatherings provided similar opportunities. Later in the fall of 1848, Bias, spokesperson for the Daughters of Zion, and Mott, participant in the women's conventions at Seneca Falls and Rochester, came together in their shared home city, Philadelphia. The occasion was an African American antislavery meeting. It was a remarkable gathering according to Mott. She later wrote to Elizabeth Cady Stanton: "We are now in the midst of a Convention of the Colored people . . . all taking an active part—and as they include women—& white women too, I can do no less . . . than be present & take a little part." For Mott, the significance of the meeting was the ambitious vision of its black leadership, one that embraced "the cause of the slave, as well as of women."[25] Here, black Methodist activists collaborated with women's rights organizers.[26] Such gatherings emerged as likely sites in which cross-race and cross-denomination discussions of church women's rights might arise. By contrast, religious culture was highly fractured by the mid-1840s. U.S. Protestant churches had been remade, first, between 1790 and 1820 by the exodus of black congregants who objected to second-class standing in white-led denominations.[27] These dissenters had gone on to found denominations such as the AME Church. The mid-1840s witnessed a second rupture when American Baptists and Methodists split into northern and southern churches over the question of slavery and slaveholding.[28] By the late 1840s, to the extent that black and white women evidenced a similar commitment to the expansion and equality of church women's authority, they did so largely in separate spaces. They sometimes glimpsed one another in antislavery circles, but their distinct currents do not appear to have come together to form a wave or singular movement for church women's rights.

Movements for Church Women's Rights in the 1870s

In the years following the 1870 ratification of the Fifteenth Amendment, the matter of church women's rights resurfaced. In African American Methodist circles after the Civil War, the campaign for church women's rights gained new momentum. By the early 1880s numerous victories had been won. Women began voting and holding office in decision-making bodies, serving as officers of home and foreign missionary societies, overseeing local church governance as stewardesses, and spreading the gospel as duly licensed preachers. These innovations resulted from shifting views about women's rights in the church. In practice, they transformed women's relationships to the rituals, deliberations, and administration of religious bodies.

The campaign was jump-started with demands for the revision of church law, the *Doctrines and Discipline*. Access to preaching licenses remained a prime objective, but postwar church women went further, insisting that all formal distinctions between the roles of men and women be eliminated. Some successes came quickly and easily. For example, in 1872, the AME Church deleted "the word 'male' wherever it occurs as a qualification of electors," and thus church women earned the right to vote.[29] Four years later, gender qualifications were struck from all provisions related to Sunday School personnel.[30] One group of female petitioners explained their proposal in explicitly political terms, noting that their aim was "giving women the same rights in the church as men."[31] Women's missionary societies were formalized in the mid-1870s. But their structure reflected ambivalences about church women's power. These bodies, which Tanner termed part of the "woman movement" of the AME Church, remained subject to male oversight.[32] In some cases, members were selected from among those women who were perceived to be most loyal to the male leadership, the "wives and daughters of our bishops and elders, and other influential ladies of our churches." In other instances male church leaders reserved final say over missionary affairs by way of governing boards that included male ministers.[33] Still, as missionary-society officers, women for the first time served as elected delegates, spoke from the podium, and presided over church conferences. They could conduct fundraising and relief work pursuant to a constitution and bylaws rather than at the discretion of male leaders. Equipped with new tools, church women stood fast, armed with changes in law that established their rights. They did not yet possess "the same rights in the church as men." Still church women used the new laws to assert decision-making authority.

Women's rights activists also reconvened in the mid-1860s under the umbrella of the Equal Rights Association. There, debates over the right to vote—who should enjoy it and under what terms—soon pitted the interests of black men against those of white women. Factions emerged over how such a goal should be realized. One view is captured by Wendell Phillips's declaration that "this hour belongs to the Negro."[34] This remark signaled acquiescence to the perceived limits of the Reconstruction era's gendered political order, in which only men would exercise formal authority. Stanton gave voice to a competing view when she decried the possibility that white women could be made into the political inferiors of black men who were "unwashed" and "fresh from the slave plantations of the South."[35] The bitterness and divisions that were produced by this debate fractured the women's rights movement going forward. Following the adoption of the Fifteenth Amendment, activists turned to one of the two resulting organizations: the American Woman Suffrage Association and the National Woman Suffrage Association.[36] As the decade proceeded, these women's organizations worked across a terrain that had been simultaneously expanded and fractured by Civil War and Reconstruction politics. Still, both offered endorsements of church women's claims to religious authority.

The campaign for women's suffrage mingled with calls for the rights of church women in the American Woman Suffrage Association (AWSA) through the affiliations of its leaders. The 1870s witnessed the elevation of prominent Protestant clergymen to leadership within the women's movement, a development that tightened the nexus between analyses of women's rights in law and politics and their rights in churches. For example, Boston's Gilbert Haven served both as president of the AWSA and as bishop of the Methodist Episcopal Church (North).[37] Haven gave voice to a multifaceted rights agenda that included women's political suffrage and the rights of female preachers. His introduction to the 1872 biography of Methodist evangelist Maggie Newton Van Cott, *Life and Labors of Mrs. Maggie Newton Van Cott*, reads much like a manifesto on the rights of female preachers. Haven took the occasion to skillfully dismantle those Bible-based arguments that were being wielded against both female preachers and women's suffrage.[38] Henry Ward Beecher also linked the AWSA to church women's rights. Both a leading Congregationalist minister and the first president of the AWSA, Beecher had been associated with radical causes since his years as an abolitionist preacher.[39] Beecher used his overall notoriety and his Brooklyn-based sanctuary, Plymouth Church, to draw attention to the effectiveness of preaching women. He praised their skills, spoke of their presence as an exercise of rights, and helped elevate many of the era's preaching women to national prominence. Like Haven, Beecher challenged the view that the Bible barred women from the pulpit. He further underscored the link between the secular and the sacred rights of women by sharing platforms with women's rights leaders.[40]

Among activists affiliated with the National Woman Suffrage Association (NWSA), church women's rights assumed a place alongside rights and politics by way of declarations and resolutions. One such example comes out of the NWSA's 1874 national convention. Among matters taken up that year were the terms of the Civil Rights Act pending before Congress. Some among the NWSA's membership strongly lamented what they saw as the enhancement of black men's civil rights in the face of Congress's continued neglect of women's rights of any sort. Thus, while urging the adoption of a civil rights bill in Congress, the NWSA penned its own civil rights agenda for women. The result was a document that awkwardly set women's rights and the rights of African American men against one another. The convention called on Congress to adopt "a civil rights bill for [women's] protection . . . that shall secure to them equally with colored men all the advantages and opportunities of life." The terms of its fifth resolution spoke directly to the question of church women's rights, urging that women be "admitted to all theological seminaries on equal terms with colored men; to be recognized in all religious organizations as bishops, elders, priests, deacons; to officiate at the altar and preach in the pulpits of all churches, orthodox or heterodox; and that all religious sects shall be compelled to bring their creeds and biblical interpretations into line with the divine idea of the absolute equality of women with the colored men of the nation."[41] Black Methodist women heard echoes of the issues they too were grappling with. But the racial framing of the NWSA's demands likely made them uneasy.

Battles over church women's rights within denominations may have been easily overlooked. Female preachers were difficult to ignore. Their activities captured the attention of black Methodist and women's rights activists in the 1870s. News coverage broadened their visibility beyond the local venues in which they preached. Stories circulated about how black and white Protestant women all faced opposition to their public work because they were women. The NWSA's weekly newspaper, the *Woman's Journal*, reported on black Methodist preacher Amanda Berry Smith, while also providing extensive coverage of white preachers, including Sarah Smiley, Phebe Hanaford, and Van Cott. African American Methodists had a similar interest in preaching women. The denomination's weekly, the *Christian Recorder*, carefully followed the work of Smith, who was a longstanding member of the denomination. Smiley and Van Cott also proved themselves newsworthy to the *Recorder*'s readership. Smiley's 1874 confrontation with her opponents in the Presbyterian Church led black Methodist leaders to declare that bars against female preachers were out of step with the times.[42]

Preaching women knew one another. They read the relevant press accounts. They encountered one another in pulpits and at camp meetings. Newspaper reports permit us to glimpse such encounters. For example, Smith preached alongside her white counterparts, including Anna Oliver, Van Cott, and Helen Brown.[43] Because we have little evidence of the lived dimension of these encounters, we are left to wonder: To what extent did these women engage one another about the form or the substance of their work, and how did they regard one another's capacities to preach the gospel and convert souls? Were they allies and of one movement and with church women activists generally? Nothing in the mere fact of these encounters between preaching women cues us into their sense of shared purpose on the matter of church women's rights.

Still, as preaching women were drawn into debates over gender and power in the church, they attempted to justify their vocations not from the pulpit but by the pen.[44] Whether through memoir, biography, or historical chronicle, preaching women of the 1870s turned to print culture. Their skills of oratory were formidable and their commitments to vocation stalwart. Pressed to justify their public work, preaching women turned to the printed word to make the case for their right to religious authority. Many of the women most admired in both women's rights and black Methodist circles published texts in the latter part of the century. Van Cott was first when in 1872 she cooperated in the publication of a biography that provided a justification of Van Cott's conversion and calling to preach.[45] In 1877, Hanaford offered a historical chronicle, *Women of the Century*, which included an extensive exploration of church women's contributions to U.S. history.[46] Finally, Smith published her spiritual memoir, *An Autobiography: The Story of the Lord's Dealings with Mrs. Amanda Smith, the Colored Evangelist*, in 1893, in which she recounted her evolution from enslaved child to worldwide evangelist.[47] These women framed themselves and one another through ideas about gender, church, and race. Their texts provide another glimpse into the shared ideas and experiences that may have bound them together in a church women's movement.

Van Cott's biography was published less than a decade after her emergence as a Methodist preacher. Its author, the Reverend John Foster, explained that after Van Cott had a serious illness, he persuaded her to memorialize her extraordinary story. The text chronicles Van Cott's spiritual journey from a privileged life free of material wants to one committed to family, labor, and the conversion of souls. Foster began his text with two testimonials authored by Haven and the Reverend David Sherman. This framing firmly situated Van Cott's life story within Methodist Episcopal Church debates over the licensing of female preachers. Van Cott was recognized for her remarkable achievements on behalf of the church. But each testimonial spent equal time addressing what Sherman termed "Woman's Place in the Gospel." For her male allies, Van Cott's story was evidence in support of broad changes in church women's authority. Sherman concluded: "Why should not such a woman be clothed with the full powers of the ministry?"[48]

Race was central to explaining Van Cott's odyssey. Haven opened his remarks with an anecdote about Van Cott's first invitation to preach at an African American church. She accepted the challenge but faltered by requesting to be lodged among white rather than black people. The African American minister in charge clarified that all guests of the congregation stayed overnight with his family. Haven deemed Van Cott's gracious acceptance of the rebuke as evidence of her willingness to follow duty "unflinchingly." He thus sets the tone for reflections on race in the biography. Van Cott's encounters with black Americans serve to highlight her depth of character, capacity to throw off prejudice, and commitment to realizing just ideals.[49] Her encounters with African Americans further suggest how black Christians may have viewed the matter of female preachers. We learn that Van Cott refused to work among black people during the early years of her ministry. Her attitude was transformed, however, when she was invited to speak before an African American prayer meeting in New York City's notorious Five Points neighborhood. She confesses that she initially refused the engagement. But her spiritual conscience intervened, and Van Cott attended the dreaded meeting. The result was that she expanded the mission's work and succeeded in making converts out of black urban residents. Most remarkable is how Van Cott's story comments indirectly on the question of female preaching. Her black audience members faced many obstacles in their strivings to be saved. Still none ever questioned either Van Cott's right to preach or the potential of her interventions. We learn, it seems, that working-class and poor black Christians did not challenge female preachers, even one who harbored misgivings about them, at least not in Van Cott's view.[50]

Van Cott's biography does not show her to be connected to church women generally or to any movement for their rights. Instead, she is a singular figure as a preaching woman and church activist. Van Cott's biographer never lost sight of the challenges she faced as a female preacher. Still, never were her struggles explained as part of campaigns being waged by similarly situated women. In the book, we never encounter female preachers such as Smith or Smiley. Van Cott's story ultimately works against the conclusion that a church women's movement existed in the 1870s. Her peers were generally white, male church leaders and she remains a singular and exceptional figure in this depiction of Protestant culture.

In contrast, Smith's memoir was a testament to the cross-racial character of church women's activism in the post–Civil War period. Although Smith was a member of the AME Church, her spiritual quest and her evangelical vocation drew her into white as well as black Protestant circles. Her earliest allies were black Methodists, male and female. Smith's effectiveness as a preacher and her personal sense of calling increasingly drew her into white-dominated settings. There, she more often than not reports having encountered those who drew no strict color line around her. Black and white lay women are depicted as Smith's most devoted benefactors and collaborators throughout her public life. Smith also places herself on the scene during some of the era's most pointed confrontations over church women's rights.

She finds herself drawn into AME debates over women's ordination in the 1870s and recalls numerous instances in which she was required to defend against those who were opposed to preaching women. Smith's voice is consistent on these matters. She endorses the ordination of women to the ministry, even as she herself disavows any desire to be formally admitted to the ministry. She stands fast on women's right to preach. Smith signals readers to her awareness of the debates that swirled around her public work and often takes occasion to weigh in on questions of biblical interpretation and female respectability. In this sense, not only does Smith's memoir serve as a justification of her own calling, but it also buttresses arguments that were being put forth in black Methodist conventions and in women's rights assemblies.

Preaching women make occasional appearances in Smith's memoir. These encounters reveal tension between black and white preaching women. Prominent among these is Smiley, whom Smith reports having encountered in a variety of instances. Smiley's presence on the evangelical scene served multiple purposes. Smith makes clear that preaching women might easily view one another as competitors rather than allies in a campaign for church women's rights. For example, Smith relates how in 1870 she was invited to hear Smiley speak during a Bible reading at Brooklyn's Twenty-fourth Street Methodist church. Upon her arrival Smith was urged to sing a hymn, and, prior to Smiley's taking the pulpit, she obliged. Subsequent to Smiley's Bible reading, Smith found herself escorted out of the sanctuary. A confidante of Smiley made it clear that Smith was not welcome to share the venue. Smith describes herself as tearful and despondent after this rebuff.[51]

Smith and Smiley encountered one another again years later when both were touring the British Isles. This meeting appears more cordial on the surface than the one just described. Smiley generously offered Smith advice about her preaching itinerary, suggesting that her next stop be Victoria Hall rather than Broadlands. But as Smith reflects on Smiley's recommendations, we learn that they were not purely benevolent: Smiley's reasoning reflects a paternalistic posture. When she advised Smith against attending the Broadlands meetings, she warned that the "deep truths" espoused there might lead to "a good deal of confusion" for Smith. Smith heeded Smiley's advice, but on arriving at Victoria Hall she understood better Smiley's objectives. Unbeknownst to Smith, church activists had long planned for and had widely publicized her appearances at Victoria Hall. Had Smith opted to travel first to Broadlands, Smiley's associates would have been disappointed and embarrassed.[52] Through both encounters between Smith and Smiley readers learn the depth of Smith's fortitude. Despite being rebuffed and misled, she repeatedly returns to a course set by her individual sense of calling. At the same time, these episodes permit us to glimpse how Smith positioned herself against other preaching women. These relationships were uneasy at best.

Hanaford's writing took another form, that of historical chronicle. Her 1877 *Women of the Century*, published to coincide with the centennial of the United States, documented the national debt owed to women. The 640-page text included biographical essays about hundreds of women and their "patriotism, intelligence, usefulness, and moral worth."[53] Twenty-seven chapters charted women's contributions to U.S. history and culture.

Hanaford takes care to rank the achievements of African American women as noteworthy evidence of the "respect and honor" that was due to the nation's women.[54] The poetry of Phillis Wheatley demonstrated women's intellectual capacities: "Even African women, despised as they have been, have intellectual endowments." The part that Wheatley's "mistress" played in the poet's education further demonstrated the virtue of white women: "Colonial women, though some of them slaveholders, were not destitute of a lively interest in those the custom of the times placed wholly in their charge." Mary Peake, an African American teacher of former slaves, was the "first" teacher at Fortress Monroe and was evidence of how the American Tract Society finally endorsed "Christian effort without regard to race or color." Frances Ellen Watkins Harper was, in Hanaford's view, an eloquent lecturer on temperance, equal rights, and religious themes. She exemplified women's work in the Civil War era and was "one of the colored women of whom white women may be proud."[55] Among those noted under the heading "Women Lawyers," is Charlotte E. Ray, an 1872 graduate of Howard University Law School. Hanaford quotes the *Woman's Journal* report of Ray's admission to the bar: "Ray . . . is said to be a dusky mulatto, possess quite an intelligent countenance." She "doubtless has also a fine mind, and deserves success," Hanaford added.[56] Finally, the sculptor Edmonia Lewis was included among "Women Artists." Here, Hanaford relied on the words of the *Christian Register*, which termed Lewis a "waif" possessed of "perseverance, industry, genius, and naïveté," all of which had earned her the admiration of white Americans.[57]

Hanaford's overall treatment of African American women is complicated. She often situates them quite unremarkably among their white peers.

However, her commentary suggests that their value comes in part from how their accomplishments highlight the relationship of white Americans to black people and to the nation. White Americans are agents of black women's achievement, they are transformed by their interactions with black women, and they are the arbiters of black women's accomplishments.

Hanaford was herself an ordained Universalist Church minister. This point of view helps explain the extensive attention that *Women of the Century* gives to church women activists of all sorts. Three separate chapters constituting nearly 15 percent of the text—"XIII. Women Preachers," "XIV. Women Missionaries," and "XIX. Women of Faith"—were devoted to chronicling the contributions of church women. Not surprisingly Hanaford's tone was laudatory, as it was throughout the text. What is remarkable, however, is the silence in these chapters. In Hanaford's lengthy and far-reaching chronicle of church women's activism, not one African American woman nor one black church women's organization is mentioned. Had Hanaford excluded black women from her text altogether, we might conclude that she had drawn a crude color line when compiling *Women of the Century*. But we know that she went to some lengths to incorporate black women into other sections of the text. It seems unlikely that she did not know about women like Smith. Even the *Woman's Journal*, a source that Hanaford frequently cites in her text, reported on Smith. And a passing review of the national press generally would have brought Smith to Hanaford's attention.[58]

Preaching women like Van Cott, Smith, and Hanaford were central to rethinking the authority of church women in the post–Civil War era. Their struggles to preach, to secure licenses, and to be ordained were dramatic and highly visible episodes in the era's campaigns for church women's rights. They were the embodiment of ideals expressed in women's rights organizations and in African American Protestant churches. Still, as we contemplate their self-fashioned narratives of race and church women's rights, their relationships appear strained, at some moments to the point of rupture. Preaching women of the 1870s generated roiling currents, but, up close, they appear to be at cross-purposes: Van Cott ignores Smith and Hanaford; Smith is uneasy with Smiley; and Hanaford erases Smith, while holding up Van Cott, Smiley, and herself as exemplars of church women's activism. If they were indeed a wave, they were brought together, not at the moment of a surfer's elegant curl, but instead just as the sea was crashing to the shore.

Conclusion

Waves obscure more than they reveal. Still the illusory moments of unison, even if lived only in the realm of ideals, point us to critiques and objectives shared across lines of race and religion for nineteenth-century women. Perhaps we can retain the metaphor, even as we redefine its meanings. Any wave is the byproduct of many cross-currents. As we gaze across the expanse of women's history, church women generated many such currents. Our work is both to ride the surfer's curl and to brace ourselves for the inevitable pounding at the shore.

NOTES

1. "The Mite Missionary Society/Women's Missionary Society," *Christian Recorder* (Philadelphia), May 28, 1874. The *Christian Recorder* was the weekly newspaper of the African Methodist Episcopal Church, but it covered a broad range of news and opinion related to African American public culture. Tanner had served as the paper's editor since 1867. Gilbert Anthony Williams, *The Christian Recorder, Newspaper of the African Methodist Episcopal Church: History of a Forum for Ideas, 1854–1902* (Jefferson, NC, and London: McFarland, 1996). On Tanner, see William Seraile, *Fire in His Heart: Bishop Benjamin T. Tanner and the A.M.E. Church* (Knoxville: University of Tennessee Press, 1998).

2. "The Mite Missionary Society/Women's Missionary Society."

3. For a discussion of preaching women in this early period, see Catherine A. Brekus, *Strangers and Pilgrims: Female Preaching in America, 1740–1845* (Chapel Hill: University of North Carolina Press, 1998).

4. Jarena Lee recounted her confrontation with the AME Church's founding bishop, Richard Allen, in her memoir: "The Life and Religious Experience of Jarena Lee, a Coloured Lady, Giving an Account of Her Call to Preach the Gospel," in *Sisters of the Spirit: Three Black Women's Autobiographies of the Nineteenth Century*, ed. William L. Andrews (1836; repr., Bloomington: Indiana University Press, 1986), 25–48. Julia A. J. Foote, another of the early black Methodist preaching women, explains how her petition for a preaching license was ignored by a church conference in "A Brand Plucked from the Fire: An Autobiographical Sketch by Mrs. Julia A. J. Foote," in *Sisters of the Spirit: Three Black Women's Autobiographies of the Nineteenth Century*, ed. William L. Andrews (1836; repr., Bloomington: Indiana University Press, 1986), 161–234.

5. Ward is among the twenty-one ministers who founded the Indiana Conference in 1840. Daniel A. Payne, *History of the African Methodist Episcopal Church* (1891; repr., New York: Arno Press, 1969), 130, 167–181.

6. Foote, "A Brand Plucked from the Fire," 216.

7. C[harles] S[pencer] Smith, *A History of the African Methodist Episcopal Church: Being a Volume Supplemental to a History of the African Methodist Episcopal Church, by Daniel*

Alexander Payne, D.D., LL.D., Late One of Its Bishops: Chronicling the Principal Events in the Advance of the African Methodist Episcopal Church from 1856 to 1922 (Philadelphia: Book Concern of the AME Church, 1922), 19–20, and, Benj[amin] T. Tanner, *An Outline of Our History and Government for African Methodist Churchmen, Ministerial and Lay, in Catechetical Form* (Philadelphia: Grant, Faires & Rodgers, 1884).

8. Martha S. Jones, *"All Bound Up Together": The Woman Question in African American Public Culture, 1830–1900* (Chapel Hill: University of North Carolina Press, 2007), 47–50.

9. Church women would make one additional attempt to gain the right to preaching licenses before the Civil War, in 1852. That petition was also defeated by an opposition led by Daniel Payne. Smith, *A History of the African Methodist Episcopal Church*, 24, and Payne, *History of the African Methodist Episcopal Church*, 27–73, 301.

10. On Payne's ideas generally, see David W. Wills, "Womanhood and Domesticity in the AME Tradition: The Influence of Daniel Alexander Payne," in *Black Apostles at Home and Abroad: Afro-Americans and the Christian Mission from Revolution to Reconstruction*, ed. David W. Wills and Richard Newman (Boston: G. K. Hall, 1982).

11. Tanner, *An Outline of Our History and Government for African Methodist Churchmen.*

12. African Americans reported on the women's conventions at Seneca Falls and Rochester in the *Liberator* and the *North Star*. "Woman's Rights Convention," *North Star*, July 14, 1848; "The Rights of Women," *North Star*, July 28, 1848; "Woman's Rights Convention," *North Star*, August 11, 1848; "Reformatory: Women's Rights Convention," *Liberator*, August 25, 1848; "Reformatory: Proceedings of the Woman's Rights Convention," *Liberator*, September 15, 1848.

13. *The First Convention Ever Called to Discuss the Civil and Political Rights of Women, Seneca Falls, N.Y., July 19, 20, 1848.* Woman's Rights Convention (n.p., 18—), 3–4.

14. Quoted in Elizabeth C. Stanton, Susan B. Anthony, and Matilda J. Gage, eds., *History of Woman Suffrage* (Rochester, NY: Susan B. Anthony et al., 1881), 1:72–73.

15. Frederick Douglass, William C. Nell, and William C. Bloss were recorded as endorsing church women's authority, while Milo Codding, Mr. Sulley, Mr. Pickard, and Mr. Colton were noted as opposed; ibid., 1:76.

16. Quoted in ibid., 1:76–77.

17. *Proceedings of the Woman's Rights Conventions, Held at Seneca Falls & Rochester, N.Y., July & August, 1848* (New York: Robert J. Johnston, 1870), 15.

18. Judith Wellman, *The Road to Seneca Falls: Elizabeth Cady Stanton and the First Woman's Rights Convention* (Urbana: University of Illinois Press, 2004), 177–182.

19. "Complexion, *n.*," *Oxford English Dictionary Online, 2008* (accessed July 1, 2008).

20. For one perspective on how calls for women's rights were not always linked to one another, see Lori D. Ginzberg, *Untidy Origins: A Story of Woman's Rights in Antebellum New York* (Chapel Hill: University of North Carolina Press, 2005).

21. "African M.E. Conference," *Cleveland Herald* (Cleveland, OH), May 13, 1848.

22. Rosalyn Terborg-Penn, *African American Women in the Struggle for the Vote, 1850–1920* (Bloomington: Indiana University Press, 1998), 14.

23. "Woman's Rights Convention," *North Star*, August 11, 1848; Nell, "Woman's Revolution," *Liberator*, September 1, 1848; and *North Star*, August 8, 1848.

24. For a full analysis of the Cleveland convention, see Jones, "*All Bound Up Together*," ch. 3.

25. Lucretia Coffin Mott to Elizabeth Cady Stanton, 3 October 1848, in *The Selected Papers of Elizabeth Cady Stanton and Susan B. Anthony*, vol. 1, *In the School of Anti-Slavery*, ed. Ann D. Gordon (New Brunswick, NJ: Rutgers University Press, 2000), 126–128. Regarding antislavery alliances between black and white women, see Ira V. Brown, "Cradle of Feminism: The Philadelphia Female Anti-Slavery Society, 1833–1840," *Pennsylvania Magazine of History and Biography* 102 (1978): 143–166.

26. Henry H. Garnet, George Galbraith, J. J. G[ould] Bias, Wm. T. Cato, and D. J. Peck, M.D., "Proceedings of the Anti-Slavery Convention Held in Philadelphia," *North Star*, November 10, 1848, and Lucretia Coffin Mott to Elizabeth Cady Stanton, 3 October 1848. In subsequent years, black Methodist leaders would take part in women's conventions, as did the Reverend Jermain Loguen, who was elected vice president at an 1853 New York State women's rights convention. "Women's Rights Convention [reprint from the *New York Tribune*]," *Frederick Douglass' Paper*, December 16, 1853.

27. Carol V. R. George, *Segregated Sabbaths: Richard Allen and the Rise of Independent Black Churches: 1760–1840* (New York: Oxford University Press, 1973).

28. Chris Padgett, "Hearing the Antislavery Rank-and-File: The Wesleyan Methodist Schism of 1843," *Journal of the Early Republic* 12, no. 1 (1992): 63–84.

29. *The Fifteenth Quadrennial Session of the General Conference of the African Methodist Episcopal Church, Nashville, Tennessee. May 6, 1872*; available at the Office of the Historiographer of the AME Church, Nashville, TN.

30. *The Sixteenth Session, and the Fifteenth Quadrennial Session of the General Conference of the African Episcopal Methodist Church. Place of Session, Atlanta, Georgia, from May 1st to 18th, 1876*; available at the Office of the Historiographer of the AME Church, Nashville, TN.

31. Reverend Mark M. Bell, *Daily Journal of the Sixteenth Quadrennial Session of the General Conference of the AME Zion Church, of America, Held at Montgomery, Alabama, May, A.D., 1880* (New York: Book Concern of the AME Zion Church, 1880), 71.

32. Lawrence S. Little, *Disciples of Liberty: The African Methodist Episcopal Church in the Age of Imperialism, 1884–1916* (Knoxville: University of Tennessee Press, 2000), 10. The AME Zion Church founded the Women's Home and Foreign Missionary Society in 1880; William J. Walls, *The AME Zion Church: Reality of the Black Church* (Charlotte, NC: AME Zion Publishing House, 1974), 376, 388. The Colored Methodist Episcopal Church authorized its Women's Missionary Society in 1890; Othal H. Lakey, *History of the CME Church* (Memphis, TN: CME Publishing House, 1996), 303.

33. Walls, *The AME Zion Church*, 376, 388. Little, *Disciples of Liberty*, 10.

34. Wendell Phillips, "Thirty-Second Anniversary of the American Anti-Slavery Society," *Liberator*, May 19, 1865.

35. Elizabeth Cady Stanton, "Address to the National Woman Suffrage Convention, Washington, D.C., January 19, 1869," reprinted in Mari Jo Buhle and Paul Buhle, eds., *The Concise History of Woman Suffrage: Selections from History of Woman Suffrage, edited by Elizabeth Cady Stanton, Susan B. Anthony, Matilda Joslyn Gage, and the National Woman Suffrage Association* (Urbana and Chicago: University of Illinois Press, 2005), 249.

36. See Eric Foner, *Reconstruction: America's Unfinished Revolution, 1863–1877* (New York: Harper & Row, 1988), 480, and Terborg-Penn, *African American Women in the Struggle for the Vote*.

37. William Gravely, *Gilbert Haven, Methodist Abolitionist: A Study in Race, Religion and Reform, 1850–1880* (Nashville, TN, and New York: Abingdon Press, 1973).

38. Van Cott's biography was first published in 1872: Reverend John O. Foster, *Life and Labors of Mrs. Maggie Newton Van Cott, the First Lady Licensed to Preach in the Methodist Episcopal Church in the United States* (Cincinnati: Hitchcock and Walder, for the author, 1872). The book was reissued in an expanded edition in 1883: Reverend John O. Foster, *The Harvest and the Reaper: Reminiscences of Revival Work of Mrs. Maggie N. Van Cott* (New York: Geo. A. Sparks, 1883). Haven's introduction was published in both editions, without revision. Regarding Haven's presidency of the AWSA, see *Constitution of the American Woman Suffrage Association and the History of Its Formation: With the Times and Places in Which the Association Has Held Meetings up to 1880* (Boston : G. H. Ellis, 1881).

39. Stanton, Anthony, and Gage, *History of Woman Suffrage*, 2:427.

40. "Woman Suffrage Meeting in the Academy of Music," *Woman's Journal*, June 6, 1874.

41. "Memorials Adopted by the National Woman Suffrage Association," 15 January 1874, in *The Selected Papers of Elizabeth Cady Stanton and Susan B. Anthony*, vol. 2, *Against an Aristocracy of Sex, 1866–1873*, ed. Ann D. Gordon (New Brunswick, NJ: Rutgers University Press, 2000), 32–34.

42. "Concerning Women," *Woman's Journal*, January 25, 1873; "[Letter from Albany,]" *Christian Recorder*, April 6, 1872; "[We Don't Wonder at Christ . . .]," *Christian Recorder*, August 21, 1873; "Proceedings of the Literary Association of the Philadelphia Annual Conference," *Christian Recorder*, November 23, 1876; "Brevities," *Christian Recorder*, February 28, 1878; Geo[rge] F. Pentecost, "Miss Smiley," *Christian Recorder*, April 17, 1873; "[Our Pastor Wants Her . . .]," *Christian Recorder*, April 17, 1873; "[Smiley in Cleveland]," *Christian Recorder*, January 27, 1876; "Female Preaching," *Christian Recorder*, March 9, 1872; "Personal Items," *Christian Recorder*, December 2, 1875; "[Bishops of the M.E. Church . . .]," *Christian Recorder*, November 5, 1874; Clarissa M. Thompson, "Woman's Work," *Christian Recorder*, February 8, 1877; "[Mrs. Van Cott and People of Color]," *Christian Recorder*, May 28, 1874; "[Bishops of the M.E. Church . . .]," *Christian Recorder*, November 5, 1874; Bishop A. W. Wayman, "Communication. Notes by the Way," *Christian Recorder*, November 30, 1876; and "Our New York Letter," *Christian Recorder*, November 21, 1878.

43. "Latest News Items," *Daily Evening Bulletin* (San Francisco), March 5, 1877 (Smith with Oliver for a Thanksgiving week revival in Passaic, New Jersey); "Summit Grove Camp-Meeting," *Baltimore Sun*, August 14, 1875 (Smith scheduled to appear with Van Cott during York County, Pennsylvania, camp meeting); and "State Items," *Trenton State Gazette* (Trenton, NJ), November 15, 1875 (Smith speaks at New Jersey Women's Christian Temperance Union meeting with Brown.)

44. Kenneth E. Rowe, "The Ordination of Women: Round One; Anna Oliver and the General Conference," in *Perspectives on American Methodism: Interpretive Essays*, ed. Russell E. Richey, Kenneth E. Rowe, and Jean Miller Schmidt (Nashville, TN: Kingswood Books, 1993); William R. Phinney, *Maggie Newton Van Cott: First Woman Licensed to Preach in the Methodist Episcopal Church* (Rye, NY: Commission on Archives and History, New York Annual Conference, United Methodist Church, 1969); and Adrienne M. Israel, *Amanda Berry Smith: From Washerwoman to Evangelist* (Lanham, MD: Scarecrow Press, 1998).

45. Foster, *Life and Labors*.

46. Phebe A. Hanaford, *Women of the Century* (Boston: B. B. Russell, 1877).

47. Mrs. Amanda Smith, *An Autobiography: The Story of the Lord's Dealings with Mrs. Amanda Smith, the Colored Evangelist*, ed. Jualynne E. Dodson (New York: Oxford University Press, 1988).

48. Reverend David Sherman, introduction to Foster, *Life and Labors*, xxxix.

49. Gilbert Haven, introduction to ibid., xiii–xvii.

50. Ibid., 115–134.

51. Smith, *An Autobiography*, 193–195.

52. Ibid., 259.

53. Hanaford, *Women of the Century*, 5.

54. Ibid., 7.

55. Ibid., 35, 168, 291.

56. Ibid., 568, 574.

57. Ibid., 264–267.

58. "Concerning Women," *Woman's Journal*, January 25, 1873 (Smith preached in Cincinnati); "About Women," *Daily Evening Bulletin* (San Francisco), February 22, 1873 (Smith preached in Cincinnati); "Personal Items," *Milwaukee Daily Sentinel*, July 17, 1873 (Smith preached in Round Lake); "Local News: Akron Items," *Daily Cleveland Herald*, November 1, 1873 (Smith preached in Akron); "General and Personal," *St. Louis Globe-Democrat*, July 15, 1875, and "People and Things," *Inter Ocean* (Chicago), July 20, 1875, and "The Round Lake Meeting," *New York Times*, July 11, 1875 (Smith preached in Round Lake); "The Ada Street Church Trial," *Inter Ocean* (Chicago), September 25, 1875 (Smith credited with a "miracle" at Ocean Grove); "People and Things," *Inter Ocean* (Chicago), February 8, 1876 (Smith conducted a revival in Wilmington, DE); *Newark Advocate* (Newark, OH), February 11, 1876 (Smith preached in Wilmington, DE); "State News," *Boston Daily Advertiser*, November 22, 1876 (Smith was at a Worcester, MA, revival); "Latest News Items,"

Daily Evening Bulletin (San Francisco), March 5, 1877 (Smith was with Oliver for a Thanksgiving week revival in Passaic, NJ); "New York: Miscellaneous," *Boston Daily Advertiser*, February 18, 1878, and "Mr. Beecher on Ritualism," *St. Louis Globe-Democrat*, February 21, 1878 (Beecher announced that Smith was to speak at Brooklyn missions); "State Items," *Trenton State Gazette* (Trenton, NJ), May 29, 1875 (Smith was at a Pitman Grove camp meeting); "Summit Grove Camp-Meeting," *Baltimore Sun*, August 14, 1875 (Smith was scheduled to appear with Van Cott during a York County, PA, camp meeting); "State Items," *Trenton State Gazette*, November 15, 1875 (Smith spoke at a New Jersey Women's Christian Temperance Union meeting with Brown); "Religious Notices," *New York Times*, December 6, 1873 (Smith was scheduled to speak at the Seventeenth Street M.E. Church); and "The Union Camp-Meeting," *New York Times*, July 11, 1873 (Smith preached at Sea Cliff Grove).

7

Labor Feminists and President Kennedy's Commission on Women

DOROTHY SUE COBBLE

Many histories of U.S. women's rights note the impact of two best-selling 1963 publications: Betty Friedan's *The Feminine Mystique* and the President's Commission on the Status of Women report, *American Women*.[1] Both texts called for a reassessment of women's place in society, and both helped spawn the new feminism that would erupt by the late 1960s. *The Feminine Mystique* resonated with the frustrated aspirations and seething resentment of millions of women, and its author, Betty Friedan, went on to launch the National Organization for Women (NOW) and serve as its first president. Similarly, *American Women*'s bold assertion of women's second-class citizenship and its call for widespread government action to end the "discriminations and disadvantages" that created this status also found a responsive audience.[2] *American Women* sold out quickly and a small but growing group of committed men and women began agitating for the implementation of its many recommendations and for the creation of commissions on the status of women in states and municipalities across the country. By January 1965, in response to the mounting political pressure, thirty-six governors had appointed commissions.[3] Betty Friedan herself was swept up in the new movement: it was at the Third National Conference of Commissions on the Status of Women in June 1966, sponsored by the Women's Bureau of the U.S. Department of Labor, that Friedan and others launched NOW.[4]

Yet despite the centrality of the President's Commission in changing attitudes, generating policy initiatives, and spurring the birth of a new women's movement, its origins remain obscure and its politics baffling.[5]

Why, for example, did President John F. Kennedy issue an executive order setting up a federal commission on women in December 1961, years before the rise of "women's liberation"? And how did a national document proclaiming its commitment to ending the secondary status of American women emerge in an era often seen as mired in conservative gender ideology and hostile to women's equality?

This article maintains that the origins and politics of the President's Commission on the Status of Women (PCSW) can only be understood by incorporating the long and robust traditions of labor feminism into our narratives of twentieth-century women's rights. As I will detail in the rest of this essay, by the 1940s, a group of women labor reformers and their allies, a group I have termed "labor feminists,"[6] reached a consensus that a presidential executive order setting up a federal commission on the status of women would be a major boost to advancing their agenda, and it was their consistent and persuasive lobbying in the decades following World War II that finally resulted in the emergence of the PCSW in the early 1960s.

I consider this group of women labor reformers and their allies "feminists" because they recognized that women suffer disadvantages due to their sex and because they sought to eliminate sex-based disadvantages. I call them *labor* feminists because they looked to the labor movement as the primary vehicle through which to end the multiple inequities women confronted. Their notion of women's rights emerged in conversation with men and women in the labor movement as well as other campaigns for social justice such as the civil rights movement; it also was shaped by their involvement in transnational and international organizations and debates. *American Women* did not fully incorporate the aims or the social policies advanced by labor feminists: political compromises were necessary. Nevertheless, the labor feminist vision is evident throughout its pages.

Within a few years of its publication, *American Women* would be challenged by a new feminist sensibility with different notions of women's needs and different ideas about how to realize those needs. For many post-1960s feminists, the President's Commission and its report would come to seem conservative and even "pre-feminist." Now, almost fifty years later, it is time to reconsider *American Women*. In that spirit, the essay ends with a rereading of *American Women* that endeavors to place it in the context of its times and to see its strengths as well as its weaknesses.

Multiple U.S. Feminisms

Ever since the word "feminism" came into common usage in the United States in the early twentieth century, there have been debates over who was and was not a feminist and what the appropriate ends and means for a movement on behalf of women should be.[7] That debate intensified after the passage of suffrage in 1920 when two groups of women reformers faced off against each other over how best to advance women's equality. The historian William O'Neill called these two groups "social feminists" and "equal rights feminists" and his categories are still useful.[8] I also find Kathryn Kish Sklar's term "social justice feminist" equally appropriate and will use it interchangeably with "social feminist."[9]

Social feminists believed that women's oppression stemmed from multiple sources and that a wide variety of interventions were necessary to remedy these disadvantages. The problems of class, for example, or of race, could be as serious a barrier to women's opportunity and advancement as restrictions based on sex. Social feminists argued that "equal treatment" under the law and in practice might not always result in moving women toward "equality." There were some sex-based distinctions, legally and socially, that were advantageous for women, particularly given women's greater responsibilities for child and elder care. "Equal rights feminists," on the other hand, stressed "equal treatment" under the law and, after the Nineteenth Amendment was passed in 1920, gathered their forces and single-mindedly pursued a second constitutional amendment, the Equal Rights Amendment (ERA). When introduced into Congress in 1923, the ERA declared that "men and women shall have equal rights throughout the United States and in every place subject to its jurisdiction."[10]

The political chasm between these two groups widened in 1923 and remained a yawning divide for the next half century. For one, the two groups failed to reach a compromise on the language of the ERA that would protect the body of fair labor standards legislation that Progressive era social justice feminists like Jane Addams, Florence Kelley, Rose Schneiderman, and Pauline Newman had made a priority. But equally revealing was the divide over the 1923 Supreme Court decision in Adkins v. Children's Hospital, which overturned the District of Columbia minimum wage law. Social feminists were distraught, believing that without such protections the majority of women's lives would be greatly worsened; equal rights feminists celebrated, believing it a victory for women's freedom and an acknowledgment of their equality with men.[11]

Underneath the conflicts over how to advance women's interests lay other profound political disagreements. The "equal rights" banner was carried primarily by the National Woman's Party (NWP). Although some working women belonged to the NWP, the majority of its members were professional women from middle-class and elite backgrounds. They also tended to be white and Republican, and their principal allies after the 1920s were Republicans and conservative Democrats as well as business groups like the Chamber of Commerce and the National Association of Manufacturers. Many of these allies supported the ERA because they, like the social feminists, believed it would mean the end of sex-based labor legislation.[12] In contrast to the NWP feminists, social feminists allied primarily with the liberal wing of the Democratic party. They disliked many of the NWP women as much for their Republican affiliation and their opposition to labor regulation as for their gender politics.[13] For labor feminists in particular, the "liberty of contract" doctrine that workers should have the right to contract or sell their labor without any government constraints or regulations such as minimum wage laws held little appeal. For those without capital, economic or cultural, labor feminists believed, the so-called free market was a source of exploitation and degradation as much as a realm of fulfillment and freedom.[14]

The NWP continued its efforts on behalf of the ERA during the so-called "doldrum years" of the post–World War II era.[15] So did the social feminists. The older social feminist network of separate-sex women's organizations, loosely gathered around the U.S. Women's Bureau, persisted and was joined by new women's organizations like the National Council for Negro Women (NCNW), founded in 1935 by Mary McLeod Bethune, and the YWCA.[16] By the 1940s, however, labor feminists took the leadership reins of the social feminist movement. Both in terms of numbers and the power of the organizations they represented, they were the dominant constituency within social feminism from the 1940s to the 1960s. They brought their ties to the economic and political resources of organized labor, the largest social movement of the day, and they brought their own ideas of how to advance the status of women.[17]

Like earlier social feminists, labor feminists continued to oppose the ERA, believing it a threat to state sex-based labor standards laws that remained, even after the passage of the 1938 federal Fair Labor Standards Act, the primary mechanism regulating the wages and hours of many low-income female wage earners.[18] At the same time, they pursued their own political agenda. Labor feminists advocated an end to sex- and race-based discriminations which they believed disadvantaged women. Yet they pointed out that ending discrimination was not enough. Many low-income women would not be able to take advantage of equal employment opportunities without additional social and economic rights and guarantees. Thus, they pressed for a wide array of positive rights and benefits—what they called "full social security"—both from the state and from employers. These included not only healthcare and pension guarantees but universal, government-funded childcare, social wages for childbearing and child rearing, and changes in workplace policies that would make it easier to combine income-earning and caregiving. They sought legislation that would raise the minimum wage and require equal pay for equal work. They also sought a fairer share of the country's wealth and a greater political voice for working people through collective organizing and bargaining. They looked primarily to the new industrial labor movement, the Congress of Industrial Organizations (CIO), to realize these reforms. Yet many labor feminists, African Americans as well as others, saw the civil rights movement as crucial to women's freedom and considered the fate of workers, women, and other marginalized groups as deeply intertwined.[19]

A Diverse Movement

The majority of labor feminists came from working-class and poor backgrounds, but some of the most prominent were from decidedly elite families. A generation earlier, many politically engaged college women moved into settlement house work, or joined the National Consumers' League, or pursued a career in social welfare. But in the context of the 1930s, they gravitated toward the labor movement. By the 1940s many held union staff jobs as lobbyists and political action coordinators, as community service representatives, and as research and education directors.

Labor feminists also were racially and ethnically diverse. Many were African American: Dorothy (Dollie) Lowther Robinson of the Amalgamated Clothing Workers and the U.S. Women's Bureau; Maida Springer-Kemp of the International Ladies' Garment Workers' Union and the International Affairs Division of the AFL-CIO; Gloria Johnson of the International Union of Electrical Workers; Addie Wyatt of the United Packinghouse Workers Union;

and Lillian Hatcher of the United Automobile Workers, for example. A few were Spanish-speaking such as Dolores Huerta of the Farm Workers or Luisa Moreno of the Food, Tobacco, and Agricultural Workers.

A number of labor feminists who were close to the Communist party like Luisa Moreno or Ruth Young, the first woman on the international executive board of the United Electrical Workers Union, disappeared from the national leadership by the early 1950s, due in large part to Cold War politics. But labor feminism persisted, rooted largely in the left-liberal industrial unions allied with the Democratic party.[20]

It would be impossible to give each of the leaders of this movement their due, but let me offer brief biographical sketches of a few of the labor feminists who figured prominently in the history of the President's Commission. Esther Eggertsen Peterson and Katherine (Kitty) Pollak Ellickson, both from middle-class backgrounds, were among the most influential. Born in 1906 into a Republican Mormon family in Provo, Utah, Esther Peterson finished a degree at Brigham Young University before heading to New York City. She earned a master's degree from Columbia Teachers' College in 1930 and was soon swept up in labor and feminist politics. She taught classes for industrial workers at the YWCA and at the Bryn Mawr Summer School for Women Workers and organized multiracial locals in the South during World War II for the Amalgamated Clothing Workers of America. In 1945, she became its first legislative representative in Washington. In 1948, when her husband, Oliver Peterson, was appointed labor attaché to Sweden, she moved her family of four abroad, continuing her trade union work in Sweden and then in Belgium where she helped found the Women's Committee of the International Confederation of Free Trade Unions, the forty-eight-million-member labor body set up by noncommunist unions as a rival world federation to the World Federation of Trade Unions. Upon her return in 1957, she became the AFL-CIO's first woman Washington lobbyist. In 1960, President Kennedy tapped Peterson for director of the U.S. Women's Bureau and then promoted her to Assistant Secretary of Labor, making her the highest-ranking woman official in his administration. It was Peterson who took on the task of convincing Kennedy to set up the Commission and it was Peterson who served as its executive vice-chair.[21]

Katherine Pollak Ellickson, a close friend of Peterson's, graduated from Vassar in 1926 with a degree in economics and then did graduate work at Columbia University. When the CIO hired her into its Research Department in 1942, Ellickson already had a decade of experience as a labor educator, speechwriter, and organizer. She stayed with the CIO Research Department during the war and moved into the AFL-CIO Research Department after the merger in 1955. In 1962, at the urging of Peterson, Ellickson took a leave from the AFL-CIO to take on the full-time job as the commission's executive secretary, coordinating its work.[22]

Three other labor feminists, Mary Callahan, Addie Wyatt, and Caroline Dawson Davis, all from working-class backgrounds, ended up serving on the commission along with other labor women like Bessie Hillman, cofounder of the Amalgamated Clothing Workers along with her husband, Sidney Hillman. Widowed at age nineteen with a two-year-old son in the middle of the Depression, Mary Callahan found a job at the International Resistance Company electronics plant in Philadelphia. Soon after, "for reasons of dignity," she later explained, she led her fellow workers out on a month-long strike for union recognition which also gained them the right to have the washrooms unlocked and a regular "relief period" (bathroom break). By 1946, she held the top position in her local union, a sizable organization with 85 percent female membership, and had successfully negotiated paid maternity leave and other innovative benefits. She moved on to chair the National Woman's Council of the International Union of Electrical Workers (IUE) and to serve as one of two women on the IUE National Executive Board. In 1961, she accepted President Kennedy's appointment to the twenty-six-member Commission, joining college presidents, senators, corporate heads, newspaper publishers, and other powerful public figures.[23]

Addie Wyatt and Caroline Dawson Davis did not serve on the Commission itself but on one of the seven advisory committees to the Commission: Wyatt sat on the Committee on Protective Labor Legislation, Davis on the Committee on Private Employment. Hired in 1941 at Armour's meat-packing plant in Chicago, Mississippi-born Addie Wyatt, like many African American women, had her first encounter with trade unionism during the war. It was not long before she filed her first grievance. The foreman had given her job to a newly hired white woman and reassigned her to a worse position on the "stew line." "I was very angry, and as I always did when there was something I didn't think was right, I spoke out." When the issue could not be resolved with the foreman, Wyatt and her union representative, a black woman steward, marched over to the plant superintendent's office. "What effect," Wyatt remembered thinking, could "two black women have talking to the two white, superior officers in the plant?" To her amazement, they won. Just as surprising was the union response when she got pregnant. The steward explained the union's maternity clause: Wyatt could take up to a year off and her job would be held for her. "I didn't really believe them. But I thought I'd try it, and I did get my job back." By the early 1950s, her local (United Packinghouse Workers of America, Local 437), the majority of whose members were white men, elected her vice-president. Later, she took over the presidency of the local and ran successfully for the national union's executive board on a platform emphasizing women's rights and the advancement of racial minorities. In 1954, she was appointed to the national union staff as the first black woman national representative, a position she held for the next thirty years.[24]

Caroline Dawson Davis, who directed the influential Women's Department of the United Auto Workers (UAW) from 1948 until her retirement in 1973, grew up in a poor white Kentucky mining family steeped in religion and unionism. In 1934, she got a job as a drill press operator in the same Indiana auto parts plant that hired her father. Caroline Davis had a strong antiauthoritarian streak, and like Addie Wyatt, had a bad habit of stepping in to stand up for anyone being mistreated. Both these traits propelled her toward union activity. "The worst thing about a job to me was authority," Davis once explained. "I loved people," she continued, and "I believed in people. I never saw the difference between someone who had a title and a lot of money, and Joe Doe and Jane Doe who swept floors and dug ditches." Thirty-year-old Davis helped organize her plant in 1941, was elected vice-president of UAW Local 764 in 1943, and shortly thereafter, "moved upstairs when the union president was drafted." By 1948, Davis had taken over the reins of the UAW Women's Department. A year earlier, *Life* magazine ran a feature story on "the strikingly attractive lady labor leader," accompanied by a four-page photo spread of Davis. In one photo, Davis lounges at home reading Freud, a thinker whose ideas, she explained to the interviewer, proved indispensable to running her local union. "If I hadn't been a union leader," Davis added, "I would have been a psychiatrist."[25]

The Global Origins of the President's Commission on Women

It is no accident that U.S. labor women began contemplating a domestic commission on the status of women in 1946 and introduced the "Women's

Status Bill," the labor feminist alternative to the NWP's Equal Rights Bill, a
year later. U.S. labor women found the language of "status," a concept
employed among feminists worldwide by the 1940s, helpful in their own
domestic policy campaigns and they adopted it. Like many women reformers
around the world, they were influenced by the global debates on women's
status that had taken place in such forums as the Pan-American Union
and the League of Nations in the 1920s and 1930s. These then burst forth
again, with pent-up intensity, after World War II, culminating in the establishment of the United Nations (U.N.) Commission on the Status of Women
in 1946.

Before World War II, U.S. and non-U.S. feminists in both the Pan-
American Union and the League of Nations called for commissions on the
status of women. Doris Stevens, who from 1928 to 1939 chaired the Inter-
American Commission of Women (CIM), a branch of the Pan-American
Union, and other feminists associated with the NWP emphasized the need
for a study of the legal and civic status of women on a country by country
basis. They hoped that such studies would lead individual countries to pass
an "Equal Rights Treaty" committing them to the eradication of sex-based
differential treatment of men and women. U.S. Women's Bureau director
Mary Anderson, a former shoe worker, union official, and Women's Trade
Union League leader, lobbied against the NWP's Equal Rights Treaty in the
CIM and in the League of Nations. She, along with other labor feminists,
feared that such a treaty would eliminate the large body of labor standards
and worker rights that by the 1930s existed not only as national and subna-
tional law but as international policy through the International Labor
Organization (ILO), the body set up by the League of Nations in 1919 to formulate international labor standards.[26]

Labor feminists, however, did support international efforts to establish
women's status commissions when such initiatives called for investigations
into the status of women without committing nations to "equal treatment"
of the sexes in their laws and policies. Labor feminists favored broad-based
studies focusing on the economic and social status of women as well as their
political and civil rights. Pre–World War II feminist agitation for women's
status investigations culminated in 1937 when the assembly of the League of
Nations approved a proposal (presented by Sweden's Kerstin Hesselgren, a
factory inspector who two years later became the first woman to preside
over the Swedish Parliament) for a committee to study the status of women

worldwide.[27] Hesselgren and Anderson had close ties throughout this period, due to their shared Swedish heritage and to Anderson's own international work with the ILO and the League.[28]

With the dissolution of the League of Nations in the aftermath of World War II, efforts to advance the study of women's status through national and regional commissions continued under the aegis of the U.N., the League's successor.[29] Labor feminist Frieda S. Miller, who took over from Mary Anderson as director of the Women's Bureau in 1944, was intimately involved in these international initiatives in the 1940s and 1950s, and their influence on her and other U.S. women reformers of the time was substantial.

Miller first found her internationalist sea legs in 1923 when she attended, along with her life-long partner veteran labor organizer and labor journalist Pauline Newman, the third conference of the International Federation of Working Women (IFWW) in Vienna. The IFWW dissolved soon after, but many of its members, including Anderson, Miller, and Hesselgren, turned to other venues like the League of Nations in search of mechanisms to raise women's global economic and social status. Miller served as an official U.S. delegate to the League's ILO gatherings in 1935, 1936, 1938, and 1941, for example, and in 1946, she chaired the ILO Constitutional Committee charged with, among other items, ensuring the ILO's transition into the U.N. and coordinating its work with the newly established U.N. Commission on the Status of Women.[30]

Miller brought back insights from her ILO and U.N. activities into her domestic work and shared them with the labor feminist network she had gathered around the U.S. Women's Bureau. In 1945, Miller set up the "Women's Bureau Labor Advisory Committee," which served for the next decade as a policy think tank for top women in the labor movement. It included, among others, Esther Peterson and Dollie Robinson of the Amalgamated Clothing Workers; Kitty Ellickson of the CIO Research Department; Caroline Davis and Lillian Hatcher from the United Auto Workers; Ruth Young of the United Electrical Workers; and Pauline Newman of the International Ladies' Garment Workers' Union. Out of these meetings sprang not only the Equal Pay Act, introduced for the first time in 1945, but also the "Women's Status Bill," introduced into both houses for the first time on February 17, 1947, and reintroduced every year until 1954. At the "heart of the bill," Frieda Miller explained, was a recommendation for a presidential commission on the status of women.[31]

The Two Equal Rights Bills

The "Women Status Bill," as Cynthia Harrison points out, was "a way to meet the threat of the ERA."[32] By 1946, the ERA was ready for a vote in both houses, having been favorably reported out of committee for the first time since its introduction in the early 1920s. But the labor feminists who supported the "Women's Status Bill" had more on their minds than simply stopping the ERA. They were pursuing a comprehensive and ambitious reform agenda to raise women's status on multiple fronts.

The Women's Status bill called for a nine-member commission appointed by the President which would investigate and review "the economic, civil, social, and political status of women, and the nature and extent of discriminations based on sex throughout the United States, its Territories, and possessions." According to the bill's preamble, the commission and its subsequent report were needed to eliminate "statutes, regulations, rules, and governmental practices which discriminate unfairly on the basis of sex" and to bring the United States "into harmony" with the principles of the U.N.'s 1945 Charter "promoting and encouraging respect for human rights and fundamental freedoms for all without distinctions as to ... sex."[33] Proponents of the bill, echoing the preamble's sentiments, often cited their desire to end unfair discrimination against women and spoke of the U.S. commission as a necessary domestic analog to the U.N. Commission on the Status of Women. As Frieda Miller explained in her 1948 congressional testimony on behalf of the bill, the U.S. commission will "enrich and expand the information on the status of women which is being prepared for the United Nations." Without such a commission, she warned, the United States might be embarrassed in front of the international community. A "comparative study is being planned by the United Nations Commission on the Status of Women," she reminded her audience, "and women in the United States are eager that American experience be presented as fully as possible for the United Nations use."[34]

Esther Peterson and Kitty Ellickson were particularly strong advocates for a U.S. commission when it was discussed in the U.S. Women's Bureau Labor Advisory Committee meetings. They and other labor feminists were influenced by Miller, who urged her committee to link their domestic reforms to the global conversation and frame the U.S. commission as a part of the U.N.-sponsored efforts to map the global status of women.[35] They also

found the President's Committee on Civil Rights, established by President
Harry Truman's executive order in December 1946, and its pending report,
"To Secure These Rights," which appeared in 1947, a useful precedent and
model. The report, "a clarion call to wipe out racial injustice," according to
civil rights historian Steven F. Lawson, provided a "comprehensive blueprint
for achieving first-class citizenship" for all and set "the federal government's
agenda on civil rights" for years to come. Although many of its recommendations were not enacted until the 1960s, the report was an important national
acknowledgment of the race problem and the need for government intervention to help solve it. The labor feminists behind the Women's Status Bill
hoped for a similar report that would stir the nation and inaugurate a
national debate over the status of women.[36]

The Women's Status Bill and its proponents are rarely mentioned in histories of women's rights in the postwar era. It is the bill labor feminists
opposed, the ERA, which is seen as carrying the banner of feminism. Yet the
actual congressional debates reveal a surprising degree of unanimity among
NWP and labor feminists on many issues. Both groups believed that the law
discriminated against women on the basis of sex, that such discriminations
should be eliminated, and that the ultimate goal was equality between the
sexes. As Frieda Miller remarked, "Everyone is for equality for women"; what
is not clear is "what in fact would provide equality for the great majority of
women."[37] Both sides also agreed that it was unclear what, if any, biological
distinctions existed between the sexes, except for pregnancy and childbirth,
and that the law should accommodate these differences in some fashion.

The angriest exchanges were often over political differences having little
to do with gender. Emma Guffey Miller, the congressional chairman of the
National Woman's Party, opened her congressional testimony on behalf of
the ERA in March 1948 by attacking her opponents as "Communists," as
"professional welfare workers," as "lady bountifuls," and as dupes of "certain
labor leaders" who "fear that women may take their jobs." Pauline Newman
and other labor feminists responded in kind, charging those who proposed
this "so-called ERA" with being "selfish careerists" who were "numerically
insignificant, industrially inexperienced, economically unsound, and intellectually confused."[38]

Most of the more reasoned debate centered not on gender per se but on
labor standards laws—specifically the woman-only state laws that still existed

in virtually every state in 1948—and whether the ERA would eliminate these laws and whether this loss would be a good thing. Labor feminists and their allies—women such as Helen Gahagan Douglas, Democratic congresswoman from California, and Mary Norton, Democratic congresswoman from New Jersey—feared the ERA would remove all such laws. Instead, they proposed that the sex-based laws be evaluated on a case-by-case basis—an approach that came to be known as "specific bills for specific ills." The laws deemed harmful to women would be removed; those deemed beneficial would be retained or amended to cover men. The presidential commission they sought would evaluate laws on a case-by-case basis and consider the broader questions of women's economic and social equality. As Peterson explained in a January 1947 meeting of the labor advisory group, the commission could list the "distinctions that should be kept, those that should not, and those in the middle ground."[39]

By the mid-1950s, political pressure for the Women's Status Bill, including its clause proposing a President's Commission on the Status of Women, subsided among labor feminists. With the return of a Republican to the White House, labor feminists and their allies turned their attention to state and local politics and to more specifically targeted federal initiatives such as the Equal Pay for Equal Work Bill and tax policies to better support childcare and mothering. Labor feminists, many of whom were women of color, also became increasingly involved in the civil rights movement and in pushing their labor unions to end race discrimination in the workplace and to take a stand against Jim Crow in all its forms.

Establishing the Commission

With the election of Democrat John F. Kennedy to the presidency in 1960 many believed a new day was dawning. Esther Peterson, an early supporter of Kennedy and a friend of his from her Washington lobbying days with the AFL-CIO, had set up a Women for Kennedy National Committee in 1959, helping elect Kennedy in an extremely close vote. She accepted Kennedy's appointment as director of the U.S. Women's Bureau and immediately went to work strategizing about how the long-stymied labor feminist agenda from the 1940s could be enacted. She quickly revived the idea of a presidential commission on women. Within two months of Kennedy's inaugural speech in January 1961, Peterson met with trade union women and convinced a small committee, including Dollie Robinson and Kitty Ellickson, to begin drafting a proposal for a presidential commission. Before approaching Kennedy, Peterson lined up Secretary of Labor Arthur Goldberg, a former labor counsel to the Steelworkers and the CIO and an old friend of Peterson, and other governmental officials and made sure she had the support of her base: women in labor organizations, in the Democratic party, and in the social feminist Women's Bureau network. President Kennedy was closer politically and socially to labor feminists than to the equal rights feminists gathered under the banner of the NWP, and may have preferred establishing a commission to pushing for the passage of the ERA. Yet in agreeing to set up the commission, Kennedy also was responding to pressure from labor feminists and their allies.

Peterson proposed the commission on women to Secretary Goldberg in June, noting that it would "help women move to full partnership and genuine equality of opportunity" and "substitute constructive recommendation for the futile agitation about the ERA." It would also make suggestions on "adopting protective laws to changing conditions," on "new and expanded services required for women as workers, wives, and mothers," and other topics. Having secured Goldberg's blessing, Peterson now convinced Ellickson to take a leave from her job at the AFL-CIO and devote herself full-time to the commission. Ellickson agreed, and in consultation with Peterson, Goldberg, trade union women, and Women's Bureau staff, she prepared a background paper detailing the rationale for the commission.[40]

In early December, Goldberg wrote President Kennedy to secure his support, relying on language drawn almost word for word from Ellickson's draft proposal. Kennedy agreed, signing Executive Order 10980 establishing the President's Commission on the Status of Women (PCSW) on December 14, 1961. Peterson asked that Eleanor Roosevelt be appointed chair, a largely honorific position, and that Kitty Ellickson be made the executive secretary, a key administrative appointment responsible for coordinating the work of the commission and its many committees and helping draft committee and commission reports. Peterson acted as executive vice-chair and took the lead in appointing the twenty-six commissioners (eleven men and fifteen women) and the dozens of others who joined the PCSW's subcommittees and consultations. She insisted that the PCSW be bipartisan and that it include high-level government officials as well as prominent public men and women from business, labor, and the university sector. On the commission itself sat

IUE's Mary Callahan, National Council for Negro Women president Dorothy Height, AFL-CIO secretary-treasurer William Schnitzler, Congresswoman Edith Green, Radcliffe College president Mary Bunting, Senator Maurine Neuberger, Attorney General Robert Kennedy, historian Caroline R. Ware, New School for Social Research president Henry David, *Ladies' Home Journal* public affairs editor Margaret Hickey, and others. Peterson selected Princeton University economics professor Richard Lester as the commission's vice-chair. The seven subcommittees and four consultations advising the commission had a similar mix of appointees, including trade union women Caroline Davis, Addie Wyatt, Bessie Hillman, civil rights activist and lawyer Pauli Murray, IUE President James Carey, Mary Dublin Keyserling, who would move into the U.S. Women's Bureau directorship in 1964, and dozens of others.[41]

The Labor Feminist Agenda and *American Women*

Given the large and diverse constituency of the PCSW, its final report, *American Women*, was not simply a restatement of the longstanding agenda of labor feminism: other political perspectives were represented. Auto worker leader Caroline Davis, for example, who served on the Committee on Private Employment, felt the commission had been unduly swayed by employer arguments against government regulation. Davis urged tough new government policies forbidding sex discrimination that would cover *all* employers in the private sector. The Commission, however, ended up recommending an executive order favoring "equal opportunity for women" that covered *only* a small minority of employers: those with federal contracts. The majority of employers were asked by the commission to initiate *voluntary* equal opportunity policies and "to examine individual qualifications rather than accept general attitudes when hiring women."[42]

Similarly, labor feminists Addie Wyatt, Bessie Hillman, and Mary Callahan, all on the Committee on Protective Labor Legislation, were dismayed when some of their recommendations were rebuffed by the commission. The commission agreed with the committee that woman-only state maximum hour laws should be "maintained, strengthened, and expanded" until other provisions were in place. But the commission *rejected* its proposal that the woman-only maximum hour laws, many of which offered *better* health and safety protection and set *mandatory* limits on work time, be used as the model for all workers. Instead, the commission favored the weaker Fair Labor Standards Act model, which eschewed mandatory hour limits and relied solely on the disincentive of "premium pay" for overtime as a "deterrent" to "excessive hours." This defeat arguably is part of the reason why work hours in the United States are among the longest in the industrial world.[43]

Nevertheless, because of Peterson's influence as executive vice-chair and the involvement of many other labor feminists, the priorities of the commission and many of its key policy recommendations reflect those animating the postwar labor feminist wing of the women's movement. The commission, for example, assumed that "women work in home and out for income and self-fulfillment," and its aim was dual: to open up opportunities for women in the market sphere and to enhance women's satisfaction in non-market endeavors. The report held that these changes, "long overdue," would not come about without societal and government action. The problems women faced were structural and social, not private and individual. "Full equality of rights" had been denied women: employers, unions, and the government had an obligation to rectify that situation.[44]

Later characterized by Peterson as an exercise in "the art of the possible," the report's recommendations provoked criticism when first released and continue to remain controversial. Yet set in the context of its time, *American Women* was a far-reaching document that condemned sex discrimination and offered a concrete set of recommendations aimed at achieving gender equality. The PCSW did not endorse the ERA, deftly sidestepping the issue by relying on Pauli Murray's contention that equality of rights under the law could be advanced through the Fourteenth Amendment and thus, the ERA, "need not now be sought." But it did assume that there were problems women faced because they were *women*, a view not widely shared at the time, and it called unequivocally for the right to employment for all women. This right, the commission pointed out, could only be achieved by eliminating the particular barriers faced by low-income women and mothers and by ending discrimination against "nonwhite" and other minority women.[45]

Ironically, the few contemporary commentators who took the report seriously—much of the popular media treatment was "humorous, condescending or tinged with sexual undertones," according to Ellickson[46]—often saw it as undermining the very behavior some later critics claimed it reinforced. By affirming women's right to employment, contemporary commentators, with few exceptions, worried that *American Women* encouraged women to abandon their home responsibilities. In contrast, later criticism faulted the commission for paying too much attention to the needs of mothers and homemakers and not enough to women's employment rights. The commission's concern for women's family responsibilities and for helping them meet the multiple demands of home, community, and the economy was viewed as undermining women's claim to paid careers and to employment equity.[47]

The report, however, was optimistic that the long list of concrete interventions they urged would not only help reconcile market work and family life but would move all women toward first-class economic citizenship. The commission sought greater respect for women's nonmarket work and "more attention to the services needed for home and community life." Specific recommendations included income guarantees for pregnant and unemployed women, childcare services for women "whether they were working outside the home or not," better tax policies for families raising children, and changes in the Social Security system that would allow housewives to build up equity as if they were earning wages. *American Women* favored opening up educational and training opportunities so that women could move into jobs traditionally held by men. At the same time, the commission recognized the need to upgrade the conditions in what labor feminists called the "woman-employing occupations," where the vast majority of women worked. As part of that effort, the commission endorsed raising minimum wages, expanding the number of jobs covered by labor laws, ending sex-based wage discrimination, and passing "equal pay for comparable work" legislation, long a labor feminist priority. Finally, the commission favored a firm governmental commitment to the right of workers to organize and bargain collectively and to programs increasing women's political and civic leadership.[48]

In contrast to the women's movement of the late 1960s and early 1970s, the commission emphasized reaching equality through revaluing the work women did rather than pulling down the walls separating men and women's jobs or rethinking the gendered division of labor. The Committee on Protective Labor Law, heavily weighted toward labor women, did question conventional notions of masculinity by arguing that many of the stronger labor rights and protections women enjoyed under state law, such as limits on involuntary overtime and shorter hours, should be extended to men. In so doing, they were unmasking the myth of male power in the marketplace, that is, the gendered *assumption* that men, unlike women, did not need protection from market forces. Yet the commission rejected this recommendation in part because no one challenged masculinity in the home: it was agreed that men, unlike women, had only a limited capacity to nurture and that their nature prevented them from taking a primary role in the home. Nor did anyone argue that men ought to have *more* domestic duties and that limiting men's work time would open up that possibility.[49] Such a wholesale assault on the gender division of labor and on notions of masculinity and femininity would not emerge until later. But that assault was made possible by the work of earlier feminists.

An Unfinished Agenda

In 1973, Kitty Ellickson wrote her own history of the President's Commission on the Status of Women. Now in her sixties and in semi-retirement, she had time to reflect, ten years later, on its limits as well as its achievements. In a remarkably charitable spirit, Ellickson welcomed the new feminism that had swept her generation's work aside. She described it "as a different wave in the long struggle for women's equality." And although it was "more representative of professional and upper middle-class groups than the larger number of wage workers," it reflected "the desire of young women to find their identity, [to have] control over their own bodies, and overcome the many discriminations the PCSW by its very nature could not handle." She listed these as "the psychological aspects of discrimination, abortion, and the sharing of household tasks." Yet the PCSW agenda, she continued to believe, still best represented the needs of wage-earning women.[50]

Today, in 2009, the problems of low-wage women and the difficulties of combining income-earning and caregiving, two central concerns of labor feminists, seem more pressing than ever. Indeed, class inequalities among women as well as men have soared to levels not known since before the New Deal, producing extremes of ostentatious wealth and grinding poverty. The economic situation for many women, particularly for women of color and for single heads-of-household, is worsening. Forty-seven percent of the nation's wage and salary workforce is now female, but many of these women continue to be relegated to the lowest-paid, least prestigious jobs. A whopping

90 percent of those earning less than $15,000 annually and over two-thirds of those making under $25,000 are women.[51]

To make matters worse, although many men of all classes engage in caring labor at home and in their communities, the rise of female-headed families and the aging of the population have resulted in increased numbers of women caring for children and elderly relatives with little help from men, financially or emotionally. The highly touted family-friendly workplace—that coveted market nook with flexible work schedules, job sharing, childcare assistance, and comprehensive health and welfare coverage—is not yet a reality for the majority of salaried employees let alone hourly workers. Those needing help the most, hourly workers stuck in low-paying jobs, are the last to benefit. They cannot afford to send their children to the on-site childcare center, even if one exists. And in workplaces where bathroom breaks are still monitored, taking time off for a child's graduation or leaving early to fix an aging parent's heater in the dead of winter can mean losing one's job.[52]

Labor feminists believed that the needs of low-income women and of those responsible for caregiving were different from those of other groups and that those needs had to be considered in formulating policy and priorities. For them, that meant redesigning workplaces to fit nonwork schedules, curtailing involuntary market work as well as involuntary domesticity; raising the pay, status, and working conditions of traditional women's work in the home and in the market; and creating social supports and benefits that made it possible for all women to have opportunities for education, leisure, and citizenship as well as satisfying work and social relationships. They believed that these advances would only come when women organized politically and economically. This was the "bread and roses" tradition of unionism that working-class women had carried forward for generations.

In October 1971, Esther Peterson penned a letter to Representative Martha Griffiths in which she explained why she no longer opposed the ERA. Hers was not a letter admitting she was wrong. She simply noted that since few woman-only state laws remained, many of the reasons to oppose the ERA had disappeared.[53] Peterson was relieved that this barrier to cross-class alliances among women was finally gone. Yet class differences had not disappeared, she stressed, and these differences should not be forgotten. She urged women like Griffiths "who have found changes in the law to be to their advantage to make every effort to assist those who still may be exploited."[54] It is for historians to assess whether her admonition was heeded.

NOTES

This article was originally published online as "The Labor Feminist Origins of the U.S. Commissions on the Status of Women" on the Scholar's Edition of *Women and Social Movements in the United States, 1600–2000*, 13, no. 1 (March 2009), at http://asp6new .alexanderstreet.com/was2. Used by permission.

1. Betty Friedan, *Feminine Mystique* (New York: Norton, 1963), and President's Commission on the Status of Women (PCSW), *American Women: Report of the President's Commission on the Status of Women* (Washington, DC: Government Publications Office, 1963). For historical treatments, see, for example, Nancy Woloch, *Women and the American Experience: A Concise History*, 2nd ed. (New York: McGraw-Hill, 2001), 482–492, and Ellen Carol DuBois and Lynn Dumenil, *Through Women's Eyes: An American History with Documents* (Boston: Bedford/St. Martin's Press, 2005), 559–562, 588–592.

2. PCSW, *American Women*, quote from 4.

3. For the list of state commissions as of January 1965, Margaret Mead and Frances Balgley Kaplan, eds., *American Women: The Report of the President's Commission on the Status of Women and Other Publications of the Commission* (New York: Scribner, 1965), 171–172. Many of the records of the commissions on the status of women are now available on the *Women and Social Movements in the United States, 1600–2000*, Scholar's Edition, database and website.

4. On NOW and the 1966 conference, Betty Friedan, *Life So Far: A Memoir* (New York: Simon & Schuster, 2000), 164–179; Cynthia Harrison, *On Account of Sex: The Politics of Women's Issues, 1945–1968* (Berkeley: University of California Press, 1988), 192–209; Susan Hartmann, *From Margin to Mainstream: American Women and Politics since 1960* (New York: Knopf, 1989), 58–69; Dorothy Sue Cobble, *The Other Women's Movement: Workplace Justice and Social Rights in Modern America* (Princeton, NJ: Princeton University Press, 2004), 182–186; and "The Founding of NOW," http://www.now.org/history/the_founding.html (accessed October 10, 2008).

5. The scholarship on the origins and the politics of *The Feminine Mystique* is also still surprisingly thin, although some excellent studies do exist. See, for example, Daniel Horowitz, *Betty Friedan and the Making of the Feminine Mystique: The American Left, the Cold War, and Modern Feminism* (Amherst: University of Massachusetts Press, 1998).

6. Cobble, *The Other Women's Movement*, 3.

7. On the history of the term "feminist," see Estelle B. Freedman, *No Turning Back: The History of Feminism and the Future of Women* (New York: Ballantine, 2002), 3–6.

8. William O'Neill, "Feminism as a Radical Ideology," in *Dissent: Explorations in the History of American Radicalism*, ed. Alfred F. Young (DeKalb: Northern Illinois University Press, 1968), 275–277, and William O'Neill, *Feminism in America: A History*, 2nd rev. ed. (New Brunswick, NJ: Transaction, 1989), xiv. I prefer using the terms "social feminist" and "equal rights feminist" to the more popular categories of "equality" and "difference" feminists. The latter labels are misleading because

both groups believed in women's "equality" and few in either group believed that men and women were the "same." I consider labor feminism a strand within a broader social feminist movement. Not every social feminist, however, was a labor feminist. Labor feminists stressed labor organizations as vehicles for lifting women's status, for example, an emphasis not shared by all social feminists.

9. Kathryn Kish Sklar, Anja Schuler, and Susan Strasser, eds., *Social Justice Feminists in the United States and Germany: A Dialogue in Documents, 1885–1933* (Ithaca, NY: Cornell University Press, 1998), 5–6.

10. The debates among feminists in the 1920s are illuminated in Nancy F. Cott, *The Grounding of Modern Feminism* (New Haven, CT: Yale University Press, 1987); Kathryn Kish Sklar, "Why Were Most Politically Active Women Opposed to the ERA in the 1920s?" in *Women and Power in American History*, ed. Kathryn Kish Sklar and Thomas Dublin (Englewood Cliffs, NJ: Prentice-Hall, 1991), 2:154–173; and Amy Butler, *Two Paths to Equality: Alice Paul and Ethel M. Smith in the ERA Debate, 1921–1929* (Albany: State University of New York Press, 2002).

11. Cobble, *The Other Women's Movement*, 60–61, 94–96. On Newman and Schneiderman, Annelise Orleck, *Common Sense and a Little Fire: Women and Working-Class Politics in the United States, 1900–1965* (Chapel Hill: University of North Carolina Press, 1995).

12. On the background of NWP members, Butler, *Two Paths to Equality*; Leila J. Rupp and Verta Taylor, *Survival in the Doldrums: The American Women's Rights Movement, 1945 to the 1960s* (New York: Oxford University Press, 1987); and Carl Brauer, "Women Activists, Southern Conservatives and the Prohibition of Sex Discrimination in Title VII of the 1964 CRA," *Journal of Southern History* 49 (February 1983): 37–56.

13. On social feminists, Jan Doolittle Wilson, *The Women's Joint Congressional Committee and the Politics of Maternalism, 1920–1930* (Urbana: University of Illinois Press, 2007), and Susan Ware, *Beyond Suffrage: Women in the New Deal* (Cambridge, MA: Harvard University Press, 1981).

14. Cobble, *The Other Women's Movement*, chs. 2, 6.

15. The phrase "doldrum years" is taken from the title of Rupp and Taylor's book, *Survival in the Doldrums*.

16. Ibid.; Harrison, *On Account of Sex*; Kathleen Laughlin, *Women's Work and Public Policy: A History of the Women's Bureau, U.S. Department of Labor, 1945–1970* (Boston: Northeastern University Press, 2000); and Deborah Gray White, *Too Heavy a Load: Black Women in Defense of Themselves, 1894–1994* (New York: Norton, 1999).

17. Cobble, *The Other Women's Movement*, chs. 1, 2.

18. Ironically, the Fair Labor Standards Act in 1938 was supposedly gender-neutral in that it covered both men and women. Yet because it covered jobs primarily in the industrial sector, fewer women than men were protected.

19. Cobble, *The Other Women's Movement*, chs. 1–6.

20. For biographical sketches and further sources on these and other labor women reformers, consult Cobble, *The Other Women's Movement*, 25–49.

21. Ibid., 34–36, 151–164, 181–182; Esther Peterson (with Winifred Conkling), *Restless: The Memoirs of Labor and Consumer Activist Esther Peterson* (Washington, DC: Caring Publishing, 1995); and Esther Peterson Papers, Schlesinger Library on the History of Women, Harvard University, Cambridge, MA (hereafter EP-SL).

22. On Ellickson, Cobble, *The Other Women's Movement*, 35–37, and Kitty Ellickson Papers, Archives of Labor and Urban Affairs, Wayne State University, Detroit (hereafter cited KPE-ALUA).

23. On Callahan, Cobble, *The Other Women's Movement*, 31–32; interview with Mary Callahan by Alice Hoffman and Karen Budd, 7 May 1976, *Trade Union Woman Oral History Project* (microfilm edition, 1979) (hereafter cited TUWOHP); and *IUE News*, October 8, 1979, and May 11, 1959, 5.

24. Quotes from Wyatt, "'An Injury to One Is an Injury to All': Addie Wyatt Remembers the Packinghouse Workers Union," *Labor Heritage* 12 (Winter/Spring 2003): 6–27, and interview with Addie Wyatt by Rick Halpern and Roger Horowitz, January 30, 1986, United Packinghouse Workers of America Oral History Project, State Historical Society of Wisconsin, Madison. See also Cobble, *The Other Women's Movement*, 31–33, 201–203.

25. On Davis, Cobble, *The Other Women's Movement*, 31–34; cites from interview with Caroline Davis by Ruth Meyerowitz, July 23, 1967, TUWOHP, 83, 112–114; and "Lady Labor Leader: To Keep Labor Peace and Prosperity in an Indiana Factory, the Boss of Local 764 Just Acts Like a Woman," *Life*, June 30, 1947.

26. See, for example, Series V, Inter-American Commission of Women, Doris Stevens Papers, 1884–1983, and Folders 7, 16, 28, 30–33, 69, 75–77, Mary Anderson Papers, both in Schlesinger Library on the History of Women, Harvard University, Cambridge, MA. For an argument that U.S. and Latin American feminists differed on the goals of CIM in its early years, Megan Threlkeld, "The Pan American Conference of Women, 1922: Successful Suffragists Turn to International Relations," *Diplomatic History* 31, no. 5 (November 2007): 801–828. See also Francesca Miller, *Latin American Women and the Search for Social Justice* (Hanover, NH: University Press of New England, 1991).

27. Carol Miller, Jean Quataert, and Marilyn Lake, among others, have recounted parts of this fascinating interwar history: Miller, "'Geneva: The Key to Equality': Interwar Feminists and the League of Nations," *Women's History Review* 3, no. 2 (1944): 219–245; Quataert, *The Gendering of Human Rights in the International Systems of Law in the Twentieth Century* (Washington, DC: American Historical Association, 2006); and Lake, "From Self-Determination via Protection to Equality via Non-discrimination: Defining Women's Rights at the League of Nations and the United Nations," in *Women's Rights and Human Rights: International Historical Perspectives*, ed. Patricia Grimshaw, Katie Holmes, and Marilyn Lake (New York: Palgrave, 2001), 254–271. On Hesselgren, Lene Buchert, "Kerstin Hesselgren, 1872–1964," *Prospects* (UNESCO, International Bureau of Education) 34, no. 1 (March 2004): 127–136.

28. Anderson emigrated from Sweden in 1889 at the age of sixteen and maintained strong links with her country of origin. See Mary Anderson's memoir, *Woman at*

Work: The Autobiography of Mary Anderson as told to Mary Winslow (Minneapolis: University of Minnesota Press, 1951), ch. 1. See also Mary Anderson Papers, Schlesinger Library on the History of Women, Harvard University, Cambridge, MA. Interestingly, Esther Peterson also became friends with Hesselgren in the 1940s and 1950s while she was in Sweden and maintained ties with her until Hesselgren's death in 1964. See, for example, Folder 361, EP-SL.

29. For a recent discussion of the early U.N. Commission on the Status of Women, Jo Butterfield, "Playing Russian Roulette: Cold War Politics, International Feminism and the Stakes over the United Nations Commission on the Status of Women," paper prepared for the 14th Annual Berkshire Conference on the History of Women, University of Minnesota, June 2008.

30. On Miller, see, for example, Box 1, Folder 1, and Series V, International Labor Organization, 1936–1967, Frieda S. Miller Papers, 1909–1973, A-37, Schlesinger Library on the History of Women, Harvard University, Cambridge, MA (hereafter, FM-SL); Cobble, *The Other Women's Movement*, 27–29, chs. 2–7. Miller remained active in international efforts to secure women's economic and social rights throughout the 1950s and 1960s.

31. Cobble, *The Other Women's Movement*, 52–54, 63–64. "Statement of Frieda S. Miller," U.S. House of Representatives, *Equal Rights Amendment to the Constitution and Commission on the Legal Status of Women: Hearings before Subcommittee No. 1* of the Committee on the Judiciary, March 10 and 12, 1948 (Washington, DC: GPO, 1948), 102 (hereafter U.S. House, *Equal Rights Hearings, 1948*).

32. Harrison, *On Account of Sex*, 26.

33. Text of H.R. 1972, H.R. 1996, H.R. 2003 (and other identical women's status bills), reproduced in U.S. House, *Equal Rights Hearings, 1948*, 89.

34. "Statement of Frieda S. Miller," in U.S. House, *Equal Rights Hearings, 1948*, 103.

35. Minutes, 9 January 1947, and 3 February 1947, Labor Advisory Committee, box 6, file 140, FM-SL; statement of Frieda Miller, 15 April 1949, box 8, file 168, FM-SL; and box 91, file 12, KPE-ALUA, pt. 1. See also "Agenda—Labor Advisory Committee Meeting," 3–4 June 1948, box 6, File 141, FM-SL, and Peterson, *Restless*, 102–114.

36. Cobble, *The Other Women's Movement*, 63. For Lawson quotes, see Steven F. Lawson, preface to *To Secure These Rights: The Report of President Harry S. Truman's Committee on Civil Rights*, edited with an introduction by Steven F. Lawson (Boston: Bedford/St. Martin's Press, 2004), iv.

37. "Statement of Frieda S. Miller," U.S. House, *Equal Rights Hearings, 1948*, 100.

38. U.S. House, *Equal Rights Hearings, 1948*, 10–11, 215.

39. Cobble, *The Other Women's Movement*, 60–66; minutes, Labor Advisory Committee meeting, 9 January 1947, Box 6, File 140, FM-SL.

40. Cobble, *The Other Women's Movement*, 145–155, 159–161.

41. Ibid., 148–161; Harrison, *On Account of Sex*, 109–126; and PCSW, *American Women*, 77–85.

42. Cobble, *The Other Women's Movement*, 170–171; PCSW, *Committee on Private Sector Employment* (Washington, DC: GPO, 1963); and PCSW, *American Women*, 27–34.

43. Cobble, *The Other Women's Movement*, 171–172; PCSW, *Committee on Protective Labor Legislation* (Washington, DC: GPO, 1963); PCSW, *American Women*, 36–37; and International Labor Organization, *Key Indicators of the Labour Market*, 5th ed. (Geneva: ILO, 2007).

44. Cobble, *The Other Women's Movement*, 169, and PCSW, *American Women*, 2, 27–34, 44–46.

45. Esther Peterson, "The Kennedy Commission," in *Women in Washington*, ed. Irene Tinker (Beverly Hills, CA: Sage Publications, 1983), 29; and PCSW, *American Women*, 4–5, 18–26, 35–39, 43, for the ERA quote and the argument that the U.S. Constitution "now embodies equality of rights for men and women," 45–46.

46. Katherine Pollak Ellickson, "The President's Commission on the Status of Women: Its Formation, Functioning, and Contribution," unpublished manuscript, January 1976, box 90, file 1A, KPE-ALUA, pt. 1, 13.

47. Cobble, *The Other Women's Movement*, 170.

48. PCSW, *American Women*, 19–23, 37, 39, 40–43, 49–52.

49. PCSW, *Committee on Protective Labor Legislation*, and PCSW, *American Women*.

50. Cobble, *The Other Women's Movement*, 196; Katherine Ellickson, "Eleanor Roosevelt's Contribution to the PCSW," n.d., box 6, file 40, KPE-ALUA, pt. 2. See also Ellickson, "The President's Commission on the Status of Women."

51. Dorothy Sue Cobble, "Introduction," 1–12, and Vicky Lovell, Heidi Hartmann, and Misha Werschkul, "More Than Raising the Floor: The Persistence of Gender Inequalities in the Low-Wage Labor Market," Table 2.1, 36, both in *The Sex of Class: Women Transforming American Labor*, ed. Dorothy Sue Cobble (Ithaca, NY: Cornell University Press, 2007).

52. Cobble, "Introduction," and Netsy Firestein and Nicola Dones, "Unions Fight for Work and Family Policies: Not for Women Only," 140–154, both in *The Sex of Class: Women Transforming American Labor*, ed. Dorothy Sue Cobble (Ithaca, NY: Cornell University Press, 2007).

53. After *Rosenfeld v. Southern Pacific Co.* (1968), in which a California district court invalidated a sex-based weightlifting law, holding that it conflicted with Title VII of the Civil Rights Act, many states followed the court's reasoning by repealing or amending their protective laws for women. See Karen J. Maschke, *Litigation, Courts, and Women Workers* (New York: Praeger, 1989), 44–45, and Cobble, *The Other Women's Movement*, 182–190.

54. Esther Peterson to Martha Griffiths, 12 October 1971, Box 54, File 1061, EP-SL.

8

Expanding the Boundaries of the Women's Movement

Black Feminism and the Struggle for Welfare Rights

PREMILLA NADASEN

The . . . dismantling of Aid to Families with Dependent Children (AFDC), the federal safety net for poor women and children, [took] place with relatively minimal protest and outrage. Local welfare rights organizations planned demonstrations, the National Organization for Women (NOW) launched a day of protest, and a network of mostly academic women known as the Committee of 100 lobbied Congress and organized a picket at the White House. Progressive think tanks and public policy institutes expressed concern about the turn of events. But compared with the response from women nationwide when the legal right to abortion was threatened in the late 1980s or when Anita Hill charged Supreme Court nominee Clarence Thomas with sexual harassment, the end of welfare as we knew it became reality with a disheartening measure of public apathy.

The lack of protest suggests that welfare, although it is the main economic support for women in need in the United States, is still not considered by most feminists a women's issue. At the same time, civil rights organizations, seeking to challenge white Americans' conflation of poverty and race, have been reluctant to make African American welfare mothers symbolic of the Black plight. And working-class movements have historically focused on workplace issues, distancing themselves from the non-wage-earning poor. These strategic choices and the deeply embedded negative stereotypes of women on welfare that permeate American culture have made welfare a difficult and unlikely issue around which progressives can organize. Yet, despite the difficulties of recruiting allies to their cause, poor Black women, along with other women of color, have fought for decades to demonstrate the connections among race, class, and gender injustice and to use the demand for welfare rights as a vehicle for developing feminist theory and action. The welfare rights movement of the 1960s and 1970s provides one example of this phenomenon.

The feminist politics of the welfare rights movement were perhaps best summed up by Johnnie Tillmon, AFDC recipient and welfare rights organizer since the early 1960s. Tillmon's 1972 *Ms.* article, "Welfare Is a Women's Issue," reflected the long struggle to define the welfare rights movement as a part of the larger women's movement. Tillmon wrote:

> The truth is that AFDC is like a super-sexist marriage. You trade in *a* man for *the* man. But you can't divorce him if he treats you bad. He can divorce you, of course, cut you off anytime he wants. *The* man runs everything. In ordinary marriage sex is supposed to be for your husband. On AFDC you're not supposed to have any sex at all. You give up control of your own body. It's a condition of aid. You may even have to agree to get your tubes tied so you can never have more children just to avoid being cut off welfare. *The* man, the welfare system, controls your money. He tells you what to buy, what not to buy, where to buy it, and how much things cost. If things—rent, for instance—really cost more than he says they do, it's just too bad for you. He's always right. Everything is budgeted down to the last penny and you've go to make your money stretch. *The* man can break into your house anytime he wants to and poke into your things. You've got no right to protest. You've got no right to privacy when you go on welfare. Like I said. Welfare's a super-sexist marriage.[1]

. . . . In her analysis, welfare combined racial, class, and gender oppressions, laying the basis for an argument that it should be defined as a feminist issue.

Black welfare activists like Tillmon formulated a distinctive and broadly based analysis of women's liberation that spoke to the needs of many women who were not traditionally considered a part of the feminist movement. They put forth an insightful critique of the welfare system and the ways in which it controlled and regulated the sexuality and lives of women. The movement was comprised primarily of poor Black women on AFDC who organized protests and planned campaigns to demand higher welfare benefits, protection of their civil rights, and better treatment from their caseworkers. But it also drew support from other poor women of color and white women who came to see gender as central to the politics of welfare and who increasingly identified as feminists.

Even welfare rights activists who were more reluctant to identify as feminists nevertheless articulated economic demands that increasingly asserted a critique of gender roles, patriarchy, and proscribed sexuality. For example, these activists sought to bring dignity to their work as mothers and defy a culture that for the most part denied them the right to be mothers. They also challenged the belief that paid work was automatically liberating and explored the exploitative conditions in the labor market under which most women, especially poor women of color, worked. Rather than prescribing that women either enter the workforce or stay home with children, choose to marry or reject marriage, welfare activists demanded that women have the power to define their own lives. . . .

Most welfare recipients, even those who became activists, cannot be called intellectuals, in the traditional sense of the word. Their analysis was forged not from a theoretical understanding of women's place but from a worldview constructed out of their day-to-day lives. The material reality of their circumstances and the culture that surrounded them shaped a distinctive notion of gender politics and identity. These women thus became organic intellectuals, theorizing the interconnections among race, class, and gender on the basis of their daily experience. In the context of other social movements of the 1960s and 1970s, they produced a counterhegemonic discourse that challenged the social position to which they, as poor women on welfare, were relegated.[2] . . .

The analyses of work, motherhood, family, and sexuality espoused by women welfare rights activists did not form a well-defined ideology at the movement's inception. It emerged haltingly and unevenly as welfare activists engaged in the struggle for improvements in public assistance. . . . Welfare activists continually appealed to other women and women's groups and identified themselves simultaneously as mothers, welfare recipients, workers, sexual partners, political activists, and women. The Washington, D.C., Welfare Alliance, for example, wrote in 1968 to all the women's organizations in the area, including feminist organizations, inviting them to a meeting to discuss President Johnson's welfare proposals.[3] In New York City, Coretta Scott King organized a similar gathering on behalf of the welfare rights movement, to discuss ways that women's groups could support the struggle.[4] One of the most interesting attempts of welfare rights activists to appeal to

women outside their ranks occurred in Michigan. There, they asked Lenore
Romney, the governor's wife, "to intercede on their behalf and as a concerned mother" to oppose proposed cuts in AFDC.[5] From the early 1960s to
1971, the threads of feminist consciousness that were evident among welfare
rights activists at the local level spread across the country, affecting the
development and dynamics of the National Welfare Rights Organization
(NWRO) and the priorities of the larger women's movement.

After 1972, the politics of welfare rights activists became more explicitly
feminist; for instance, they advocated not just mothers' rights but women's
rights and not just personal choice but reproductive rights. Moreover, rather
than simply allying with women's organizations, by 1972, NWRO was calling
itself a women's organization. This transformation from an implicit to an
explicit feminist agenda was a product of the day-to-day struggles waged by
women on welfare, the internal tension between women and men in the
movement, and the larger political climate of the period in which feminism
was becoming a more visible dominant force.

The conflict between women and men leaders within NWRO profoundly
shaped the feminism of welfare rights activists. Throughout the late 1960s
and early 1970s, leaders struggled over who had control of the organization
and the degree to which women's issues ought to take precedence. These
conflicts led women to take over formal leadership of the organization by the
end of 1972 and to put forth a more explicitly woman-centered agenda. Their
struggle for economic security, then, was increasingly tied to their desire for
autonomy as women. Overall, their struggle represented a unique brand of
feminism, one that contributed to and expanded the boundaries of the
women's movement. This article traces the development of a feminist welfare rights movement and the role of poor Black women in its creation.[6]

The Emergence of Welfare Rights

The welfare rights movement began in the early and mid-1960s when hundreds of recipients of AFDC began to express dissatisfaction with the system
of welfare. Disgruntled recipients initially came together in small neighborhood and community groups across the country[,] . . . primarily in response
to local problems with welfare departments, such as a recipient unjustly
removed from the welfare rolls, unable to buy basic necessities, or treated
unfairly by caseworkers. . . .

Many of the local groups ... were headed by women. In Detroit, for example, a group of recipients calling themselves Westside Mothers ADC got involved in practical, problem-oriented campaigns. During its first year, the group met with postal authorities to get locks put on mailboxes in apartment buildings to prevent the theft of welfare checks, negotiated with the welfare department to pay for babysitters for mothers involved in the work experience program, requested special clothing allowances from the welfare department, and persuaded utility companies to eliminate deposits for low-income families.[7] The Englewood Welfare Rights Organization in New Jersey started when "many welfare recipients, through meeting and talking generally with one another, found that they were experiencing some of the [same] difficulties with the Bergen County Welfare Board." This included disrespect from caseworkers and a lack of communication between client and caseworker. When their complaints went unheeded, they began to recruit other recipients to join their newly formed group.[8]

Some individuals drawn to welfare rights activity had a long history of political organizing. Tillmon, a mother of six in Los Angeles who formed Aid to Needy Children-Mothers Anonymous (ANC), worked in a laundry and was also a union shop steward. Tillmon joined the welfare rolls in 1963 because of illness but found the system so degrading that she decided to form a welfare rights group. She visited more than five hundred recipients living in her housing project to get them involved in ANC.[9] A tireless advocate of poor women, Tillmon was instrumental in founding NWRO and served on its executive board until 1972, when she became the first welfare recipient to be elected executive director of the organization.[10] Other welfare recipients traced their political activity to the civil rights movement. Mothers for Adequate Welfare (MAW) in Boston, a multiracial group not affiliated with the national organization, was formed after several mothers in the area attended the 1963 March on Washington. . . .[11] Sometimes these grassroots activists came together on their own; sometimes they got assistance from local churches, students groups, civil rights organizations, or Community Action Agencies, which were funded as part of the War on Poverty to encourage political participation by the poor.

These local groups eventually coalesced in 1967, with the help of middle-class organizers, to form the NWRO, the first national body to represent AFDC recipients. NWRO chapters and other unaffiliated welfare rights groups around the country were highly successful at winning concessions for poor women from state and local welfare departments. Recipients were granted additional allowances for household items, forced the creation of client advisory groups, and overturned some welfare regulations that were considered especially oppressive. On the national level, they won legal victories guaranteeing them the right to due process. The movement, funded largely by churches and foundations, reached its peak in 1968 with thirty thousand members.

The welfare rights movement as a whole, including members, paid organizers, and staff, was diverse and included women and men, African Americans, other people of color, and whites. These diverse groups brought competing notions of liberation and empowerment into the movement. The elected leaders of NWRO were drawn from the ranks of the membership, which was limited to welfare recipients and later broadened to include any poor person. The National Coordinating Committee, which met four times a year, included delegates from each state. The nine-member Executive Committee, which met eight times a year, was elected at the annual conventions and charged with carrying out policies set by the membership. Although this structure was designed to ensure recipient participation, in reality most of the political power in NWRO rested with the paid field organizers and staff in the national office, most of whom were middle-class men, often white.[12] The first executive director of NWRO was George Wiley, an African American who grew up in a predominantly white, relatively privileged community in Rhode Island. . . . In 1967 he was instrumental in the formation of NWRO. By 1970, questions of leadership and political direction of the movement would come to plague the organization, diminishing its political clout, but opening up opportunities for a more vocal Black feminist politics. Then in the mid-1970s internal tensions, severe financial difficulties, and a more hostile political climate, led the NWRO, like most welfare rights organizations, to fold.

The best estimates suggest that the membership of the movement was roughly 85 percent African American, 10 percent white, 5 percent Latina, with a small number of Native American participants as well. Although a handful of men became members, the organization was comprised almost exclusively of women—perhaps 98 percent.[13] In addition to the differences of race/class/gender backgrounds of those involved in the welfare rights movement, political controversies were common between different chapters and even within local groups that were relatively homogeneous in terms of race and gender.[14] Despite the difficulties of speaking of a single movement, certain generalizations about the interests of grassroots members can be made.

In its early years, welfare rights advocates articulated what in practice was a feminist agenda. . . .

Welfare rights activists demanded the right to choose to be mothers or to enter the world of work outside the home; to date and have intimate relationships or to remain single; to have a child or not. They opposed welfare regulations that circumscribed their social lives and told them who they could or could not see. They opposed work requirements forcing women to accept employment when they preferred to stay at home. They opposed the arbitrary power of caseworkers and demanded the right to a fair hearing when caseworkers made decisions they believed were unfair. They demanded higher welfare benefits or "special" grants for items they needed so they could properly take care of themselves and their children. They demanded the right to control their own reproduction, choosing for themselves when and how to take birth control, have an abortion, or be sterilized. And they demanded the right to control their own organizations.

Contesting Motherhood

One of the most important elements of the feminism advocated by early welfare rights advocates was support for women's role as mothers. Many white and Black feminists in the 1960s viewed motherhood as a source of oppression. One of the central goals advanced by radical white feminists such as Shulamith Firestone was "the freeing of women from the tyranny of reproduction."[15] Frances Beal, an important early voice of Black feminism and a founder and leader of the Student Non-Violent Coordinating Committee (SNCC) Black Women's Liberation Committee, initiated in 1966, had a similar view. She argued in her path-breaking article "Double Jeopardy" that "black women sitting at home reading bedtime stories to their children are just not going to make it." She believed that full-time mothers lead an "extremely sterile existence."[16] Beal was responding in part to calls from Black nationalists who claimed Black women could best aid the struggle for racial liberation by having babies. . . . Like Firestone, she wanted to open up rather than limit opportunities for women. In the process, however, their views implied to many that the work that mothers did was not by itself rewarding and ought to be replaced or supplemented with work outside the home. . . .

In contrast to many other feminists in the 1960s, women in the welfare rights movement valued the work that mothers did. Their concerns for their children often spurred their involvement in the welfare rights struggle and their status as mothers was inseparable from their activism.[17] From the inception of the struggle, welfare rights activists referred to themselves as "mothers" or "mother-recipients" and sought to bring dignity and respect to their work as family caregivers.[18] . . . In 1968, reporter Gordon Brumm wrote that "MAW's leaders hold that motherhood—whether the mother is married or not—is a role which should be fully supported, as fully rewarded, as fully honored, as any other."[19] Vera Walker, a welfare rights activist in Kansas and a thirty-year-old mother of five who grew up in a rural Mississippi shack, explained her involvement in welfare rights: "The white man told us what school to go to and when. If he said go to the fields, that is where we went. We worked behind the mule, plowed the white man's land, and made the white man rich. . . . Now I want to see to it that my children get better schooling and better clothes—everything that I didn't have a chance to get."[20] . . .

More than simply exalting motherhood as meaningful and important work or acknowledging the centrality of their children in their lives, welfare recipients also demanded that their labor as mothers be recognized and compensated financially. . . . The movement's slogan "welfare is a right" challenged the long-standing belief that AFDC should be given only to mothers who welfare officials determined were worthy. Instead, welfare rights activists suggested that all poor mothers deserved assistance. . . .

This would best be achieved, they believed, with the implementation of a guaranteed annual income. For the women in the welfare rights movement, this guarantee was necessary as both an avenue to achieve women's economic independence and as compensation for their work as mothers. . . . For poor women to have real autonomy, they had to have the financial support that allowed them to make the same choices that middle-class women were able to make. Welfare rights activists did not just look at the social pressures and norms governing women's lives but also at the financial constraints restricting women's choices. Endorsing the concept of a guaranteed annual income served several purposes at once. It forced the state to recognize housework and childcare as legitimate work, freed women from dependence on men, debunked the racial characterizations of Black women as lazy by acknowledging the work they did as mothers, and gave women a viable option to degrading labor market conditions. . . .

The value welfare rights activists placed on motherhood was a counterpoint to the experiences most African American women had with work and motherhood. Few Black women had the "luxury" of being full-time mothers, and most worked outside the home out of necessity. The majority of white women, even with rising employment rates following World War II, were able to avoid wage work during their peak childbearing and child-raising years. Wage work for poor women and most Black women often meant long hours, drudgery, and meager rewards, not a fulfilling career. As late as 1950, 60 percent of gainfully employed Black women worked in private households or as cleaning women and "help" in hotels, restaurants, and offices.[21] Given the opportunity, many poor African American women preferred to stay home. Thus, for Black women, the struggle to preserve their right to be mothers was viewed historically as a challenge to the subordination of African Americans.[22]

Alternative Family Models

Welfare rights activists were also critical of the ways in which domestic relationships with men could be oppressive to women and especially to mothers. In their exaltation of motherhood, they were not proposing that women on welfare simply marry and accept a subordinate status as mother and homemaker. They condemned the subordination of women in traditional family formations and suggested alternative models. Moreover, they defended their status as single mothers and disputed stereotypes vilifying them. Ultimately, they believed that women should have control over their sexuality and reproduction and autonomy in choosing their partners.

Women in the welfare rights movement responded to widespread attacks on Black single motherhood, views popularized by Daniel Patrick Moynihan's famous 1965 report, *The Negro Family*. In it, Moynihan claimed Black women were domineering, Black men failed to provide for their families, and that the increase in single motherhood in the African American community created a social crisis.[23] . . .

Like other Black feminists, women in the welfare rights movement challenged the idea that strong Black women were dysfunctional. But they went one step further, questioning the primacy of the two-parent family model that Moynihan and most of his critics embraced. They attempted to debunk the notion that single motherhood was a sign of cultural deficiency and challenged the assumption that poor single mothers needed a male breadwinner. . . . Tillmon argued that if a woman was not married, people assumed she had "failed as a woman because [she has] failed to attract and keep a man. There's something wrong with [her]." The meager benefits and stigma attached to welfare served as an "example" to let any woman know what would happen "if she tries to go it alone without a man."[24] Brumm reported that MAW believed that marriage with its "fixed rules and obligations" was a "means for domination more than a means for expressing love."[25] These women argued that social pressures, the welfare system, and the institution of marriage all worked to discourage autonomy by forcing women into subordinate relations with men. For them, liberation meant preserving their right to be women and mothers independent of men.

Welfare activists did not, however, reject men. Instead, they proposed alternative models for female-male relationships. . . ."Instead [of institutional marriage]," Brumm explained, members of MAW "favor love, . . . responsibility toward other persons, and freedom to whatever extent that responsibility allows."[26] An important component of the eligibility criteria for AFDC was that mothers were not to date or be intimately involved with men. Welfare caseworkers believed such relationships would compromise the mother's moral standing or indicate that she no longer needed assistance because the man with whom she was involved could support her. Welfare rights activists asserted their right to date or develop relationships with men without negative repercussions from the welfare department.

Since the AFDC program's inception, caseworkers had conducted investigations to determine recipients' worthiness, sometimes showing up unexpectedly in infamous "midnight raids" to determine if clients were engaged in what they believed was unethical behavior. To counter this pattern of harassment, welfare recipients in Morgantown, West Virginia, wrote a handbook instructing others that "an AFDC mother can have male visitors as often as she wants and go out on dates if she leaves her children in the care of a responsible person." Later, they wrote that although the welfare department will not pay for a divorce, you can get a "pauper's divorce," suggesting women could separate from their husbands and plead ignorance about their whereabouts.[27] When women did marry someone who was not the father of their children and therefore not obligated to provide support, they ideally wanted to continue to receive welfare and maintain their economic independence. Westside ADC Mothers of Detroit sought to overturn a policy which made the new husband financially liable for the children of the recipient.[28] Through such strategies, welfare rights activists attempted to legitimate their status as single parents and assert their right to enter or reject the institution of marriage on their own terms. As Barbara Omolade argues, the survival of single mothers represented a challenge to the patriarchal ideal.[29] Welfare rights activists, by refuting the claim that single motherhood was pathological, similarly attempted to transform dominant notions of who and what comprised a functional family.

Reproductive rights were also an important concern for women on welfare, as they were for many women in this period. . . . Yet within the Black power movement, some people repeatedly called for Black women to refrain from using birth control and to do their "revolutionary duty," which was to have babies to perpetuate the race. . . . In response . . . , Black feminists asserted the benefits of reproductive choice, claimed their right to use birth control, and were adamant that their role in the revolution not be confined to procreation.[30]

. . . For Black women on welfare the problem was compounded by a public outcry about welfare "abuse" that coupled "reform" with efforts to prevent poor women from bearing more children. In some cases, acceptance of welfare benefits was tied directly to sterilization, for instance. This made it necessary and logical for women on welfare to frame reproductive issues not in terms of access to abortion and birth control but choice, a term that would only come into vogue among middle-class white feminists in the mid-1970s. . . . In 1969, when United Movement for Progress (UMP), a predominantly Black antipoverty coalition in Pittsburgh, refused federal funds for six Planned Parenthood clinics that served the poor community, women in the NWRO mobilized against community leaders. Speaking of William Haden, head of the UMP, mother Georgiana Henderson charged, "Who appointed him our leader anyhow? . . . He is only one person—and a man at that. He can't speak for the women of Homewood. . . . Why should I let one loudmouth tell me about having children?"[31] Through their organizing, the mothers had Haden removed as a representative on the antipoverty board and the funds restored to the clinics.

The struggle around the Planned Parenthood clinics in Pittsburgh indicates one way in which women on welfare struggled to keep birth control options open so they could assert their sexual and familial autonomy. Some manuals created by local welfare rights organizations to educate recipients informed them about birth control but stressed that "this is your choice."[32]

In 1971 the NWRO national convention included a panel on abortion, but, as Tillmon explained, "We know how easily the lobby for birth control can be perverted into a weapon against poor women. The word is choice. Birth control is a right, not an obligation. A personal decision, not a condition of a welfare check."[33] The political positions the welfare rights movement took around family and sexuality were an important departure from previous Black women's activism. As Deborah Gray White argues, prior to the 1960s, national leaders attempted to counter racist and sexist characterizations of Black women by portraying them as asexual beings.[34] Women welfare rights activists, on the other hand, vocally asserted their right to sexual freedom.

Work and Liberation

Women in the welfare rights movement also questioned feminist assertions that employment led to liberation. . . . Welfare rights activists, many of whom worked out of necessity, believed that wage labor ought to be a matter of choice. They came to this conclusion because for them, as for most poor women, work was more often a source of oppression than a means of empowerment. Poor women found little that was rewarding or fulfilling in jobs that were physically taxing, unpleasant, and afforded them no autonomy or flexibility.

The different social expectations for Black and white, poor and middle-class women regarding employment were institutionalized when in 1967 welfare "reforms" required recipients to seek work. The Work Incentive Program (WIN) departed from the original premise of AFDC, which insisted that mothers stay home and care for their children; it penalized welfare recipients who did not register for jobs or job training. Welfare rights activists challenged the artificial dichotomy between work and welfare and realized that welfare policies forcing mothers to work contradicted popular notions about their proper role as caretakers. They argued that the work ethic created a double standard; it applied only to men and to women on welfare. In a local Ohio newsletter, one welfare recipient cleverly contrasted her situation with the era's reigning symbol of womanhood: "Jackie Kennedy gets a government check. Is anyone making her go to work?"[35] . . . Women in the welfare rights movement thus analyzed and scrutinized the different expectations society had of white middle-class women and poor women of color. Their demands to be viewed more like their white counterparts illustrates the very different perceptions and realities of gender, domesticity, and motherhood across racial lines.

Welfare rights activists opposed forcing women into a labor market where they were unable to earn enough to support their families. Gender, they argued, was a powerful determinant in pay scales, and women's lower wages created an impossible predicament for single working mothers trying to raise a family. Tillmon pointed out that . . ."a woman with three kids . . . earning the full Federal minimum wage of $1.60 an hour, is still stuck in poverty."[36] Women in the welfare rights movement analyzed the ways in which the family wage system provided for married middle-class women but undercut the wages of their working-class counterparts. Members of MAW, for instance, according to Brumm, argued that working mothers "need nearly the same income as a family man, yet they are expected to take jobs ordinarily occupied by young unmarried women." . . . [37]

Yet welfare rights activists also sought to ease the problems of women who, out of choice or necessity, entered wage work. In particular, they supported the creation of childcare centers. This was, in fact, "one of the first priorities" of Tillmon's welfare rights organization in California.[38] The NWRO office produced a guide for local welfare rights groups on how to organize a comprehensive community-controlled childcare program, giving them advice on raising money, hiring staff, and planning meals.[39] . . . Although proponents of daycare centers, women in the welfare rights movement were, nevertheless, critical about the dynamic created when poor women were hired to care for other women's children. Afraid of the way institutionalized childcare could be used to oppress women, Tillmon warned that the fight for universal childcare should not be used to create "a reservoir of cheap female labor" that "institutionalized partially self-employed Mammies."[40] . . . Thus, although daycare centers could potentially free some women from the constraints of childcare, it could just as likely create an exploitative situation for other women.

Because Black and white women . . . had different experiences, they came to different conclusions about the necessity of paid employment, the scope of sexual and reproductive freedom they desired, and the value placed on motherhood. For poor Black women, paid employment was not necessarily a challenge to sexual inequality. On the contrary, encouraging women to enter the world of work would only reinforce the kind of exploitation and oppression that many of them faced on a daily basis. Instead, they proposed that women have the option of staying home by providing adequate public support. This, in itself, was a radical challenge to the socially defined gender roles of poor Black women, who had never been seen primarily as homemakers or mothers. Although some may argue that the welfare rights movement did not pose a challenge to the conventional wisdom that "women's place is in the home," it did question the popular belief that "Black women's place is in the workforce."

Autonomy within NWRO

By the early 1970s, the distinctive feminist analysis that had been gradually formulated at the grassroots level became a more defined element within NWRO, leading to clashes with the national staff, who were predominantly male and mostly white. . . . This struggle for power within the welfare rights movement helped women define and assert their feminist outlook even more clearly.

One of the fundamental issues that divided staff and recipients was how the two groups defined the movement. For the staff, NWRO was a movement of poor people with the primary goal of eradicating economic injustice. . . . Staff members had one goal—to win greater benefits for welfare recipients. For recipient leaders, especially Black women, the issues of power and economic justice were significant; but their struggle was also about racist and sexist ideology, the meaning of welfare, and self-determination. The meager monthly checks, the persistent efforts to force recipients to work outside the home, the poor treatment they received from caseworkers, and the stigma associated with their assistance could not be separated from what society expected of them and how society demeaned them as Black women.

The struggle over the WIN Program exemplified this difference. The women opposed the basic premise of WIN because it required mothers to work. They argued: "This means that a mother with school-age children will be forced (if they do not volunteer) to accept the same old inferior training or jobs that have always been left for poor people."[41] The desire of welfare mothers to have a choice whether to work at home raising their children or to take paid employment outside the home was not always respected by the predominantly male staff of NWRO. Indeed in late 1968, middle-class staff members reversed the organization's earlier stand opposing WIN and accepted a $434,000 contract with the Department of Labor to educate and train participants in the program. This deal was bitterly opposed by women involved in the movement, especially those at the grassroots level. The Philadelphia Welfare Rights Organization, led by Roxanne Jones and Alice Jackson, denounced the national leadership for supporting and helping to implement "the most reactionary program in decades."[42] Challenging society's assumptions about poor mothers, putting forth a morally defensible position, and protecting their dignity and worth as mothers were more important to these women than the infusion of cash to build up the national organization. . . .

NWRO was theoretically structured to ensure control by welfare recipients, but in practice, staff members—who took charge of fund-raising, coordinating welfare rights groups, managing the budget, planning programs, and devising strategy—wielded power in the organization. . . . These middle-class men, were, in effect, the leaders. . . .

Tillmon was one of those asserting women's right to control NWRO and determine its political direction. As Guida West recounts, Tillmon proposed that the nonpoor serve only in supportive roles and advocated a strategy in which women on welfare organize "to try and do something for ourselves and by ourselves to the extent that we could."[43] Central to Tillmon's vision was that women, in addition to challenging the welfare bureaucracy, should develop autonomy and self-sufficiency. . . . For recipient leaders, the methods of organizing and the process of empowering one of the most oppressed sectors of society were as important as demanding that the state provide adequate assistance for the poor. . . .

The issue that in early 1970 led to a permanent division between NWRO staff and recipients and the resignation of many staff members was how to revive the floundering organization. Internal conflict intensified as membership rolls shrank, donations slowed to a trickle, and the political climate became increasingly hostile. The male staff . . . sought to broaden the movement to include the working poor and unemployed fathers. . . . Many recipient leaders opposed this change because they believed the political focus on the needs of women and children would be diluted. As a result of these irresolvable differences, women leaders became convinced of the need for an organization run by and for welfare recipients, meaning mainly poor Black women. [George] Wiley resigned from NWRO in 1972 and began another organization called the Movement for Economic Justice, which included the working poor. Tillmon succeeded him as executive director of NWRO and after that point, the organization was in the hands of the female recipients.

... The welfare rights movement was not sheltered from the politics of the dominant culture, and there was a constant battle over goals, aspirations, and organizational style. Whatever good intentions motivated the national staff, they ended up replicating the very power relations they sought to eradicate. . . . Thus, Black women on welfare had to wage a struggle not only against dominant political institutions and cultural forces but their radical allies as well. This process of seeking empowerment within their organization, in addition to their battles with the state and the labor market, helped crystallize welfare recipients' feminist outlook.

Welfare Is a Women's Issue

By the early 1970s, the ideas that had germinated among welfare rights activists on the local level became part of an analysis that reflected NWRO's place in the larger women's movement. Because of their earlier conflicts with male allies and the growing visibility of women's liberation, women in the welfare rights movement more directly and with greater frequency spoke of themselves as a part of the feminist movement. . . . Even those who did not explicitly characterize their organization as feminist clearly saw the empowerment of women on welfare as their ultimate goal. Rather than eclipsing the struggle for economic justice, the identity of NWRO as a women's group was firmly rooted in members' desire to mitigate the effects of poverty. Far from being contradictory, the diverse goals of the movement reinforced its strength and supported a universalist agenda.

Upon assuming control of NWRO, recipient leaders immediately issued a "Women's Agenda," which defined poverty and welfare as women's issues. The official shift in focus was signaled by changes in procedures as well as priorities. Members, for example, began to refer to the convention chair as chairwoman rather than chairman.[44] At the national convention in 1974, the organization offered a panel on feminist politics at which Margaret Sloan of the newly organized National Black Feminist Organization (NBFO) spoke. Women in the welfare rights movement also endorsed the Equal Rights Amendment; and at one point, welfare leaders on the Executive Committee considered changing the name of the organization to the National Women's Rights Organization.[45] . . .

Perhaps most indicative of the change in the organization at the national level was a pamphlet issued by the national office entitled "Six

Myths about Welfare." The pamphlet wove together an analysis of poverty, welfare, and motherhood from threads that had emerged earlier among grassroots constituencies. Now the NWRO articulated a full-fledged feminist vision of welfare:

> Whether or not one accepts the notion that child-raising should be "woman's work," the fact is that in most American families childraising is woman's work—and hard work, at that. If a woman's husband dies or leaves home, does childraising suddenly cease to be "work"? In effect, that's what the welfare department is saying when it defines "work" solely as a job outside the home. The reality, of course, is that a woman who becomes the head of a household is doing more work, being both the father and the mother of her children. It's at least paradoxical, perhaps cruel, that a society which traditionally extols the virtues of motherhood is simultaneously forcing some mothers to leave their homes and children for low-wage, dead-end, outside jobs.[46]

After women officially took control of NWRO, political activity around reproductive choice expanded as well. The organization took more proactive measures in regard to the forced sterilization of African American, Native American, and Puerto Rican women. . . . In the mid-1970s, the sterilization rate for women on public assistance with three children was 67 percent higher than for women with the same number of children but not on public assistance.[47] Thus, sexual freedom for welfare recipients was defined not only by access to birth control and abortion but also by complete control over one's reproduction, including the right to oppose sterilization and bear healthy children. In 1973 Tillmon, as executive director, issued a statement jointly with Charles Fanueff, executive director of the Association for Voluntary Sterilization, opposing forced sterilization of welfare recipients.[48]

NWRO's position on reproductive rights . . . preceded mass movements of white and Black women around this issue. As early as 1969, the Citywide Welfare Alliance in Washington, D.C., challenged restrictive eligibility procedures for free abortions at the city's only public hospital. . . . After picketing and filing a lawsuit, welfare activists were appointed to a committee to review the hospital's abortion policy.[49] For these activists, access to abortion meant not just demanding its legality but assuring that public funding be available to poor women who otherwise would not be able to afford the service. The concerns of welfare recipients with reproductive rights soon developed into a more widespread political movement. In the mid- and late-1970s several local organizations to end sterilization abuse and protect women's right to abortion were formed, including the Committee for Abortion Rights and against Sterilization Abuse, an interracial group in New York City. In 1981 a group of mostly white socialist feminists formed the Reproductive Rights National Network, which embodied NWRO's goals for both abortion rights and prevention of sterilization abuse.

In the early 1970s mainstream white women's organizations also began to take a greater interest in poverty and welfare. As early as 1970, NOW passed a resolution expressing support for NWRO and recognizing the importance of poverty as a woman's issue: "The poor in the United States are predominantly women. . . . NOW must, therefore, work particularly hard to free our sisters in poverty from the intolerable burdens which have been placed on them. The system must work for the most oppressed if it is to succeed. The National Organization for Women, therefore, proposes to establish at the national level immediate and continuing liaison with the National Welfare Rights Organization and similar groups and urges each chapter to do the same at the local level."[50] The following year, NOW endorsed NWRO's goal of a guaranteed income, which Merrillee Dolan, chair of NOW Task Force for Women in Poverty, said, "is *the* most important women's issue for which we should be fighting."[51] . . .

This success, however, was both temporary and superficial. . . . Once the welfare rights movement folded in 1975, mainstream women's organizations took little action on behalf of women on welfare. Interaction between welfare rights organizations and middle-class white women's organizations was limited largely because of their divergent views about work, family, and independence. . . . Martha Davis argues that the efforts within NOW to address poverty originated mainly with the leadership and that the middle-class membership remained "fixed on formal, legal equality for those already in the workplace as the proper instrument for addressing women's poverty."[52] This was not a strategy that women on welfare, who were fighting for the right to stay home and care for their children, would find useful or appealing. Although a common interest in empowering women brought NWRO and NOW together in the late 1960s and early 1970s, the boundaries of class and race continued to inhibit a long-term alliance as Black welfare activists and white middle-class NOW members developed different strategies to address their own particular experiences of sexism. . . .

Although a successful long-term relationship between NWRO and NOW never developed . . . , the attempts at cooperation reveal the possibilities for alliances across race and class among women. Poor Black women on welfare were positioned at the bottom of the social hierarchy, and this may have inspired their efforts to recruit white and middle-class women as allies. Similarly, they could work with men committed in a practical way to the eradication of poverty—so long as this did not impede the goal of women's autonomy. And they identified with and reached out to the ongoing movement for Black liberation—so long as this did not subsume their concerns as women. . . . Indeed, from their vantage point, such alliances were necessary if a successful struggle was to be waged. But at the same time, they took care to ensure that their integrity and political vision were not compromised.

Conclusion

Poor Black women are positioned at the nexus of race, class, and gender oppression.[53] These women often understood the importance of gender in shaping their lives, but they also realized that all women were not treated in the same way. They believed that how they were treated was determined not just by their sex but by their race and class as well. For poor Black women to decide if racism or sexism or poverty was more important in their lives was both impossible and nonsensical. . . . This reality enabled activists in the welfare rights movement to understand not just how these oppressions coexist, but, for example, how the meaning of class is transformed by and lived through racism and sexism.

Through their struggle to reform the welfare system, poor women formulated a vision of Black feminism. . . . They incorporated aspects of class empowerment, racial liberation, gender equity, and sexual autonomy. Consequently, they were able to organize around welfare rights and understand this work as partly about women's liberation. Their example provides us with a broader definition of women's rights and suggests that the struggle for welfare rights should be considered part of the feminist movement.

Like many other feminists of the 1960s, these women ultimately wanted autonomy, although what that meant for them in concrete terms was quite different from what it meant to women of other class and racial backgrounds. For them, this goal was coupled with both ideological and practical demands. They fought for an increase in welfare benefits or a guaranteed annual income, which would provide the means to make choices about parenthood, employment, and sexuality otherwise closed to them. They believed that economic assistance was not a form of dependency but a source of liberation. They also constructed a political platform that challenged the racist and sexist stereotypes associated with Black single motherhood. The movement, then, was as much a women's movement as a poor people's movement, as much about feminism as Black liberation.

The welfare rights movement, like other Black women's political struggles, has been rendered invisible in most accounts of feminism in the 1960s. . . . But researchers are increasingly turning to the welfare rights movement to better understand women's politics. Annelise Orleck and Anne Valk have examined the role of motherhood as a justification of and motivation for Black women's political involvement in the movement. Felicia Kornbluh has suggested that the movement can help expand our notion of rights beyond a work-centered conceptualization and toward recognition of the rights of consumers. Some historians of the welfare rights movement, in particular Guida West, Jacqueline Pope, and Susan Handley Hertz, have produced pathbreaking work that analyzes the gender politics of the movement.[54] They assert that welfare rights was a social protest of poor women, not simply poor people. But . . . it is not enough to suggest that women in the welfare rights movement identified as consumers, mothers, or addressed issues of concern to women and feminists. In addition, we need to examine whether women in the welfare rights movement—on their own terms—considered themselves feminists and what particular kind of feminism they espoused. . . .

Understanding the welfare fights movement as a part of the struggle for women's liberation in the 1960s forces us to rethink our definition of what constitutes "women's issues." If, as White argues, NWRO, along with the National Black Feminist Organization, was important politically because it put Black women "back at the center of race progress,"[55] then I would argue that NWRO was also significant because it brought a race and class analysis to gender issues. . . . Welfare advocates attempted to define welfare and poverty as women's issues. This gave them a springboard to explore in a more sophisticated way issues of race and class in relation to gender. The Black women in the welfare rights movement were not plagued by the same dilemmas that many middle-class white feminists struggled with: Do we work within the system or outside of it? Do we form a movement of women dedicated to issues of importance only to women; or can we work in organizations that address problems such as poverty, racism, and militarism? As Patricia Hill Collins notes, Black feminists often rejected the oppositional, dichotomized model of organizing.[56] These Black women could simultaneously work on issues of race, class, and gender. They were working for their own benefit and to improve their community. They worked both to make the system work for them as well as to challenge it.

Women in the welfare rights movement opposed essentialized notions of race and gender and formed alliances with Black and white men and white women. Through their organizing efforts they learned that not all women (Black or white) would be their allies and not all African Americans (women or men) would support their political positions. . . . Their "multiple consciousness" encouraged them to become advocates of feminism, proponents of a guaranteed annual income, and combatants in the struggle for Black liberation—all at the same time.

Women in the welfare rights movement were certainly not the first Black women to address the issues of race, class, and gender. But the welfare rights movement was one of the most important organizational expressions of the needs and demands of poor Black women. Predating the outpouring of Black feminist literature in the 1970s, women in the welfare rights movement challenged some of the basic assumptions offered by other feminists—white and Black—and articulated their own version of Black feminism. The problem of economic survival and day-to-day experiences with poverty separated them from some other Black feminists.[57] Black women in the welfare rights movement never sought solutions in self-improvement, racial uplift, or individual assistance. They rejected traditional notions of female respectability—and all of its class trappings—as a condition for their political demands. Rather, they called for a national safety net and demanded that such assistance be a right. Relying on the Black community, although historically important, was still charity; self-empowerment and the guarantee of rights assured long-term solutions.

The process of trying to understand and take seriously the ideas put forth by welfare recipients is part of a long tradition among Black feminists to look to "African-American women not commonly certified as intellectuals by academic institutions [who have nevertheless] functioned as intellectuals." . . . By interpreting their experiences and "clarifying the Black women's standpoint," women in the welfare rights movement contributed in an important way to the development of Black feminist thought and feminist thought more generally.[58] . . . To challenge their position in society effectively, they had to confront racism, sexism, and class oppression. And it was through this effort that they succeeded in creating a movement that was as much a feminist movement as a movement for racial equality and economic justice.

NOTES

The original version of this essay appeared in *Feminist Studies* 28, no. 2 (Summer 2002). Thanks to Betsy Blackmar, Eileen Boris, Eric Foner, Tami Friedman, Bill Gladstone, Barbara Ransby, Daryl Scott, Robyn Spencer, Ula Taylor, and the Oakley Center Faculty Seminar at Williams College for providing valuable feedback and comments on this article. In addition, special thanks to Guida West for sharing her interviews of welfare rights activists. This article was written while I was on a grant provided by the Aspen Institute Nonprofit Sector Research Fund.

1. Johnnie Tillmon, "Welfare Is a Women's Issue," *Ms.* 1 (Spring 1972): 111.

2. For the role of experience in producing counterhegemonic discourse, see Shari Stone-Mediatore, "Chandra Mohanty and the Revaluing of Experience," *Hypatia* 13 (Spring 1998): 116–133, and Paula Stewart Brush, "The Influence of Social Movements on Articulations of Race and Gender in Black Women's Autobiographies," *Gender and Society* 13 (February 1999): 120–137.

3. Etta Horn, of the Washington, D.C., Welfare Alliance, "Letter to D.C. Women's Groups," 23 February 1968, box 24, George Wiley Papers, State Historical Society of Wisconsin, Madison (hereafter cited as Wiley Papers).

4. Coretta Scott King, "Special Message to Mrs. Beulah Sanders and Leaders of Women's Organizations in the New York Area," 23 July 1968, box 24, Wiley Papers.

5. Michigan Welfare Rights Organization, press release, prior to 17 March 1968, box 25, Wiley Papers.

6. The welfare rights movement was a multiracial movement that included other women of color and white women. In some cases, the women described may have been Latina, Native American, white, or their racial background may not have been evident to the writer. Nevertheless, the vast majority of women in the movement were African American.

7. Westside Mothers (ADC), "The Challenge," newsletter, 21 January 1968, box 25, Wiley Papers.

8. Englewood Welfare Rights Organization, report, 16 August 1968, box 25, Wiley Papers.

9. Hobart Burch, "Insights of a Welfare Mother: A Conversation with Johnnie Tillmon," *The Journal* 14 (January–February 1971): 13–23, and Robert McG. Thomas Jr., "Johnnie Tillmon Blackston, Welfare Reformer, Dies at 69," *New York Times*, November 21,1995.

10. The executive director was elected by the Executive Committee.

11. Jeanette Washington, interview by Guida West, New York, September 25, 1981.

12. For an extended discussion, see Guida West, *The National Welfare Rights Movement: The Social Protest of Poor Women* (New York: Praeger, 1981), 57–64. West states that most staff were college-educated white men but included some Black men and white women. There was also, occasionally, a Black woman on staff. The staff was hired and fired by the executive director.

13. David Street, George T. Martin Jr., and Laura Kramer Gordon, *The Welfare Industry: Functionaries and Recipients of Public Aid* (Beverly Hills, CA: Sage Publications, 1979), 124, cited in West, *National Welfare Rights Movement*, 45–46.

14. On local chapters, see Lawrence Nell Bailis, *Bread or Justice: Grassroots Organizing in the Welfare Rights Movement* (Lexington, MA: Heath, 1972); Susan Handley Hertz, *The Welfare Mothers Movement: A Decade of Change for Poor Women* (Lanham, MD: University Press of America, 1981); Larry Jackson and William Johnson, *Protest by the Poor: The Welfare Rights Movement in New York City* (Lexington, MA: Lexington Books, 1984); and Jacqueline Pope, *Biting the Hand That Feeds Them* (New York: Praeger, 1989).

15. Shulamith Firestone, *The Dialectic of Sex: The Case for Feminist Revolution* (New York: Morrow, 1970), 193.

16. Frances Beale [*sic*], "Double Jeopardy: To Be Black and Female," in *Words of Fire: An Anthology of African American Feminist Thought*, ed. Beverly Guy-Sheftall (New York: New Press, 1995), 146–155.

17. For an excellent overview of the connection between mothering and activism, see Alexis Jetter, Annelise Orleck, and Diana Taylor, eds., *The Politics of Motherhood: Activist Voices from Left to Right* (Hanover, NH: University Press of New England, 1997).

18. Massachusetts Welfare Information Center Newsletter, 7 April 1969, box 2, Whitaker Papers, Ohio Historical Society, Columbus (hereafter cited as Whitaker Papers).

19. Gordon Brumm, "Mothers for Adequate Welfare—AFDC from the Underside," *Dialogues* (Boston) 1 (January 1968): 11.

20. Quoted in Bob Agard, "Welfare Rights Group Seeks Charge Accounts," newspaper article (newspaper unknown), 6 December 1968, box 25, Wiley Papers.

21. Jacqueline Jones, *Labor of Love, Labor of Sorrow: Black Women, Work, and the Family, from Slavery to the Present* (New York: Vintage Books, 1986), 257–258.

22. Herbert Gutman, *The Black Family in Slavery and Freedom, 1750–1925* (New York: Vintage Books, 1976), 166–168; Jones, *Labor of Love, Labor of Sorrow*, ch. 2; Eileen Boris, "The Power of Motherhood: Black and White Activist Women Redefine the 'Political,'" in *Mothers of a New World: Maternalist Politics and the Origins of Welfare States*, ed. Seth Koven and Sonya Michel (New York: Routledge, 1993), 213–245; and M. Rivka Polatnick, "Diversity in Women's Liberation Ideology: How a Black and a White Group of the 1960s Viewed Motherhood," *Signs* 21 (Spring 1996): 679–706.

23. See Ricki Solinger, "Race and Value: Black and White Illegitimate Babies, 1945–1965," in *Mothering: Ideology, Experience, and Agency*, ed. Evelyn Nakano Glenn, Grace Chang, and Linda Rennie Forcey (New York: Routledge, 1994), 287–310, and

Regina Kunzel, "White Neurosis, Black Pathology: Constructing Out-of-Wedlock Pregnancy in the Wartime and Postwar United States," in *Not June Cleaver: Women and Gender in Postwar America, 1945–1960*, ed. Joanne Meyerowitz (Philadelphia: Temple University Press, 1994), 304–331.

24. Tillmon, "Welfare Is a Women's Issue," 112.

25. Quoted in Brumm, "Mothers for Adequate Welfare," 11.

26. Ibid.

27. "Your Welfare Rights," handbook written by the Welfare Rights Committee, Monongalia County, Morgantown, WV, n.d., box 3, Whitaker Papers.

28. Allan Becker, Robert Daniels, and Susan Wender, "Proposed Action: Public Assistance," paper submitted to Metropolitan Detroit Branch, ACLU, 17 November 1968, boxes 1134–1136, ACLU Archives, Mudd Library, Princeton University.

29. See Barbara Omolade, *The Rising Song of African American Women* (New York: Routledge, 1994).

30. See especially essays by Beale, "Double Jeopardy" (146–155), Pauli Murray, "The Liberation of Black Women" (186–197), and Michele Wallace, "Anger in Isolation: A Black Feminist's Search for Sisterhood" (220–227), all in *Words of Fire: An Anthology of African American Feminist Thought*, ed. Beverly Guy-Sheftall (New York: New Press, 1995).

31. Quoted in Loretta Ross, "African American Women and Abortion, 1800–1970," in *Theorizing Black Feminisms: The Visionary Pragmatism of Black Women*, ed. Stanlie James and Abena P. A. Busia (New York: Routledge, 1993), 155.

32. Chicago Welfare Rights Organization, handbook, June 1968, box 3, Whitaker Papers, and Mothers for Adequate Welfare, "Your Welfare Rights Manual," n.d., box 3, Whitaker Papers.

33. Tillmon, "Welfare Is a Women's Issue," 115.

34. Deborah Gray White, *Too Heavy a Load: Black Women in Defense of Themselves, 1894–1994* (New York: Norton, 1999), ch. 4.

35. "Ohio Adequate Welfare News," 18 April 1968, box 1, Whitaker Papers.

36. Tillmon, "Welfare Is a Women's Issue," 112.

37. Brumm, "Mothers for Adequate Welfare," 5.

38. West, *National Welfare Rights Movement*, 253.

39. NWRO, "How to Organize a Comprehensive Community Controlled Child Care Program," pamphlet, n.d., box 16, Wiley Papers.

40. Tillmon, "Welfare Is a Women's Issue," 115.

41. Massachusetts Welfare Information Center Newsletter, 7 April 1969, box 2, Whitaker Papers.

42. Francis X. Clines, "Welfare Protest Group Accused of Joining the Establishment for a $434,930 Contract," *New York Times*, May 29, 1969.

43. Johnnie Tillmon, interview with Guida West, quoted in West, *National Welfare Rights Movement*, 101.

44. NWRO, "Strategies for Survival," 1973, box 7, Wiley Papers.

45. West, *National Welfare Rights Movement*, 243, 49.

46. NWRO, "Six Myths about Welfare," pamphlet, 1971, Citywide Coordinating Committee of Welfare Rights Groups Papers, Lehman Library, Columbia University, New York, 5.

47. Thomas Shapiro, *Population Control Politics: Women, Sterilization, and Reproductive Choice* (Philadelphia: Temple University Press, 1995), 103–104.

48. NWRO, "Strategies for Survival." The Association for Voluntary Sterilization was not formed for the prevention of sterilization abuse. Rather, it had its roots in the eugenics movement but was moving toward a position of voluntary sterilization.

49. Anne M. Valk, "Mother Power: The Movement for Welfare Rights in Washington, D.C., 1966–1972," *Journal of Women's History* 11 (Winter 2000): 41–42.

50. "Women in Poverty," statement adopted by the Executive Committee of the National Organization for Women, 29 November 1970, box 21, Wiley Papers. See also Martha Davis, "Welfare Rights and Women's Rights in the 1960s," *Journal of Policy History* 8, no. 1 (1996): 144–165.

51. Merrillee Dolan, chair, Task Force for Women in Poverty, to George Wiley, 1 October 1971, box 36, Wiley Papers.

52. Davis, "Welfare Rights and Women's Rights," 157.

53. See Deborah King, "Multiple Jeopardy, Multiple Consciousness: The Context of a Black Feminist Ideology," *Signs* 14 (Autumn 1988): 42–72, and Evelyn Brooks Higginbotham, "African American Women's History and the Metalanguage of Race," *Signs* 17 (Winter 1992): 251–274.

54. Annelise Orleck, "Political Education of Las Vegas Welfare Mothers," in *The Politics of Motherhood: Activist Voices from Left to Right*, ed. Alexis Jetter, Annelise Orleck, and Diana Taylor (Hanover, NH: University Press of New England, 1997), 102–118; Valk, "Mother Power"; Felicia Kornbluh, "To Fulfill Their 'Rightly Needs': Consumerism and the National Welfare Rights Movement," *Radical History Review* 69 (Fall 1997): 76–113; West, *National Welfare Rights Movement*; Pope, *Biting the Hand That Feeds Them*; and Hertz, *Welfare Mothers Movement*.

55. White, *Too Heavy a Load*, 215.

56. Patricia Hill Collins, *Black Feminist Thought: Knowledge, Consciousness, and the Politics of Empowerment* (New York: Routledge, 1990), ch. 4.

57. Lisa Albrecht and Rose Brewer have urged scholars to look at class differences among women, including Black women; see "Bridges of Power: Women's Multicultural Alliances for Social Changes," in their edited collection, *Bridges of Power: Women's Multicultural Alliances* (Philadelphia: New Society, 1990), 5. See also E. Frances White, "Africa on My Mind: Gender, Counter Discourse, and African American Nationalism," *Journal of Women's History* 2 (Spring 1990): 73–97, for an excellent discussion of Black nationalism and feminism.

58. Collins, *Black Feminist Thought*, 14, 15.

9

Rethinking Global Sisterhood

Peace Activism and Women's Orientalism

JUDY TZU-CHUN WU

In April 1971, approximately one thousand female activists from throughout North America gathered in Vancouver and Toronto, Canada, to attend the Indochinese Women's Conferences. The U.S. and Canadian women came from large metropolitan centers, small towns, and even rural communities to meet a delegation of women from Viet Nam and Laos. Some North American antiwar protestors had previously traveled to Southeast Asia. Others had learned through movement newspaper stories and photographs to empathize with the sufferings and to respect the heroism of Indochinese women who were fighting for national liberation. However, the Indochinese Women's Conferences of 1971 presented the first opportunities for large numbers of American and Canadian women to have direct contact with their "Asian sisters."

This essay examines the Indochinese Women's Conferences (IWC) of 1971 as a case study that illuminates how North American women sought to build an international, multigenerational, and multiracial movement based on antiwar politics. It expands on existing scholarship on social activism of the long decade of the 1960s in three ways. First, it highlights the variety of women's activism in the antiwar movement. Feminist scholars have identified the chauvinism within these circles as a catalyst for the emergence of a separate women's liberation movement.[1] Yet the IWC indicate that despite this disaffection with the male-led antiwar cause, women continued to pursue peace activism alongside new feminist initiatives. Furthermore, the conference was organized and attended by diverse groups of women. The cosponsors of the conference included "traditional" women's organizations,

"Third World" women, as well as women's liberation activists who themselves ascribed to a variety of political viewpoints.[2] Second, the conference offers an opportunity to analyze the hopes for and the obstacles limiting the formation of multiracial and transnational alliances—that is, "global sisterhood." Tensions among conference organizers and delegates tended to coalesce around race, sexuality, and nationality. Nevertheless, some American women regarded these conferences as life-transforming events; they experienced profound emotional and political connections with one another and, particularly, with the women from Indochina.

Finally, this study examines how North American activists both challenged and were influenced by Orientalist understandings of Asia and Asian women. Edward Said conceptualized Orientalism as a system of knowledge that the West developed about the East as the Occident colonized the Orient.[3] Within this framework, the East historically serves as a contrasting and not coincidentally inferior image to the West. This polarization not only created the Orient in the Occidental imagination but also defined the West to itself. Leila Rupp, in her study of interwar female internationalism, identifies a particularly female form of Orientalism that Western women exhibited toward their non-Western sisters. In their efforts to condemn repressive gender practices in these societies, Western women tended to reinforce colonial perceptions that these practices exemplified the essence—that is, the backwardness—of traditional non-Western societies.[4] In addition, they highlighted the need for Western women to rescue and modernize their less fortunate sisters.

This "politics of rescue" was also present during the movement to end the U.S. war in Viet Nam. However, during this period, North American women of varying racial backgrounds also exhibited what I characterize as a radical *Orientalist* sensibility. Through travel, correspondence, and meetings, they learned to regard Asian female liberation fighters, especially those from Viet Nam, as exemplars of revolutionary womanhood. These idealized projections countered classical Orientalist depictions of exotic, sexualized, and victimized Asian women. Nevertheless, these radical portrayals also tended to serve an Orientalist purpose in which the Orient again served as a mirror for Western self-definition. Now representing a contrasting image of revolutionary hope to oppressive gender roles in North American societies, Asian women helped female reformers in the West to redefine their aspirations and political goals.

Sisterhood across Borders

The IWC in Canada resulted from a long history of North American and Southeast Asian women engaging one another politically. Through face-to-face meetings that took place in Europe, Asia, Cuba, Africa, and Canada, they had cultivated personal and political connections that laid the basis for fostering an international sisterhood rooted in the common goal of ending the U.S. war in Viet Nam.[5] The sponsors of the IWC—designated "old friends," "new friends," and "Third World" women—reveal both the variety of women engaged in this effort and also their unequal experience in traveling across national boundaries to foster women's internationalism.

The term *old friends* referred to the U.S.-based Women Strike for Peace (WSP), the Canada-based Voice of Women (VOW), and the Women's International League for Peace and Freedom (WILPF). These organizations were designated *old* not because of the age of their constituency—although all three did attract largely middle-aged to elderly women—but rather because of the history of friendship that these North American women established with Vietnamese women. For example, WSP had a history of contact going back to 1965, when two members of the group were among the first Americans to visit Hanoi after the commencement of U.S. bombing of North Viet Nam. That same year, a ten-person delegation from WSP met with representatives from North and South Viet Nam in Djakarta, Indonesia, to affirm women's unique abilities to cross Cold War barriers and foster peace.[6] Although differences existed among WSP, VOW, and WILPF, they could be characterized as expressing a form of maternalist peace politics. For example, WSP originated in 1961 from the efforts of predominantly middle-class and middle-aged white women. As Andrea Estepa has argued, although the members of the organization had "wide-ranging professional identities," the group chose to publicly identify themselves as "housewives and mothers."[7] These women proclaimed their right to condemn the threat of global and nuclear warfare based on the desire to protect their families. In other words, they were not rejecting gender difference but embracing it to define a special role for women on the global stage. The roots of this maternalist form of peace politics can be traced back to Victorian and Progressive-era notions of gender difference. WILPF, an organization founded in 1919 under the leadership of Jane Addams, has a direct connection to this previous expression of maternalist activism.[8] Such an approach regained its political utility in the early Cold War period as a seemingly "commonsense," or nonideological, approach to defusing global conflict.[9]

The women from North and South Viet Nam who cultivated and encouraged these international contacts also articulated a unique gender role for women in the struggle for peace and national liberation. They represented women's organizations in their respective regions, specifically the Vietnam Women's Union (VWU) in the North and the South Vietnam Women's Liberation Union. Although the phrase *women's liberation* in the U.S. context referred to activists who sought to identify and subvert the workings of patriarchy, these Vietnamese organizations mobilized women primarily for anticolonial struggles. Because of the long history of political repression in their country, by both French and American colonizers, these women had an array of life experiences that generally exceeded those of their Western counterparts.

For example, Nguyen Thi Binh, who was present in Djakarta, became one of the most recognizable Asian female figures in Western women's political circles. Like WSP members, she came from a relatively elite and educated background. However, unlike most WSP members, she also became an authorized political leader, eventually serving as the foreign minister of the Provisional Revolutionary Government of South Viet Nam and its chief negotiator at the Paris peace talks. Amy Swerdlow, an activist in WSP as well as the organization's historian, noted the unequal status between the American and Asian women. While WSP publicly identified itself as consisting of "nonprofessional housewives, . . . the women who represented North and South Vietnam presented themselves as workers, students, professionals, and artists."[10] Despite the disjuncture, Southeast Asian women like Binh also articulated their common connections in the language of sisterhood and motherhood. For example, in a fifteen-minute film produced in 1970 and intended for an American female audience, Binh explained:

> I am so happy as a South Vietnamese woman and mother to have the opportunity to speak to you. . . . May I express my sincere thanks to the Women Strike for Peace for its contribution to the anti-war movements and its sympathy and support to our people, particularly the South Vietnamese women. . . . Our aspirations for peace are all the more ardent for over twenty-five consecutive years now, our compatriots, we women included, have never enjoyed a single day of peace.

Let me tell you that in my own family, several members have been killed while some others are still jailed by the Saigon regime. I myself have had not much time to live with my husband and my children. The moments my son and daughter were allowed to be at my side have become so rare and therefore so precious to them.[11]

Her emphasis on the destructive impact of warfare on family life both reflected the actual experiences of women in Viet Nam and also resonated effectively with maternalist activists in the West who valued the sanctity of motherhood and home life.

The unique role that women performed in political revolution resonated differently for the "new friends" who cosponsored the IWC. This designation generally referred to a younger generation of women who became politically active through the civil rights, the New Left, and eventually the women's liberation movements. For example, Vivian Rothstein, who was an activist in Students for a Democratic Society, traveled to Hanoi in 1967. When she returned to the United States, she helped form the Chicago Women's Liberation Union, which she modeled on the VWU.[12] She viewed her trip to Viet Nam as a major influence on her political development in at least two ways. First, she noted that her invitation to Hanoi was at the insistence of the VWU, which at the time had a clear understanding of how women could and should perform important roles in political movements. She recalled that in fact the North Vietnamese women had a greater understanding of women's potential than she or her fellow male New Left organizers did. Second, her exposure to what she describes as the "majoritarian" approach to political organizing in Viet Nam, characterized by an emphasis on building broad political movements, reinforced her desire to avoid sectarianism.[13] In cofounding the Chicago Women's Liberation Union, Rothstein attempted to create an organization that could engage women in a variety of ways by creating committees that examined diverse issues ranging from health, politics, and economics to culture.

Just as American activists learned from the Vietnamese, their hosts in Viet Nam were eager to learn from them. Charlotte Bunch-Weeks, a student and civil rights activist who joined the women's liberation movement in the Washington, D.C., area, traveled to Viet Nam as part of a multiracial and mixed-sex group in 1970. During her trip, she received a request to give a presentation on the origins, status, and goals of the women's liberation movement.[14] Consistent with the "majoritarian" approach, the North Vietnamese were interested in understanding and broadening their contacts with a variety of political movements.

Rothstein, Bunch-Weeks, and other women's liberation activists who met with the Vietnamese in Asia or through travels to Cuba, Europe, and Africa became key organizers for the IWC. These face-to-face encounters inspired U.S. women profoundly. One individual, after meeting North Vietnamese women in Budapest, Hungary, in 1970, explained in a letter:

> We have just had our first formal meeting with the Vietnamese & Cambodians. They are incredible out of sight people. Yesterday, when I first met them, I filled up with tears & wanted to take them in my arms & say 'I'm sorry.' . . . No matter how much you read & how much you know in your head what a monster imperialism is, it comes home to you with an emotional force that seems physical, meeting women who live under the threat of death. It seems impossible to think that I could ever, even for a minute, contemplate withdrawing or dropping out.[15]

By helping to organize the IWC, women's liberation activists had the opportunity to re-create their political intimacy with Southeast Asian women for larger numbers of women who did not have the privilege or opportunity to travel to Asia and other parts of the world.

The final group of cosponsors of the IWC were "Third World women," women from racially oppressed groups in North America who identified their status in the West as being akin to the status of Third World peoples globally. The category of Third World women, which could have been used to describe nonwhite individuals involved in mainstream women's organizations, included instead women who were active during the late 1960s in identity-based liberation movements in race-based communities. Along with other antiwar activists, some of these women of color also traveled to Viet Nam. They included Elaine Brown of the Black Panther Party and Pat Sumi, who would emerge as a leader in the Asian American movement. These two women of color were part of an eleven-person delegation that visited North Korea, North Viet Nam, and the People's Republic of China in 1970.[16] The Vietnamese were particularly aware of the vanguard role that the African American liberation movement played in the United States and sought to cultivate connections with key individuals and organizations.

The Vietnamese also were eager to learn about emerging liberation movements. For example, Betita Martinez, a Chicana activist based in New Mexico who was in the same delegation as Bunch-Weeks, was asked to answer questions about the Chicano movement in the United States.[17] For these "Third World" women, their sense of commonality with Vietnamese women was due not only to gender but also to what they perceived as a shared racial and colonized status. In her study of the Chicano antiwar movement, Lorena Oropeza quoted Martinez's reflections about her journey:

> "There are mountains and valleys and caves and big skies and glowing sunsets, as in New Mexico." ... The Vietnamese were *campesinos* (literally, people of the *campo* or countryside) who loved their land. Eastern medicine was like our *curanderismo* (folkhealing). ... "The spirit of the people was like a force of nature itself, creating life in the shadow of death. The white people of the West with their unnatural soul and their unnatural weapons are a death people. ... The Vietnamese are a life people [like Chicanos]. And anyone who thinks that a life people can really be conquered is a fool."[18]

All three sponsoring groups of the IWC—old friends, new friends, and Third World women—were eager to re-create their intense political experiences for their fellow activists.[19] However, the three groups had varying degrees of experience in facilitating international contacts, internal coherence, and resources. In addition, they had limited interactions with one another, and the tensions that existed within North American movements were not overcome but in fact were magnified as they attempted to cosponsor and co-attend the IWC.

Factions, Not Unity

On the last night of the IWC in Vancouver, North American women met for a criticism and evaluation session. A guerrilla theater group set up a sign announcing themselves to be "C.U.R.S.E. (Canadian Union of Rabid Senseless Extremists)" and attempted to perform a skit to express their critique of the conference. The reaction of the audience reflected the tense atmosphere of the entire event:

> Immediately a woman stood up grabbing away the sign. She demanded the C.U.R.S.E. women leave. Other women then came forward shoving

and pushing, trying to get the guerrilla theatre woman out of the meeting. The C.U.R.S.E. woman linked arms and refused to leave. At this point, a couple of woman began beating on one woman in the theatre group; the other woman in the skit shouted "Don't hit her she's pregnant." But the American women kept on slugging her shouting "She shouldn't be here then." The five C.U.R.S.E. women then formed a circle so as to protect their pregnant sister.[20]

The audience finally allowed the performance to take place. The skit consisted of a series of vignettes that followed one woman's experiences of denigration in the male-dominated work environment, the double standard and sexual abuse that she experiences in the home, and the political repression that she faces in protesting for abortion. Although she is able to recover from these efforts to wound and humiliate her, she is not able to overcome the hostility that she faces from other women when she attends the IWC:

[First, the] heroine is stopped at door by a stern-faced security guard demanding her revolutionary credentials. The security guard begrudgingly lets her pass. She is met by three women mechanically chanting "Off the Pig." And raising their fists in synchronized time. She innocently offers her [hand] in friendship to a delegate wearing a sign saying "Third World."

The chanting stops as the Third World delegate screams "Racist" and then hits her with a sign reading "Guilt." Somewhat beaten, she timidly approaches the next delegate with "Gay Lib" on her T-shift, who says "Heterosexual!" Again she is clobbered with guilt. Beaten to her knees she crawls to the USA Women's Lib delegate but, as she reaches out to touch her, she's accused of being a "Liberal." This final blow of guilt knocks her flat to the floor where she drags herself off-stage, completely beaten.[21]

This theatrical depiction illuminated three axes of difference—race, sexuality, and nationality—which precipitated great hostility among North American women at the conference.

Racial tensions emerged early on. Unlike the old and new friends, Third World women were not initially and consistently part of the planning process for the conference. The women from Southeast Asia as well as women's liberation activists expressly desired Third World women to be represented.

When women's liberation representatives gathered in New York City in September of 1970 to select delegates to attend a planning meeting in Budapest, they discussed ways to avoid the exclusivity that characterized previous international teams. International delegations were often selected "through personal contacts, choosing known individuals rather than groups, choosing friends, etc.," and they "felt it was of utmost importance to the success of the Canada conference to get away from this kind of elitism and to involve as many women as possible in the planning for the Conference . . . through broad, grass-roots representation and collective responsibility."[22]

In order to involve Third World women, women's liberation organizers decided to contact the Third World Women's Alliance (TWWA), a New York–based African American and Puerto Rican organization, and the Black Panthers, whose national headquarters was in Oakland, California. They asked whether these groups wanted to participate in planning the conference and whether they were interested in sending representatives to Budapest, with the financial support of women's liberation groups. In one of a series of criticism/self-criticism statements following the conference, women's liberation organizers acknowledged their good but misguided intensions in these efforts. After all, "we knew early that we did not want to be put in the position of 'choosing' which third world women should go, be represented, etc. We even had trouble with our decision that we should contact the Third World Women's Alliance and the Panthers for we felt that we were making the organizational choices for third world women."[23] Neither TWWA nor the Panthers sent representatives to Budapest, but TWWA did eventually participate in the planning process, although they generally organized with other Third World women: "[Initially] three or four third world women did attend New York planning meetings in the Fall. [However] they finally stopped attending, probably because the WL [women's liberation] women were struggling among themselves for the most part. [Instead] by December a number of third world groups were meeting separately and regularly in NYC. Sometimes third world representatives would come to the New York WL meetings."[24] Brown of the Black Panthers never responded to the letter sent to her. She had returned from visiting socialist Asia in the summer of 1970 to the volatile and contentious split between Huey Newton, who was released from prison during her travels, and Eldridge Cleaver, who had led the delegation of travelers. However, other Third World women, particularly in Los Angeles and San Francisco, began meeting on their own to discuss the conference.

On the West Coast, the political determination and organizational efforts of Third World women eventually resulted in a decision to divide the Vancouver conference into three segments. The Vietnamese initially suggested a division into two meetings, one for old and one for new friends because the two groups of women had such different political backgrounds and would want to engage in different types of discussion. Third World women from Los Angeles, led by Sumi (who had traveled to socialist Asia with Brown), demanded time in the conference schedule so they could engage with Indochinese delegates autonomously. As their statement explained, "Since we have been denied an equal participation *with* white groups, we can only ask for equal but separate conferences. The possibility of a confrontation between Third World and white women's groups at a joint conference would be disrespectful to the Indochinese women and would further reinforce the tensions that exist among North American women."[25] Their proposal received the support of white women from Los Angeles, who explained, "Why should Third World women unify with white women who claim to recognize the need of self-determination for the Indochinese, but who do not recognize the right of self-determination of all peoples in this country, as manifested in the 'small' way of planning a conference for people instead of with them."[26]

There were similar suggestions for a separate conference for Third World women in Toronto, but the effort did not appear to be as organized as the one in Vancouver. Neither Third World women or women's liberationists on the East Coast formulated an identifiable position statement acknowledging the need for political autonomy. There also did not appear to be sustained coordination between the Vancouver and Toronto conferences so that the organizers on the two coasts could share their decisions. Only afterward, in another criticism/self-criticism statement, did women's liberation organizers on the East Coast recognize the problem:

> We didn't know and didn't consciously try to find out what third world women's needs might have been with respect to the conference. On some levels we always saw the conference as "ours" with third world "participation." . . . When we talked about joint sessions with the third world women we were mostly considering our interests—that is to force women's movement women to see their racism, to learn from third world women, etc., etc. We seldom were conscious of whether a

joint conference would in fact meet their needs; whether in fact they had a reason or need to meet with us. In addition, our vision of the potential of women from different race and class backgrounds coming together and struggling together in a sisterly way was far ahead of our practice and the practice of third world women. If we had considered all these factors and if we had had some real practice with third world women at the time the conference was initiated, we might have decided then that the most useful arrangement would be for separate conferences of third world and white women with the Indochinese— that separate conference would be O.K. politically.[27]

On the East Coast, where activists tried to work across racial lines, and even on the West Coast, where a degree of autonomy was validated, tensions surfaced particularly around issues related to security. Given the destructiveness of COINTELPRO (the Federal Bureau of Investigation's Counter Intelligence Program) in targeting organizations like the Black Panthers, Third World women tended to be highly sensitive to potential harassment of themselves as well as of the Indochinese delegation.[28] All U.S. participants, regardless of race, were issued instructions about how to cross the border safely: "You should 1) be prepared to look as straight as possible (there is no way of getting around this) 2) have $15 to $20 per day for the length of time you are planning to stay . . . 3) have good I.D. . . . 4) have *no dope*. People are often thoroughly searched, stripped, etc. 5) no literature, especially anything pertaining to border crossing."[29] However, Third World women received additional advice about getting to Canada and being safe in another country:

All of us from the U.S. and Hawaii are foreigners in a nation colonized and exploited by U.S. imperialism. . . . Since the Indochinese are not guests of the Canadian government, the Third World advance group decided that delegates themselves would take on the responsibility for the safety for the Indochinese friends with no dependency on the Vancouver or national Canadian pig forces. . . . If your delegation is fairly large, break down into brigades of ten women each. Each brigade should have a leader who will be responsible for getting everyone up on time, and keeping track of sisters so everyone is accounted for at all times. . . . Don't go around by yourself. Always take someone

with you. And don't wear your delegate card as a badge. Canada has a
large group of fascist racists who may gather around the conference to
hassle delegates, so be careful.[30]

The concerns were not simply a product of paranoia. Some Asian
American women recalled, "In Vancouver, we were reminded that racism is
not confined to the United States. Throughout our stay there, the Third
World candidates were followed whenever we traveled in our chartered
buses. One night when we visited Chinatown, the delegates were harassed by
Canadian police for charges such as jaywalking."[31]

This concern for security extended to policies regarding all conference
participants. For example, Third World women "wanted no personal cameras
at all" because photographs of conference attendees could be subsequently
used to target activists.[32] They also warned white women that they "must be
prepared for agents and provocateurs in our midst." Finally, Third World
women took their responsibilities on the security force seriously, too seriously for many of the other delegates. Naomi Weisstein, a pioneer feminist
scholar, recalled being body searched before her Chicago Women's
Liberation Rock Band was finally allowed to perform as part of the Cultural
Exchange Night at the Toronto conference. Her attempt to protest this action
through humor by chanting "Don't touch me unless you love me" was not
well received.[33] Even in Vancouver, the policies instituted regarding security
led women's liberation activists to "feel that in some ways the whole 'show'
of security was a way for groups to flex their muscles and gain power positions at the conference. By the third day the disputes over security between
the Third World and white women were becoming so divisive that it was
decided (partly as a result of discussion with the Indochinese) that the security would be much relaxed. Immediately the tension was reduced."[34]

The tensions concerning security were particularly intense between
women of color and women's liberation activists because the women's liberation activists believed in the principle of involving everyone in planning
and managing the conference. Although the old friends acceded to the
cosponsorship by Third World women, WSP, VOW, and WILPF had less direct
contact with actual women of color. However, even the old friends expressed
criticism of what they perceived to be the militancy, arrogance, and dictato-
rial nature of the Third World women.[35] In turn, women of color criticized
the manipulation that they perceived on the part of some white women who

had "direct contact with the Indochinese women . . . [and] used this privilege as a source of power and status for their own groups. . . . Because we do not have the direct contacts ourselves, we have . . . been left dependent on the whim of groups who apparently disseminate information only if and when it is advantageous."[36] Both Third World women and white women perceived each other as seeking to assert "control" and "power." The tensions can be traced to profound differences between white and nonwhite women's histories of involvement in the conference planning as well as to their diverse life experiences and political perspectives. Although some women were able to engage in political conversation across racial lines, it was extremely difficult for larger groups and especially those who were new to these encounters or unused to sharing authority to recognize and understand different approaches. Instead, because of the urgency of organizing and executing the conference, their differences exploded into hostile and derogatory interactions.

Another volatile set of tensions emerged around issues of sexuality, specifically whether lesbianism should be a point of discussion at the antiwar gathering. Like the racial-identity liberation movements, lesbianism as a sexual-identity liberation movement emerged in the late 1960s and early 1970s.[37] The debates concerning sexuality at the IWC revealed the variety of ways that the women's liberation movement understood colonialism and liberation.

In a memo issued to IWC attendees in Vancouver, members of the San Francisco branch of Radicalesbians criticized the organizers of the conference for eliminating lesbianism as a topic of discussion. The statement decried that "lesbianism apparently is not seen as a primary or relevant subject at an Indochinese Women's Conference."[38] This set of conflicts reflected broad tensions within the women's movement. In 1969, the National Organization for Women president Betty Friedan infamously denounced lesbians as a "lavender menace" for providing "enemies with the ammunition to dismiss the women's movement as a bunch of man-hating dykes."[39] In response to these charges, which were raised in multiple movement circles, lesbians criticized gay baiting as a form of false consciousness. The group Radicalesbians, initially formed in New York City in 1970, issued the now-classic statement "Woman-Identified Woman," which the San Francisco branch reproduced for IWC attendees and quoted in its own memo. For them, "lesbianism is not a sexual preference but a lifestyle in which women get their love, identity, and support from other women."[40] In other words, lesbianism represented the ultimate expression of a separatist women's movement that sought to subvert male domination.[41] The Radicalesbians argued that lesbianism was thus a subject particularly appropriate for a conference devoted to anti-imperialism. Using the anticolonial analogy of the Third World being dominated by the West, the Radicalesbians argued that women were colonized subjects under male domination. By extension, lesbians as women-identified women were de facto anti-imperialists because of their efforts to obtain female liberation from male control.[42]

Those who opposed addressing lesbianism at the conference ranged widely in their motivations. Some were no doubt fearful of lesbianism and dismissed the issue as irrelevant because of their own heteronormativity. The old friends, who tended to base their peace activism on their identities as housewives and mothers, were not particularly inclined to discuss lesbianism, for instance, even though some later identified themselves as lesbians. The Third World contingent also tended to distance themselves from this issue. Again, although some women of color attending the conference were lesbians, the dominant perspective in these circles emphasized gay liberation as a white women's issue. Maria Ramirez and Nina Genera, two Chicana antiwar activists from the San Francisco Bay Area, recalled that they and other Mexican American women activists tended to be "traditional" in their appearance. They experienced culture shock while being housed with women's liberation activists in a large auditorium in Vancouver. As they and their Chicana friends were trying to put on makeup to get themselves "dolled up" for the conference, they saw "white" women sporting unshaved legs, fatigues, and combat boots.[43] This dichotomy between "femme" and "butch" gender presentations did not necessarily distinguish heterosexuals and homosexuals. However, in the minds of Ramirez and Genera, these differences concerning body adornment were not only indicative of distinct gender identities but also mapped onto racial divides.

Other Third World women did not comment on racial gender differences. Instead, they argued that lesbianism should not be a central issue for a conference focused on ending the war. In fact, they viewed the insertion of this topic as another expression of white Western women's chauvinism. Judy Drummond, an antiwar activist who was involved with the San Francisco Bay Area Chicano movement and traced her ancestry to Native American communities in California, recalled that "some of the radical lesbians just pissed me off. They pissed everybody off. . . . They had asked if the [Vietnamese] women had sex together in the fields. . . . And, it was, like, how rude. I mean, you know, these women are fighting for their lives and you're asking what we thought was a trivial question." Drummond subsequently acknowledged that the question was not trivial, but at the conference she and other women of color sought to silence these questions from radical lesbians. Drummond recalled that she did so at the request of the Indochinese female representatives, some of whom "walked off the stage . . . when they [the Radicalesbians] asked that question. You know, you don't ask those kinds of questions to these women. It is sort of inappropriate. You need to think. . . . You have your own agenda but . . . we're here for their agenda."[44] While the Radicalesbians regarded themselves as anti-imperialists, the Third World Women from North America and Indochina regarded lesbianism as secondary to the efforts to obtain national liberation in Southeast Asia.

Even some lesbian antiwar activists had concerns about raising lesbianism at the conference. Bunch-Weeks was in the process of coming out as a lesbian when she helped to organize the Toronto IWC. She recalled experiencing enormous pressure, particularly from her lover, Rita Mae Brown, to place lesbianism on the agenda.[45] However, because of Bunch-Weeks's previous trip to Hanoi and her prior contact with Southeast Asian women, she recalled: "I did not feel that it was the right time and place to try to raise lesbian feminism, but I felt enormous guilt because I was just a new lesbian. . . . So what happened to me, which I now understand, . . . is that I got sick. . . . I couldn't handle it. . . . I couldn't see a way to make it better . . . and I just . . . withdrew from the process. . . . I felt very guilty about not going because I also felt like I should try and make it better, but I couldn't see any way to make it better and so my whole body just collapsed."[46] The tensions that exploded at the IWC literally imploded in Bunch-Weeks. Just as different factions at the conferences could not reconcile their different interpretations of anti-imperialist politics, Bunch-Weeks could not intellectually or emotionally process her own conflicting understandings of what constituted liberation.

In addition to the conflicts surrounding race and sexuality, nationality constituted a third flash point. Although the IWCs were held in Vancouver and Toronto, Canadian organizers and attendees criticized their U.S. guests for their chauvinistic and imperialist behavior toward their hosts. Because of these dynamics, the Canadian female activists, irrespective of their racial backgrounds, tended to identify themselves as colonized subjects whose status was akin to Third World women from Southeast Asia and the United States.

The selection of Canada as a site for the IWCs reflected a general practice within the North American antiwar movement. During the course of the U.S. war in Viet Nam, representatives from North Viet Nam and from the resistance movement in South Viet Nam could not enter the States. However, Canada, as an officially neutral country, served not only as a refuge for U.S. draft dodgers but also as a communication node that facilitated face-to-face contact between Southeast Asian anticolonial spokespersons and the North American antiwar movement.[47] In fact, the idea for the 1971 IWC originated at a 1969 gathering in Eastern Canada of WSP, VOW, and female representatives from the North and South Vietnamese women's unions. Because the U.S. peace movement encouraged travel and relocation across the Forty-Ninth parallel, some of the Canadian organizers of the IWC were in fact former U.S. residents and veterans of the civil rights, New Left, and women's movements in the States.

Despite the existence of these international alliances and transnational connections, the Canadian organizers, particularly those who were identified as new friends, believed they were unequal partners in organizing the IWC. Fewer criticisms were raised by the old friends than by the new friends from Canada, most likely because VOW had worked closely with WSP. However, the Canadian women's liberation activists, especially those in Vancouver, who did not have a history of ongoing political partnerships with their U.S. "sisters," expressed a sense of frustration and imposition. For example, Liz Breimberg, a British Canadian women's activist who had participated in the Berkeley Free Speech Movement, recalled:

> This conference was in April of 1971 and we only heard of it in December of 1970. And we only heard of it by accident by a woman from . . . the United States, I think from California, [who] was up visiting someone here and came to one of our women's caucus meetings. . . . [She] told us . . . that this was being organized by women in the United States and it was like we were just being used. . . . They never even bothered to let us know. . . . The conferences were to be for the Indochinese people to meet the . . . women from the United States who were involved in the women's liberation movement. . . . I mean, we were treated as if we didn't exist.[48]

The lack of communication resulted partly from the difficulties of organizing across national boundaries and coordinating the efforts of women from Southeast Asia, the United States, and Canada. After all, these political networks were being created as part of the conference organizing process. However, the conference planning also revealed power inequalities. Breimberg recalled that she and other women's liberation activists in Vancouver became responsible for arranging the conference venue and housing for several hundred delegates. They also assumed many of the financial costs associated with the event. In other words, they performed much of the "grunt" work for the conference, even though they had limited input into the decision-making process.

Despite the fact that Canadian women served as hosts for the IWC, their presence remained marginal. Conference organizers decided early on to establish a quota system so that they could ensure diversity among the attendees. Half the U.S. quota was allocated to women of color. Cities with large activist populations, like San Francisco, Los Angeles, New York City, Boston, and Washington, D.C., received higher allocations. However, not everyone who wanted to attend could do so because other spots were reserved for participants from smaller towns and from the interior and southern states. Strikingly, Canada, the site of the conferences, was granted a small fraction of the overall slots. As Breimberg emphasized, the events were intended for U.S., not Canadian, women.

To add insult to injury, the female activists from south of the border did not always recognize that they had crossed into another country. Breimberg recalled: "One of the problems we had with the whole thing was the total chauvinism of the United States delegation. It was just absolutely astounding to the point where . . . when they spoke in the conference they would talk about this country as if this country was their country." In contrast, Breimberg recalled being painfully aware of the Forty-Ninth parallel. She and other Canadian activists crossed over to the United States in February 1971 for a preconference planning meeting in Portland, Oregon. Because they brought activist literature with them, the U.S. border patrol ordered a strip search, which took place in front of a giant poster of President Richard Nixon.[49] Based on these preconference interactions, some of the Canadian women anticipated the need to educate their U.S. sisters and to curb their sense of entitlement. Toward that end, the Canadian organizers authored a cartoon history of their nation that highlighted women's contributions.

This forty-page publication, entitled *She Named It Canada: Because That's What It Was Called*, was subsequently distributed to the conference attendees.[50]

As a result of the dynamics between white American and Canadian women, the Canadians identified themselves as colonized subjects. They tended to regard themselves as occupying a status similar to women of color from the United States because both groups suffered from the chauvinism of the U.S. women's liberation movement. The Canadian women also sympathized strongly with Southeast Asian women as colonial subjects. This analogy was particularly intense for activists who supported the French separatist movement based in Quebec. Initially, the IWCs were to take place in three cities, Toronto for East Coast participants, Vancouver for West Coast activists, and Montreal for those from the Midwest. Advocates for the last site noted the similarities between Quebec and Viet Nam as colonies seeking self-determination and liberation; they also highlighted the significant population of Afro-Caribbeans in Montreal and emphasized a sense of racial camaraderie with the black liberation movement in the United States.[51] In the end, the Montreal conference did not take place because the escalation of separatist protest and government repression resulted in the imposition of martial law in Quebec in 1970. Thus, even the cancellation of the conference emphasized the similarities between the political persecution of the Front de Liberation Quebecois and the sufferings of the Vietnamese National Liberation Front.

Yet even as white Canadian women regarded themselves as colonized subjects, women of color in Canada distinguished themselves from their white counterparts. Gerry Ambers, a Native Canadian, or First Nations, activist, recalled that she and other members of her community received a request from IWC organizers to cook for the Indochinese delegates.[52] She remembered that the Indochinese appreciated the meals that she and other First Nation women prepared, which tended to feature foods "traditional" to her community, such as salmon and other seafood. In Ambers's mind, it was not just a coincidence that these items were familiar to and well-liked by the Vietnamese; their dietary similarities symbolized a deeper rapport between the First Nations and the Third World. In contrast, Ambers recalled that the white Canadian women offered unpalatable food, like raw carrot sticks, that were both unfamiliar to the Vietnamese and difficult to digest, especially given the poor dental health of some of the Southeast Asian representatives who resided in rustic revolutionary base camps. This disconnect suggests that the First Nations women did not readily accept the Canadian women's claim to being colonized subjects.

Meeting Woman Warriors

As much as the North American women critiqued one another, they expressed adulation for their Indochinese sisters. The delegation from Southeast Asia consisted of three teams of two women and one male translator each for North Viet Nam, South Viet Nam, and Laos.[53] A fourth delegation from Cambodia had intended to travel to Canada as well but was unable to do so. The inclusion of the Laotians and the planned presence of Cambodians reflected a pan-Indochinese strategy that was increasingly necessary as the U.S. war in Viet Nam spread to all of Southeast Asia. The Indochinese women, whose ages ranged from twenty-nine to fifty and who included a housewife, several teachers, a literature professor, and a physician, presented themselves to North American women in large plenaries, smaller workshops, and discussions over meals. Because the conversations occurred via translation, some North American women questioned why the Indochinese chose to send male interpreters. Other women thought little of this gendered division of labor because the Indochinese women made such a powerful impression not only through presentations and responses to questions but also through their laughter and physical intimacy. One Canadian conference organizer recalled:

> Most remarkable about these women were their gentle dignity, self command, and deep concern for others, both individually and as nations. They laughed often with the women they met, hugged them when they felt common feelings, wept a little as they heard of each others' sufferings, and comforted us when (as too often happened) we ran late with the program or failed with the conference arrangements. Although their competence and dedication awed us, we felt that we, too, might cope better in future, as women and as citizens, for having met them.[54]

The newspaper coverage of the conference in North American women's publications revealed both Western women's desire to "rescue" their sisters as well as their tendency to place the Indochinese on idealized political pedestals. The delegates from Southeast Asia who tended to receive the most

attention in these publications were the women who either suffered trau-
matic abuse or could testify to wartime atrocities. Dinh Thi Hong received
featured coverage. Hong, a forty-six-year-old housewife from South Viet
Nam, had not been politically engaged in the movement for liberation, but
she was arrested, tortured, and detained in a series of the most notorious
prisons in the South. Her detailed account of her experiences appeared in
several movement publications produced by the New Left and Third World
communities and by women's organizations.[55] She recalled having "pins
[planted] in my fingertips," having "electrodes . . . attached to my ears and to
my fingers, nipples and genitals . . . and [being] tortured with electricity until
I was unconscious." In addition, her interrogators "forced water, lye and salt
into my stomach and trampled on my stomach until I vomited blood and was
unconscious." These dramatic episodes illustrated the visceral and sexualized nature of militarized violence to her audience. In addition, her accounts
conveyed the dehumanizing day-to-day indignities of trying to survive in
crowded cells with inadequate facilities and either little food or "rotten rice."
One cell that measured approximately 9 feet by 4½ feet held "15 to 32 people
at a time—women and men in the same cell. In this cell the prisoners eat, go
to the bathroom. Prisoners could only stand. I was not allowed to bathe from
November 1955 to August 1956."[56] After nearly six years, Hong was finally
found "not guilty" and released. During that time, her weight dropped from
108 to 78 pounds.[57] In addition, other family members had died or were
imprisoned. Following her release, Hong decided to "join my people to fight
against the Americans and puppets." As she surmised, "The more barbarous
the army is, the stronger the struggle of the people."[58]

Another delegate who received extensive coverage was Nguyen Thi
Xiem, a physician from South Viet Nam, who worked in Hanoi for the
Institute for the Preservation of Mothers and Newly Born Children. While
Hong offered personal testimony regarding the brutality of the South
Vietnamese government, Xiem provided an analysis of the widespread and
long-term impact of the war on the Vietnamese people and land. North
American attendees recalled:

> Dr. Xiem presented an account, including pictures, of the Vietnamese
> wounded by pellet bombs, napalm and defoliants. Tremendous pain
> and mutilation, as well as death, have resulted from the use of bombs
> that release thousands of tiny pellets to become embedded in vital

organs—napalm that burns and suffocates—defoliant sand that cause[s] blindness, genetic damage and other destruction to human beings, in addition to . . . devastating the countryside. 44% of the forests and cultivated land of South Vietnam have been affected by toxic chemicals.[59]

Xiem's status as a physician gave her report an air of authority. However, she also underscored that expert forms of testimony were not always necessary When asked about the psychological effect of bombing on young children, the doctor replied, "This bombing is not suitable for their development. It is not necessary to make an analysis. Our experiences as mothers should indicate this. Thank you for your attention to our baby children."[60] These accounts of atrocities reminded North American women of the atrocious nature of the U.S.-supported warfare in Southeast Asia. Although many antiwar activists no doubt had absorbed similar information from movement publications, the impact of hearing these stories in person was profound.

However, reports of oppression in Viet Nam sometimes reinforced a sense of moral obligation that resembled a politics of rescue. In a series of letters published in *Memo*, the newsletter of WSP, a statement by the president of VOW, Muriel Duckworth, bore the headline "They Must Be Saved."[61] The phrase suggests that Duckworth or the editor of *Memo* regarded North American women as the saviors of their Asian sisters. In contrast, the Indochinese women tended to highlight their own political agency as well as the ways in which the U.S. war in Southeast Asia also victimized Americans and damaged U.S. society more broadly. The sense of "paternalistic" maternalism that Duckworth's letter conveyed in many ways resonated with the political and cultural orientation of "older" women's peace organizations.

In contrast, Third World women, women's liberation activists, and even other maternalist peace advocates tended to regard the Indochinese as idealized revolutionary figures. In contrast to the divisiveness and factionalism among North American women, who were in many ways engaged in a politics of "blame," the Indochinese "never let us feel guilty of the crimes they described. Furthermore, they expressed sincere compassion for the suffering the war has brought to Americans. These women, whose families were scattered by our armies, whose villages were leveled, whose loved ones were murdered, these women recognized that 'young Americans are scapegoats' forced to fight the war. Over and over the Indochinese women reiterated their confidence that if the American people only knew what was going on in Indochina, Americans would demand an end to atrocities and the war."[62] The ability of the Indochinese to forgive and to distinguish between the people of the United States and their government led many conference attendees to "place them on a pedestal because of their revolutionary courage, spirit and warmth."[63] For Third World women in particular, the opportunity to interact with and learn from nonwhite female leaders was especially empowering. As Ramirez and Genera recalled, this was the first time that they had witnessed such strength and leadership from Third World women; the Indochinese women represented the first women of color role models who were in the vanguard of an actual revolution.[64]

This idealization of Southeast Asian women reflects what I have defined as a radical Orientalist sensibility. The revolutionary social movements of the late 1960s and early 1970s tended to endow the most oppressed with the greatest political capital. In the minds of many North American activists who attended the IWC, the Indochinese women, as targets of Western militarism, imperialism, racism, and sexism, represented the ultimate underdogs. Furthermore, they fought against nearly impossible odds with a sense of strength, clarity, and unity. As warm, dedicated, courageous, and revolutionary heroines, the Southeast Asian representatives reminded North American women what it was possible to achieve both individually and collectively. After all, women of color, lesbians, and Canadians all utilized the colonial analogy to conceptualize and resist oppression. Following in an Orientalist tradition, the imagined East helped to redefine the imagined West.

It should be noted that the exemplary status of Southeast Asian female revolutionaries was promoted by the Indochinese delegates themselves. As one representative explained, "Cadres must make the masses love them. This is a question of principle. If the masses love the cadres, they will listen to what they say and give them protection. That is why you must be exemplary. You must be exemplary in sacrifices. You must be the first to give your life, and the last to get rewards."[65] The heroism and humanity of the Indochinese women, which resulted from concerted political effort, ironically led North American women to examine themselves even more critically than before for their failure to achieve that ideal.

Conclusion

In Benedict Anderson's now famous account of the nation, he argues that the nation is an "imagined community" because "all communities larger than primordial villages of face-to-face contact . . . will never know most of their fellow-members . . . yet in the minds of each lives the image of their communion."[66] During the U.S. war in Viet Nam, as in all wars, a sense of nationalism was intensely promoted by mainstream culture and government agencies. However, the North American activists who traveled to Vancouver and Toronto sought to imagine themselves as members of an international community. Their face-to-face interactions and their shared identities as women helped to foster communion across national boundaries.

Ironically, the ability of North Americans to espouse a sense of sisterhood with Indochinese women was greater than their capacity to generate solidarity among themselves. In some ways, the racial, sexual, and national differences among North American women were more contentious because these activists lived and worked in closer proximity to one another. In contrast, they encountered briefly a very select group of female political leaders from Indochina who could fulfill and exceed their romantic visions of victimhood and heroism. As much as the North American delegates brought home with them stories of conflict with one another, they also carried and nurtured revolutionary hopes for political change. Although some became disillusioned by the tensions among North American women, others became even more dedicated than they had been to exposing and ending the horrors of the war in Southeast Asia.

Although the male-dominated antiwar movement has commonly been regarded as a catalyst for the emergence of female separatism, the IWC reveal the passionate engagement for peace and liberation by women of varying generations, racial backgrounds, sexual orientations, and nationalities. One indication of the importance of this female internationalism can be gleaned by a celebration in Hanoi that marked the official end of the U.S. war in Southeast Asia. On January 19,1973, the Washington, D.C., branch of WILPF received an urgent cable from the VWU. The message, written in French and translated into English, invited a small delegation from WILPF to visit the capital of North Viet Nam for a week, beginning on January 27.[67] Even though the travelers had only eight days to prepare for their journey and were not provided with a reason for their visit, WILPF accepted the invitation. On their arrival, the delegates were joined by "five women representing the Women's International Democratic Federation, one each from Argentina, Russia, India, France, and the Republic of Congo. To our knowledge, we were the only two visiting Americans in Hanoi for the signing of the Peace Accord."[68] The staging of this international female celebration to mark the end of the U.S. war in Viet Nam conveys the significance of women's peace activism. The invitation from the Vietnamese indicates how much they valued and consciously fostered global female networks as part of their campaign to obtain national liberation and reunification. The acceptance of the invitation by WILPF representatives, given the limited information provided to them and the enormous resources necessary to travel across the world on such short notice, reveals how much U.S. women believed in the profound possibilities of global sisterhood.

NOTES

1. Sara M. Evans, *Personal Politics: The Roots of Women's Liberation in the Civil Rights Movement and the New Left* (New York: Random House, Vintage Books, 1979).

2. Scholars of sixties radicalism are increasingly emphasizing the diversity of backgrounds and political perspectives of activists from this era. For examples, see Stephanie Gilmore, ed., *Feminist Coalitions: Historical Perspectives on Second-Wave Feminism in the United States* (Urbana: University of Illinois Press, 2008), and Cynthia A. Young, *Soul Power: Culture, Radicalism, and the Making of a U.S. Third World Left* (Durham, NC: Duke University Press, 2006).

3. Edward W. Said, *Orientalism* (New York: Vintage Books, 1979).

4. Leila J. Rupp, *Worlds of Women: The Making of an International Women's Movement* (Princeton, NJ: Princeton University Press, 1997).

5. For discussions of travel and the antiwar movement, see James W. Clinton, *The Loyal Opposition: Americans in North Vietnam, 1965–1972* (Newt: University Press of Colorado, 1995); Mary Hershberger, *Traveling to Vietnam: American Peace Activists and the War* (Syracuse, NY: Syracuse University Press, 1998); and Judy Tzu-Chun Wu, "Journeys for Peace and Liberation: Third World Internationalism and Radical Orientalism during the U.S. War in Viet Nam," *Pacific Historical Review* 76, no. 4 (November 2007): 575–584.

6. Amy Swerdlow, *Women Strike for Peace: Traditional Motherhood and Radical Politics in the 1960s* (Chicago: University of Chicago Press, 1993), 214–215.

7. Andrea Estepa, "Taking the White Gloves Off: Women Strike for Peace and 'the Movement,' 1967–73," in *Feminist Coalitions: Historical Perspectives on Second-Wave Feminism in the United States*, ed. Stephanie Gilmore (Urbana: University of Illinois Press, 2008), 87.

8. Harriet Hyman Alonso, *Peace as a Women's Issue: A History of the U.S. Movement for World Peace and Women's Rights* (Syracuse, NY: Syracuse University Press, 1993), 83. The organization evolved from the Women's Peace Party, which was founded in 1915.

9. Estepa, "Taking the White Gloves Off," 88.

10. Swerdlow, *Women Strike for Peace*, 216.

11. "Madame Nguyen Thi Binh Speaking to American Women," text of film, October 1970, Women Strike for Peace Collection (WSPC), Series A, 2, Box B, 2, Swarthmore College Peace Collection, Swarthmore, PA, p. 1 (hereafter cited as SCPC).

12. Vivian Rothstein, telephone interview with author, Los Angeles, March 9, 2007.

13. Amy Kesselman, a close friend of Rothstein's and a fellow member of the Chicago Women's Liberation Union, believed that Rothstein already had a "majoritarian" approach to politics prior to her trip to North Viet Nam. In other words, in Kesselman's eyes, Rothstein's travels there tended to confirm rather than transform her politics. Amy Kesselman, conversation with author, Boston, June 26, 2008.

14. Charlotte Bunch, interview with author, New York City, November 30, 2006.

15. Alice Wolfson to "Companeras," n.d., Accession Number 87-M149–88-M18, Box 1, F. 34, Charlotte Bunch Papers, Schlesinger Library, Radcliffe College, Cambridge, MA, 1–2 (cited hereafter as Bunch Papers).

16. The group was led by Black Panther Leader Eldridge Cleaver and *Ramparts* editor Robert Scheer. The delegation included five white women as well: Jan Austin, Regina Blumenfeld, Ann Froines, Janet Kranzberg, and Randy Rappaport.

17. Betita Martinez, telephone interview with author, San Francisco, December 7, 2006.

18. Lorenz Oropeza, *Raze Si! Guerra No!: Chicano Protest and Patriotism during the Viet Nam War Era* (Berkeley: University of California Press, 2005), 99–100.

19. For example, WSP leader Cora Weiss played an instrumental role in arranging trips for American antiwar activists to visit North Viet Nam through the Committee of Liaison with Families of Prisoners Detained in Vietnam. In addition, WSP was aware of its primary demographic base and attempted to involve women of color and younger women, as well as working-class women.

20. "Curses," *Georgia Straight*, April 8–13, 1971, 17.

21. Ibid.

22. "Projected Conference in North America with Indochinese Women," F-III, Subject Files, Folder "Indochinese Women Conference," Kathleen Hudson Women's Bookstore Collection, Simon Fraser University, Vancouver, British Columbia, 1–2 (cited hereafter as Women's Bookstore Collection).

23. "An Evaluation of the Canadian Conference Process," Access. No. 87-M149–88-M18, Box 1, Folder 34, Bunch Papers, 11.

24. Ibid., 10.

25. "We as Third World Women . . . ," statement, F-111, Women's Bookstore Collection.

26. "Statement from a Number of the White Women in Los Angeles Who Are Working on the Indochinese Women's Conference," F-111, Women's Bookstore Collection, 2.

27. "An Evaluation of the Canadian Conference Process," 11.

28. Jeremy Varon points out that white activists in the United States tended to not face the same type of state-sponsored repression as activists of color; *Bringing the War Home: The Weather Underground, the Red Army Faction, and Revolutionary Violence in the Sixties and Seventies* (Berkeley: University of California Press, 2004). For an account of Canadian state surveillance of IWC, see Steve Hewitt and Christabelle Sethna, "'Sweating and Uncombed': Canadian State Security, the Indochinese Conference and the Feminist Threat, 1968–1972," paper presented at the Canadian Historical Association, University of British Columbia, Vancouver, May-June 2008.

29. Letter to "Dear Sisters" from the Indochinese Conference Committee, F-166, Folder "Indo-Chinese Women's Conference" # 3, Anne Roberts Women's Movement Collection, Simon Fraser University, Vancouver, British Columbia (cited hereafter as Women's Movement Collection), 1–2.

30. "General Information for All Third World Delegates," F-166, Folder "Indo-Chinese Women's Conference" # 3, Women's Movement Collection, 1–2.

31. "Indochinese Women's Conference," *Asian Women* (University of California, Berkeley) (1971), 79.

32. "An Evaluation of the Canadian Conference Process," 12.

33. Naomi Weisstein, telephone interview with author, New York City, February 5, 2007.

34. Anne Roberts and Barbara Todd, "Murmurings after the Indochinese Conference," *Pedestal* (May 1971): 6.

35. Madeline Deckles, interview with author, Berkeley, California, October 21, 2006.

36. "We as Third World Women . . ."

37. Ruth Rosen, *The World Split Open: How the Modern Women's Movement Changed America* (New York: Viking Penguin, 2000), 164–175.

38. "Hello sisters! We are Radicalesbians . . . ," F-166, Folder "Indo-Chinese Women's Conference" # 3, Women's Movement Collection, 1.

39. Quoted in Rosen, *The World Split Open*, 166.

40. "Hello sisters!," 1.

41. Ibid., 2.

42. The San Francisco Radicalesbians incorporated this analysis from the "Fourth World Manifesto," a lengthy statement issued by a group of women's liberation activists based in Detroit; "Fourth World Manifesto," F-166, Folder "Indo-Chinese Women's Conference" # 1, Women's Movement Collection.

43. Maria Ramirez and Nina Genera, interview with author, Chabot, California, February 27, 2007.

44. Judy Drummond, interview with author, San Francisco, March 21, 2007.

45. For Brown's critique of women's involvement in the antiwar movement and the need to center lesbianism as a primary political issue, see Rita Mae Brown, "Hanoi to Hoboken, a Round Trip Ticket," in *Out of the Closets: Voices of Gay Liberation*, ed. Karla Jay and Allen Young (New York: Douglas, 1972), 195–201.

46. Bunch interview.

47. Canada's support for the U.S. antiwar movement should not be overstated. Although the country was officially neutral, Canadian citizens volunteered to fight in the U.S.-led war in Southeast Asia; in addition, the Canadian government engaged in "secret missions, weapons testing and arms production": http://archives.cbc.ca/IDD-1-71-1413/conflict_war/vietnam/

48. Liz Breimberg, interview with author, Vancouver, British Columbia, November 2, 2005. For related accounts of U.S.-Canadian tensions, see Hewitt and Sethna, "Sweating and Uncombed."

49. Breimberg interview.

50. The original publication was authored by the Vancouver Corrective Collective in 1971. The members were identified as Karen Cameron, Collette French, Pat Hoffer, Marge Hollibaugh, Andrea Lebowitz, Barbara Todd, Cathy Walker, and Dodie Weppler.

51. The Montreal International Collective, "Memorandum to the Interim Work Committee," 19 December 1970, F-166, Folder "Indo-Chinese Women's Conference" #2, Women's Movement Collection. The signers of the memo were Anne Cools, Marlene Dixon, Estelle Dorais, Susan Dubrofsky, Vickie Tabachnik, and Eileen Nixon.

52. Gerry Ambers, telephone interview with author, Vancouver, British Columbia, April 4, 2007.

53. "The Indochinese Women's Conference," *Goodbye to All That* ("The Newspaper by San Diego Women"), no. 13, April 20–May 4, 1971, 3.

54. Kathleen Gough, "An Indochinese Conference in Vancouver," F-166, Folder 1, Women's Movement Collection, 2.

55. A dissertation by Agatha Beins examines how women's movement periodicals created political meaning and fostered a sense of community among activists; Agatha Beins, "Free Our Sisters, Free Ourselves! Locating U.S. Feminism through Feminist Publishing" (PhD diss., Rutgers University, 2008), and Agatha Beins, "Sisters Rise Up! Feminist Identities and Communities in the Women's Liberation Movement," seminar paper, NEH Summer Institute: "Sequel to the 60s," Schlesinger Library, Radcliffe College, Cambridge, MA, 2008.

56. "Dinh Thi Hong: A Prisoner of War," *Goodbye to All That*, no. 13, April 20–May 4, 1971, 4.

57. "Indochinese Women's Conference," *Asian Women*, 84.

58. Ibid.

59. "Indochinese Women's Conference," *Goodbye to All That*, 3.

60. "A Reaction," *Goodbye to All That*, no. 13, April 20–May 4, 1971, 2.

61. Muriel Duckworth, in "Impressions from the Conference of Indochinese and North American Women, April 1971, Sponsored by Voice of Women, WILPF, WSP," *Memo* 2, no. 1 (Fall 1971), 16.

62. "A Reaction," 2.

63. "Indochinese Women's Conference," *Asian Women*, 78.

64. Ramirez and Genera interview.

65. "Learning How to Do It," *Pedestal* (May 1971): 11.

66. Benedict Anderson, *Imagined Communities: Reflections on the Origin and Spread of Nationalism*, rev. ed. (London: Verso, 1991), 6.

67. Vietnam Women's Union, cable to Women's International League for Peace and Freedom (WILPF), 1 January 1973, DG 043, Part III: U.S. Section, Series A, 4, and Series H, 4, box 20, F, Women's International League for Peace and Freedom Collection (hereafter WILPF Collection). "WILPF delegation to Hanoi (Vietnam), Feb. 1973," SCPC.

68. "Statement of Dorothy R. Steffens, National Director of Women's International League for Peace and Freedom," on her return from Hanoi, and "Visit to Hanoi (Vietnam), Jan. 1973.," 7 February 1973, 1, Part II, H, 4, box 20, F, WILPF Collection.

10

Living a Feminist Lifestyle

The Intersection of Theory and Action in a Lesbian Feminist Collective

ANNE M. VALK

In a 1972 memo to the Furies, member Charlotte Bunch articulated her dream for fifty years in the future. Bunch foresaw that "women will have taken power in many regions in the US, [and] are governing and beginning to create a new feminist society." This new society entailed a long-term view of lesbian feminist separatism: "[W]e have built alliances in which we are the dominant power, with some minority groups and with a few male groups (especially gay males). We have minimal, but not warring, relations with some other US regions where minority groups have taken power and where the women are advancing rapidly but not yet in total control." The former United States had become "A Federation of Feminist States," governed by a lesbian feminist party.[1] Building on Bunch's vision, members of the Furies, a lesbian feminist collective based in Washington, D.C., in the early 1970s, proceeded to plan how they could eventually bring about this political goal. Their short-term strategy involved creating a collective where a small number of white lesbian feminists lived and worked together, separated both from heterosexual women and men. As in the proposed Federation of Feminist States, the collective members accepted that they would interact with some men and with women of color in a limited, but not necessarily antagonistic, fashion. So situated, the Furies distanced themselves from what they perceived as a hostile world in order to analyze their experiences as women, question their own principles and assumptions, and subsequently develop a base from which they could mobilize other women for social change.

. . . The Furies formulated their collective as a place where they could immediately enact their political beliefs and, at the same time, focus on how best to gradually and completely eradicate women's oppression. . . . They focused their efforts in three interconnected areas: analyzing and transforming individual behavior and everyday relations, particularly within their own collective; publishing theory in their monthly newspaper, *The Furies*; and developing local educational programs intended to empower women. By concentrating on these projects, the members believed they would inspire a mass movement to end sexism. Occupying a common living space, they reasoned, would enhance their theoretical insights by encouraging them to work through new models of interaction, create a supportive environment for political and personal change, and insulate them from activists who denigrated or ignored lesbianism. The newspaper and educational workshops, in turn, provided forums where the group could discuss and disseminate ideas developed within the collective. The record of their experiences and ideas would create a model for feminists in the 1970s and leave a lasting legacy for activists in the future.

The Furies, existing as a collective from 1971 to 1972, were not the first or the only lesbian feminist group of the time.[2] . . . Yet the Furies differed from . . . other initiatives in several ways. Living and working together, collective members sought to exercise feminist politics within a communal household. Unlike most collectives, the members wrote extensively about their living arrangements. For more than a year they produced a newspaper, and the publication became a vehicle for promoting feminist analysis, thereby shaping the direction and emphases of the women's movement. At a time when many feminists opposed the concept of political leadership and sought to create a nonhierarchical movement, the Furies embraced the opportunity to direct the struggle for women's liberation.

Dana Shugar, who analyzed a broad range of lesbian feminist writings from the 1970s, argues that the discourse of separatism "in many ways required women to live and/or work in collectives as the full realization of their political analyses." Shugar notes, however, that such ventures were "repeatedly undercut by ideologies of difference and unity that divided women within the collectives themselves" and ultimately led to their dissolution.[3] Among the Furies, personal differences and political disagreements regarding how to organize a mass movement caused conflict both within the collective and with other women. Dissension disrupted the collective's productivity and, following the pattern noted by Shugar, eventually contributed to its collapse. Nonetheless, the Furies collective was an important incubator for activists and ideas that became significant to the broader feminist movement. Charlotte Bunch, Joan E. Biren, Rita Mae Brown, and other members went on to forge several important feminist initiatives.[4] Moreover, the record of activities left by the group offers an important example of feminists' efforts to transform society. Thus, although the Furies collective was not long lived, its influence was extensive.

This article . . . aims to complicate the story of second wave feminism by taking into account the importance of both theory and practice in the development of lesbian feminism and their impact on the larger movement.[5] Considering the collective on both a theoretical and pragmatic basis, this analysis explores participants' conception of the connections between lesbianism and feminism, the activities they undertook to advance the movement's goals, and the unintended consequences of their ideas and projects. Like other radical feminists, the Furies emphasized the connections between the personal and the political: their own experiences became the basis for their analysis, and they believed they could change the world by creating institutions and models of living that would bring forth a new society. . . . For the Furies, this entailed an intense scrutiny of relationships, daily living, household politics, and emotions.

Notwithstanding their conjoined significance as forces for social change, theory and action sometimes inadvertently worked in conflicting ways and toward contradictory ends, for the Furies as they did for other radical groups. In particular, the women's decision to work within a small, separatist collective where they promoted a narrow set of prescribed behaviors led to burnout and myopia that hampered the group's achievements and made it impossible to mobilize feminists on a large scale. Certain aspects of their politics, such as the priority granted to theory, generated criticism from other women activists and opened the collective members to charges of elitism. Thus, the collective's long-term goal of creating a mass movement was undermined by the complications of trying to connect personal and political lives, by making theory and action conform. Ultimately, a history of the Furies demonstrates how lesbian feminism was driven forward by energies and experiments that also limited the movement's influence and undermined its impact. . . .

The Furies emerged as part of the more radical branch of the [feminist] movement that developed after 1968. Reflecting participants' prior background in civil rights and New Left movements, radical feminists did not focus solely on legal, economic, and political rights; instead, they sought transformation on a personal level as well as broader changes in the country's political and economic structures. At the same time, radical feminists identified male supremacy and capitalism as the root causes of women's oppression and viewed women as a "sex class." Believing that sex-based oppression united women, and that other "isms"—racism and classism—derived from male supremacy, radical feminists sought to "smash the patriarchy." . . . Although concerned with race as well as gender issues, most radical feminist groups remained predominantly white; the class affiliations of members were more varied and, indeed, became one source of tension within many groups. In Washington, the women's liberation movement became an umbrella under which radical feminists from all backgrounds worked on projects such as a daycare center and the publication of the newspaper *off our backs*, participated in consciousness-raising (CR) groups, and undertook political protest.[6] These projects were typically set up in a nonhierarchical fashion and, unlike NOW, excluded men. Radical feminism thereby transformed the movement's theory and praxis and brought waves of new women to the struggle.

By 1970, feminists who had been movement activists for nearly a decade strove to build and sustain their organizations as they faced an influx of participants who lacked previous political experience. At the same time, feminists confronted internal challenges. . . . Concerns over racial differences had plagued the predominantly white movement from the beginning, but in 1970, the split that developed over issues of sexuality seemed even more devastating. . . . In one often-repeated story, Rita Mae Brown claimed that Betty Friedan maneuvered her out of a New York City chapter of NOW after Brown came out as lesbian. According to Brown and later historians, this incident marked the beginning of identity-based organizing by lesbians in the feminist movement. Brown's ouster served as the impetus for a protest by a group of lesbians at the Second Congress to Unite Women in May 1970, when Brown and other members of Radicalesbians distributed their essay "Woman-Identified Woman," articulating an ideological foundation for lesbian feminism.[7]

Scholars have used the history of lesbian feminist groups in the 1970s . . . primarily to mark the evolution of second wave feminism from a movement focused on legal rights and political transformation to one that increasingly emphasized culture. Historian Alice Echols has associated the emergence of lesbian feminism with a shift away from radicalism by highlighting changes in lifestyle rather than politics. With the rise of lesbian feminism, Echols argued, "the focus shifted from building a mass movement to sustaining an alternative woman's culture and community." Subsequently, she claimed, cultural feminism became the movement's dominant ideology: "Cultural feminism with its insistence upon women's essential sameness to each other and their fundamental difference from men seemed to many a way to unify a movement that by 1973 was highly schismatic."[8]

Other scholars, although not faulting lesbian feminists for a conservative turn from politics, have nonetheless emphasized their cultural concerns. Sociologist Arlene Stein, for example, examined the conceptualizations of identity that emerged as lesbian feminists contributed to a normalization of women's relationships with each other by "deprecating heterosexual relationships and by generating a culture and vocabulary that valued and even idealized lesbianism."[9] Sociologist Verta Taylor and historian Leila Rupp have countered Echols, arguing that cultural feminism represented only one tendency among lesbian feminists and that those who emphasized female values, separatism, the primacy of women's relationships, and feminist ritual actually helped sustain feminist activism throughout the 1970s and 1980s. . . .[10] Nonetheless, the Furies and other lesbian feminist groups of the time continue to be associated with the transformation of feminism away from an earlier radicalism.

This emphasis on cultural aspects of lesbian feminism stands in contrast to scholars' characterizations of other radical movements of the period, movements that also sought to merge theory and action into an effective plan for social change. In particular, the Black Power movement, [which] developed in the United States during these same years, shared with lesbian feminism a commitment to political and personal transformation.[11] Despite the parallels between these simultaneous movements, lesbian feminism has not been considered in the context of the Black Power movement. Doing so suggests a way to understand the role that so-called cultural activities play as part of a militant political agenda. As Charlotte Bunch's opening statement reveals, lesbian feminists addressed more than issues of lifestyle, identity, and cultural transformation. Political and social transformation remained central to the long-term vision of the Furies. . . . Such ideas need to be analyzed more fully in order to understand lesbian feminists' political agenda and how its components fostered both new directions and new divisions in the women's movement.

Lesbianism and Feminism: Theoretical Connections

The varied backgrounds of members of the Furies reveal many of the roots of second wave feminism and allow us to trace the movement's evolution from the 1960s to the early 1970s. As historians Sara Evans and Echols have noted, many of the women who became radical feminists had earlier experiences in the civil rights, antiwar, gay liberation, and women's movements.[12] Disillusioned by a turn toward racial separatism within Black liberation movements and the sexism of male activists, scores of white women turned their political concerns and skills to feminist movements. Those who formed the Furies collective in the spring of 1971 brought a commitment to social change and a willingness to make political activism the center of their lives. All white and younger than thirty years old, the twelve women believed that their similarities as lesbians would override other characteristics that differentiated them—namely, educational background, socioeconomic class, and their status as parents. Prior to moving to Washington, D.C., and engaging in feminist politics, Bunch and Nancy Myron had been involved in civil rights activities, while Tasha Peterson, Ginny Berson, Joan Biren, Helaine Harris, and Susan Hathaway had taken part in antiwar rallies, anti-imperialist groups, and neighborhood development projects. Brown, Myron, and Jennifer Woodul worked in earlier groups in New York to mobilize lesbians against discrimination, while several women belonged to an earlier lesbian collective in Washington, D.C. Radical feminism then became their primary political commitment. Bunch had helped found D.C.'s primary women's liberation group; and Joan Biren and Sharon Deevey joined that organization shortly afterward, participating in project groups and coordinating the office. Coletta Reid, Lee Schwing, and Tasha Peterson had belonged to the collective that produced the radical feminist newspaper *off our backs*.

Significantly, even as future members of the Furies concentrated their political efforts around women's issues, they retained a concern with ending racial discrimination. . . . Biren and Deevey became aware of lesbian feminism in September 1970 when they attended the Revolutionary People's Constitutional Convention organized by the Black Panther Party. . . . These experiences would play a role in how the Furies, and other women activists, perceived their position in the larger revolutionary movement.

In addition to prior activist experiences, other aspects of their personal lives led women to lesbian feminist organizing. Before coming out as lesbian, several members had been married. For these participants, the experience of living without husbands and male partners enhanced their understanding of the connections between women's economic status and family structure. In contrast, for those women who had identified as lesbian prior to their involvement in the movement, lesbian feminism provided a way to overcome the shame they had internalized as a result of their sexual orientation. In this sense, lesbian feminism functioned in ways that echoed Black Power by emphasizing the positive value of and personal pride in an identity otherwise demeaned by the dominant society.[13]

As lesbians embraced their sexuality, they formed separatist groups in New York, Washington, Chicago, and other cities. In Washington in the spring of 1971, Reid, a mother of two young children and a founder of a daycare center for the children of women's liberationists, claimed that her coworkers reacted with hostility when she separated from her husband and came out as a lesbian. According to Reid, other daycare workers and parents behaved as though she might molest young girls and insinuated that her "angry and manhating" attitude was inappropriate around children.[14] Galvanized by what she considered discriminatory and narrow-minded behavior, Reid joined with other lesbian activists to form the Furies. In doing so, they temporarily severed their ties with the larger radical feminist movement in Washington. By constituting their own collective, members of the Furies both served their immediate need to insulate themselves from antagonism and established the groundwork for their plan to unite lesbian feminists and transform the women's movement.

Yet having separated from women's liberation, members set out to articulate lesbianism's significance to feminism and other radical movements. They did so by focusing on the institution of heterosexuality. Engaging other activists through writing and intellectual debate, the Furies argued that heterosexuality constituted the basis of patriarchy. Lesbian feminism, conversely, contained the potential for revolutionary change. . . . By rejecting relationships with men, repudiating male privilege, abandoning patriarchal institutions, and developing female-centered organizations and worldviews, lesbian feminists would constitute a vanguard in the revolution against capitalism and male supremacy, just as Black nationalists viewed themselves as leaders in the struggle against white supremacy and imperialism.

At least initially, however, Furies members suggested that separatism from men and heterosexual women was necessary only because other groups

failed to take lesbianism seriously. Moreover, the Furies emphasized conflicts with straight women as much as with men: "Lesbians must get out of
the straight women's movement and form their own movement in order to
be taken seriously, to stop straight women from oppressing us, and to force
straight women to deal with their own Lesbianism. Lesbians cannot develop
a common politics with women who do not accept Lesbianism as a political
issue."[15] Rather than deplete their energies through continued battles over
the legitimacy of lesbianism, the Furies turned to separatism as a means of
strengthening their arguments and consequently winning support for their
position.

Within their collective, the Furies constructed lesbian feminist identity
as positive, claiming that such an identity constituted a political act in
itself. . . . In a founding "Statement of the Furies," the group argued that
"revolutionary lesbians are not only fighting against the institutions of male
heterosexual power and privilege but are attacking the very foundations of
the male world view—a view which is based on competition, aggression, and
acquisitiveness. Lesbians choose to reject that world view and to live apart
from men who have perpetuated those values for thousands of years. We
have broken our last dependence on male privilege which kept us from
being revolutionary."[16]

According to the collective, male supremacy compelled women to submit to men; enforced heterosexuality; and divided people by class, race, and
nationality. Lesbian feminism represented the means to end such oppression because women thereby renounced the privileges of heterosexuality,
challenging all forms of supremacy and rejecting cultural imperatives that
socialized women to shape their lives around relationships with men. Bunch
asserted that a lesbian rejected "the male definitions of how she should feel,
act, look and live. To be a lesbian is to love oneself, woman, in a culture that
denigrates and despises women."[17] Moreover, because lesbian feminism led
women to denounce the advantages they derived as wives, lovers, and daughters and thereby "threatens male supremacy at its core," lesbians were
uniquely qualified to lead the movement to end capitalism, racism, and
imperialism. As Brown wrote in a 1972 essay, once a woman embraced lesbian feminism and became strengthened through uniting with other
women, her view of the world would change: "Once you feel your strength
you cannot bear the thought of anyone else being beaten down. All other
oppressions constructed by men become horrible to you, if they aren't

already. Class and race, those later day diseases, sprung from sexism, maim and destroy people every bit as much as sexism itself. No oppression is tolerable. All must be destroyed. Once you have come out you can no longer fall back on race and class privilege, if you have any." . . . Brown conceded that "becoming a lesbian does not make you instantly pure, perpetually happy and devotedly revolutionary."[18] Racism and classism divided lesbians, as they did other women, but because the collective conceived male supremacy as the foundation of all forms of oppression, separate action to eliminate race and class oppression would prove unnecessary.

For the Furies, as for other activists, the feminist adage "the personal is political" contained an equally influential counternotion, "the political is personal." This . . . translated into a set of prescribed beliefs about how women should demonstrate their commitment to women's liberation. The collective's claim that embracing lesbian feminism demonstrated the depth of one's commitment to ending male supremacy exemplified this tendency. The Furies argued that liberation would come from a renunciation of worldviews that devalued women and reinforced female dependence on men. In their 1970 essay, "Woman-Identified Woman," the New York–based Radicalesbians argued that "until women see in each other the possibility of a primary commitment which includes sexual love, they will be denying themselves the love and value they readily accord to men, thus affirming their second-class status."[19] But, unlike the New York group, which viewed lesbianism as only one path to women's liberation, the Furies emphasized lesbianism as a political imperative: "Lesbianism is not a matter of sexual preference, but rather one of political choice which every woman must make if she is to become woman-identified and thereby end male supremacy. . . . Lesbians must become feminists and fight against woman oppression, just as feminists must become Lesbians if they hope to end male supremacy."[20] Thus, lesbian feminism represented not simply a personal preference but also a political commitment that all women could and should make in order to end oppression.

Sexual activity clearly fit in the collective's definition of lesbian identity, and members engaged in sexual relationships with each other and with women outside the group. But their writings and analysis primarily stressed the political implications of lesbianism and paid little attention to sex itself. Indeed writings by the Furies revealed an ambivalence regarding sexual pleasure as a determining factor in lesbian feminist identity. Any woman could be a lesbian; conversely, they contended, any woman's failure to feel sexually attracted to women indicated an acceptance of the male world view. . . . This ideology . . . contradicted feminists' view that liberated women would find sexual satisfaction and empowerment by exploring their own sexuality.

Not surprisingly, such ideas provoked conflict and disagreement among radical feminists. . . . Some responded negatively to the emphasis on separatism, which they considered unnecessarily strident and particularly difficult for women's liberationists who were mothers. Others considered the Furies too narrowly focused on the issue of male supremacy, too anti-male in tone, and too focused on conformity to a single ideology.[21] One member of the D.C. women's liberation movement objected that the Furies' ideology required that sexual preferences be subsumed to politics. "If it is true, and I suspect it may be, that lesbianism generates energy, assertiveness, and strength," the local critic charged, "to demand that women 'become' lesbians so that they may be more useful to the women's movement seems only slightly less inhuman than demanding that 'mentally ill' people submit to behaviorist manipulation so they can more quickly become useful members of society."[22] . . .

That the Furies never acknowledged the parallels between their own political program and that of Black Power organizations seems a puzzling oversight given some of the Furies members' prior connections to the Black liberation movement. Both radical movements combined political transformation with changes in individual lifestyle and collective culture. Each voiced suspicion and disdain for those perceived as traitors to the cause: heterosexual women in the case of lesbian feminism, and advocates of integration in the case of Black Power. Each insisted on the importance of rejecting the broader society's views and replacing them with love for self and others of one's group. . . . Similarly, lesbian feminists and Black Power advocates shared a sense that they comprised the revolutionary vanguard. This last characteristic, perhaps, explains why the Furies never indicated any awareness of the ways in which lesbian feminism mirrored Black Power politics, because doing so might suggest a lack of originality or of ideological purity that could call into question their leadership status. Nonetheless, given the background of collective members and the high degree of visibility of the Black power movement, other radical movements almost certainly influenced lesbian feminists' ideas about what revolutionary change entailed.

Putting Theory into Practice

The Furies claimed to understand the theoretical importance of lesbianism to feminism, but they faltered in figuring out how to move from the idea that all women should be lesbians to creating new models of living that would transform the larger society. In their struggles to bring more women to lesbian feminism and to plant seeds that would shape the direction of feminism, the Furies faced three major challenges. First, although they sought to build a mass movement, the Furies established practices that inadvertently worked against this goal. Second, the analysis and actions the Furies advocated through their projects alternately mobilized and excluded other women. . . . Finally, interpersonal dynamics, essential to personal and political transformation, made it difficult to enact their ideas for social change outside the collective. Thus, like the Black Panther Party, the Weather Underground, and other radical groups of the era, the priorities of the Furies were undermined by the effort required to simply maintain their own community in the face of internal dissension and external hostility.[23]

Within the collective, members wrestled with the problem of how to build a mass movement. . . . They drafted a five-year plan to organize women in other cities: with the Furies taking a leadership role, the plan included an outline for how to help the movement develop ideology, devise a plan to take power, and put together a functioning political party.[24] The collective never published this plan, however, and their publications offered few concrete proposals for organizing feminists on a large scale. But even though they devoted tremendous attention to dynamics within their collective, the Furies understood the limitations of small groups, and their articles clearly reflected an imperative that feminists build a mass movement. Paradoxically, they envisioned the larger movement developing in ways that later failed their own collective. . . .

Clearly for the Furies, lesbian feminism offered no retreat into "culture and community." In an effort to generate extensive political change, the Furies developed projects to reach large numbers of women and to "help us see what the roots of our oppression were, what kind of new society we wanted to create, and how to get from here to there."[25] The *Furies* newspaper, for instance, presented a forum for ideological exchange. Workshops to teach skills and theory to local women constituted other primary ventures. . . . The presentation of [the Furies'] ideas outside the collective, however, was fraught with conflict. Their insistence that lesbian feminism—personified in their own group—represented the revolutionary vanguard provoked controversy and failed to appeal to many women activists. . . . In addition, vanguardism became institutionalized in projects that left little opportunity for the development of others' leadership and perpetuated divisions between the movement's "thinkers" and "doers." Like dissension within the collective, the resistance which their ideas generated in others ultimately limited the group's ability to mobilize women as they intended.

The Furies initially emphasized the political education of local women as the main venue for interaction outside the collective. They organized seminars and workshops to inspire, educate, and mobilize diverse groups of women, including African American and Hispanic residents of their neighborhood, members of the National Welfare Rights Organization, women's liberationists, and lesbians they met at the city's gay bars. The workshops focused on mechanical know-how, such as electrical wiring, and survival skills, such as self-defense. The Furies considered these efforts examples of how "women with economic privilege . . . should organize to meet the survival needs of women without economic privilege."[26] . . . Like community schools established by the Black Panther Party, the collective's educational programs intended to facilitate long-term goals while also meeting short-term needs. In addition to fostering independence from men and thereby weakening male supremacy, these educational projects could draw new women into the feminist movement.[27]

. . . Although the Furies targeted a broad audience for their workshops, these attempts at outreach and education never met their own expectations. Instead, their programs demonstrated the distance between the collective's ideas and their capabilities, as well as the degree of separation between the Furies and other local women. Biren recalled that before she could teach an electrical wiring workshop, she first borrowed books from the local library in order to learn the skill herself. . . .[28]

Other forms of outreach, which drew on the group's analytical strengths, although controversial, were more sustained and successful. . . . Members of the Furies coordinated a series of public discussions, held poetry readings, arranged film screenings at a lesbian bar, and directed a lesbians-only theory workshop. Unlike the skills workshops, these sessions were directed toward a narrower audience and . . . emphasized the unification of women around a program of shared analysis. The difference in purpose coincided with a distinction in the audience sought for the two types of workshops. The collective advertised the survival workshops by posting signs in establishments located in racially and economically diverse neighborhoods; the film screenings and seminars, however, were advertised through announcements in the city's gay, women's, and alternative newspapers. In this case there was no concerted effort to reach out to women of color, poor women, or those not already involved in radical politics.[29]

Educational workshops and skills seminars played a secondary role to the collective's major project, writing and publishing. . . . The group initiated *The Furies*, their most significant endeavor. Produced from January 1972 to June 1973, the publication outlived the actual collective. . . . *The Furies* concentrated on theoretical articles so as to provide "intellectual leadership for the women's movement" and to claim critical analysis as central to radical feminism.[30] In a January 1972 statement, the Furies charged that feminists, in trying to sever their connections to the male New Left, had neglected the importance of theory. The consequent lack of clear thinking impeded feminism. "For too long," they contended, "women in the Movement have fallen prey to the very male propaganda they seek to refute. They have rejected thought, building an ideology, and all intellectual activity as the realm of men, and tried to build a politics based only on feelings—the area traditionally left to women. . . . This is not to say that feelings are irrelevant . . . [but] a political movement cannot advance without systematic thought and practical organization."[31] . . .

The determination to guide feminism brought the members of the Furies into conflict with other women activists who viewed theory, hierarchy, and leadership with suspicion. Certainly other radicals disagreed over who should hold leadership positions within their organizations. But only radical feminists systematically challenged the concept of leadership itself. . . . Misgivings about leaders' motivations and a concurrent concern with a few women monopolizing skills led radical feminists to rotate tasks like leading meetings or running an office. Radical feminists also challenged the notion of ownership of ideas and instead stressed a lack of intellectual property by not signing articles in women's publications. Many of these ideas were more easily articulated than put into consistent practice, but such efforts indicate many radical feminists' commitment to an egalitarian and inclusive movement.[32]

In contrast, the Furies . . . argued that such concerns resulted in a lack of direction that undercut the effectiveness of the feminist movement. Addressing this issue, Brown urged feminists to distinguish between "leaders" and "stars." According to Brown, movement "stars" were those individuals selected as token spokespeople by the "white, rich, male media establishments." True "leaders," however, rose from the movement's ranks through their hard work and sought to foster initiative in others. . . . By thus reconceptualizing leadership, the Furies could create a role for themselves at the front of the movement but insulate themselves from others' perceptions that power or prestige served as their primary motivation.[33]

Comfortable with their role as leaders, the Furies initially managed every aspect of their paper, including the determination of content and the distribution process. . . . Two collective members attended typesetting classes at local trade schools, and others maintained the subscription lists and coordinated mailings. Their willingness to acquire complicated skills suggests that they considered publication a long-term project and viewed the investment in technical expertise as a component of a serious commitment to political change.[34] This strategy contrasted sharply with the earlier workshops, [which] were intended to empower women individually but would not necessarily serve the revolutionary cause. The group's investment in *The Furies* suggested a direct application to mobilizing women into a lesbian feminist movement. Thus, although the collective articulated the development of both ideology and practical skills as essential steps to an organized struggle, they faced difficulties in embedding these processes in the projects that disseminated their ideas outside the collective. In particular, the group reserved theory as the domain of a small coterie of women—those who produced the paper—and conceived their readers as "students" rather than as collaborators in movement building.

Consistent with their view that theory would derive from within the collective, the Furies generally disengaged their intellectual development from dialogue with other women and, as a result, alternative views received little coverage in their writings and publications. But as their ideas about sexuality, leadership, and political organization gained a readership, they also engendered dissent, as revealed in an exchange with the women who produced the Ann Arbor–based newspaper *Spectre*. The Michigan publication differed from *The Furies* in several ways. Its authors never signed their articles or indicated their identity in their publication, conveying the message that feminists' ideas derived from a collaborative process and could not be claimed by any individual. Their writing style and spelling deviated from correct usage and thereby suggested an attempt to appeal to a broad audience in a voice not tainted with traditional, male-determined standards. Also unlike the Furies, the *Spectre* women argued that theory, in and of itself, was a tool of the male-dominated Left; therefore, the emphasis of the Furies on developing "correct analysis" indicated their continued ties to male behavior. . . . In contrast, *Spectre* advocated personal experiences as the basis for a more inclusive feminist movement. In their November-December 1971 issue, the "white revolutionary lesbians" of *Spectre* claimed: "We think that 'correct analysis' is somethin only a few people can have . . . not all of us . . . and for that reason men and stars and privileged people like to say that you have to be 'historical' or things like that . . . because then us women and lesbians who don't know all that abstract big-shit talk can't be a part of anythin . . . and that's just what they want to see. But experiences? Well, everyone has those, and if everyone can begin to understand and change thru our experiences . . . where would all those stars and men and big-shits be?"[35]

In response, one member of the Furies wrote to *Spectre* to clarify and reassert the D.C. collective's position.[36] These letters, published in *Spectre*, reveal how the two groups conceived the intersection of class, personal experience, and analysis and the relationship of these factors to political mobilization. As the unnamed member of the Furies stated: "You can't build a movement on random experiences"; rather, "you have to collect the experiences, analyze them and come up with ideology and a line of action." . . . Answering *Spectre*'s charges of elitism, the writer conceded that concentrating on theory "gives educated women a verbal advantage." Therefore, "we need both to balance each other or we will be totally taken in by the most undesirable petty opportunists." In turn, the *Spectre* women responded that social change would best happen through expression of feelings and the investigation of experiences; as women worked together in small groups to "get thru to the rage and anger that is bottled up inside of us and to learn to direct that energy . . . if all of us really started confronting our experiences and really working thru them—well we would all be making those connections and changin things[;] . . . for that kind of thing—you don't need leaders . . . and if you don't have leaders . . . well then you don't have followers."[37]

As this interchange revealed, the collective's view of its ideological importance and vanguard leadership alienated other activists and restricted outreach efforts. The exchange also exemplified the unwillingness of the Furies to engage in actual debate outside the collective. Tellingly, the collective did not allocate space in *The Furies* to the criticisms of *Spectre* or, for that matter, any other readers. In contrast, the Michigan women wrote publicly about their disagreements with the Furies, and published responses to their articles. . . .[38]

The Furies justified their doctrinal dogmatism by indicating that a hard edge was required to overcome the extensive hostility to their message, but their vehemence also contributed to the group's downfall. To outsiders, their message, and their means of delivering that message, reminded feminists of the very traits they abhorred in the New Left, among male activists, and in the society they sought to change. Elitism, conformity, hierarchy, and imposed behaviors, even if they were adopted only for the short term, contradicted prevalent feminist definitions of liberation.

The Debilitating Impact of Internal Dissension

The exchange with *Spectre* over issues of theory and leadership challenged the collective's idea that they would be insulated from a hostile world. Similarly, the reality of their communal experience abruptly upset the notion that collective living would provide a supportive atmosphere in which lesbian feminists could work out their ideas. Despite their ideals, the Furies discovered that the failure of their small collective provided some of the best insights into how to mobilize a mass movement.

The Furies conceived their collective as a means to domesticate political life and politicize domestic life. Believing that "revolution begins at home," the collective became a kind of laboratory where each member would interact in ways intended to overcome patterns of behavior that reflected both their class status and internalized hatred of women.[39] Members of other radical movements shared living space and established communes, but the motivation of the Furies extended beyond convenience, comfort, or an attempt to share resources. . . . For the Furies, political transformation, growing out of personal change, became the primary reason people lived together and, at least in principle, the focus of domestic life. . . . They questioned every aspect of collective living; all matters became political issues to be resolved through frequent and lengthy meetings, often lasting late into the night. The decisions they made and the theoretical insights they reached would be written up and published, thus becoming the basis for their long-range political strategies. By working as a group to build lesbian feminist politics, they believed they could expand their understanding of oppression beyond their own experiences and, with a shared goal, would increase their willingness to confront divisive issues such as class privilege.[40]

Adopting diverse methods to address the economic differences among collective members—sharing material resources, for example—the Furies demonstrated their desire to develop behavior divorced from standard (male) norms. Theoretically, they considered classism a form of oppression that derived from male supremacy and thus would disappear with the end of sexism; in the meantime, however, differences based on class privilege emerged as an area of conflict within the group. . . . Some held jobs where they could directly challenge patriarchy and capitalism, as in the salaried positions Brown and Bunch occupied as political organizers. But the majority of women in the collective worked at low-income service jobs or were students who possessed limited time to attend meetings and demonstrations. To compensate for the differential earning potential and types of jobs held by members, the Furies pooled their wages through a percentage-based system that accounted for the amount earned and individual economic potential judged by past "heterosexual privilege." . . .[41]

The group also theorized that class fundamentally shaped behavior in ways that negatively influenced feminism. In particular, the Furies concerned themselves with the ways that middle-class women's oppression of working-class women crippled the feminist movement. In discussion sessions and then published articles, the group identified as typical middle-class behaviors expressions such as guilt and denial that were used to control working-class activists.[42] The socialization of middle-class women, they implied, supported patriarchy and capitalism to a greater extent than that of working-class women. Former members now believe the group romanticized the radicalism of working-class women and stereotyped middle-class women as complaining and self-indulgent. Nonetheless, their critiques of class privilege were necessary to building a broader women's movement.[43]

Criticism of middle-class women's emotional manipulation directly connected to the collective's critique of CR. . . . Furies members agreed that CR could effect both individual and collective change, but they believed that the technique risked reinforcing the status quo. . . . Emotions evolved from experiences that were limited by class and race, and feelings could be "used to excuse inaction and inability to change." . . . Thus, feminists must combine discussion of personal experiences and feelings with the study of political theory and the history of social movements and women's condition throughout the world. In addition, the Furies contended that patriarchal culture trained women to prioritize their relationships and to manipulate each other through emotions. They concluded that in order to overcome their connection to patriarchy, lesbians should use theory to guide their actions, view relationships in political terms, and develop independent self-identities.[44]

Despite the group's insistence that feminists should minimize the significance of personal relationships and emotions, these forces ultimately contributed to the collective's dissolution. Women in the Furies experienced tremendous stress due to their separation from family and friends, their suspicion of outsiders, and their distrust of the emotive side of relationships. The collective was challenged to implement their ideas within the context of their passionate, often sexual, and sometimes antagonistic relationships.[45] At times the collective itself caused emotional distress, particularly when members critiqued each others' behavior. In the view of participants, the middle-class women who exhibited objectionable or manipulative behavior should be forced to change for the good of the collective and the movement. But such ideas sometimes revealed contradictory impulses. Biren's graduate education in political science at Oxford University, for example, should have enabled her to make important contributions to the collective's ideology and become a movement "leader" in the collective's definition of that term. But instead, members charged that Biren's elite education had trained her to verbally take advantage of others and they insisted that she needed to develop modes of communication free from such "patriarchal taint." . . . In what some later considered the most extreme instance of distress caused by the collective's actions, the group sent away the three small children who lived with them, arguing that childcare diverted too much attention from other political activities. . . . .

Perhaps the issue that most strained members' patience was the collective process itself. Because they sought to closely analyze all aspects of their group dynamics, every practice was subjected to scrutiny and extensive discussion. As Biren remembered: "We would spend months figuring out how to divide the money. We knew we had to put it all in—all the cars, all the money, all the clothes, everything was pooled. That we knew. It was how it got divided out that was the problem. Could we have individual toothbrushes?

. . . Nothing was assumed about anything and it was just exhausting to figure it all out." Thus, the Furies faced a paradox: even as they sought to diminish the centrality of personal relationships and emotions in their lives, the work of maintaining their household, studying and writing, making money, guarding against FBI infiltration, and coordinating projects drained the women's energy, intensified their feelings about each other, and ultimately made it difficult to accomplish their larger goals. Under such circumstances, the group frequently reverted to behavior that was inconsistent with their ideas.[46]

As the Furies . . . attempted to reject their socialization as women and as members of a class, the group substituted one set of prescribed behaviors with others that some considered equally exploitative. . . . Brown reflected that the Furies "began to create within ourselves the dynamic of a fascist state." The collective expelled Biren and Deevey for allegedly refusing to repudiate behaviors tainted by their class status; several months later, Brown was also kicked out. . . . Believing that attention to personal relationships should accede to political analyses did not ensure that such a practice could be followed.[47]

As the above discussion makes clear, the Furies strove to develop theory, projects, and even a political party that would influence feminism as a political movement. Their success was muted, however, by the effort to merge theory and action in a manner that would further their long-term goals. Despite the conflicts they encountered and even as the collective imploded under the weight of internal and external pressures, members of the Furies remained sure of their contribution to feminism. Bunch predicted that "in five years, many of our assertions will be daily discussions and accepted by large numbers of people. . . . While we are now treading on territory deeply socialized in people—the absolute sanctity of heterosexuality—I think that [when] we do connect with the lives of enough people, especially young women, that this will take hold."[48] Along with Radicalesbians in New York, the Washington, D.C., collective played a pivotal role in bringing attention to lesbians' existence in the women's movement and legitimating lesbian feminism as a political issue. . . . In addition, the members' accounts of their collective provide a critical example of how women tried to bring about a political revolution. Finally, by taking pride in their identities as lesbians and political women, their theory and action provided a powerful model for future activists.[49]

Moreover, after they left their collective, former members devised new means to spread feminist theory and culture throughout the country and into mainstream America. In doing so, they not only helped sustain the feminist movement but also served to substantively broaden both the movement's ideological foundations and the diversity of its adherents.[50] Former members focused particularly on publishing and the development of media as a method of political action. In 1974, Brown and Bunch established the journal *Quest* to publish writings that explored the connections between feminist theory and activism. . . . *Quest* represented a broad vision of women's liberation that included writers with a range of organizational and movement affiliations; even though former members of the Furies helped publish the journal, it was not devoted exclusively to lesbian feminism. . . . This publication thereby . . . moved away from the vanguardism of the Furies to a more inclusive consideration and representation of alternative perspectives on social change.[51]

Former members disseminated feminist theory and supported the women's movement in a variety of other ways. Biren published her photographs and established Moonforce Media to produce and distribute feminist films.[52] Schwing, Harris, Woodul, and Berson started the women's recording company Olivia Records. Bunch and Brown each published collections of their theoretical essays.[53] Reid worked with Diana Press publishers in Baltimore where she helped produce *Quest* and two anthologies of articles from *The Furies*. Former members also published numerous essays and interviews where they reflected on the importance of their collective experiment. These retrospective accounts reflected their continued sense of their contribution and shaped deeper knowledge and understanding of the group among feminists. They also became part of the foundation on which (and against which) a broader lesbian feminist culture emerged in the mid-1970s.[54]

These later endeavors took lesbian feminism and feminist activism in new directions, but the imprint of the Furies remained evident. In their work after the collective collapsed, former members continued to advocate feminist separatism and to herald the revolutionary potential of lesbian feminism, but strikingly they all emphasized outreach rather than isolation. . . . Along with encouraging the expression of diverse views, the post-Furies efforts focused on ways to mobilize large numbers of women and implicitly rejected the collective living model that they had earlier attempted. By abandoning their dogmatic approach and extending themselves to both lesbian and heterosexual women, the Furies strengthened their place in the center of the feminist movement, although the broader political movement envisioned by Bunch never developed.

For contemporary readers the collective's experiment can illuminate the unexpected consequences that can develop from an attempt to merge political and personal change. For the Furies, the intimacy and intensity of collective living prompted new understandings of the ways that personal identity shaped women's relationships and, moreover, how such interactions could be altered to pursue revolutionary aims. Through their activities, particularly their analytical writings, collective members demonstrated intellectual creativity and political passion that contributed immeasurably to understanding the roots of women's oppression. But at the same time that their endeavors opened up innovative avenues for change, they also closed off options for political action. In this way, theory and action operated as contradictory forces. Seeking to move radical feminism beyond an emphasis on individualism and small-group structures to nationwide organization, the Furies criticized the movement's tendency to promote conformity and to emphasize personal relationships. Ironically, however, the collective imposed new, restrictive imperatives on feminists, advocating a singular ideological path as the solution to women's oppression. In particular, the collective members' scrutiny of women's actions as indicators of political commitment reinforced homogeneity and, in the end, limited their attempts to extend their movement either within the racially and economically diverse city where they lived or throughout the country.

The Furies collective's attempts to impose both theoretical and behavioral litmus tests on feminists, coupled with the exclusivity of their collective, inspired conflict both from inside and outside the group. This resistance generated energy and anger that sparked the creative process and encouraged the growth of lesbian feminism; but at the same time, the resulting conflicts enervated the collective. Although the Furies fostered an environment where members' commitment to each other, and to feminism, facilitated personal change, members could not translate their insights into a blueprint for a larger movement to end male supremacy. Their writing and the projects they initiated demonstrate that they saw their collective as the first step in a broad revolutionary movement. They had formed their collective in response to their own sense that feminism had focused too much on personal issues and experience, and not enough on theory. Still, that their collective failed to provide the basis for such a mass movement reveals more about the challenges feminists and other advocates of radical change faced than about the shortcomings in their vision.

NOTES

The original version of this essay appeared in *Feminist Studies* 28, no. 2 (Summer 2002).

1. Charlotte Bunch, "Notes for the Cell Meeting, January, 1972," box 1, Joan E. Biren Papers, Lesbian Herstory Archives, New York (cited hereafter as Biren Papers).

2. Studies of feminist and lesbian feminist organizations include Alice Echols, *Daring to Be Bad: Radical Feminism in America, 1967–1975* (Minneapolis: University of Minnesota Press, 1989); Michele D. Dominy, "Lesbian-Feminist Gender Conceptions: Separatism in Christchurch, New Zealand," *Signs* 11 (Winter 1986): 274–289; Trisha Franzen, "Differences and Identities: Feminism and the Albuquerque Lesbian Community," *Signs* 18 (Summer 1993): 891–906; Becki L. Ross, *The House That Jill Built: A Lesbian Nation in Formation* (Toronto: University of Toronto Press, 1995); Michal Brody, ed., *Are We There Yet? A Continuing History of Lavender Woman, a Chicago Lesbian Newspaper, 1971–1976* (Iowa City: Aunt Lute Books, 1985); Saralyn Chesnut and Amanda C. Gable, "'Women Ran It': Charis Books and More and Atlanta's Lesbian-Feminist Community, 1971–1981," in *Carryin' On in the Lesbian and Gay South*, ed. John Howard (New York: New York University Press, 1997), 241–284; and Margaret Strobel, "Consciousness and Action: Historical Agency in the Chicago Women's Liberation Union," in *Provoking Agents: Gender and Agency in Theory and Practice*, ed. Judith Kegan Gardiner (Urbana: University of Illinois Press, 1995), 52–68.

3. Dana Shugar, *Separatism and Women's Community* (Lincoln: University of Nebraska Press, 1995), 57–60.

4. The twelve members of the Furies were Ginny Berson, Joan Biren, Rita Mae Brown, Charlotte Bunch, Sharon Deevey, Susan Hathaway, Helaine Harris, Nancy Myron, Tasha Peterson, Coletta Reid, Lee Schwing, and Jennifer Woodul.

5. Alice Echols, "We Gotta Get Out of This Place: Notes toward a Remapping of the Sixties," *Socialist Review* 22 (April–June 1992): 14–15, and Barbara Epstein, *Political Protest and Cultural Revolution: Nonviolent Direct Action in the 1970s and 1980s* (Berkeley: University of California Press, 1991).

6. For further information about the women's movement in Washington, D.C., see Anne M. Valk, "Separatism and Sisterhood: Race, Sex, and Women's Activism in Washington, D.C., 1963–1980" (PhD diss., Duke University, 1996), and Anne M. Valk, *Radical Sisters: Second Wave Feminism and Black Liberation in Washington, D.C.* (Urbana: University of Illinois Press, 2008).

7. Rita Mae Brown, *Rita Will: Memoir of a Literary Rabble-Rouser* (New York: Bantam Books, 1997), 228–238.

8. Echols, *Daring to Be Bad*, 240–244.

9. Arlene Stein, *Sex and Sensibility: Stories of a Lesbian Generation* (Berkeley: University of California Press, 1997), 73.

10. Verta Taylor and Leila J. Rupp, "Women's Culture and Lesbian Feminist Activism: A Reconsideration of Cultural Feminism," *Signs* 19 (Autumn 1993): 32–61.

11. An in-depth comparison of Black Power and lesbian feminist organizations remains to be written. For an extended discussion of Black Power organizations and the various ideologies to which they adhered, see William L. Van Deburg, *New Day in Babylon: The Black Power Movement and American Culture, 1965–1975* (Chicago: University of Chicago Press, 1992), and Komozi Woodard, *A Nation within a Nation: Amiri Baraka (LeRoi Jones) and Black Power Politics* (Chapel Hill: University of North Carolina Press, 1999). The best . . . scholarship on the Black Panther Party is collected in Charles E. Jones, ed., *The Black Panther Party Reconsidered* (Baltimore: Black Classic Press, 1998).

12. Sara Evans, *Personal Politics: The Roots of the Women's Liberation Movement in the Civil Rights Movement and the New Left* (New York: Vintage Books, 1979); Echols, *Daring to Be Bad.*

13. Charlotte Bunch, interview by author, New York, February 15, 1995; Joan E. Biren, interview by author, Takoma Park, MD, December 30, 1992; Sharon Deevey, interview by author, Columbus, Ohio, September 25, 1993; Helaine Harris, interview by author, Hyattsville, MD, August 16, 1993; Sue Fox, "The Furies," *Washington Blade*, June 16, 1995, 63, 65, 67; and Tasha Peterson, "Class Will Tell," *off our backs*, April 15, 1971, 7. See also autobiographical articles by Coletta Reid, Helaine Harris, and Nancy Myron in *Motive* 32 (January 1972).

14. Coletta Reid, "Coming Out in the Women's Movement," in *Lesbianism and the Women's Movement*, ed. Nancy Myron and Charlotte Bunch (Baltimore: Diana Press, 1975), 95.

15. This idea is expressed elsewhere in Ginny Berson, "The Furies," *The Furies* 1 (January 1972): 1; Rita Mae Brown, "Roxanne Dunbar: How a Female Heterosexual Serves the Interests of Male Supremacy," *The Furies* 1 (January 1972): 5–6; Rita Mae Brown, "Hanoi to Hoboken: A Round-Trip Ticket," *off our backs*, March 25, 1971, 4–5; Charlotte Bunch, "Out Now," *The Furies* 1 (June-July 1972): 12–13.

16. "Statement of the Furies," May 1971, carton 2, folder 54, Charlotte Bunch Papers, Schlesinger Library, Radcliffe College, Cambridge, MA (cited hereafter as Bunch Papers); Those Women, "Lesbians and DayCare," *Rat*, June-July 1971, 13.

17. Charlotte Bunch, "Lesbians in Revolt," *The Furies* 1 (January 1972): 8–9.

18. Rita Mae Brown, "The Shape of Things to Come," *Women: A Journal of Liberation* 2 (Winter 1972): 44–46, reprinted in her *Plain Brown Rapper* (Oakland: Diana Press, 1976), 110.

19. Radicalesbians, "Woman-Identified Woman," *Women: A Journal of Liberation* (Summer 1970): 39, and Echols, "We Gotta Get Out of This Place."

20. Berson, "The Furies," 1.

21. Bev Fisher, interview in *off our backs*, November 1972, 2–3, and Fran Chapman, "Commentary," *off our backs*, January 1972, 7.

22. Chapman, "Commentary," 7.

23. Ron Jacobs, *The Way the Wind Blew: A History of the Weather Underground* (London: Verso, 1997).

24. Bunch, "Notes for the Cell Meeting."

25. Coletta Reid, "Details," *The Furies* 1 (June-July 1972): 7.

26. Brown, "Shape of Things to Come," 45.

27. "Teach Each Other, Teach Ourselves," pamphlet, 1971, Addenda, carton 2, folder 49, Bunch Papers. Information regarding turnout at these events is not available.

28. Biren interview. Although as a group the Furies discontinued their skills workshops as they concentrated on writing and as their collective foundered, Bunch's notes from the January 1972 cell meeting indicate that the group still considered skills centers an important activity.

29. Charlotte Bunch to parents, 14 October 1971, carton 1, folder 23, Bunch Papers, and *Gay Blade* 3 (March 1972): 1–2.

30. Rita Mae Brown to the Furies, n.d., circa 1972, Sharon Deevey, personal papers, privately held.

31. Berson, "The Furies," 1.

32. This suspicion of leaders, especially feminist authors like Kate Millett and Susan Brownmiller, led to some of the movement's most destructive behavior. See Susan Brownmiller, *In Our Time: Memoir of a Revolution* (New York: Dial, 1999).

33. Rita Mae Brown, "Leadership vs. Stardom," *The Furies* 1 (February 1972).

34. Deevey interview.

35. *Spectre* 5 (November-December 1971): 7. The misspellings are in the original. Two women from *Spectre* visited the Furies in Washington in September 1971 in order to discuss their analyses and solidify a bond as lesbian feminists. The discussions published in *Spectre* followed this disastrous visit between the two groups; Box 1, "Jeanne and Lois" folder, Biren Papers.

36. *Spectre* published letters from readers but did not identify any author's name. Based on evidence within the letters, Rita Mae Brown was unquestionably the author of the reprinted letters regarding ideology described here.

37. *Spectre* responded to Brown's articles "Roxanne Dunbar" and "Leadership vs. Stardom"; Rita Mae Brown, "Gossip," *The Furies* 1 (January 1972): 11–12. For *Spectre* responses, see "Parts of a Letter to Us—From a 'Star' in the Lesbian Movement," *Spectre* 5 (November–December 1971): 7, 9, 14; letters from readers, *Spectre* 6 (January–February 1972): 13.

38. Charlotte Bunch to parents, 5 February 1972, carton 1, folder 23, Bunch Papers, and Brown, "Shape of Things to Come."

39. Charlotte Bunch and Coletta Reid, "Revolution Begins at Home," *The Furies* 1 (May 1972): 2–4.

40. Ginny Berson, "Only by Association," *The Furies* 1 (June-July 1972): 5–6.

41. Harris interview.

42. Bunch and Reid, "Revolution Begins at Home."

43. Biren attended graduate school in political science at Oxford University prior to moving to Washington, D.C. No articles in *The Furies* newspaper appear with her name. Susan Fox, "After the Revolution," *Washington Blade*, June 23, 1995, 45, 47; Biren interview.

44. Berson, "The Furies," and Sharon Deevey and Coletta Reid, "Emotionalism—Downward Spiral," *The Furies* 1 (February 1972): 11.

45. Fox, "After the Revolution," and journal entry, n.d., Sharon Deevey, personal papers, privately held.

46. Harris interview; Deevey interview; Fox, "The Furies"; and Biren interview.

47. Fox, "After the Revolution"; Harris interview; Biren interview; and Brown, *Plain Brown Rapper*, 17–19.

48. Charlotte Bunch to parents, 5 February 1972, carton 1, folder 23, Bunch Papers. Responses to the Furies from activists in Washington and elsewhere were mixed. In addition to *Spectre*, see Chapman, "Commentary."

49. The North Carolina lesbian feminist group, Feminary, acknowledged the role of the Furies in shaping their ideas about lesbianism and collective living. See Elizabeth Knowlton, "Rita Mae Brown," *Feminary* 10, no. 1 (1979): 74.

50. Taylor and Rupp, "Women's Culture and Lesbian Feminist Activism."

51. Karen Kollias, "Spiral of Change: An Introduction to Quest," *Quest* 1 (Summer 1974): 6.

52. Biren's photographs appear in numerous publications, including two collections she published of her own work: Joan E. Biren, *Eye to Eye: Portraits of Lesbians* (Washington, DC: Glad Hag Books, 1979), and *Making a Way: Lesbians Out Front* (Washington, DC: Glad Hag Books, 1987).

53. Charlotte Bunch, *Passionate Politics: Feminist Theory in Action, 1968–1986* (New York: St. Martin's Press, 1987), and Brown, *Plain Brown Rapper.*

54. For further discussions of individual members' goals after they left the collective, see Coletta Reid, "Taking Care of Business," *Quest* 1 (Fall 1974): 6–23, and "The Muses of Olivia: Our Own Economy, Our Own Song," *off our backs*, August–September 1974, 2–3.

11

Strange Bedfellows

Building Feminist Coalitions around Sex Work in the 1970s

STEPHANIE GILMORE

Feminists in the United States have long recognized sexuality as a site and source of women's oppression and of women's liberation. This has been the subject of intense debate for more than a century.[1] In the post–Civil War era, feminists sought to address economic realities, which at times put women in the position of engaging in sexual commerce. During the Progressive era, activists drew attention to "white slavery," that is, the physical coercion of women into prostitution; feminists pursued moral and economic uplift that would rescue those they believed to be "fallen girls." Although feminists acknowledged that some women "treated" men to sexual favors in exchange for material goods, or simply a nice evening, many assumed that women were in a state of constant danger from male violence. This construction of women-as-victims did not take into account that some women enjoyed the sense of sexual agency, even though it did acknowledge the realities of sexual oppression.[2] In the aftermath of two world wars, however, prostitutes became identified as a social and moral evil, and social anxieties about female sexuality were apparent in the postwar United States.[3] Into the twenty-first century, feminists still debate the cultures of female and male sexuality. Although many oppose structural forces that continue the commodification of women and seek to draw attention to human sexual slavery, sex tourism, and trafficking, many also acknowledge that prostitutes have gone from being fallen women to "fall girls" and lament any sense of women's sexual agency and liberation.[4]

In the era of "second wave" feminism—a term used to denote mass mobilization of feminist activists between the mid-1960s and early

246

1980s—feminists grappled with the politics of sexuality. They disputed the points at which women possessed sexual power and the ability to consent to sex; they challenged hypersexual representations of women in the media; and they fought for women's sexual agency and autonomy. In the early 1980s, feminists engaged in "sex wars" around the issue of pornography and feminist-backed legislation to censor it in order to protect women.[5] So-called antisex feminists targeted pornography and commercial sex, arguing that they were fundamentally oppressive to women.[6] According to this perspective, sex was rooted in men's desire to dominate women, and sexual relations outside of patriarchy thus were, and remain, impossible because sex is a byproduct of unequal power relations. On the other side of this debate, so-called prosex feminists suggested that women's liberation was possible only when women were free to talk about and explore sex and sexuality without shame or stigma. As is the case with most dichotomies, the labels do not suggest the complexity of the issues, and, as a result, there has been a proliferation of important scholarship on women's sexualities, sexual experiences, and the structural relationships among sex, gender, economics, politics, and culture, all of which pushes us to understand sexuality as a category of historical analysis.[7]

The sex wars of the 1980s have been identified by most feminist scholars as the province of radical feminists and sex radicals.[8] This framework obscures other contemporary activists who theorized, debated, and acted on issues of female sexuality, including the power dynamics inherent in sexual relations. For instance, the National Organization for Women (NOW), identified generally with liberal feminism, is often distinguished from radical feminist groups and assumed to be marginal to the sex wars. Yet in a number of local chapters, NOW women debated who was an appropriate sex partner and what constituted feminist sex.[9] During the 1970s, NOW members organized alongside prostitutes' rights activists, advocates for battered women, and women pushing for wages for housework to decriminalize prostitution; together, they also criticized and sought to dismantle patriarchal structures that oppressed women and forced them into sex work.

A few scholars have noted that NOW addressed the issue of prostitution and called for its decriminalization, although not without some hesitation. For example, sociologist Ronald Weitzer has argued that although NOW endorsed decriminalization of prostitution in 1973, it never lent its full support to the rights of prostitutes as workers or to COYOTE (Call Off Your Old

Tired Ethics), the U.S.-based prostitutes' rights organization founded in 1973. In a footnote, however, he notes that local chapters, especially those in the San Francisco area, were more actively involved with COYOTE than the national organization was.[10] Sociologist Valerie Jenness argues that COYOTE's affiliations with NOW and other feminist groups were "conducive to COYOTE's entrance into contemporary feminist discourse."[11] These scholars suggest that COYOTE did not operate independently, but they do not elaborate on how or why this group found common cause with NOW chapters. Moreover, Weitzer in particular concludes that the prostitutes' rights movement failed because it did not achieve its stated goal, namely the decriminalization of prostitution.

Despite failure in this conventional sense, much can be gained from digging deeper than Weitzer has to understand the coalitions that developed among NOW chapters and prostitutes' rights activists. This article traces the political and philosophical networks that NOW members and sex workers created and sustained as they mobilized to bring sex work as work into the heady feminist debates over women's rights and women's liberation. This examination both broadens the scope of the "sex wars" and allows for a more nuanced understanding than we now have of how feminists grappled with what historian Heather Lee Miller has termed "the nexus of sex and work."[12]

In overviews of 1970s feminism, NOW is often painted in broad strokes as a liberal feminist organization that operated mainly on the national level and in juxtaposition to radical feminists. If NOW is mentioned in the context of women's sexualities, it is usually vis-à-vis Betty Friedan's grousing about the "lavender menace"—that is, lesbians who threatened the political efficacy of "her" organization. In response to this epithet, about forty lesbians and allies, many from the New York City chapter of NOW, stormed the stage of the 1970 Congress to Unite Women wearing "Lavender Menace" tee-shirts and read the now-famous manifesto "The Woman-Identified Woman."[13] In 1971, NOW passed a resolution (that had been defeated and then tabled the year before) acknowledging lesbians' issues as feminist issues. This episode is usually considered NOW's entrance into—and exit from—historical analyses of feminist debates over sex and sexuality.[14]

Most troubling about the standard narrative is the underlying assumption that NOW operated only at the national level. National leaders of any organization or movement can never represent the whole, as scholars who study the black freedom and gay and lesbian rights movements make clear.

Analyzing NOW from a grassroots angle rather than as a national organization yields a much more complex picture of this largest second wave feminist organization. It also reveals how NOW members grappled with, debated, united over, and divided over many issues, strategies, goals, and objectives, including sex as work. Focusing on NOW chapters in the South, Midwest, and West Coast also challenges the hegemony of U.S. women's history and U.S. feminism as rooted in the lives of women on the East Coast.[15] This history reveals many and varied debates over lesbian sex and sexuality, both before and certainly well after 1971; fascinating explorations of feminist kinky sex with men and with women; and intense consideration of whether women could be liberated while in relationships with men.[16] NOW members also debated whether feminists should advocate for prostitutes on the job and should work to decriminalize prostitution.

To be clear, there was never full consensus on issues surrounding sexuality, and not all NOW chapters took up these concerns. Furthermore, not all members in those chapters that did address prostitutes' rights agreed with their sisters' agenda; some chose to focus on other issues. Still, it is important to recognize that NOW feminists across the country were grappling with issues of prostitution, sex as work, and on-the-job protections for prostitutes. NOW chapters also forged coalitions with sex workers' rights activists and other feminist groups concerned with women's "intimate labors."[17]

Women in NOW first raised challenges about the disparate treatment of female prostitutes and male johns under the law. This perspective fit well with NOW's general efforts to mobilize around issues of women's economic discrimination and to pursue legal remedies.[18] Indeed, NOW formed in part because the Equal Employment Opportunity Commission (EEOC), charged with addressing formal complaints of sex and race discrimination under Title VII of the 1964 Civil Rights Act, refused to hear cases of sex discrimination. Two original EEOC commissioners, Richard Graham and Aileen Hernandez, were among the conveners of NOW in 1966, and Hernandez was elected NOW's national president in 1970. One of NOW's earliest projects was to "desexegrate" newspaper want ads, which separated employment advertisements for men from those for women. The organization also led legal battles at local and national levels against sex discrimination on the job, including major class-action lawsuits against AT&T and Sears.[19] NOW members always—although not exclusively—wielded liberal rhetoric and pursued liberal strategies of equality under the law. Given the organization's early history in the arena of workplace discrimination against women, it is logical that NOW feminists would take up the issue of prostitution in the context of labor and inequitable legal treatment.

In 1970, city leaders in San Francisco proposed to curb what seemed to be rampant prostitution by arresting whores. In response, San Francisco NOW (SF NOW) member Del Martin (who later became a member of the national board) demanded full equality for women and men, recommending to Mayor Joseph Alioto that "no woman will be prosecuted under the law without the same sentence being given to the male partner."[20] Her focus on legal equality between women and men and her challenge to a sexual double standard are not surprising—she and her lover Phyllis Lyon had long advocated equal treatment for all under the law.[21] Speaking out as a NOW member, Martin put prostitution on the organization's agenda, and the San Francisco chapter led the way for others to confront police and a legal system that treated whores and johns differently.

In 1973, prostitutes and feminist allies founded COYOTE, which called for an end to discriminatory practices against prostitutes. COYOTE activists charged that "the sexual double standard involving prostitution is blatantly unfair and illegal, since the men who create the market and buy bodies are untouched, [but] the women who supply the demand and sell their bodies pay the penalty."[22] Arrest statistics suggest that in San Francisco, where both prostitution (selling sexual activity for a fee) and solicitation (purchasing sexual activity for a fee) were criminal offenses, prostitutes were arrested at rates three times that of johns. According to the *Sourcebook of Criminal Justice Statistics*, in 1973, thirty-five thousand people in San Francisco were arrested on prostitution-related charges, 75 percent of whom were women.[23] COYOTE and SF NOW member Gail Gifford pointed out that this prosecutorial double standard meant that "women convicted of prostitution make up 30% or more of most county jail populations and . . . 70% of the women in prison received their first criminal conviction on a prostitution charge."[24] COYOTE also charged that "the white male clubs known as Congress and our State Legislatures" are passing laws "that will protect males from predatory females," an obvious tongue-in-cheek jab at what they saw to be ridiculously discriminatory views on and legal harassment of prostitutes. The organization also emphasized that the costs were "*only* $575 per prostitute arrest," suggesting that taxpayer funds should not be spent on what it believed to be a victimless crime.[25]

Whether prostitution was a "victimless crime" was the subject of continued debate, and the issue was vociferously argued in the early days of the women's liberation movement. In New York City, some NOW members joined New York Radical Feminists, The Feminists, and other women's liberationists in a 1971 conference on prostitution. The flyer for this event featured a line drawing of a naked woman on her knees, arms wrapped around a dollar sign, head tilted upward as if pleading to the dollar sign not to leave her. Her foot is shackled and chained to the dollar sign, an image suggesting that even if the dollar sign left, it would drag her with it. The flyer thus highlighted the conference organizers' analysis that women are reduced both to sexual objectivity and to financial dependence on men.[26] Susan Brownmiller, a member of New York City NOW and founder of New York Radical Women, noted in her commentary to the New York State Legislature hearing on "prostitution as a victimless crime" that "the buyers, the ones who hold the cash in their hand, the ones who create the market by their demand, they are all men, gentlemen, the same sex as yourself."[27]

COYOTE activists would not disagree, but discord among feminists developed over whether women could participate in such an economic exchange legally and freely. Brownmiller agreed with COYOTE that laws around prostitution were applied unevenly: "The law in this city is applied to punish the woman and to let the man go scot-free."[28] But, on the issue of "victimless crime," she took a different stance: "Prostitution is a crime, gentlemen, but it is not victimless. There is a victim, and that is the woman." She further disputed the "myth" that "the female prostitute is a free participant in her act [and] has made a conscious choice to sell her body," arguing that prostitution was little more than sexual slavery.[29] Moreover, in her analysis, women were doubly victimized by the practice of prostitution and the prosecution of the crime; she argued that men needed to be prosecuted for "the criminal act of purchasing another's body."[30] Her words mirror those of The Feminists, who openly protested "renewed police drives against prostitutes" in New York City: "The very essence of prostitution is degradation—not only of the prostitute herself but of all women."[31] All women, in this analysis, were victims in the practice of prostitution.

NOW members continued this debate. Was prostitution a form of sexual slavery? Was it exploitation that victimized both prostitutes in particular and women in general? Should laws be changed to legalize or decriminalize prostitution? Many feminists in NOW agreed that female prostitutes were targeted unfairly vis-à-vis male solicitors and that laws criminalizing prostitution were applied unfairly. Many likely agreed with Brownmiller, who acknowledged that "as with most other issues of women's liberation, the problem of prostitution is unbelievably complex, resting as it does on economics, psychology, sexuality, and the male power principle."[32] But the solution was not so clear. In order to pass a national resolution affirming national NOW's official position on a given issue, members must introduce a resolution at a chapter or state meeting. If the resolution is successful there, the originating chapter then introduces it at the regional meeting, and after that, a vote is taken at the national meeting. This "governance structure" requires grassroots mobilization; resolutions cannot be introduced from the leadership down to the membership.[33] Successful resolutions at national meetings do not always translate into direct action on the part of the organization. But the fact that resolutions originate in the face-to-face meetings of local chapters and require members to build common cause with others in the organization underscores the importance of grassroots activism in NOW.[34]

On the issue of prostitution, Tish Sommers of Berkeley NOW initiated a resolution urging the organization to go on record in opposition to "both present discriminatory treatment of prostitutes under law, and so-called 'legalized prostitution,' which is only a mask for greater exploitation of women's bodies." She also insisted that the group end all laws "aimed at government (male) control of women's sexual life" and "fight for real job alternatives for women, which will make prostitution a less desirable economic solution."[35] Her argument suggested that prostitution is only about male sexual satisfaction and that women choose it only because they have no other alternatives, thereby denying it is a choice at all. She also recognized the larger context of gender, labor, and sexuality as interrelated facets in women's lives. Sommers's resolution passed in the Berkeley chapter, and she advanced her argument at the national NOW convention in February 1973.

At the same meeting, anthropologist and Seattle NOW activist Jennifer James penned a different resolution in collaboration with Margo St. James, founder of a group called WHO (Whores, Housewives, and Others).[36] St. James, who coined the term *decriminalization* in the context of prostitution, proposed that NOW support the removal of "all laws relating to the act of prostitution per se, and as an interim measure, [should favor] the decriminalization of prostitution."[37] The organization voted overwhelmingly in

favor of St. James's resolution. Like other groups within the liberal establishment, such as the American Civil Liberties Union (ACLU), NOW had
an official perspective on prostitution that was "anchored in a belief that . . .
sexual behavior between consenting adults should remain outside the
purview of the law."[38] Moreover, it acknowledged that prostitution should be
understood as paid labor: prostitutes earn money as they "enter into an
agreement, contractual in nature, with a consenting adult, to perform a
service."[39] National NOW did not respond again to prostitutes' rights until
the 1980s. Moreover, in the 1990s and early 2000s, NOW had articulated
positions on prostitution only in the context of condemning international
sex trafficking.[40]

Unlike the national organization, however, local chapters continued to
engage the issue. In several chapters, members maintained an interest in
legal and health issues related to prostitution and allied with sex workers
and their advocates to decriminalize prostitution and acknowledge sex work
as labor. In Nevada, for example, the state NOW chapter undertook a study of
legal brothel prostitution in 1973. The state had passed a law in 1970 that
mandated the licensing of brothels and prostitutes; the law placed responsibility on prostitutes who operate as "independent contractors" to pay for
their own health care and mandatory testing for sexually transmitted diseases. NOW activist Priscilla Alexander noted that the law also limited prostitutes' activities beyond the workplace: "They are not allowed to be in a
gambling casino or a bar at all, or be in the company of a man on the street
or in a restaurant. They are also not allowed to reside in the same community
in which they work (they generally work a three-week shift in the brothel,
after which they are 'off' for a week or more). Since the women are required
to register with the sheriff as prostitutes, these restrictions are easy to
enforce."[41] Although lawmakers suggested that licensing whores "resolved
[the state's] prostitution 'problem,'" Nevada NOW members insisted that
licensing was an incomplete and unfair solution because it did not protect
the women as workers. Specifically, there was "no limitation on the 'house
cut' of their salaries, no restriction on the length of their working hours;
even no assurance that they can collect their earnings." Moreover, the licensing law, they argued, "effectively relegates the prostitute to the position of
slave to the owner and opens the situation to oppressive extra-legal restrictions which may demoralize the women. . . . [In this] strictly controlled and
confined environment [women do not have the] right to refuse or accept

clients or to perform any requested services." Thus COYOTE's stated goal was to "remove prostitution from the criminal code and from any government control. Making prostitution legal is NOT Coyote's stand because it would still involve and enable the government to license and regulate what a woman does with her body."[42]

Prostitutes' rights advocates in COYOTE and NOW pursued full decriminalization of prostitution, a goal that has yet to be achieved. Sociologist Weitzer suggests that because COYOTE (and, by extension, other prostitutes' rights groups) push for decriminalization, they have remained marginalized in the feminist movement and their *"movement has had no positive effect on public attitudes regarding prostitution."*[43] Yet the prostitutes' rights movement in the 1970s, spearheaded by COYOTE and joined by activists in NOW, ACLU, and Wages for Housework (an international organization with chapters in Toronto, London, Italy, Los Angeles, and Brooklyn), made significant strides in pushing both the public discourse on and feminist analysis of women's autonomy and agency not only around the issue of prostitution but also on feminist issues such as sexual health, rape, domestic violence, labor, poverty, racism, and the Equal Rights Amendment (ERA).

St. James knew the power of coalitions to advance the cause of prostitutes' rights. In the mid-1970s, she traveled around the country to attend trials of prostitutes and "meet with lawyers committees, women's groups, as many women as possible, to see if I can't get them interested in the issue of decriminalization of prostitution, building a political network across all class lines, color lines, economic lines. The discrimination against women as a class is blatant in the case of prostitutes."[44] In her efforts, she reported that prostitutes' rights feminists were "trying to educat[e] the public to create a community exchange and dialogue" about decriminalization but that this dialogue extended well beyond the issue of prostitution. While observing the trial of a prostitute arrested for solicitation in Kansas City in 1976, she commented on sexist and racist prosecution practices: "Most women will agree that being called a whore is the worst thing that can happen to a woman. A whore is something there is no equal to for a man. And if you will notice, most women who are prosecuted for prostitution here are black. The law, in this regard, is both sexist and racist."[45]

Kansas City lawyer Sally Wells, a NOW member who represented the local COYOTE chapter, pointed out that in 1975 city police arrested 746 women and 46 men under prostitution laws. Men, she argued, were able to plead guilty to a different charge (so that "solicitation of a prostitute" would not appear on their records) if they testified against the woman. She also argued that criminalization of prostitution "invades the individual's right to control her or his body" without the interference of the state.[46] Councilman Joel Pelofsky agreed that prostitution was "an act of commerce" but opposed its decriminalization, stating, "In the interest of the public welfare of the city of Kansas City we are not going to permit acts of commerce involving this particular subject to be perpetrated on the streets of the city."[47] Confronting the sexism of the culture—and how it was perpetuated by lawmakers—local COYOTE organizer "Ocelot" stated that the current ordinance criminalizing prostitution did nothing to stop the fact that "women are constantly solicited by men in one form or another, whether or not a price is actually quoted. . . . You can do anything to a prostitute and get away with it."[48]

Although St. James, Wells, and "Ocelot" acknowledged sexism, and to some extent racism, in the context of the case in Kansas City, the Seattle–King County chapter of NOW had been seeking to move the national organization beyond its 1973 resolution. At the Western Regional Conference of NOW in September 1973, chapter copresident Jean Withers proposed a national task force on prostitution in order to "indicate NOW's deep and continuing concern for the poor and minority women who are prostitutes." Recognizing that poverty was a reality in many women's lives and connecting poverty to race, Withers noted that "it is these women, often too poor to enter the less overt forms of prostitution (such as call girls) who become streetwalkers. As such, they are most often the victims of customer brutality and repeated police harassment and arrest."[49] Others agreed, and the regional conference called for a national task force, which came to fruition six years later. Although the time it took to implement the call suggests the limits on direct action, the issue of prostitution nonetheless served as the impetus for understanding the interconnectedness of race, gender, class, and sexuality—not only for prostitutes but for all women.

The issue of harassment and the assumed availability of prostitutes'— and women's—bodies to men was paramount in discussions in and beyond NOW and was fundamental to feminists' calls for decriminalization. For example, Lisa Fenton, a member of Dallas NOW, penned "Some of My Best Friends Are Streetwalkers" for *Coyote Howls*, the official publication of COYOTE. In it, she confessed that "before I became involved in the Dallas area feminists' campaign to end harassment of local prostitutes, my attitudes were pretty condescending. In fact, I felt downright superior! Why, I wondered, would any woman want to be a prostitute?" Once she started talking to the women she sought to help, Fenton realized that "all these women are no different than me; all these women are my sisters." At bottom, she recognized that "prostitutes deal with the same sexist pigs all women deal with[;] perhaps just by their professions, however, they are called upon to take more shit than other women because many of their customers refuse to see them as human beings."[50] Although her new "sisters" were black, Chicana, and white, she acknowledged that "the only generalization that I could apply to most of the women I talked to is that prostitution is a means to transcend the poverty many of them grew up in."[51] Fenton found herself on the margins between activist and prostitute when financial hardship hit; however, "a bearable job came my way and I did not hit the street and join the business." In becoming an activist and ally, she merged prostitutes' rights with all women's rights: "They are tired of having their most basic rights violated: the control of their own bodies."[52]

In this vein, some NOW feminists found common ground with COYOTE, but they were not the only ones. In 1975, COYOTE welcomed Wages for Housework into their fold. The summer 1975 COYOTE newsletter identified Wages for Housework as "part of an international movement demanding wages for housework for all women from the state, and [it] feels that sexuality is part of the housework that women want to be paid for.... It is an organization that emphasizes the solidarity of women, and Coyote applauds."[53] And understandably so: like NOW in 1973, Wages for Housework issued a firm "demand [for] the abolition of all laws against prostitution."[54]

In 1977, women from the San Francisco and Los Angeles committees of Wages for Housework identified all work as prostitution: "We are forced to sell our bodies—for room and board or for cash—in marriage, in the street, in typing pools or in factories."[55] This statement may not have seemed particularly new. For example, in 1971, The Feminists made similar statements about the relationship between marriage and prostitution. The group wrote: "Both wives and prostitutes have the job of providing sexual services for men. The wife, in addition, is required to perform innumerable other tasks—she has to wash his clothes, clean his house, cook for him, bear and raise his children. In return for all of this, instead of pay, she gets a certain amount of social respectability. The prostitute, on the other hand, in many cases is actually freer than the wife, in that she is not dependent on one man for survival.

She is, however, a social outcast and subjected to abuse, harassment and even arrest and imprisonment."[56] The Feminists recognized similarities between wives and prostitutes but focused on the social and cultural differences. Rather than reinforce such cultural distance, COYOTE and Wages for Housework focused on common ground: "Whenever we are demanding our wages—from the Welfare Department, in the street, at the job, outside the home—we are fighting for money for all our work. Prostitution is one way of getting our wages. Although the government tries to isolate our struggles, we refuse to be divided."[57] This refusal to be divided created another compelling coalition among feminists engaged in prostitutes' rights and drew attention to women's common plight across racial and class lines.

Prostitutes in COYOTE, Wages for Housework, and NOW also mobilized around the issue of domestic violence. When "L. Lion" reviewed NOW board member Martin's 1976 book *Battered Wives*, she underscored the author's main point: "The battered wife has little legal recourse, scant protection, and negligible support." Furthermore, she extended Martin's analysis: "Wife battering is on the other side of the coin from prostitution. Where prostitution is a 'moral' crime on which taxpayers' money is spent to further men's political careers, wife battering is a violent and vicious crime that is rarely prosecuted, and when it is, it is a misdemeanor. While the act of prostitution can affirm a woman's right to her body, wife battering epitomizes male usurpation of women's bodies." She even suggested that prostitution could free women from male domination: "Prostitution can be a source of economic freedom for women; wife battering is the most literal example of women's enslavement by men. Yet prostitutes are thought to deserve the worst and wives the best."[58] "L. Lion" then encouraged women to contact either Martin or Betsy Warrior, cochairs of NOW's National Task Force on Battered Women/Household Violence, suggesting a connection between prostitutes' rights and issues that some feminists found more acceptable or pressing than those rights.

On May 9, 1977, NOW, Wages for Housework, and COYOTE protested various kinds of violence against women at a public demonstration. St. James spoke while a group of black and white women surrounded her; a black woman from Wages for Housework held a sign, "Amnesty for All Prostitutes." Later that year, COYOTE addressed in its newsletter the prevalent "myth" that "a prostitute can't be raped." In an article entitled "The 'Legitimate' Victim?" an activist confronted this myth directly: "The prostitute like any other woman can be raped, like any other woman, for example—while she is on her way to the store for a pack of cigarettes [and] is abducted at knife-point. In fact, the incidence of sexual assault among prostitutes, particularly streetwalkers, is much greater than it is for other women (although they rarely report it to the police) because of their vulnerability." Continuing to draw connections among women, she continued, "Prostitutes have been isolated from nonprostitute women and they rarely have the support systems that other women have developed in recent years."[59] Rather than bemoan this isolation, however, the newsletter listed feminist resources in the Bay Area, from general women's centers and switchboards and feminist book-stores to specific hotlines for battered women and rape victims. It also pro-vided contact information for chapters of Wages for Housework and NOW as well as gay and lesbian groups and employment services. By 1977, then, the prostitutes' rights movement in San Francisco was firmly entrenched in the liberal feminist network, promoting the rights of whores as women and of all women to control their bodies and have financial freedom.

Yet prostitutes' rights remained controversial. In the mid-1970s, the San Francisco NOW chapter suffered a rift, and several women left to form the Golden Gate chapter of NOW. Under the nom de plume Virtue Hathaway, Shirley Boccaccio penned an "advice column" for the new chapter's newslet-ter, highlighting various issues members were addressing. In September 1974, a "moral feminist" voiced her disapproval that the Golden Gate chapter cosponsored with COYOTE the first Hookers' Convention, held at Glide Memorial Church. She wrote, "Personally, I don't sympathize with hookers. I find it degrading that women should sell their bodies. My friends would rather go on welfare than be street walkers." She asked Virtue, "Just how does NOW justify supporting these loose women?" Virtue responded by pointing out that national NOW had supported a resolution in favor of decriminaliz-ing prostitution a year before. Moreover, Virtue suggested that "in the realm of feminist ideology, we have made a fundamental commitment to uphold the right of a woman to do with HER body as SHE chooses." This was the basis of feminist efforts to repeal abortion laws and NOW's bottom-line stance on women's rights.[60]

This exchange between a "moral feminist" and Virtue may well have been a clever device to address a longer-standing discussion or a heated face-to-face argument within the chapter; it may have been Boccaccio's way of speaking out on behalf of herself and the chapter about feminism and prostitution. (Boccaccio was never one to mince words: she drew the famous poster of a witchlike woman holding a broom, broken in half, under the words "fuck housework.") Whatever the underlying impetus, the message was clear: if NOW was going to support a woman's right to free and unfettered choice as the road to equality and liberation, it would have to support the choice to enter into prostitution. Decriminalization of prostitution was part and parcel of a woman's right to choose, and at bottom, women's choices, under whatever circumstances, had to be respected.

This sentiment was echoed in June 1977, when NOW, COYOTE, and numerous other groups and individuals convened in Los Angeles at the California Conference for the International Women's Year (IWY). IWY delegates endorsed a resolution calling for the complete decriminalization of prostitution and "that all criminal records relating to prostitution be destroyed." It affirmed that "all people have the right to control the use of their bodies" and continued to merge related issues around the subject of prostitution, including poverty, violence, and the diversion of police resources and taxpayers' monies for what delegates considered victimless crimes. The California conference also affirmed its support for the ERA, daycare for children, reproductive freedom for all women, and gay rights, leaving COYOTE activists energized: "Now if the national conference in Houston turns out as well as the California conference, the legislature just may wake up!"[61]

NOW and COYOTE activist Alexander was a California delegate to the Houston IWY conference. Her report back to COYOTE took up three newsprint pages. She proclaimed, "History was made in Houston at the National Women's Conference, held November 18–21, 1977. Neither the women's rights nor the civil rights movement will ever be the same—after Houston they are permanently linked." She commented on the "anti-change delegates" from Mississippi, Utah, Indiana, Hawaii, and Washington, who "wanted any programs dealing with violence against women and children to be voluntary, so that only if the batterer or molester 'wanted' help and asked for it would it be available." These women explicitly opposed "the intrusion of the federal government into their lives."[62] She then offered a resolution-by-resolution account of the conference, commenting repeatedly on women's rights to personal, individual autonomy and choice. COYOTE and Wages for Housework shared a booth at the convention center, where they distributed literature and talked with members of other political organizations, state delegations, and feminist groups. COYOTE also held a prostitution caucus at the conference; and San Francisco NOW member and COYOTE activist Ginny Durrin introduced her film *Hard Work*, which she made during the 1976 Hookers' Convention in Washington, D.C.[63] Feminist Party leader, black feminist lawyer, and NOW member Flo Kennedy led everyone in singing "Everybody Needs a Hooker." At the end of the Houston conference, Bella Abzug read a list of resolutions that had been submitted for discussion but not brought to the floor (ten states had to bring a resolution to the floor before it could be voted on by the entire delegation). Oregon and California both submitted resolutions calling for the decriminalization of prostitution, and, according to Alexander, when these resolutions were announced, "women from all over the country began to applaud. It was clear that if the resolution had reached the floor, it would have passed."[64] Even though such a resolution was not introduced, prostitutes' rights feminists continued to bring the issue of decriminalization to the fore as a part of a women's equal rights agenda.

After the Houston conference, COYOTE changed its focus. Alexander and St. James formed a National Task Force on Prostitution (NTFP). Acknowledging that "COYOTE served its purpose [and] prostitution is being discussed nationwide," the NTFP would "form a strategic force to overturn the prostitution laws." The goal: legislation to decriminalize prostitution: "When legislators are asked how they feel about decrim[inalization], they often say that they, personally, are in favor but 'the women' would never go for it. It is time for women to let legislators know that we will no longer stand for our sisters paying the price of inequality, no matter what its form."[65] NTFP boasted a large and diverse list of organizations in support of decriminalization, from the ACLU, Wages for Housework, NOW, and the Feminist Party to the California Democratic Council, the California Corrections and Parole Officers Association, and the National Pre-trial Services Division of the American Bar Association.[66] Moreover, it implored "organizations concerned with criminal justice, women's rights, violence, and gay rights . . . to make prostitution a primary issue."[67]

Feminists were optimistic about the Houston conference as a significant boost for the women's movement. If, as COYOTE editorialist "Galloping Horse," suggested, "tradition is the bulwark of sexism and hypocrisy," the 1977 IWY convention signaled that feminists would no longer tolerate the tradition of inequality. "Galloping Horse" further commented that "Houston hopefully will mark the end of the ostracism of prostitution by other women. . . . The response of women to the proposal to decriminalize was overwhelming[ly] positive."[68] COYOTE and the NTFP continued support of other feminist issues, including the ERA, reproductive rights, childcare, ending violence against women, and welfare rights, recognizing these issues as integral to the liberation of all women, including prostitutes.[69]

In addition to the extensive network of groups supporting prostitutes' rights, the 1974 Hookers' Convention and subsequent Hookers' Balls in San Francisco reveal the racial, ethnic, and class diversity of the prostitutes' rights movement. Golden Gate NOW, along with the Feminist Party, ACLU, and Glide Memorial Church, was a primary sponsor of the first Hookers' Convention, the theme of which was "We're Sisters and You Ain't Walkin' on Us No More." Flo Kennedy gave the keynote address to a crowd of more than one thousand, as reported in the feminist journal *off our backs*:

> Wearing a green pith helmet and floor length lavender cape, she [Kennedy] demanded to know "what is this shit that's going on between the whores and the police?" She explained that police arrest and harass prostitutes, homosexuals, minorities, and women because it pads arrest statistics and diverts the public's attention from the real criminals: politicians and rich white businessmen. "In this society you have to suck your way to power and the politicians are the real whores and pimps." At the end of her speech she summoned several women to the stage and led them in singing "My Ass Is Mine" and the feminist party song "Move on Over or We'll Move on Over You."[70]

As others had done before, Kennedy targeted police harassment, alluding to the ways in which laws were enforced unevenly to persecute nonwhite males. But Kennedy also openly confronted hypocritical lawmakers and businessmen who harassed prostitutes and overlooked "real criminals." Indeed, challenging lawmakers became an important strategy in the prostitutes' rights movement. San Francisco lawmakers had been "openly and sincerely" supportive of COYOTE; in 1973, St. James identified sheriff Dick Hongisto as "an entirely new breed of lawman" who eased prosecution of prostitutes in the city and ushered in an atmosphere "so free that there is an overpopulation of prostitutes in San Francisco."[71] But she also admitted that "San Francisco is probably the only city in the world from which COYOTE could spring."[72]

As the prostitutes' rights movement went into full swing in San Francisco, Seattle, and other West Coast cities, advocates sought to expose those whom Kennedy considered the "real whores and pimps." With the support of Seattle–King County NOW activists, including Jennifer James and Jean Withers, prostitutes' rights activists and sex workers organized the second prostitutes' rights group in the United States, the Association of Seattle Prostitutes (ASP), in June 1974. The annual meeting of state governors had recently taken place in the city, and the ASP newsletter editor hoped that anyone who "turns an interesting, illustrious trick" would share the information (anonymously, of course). Keenly aware that the same politicians who criminalized prostitution also participated in it, ASP promoted the slogan "Better an honest hooker than a crooked politician."[73]

At times, prostitutes' rights advocates in and beyond NOW poked fun at the contradictory actions of politicians who would, by night, break the very laws they enforced by day. One particularly campy example occurred at the 1975 Hookers' Masquerade Ball. A woman identified only as Kathy donned elbow-length black gloves, a garter belt on her upper arm, nipple pasties, string-bikini panties, and a Richard Nixon mask. Her nametag read: "I'm not a crook, I'm a hooker."[74] But far more often prostitutes' rights advocates challenged politicians who ignored crimes committed against prostitutes or threatened women's equality and right to work as prostitutes.

In the tradition of "honoring" sexists, as NOW did with its "Barefoot and Pregnant Award" in the late 1960s and early 1970s, COYOTE awarded a "jerk off award" to San Francisco District Attorney Joseph Freitas in 1976 because he refused to prosecute a case where the complainant was a prostitute. Although she had been beaten and robbed by four men, he commented, "I won't try a case where the jury wouldn't convict[;] . . . a whore's word is no good in court."[75] (It also sent "Coyote Kisses" to politicians who supported the group, including Alameda County assistant public defender Michael Milman and ACLU attorney Margaret Crosby, who defended 143 women arrested for prostitution in Oakland.[76]) The next year, the "jerk off award" went to the San Francisco Police Officers Association for its "sluggish enforcement of the laws against real crime in the city." COYOTE charged that the San Francisco police employed "gestapo tactics and trappings" to harass and intimidate prostitutes, thereby contributing "daily to the frightening situation" faced by women trying to earn a living without protection in a city where crime ran rampant.[77] In issuing these kinds of "awards," COYOTE pressed the idea that prostitution was a feminist issue because it has a universal effect on women socially, economically, and politically.

But as the 1970s wore on, tides were changing. Delegates at the 1977 Houston conference overwhelmingly affirmed the ERA, and, indeed, it appeared that it would be added to the U.S. Constitution. Thirty-five states had already ratified the amendment, and although only three more were needed, none had done so since 1975. With time drawing short, feminists started to mobilize around an extension campaign to allow additional time for states to ratify the amendment. But a strong anti-ERA force also mobilized and ultimately defeated the amendment. As national feminist organizations, NOW most prominently among them, rallied behind the amendment, COYOTE complained that "they have temporarily shed their buddies, the lesbians and the whores . . . feeling, perhaps correctly, that Houston lost them some male supporters."[78]

In direct response to the ERA campaign and in continued response to politicians who denied prostitutes the opportunity to work freely, without harassment and with protection, COYOTE and California NOW launched a "Kiss and Tell" campaign "designed to strengthen lobbying efforts for the passage of the Equal Rights Amendment." Working women were asked to identify anti-ERA legislators, especially in unratified states, who had utilized the services of prostitutes.[79] The idea originated in Western Europe, where women in Spain publicly identified adulterous lawmakers in order to rid the country of its adultery laws, which had been enforced only against women. Similarly, to keep abortion and prostitution laws out of the new legal code in Portugal, women named lawmakers who had funded then-illegal abortions or frequented prostitutes.[80] Closer to home, feminists in Michigan NOW called out six antiabortion legislators who had secretly paid for abortions. COYOTE called on prostitutes to follow suit and send in names of "these hypocrites" who opposed the ERA to St. James or "your local NOW chapter."[81] Pushing prostitution as the rallying cry for equality, the organization argued that "prostitution should be on the agenda of every national woman's conference around the world because it epitomizes women's position in a man's world." It noted, moreover, that "punishing prostitutes publicly is the means for maintaining control over women as a class by stigmatizing her sexual organs. This is the bulwark for the rise in violence against women and the backlash against the ERA." And this backlash affected all women—"a Harvard graduate, a social worker, a Manhattan housewife, or 'working' women."[82] "Kissing and telling" was a radical zap-action tactic, and COYOTE and NOW members joined forces as a radical flank while also pushing for the ERA.

The Kiss and Tell campaign was not without ethical problems for prostitutes however. Naming names violated COYOTE's code of ethics—"the prostitute will never divulge the name of a client"[83]—but "the urgency of the ERA usurped this particular ethic."[84] Alexander confronted the ethical dilemma in the COYOTE newsletter, indicating that the code of ethics is "a good policy, all things being equal, analogous to the code which covers doctors and lawyers and privileged information about their patients and clients."[85] But, as Alexander quickly noted, "all things are not equal. Prostitution is against the law, with the law being enforced primarily against women, and customers are witnesses against them in court. Men have always kissed and told."[86] Even in Nevada, where prostitution was legal, Alexander explained, women are subject to the state and unable to work independently. Furthermore, the Nevada legislature had recently rejected the ERA, which "is not really surprising, considering the legislative system of prostitution which allows the state to make a fortune off of prostitution by luring tourists to the state with the promise of easy sex, but which confines the prostitute women to prison-like brothels." So Alexander admonished prostitutes in Nevada "who serve those anti-woman legislators; it is time that they named names to the local chapters of the National Organization for Women."[87]

Although NOW chapters supported the Kiss and Tell campaign, many U.S. feminists were reluctant to support prostitution as an issue and "even slower still in reaching agreement on the place of prostitution in the pursuit of women's liberation."[88] Feminist commitment to choice became problematic in the context of female sex and sexuality, as the sex wars soon made clear. But prostitutes' rights advocates continued to insist that "putting prostitutes first would give the women's movement a whole dimension of strength, as yet unrecognized."[89] Alexander and prostitutes' allies in NOW, COYOTE, and other feminist groups understood that "some feminists have been afraid that a mere mention of more controversial issues—abortion, gay rights, prostitution—would damage the fight for the ERA."[90] To be sure, anti-ERA forces mobilized around precisely those issues: Anita Bryant launched a national boycott of Florida orange juice in response to a Dade County ordinance that prohibited discrimination on the basis of sexuality;

Phyllis Schlafly and the "moral majority" attacked gay and lesbian rights; a growing "right-to-life" movement challenged reproductive rights at every turn. Although prostitutes' rights advocates tried to harness the positive spirit of Houston, the reality was that the political and cultural tide had turned, and many feminists abandoned other struggles to pursue the ERA. Still, Alexander demanded that "all women's issues must be fought loudly and clearly in this battle for our civil rights. Any other tactic will only divide us by pitting good women against bad. Equal rights will mean nothing if women are forced to be pregnant, jailed for loving each other, or jailed for fucking men and getting paid for it."[91]

The Kiss and Tell campaign failed, but only to the extent that the ERA failed. After the defeat of the ERA, NOW chapters around the country saw sharp declines in membership; the organization as a whole suffered under the weight of a politically and culturally conservative wave. But NOW feminists continued to talk about prostitutes' rights precisely because feminist gains were quickly becoming feminist losses. Writing from California, Alexander noted that "our experience with the Equal Rights Amendment and abortion—not to mention sexual assault, domestic violence, sexual harassment, comparable worth, and the rest of the issues on our agenda—should tell us that if we leave the issues up to male legislators and pressure groups, the resulting legislation will not be in our interests. The same is true with prostitution."[92] She castigated national NOW for doing little after calling for the decriminalization of prostitution in 1973. But she also noted that chapters from San Francisco to Detroit and Baltimore were addressing prostitutes' rights through task forces and that California NOW resolved to affirm the right of women to work as prostitutes when it was of their choice.[93] Insisting that NOW pay attention to the "work" in "sex work," she concluded her report:

Whatever one thinks of prostitution, women have the right to make up their own minds about whether or not to work as prostitutes, and under what terms. They have the right to work as free-lance workers, just as do nurses, typists, writers, doctors, and so on. They also have the right to work for an employer, a third party who can take care of the administration and management problems.... They have the right to a full, human existence. As women, we have to make that clear, we have to end the separation of women into whores and madonnas that hurts all of us.[94]

Before much could be done to help prostitutes, Alexander observed that the laws must be changed. This has not happened. As of 2009, prostitution is legal only in some counties in Nevada; Rhode Island is the only state that does not have a law against prostitution per se. As we have seen, Weitzer argues that the lack of change suggests a failure of the prostitutes' rights movement. Yet such an analysis ignores victories within the movement, namely the coalition building that occurred around the insistence that prostitution was, and is, a feminist issue. Many second wave feminists acknowledged the nexus of women's sexuality and the capitalist economy, and they aligned housework and prostitution in order to argue how both demeaned women. Moreover, although few attended to prostitutes' on-the-job rights, many feminists moved beyond drawing cultural parallels between whores and housewives and forged a coalition to protect all women as laborers, including prostitutes.

As this essay argues, coalitions were—and are—necessary when opponents of change mobilize. The longevity and diversity of feminist activism around the issue of decriminalization of prostitution suggest that the movement made gains, even if it did not achieve its explicit goal. Prostitutes' rights were a significant bridge issue, creating what appears on the surface to be strange bedfellows. Furthermore, this history broadens and deepens our understanding of the "sex wars." In their aftermath, feminist scholarship has continued to explore female sexuality in the contexts of sexual pleasure and sexual danger, and many scholars are examining the complexities and lives of sex workers and feminists, recognizing that these are not mutually exclusive categories.[95] If we push beyond the dichotomies of antisex and prosex feminists and into the histories of these overlapping identities, we find an array of activists who mobilized around the idea that women's sexuality was a source of oppression and liberation and that women must control their sexuality—in every aspect—in order to be equal and free.

NOTES

Thanks to Charlotte Brooks, Sarah Elizabeth Cornell, Linda Gordon, Maria Lizzi, Sigrid Pohl Perry, and Kim Warren for providing research assistance in places I could not get to immediately; I am truly indebted. Laura Agustín, Eileen Boris, Nancy Hewitt, Elizabeth Kaminski, Jo Reger, Becki Ross, and Leila Rupp read this work in different forms and drafts and provided thoughtful and insightful comments.

  1. Elise Chenier, "Lesbian Sex Wars," *glbtq: An Encyclopedia of Gay, Lesbian, Bisexual, Transgender, and Queer Culture*, www.glbtq.com/social-sciences/lesbian_sex_wars .html, accessed October 3, 2007; see also Lisa Duggan and Nan Hunter, *Sex*

Wars: Sexual Dissent and Political Culture (New York: New York University Press, 1995), and Gayle Rubin, "Thinking Sex: Notes for a Radical Theory of the Politics of Sexuality," in *The Lesbian and Gay Studies Reader*, ed. Henry Abelove, Michele Aina Barale, and David M. Halperin (New York: Routledge, 1993), 3–44.

2. Ellen Carol DuBois and Linda Gordon, "Seeking Ecstasy on the Battlefield: Danger and Pleasure in Nineteenth Century Thought," *Feminist Studies* 9, no. 1 (1983): 7–25; Brian Donovan, *White Slave Crusades: Race, Gender, and Anti-vice Activism, 1887–1917* (Urbana: University of Illinois Press, 2007); Mary E. Odem, *Delinquent Daughters: Protecting and Policing Adolescent Female Sexuality in the United States, 1885–1920* (Chapel Hill: University of North Carolina Press, 1995); and Elizabeth Clement, *Love for Sale: Courting, Treating, and Prostitution in New York City* (Chapel Hill: University of North Carolina Press, 2006).

3. Clement, *Love for Sale*; Marilyn Hegarty, *Victory Girls, Khaki-Whackies, and Patriotutes: The Regulation of Female Sexuality during World War II* (New York: New York University Press, 2007); and John D'Emilio and Estelle B. Freedman, *Intimate Matters: A History of Sexuality in America* (1988; repr., Chicago: University of Chicago Press, 1997).

4. Christine Stark and Rebecca Whisnant, *Not for Sale: Feminists Resisting Prostitution and Pornography* (North Melbourne, Victoria: Spinifex Press, 2004); Jill Nagle, ed., *Whores and Other Feminists* (New York: Routledge, 1997); Mark Benjamin, "Fall Girls," *Ms.*, Summer 2008, online: http://www.msmagazine.com/Summer2008/fallgirls.asp; and Jaclyn Friedman and Jessica Valenti, eds., *Yes Means Yes: Visions of Female Sexual Power and a World without Rape* (New York: Seal Press, 2008).

5. Lisa Duggan acknowledges that the term *sex wars* is "the casual, although bitter reference people use for this time." Lisa Duggan, "Feminist Historians and Antipornography Campaigns: An Overview," in *Sex Wars: Sexual Dissent and Political Culture*, ed. Lisa Duggan and Nan Hunter (New York: New York University Press, 1995), 69. Joan Nestle also comments on the use of this terminology in "Wars and Thinking," *Journal of Women's History* 15, no. 3 (2003): 49–57.

6. By using the language of "prosex" and "antisex" as well as "sex-positive," sex radicals claimed and defined the language of the debate. Duggan and Hunter, *Sex Wars*; Rubin, "Thinking Sex"; DuBois and Gordon, "Seeking Ecstasy"; Jane Gerhard, *Desiring Revolution: Second Wave Feminism and the Rewriting of American Sexual Thought, 1920–1982* (New York: Columbia University Press, 2004).

7. Chenier, "Lesbian Sex Wars." See also Christine Stansell and Ann Snitow, eds., *Powers of Desire: The Politics of Sexuality* (New York: Monthly Review Press, 1983); Adrienne Rich, Joan Nestle, Judy Tzu-Chun Wu, Mattie Richardson, and Alison Kafer, "Women's History in the New Millennium: Adrienne Rich's 'Compulsory Heterosexuality and Lesbian Existence,'" *Journal of Women's History* 15 (Fall 2003); Adrienne Rich, "A Response," *Journal of Women's History* 16 (Spring 2004); Donna Guy, "Sex Work and Women's Labors around the Globe," *Journal of Women's History* 15 (Winter 2004); Duggan and Hunter, *Sex Wars*.

8. Rubin, "Thinking Sex"; Rosalyn Baxandall and Linda Gordon, eds., *Dear Sisters: Dispatches from the Women's Liberation Movement* (New York: Basic Books, 2000);

Rosalyn Baxandall and Linda Gordon, "Second Wave Feminism," in *The Blackwell Companion to American Women's History*, ed. Nancy A. Hewitt (Oxford: Blackwell, 1999); Ruth Rosen, *The World Split Open: How the Modern Women's Movement Changed America* (New York: Viking Penguin, 2000); Sara M. Evans, *Tidal Wave: How Women Changed America at Century's End* (New York: Free Press, 2003); Duggan and Hunter, *Sex Wars*. Much of this analysis is from the perspective of white women, although women of color were grappling with women's sex and sexualities beyond the boundaries of so-called second wave feminism. In the context of sex work per se, see Mireille Miller-Young, "A Taste for Brown Sugar: The History of Black Women in American Pornography" (Ph.D. diss., New York University, 2004).

9. Stephanie Gilmore, "Bridging the Waves: Sex and Sexuality in a Second-Wave Organization," in *Different Wavelengths: Studies of the Contemporary Women's Movement*, ed. Jo Reger (New York: Routledge, 2005), 97–116.

10. Ronald Weitzer, "The Politics of Prostitution in America," in *Sex for Sale: Prostitution, Pornography, and the Sex Industry* (New York: Routledge, 2000), 176.

11. Valerie Jenness, *Making It Work: The Prostitutes' Rights Movement in Perspective* (New York: Aldine de Gruyter, 1993), 70–76, quotation on 73.

12. Heather Miller, "Trick Identities: The Nexus of Work and Sex," *Journal of Women's History* 15 (Winter 2004): 145–152. See also Eileen Boris, Stephanie Gilmore, and Rhacel Parrenas, eds., "Sexual Labors: Interdisciplinary Perspectives toward Sex as Work," *Sexualities* (forthcoming).

13. See Sidney Abbott and Barbara Love, "Is Women's Liberation a Lesbian Plot?" in *Radical Feminism*, ed. Barbara Crow (New York: New York University Press, 2000), esp. 319.

14. Stephanie Gilmore and Elizabeth Kaminski, "A Part and Apart: Lesbian and Straight Activists Negotiate Feminist Identity in a Second-Wave Organization," *Journal of the History of Sexuality* 16, no. 1 (2007): 95–113. Jenness and Weitzer do acknowledge NOW in formal, "paper" coalition with COYOTE, but it is scant; in the case of Weitzer, it is also dismissive.

15. Albert Hurtado, "Settler Women and Frontier Women: The Unsettling Past of Western Women's History," *Frontiers* 22, no. 3 (2001): 1–5.

16. Gilmore, "Bridging the Waves."

17. Eileen Boris and Rhacel Parrenas, *Intimate Labors: Interdisciplinary Perspectives on Domestic, Care, and Sex Work* (Stanford, CA: Stanford University Press, forthcoming).

18. On NOW's origins and early history vis-à-vis economic discrimination, see Evans, *Tidal Wave*; Rosen, *The World Split Open*; Myra Marx Ferree and Beth Hess, *Controversy and Coalition*, 4th ed. (New York: Routledge, 2000); Cynthia Harrison, *On Account of Sex: The Politics of Women's Issues, 1945–1968* (Berkeley: University of California Press, 1989); Dorothy Sue Cobble, *The Other Women's Movement: Workplace Justice and Social Rights in Modern America* (Princeton, NJ: Princeton University Press, 2004); Maryann Barakso, *Governing NOW* (Ithaca, NY: Cornell

University Press, 2005); Stephanie Gilmore, *Groundswell: Grassroots Feminist Activism in Postwar America* (New York: Routledge, forthcoming).

19. On NOW and legal battles against AT&T, see Lois Herr, *Women, Power, and AT&T* (Boston: Northeastern University Press, 2003). On NOW and fights against Sears, see Emily Zuckerman, "The Cooperative Origins of EEOC v. Sears," in *Feminist Coalitions: Historical Perspectives on Second-Wave Feminism in the United States*, ed. Stephanie Gilmore (Urbana: University of Illinois Press, 2008).

20. Del Martin to Mayor Alioto, Box 55, folder 9, SF NOW Papers, Lyon and Martin Papers, LGBT Historical Society, San Francisco.

21. "No Secret Anymore," DVD, 2003; Marcia Gallo, *Different Daughters* (New York: Seal Press, 2006).

22. Gail Gifford, "A Commentary by Gail Gifford," 29 October 1976, part of "Press Kit," 1976, "WEF," Femina Collection, Charles Deering Library, Northwestern University (hereafter cited as Femina).

23. Margo St. James and Priscilla Alexander, "Testimony on Prostitution," 30 October 1985, "Coalition on Prostitution," Ephemeral Materials, Wilcox Collection of Contemporary Political Movements, Kansas University Library, 1992 (hereafter cited as Wilcox Collection).

24. Gifford, "A Commentary by Gail Gifford."

25. Gina Allen, "Prostitutes and Politicians," 29 October 1976, part of "Press Kit," Femina.

26. Flyer, "Come to a Women's Conference on Prostitution," n.d. [1971], New York City NOW papers, Series VII, Box 27, folder 25, Tamiment Library/Robert L. Wagner Archives, New York University.

27. Susan Brownmiller, "Speaking Out on Prostitution," 1971, Femina.

28. Ibid.

29. Ibid. See also Kathleen Barry, *Female Sexual Slavery* (New York: New York University Press, 1984).

30. Brownmiller, "Speaking Out on Prostitution."

31. "Feminists Forum on Prostitution," excerpted from *Goodbye to All That*, no vol. no., 1971, 5, Femina.

32. Brownmiller, "Speaking Out on Prostitution."

33. Barakso, *Governing NOW*, uses the language of "governance structure" and attributes this structure to NOW's longevity.

34. On grassroots activism that operated within, but also beyond, this governance structure, see Gilmore, *Groundswell*; Jo Reger and Suzanne Staggenborg, "Grassroots Organizing in a Federated Structure: NOW Chapters in Four Local Fields," in The *U.S. Women's Movement in Global Perspective*, ed. Lee Ann Banaszak (New York: Rowman & Littlefield, 2005).

35. Tish Sommers, writing on prostitution in the Berkeley NOW Newsletter, 1971.

36. WHO was the predecessor to COYOTE. According to St. James, "The forerunner of COYOTE was WHO: Whores, Housewives, and Others. 'Others' meant lesbians but it wasn't being said out loud yet, even in those liberal bohemian circles." She attributes her feminist activism to her daily socialization with "the housewives who were participating in consciousness-raising groups." Margo St. James, "Preface," *A Vindication of the Rights of Whores*, ed. Gail Pheterson (Seattle: Seal Press, 1989), xvii–xx, quotations on xvii.

37. "Prostitution Resolution, as Amended by the 6th Annual Conference of the National Organization for Women in Washington, DC, February, 1973," Box 58, folder 21, SF NOW papers, Lyon and Martin Papers.

38. Jenness, *Making It Work*, 32. On the ACLU, see Weitzer, "The Politics of Prostitution in America," 176; he states that decriminalization of prostitution "is a very low-priority issue for the ACLU" (176).

39. "Prostitution Resolution."

40. See www.now.org for stories and details. In 2005, a resolution proposed by Stacey Cleveland called for a public and unified stand against pornography and its harmful effects on women (text can be found at http://www.bestpracticespolicy.org/subpage1.html); Stacey Swimme, a NOW member and sex worker, circulated a petition and resolution by sex workers rejecting the original resolution in favor of one protecting free speech and proposing that NOW recognize "that women who work in the sex industry, including pornography and prostitution, are entitled to the same basic human rights as other women" (http://www.bestpracticespolicy.org/subpage.html). Neither resolution has been passed at the national meetings, but they are evidence that some feminist sex workers in NOW are still fighting for rights as workers.

41. Priscilla Alexander, "Working on Prostitution," California NOW, July 1983, Wilcox Collection. Although this paper was written in 1983, Alexander noted that these restrictions had been in place since the licensing law was passed in Nevada in 1970; these restrictions remain in place.

42. "Background," part of "Press Kit," 29 October 1976, Femina.

43. Weitzer, "The Politics of Prostitution in America," 177, emphasis in original.

44. Jean Haley, "Farmer's Daughter Fighting for Prostitutes," *Kansas City Times*, 20 April 1976, Wilcox Collection.

45. David Zeeck, "Prostitution Law Racist, Sexist," *Kansas City Star*, 20 April 1976, Wilcox Collection.

46. Robert L. Carroll, "Leave Us Alone, Prostitutes Say," *Kansas City Times*, 30 April 1976, Wilcox Collection.

47. Ibid.

48. Ibid. "Ocelot" was a pseudonym; COYOTE encouraged organizers who were active sex workers to use pseudonyms to help protect themselves against harassment.

49. "Proposal for a NOW National Task Force on Prostitution," pamphlet, 1979, California NOW, Wilcox Collection.

50. Lisa Fenton, "Some of My Best Friends Are Streetwalkers," *Coyote Howls* 3, no. 2 (1976): 2. COYOTE newsletters are housed in the organization's papers at the Schlesinger Library, Radcliffe College, Cambridge. MA; my copies of COYOTE newsletters are from the Femina Collection.

51. Fenton, "Some of My Best Friends Are Streetwalkers."

52. Ibid.

53. *Coyote Howls* 3, no. 1 (Summer 1975): 5, Femina.

54. *Coyote Howls* 4, no. 1 (Winter 1977), Femina.

55. *Coyote Howls* 4, no. 1 (Winter 1977): 1, Femina.

56. "Feminists Forum on Prostitution."

57. *Coyote Howls* 4, no. 1 (Winter 1977): 1, Femina.

58. *Coyote Howls* 4, no. 1 (Winter 1977): 10, Femina.

59. *Coyote Howls* 4, no. 2 (Autumn 1977): 12, Femina.

60. Golden Gate NOW Newsletter, September 1974, Box 55, folder 14, Lyon and Martin Papers,.

61. *Coyote Howls* 4, no. 2 (Autumn 1977): 11.

62. Priscilla Alexander, "The Houston Conference," *Coyote Howls* 5, no. 1 (1978): 4, Femina.

63. "Presence in Houston," *Coyote Howls* 5, no. 1 (1978): 5, Femina.

64. Ibid.

65. "NTFP," *Coyote Howls* 5, no. 1 (1978): 6, Femina.

66. Ibid.

67. Ibid.

68. Galloping Horse, "Chief Shots," *Coyote Howls* 5, no. 1 (1978): 7, Femina.

69. Galloping Horse, "National Tattle," *Coyote Howls* 4, no. 2 (1977): 5, Femina.

70. Janine Bertram, "Hookers' Convention," *off our backs*, September 30, 1974, 12.

71. First quotations from "Call Off Your Old Tired Ethics: A Loose Woman's Organization," Femina; last quotation from Haley, "Farmer's Daughter Fighting for Prostitutes."

72. "Call Off Your Old Tired Ethics: A Loose Woman's Organization," Femina.

73. Association of Seattle Prostitutes, newsletter, vol. 1, no. 1 (June 1974), Femina. In Vancouver, prostitutes were also mobilizing against city lawmakers who were driving them out of the city's West End. Becki L. Ross, "Sex and (Evacuation from) the City: The Moral and Legal Regulation of Sex Workers in Vancouver's West End, 1975–1985," in Eileen Boris and Rhacel Parrenas, *Intimate Labors: Interdisciplinary Perspectives on Domestic, Care, and Sex Work* (Stanford, CA: Stanford University Press, forthcoming).

74. *Coyote Howls* 3, no. 2 (Summer 1976): 1, Femina.

75. *Coyote Howls* 3, no. 2 (1976): 6, Femina.

76. Ibid.

77. *Coyote Howls* 5, no. 2 (1978): 7, Femina.

78. *Ibid.*, 10.

79. Quotation from Jenness, *Making It Work*, 73.

80. Ibid.; on the Spanish and Portuguese campaigns, see *Coyote Howls* 6, no. 1 (1979): 1, Femina.

81. *Coyote Howls* 5, no. 2 (1978): 10, Femina.

82. Ibid.

83. Priscilla Alexander, "ERA Strategy," *Coyote Howls* 6, no. 1 (1979): 15, Femina, quoted in Jenness, *Making It Work*, 73.

84. Jenness, *Making It Work*, 73.

85. Priscilla Alexander, "Kiss and Tell Campaign: A Question of Ethics," *Coyote Howls* 6, no. 1 (1979): 7, Femina.

86. Ibid.

87. Ibid.

88. Jenness, *Making It Work*, 74.

89. "The Big Apple," *Coyote Howls* 5, no. 2 (1978): 10, Femina.

90. Alexander, "ERA Strategy," 15.

91. Ibid.

92. Alexander, "Working on Prostitution," 15.

93. Ibid.

94. Ibid.

95. Nagle, *Whores and Other Feminists*; Frederique Delacoste and Priscilla Alexander, eds., *Sex Work: Writings by Women in the Industry* (San Francisco: Cleis Press, 1987); Miller-Young, "A Taste for Brown Sugar"; and Siobhan Brooks, "Feminist and Antiracist Organizing at the Lusty Lady," in *Feminism and Anti-racism: International Struggles for Justice*, ed. Kathleen Blee and France Winndance Twine (New York: New York University Press, 2001), 59–70. See also the launch and success of *$pread*, a magazine for, by, and about sex workers.

12

From Sisterhood to Girlie Culture

Closing the Great Divide between Second and Third Wave Cultural Agendas

LEANDRA ZARNOW

Sporting a bedazzling black tee-shirt embossed with the slogan "F Word," cover model Gloria Steinem donned an updated look reflective of the do-it-yourself culture championed by *Bust* magazine. Billing her as the beacon of third wave feminist cool, *Bust*'s editors selected the founder of *Ms.* magazine to represent the second wave in their 2000 issue devoted to feminism. Consider *Bust* cofounder Debbie Stoller's public slight four years prior: "Steinem has gotten so lame[;] . . . if she was cool *Ms.* would have a cover story on *Bust*."[1] Regardless, Stoller singled out Steinem, along with Bikini Kill band leader Kathleen Hanna, as the "*de facto* poster girls for their respective generation's women's movements."[2]

If Stoller was correct in depicting these two feminists as media-appointed stars, her assumptions about their cultural politics were quickly debunked. Stoller asked Hanna, a frontrunner in the 1990s Riot Grrrls feminist punk-music scene, whether she drew inspiration from Cyndi Lauper or Madonna. "I'd rather talk about Shulamith Firestone than Madonna," she replied.[3] "So we've changed places!" Steinem exclaimed, reflecting on Madonna's powerful appropriation of "all the symbols of Marilyn Monroe," whose "real" story was reclaimed by *Ms.* in 1972.[4] Reminding Stoller that she wore miniskirts in the 1970s, Steinem remarked, "It's always seemed to me that the point was to be able to wear what you fucking well please." Hanna, however, dismissed the girlie culture first popular among Riot Grrrls, asserting that at thirty-one, she was over "dressing like a little girl."[5] Steinem's and Hanna's responses demonstrate that dichotomous characterizations of so-called second and third wave feminists—politically rigid versus apolitical, puritanical versus

hypersexual, culturally unsophisticated versus self-absorbed and entitled—
preclude complex analysis of current feminisms.

One could read both Hanna's and Steinem's takes on cultural politics
and Stoller's slight of Steinem as uncool as indicators of cross-generational
infighting. As this story goes, the dialogue between second and third wave
feminists is best described as a mother-daughter dispute. Indeed, feminists
on both sides of the generational divide describe their disagreements using
familial terms. For instance, responding to Phyllis Chesler's reproach of
younger women's commitment to feminism in *Letters to a Young Feminist*
(1997), Jennifer Baumgardner and Amy Richards bemoaned, "Stop treating us
like daughters." Instead, "read our books, buy our records (and read the
lyrics), and support our organizations."[6] Yet, not all Richards's and
Baumgardner's peers are willing to maintain this daughter complex. As
Hanna suggested, "Things aren't going to change until we have a continuum"
and stop "reinventing the wheel over and over again."[7] And "similarities are
much more difficult" than generational differences, observed *Bitch* magazine
cofounder Lisa Jervis.[8]

If historians appropriate the discourse of mothers and daughters in first
histories of contemporary feminism, then we will affirm what Deborah Siegel
calls a "generational disconnect," which ultimately causes multiage feminists to "splash about in separate pools."[9] Using generational tropes—and
especially the wave metaphor—compresses the highly nuanced reworking of
feminist thought and practice during the late twentieth and early twenty-
first centuries. Just as many of the revisionist essays in this volume broaden
the history of the 1960s' and 1970s' feminist resurgence, this study contem-
plates what third wave history would look like without the wave.

This essay serves two purposes. First, it places the 1990s' and early
2000s' feminist moment squarely on the historical map. Considered are why
historians have arrived late to the interdisciplinary study of third wave feminism and how historical analysis would enrich first studies of contemporary
feminism. Second, this article explores how to historically analyze contemporary feminist activism, considering lessons learned about the inadequa-
cies of waving feminist history. Rather than crafting a new synthesis or
a solely conceptual piece, I look at one strand of feminist thought and
practice—popular feminism. My aim is to show links among *Ms.*, *Bust*, and
Bitch magazines without valuing the product of a prior historical moment—
Ms.—over more recent contributors to this ideological current—*Bust* and

Bitch. Equally, this comparative case study demonstrates the importance of analyzing how inherited ideologies and institutions shape later feminist ventures in acknowledged and hidden ways. This approach is not about who came first and who did it better, but why choices are made to fit one's time. Certainly not a definitive history of these popular feminist magazines, this study instead offers an initial musing about how to do 1990s' and 2000s' feminist history differently from the start.

Bridging the Historical Divide

Historians have left the documentation of contemporary feminisms—what some activists have described as the third wave—to scholars in other disciplines and to activists themselves. An ever-expanding number of articles, collections, and monographs have been published by scholars engaged in women's studies, communications, English, American studies, and sociology. These first academic studies, from *Third Wave Agenda* (1997) to *Feminist Waves, Feminist Generations* (2007), seek to define the movement as well as to serve notice that current feminisms merit scholarly attention.[10] Lacking sophisticated historical grounding, they often take at face value the origin stories promoted by self-identified third wavers.

The narrative of third wave exceptionalism first appeared in popular-press anthologies published in the 1990s and early 2000s. With the proliferation of desktop and on-line publishing, the increased popularity of memoirs, and the support of small publishing houses such as Seal Press, third wave anthologies abound. Personal narratives presented in collections, such as *To Be Real* (1995) and *We Don't Need Another Wave* (2006), engage in consciousness raising on issues including body image, racial/ethnic inclusiveness, and queer politics. In many ways, they are reminiscent of *Notes from the First Year* (1968) and *The Black Woman: An Anthology* (1970).[11] Determined to be different from previous feminists, contributors are not always self-reflective about when and how their theoretical approaches and organizational strategies draw on prior feminisms.

Historical amnesia may be no fault of their own. The only two monographs that analyze connections between the 1960s'–1970s' feminist resurgence and more recent feminisms are not written by historians—Astrid Henry's *Not My Mother's Sister* (2004) and Deborah Siegel's *Sisterhood, Interrupted* (2007). Although Henry and Siegel are preoccupied with what they see as younger and older feminists' generational disconnect, they do offer a sophisticated take on the "I'm not a feminist, but . . ." phenomenon. Meanwhile, women's historians remain fixated on what Sara Evans calls the long "tidal wave" of second wave feminism, unable to gain distance from personal movement experience.[12]

Henry correctly challenges current feminist activists to acknowledge and access their usable past. For instance, she takes on the common belief among proponents of the third wave that women's liberationists were anti-sex. Instead, she argues, they "considered some of the issues that the third wave now champions as its own: masturbation, non-monogamy, bisexuality, pornography, sex work, and of course, orgasm."[13] Likewise, she demonstrates how young feminists determined to critique "mother feminism" as a white women's movement often overlook the roles of women of color in the 1960s' and 1970s' feminist resurgence.[14] Last, she draws attention to simplistic feminist origin stories: "It is unfortunate that formulating feminisms' history in this manner—a trajectory in which the struggle for racial equality inevitably leads to the struggle for gender equality—tended to obliterate the intersections between race and gender."[15] Ironically, though, she reinscribes this model, naming the 1991 Anita Hill–Clarence Thomas hearings and Rebecca Walker's 1992 declaration, "I am the third wave," as the main catalysts for 1990s' feminist activism.[16] In so doing, she obscures the multifarious roots of current feminisms.

Less attentive to race and class than Henry, Siegel instead focuses on the cultural transmission of the consciousness-raising slogan "the personal is political." Focusing on "the women's movement's consummate mainstreamer[s]," she historicizes both the critiques by women's liberationists of Steinem's and Betty Friedan's efforts to popularize feminism and the media's misrepresentation of this important ideological debate as a cat fight.[17] "Many younger women are not in touch with even this most popular vision of feminism's past," she argues.[18] Yet in Siegel's attempt to counter the "so-called death of feminism" by tracing "its actual life," she, like Henry, maintains the very discourse and narrative frameworks that she critiques.[19] Contemporary public debates about feminist thought and practice thus become the ultimate brawl between mothers and daughters.

As historians begin to document current feminisms, we should not reinscribe the generational framework applied in first treatments of third wave activism. At this juncture, scholars need to be self-reflective about why feminist history remains generationally bound. As pioneers in the field, women's historians engaged in women's liberation have been the primary architects of U.S. feminist history. The uneasy byproduct of this intimacy, however, is that most histories of the 1960s' and 1970s' feminist resurgence are shaped by participants with strong emotional investments in the stories they tell. "This personalization of waves," sociologist Nancy Naples aptly argues, "complicates the view of feminist activism by reducing the difference between waves to personal intergenerational struggles over definitions of feminism."[20] Accessing their own feminist memory banks, some historians easily fall into the narrow comforts of memoir, foreclosing broad historical analysis.

Synthetic histories of the modern women's movement such as Ruth Rosen's *The World Split Open* (2000) and Evans's *Tidal Wave* (2003) reveal how generational blinders can narrowly frame feminist historical thought. Referencing classroom experiences, Rosen cautioned, women who "grew up believing they could do anything" needed to remember the movement that "these young people now took for granted."[21] Likewise, Evans hoped to "affirm for future generations that they do indeed have a history . . . on which they can build."[22] Although their pedagogical purpose is admirable, both historians examine contemporary feminisms from the premise that the third wave moment is solely a reflection of their political generations' resilience. That many of the third wave's media-appointed spokeswomen are daughters of second wave notables—Alice Walker's daughter Rebecca Walker, for instance—bolsters this genealogical reading of recent history. Recognizing the insularity of the first second wave histories, historians are beginning to cast a wide net to include overlooked activists, organizing sites, and ideological currents.[23] Treating 1990s' and early 2000s' feminist activism as a viable historical subject, rather than another generation's end game, will further this revisionist project. But what might historical study of current feminisms look like?

Reframing Feminist History:
Ms., *Bust*, and *Bitch* Transmissions

When I first began documenting the organizational history of *Bust* and *Bitch* in 2004, I could not help but think of these magazines in sisterly association. Initially, I assumed that *Bitch*, like a younger sister, looked up to her older sibling *Bust*, eavesdropping on conversations about sex and girlie fun until college years fostered disapproval of her materialism and preoccupation with celebrity. Of course, I argued, this sisterly love could not come about without the hovering presence of *Ms.*, the ultimate mother figure.

Why is this happy union of mother and daughters not good enough? With some critical distance, I came to realize that my initial storyline revived a tired familial narrative. I searched for a conceptual framework that would both shed generational tropes and fight the impulse to write histories of progress and decline. Just because I chose not to look at *Ms.* as the popular embodiment of "mother feminism," however, does not mean that the magazine should be excluded from the story. Rather, it is necessary to look at *Ms.* business practices and content decisions to understand how *Bust* and *Bitch* worked within an inherited ideological paradigm of popular feminism. How aware were *Bust* and *Bitch* founders of prior popular feminist magazine ventures and in what ways did they retool this usable past? Were publishing and editorial difficulties experienced by these magazines endemic to popular feminist enterprises, or were these constraints specific to the dot.com age and a politically conservative moment? These questions require a comparative approach that moves across waves, focusing on the transmission of feminist ideas and practices among individuals and organizations that share similar ideological grounding.

The founders of *Ms.*, *Bust*, and *Bitch* all grappled with a central dilemma facing creators of popular feminist magazines—how far feminism can be mainstreamed before selling out.[24] They believed that commercial media could be used as a politicizing force, what Amy Erdman Farrell calls "the promise of popular feminism."[25] Farrell writes in her history of *Ms.*, the magazine "did not so much repudiate the genre of mass market women's magazines as try to revise it; a rhetorical move from 'us girls' in the mainstream women's magazines to 'we sisters' in *Ms.*"[26] Likewise, *Bust* determined to move from "us girls" to "we, the New Girl Order," and *Bitch* to "us culturally savvy girls." Each struggled with the balancing act of attracting advertisers and meeting the demands of an engaged readership, making these magazines "contested terrain."[27] And although *Ms.*, *Bust*, and *Bitch* staff hoped to create an oppositional feminist space within consumer culture, the capitalist markets they worked within were inherently different from the alternative feminist press of the 1970s or the 'zines of the 1990s.

When *Ms.* hit newsstands in 1971, its founders bravely launched their popular feminist venture in a flailing commercial magazine market. Not only did the growing television industry continue to steal advertisers, but an expanding suburban consumer market brought the adverse effect of sky-rocketing mailing costs.[28] By the end of the 1960s, women's magazine main-stays from *Good Housekeeping* to *Redbook* reacted to these constraints by catering to smaller, affluent specialty markets, what Ellen McCracken calls "'class' rather than 'mass' publication."[29] *Ms.* fit the bill, catering to "liberated" middle-class women, just as *Essence* (1970) first intrigued African American middle-class women and *New Woman* (1970) attracted working professional women.[30] "On the cutting edge of business thinking," according to Patricia Bradley, *Ms.* sold readers on the idea "that overturning tradition could be accomplished speedily, by personal transformation that mimicked the speed of change of the times."[31] *Ms.* staff focused on defying industry norms during the 1970s, trailblazing with firsts such as having the first all-women advertising team at a time when men filled many advertising positions at women's magazines.[32] Inside the fold, *Ms.* staff sought to turn the "how-to" model of women's magazines into a transformative vehicle, wrap-ping a consciousness-raising rap session into each issue.

Likewise, *Bust* and *Bitch*—created in 1993 and 1996 respectively—entered a commercial magazine market undergoing seismic shifts. If the 1970s signaled a turn toward specialty magazines, the 1990s marked their satu-ration of the market, with 789 new magazines created in 1993 alone.[33] Launching an alternative magazine in glossy form still required capital, and many entrepreneurs were thus compelled to first create a 'zine—a self-made magazine requiring no more than scissors and a Xerox machine for produc-tion. Just as *Ms.* harnessed the vibrant pamphlet culture of women's libera-tion, *Bust* and *Bitch* founders tapped into the rich feminist 'zine culture associated with the Riot Grrrls movement.[34] Although not necessarily lucra-tive, desktop publishing enabled both popular feminist enterprises to move relatively seamlessly from 'zine to full magazine form.[35] Thus, both maga-zines helped crack open the male-dominated worlds of underground 'zine culture and computer self-publishing, and later they ensured that cyber-space would be a feminist domain.[36]

Troubled Times for *Ms.* and *Sassy*

Considering the shared interest in political function, why did *Bust* and *Bitch* founders not immediately look to *Ms.* as a model form? A natural starting place for these magazine hopefuls, one might think, would be reading back issues of *Ms.* or seeking out Steinem's publishing advice. Yet *Ms.* remained largely off *Bust* and *Bitch* founders' radar because the *Ms.* they knew in the late 1980s and 1990s was a magazine far more lackluster than it was in its original glossy form.

The 1980s were rough years for *Ms.*, with paper costs and postal fees skyrocketing just as recession plagued the economy.[37] Even with a record readership of five hundred thousand, newsstand sales up 13 percent, and ad pages up 19 percent in 1984, *Ms.* remained in precarious financial shape.[38] In 1987, Steinem and company felt they were leaving *Ms.* in good hands when they entered a deal with John Fairfax, Ltd., to place their magazine under the direction of Australian feminists Sandra Yates and Anne Summers.[39] However, Yates and Summers's main focus was the U.S. launch of teen magazine *Sassy*, and their feminist touch fell on the "lighter side." As Summers put it, "We [feminists] like to do something other than sit around feeling oppressed."[40] Ironically, it was not *Ms.*'s political stance but her younger counterpart that brought both magazines down. Summers and Yates lost ownership in May 1989, unable to recover from the advertiser pull-out after Christian Right groups banned *Sassy*, protesting its overt sex talk.[41] Ultimately, Dale Lang, owner of *Ms.* competitor *Working Woman*, purchased both magazines, causing *Sassy* to go "lite" while overseeing *Ms.*'s 1990 transformation into an adless, journal-like subscription magazine.[42]

Although *Ms.* and *Sassy* shared office space between 1987 and 1994, their staffs did not mingle. Nonetheless, a subtle transmission of ideas did occur under shared ownership. As one *Sassy* staff member, Karen Catchpole, reflected, "I think there was definitely this idea that *Sassy* would be this sort of prep school for future *Ms.* readers." She looked up to the feminist activists down the hall but also recognized that "we were doing our own thing" because *Ms.*'s content and prose "wouldn't be right for our readers."[43] Geographic proximity nevertheless led to subconscious fusion of content so much that the public took note. "When you pick up *Ms.* magazine these days, expect to find weighty adult issues, interspersed with healthy doses of fun," observed journalist Tom Dial, "When you buy a copy of *Sassy*, expect to find pages of fun, laced with weighty teen issues."[44]

If the founders of *Bust* and *Bitch* barely noticed *Ms.*'s new look in the early 1990s, it was because they were busy devouring *Sassy*. Teen readers discovered in *Sassy* what adult readers had first found in *Ms.*—a magazine that encouraged them to be independent, inquisitive, and opinionated. *Sassy* readers felt personally connected to staff members, who used their first names in print and included office gossip in article copy as freely as conversational quips about dating, frank talk about sex, or their latest "indie" music or film discovery. *Sassy* staff schooled their readers in oppositional cultural politics, encouraging teens to talk back to popular media just as they avidly consumed it. *Sassy* also introduced readers to 1990s' feminist activism, featuring homemade 'zines in a regular "Zine Corner," reporting on the Riot Grrrls, and redefining girlhood as something cool. "These days you may as well eat dirt as admit to being a feminist," the staff revealed in one editorial. "We're not embarrassed to admit in print that we all be feminists."[45] When Dale Lang sold *Sassy* in early 1994, however, the teen magazine quickly lost its feminist edge as new owners transformed the beloved magazine into a "Stepford *Sassy*."[46]

Although the *Sassy* moment had passed, its impact was lasting. More than a cult classic, the magazine served as a training ground for young feminists interested in alternative publishing. In the early 1990s, *Sassy* hosted a reader-made issue that brought young talent to the magazine, such as Tali Edut. She later cofounded the multicultural feminist magazine *Hear Us Emerging Sisters (HUES)* while a student at the University of Michigan.[47] Likewise, many future 'zine publishers interned at *Sassy*, including Andi Zeisler and Lisa Jervis, cofounders of *Bitch*. "Everyone who read *Sassy* started a zine," recalled Rita Hao, an avid *Sassy* reader and later contributor to *Bitch*.[48] Certainly, this statement held true for *Bust* cofounders Debbie Stoller and Marcelle Karp.

Bust: Defining the New Girl Order

Bored at work, Stoller and Karp shared adjoining cubicles at Nickelodeon headquarters in New York City. Just shy of thirty, they bonded over their secret obsession for the teen sensation *Sassy*, lamenting that "there was nothing like it for women who are educated, funny, smart, angry—but out of high school."[49] In 1992, they started to consider developing an adult version of *Sassy*. Stoller later recalled she "just wanted to be involved in making some kind of better media for women. . . . Whether it was magazines or TV or movies . . . it didn't matter so much what way it was done."[50] Yet this offhand statement does not reflect Stoller's substantial training in women's studies.

She earned a Ph.D. in social psychology from Yale in 1988, completing a dissertation that analyzed images of women in the media. Karp's cultural politics were informed by her B.A. degree in film and television from Queens College in 1982. Thus, while *Sassy* provided Stoller and Karp with inspiration, their cultural awareness and education also shaped the venture. Their particular articulation of feminism stemmed from the contradictory impulses of feminist institutionalization, the backlash against feminism, and a burgeoning indie feminist counterculture.

When the first five hundred copies of *Bust*'s inaugural issue hit a few select New York City newsstands in July 1993, Stoller and Karp hoped other like-minded, single, urbanite feminists might find in it a welcome refuge from magazines like *Glamour* and *Cosmopolitan*. Although they had big ideas for *Bust* from the get-go, staff, time, and money constraints limited their first production to cut-and-paste, Xeroxed form. With no capital and few connections in the magazine business, Stoller and Karp found that *Bust*'s first issue did not make the splash that *Ms.* had in 1971. Steinem had had a strong relationship with Clay Felker of *New York* magazine, who agreed to take on the publication and circulation costs of three hundred thousand *Ms.* preview issues; Stoller and Karp lacked any such ties.[51] Nor could they dream of pulling off the financing coup that Steinem and *Ms.* cofounder Patricia Carbine did in spring 1972, when they persuaded Warner Communications to invest $1 million.[52] Leasing space in mid-town and bringing on a full-time staff was out of the question for *Bust*.[53]

More of a weekend hobby than a business venture, *Bust*'s publication occurred after hours and among friends. Stoller and Karp called on eleven nonprofessional writers to contribute, encouraging them to use pseudonyms in order to feel unrestrained about the personal stories they told, in imitation of *Sassy*'s tradition of using first-name by-lines. Collectively, they wrote the "Bust Manifesta." As Karp recollected, "We came up with lots of different things we were going to do to revolutionize the way men and women looked at women's magazines."[54] And from the start they knew "we'd call it Bust: a name that was both sexy and aggressive; a joke inside a mystery wrapped in an enigma."[55]

Shaping their opening editorial in the form of a bulging bra, *Bust* founders announced their entrance into feminist culture. Foremost, they responded to media characterizations of Generation X as a bunch of entitled slackers and of working women as failures unable to juggle marriage, motherhood, and career. They also reacted to the late 1980s' feminist prosex-versus-antisex debate that coalesced around the issues of sexual harassment, pornography, and rape culture.[56] "There has been very little talk about Generation XX, we women slackers, the girls having a difficult time being women," they proclaimed. They were fed up with being the subject of conversation without being part of the conversation. Their generation, the editors complained, faced the pressures of being superwomen at the same time their peers who were childless and single were deemed lazy and apathetic. Internalizing the media's portrayal of older feminists as sexless, humorless Puritans, they asserted that hip, fun, prosex (mainly white, heterosexual) feminists like themselves needed a new forum. Their magazine would speak to women who "were raised on feminism, who pitied our mothers for being choicelessly house bound, and looked down on those girls we went to high school with who got married to the first guy they fucked, had kids, and worked in shoe stores." At the same time, they felt entitled to "have choices, to have careers, to not be tied down, to hold onto our freedom, and to become sexually 'experienced.'" Signing off as "the left one & the right one," Stoller and Karp poked fun at their own sexuality just as they reclaimed their right to be sexual.[57] In so doing, they deemed sexual politics to be *Bust*'s feminist mission.[58]

The 'zine's first cover image established visually this joining of sex and feminism, paying tribute to women's sensuality. The black-and-white silhouette of a voluptuous woman with a mod short bob and flashy lipstick proclaimed to readers that real women have attitude and curves. Arching down the female form, readers traced a bold "Bust" with the "B" turned on its side to look like breasts, reworking the woman power symbol popularized by women's liberationists.[59] It would take the staff addition of Nickelodeon co-worker and artist Laurie Henzel to fully inaugurate *Bust*'s signature kitsch style, but *Bust*'s first cover already reminded readers of voluptuous B-movie babes and rock-star vixens.

Mirroring its hodge-podge visual style, *Bust*'s content offered disparate personal confessions loosely joined by a common pursuit—navigating single, heterosexual love in a world where the societal expectation of family and motherhood still reigned. Participating in consciousness raising reminiscent of the practice in women's liberation groups, contributors spoke candidly about issues from discomfort over first low-paying jobs to interest in erotic and spontaneous sex.[60] Most articles maintained a prosex tone. For instance,

Scarlett Fever demystified the labors of nude dancing, criticizing those who "think of us as whores and sluts—traitor to the feminist cause." And Jane Hanauer wrote *Bust*'s first erotica piece, imaging what it would be like to get with "Jolly Old St. Nick."[61] Yet workplace issues were explored as well. Dreaded Sister denounced former employer MTV for its token diversity-hiring practices and commercialization of black culture, while Tabitha Rasa mustered up the courage to switch gears by taking up art.[62] Karp (Betty Boob) and Stoller (Celina Hex) did not offer readers a political strategy for change. They did, however, envision their 'zine as embodying the collective purpose of linking women who were, as Stoller put it, "part of the same underclass, the same underground army."[63] Women who "may or may not be fed up with glossy magazines perpetuating myths about the body electric and submissive sexual relationships" should form a "girl/woman sisterhood," Karp argued, to commiserate over shared grievances.[64]

After five hundred letters with subscription requests poured in, *Bust* founders were reassured that other women pushing thirty shared their vision for a "girl/woman sisterhood." Just as *Ms.* sought to be a forum for many different viewpoints, *Bust* told readers: "We need to speak to each other. So speak. We wanna read you. We wanna recognize ourselves and laugh. We wanna have fun. We wanna get mad. We wanna Bust!"[65] Although *Bust* hardly garnered the twenty thousand "long, literate, simple, disparate, funny, tragic, and very personal letters" that the *Ms.* office received after their preview issue, the magazine reached broad audiences from Austin, Texas, to Dublin, Ireland.[66] Early letters to the editors suggest a readership of women and men highly engaged in the 'zine culture and ecstatic to find, as letter writer Pam of Massachusetts put it, an "interesting, intimate, friendly ['zine] I could have written myself."[67] Others commented on *Bust*'s feminist intervention, such as Mary Taylor of San Francisco, who gushed, "BUST is like that classic postcard 'It's really great to be a girl!'" and Theresa Kimm of Minneapolis, who wrote, "I find your embracing of feminism—third wave—do me feminism—to be exciting, truly."[68] Jessica Morris of Ohio commented, "*Bust* is honest. It's kind of like a new magazine for us ex-*Sassy* subscribers—*Bust* is raw power."[69] And another reader remarked on the consciousness-raising format of the 'zine, taking comfort in the "variety of women's voices" that illustrated "the importance of core experiences among women."[70]

With their first issue off the ground, *Bust* founders determined to establish a business structure and editorial direction for future issues. They kept some aspects of the *Ms.* model in mind. For example, just as *Ms.* sought to create an egalitarian working environment, Karp, Stoller, and Henzel divided business, editorial, and artistic responsibilities, respectively, but chose not to take job titles.[71] However, in other instances, *Bust* editors went their own way without acknowledgment (and possibly awareness) that *Ms.* had covered similar territory. *Bust* staff determined to explore thematic issues—fashion, sex, girlhood, men, goddesses, motherhood—that they believed were both significant for their peer group and previously neglected by feminists. During its golden years, *Ms.* too had devoted special attention to *Bust* interests including men and sex, respectively, in the 1975 "Special Issue on Men" and the 1976 special report, "How's Your Sex Life? Better, Worse, I Forget."[72] Finally, they focused intently on increasing their circulation, hoping to soon be a contender in the coveted commercial women's magazine market inhabited by *Ms.* in the 1970s.

Making the leap from five hundred to three thousand 'zines with their second issue, they invested $900 to create a sleek look using desktop publishing and offset lithographic printing. Upon doubling *Bust*'s page count with their third issue, they declared: "As you can see, we've grown a cup size since our last issue, and hope to keep doing so." Yet, despite *Bust* founders' mantra, "We must, we must, we must increase our BUST," their growth was slow, hindered by having little capital.[73] Although the third *Bust* issue included the 'zine's first advertisements, only independent businesses and media ran ads.[74] And although *Bust*'s fourth issue marked the 'zine's transformation into a four-color glossy, the magazine, relegated to bi-annual production, still could not compete with monthlies. Perhaps, if *Bust* could gain media attention, its precarious financial position would improve.

It took a pregnant belly adorned in body paint spelling "sex," *Bust*'s fourth cover shot, to attract the interest of mainstream media.[75] With this scintillating cover garnering attention, reporter Kristin Tillotson's nationally syndicated feature in the *Minneapolis Star Tribune* publicly shaped *Bust*'s niche market. Catering to "the female urban hipster aged 25–35, who likes thinking, laughing, sex, and men (often in that order)," Tillotson reported, this "loosely basted crazy quilt of stream-of-consciousness fantasies and harangues" intrigued.[76] Subscriptions jumped to two thousand as a result of this article, and public interest climbed further after the launch of Bust.com in 1995. The circulation doubled between 1996 and 1997, from seven thousand to fifteen thousand, and soared in 1999 to forty-nine thousand with an estimated readership of 196,000 when Big Top Newsstand Services started shipping *Bust* to corporate bookstores like Virgin Records and Borders.[77] Skyrocketing sales did not immediately engender popular feminist fame. *Bust* founders continued necessarily to maintain a magazine-to-magazine growth strategy: "All of the funds that come into the plush, non-existent offices of *BUST* central go to pay for one thing and one thing only: printing and distributing this little magazine of ours." Nonetheless, they inched closer to their ultimate goal: that *Bust* "take its rightful place, front and center, where you usually find those lame, ladies glossies."[78] After *The Bust Guide to the New Girl Order*—a compilation of the first six years of *Bust*—hit 1999 bestseller lists, investors finally came knocking.[79]

At the dawn of the new millennium, *Bust* founders took a leap of faith into the dot.com industry, entering an agreement with start-up company Razorfish, Inc., to publish their first full-fledged, ad-driven monthly. Their August 2000 contract seemed like the golden start that *Ms.* had achieved almost thirty years earlier. The staff maintained complete editorial control, gained office space on New York City's East Side, and could finally hire eight full-time staff and an advertising manager, while Razorfish handled publication costs. At the same time, *Bust*'s gains in staff and stature were accompanied by the dismantling of the Karp, Stoller, and Henzel union. When Karp left the magazine in April 2001 to focus on parenting, Stoller and Henzel dropped their publishing pseudonyms (Betty Boob and Aureola) and took on the titles of editor-in-chief and creative director. Indeed, as *Bust* moved closer to the commercial magazine mold, Stoller opted out of feminist egalitarian business models, asserting, "I have no interest in doing a collective-thing. I don't think it works."[80]

On September 11, 2001, plans for *Bust*'s January relaunch came to a screeching halt. Just one day prior, Stoller and Henzel were featured in the *New York Times* business section, signaling their position as a competitor in the women's magazine market. Unbeknownst to Henzel and Stoller, however, Razorfish was already hurting from the dot.com industry's 2000 downturn, and the 9/11 terrorist attacks further tanked the start-up company's stock values. When Razorfish looked to cut back investments and staff, the *Bust* agreement was among the first to get the ax.[81]

Bust remained in name only, with publishing rights up for grabs. Stoller and Henzel could not look to advertising funds to revive the magazine because their highly specialized focus on indie culture and embrace of sexually provocative content attracted few corporate advertisers other than record labels.[82] Instead, they decided to go independent, hoping to sustain their publication through subscription drives and their loyal small-business advertising niche. Updating *Ms.*'s 1980s' postage campaign, they held an on-line subscription drive, persuading three thousand supporters to buy the magazine and donate to the cause.[83] Determined to "fight like a girl"—as their comeback spring 2002 issue was titled—Stoller and Henzel have maintained an edge in the women's magazine market since regaining ownership.

Under their direction, *Bust* took seriously its role as the "voice of a brave new girl: one that is raw and real, straightforward and sarcastic, smart and silly, and liberally sprinkled with references to our own Girl Culture."[84] *Bust*'s articulation of its "own Girl Culture," one that aspired to be edgy, feminine, and fun, reflected the founders' grappling with the ambiguities of popular culture in the 1990s and early 2000s. How could they gain inclusion in a highly saturated mass-media market that promoted a feminist backlash as it commercially packaged feminist slogans and imagery devoid of politics?[85] *Bust*'s answer was to beat women's magazine producers at their own game by applying a feminist edge to staple features: the advertorial, "The Shit"; the celebrity cover, Cher to Cynthia Nixon; the gossip column, "Pop Tart"; the quiz, "Pop Quiz"; the craft corner, "She's Crafty"; the sex-advice column, "Suzie Q's"; and the fashion spread, "Off Our Racks."[86] *Bust* also referenced *Ms.* more openly than before, retooling features of this popular feminist magazine. In their "Broadcast" news department, reminiscent of *Ms.*'s "The Gazette," for example, the news brief feature "Notes from A Broad" parodied "Notes from Abroad." And "Museum of Femorabilia" reintroduced readers to consumer objects of the feminine and feminist past, but in so doing discounted that feminism as quaint.

Most notably, *Bust* tapped into a tradition of commodifying feminism, a path well paved by *Ms.* with ventures such as the women-made product clearinghouse "Ms. Classified," the holiday advertorial "Gifts for the People," the public broadcasting show *Women Alive*, and products from the *Ms. Iron-On Book* to *The Ms. Guide to Women's Health*.[87] In regular features such as "Buy Curious," "Thrift Score," "Booty Call," "Bust Test Kitchen," and "Bust Shop," *Bust* staff directed readers to vintage shops, fashion designers, and on-line stores that met their standard of feminist cool.[88] Purchasing power is political power, they told readers, carrying on the 1970s' cultural feminist tradition of promoting women-run businesses. *Bust*'s sale of "Great Girlie Gear," however, caused the magazine to fall short of its goal of accessibility to all but economically privileged urban hipsters. Just as *Ms.*'s attention to the "'sameness' of women also allowed *Ms.* to gloss over the contradictory positions of sisterhood and liberal individuality," *Bust* fashioned a feminist culture that was diverse in lifestyle choice only for those who could buy in.[89] Thus, the magazine's consumerist core overshadowed its founding political purpose—to provide a thoughtful forum for the "girl-woman" fed up with a restrictive cultural climate in which claims of postfeminism accompanied constriction of women's rights. Some readers took note. Sarah Bainbridge of New York City lamented in 2000, "I've bought my last issue of *Bust*. . . . Discussions of jeans . . . to aged feminists who Xerox their clits to 'raise female awareness' is so lacking in depth that I literally threw your magazine in the air in utter despair."[90]

Bitch: Popular Feminism's Critical Edge

For a time, *Bust* reprinted Jervis's critiques of consumer products and ads in "Media Whore," but its founders did not exhibit long-term interest in cultural criticism. In contrast, the founders of *Bitch*—Jervis and Andi Zeisler—believed feminists needed to expand their critique of popular culture. Zeisler and Jervis had not read *Bust* before publishing their first issue in 1996.[91] Instead, they channeled memories of women's studies courses they took during college (Jervis attended Oberlin College and Zeisler attended Colorado College). Both Susan Bordo and bell hooks honed their "oppositional gazes," which were required for critical consumption of popular texts.[92] Yet, nothing set Zeisler and Jervis off more than a publication they read shortly after graduation. When they compared notes on *Listen Up: Voices from the Next Generation* (1995), among the first collections defining third wave feminism, they asked each other: "How come people aren't asking our questions?"[93] How could contributors remain virtually silent on the persistence of sexism in popular culture? They were dumbfounded. Their mission clearly before them, they determined to create a forum for feminist cultural criticism.

If feminist theorists provided Jervis and Zeisler with the language and tools needed for cultural criticism, they looked to *Sassy* as a model magazine. While *Bust* founders devoured *Sassy* in their thirties, Zeisler and Jervis were the teen magazine's target audience. As interns at *Sassy*, both saw firsthand how difficult it was to keep this provocative and indie-focused magazine afloat.[94] Nonetheless, they sought to revive the magazine's political edge and frank tone. Unlike *Bust* founders' reluctant embrace of *Ms.*, Zeisler and Jervis openly combined the "fresh, irreverent voice it [*Sassy*] brought to teen media . . . with *Ms.*'s straightforward activism."[95]

As with *Bust*, the creation of *Bitch* began as a weekend project. With their careers in copyediting and illustration barely off the ground, Jervis and Zeisler were "bored enough and inspired enough to make a project out of [*Bitch*]." Both recognized that 'zines served as a channel for feminist activism, but they saw these make-shift magazines as "a visual disaster."[96] Although new to the Bay Area, they were aware of San Francisco's burgeoning specialty-magazine industry. For instance, Benjamin Shaykin, Jervis's boyfriend at the time, worked as a design intern at *Mother Jones*. He agreed to help Zeisler and Jervis navigate the new world of desktop publishing as *Bitch*'s art director, while attendance at a Media Alliance workshop on self-publishing fostered their business know-how.[97] The first issue of *Bitch* was a family affair, with Jervis's grandfather providing start-up capital of $350 for three hundred 'zines; "special thanks to the Jervis foundation for the relief of indigent scholars," the masthead duly noted.[98] Although a few independent book and music stores agreed to carry *Bitch*, Jervis, Shaykin, and Zeisler did not expect a major response. "We put the first issue out there with the idea of doing a second one, sure, but we didn't really think beyond that," Jervis recalled. "We just figured we would see what the reaction was."[99]

Bitch was a head turner. The magazine title captured the wit and irony with which contributors approached their mission—providing a "feminist response to popular culture." *Bitch* founders joined feminists in their campaign to positively redefine words used to denigrate women—such as Inga Muscio's reclamation of "cunt."[100] Downplaying this political purpose, Jervis revealed, "It was either Bitch or like Women's Media Critic."[101] "It was clear," she added, "we weren't going to soft peddle anything. . . . What's the point of a softer name?"[102]

Zeisler's illustration on *Bitch*'s first cover had an equally bold effect. A lady with medusalike hair and a matter-of-fact expression asked, "You Talkin' to Me?"[103] Although surrounded by books, this diva had an equal penchant for popular entertainment as reflected in the presence of fashion magazines and a tuned-in tube. Jervis continued to blur high- and low-brow culture in her opening editorial. Although a self-proclaimed "media junkie," she signaled that *Bitch* would be about thinking critically and "about speaking up." "[We need to stop] indiscriminate media consumption," she asserted, and instead "formulat[e] replies to the sexism" inherent in popular texts. By creating "girl-friendly places in the mass media," *Bitch* could become an oppositional feminist space that confronted popular culture from within, thereby "theorizing and fostering a transformation of pop culture."[104] If hooks considered rage to be a "necessary aspect of resistance to struggle," Jervis claimed, then highly charged cultural commentary was a necessary step in feminist politicization.[105]

In their first articles Zeisler and Jervis pulled their punches, soft-peddling feminist theorists' ideas with light girlfriend lingo, thereby priming readers for their underlying structural critique of popular texts. Take, for example, "Bait and Switch Sassy," in which Jervis demonstrated how the new *Sassy* deviously sold apolitical commercial feminism. Initially *Sassy* admitted its readers had sex, some "with other girls," and recognized "that racism is a reality." "But now the magazine was "chock full of pernicious, regressive advice and the message that feminism is bad, no one is ready for sex," she wrote. "It's the same shit that's in *YM* and *Teen* and all the others, but here it's worse because they've kept the feminist rhetoric."[106] *Bitch* took equal note of the positive potential of popular culture. Zeisler recalled the playful disruption of masculinity by early MTV video stars such as Joan Jett and Pat Benatar. These pop-music icons, who "inspired us to rock out," Zeisler remembered, "provided young girls with ideas of rebellion, sex, and self-sufficiency."[107]

Bitch founders brought into the fold much of the cultural criticism relegated to *Ms.*'s "No Comment" feature and letters to the editor section. Clearly taking their cue from *Ms.*, Zeisler and Jervis inaugurated their signature feature, "Our Love/Hate Relationship with the Media" (later renamed "Love It/Shove It"), in their first issue. Here, *Bitch* staff went beyond the *Ms.* "No Comment" model, which featured antiwomen ads without commentary. *Bitch* joined sharp textual critique with reprints of sexist ads. One such condemnation of a Sunny Delight orange-juice advertisement picturing a smiling golden babe read, "Why is it that the only Sunny Delight ads that have girls in them at all are the ones for Sunny Delight Lite?"[108] In later issues, staff would direct readers "Where to Bitch" about particular advertisements, further linking their cultural-awareness campaign to direct political action.[109]

Although *Bitch* made a quiet entrance in early 1996, the magazine received a big endorsement in the *Chicago Tribune* before the year was out. Called by the newspaper "irreverent" and a "breath of journalistic fresh air,"

Bitch found itself on the map in circles beyond 'zine traders.[110] By 1998, Katha Pollitt described the magazine as "a cheerfully attitudinous updated feminism to popular culture and daily life."[111] Readers sang praise as well. Some such as Leanda of North Carolina commiserated over the new *Sassy,* which "turned evil and very degrading," while others such as Michele McGrady of Ohio connected with *Bitch*'s "humor . . . intelligence . . . activism . . . ability to reach across class, age, race and talk about the bullshit that affects us."[112] Like the engaged consumers of *Ms., Bitch* readers treated the magazine as a political forum, sharing letters they wrote to offending corporations and signaling to staff egregious ads they should feature.[113]

Positive reader and media response enabled *Bitch* founders to transform their little magazine into a full-size newsstand regular. Like *Bust* founders, they used all profits to expand their magazine, hoping to "get to the point where *Bitch* is self-sustaining."[114] Quickly selling out one thousand copies of their second issue, they determined to publish tri-annually, hiring the two-person union collective New Earth Press to print fifteen hundred copies and then twenty-five hundred copies of their subsequent issues.[115] Although *Bitch* began featuring outside contributors in its third issue, these writers were largely Jervis's and Zeisler's friends; they continued to write the bulk of the stories until starting to solicit articles in 1998.[116] And although *Bitch* mirrored *Bust*'s thematic choices, devoting early issues to sex, fashion, and puberty, they branched out after 1998 to consider topics such as "Fame & Obscurity" and "Is Biology Destiny?"[117]

With its glossy, full-color cover and its black-and-white interior, the 1998 Puberty Issue marked *Bitch*'s commercial ascension. With this issue, *Bitch* inched away from its journal-like aesthetic, phasing out the footnotes that speckled early articles in favor of informed satire. Finally breaking even the previous year, the magazine saw its production more than double in 1998 when its distributor, Desert Moon, struck a deal with Barnes & Noble.[118] And when it switched to distributor Big Top Newsstand Services the following year, its readership skyrocketed from eight thousand to twenty thousand because of increased circulation in corporate stores.[119]

Bitch staff's unwillingness to subvert their political edge, however, kept their popular feminist enterprise teetering at the edge of the commercial magazine market. Zeisler and Jervis considered this instability in their first "Near Death Experience 2001."[120] They should have been on cloud nine, having achieved a distribution of thirty-four thousand and gaining nonprofit status.[121] Instead, they were "pretty close to hanging up our red pencils" because they did not have the time or staff to sustain the magazine. In a poignant "Editors' Letter," they appealed to Gloria Steinem to "take heart," seeing their struggle to expand *Bitch* as similar to prior popular feminist magazine ventures. Only by hiring help, quitting their day jobs (Shaykin left at this point), and expanding to a quarterly, they believed, would they be able to ensure the magazine's lasting commercial viability.[122] With their livelihoods at stake, Zeisler and Jervis effectively used feminist networks to sustain their production during difficult financial times. Concerned that they would fall short in 2003, for instance, *Bitch* founders posted an open letter to feminist organizations that brought in three thousand additional subscriptions, enabling a print run of 43,500 and an estimated readership of 155,000.[123] Although consistently financially strapped, *Bitch* has remained a viable competitor in a growing specialty-magazine market. Holding fundraising drives and obtaining nonprofit status, as well as relocating the *Bitch* offices to less expensive Portland, Oregon, in 2007, have continued to sustain the magazine.[124]

Bitch's liminal status on the outer reaches of the commercial women's magazine market enabled the magazine's staff to serve as industry whistle-blowers. If *Ms.* founders focused on pushing open advertising markets closed to women, *Bitch* founders sought to monitor and close particularly sexist advertising and media campaigns. As a relatively small enterprise, *Bitch* could not attract great interest from corporate advertisers. With less dependence on and expectation of a large advertising portfolio, *Bitch* staff have enjoyed greater freedom than the *Ms.* staff once had to reject advertisements they deem bad for women. Take this comparative example. *Ms.*'s advertising staff successfully achieved their goal of attracting advertisers from traditionally male markets such as automobiles, electronics, and credit, reshaping women's consumer culture in the process.[125] Because the magazine was utterly dependent on national advertisers, however, the staff's critical eye could be tempered. When *Ms.* ran a Club Pina Colada ad with the slogan "Hit Me with a Club," one reader, author Del Martin, suggested it made "your 'No Comment' section look utterly ridiculous."[126] In contrast, *Bitch* focused squarely on monitoring the markets to which its readers were exposed. When the staff received an ad for a CD titled *Nashville Pussy*, they decided to run a full page of commentary on the ad in its place, telling readers they chose not to print "yet another gross usage of women's bods to move the units" despite their financial loss. Readers responded to this decision with praise, even using their published response to advertisers as a women's studies lesson.[127]

While holding their magazine in high esteem, *Bitch* readers demanded that the content reflect its goal of inclusiveness. Responding to a survey question—"What do you like least about *Bitch*?"—one self-proclaimed "urban grrl" lamented, "There is a *sad* lack of racial and cultural diversity in the pages of *Bitch*." Alena Schiam of Ohio also critiqued the magazine's representation of women of color, highlighting a cover illustration that portrayed a black woman with "distinctly white facial features."[128] Jervis and Zeisler attempted to make editorial choices that moved beyond their white, middle-class, urban perspective, but they did not always meet this goal. In the "Editor's Letter" of their third issue, Jervis apologized for overlooking *Essence* in a recent review of women's magazines. "Something's really been bothering me," she stated candidly. "I've gotten pretty good about recognizing and challenging racism when I see it somewhere else—but in myself, that's another matter." Jervis pledged, "The only thing that matters is for *Bitch* to be a magazine that media-critical women of all color[s] can pick up and see articles that speak to them, that include them, that rail against the things that they hate too."[129]

If *Bitch* did not always reflect racial diversity, the magazine gave more attention than *Bust* to queer politics and class privilege. Like *Bust*, *Bitch* criticized the 1980s' feminist sex wars, arguing, "Sex is a favorite topic almost everywhere—but within the movement, we don't seem to be getting anywhere with it."[130] Its coverage of sexuality, however, moved beyond discussing what vibrator would bring the most pleasure to women to articles such as Donna Jean Troka's "When We Were Kings," an account of Troka's experience as a drag king in Columbus, Ohio, and a roundtable on the Michigan Womyn's Music Festival, "A Fest in Distress."[131] Likewise, although *Bitch* did not dismiss consumption wholesale, its founders revealed the "core mission of this magazine is to actively work against" commercialism and to "encourage readers to be critical of commercial media."[132] This founding purpose placed *Bitch* and *Bust* in tension. *Bitch*, for instance, countered *Bust*'s product pitch "The Shit," with its "The Bitch List," which featured favorite books, activists, and organizations.[133] And *Bust* founder Stoller took offence at *Bitch* features like Rita Hao's "Now a Word from Our Sponsors," which critiqued "capitalist feminism" for welcoming a certain type of "woman whose Visa card will be accepted at the door."[134] Shortly after the publication of this 1998 article, Stoller scolded in a review, "*Bitch* toes some old-school party lines. For Jervis and her colleagues, it seems, there is just no way to reconcile a feminist consciousness with beauty culture."[135] However, Jervis reflected, "*Bust*'s focus on DIY and small women's businesses is awesome, but it's still here's some cool stuff you want to buy."[136]

Comparative Feminist History

A comparative examination of *Ms.*, *Bust*, and *Bitch* brings into focus the fundamental tension endemic to popular feminist enterprises: how to popularize feminism without losing one's political edge. Feminists engaged in these commercial magazine ventures aspired to create a vehicle for transformative change that was also a competitive product. Although facing demands specific to the dot.com age, *Bust* and *Bitch* founders revived different elements of *Ms.*'s usable past. While *Bust* channeled *Ms.*'s commitment to making its readers independent, superior consumers, *Bitch* looked to the magazine's oppositional roots, aspiring to create a feminist site for cultural critique.[137] Despite their distinct interpretations of the *Ms.* venture, both set out to deflect stereotypes of feminists that compelled women to sheepishly state, "I am not a feminist, but . . ." And they aspired to reflect better than *Ms.* the hybridity of women's experience, coming to feminism as they did at the height of academic debate concerning white, neoliberal, hegemonic feminism. Nonetheless, *Bust*'s promotion of an exclusive girlie culture and *Bitch*'s uneven attention to diversity demonstrate this central problem of popular feminism—selling feminism works best in a normative and privileged package. It remains commercially effective to "gloss over the contradictory positions of sisterhood and liberal individuality."[138]

What do we learn by bridging the divide between popular feminist magazines of the 1970s and 1990s? By following the long trajectory of an ideological strand—in this case popular feminism—we can see how feminists work within inherited intellectual and organizational spaces. We can consider the political, economic, and cultural back story that frames activists' emotional investment in "their" feminism. We can assess how theoretical imagination consistently reshapes feminist ideological traditions anew. And we can develop transformational strategies for the future if we know how to use our past.

Rather than diving into separate waves, historians need to develop new methods of analyzing feminist history that foster fresh thinking about the broad links and subtle shifts in U.S. feminist thought and practice. When we compartmentalize feminist history into artificial designations of first, second, and third wave, we taper the mosaic of feminisms. Instead, we should think comparatively, analyzing how feminists both work within inherited frameworks and respond to the demands of their time.

When developing first studies of current feminisms, it is also imperative to look for feminism beyond the obvious places. Although it is important to document popular feminism, this ideological strand is also the most known and easiest to trace. Indeed, *Bust* and *Bitch* are among a handful of third wave organizations with university archives. Future studies need to apply a kaleidoscopic lens to bring a broad spectrum of actors and organizations engaged in gender-justice work into comparative feminist history. Only then will we move beyond the limitations of the wave paradigm.

NOTES

1. Quoted in Geraldine Baum, "At *Bust*, It's Not Sex Quizzes and Lingerie. It's Tequila and Black Boots," *Los Angeles Times*, February 15, 1996, sec. E.

2. Curiously Hanna was not pictured on *Bust*'s cover alongside Steinem. Debbie Stoller, "Fierce, Funny, Feminists," *Bust* 16 (Winter 2000): 54.

3. Quoted in ibid., 54.

4. Quoted in ibid., 55. For the Marilyn Monroe cover, *Ms.*, August 1972.

5. Hanna and Steinem quoted in ibid., 56.

6. Phyllis Chesler, *Letters to a Young Feminist* (New York: Four Walls Eight Windows, 1997). Jennifer Baumgardner and Amy Richards, "Letter to an Older Feminist," *Bust* 16 (Winter 2000): 57; see extended argument in Jennifer Baumgardner and Amy Richards, *Manifesta: Young Women, Feminism, and the Future* (New York: Farrar, Straus & Giroux, 2000).

7. Quoted in Stoller, "Fierce, Funny, Feminists," 55.

8. Lisa Jervis, "The End of Feminism's Third Wave," *Ms.* 14, no. 4 (Winter 2004/2005): 57.

9. Ironically, Siegel sustains this discourse, dividing her book into sections entitled "Mothers" and "Daughters" even as she criticizes the "generational disconnect" that inhibits alliances; Deborah Siegel, *Sisterhood, Interrupted: From Radical Women to Grrls Gone Wild* (New York: Palgrave Macmillan, 2007), 161.

10. Numerous anthologies, monographs, special issues or forums, and essays analyze feminist waves and specifically the third wave. These include Leslie Haywood and Jennifer Drake, eds., *Third Wave Agenda: Doing Feminism* (Minneapolis: University of Minnesota Press, 1997); Rory Dicker and Alison Piepmeier, eds., *Catching a*

Wave: Reclaiming Feminism for the 21st Century (Boston: Northeastern University Press, 2003); Hokulani K. Aikau, Karla A. Erickson, and Jennifer L. Pierce, eds., *Feminist Waves, Feminist Generations: Life Stories from the Academy* (Minneapolis: University of Minnesota Press, 2007); Astrid Henry, *Not My Mother's Sister: Generational Conflict and Third-Wave Feminism* (Bloomington: Indiana University Press, 2004); *Feminist Studies* 23, no. 1 (Spring 1997); and Kimberly Springer, "Third Wave Black Feminism?" *Signs* 27, no. 4 (Summer 2002): 1059–1082. For additional information on these and related works, see Leandra Zarnow, "Bringing the 'Third Wave' into History," *NWSA Journal*, August 2009.

11. Melody Berger, ed., *We Don't Need Another Wave: Dispatches from the Next Generation of Feminists* (Emeryville, CA: Seal Press, 2006); Rebecca Walker, ed., *To Be Real: Telling the Truth and Changing the Face of Feminism* (New York: Anchor Books, 1995); New York Radical Women, ed., *Notes from the First Year* (New York: New York Radical Women, 1968); and Toni Cade, ed., *The Black Woman: An Anthology* (New York: New American Library, 1970).

12. Sara M. Evans, *Tidal Wave: How Women Changed America at Century's End* (New York: Free Press, 2003).

13. Henry, *Not My Mother's Sister*, 106.

14. Ibid., 167–168.

15. Ibid., 76.

16. It is true that the media have focused more on white forms of third wave activism, such as the Riot Grrrls, but Walker has received a fair share of press attention as well. Rebecca Walker, "Becoming the Third Wave," *Ms.*, January/February 1992, 39–41.

17. Siegel, *Sisterhood, Interrupted*, 75.

18. Ibid., 17.

19. Ibid., 170.

20. Nancy A. Naples, "Confronting the Future, Learning from the Past: Feminist Praxis in the Twenty-First Century," in *Different Wavelengths: Studies of the Contemporary Women's Movement,* ed. Jo Reger (New York: Routledge, 2005), 221.

21. Ruth Rosen, *The World Split Open: How the Modern Women's Movement Changed America* (New York: Viking Penguin, 2000), xiii; see also Evans, *Tidal Wave*, 230.

22. Evans, *Tidal Wave*, 17.

23. Examples of revisionist histories of 1960s' and 1970s' feminisms include Stephanie Gilmore, ed., *Feminist Coalitions: Historical Perspectives on Second-Wave Feminism in the United States* (Urbana: University of Illinois Press, 2008), and Anne M. Valk, *Radical Sisters: Second-Wave Feminism and Black Liberation in Washington, D.C.* (Urbana: University of Illinois Press, 2008).

24. This article considers primarily the first ten years of the production of each magazine—*Ms.* (1972–1982), *Bust* (1993–2003), and *Bitch* (1996–2006). *Bust* and *Bitch* production records were archived through 2001 and unprocessed when I accessed them in 2004; box numbers reflect their organization at that point. For *Ms.*, Series V, Gloria Steinem Papers, Sophia Smith Collection, Smith College, Northampton,

MA (cited hereafter as Steinem Papers). For *Bust*, Bust Magazine (New York, NY) 1993–2000 (cited hereafter as Bust Papers); for *Bitch,* Bitch Magazine Records, 1996–2001 and n.d., Sallie Bingham Center for Women's History and Culture, Duke University, Durham, NC (cited hereafter as Bitch Papers). My study focuses solely on *Bust* and *Bitch* in print form; for on-line readership, see Janina Chandler, "Chicks Clicks and Politics: An Exploration of Third Wave Feminist Ezines on the Internet" (M.A. thesis, Carleton University, Ottawa, 2002), and Barbara Duncan, "Searching for a Home Place: Online in the Third Wave," in *Different Wavelengths: Studies of the Contemporary Women's Movement,* ed. Jo Reger (New York: Routledge, 2005), 161–178.

25. Amy Erdman Farrell, *Yours in Sisterhood: Ms. Magazine and the Promise of Popular Feminism* (Chapel Hill: University of North Carolina Press, 1998), 5–7.

26. Ibid., 7.

27. Ibid., 2.

28. Mary Ellen Zuckerman, *A History of Popular Magazines in the United States, 1792–1995* (Westport, CT: Greenwood Press, 1998), 205.

29. Ellen McCracken, *Decoding Women's Magazines: From Mademoiselle to Ms.* (New York: St. Martin's Press, 1993), 196.

30. Ibid., 224–229, and Julie L. Andsager, "New Woman," in *Women's Periodicals in the United States: Consumer Magazines,* ed. Kathleen L. Endres and Therese L. Lueck (Westport, CT: Greenwood Press, 1995), 253–258.

31. Patricia Bradley, *Mass Media and the Shaping of American Feminism, 1963–1975* (Jackson: University of Mississippi Press, 2005), 169, 181.

32. On *Ms.*'s collectivist editorial process, "Editorial Opinion Circulation Sheet," folder 5, box 156, Steinem Papers, and Farrell, *Yours in Sisterhood,* 116–126. On advertising, Philip Dougherty, "Advertising: Roles of Women," *New York Times,* December 20, 1972, 73.

33. Lisa E. Phillips, "Battle for the Newsstand," *Folio* 23, no. 5 (March 15, 1994): 66, and Mike Hayes, "The Ripple Effect," *Folio* 27, no. 18 (September 15, 1998): 18.

34. Chelsea Starr, "Because: Riot Grrrl, Social Movements, Art Worlds, and Style" (PhD diss., University of California, Irvine, 1999), and Jennifer Bleyer, "Cut-and-Paste Revolution: Notes from the Girl Zine Explosion," in *The Fire This Time: Young Activists and the New Feminism,* ed. Vivien Labaton and Dawn Lundy Martin (New York: Anchor Books, 2004), 42–60. See also Nadine Monem, ed., *Riot Grrrl: Revolution Girl Style Now!* (London: Black Dog, 2007)), and 'zine archival collections such as Sara Dryer Papers, Sallie Bingham Center, Duke University, Durham, NC.

35. On desktop publishing's impact on the magazine market, Fred Ferris, "Magazines in Transition," *American Printer* 212, no. 2 (November 1993): 48. *Bust* and *Bitch* were not the only popular feminist magazine ventures in the 1990s, although they were the most commercially successful. See Tali Edut with Dyann Logwood and Ophira Edut, "HUES Magazine: The Making of a Movement," in *Third Wave Agenda: Being Feminist, Doing Feminism, ed.* Leslie Heywood and Jennifer Drake (Minneapolis: University of Minnesota Press, 1997), 83–102, and *Venus* magazine at http://www.venuszine.com/.

36. See Duncan, "Searching for a Home Place."

37. "What Is a New *Ms.*?" *Ms.*, November 1979, 10.

38. See draft "Dear Friend" letter, 11 December 1984, folder 22, box 161, and Steinem to Dr. Franca Binello, 3 January 1986, folder 1, box 162, Steinem Papers.

39. Memorandum from Steinem to staff, 9 November 1987, folder 8, box 162, and "Ms. Magazine Chooses Australians," n.d., folder 15, box 161, Steinem Papers.

40. Quoted in Marjorie Williams, "The Up-to-Date Ms.: Anne Summers, Remaking the Feminist Journal," *Washington Post*, February 17, 1988, sec. C, 1; and see Marjorie Williams, "The Ms. Mystique: Feminism Puts on a Pretty Face," *Washington Post*, August 3, 1988, sec. D, 1.

41. Kara Jesella and Marisa Meltzer, *How Sassy Changed My Life: A Love Letter to the Greatest Teen Magazine of All Time* (New York: Farrar, Straus and Giroux, 2007), 33–41, and Molly Simms, "The Secret History of Sassy," *Bust* 29, Fall 2004, 71.

42. For Lang agreement, Steinem to Lang, 30 December 1989, folder 1, box 58, Robin Morgan Papers, Sallie Bingham Center, Duke University, Durham, NC; Mary Thom, *Inside Ms.: 25 Years of the Magazine and the Feminist Movement* (New York: Owl, 1998), 224–227; and Farrell, *Yours in Sisterhood*, 179–190.

43. Quoted in Jesella and Meltzer, *How Sassy Changed My Life*, 28.

44. Tom Dial, "*Ms.* Chief Magazine's New Owner 'Discovered Sales," *Post-Standard*, August 30, 1988, Lifestyle sec.

45. Quoted in Jesella and Meltzer, *How Sassy Changed My Life*, 69. This popular history of *Sassy* contains extensive staff interviews; the magazine has not established a public archive.

46. Ibid., 103.

47. Ibid., 84.

48. Quoted in ibid., 111.

49. Stoller quoted in Kristin Tillotson, "Busting a Move: Women's 'Zine Fills the Fun Void Left by the Mainstream," *Star Tribune* (Minneapolis), December 10, 1994, sec. E, 1.

50. Quoted in Lettie Conrad, "Third Wave Feminism: A Case Study of *Bust* Magazine" (master's thesis, California State University, Northridge, 2001), 82.

51. Elizabeth Forsling-Harris to Clay Felker re: promotion of Preview Issue, 27 November 1971, folder 11, box 163, Steinem Papers. For *Ms.*'s founding story, Farrell, *Yours in Sisterhood*, 26–36, and Thom, *Inside Ms.*, 7–13.

52. Thom, *Inside Ms.*, 31–33.

53. "A Personal Report from *Ms.*," *Ms.*, July 1972, 7.

54. Quoted in Conrad, "Third Wave Feminism," 85. For editorial collaboration on *Bust*'s first issue, see "Bust! First Issue" and "Sticker Lines," 1993, box 2, Bust Papers.

55. Debbie Stoller, "10 Years of Bust: We've Come a Long Way Baby," *Bust* 24 (Summer 2003): 36.

56. Nancy Whittier, "From the Second to the Third Wave: Continuity and Change in Grassroots Feminism," in *The U.S. Women's Movement in Global Perspective*, ed. Lee Ann Banaszak (New York: Rowman & Littlefield, 2005), 45–68.

57. All quotes in this paragraph, "Editor's Letter," *Bust* 1, no. 1 (July 1993): 2–3.

58. "Editor's Letter," *Bust* 1, no. 4 (Summer/Fall 1994): 2.

59. *Bust* 1, no. 1 (July 1993): 1.

60. Girl, "Blowjobs, Lipstick, Sidekicks," *Bust* 1, no. 1 (July 1993), 8, and Cassandra O'Keefe, "Girlfriend, Listen Up . . ." *Bust* 1, no. 1 (July 1993), 9.

61. Scarlett Fever, "R.E.S.P.E.C.T.," *Bust* 1, no. 1 (July 1993), 18; and Jane Hanauer, "Santa I Know—One Girl's Intimate Story," *Bust* 1, no. 1 (July 1993), 14.

62. Dreaded Sister, "Negroes 'R Us," *Bust* 1, no. 1 (July 1993), 22–23, and Tabitha Rasa, "You Can Get There from Here," *Bust* 1, no. 1 (July 1993), 20–21.

63. Celina Hex, "Fear of a Boy Planet," *Bust* 1, no. 1 (July 1993), 6–7.

64. Betty Boob, "Tales of Me," *Bust* 1, no. 1 (July 1993), 4.

65. "Editor's Letter," *Bust* 1, no. 1 (July 1993), 3, and "A Personal Report from *Ms.*," *Ms.*, January 1973, 97.

66. "A Personal Report from *Ms.*," *Ms.*, July 1972, 6.

67. Pam to *Bust*, postcard, 30 November 1993, box 2, Bust Papers.

68. Mary Taylor, "Dear Bust," *Bust* 1, no. 2 (Fall/Winter 1993), 3, and Theresa Kimm to *Bust*, 7 June 1994, box 2, Bust Papers.

69. Jessica Morris to *Bust*, n.d., box 2, Bust Papers.

70. Unknown author to Bust, 11 October 1994, box 2, Bust Papers.

71. In addition to rejecting titles, *Ms.* maintained a collective editorial process best exemplified by the "Editorial Opinion Circulation Sheet," a form soliciting input from all staff editors, folder 5, box 156, Steinem Papers.

72. *Ms.* addressed these themes regularly. Just a few examples: "How's Your Sex Life? Better, Worse, I Forget," *Ms.*, November 1976, 82–83, 114–118; Letty Cottin Pogrebin, "Motherhood," *Ms.*, May 1973, 49–51; "Special Issue on Men," *Ms.*, October 1975; and see generally the monthly feature "Stories for Free Children."

73. "Editor's Letter," *Bust* 1, no. 3 (Spring 1994): 1.

74. Ibid., and *Bust* 1, no. 2 (Fall/Winter 1993).

75. *Bust* 1, no. 4 (Summer/Fall 1994).

76. Stoller and Karp quoted in Tillotson, "Busting a Move." Other notable press coverage included Baum, "At *Bust*, It's Not Sex Quizzes and Lingerie," and Geraldine Baum, "Gutsy Writing for Women," *Glamour*, September 1996, 162; see, generally, "Press," Box 1, Bust Papers.

77. *Bust* ad-rate sheets, 1996 and 1997, "Miscellaneous folder," and "*Bust* Marketing Package," 1999, box 1, Bust Papers; for distribution, see *Bust* 12 (Spring 1999): 3.

78. "Editor's Letter," *Bust* 12 (Spring 1999): 4. On *Bust*'s failed MTV pilot, "Issue #10," box 1, Bust Papers.

79. Debbie Stoller and Marcelle Karp, eds., *The Bust Guide to the New Girl Order* (New York: Penguin Books, 1999).

80. Quoted in Conrad, "Third World Feminism," 90. See also Marcelle Karp, "Editor's Letter: When Two Becomes One," *Bust* (Summer 2001): 4.

81. Debbie Stoller, "Editor's Letter: Fightin' Words," *Bust* (Spring 2002): 4. See also Nina Willdorf, "Bust Goes Bust," *Phoenix*, November 15, 2001, http://www.bostonphoenix.com/boston/news_features/this_just_in/documents/02006468.htm, accessed April 28, 2004.

82. Ad sales for issue 13 in 2000 grossed $18,100.98, demonstrating increased revenue but no where near matching *Ms.*'s figures: "Bust Ad Sales Issue #13," "Issue 13," box 1, Bust Papers; see also "Bust Database: Ads, January 30, 1999," "Issue 12," box 1, Bust Papers, and "Memo to Debbie/Laurie," 9 May, year unknown, "Bust 6, Submissions," box 2, Bust Papers.

83. Stoller, "10 Years of Bust," 37.

84. Stoller and Karp, *The Bust Guide*, xv.

85. Leandra Zarnow, "The Politics of Beauty: Tensions between Feminism and Popular Culture," (bachelor's thesis, Smith College, Northampton, MA, 2001), 20–46, 76–127.

86. See these features in *Bust* 16 (Winter 2000).

87. "Ms. Classified," *Ms.*, December 1972, 129; "Gifts for the People," *Ms.*, December 1972, 42; *Ms. Iron-On Book*, ad, *Ms.*, November 1976, 123; and, generally, "Promotional Materials, 1972–87, n.d.," folder 3, box 150, Steinem Papers.

88. For the first "Bust Classified," later renamed "Great Girlie Gear," and other product features, see *Bust* 15 (Fall 2000).

89. Farrell, *Yours in Sisterhood*, 78.

90. Sarah Bainbridge to the Editors, *Bust* 14 (Spring 2000): 8.

91. Andi Zeisler and Lisa Jervis, interview by the author, August 9, 2004, Oakland, CA (transcript in author's possession; hereafter Zeisler and Jervis interview).

92. bell hooks, *Black Looks: Race and Representation* (Boston: South End Press, 1992), and Susan Bordo, *Unbearable Weight: Feminism, Western Culture, and the Body* (Berkeley: University of California Press, 1995).

93. Zeisler and Jervis interview; Barbara Findlen, ed., *Listen Up: Voices from the Next Generation* (Seattle: Seal Press, 1995).

94. Jervis's disillusionment with commercial women's magazines was further bolstered by her summer interning at *Sassy*'s mainstream competitor; see Ariella Cohen, "Off the Cuff: Lisa Jervis," 19 March 2004, http://www.oberlin.edu/stupub/ocreview/2004/3/19/news/offthecuff.html, accessed April 27, 2004.

95. Zeisler and Jervis interview.

96. Ibid.

97. Ibid.

98. Ibid., and Mary Ellen Slayter, "Circulating the Feminist View—on Her Terms," *Washington Post*, April 25, 2004, sec. K, 1.

99. Quoted in Jan, "The Power of a Little Bitching," *CraftyGal*, September 2001, Porch sec., http://www.craftygal.com/archives/901/porch901.htm, accessed April 27, 2004.

100. Inga Muscio, *Cunt* (Seattle: Seal Press, 1998).

101. Quoted in Cohen, "Off the Cuff."

102. Zeisler and Jervis interview.

103. *Bitch* 1, no. 1 (1996).

104. All quotes in this paragraph, "Editors' Letter," *Bitch* 1, no. 1 (1996): 1–2. For draft mission statements and articles, folder 8, box 1, Bitch Papers.

105. hooks quoted in "Editors' Letter," *Bitch* 1, no. 1 (1996): 2.

106. Lisa Jervis, "Bait and Switch Sassy," *Bitch* 1, no. 1 (1996): 3.

107. Andi Zeisler, "Amazon Women on the Moon: Images of Femininity in the Video Age," *Bitch* 1, no. 1 (1996): 21.

108. "Mad as a Whet Hen," *Bitch* 1, no. 1 (1996): 10.

109. See, for instance, "Where to Bitch," *Bitch*, 14 (2000): 95.

110. "Womanews," *Chicago Tribune*, March 21, 1996, sec. 13. For other press, folder 1, box 4, Bitch Papers.

111. Katha Pollitt, "Tidings of Discomfort and Joy," *Nation*, January 5, 1998, 9.

112. Leanda to Jervis, 25 October 1996, folder 3, box 1, and Michele McGrady to *Bitch*, 29 January 1997, folder 3, box 2, Bitch Papers.

113. Letters include Christine Beuse to Jervis, 5 December 1996, folder 3, box 1, and Judith Almgren Ferry to *Bitch*, 10 February 2001, folder 5, box 2, Bitch Papers. For comparison, see Mary Thom, ed., *Letters to Ms., 1972–1987* (New York: Henry Holt, 1987).

114. Steve Rhodes, "You're Welcome to Bitch," *MediaFile* (March/April 1997), folder 1, box 4, Bitch Papers.

115. Zeisler and Jervis interview.

116. Ibid.

117. "Fame and Obscurity," *Bitch* 19 (Winter 2003), and "Is Biology Destiny?" *Bitch* 15 (Winter 2002).

118. Ellen Cavalli, "Barnes & Nobles Deal Boosts Small Magazines," *Folio*, October 1998, 12.

119. Zeisler and Jervis interview.

120. "Table of Contents," *Bitch* 14 (2001): 3.

121. Zeisler and Jervis interview.

122. "Editors' Letter," *Bitch* 14 (2001): 5.

123. "Stats and Facts," n.d. (provided by Jervis; in author's possession).

124. Debbie Rasmussen took over as publisher from Jervis in 2006. Although no longer active in daily production, Jervis remained involved as a founder; Andi Zeisler remained the central editor. In 2007, *Bitch* moved its offices from Oakland to Portland to keep publication overhead down. See "Our History," http://bitchmagazine.org/about/history, accessed December 19, 2008, and Judith Spitzer, "Bitch . . . a noun . . . a verb . . . a magazine?" September 12, 2007, http://blog.oregonlive.com/womenoutloud/2007/09/bitch_a_noun_a_verb_a_magazine.html, accessed December 19, 2008.

125. For the range of *Ms.* advertisers, "Our Advertisers," n.d., folder 3, box 150, Steinem Papers, and Gloria Steinem, "Sex, Lies, and Advertising," *Ms.,* July/August 1990.

126. Del Martin to Steinem, 21 May 1980, and "Correspondence: Letters to Editor and Reader Response: Club Ad, 1980," both in folder 3, box 151, Steinem Papers.

127. For *Bitch* commentary, "There Was Supposed to Be an Ad on This Page," *Bitch* 14 (2000): 91. For the ad, folder 9, box 3. See generally "Bitch Advertising Package," loose folder, box 1, Bitch Papers. For a representative reader's response, Sarah Reid to *Bitch*, 16 June 2000, folder 5, box 2, Bitch Papers.

128. "An Urban Grrl Who Wants to Remain a Loyal Reader" to Jervis, 5 June 2000, folder 5, box 2, and Alena Schaim to *Bitch*, 10 January 1999, folder 4, box 2, Bitch Papers.

129. "Editor's Letter," *Bitch* 1, no. 3 (1996): 2.

130. "Editor's Letter," *Bitch* 2, no. 1 (1997): 1.

131. Donna Jean Troka, "When We Were Kings: On Being a Midwestern Drag King," *Bitch* 12 (2000): 42–47, and Robin Finkelstein, Emi Kayama, Grover Wehman, and moderator Lisa Jervis, "A Fest in Distress," *Bitch* 17 (2002): 68–102. *Bust* introduced Suzie Bright's sex column to address critiques of their straight-centric content: "Publisher's Desk," *Bust* 12 (Spring 1999): 4.

132. Zeisler and Jervis interview.

133. "The Bitch List," *Bitch* 3, no. 1 (1998): 35–39.

134. Rita Hao, "Now a Word from Our Sponsors: Feminism for Sale," *Bitch* 3, no. 2 (1998): 32.

135. Debbie Stoller, "Femorabilia: The World of *Bitch* and *Mystery Date,*" *Village Voice Literary Supplement,* September 1998, http://www.villagevoice.com/vls/157/stoller.shtml, accessed April 28, 2004.

136. Zeisler and Jervis interview.

137. Farrell, *Yours in Sisterhood*, 72, 88.

138. Ibid., 78.

PART THREE

Rethinking Agendas/ Relocating Activism

13

Staking Claims to Independence

Jennie Collins, Aurora Phelps, and the
Boston Working Women's League, 1865–1877

LARA VAPNEK

During the Gilded Age and Progressive era, white, working-class women in the nation's industrializing cities launched a series of campaigns to gain economic as well as political equality. Individually and collectively, they challenged long-held assumptions about women's dependence on men as inaccurate and damaging to the growing numbers of women who worked for wages in order to support themselves and their families. Some of these women organized to gain the same benefits being won by organized working men: shorter hours, higher wages, and greater respect at work. In addition, white, working-class women rejected their relegation to jobs as domestic servants and demanded access to a broader range of occupations. Defining themselves as breadwinners, they challenged their second-class status in the labor market and the polity, making radical new claims for female independence.

The intertwined stories of Jennie Collins, Aurora Phelps, and the Boston Working Women's League illuminate the development of northern, white, working-class women's distinctive political ideology, revealing coalitions and conflicts with laboring men and with educated, affluent women eager to expand their social influence. Collins, Phelps, and the wage-earning women who joined them in the Boston Working Women's League seized on the discrepancies between a national political ideology promising freedom and equality to all people and the circumstances of their own lives. Their petitions and public statements explained that women who had no choice but to work as domestic servants or underpaid needleworkers could hardly be considered "free." Asserting their own entitlement to freedom, these women sought to increase their independence by joining labor organizations, demanding land, and calling for full rights of citizenship.

Like many working-class women, Jennie Collins learned about the high costs of women's second-class status firsthand. Collins began working in a textile mill in Lawrence, Massachusetts, in 1842, at age fourteen. Orphaned as a young child, she had been raised by her Quaker grandmother, who provided her with an unusual degree of liberty but only a limited education and no property. Like most girls, Collins must have learned basic domestic skills such as sewing and cooking with the expectation that she would marry and have a family of her own. When family support failed, however, Collins's domestic training had little market value. Like many girls and young women in New England, she made her way to the mills to take a position as a machine operative.[1]

When she reached Lawrence, Collins quickly realized that the popular sentimental view of young, white women stopped at the factory gate. She later described the typical experiences of a young woman entering the mill. In seeking out the employment agent, she was "treated neither with politeness nor consideration." She faced him on her own and made "her own bargain with him." Earning "her own money," she was left to "hire her own board, buy her own clothes." She received no deference as a woman, and she knew that she "must work as hard and do her task as well as a man, or . . . be discharged, without ceremony or apology." Indeed, her sex entailed a burden, rather than a privilege; Collins earned only half of a man's wages and had none of his "perquisites." She could never become eligible for a skilled position because these were reserved for men.[2] Collins found herself outside the bounds of family and domesticity, yet compromised in her ability to negotiate the labor market.

As a young woman "cast on her own resources," Collins found herself in a situation that anticipated that of hundreds and thousands of northern women forced to become self-supporting after the Civil War. Not only did many women lose sons, husbands, fathers, brothers, and prospects for marriage, but the intensification of industrialization after the war strained the viability of family farms and artisan workshops, increasing pressure on working-class daughters and wives to earn money. By the early 1870s, daughters of farmers and craftsmen flooded into the labor force, joining orphaned girls and widowed mothers seeking employment in order to contribute to the family economy or to support themselves if their families had dissolved.

Finding few opportunities in the countryside, or in the prospect of westward migration, these women flocked to cities, where they formed an increasingly visible and impoverished class.

In Lawrence and then in Lowell, Collins became part of a group of factory operatives who saw themselves in collective terms. Like her, these women were young, white, single migrants from the New England countryside. They not only worked together but also lived together in company boarding houses, and they spent their free time together, whether attending church, listening to a lecture, or reading aloud in the evenings as they did their mending. Collins found that the women she worked with subscribed to "as many papers, and ha[d] as much interest in public affairs as any of the men who work[ed] beside" them.[3] Despite the monotony of standing for twelve or thirteen hours and the pressure of keeping "pace with belts, drums, and cylinders, and other parts of the machinery," the factory girls and women Collins met "retain[ed] their vivacity and spirit of independence" through their political engagement and their mutual concern for one another.[4] Textile workers also tried to organize in the face of mill owners' efforts to increase their profits by cutting wages, lengthening hours, and intensifying the pace of production. As conditions in the mills worsened, single, native-born women began moving to larger cities in search of better work.[5]

Collins joined this exodus, arriving in Boston in 1850. Possessing few transferable skills and lacking a family of her own to live with, she took a job as a domestic servant. In Boston, as in other large cities such as Philadelphia and New York, 60 percent of female wage workers found positions in domestic service and 30 percent in the garment industry. The remaining 10 percent worked in a small group of trades open to women at the lower levels, including printing, bookbinding, and clerking at dry-goods stores.[6] Educated women might find jobs as teachers, but they, too, earned only half of men's wages. Depending on whether they had husbands present or children or aging parents to care for, urban women also engaged in a range of casual labor to generate income, such as taking in boarders, laundry, or sewing, or going out to work for the day scrubbing or washing.

Collins may have worked as a general household servant before finding a position as a nurse in the family of John Lowell, an attorney whose grandfather, Francis Cabot Lowell, had become extremely wealthy by establishing the textile mills in the town that bore his name.[7] Although no direct record of Collins's work for the Lowell family survives, her time spent in this privileged household, which owed much of its wealth to the textile mill where she had once worked, may have sharpened her belief that workers were poor because they were deprived of a just share of the value they produced. Her position in the Lowell household also convinced her that "American girls" who valued their independence could not tolerate domestic service for long. Although Collins had experienced the fast-paced labor and tight regulations of the Lowell mills as oppressive, she found the new limitations on her leisure time intolerable. Servants were not even allowed to "go out and buy a spool of thread until their appointed afternoon or evening."[8] Like other servants, Collins complained of "incompetent mistresses" who knew nothing of housekeeping but were determined to wring as much work as possible out of their household help.[9] To explain native-born, white women's increasing rejection of domestic service, Collins quoted Patrick Henry's famous motto, "Give me liberty or give me death."[10] By invoking Henry, she cast women's rejection of service in revolutionary terms.

Collins's critique of domestic service was widely shared. An 1869 investigation of the conditions of sewing women in Boston by the New England Women's Club revealed a strong animosity toward domestic service among the entire working-class community. Investigators reported that "poor girls" struggled "under a weight of debt and poverty" rather than work as servants. Native-born, white women spoke with pride of the fact that they had "never had to live out yet." More shocking still, some chose prostitution rather than domestic service as a way to preserve their independence.[11] Although middle-class labor reformers used the prostitute to symbolize the dangers of women's dependence on men, some working-class women used the trade to gain higher wages than they could earn from either service or sewing and to free themselves from what they considered to be the oppressive conditions of living in others' households and being at their beck and call twenty-four hours a day.[12]

The fact that the Lowell family could find a white, native-born woman like Collins to work for them during the 1850s reflected their wealth and status. By this time, middle-class families with one "maid of all work" were far more likely to hire an Irish immigrant for the job. Young Irish women fleeing the potato famine (which began in 1845) often migrated alone, leaving behind parents and siblings in desperate poverty. The assurance of steady work, combined with employers' provision of room and board, appealed to Irish women, who felt a strong obligation to save money to send back home. Although Collins calculated the sole benefit of domestic service as having enough to eat, food and shelter may have recommended the occupation to Irish women who had faced starvation.[13] Some German women entered service, too, but those who did not speak English were considered less desirable household workers. German women were also more likely than the Irish to migrate with their families, and so they were less likely to work as servants.[14] For mistresses seeking pliant household workers, however, the fix from immigrant labor proved temporary. As Catharine Beecher, a leading purveyor of domestic advice complained in 1869, "The Irish and the German servants . . . become more or less infected with the spirit of democracy," and they soon became as difficult to manage as native-born Americans.[15]

Radical members of the working class associated the growing demand for servants with the growth of a pretentious and parasitic middle class that thumbed its nose at manual labor. Collins and other working-class labor reformers accused employers of skimping on food and wages for their domestic employees. A song titled "The Bell Goes A-ringing for Sai-rah," published in the *American Workman*, a Boston labor-reform paper, documented overwork, low pay, and stingy rations. The singer introduces herself as "the general slave round the corner," with a wage of "a hundred a year." While her employer, a man who worked downtown, earned "a thousand," the servant found her "own sugar and beer." Sarah described herself as "lady's maid, housemaid, and cook," explaining, "I do everything, honor, no joking; I scarcely have time to draw a breath, For she'll ring if the fire wants poking."[16]

Although Collins bristled at the subservience expected of domestic servants, she must have used her time in the Lowell household to gain the connections she needed to secure more satisfying employment. By 1860, Collins was working as a garment maker for a downtown Boston firm. A year later, she had gained a skilled position as a vest maker at Macular, Williams, and Parker, a Washington Street merchant known for its high-quality work.[17]

Within ten years of arriving in Boston, Collins had worked her way into a relatively secure position in the female labor market. Her ability to make this transition rested not just on her determination and ability but on the fact that single, native-born, white women had the widest degree of choice in the narrow field of female labor. By 1860, just one-third of native-born, white women worked as servants, in contrast to 78 percent of foreign-born, white women (most of whom were Irish), and 87 percent of African American women.[18] While Irish women took domestic jobs because they wanted to save money to send back home, African American women took domestic jobs simply because they could obtain no other work.

Although African Americans constituted only one percent of the population of Boston in 1860, their extremely constrained opportunities for earning a living reveal the racial segregation that structured the northern labor market.[19] As "A Colored Woman" explained in a letter to the *Philadelphia Morning Post* in 1871: "When respectable women of color answer an advertisement for a dressmaker, . . . they are invariably refused, or offered a place to cook or scrub, or do housework; and when application is made at manufactories immediately after having seen an advertisement for operators or finishers, they meet with the same reply." Black women who refused to work as domestics were left to "eke out a scanty livelihood sewing at home."[20] An African American woman from Rhode Island complained that "colored females" were "compelled to accept the meanest drudgeries or starve" because they were excluded from places where native-born, white women could find work, like "the milliner, the dressmaker, tailor, or dry good store."[21]

Although the Civil War ended slavery, it did not fundamentally change the racial segregation of the labor market in the industrializing cities of the Northeast and Midwest. White female workers became increasingly class-conscious during the war, but this consciousness did not extend to addressing racial inequality. In fact, the substitution of white, working-class women for slave women in labor-reform discourses invoked the degradation of women of color only to erase them as real people. The language of white slavery, used by Collins and other Boston labor reformers, relegated African American women to the margins of northern reform as symbols of degraded womanhood rather than as participants in postwar efforts to improve, or even transform, women's economic conditions. Yet Collins had been an ardent abolitionist since childhood. Her hatred of slavery fueled her support for the Union cause. She organized her co-workers at Macular, Williams, and Parker to make keepsakes for Union soldiers. Collins also volunteered in a Boston military hospital and helped establish a soldiers' relief association.[22] Like many middle-class volunteers who went on to form women's clubs and organizations, Collins acquired significant organizational experience through her war work.[23]

Although she supported the fight against slavery, the war heightened Collins's sense of class rather than of racial injustice. She believed that the government acted to protect corporations and property owners at the expense of workers. From returning soldiers, Collins heard stories of "the same great gulf between the rich and the poor" throughout the nation. Together on the battlefield and in military hospitals, soldiers from modest backgrounds "felt how much more they had to pay for their liberty than did the law-protected man of wealth, who sat in his home and smoked his cigar, while a hired substitute fought his battles."[24] Many workers around the country shared Collins's impressions of class inequity, and numerous strikes flared during the war. Labor activity peaked in 1865 and continued at an intense level until the depression of 1872.[25]

Like many former abolitionists, Collins saw the labor question as the nation's next major political issue. She first took the stage as a public speaker in 1868, when she presented a working woman's point of view on the labor question during public debates. The next year, she appeared at one of many conventions called by workers who advocated an eight-hour workday, earning a reputation as an engaging public speaker who "entered into the leading political and social questions of the day in a remarkably intelligent manner."[26] Collins soon joined the New England Labor Reform League, a mixed group of trade unionists, former abolitionists, and advocates of the eight-hour day led by Ezra Heywood, an anarchist who later became notorious for his advocacy of free love. Once dismissed as a motley group of "sentimental reformers," the members of the New England Labor Reform League not only made room for women but actively sought their participation and included them as officers.[27] The group's strategies for social change included strikes, boycotts, petitions, and the formation of workers' cooperatives.

In April 1869 Collins joined Aurora Phelps and Elizabeth Daniels, whom she met in the New England Labor Reform League, in establishing the Boston Working Women's League. Phelps, who had been a hospital nurse during the war, was known for her advocacy of free land for working women. Although her life had been "laborious," including stints as a servant and an outworker, she had attended college at Oberlin before moving to Boston. Phelps presented herself as having been married and widowed in England, where she had borne a child. Daniels was married to a laborer but had no children; she had worked as a sewing-machine operator and an artist before becoming a leader of Boston's eight-hour movement.[28]

Although the League lasted only a year, it provides a rare glimpse into working-class women's self-conceptions and political aspirations. The group's members presented themselves as "working women" with a right to participate in public debates on the basis of their status as self-supporting, productive citizens. They advocated homesteads for working women, increased wages for needlework, and establishment of a nonprofit employment bureau.[29] Although supported by the general movement for labor reform and receptive to alliances with elite women devoted to women's rights, members of the Boston Working Women's League expressed a determination to speak for themselves that reflected an independence of thought and action that many found surprising.

Phelps formulated her idea for Garden Homesteads in 1864, two years after the Homestead Act promised 160 acres of public land to any adult citizen who could pay a small registration fee and live on the land continuously for five years. Although the offer of free land was supposed to ensure the republican future of the country by enabling men to leave wage work and become farmers, the costs of establishing homesteads were beyond the means of most working-class families and even more out of reach for families without a male breadwinner. By establishing homesteads close to Boston, Phelps hoped to give women the means to become independent proprietors, while enabling them to remain closely connected to their families and communities. Like most people at the time, Phelps believed that wages were governed by supply and demand, meaning that urban women's rates of pay would increase if a significant number of female workers left the city. Her advocacy of land reform reflected a long tradition of British, American, and Irish labor activists' demanding rights to land in order to restore the independence lost through the deskilling of labor and the introduction of machinery. Although most proponents of land reform associated the redistribution of land with the restoration of patriarchal family values, Phelps viewed Garden Homesteads as creating new opportunities for female independence.[30]

Possibly with help from Collins, Phelps wrote a petition for Garden Homesteads that the Boston Working Women's League circulated in the spring of 1869. The petition presented a carefully formulated list of what women needed to become homesteaders, including "rations, tools, seeds and instruction in gardening, until such time as the women would be able to raise their own food, or otherwise become self-supporting." No rent would be due for the first three years. After that, each woman's rent would be applied to purchasing her plot, which could be passed along to her female heirs on her death. Inspired by state homestead exemption laws, they asked that their property be protected from seizure for debt. The petitioners identified themselves as impoverished, overworked Boston women, "dependent for our daily bread upon the daily labor of our own hands." The petition played on the chivalrous ideal, casting the legislature as the protector of last resort for Boston working women and pleading, "You should think for us, and take counsel from your own kind ears to do for us better than we know how to ask."[31]

Although the tone of the petition echoed familiar narratives of female dependence, it mixed these traditional appeals with a new consciousness of citizenship gained by patriotic sacrifice during the Civil War. Not only had many Boston working women lost fathers, brothers, and husbands in the conflict, but thousands had worked "on contract army shirts at eight cents each, from dawn to midnight." Given their sacrifice, Phelps believed that the commonwealth and "the nation" owed these women "a debt it [could] never pay."[32] From this perspective, a demand for state provision of land and simple homes might not be so radical, especially when the federal government was giving away large tracts out West not only to homesteaders but to railroad corporations. In presenting her proposal for Garden Homesteads at a labor-reform convention, Phelps argued that working women had a "righteous claim" on the government for relief. If, indeed, democratic government was instituted "for the people," then it should aid in "protecting all [its] . . . citizens in the enjoyment of life, liberty, and happiness."[33]

Equally as bold as these women's request for land was their demand that they be allowed to speak for themselves. Rebelling against elite assumptions that working-class women needed "thinking women" to act on their behalf, the Boston Working Women's League asked the legislature to allow "no one . . . except at our own express desire, to speak before your committee in our name."[34] The petition called for independence for working-class women on several levels. By living in homes that they owned, on land where they could grow food to support themselves, these women would fulfill the Jeffersonian dream of a republic populated by independent proprietors. By owning this property themselves, women would upend republican ideology, which posited women, like children, as dependent on men. They would escape dependence on employers for an insecure livelihood, and they would no longer have to seek charity or take recourse to prostitution, each of which implied a morally compromising dependence.[35] Furthermore, these women claimed political independence, including the right to think and to speak for themselves and to make new claims as citizens.[36]

Collins, Phelps, and Daniels called a meeting to discuss their petition for Garden Homesteads and to introduce the Boston Working Women's League to the public on April 21, 1869. Parker Pillsbury, who attended the convention and wrote about it for the *Revolution* (Elizabeth Cady Stanton and Susan B. Anthony's women's suffrage newspaper), considered the gathering in "every way peculiar." Not only was it called by "working women, in the severest sense of the word," but it was called primarily *for* working women.[37] An equally surprised correspondent from the *American Workman* noted that the meeting was managed by the working women themselves, "and the gentlemen or [ladies] other than working-women were not allowed to take up time, except by their permission." The journalist found it "quite amusing to see how some of the old stagers among the men were snubbed by the application of this rule so opposed to ordinary usage."[38]

The meeting, held in a basement room, began that Wednesday morning with about twenty-five people. By noon, the crowd reached a hundred, and by the evening, when women were released from work, it rose to three hundred. The organizers estimated the average wages of Boston's forty thousand women with full-time, weekly employment at about three dollars per week, "out of which they had to board, clothe, and lodge themselves" and often support "dependent children." About half these women worked in the needle trades, where wages varied greatly. Although skilled women with steady positions in custom shops, like Collins, could make a decent living, women who sewed at home for clothing contractors fared much worse. The organizers estimated at least two thousand needlewomen in Boston earned no more than twenty-five or thirty cents a day.[39] At times, Phelps admitted, she herself had been so poor she was unable to afford the soap and fuel necessary to wash her clothes. In these conditions, she remarked, working women would be "less than human" if they did not "feel the difference between their condition and that of the rich, well-dressed ladies who pass them."[40]

The meeting concluded with a number of resolutions. The women described the system of "divided labor" and the increasing use of machinery as monotonous and degrading to both the minds and bodies of female workers. However, they admitted that a return to older, household or artisan forms of production was both "impossible and undesirable." Instead, poor working women should be given land and "houses of which they themselves are mistresses, where they may regain their natural health of soul and body."

They went on to specify that not all working women wished to move out of Boston and leave the paid labor force, explaining, "Those of us who are skilled workwomen, in the receipt of good wages, and therefore in the enjoyment of a high degree of independence" are "not discontented with our present condition and not desirous of settling on the land." However, they endorsed Garden Homesteads as a good option for women unable to make ends meet in the city, especially those supporting dependents.[41]

The idea of Garden Homesteads gained enough public attention to be granted a hearing before the state legislative committee on the hours of labor. About a hundred women attended, half working women "in the technical sense of the phrase" and half "ladies of culture and wealth with a liberal representation from the New England Women's Club."[42] Members of the club, who came from elite families, initially shared demands for the abolition of slavery and the expansion of women's rights. After the Civil War, they turned their attention to improving women's position in the labor force as an important step toward women's progress.[43]

Just ten days prior to the hearing, the New England Women's Club had issued its own report on the conditions of the city's needlewomen. Drawing from city records and personal interviews, their privately printed report was a landmark in social investigation. Like the Boston Working Women's League, they noted the increasing subdivision of labor, low wages, high prices for board, and dangers of prostitution. Their solutions to these problems reflected their own class position. They called urgently for something to be "done to dignify domestic service," bemoaning the fact that so many women "have been slaves to the unproductive needle all their lives, because they never had any opportunity to learn the work for which they were best fitted by nature!"[44] Ironically, this group of elite women devoted to social progress and determined to forge lives that reached beyond the domestic sphere prescribed domestic service as the best solution to working women's poverty. While the working-class women who proposed Garden Homesteads hoped to turn pieceworkers into independent proprietors organized within a collective, the leaders of the New England Women's Club hoped to turn these predominantly native-born women into servants. United in their mutual concern for the conditions of Boston's poorest wage-earning women, they proposed dramatically different solutions, although Lucy Stone, a radical member of the New England Women's Club, offered her support for Garden Homesteads.

The hearing at the statehouse opened with Phelps presenting her petition. She noted that many of the women who signed it "were deterred from coming by threat of employers; some were persuaded to keep away by increase of pay; many who came were too timid to take a part." Phelps discussed women's limited options for earning a living, noting the declining value of skill and the low rates paid for piecework. To make matters worse, out-workers could not find steady employment but paid weekly for their board. During slack periods, those without families to fall back on turned to "soup-houses." Phelps saw charity as problematic, warning that women who depended on it "feel degraded, lose self-respect, and, by and by go *down*." Alternately, she presented Garden Homesteads as providing women with the chance to become economically independent. She recommended tracts of land just outside the city, in Medford, Dorchester, and Swampscott, as good places to try the experiment, estimating that "five thousand women would avail themselves of this plan at once, if it could be inaugurated."[45]

The legislators asked Phelps why poor women did not try housework. She responded by explaining that women who entered service were "treated as strangers and aliens," adding that she knew of cases "where the very food was grudged to them and hunger was kept off by buying outside, and this in aristocratic circles." She knew what she was talking about, having "tried it herself, both as domestic and as nurse." She might have added that domestic jobs were available only to women without children or other dependent relatives to care for, while her scheme allowed working-class women room for families of their own. As Phelps described the conditions of working-class women in Boston, not just in the needle trades but also in the households of elite statesmen and clubwomen, class tensions were revealed in the "hushed and muffled silence" that "brooded over the room."[46]

As the legislature considered the petition for Garden Homesteads, the Boston Working Women's League continued to pursue a broad agenda. In a letter to the *Revolution* Daniels wrote: "The organization means something more than mere surface work, and will accept for woman nothing less than the ballot, and the right to hold any office."[47] Although members of the group worked to build alliances with suffragists like Stanton, Anthony, and Stone, they also asserted their own authority on the problems of working women. At an early meeting held at the house of Daniels, the women described themselves as "the natural counselors of their less skillful sisters, to the almost utter exclusion of men, and to the absolute exclusion of ladies of refined leisure." Given the interest expressed in working women by the New England Women's Club, this statement can be read as a polite but firm suggestion that female reformers concerned with the conditions of the city's working women mind their own business. Indeed, this declaration of class difference denied the possibility of "class bridging" so important to the self-conceptions of Boston's female reformers.[48]

Members of the Boston Working Women's League hoped to intervene in the market for women's labor by establishing their own employment agency. They criticized current agencies, run for profit, as preying on women who needed work and misleading both employers and employees. Their non-profit bureau, run by the women themselves, would "be established on entirely new principles," seeking to match potential employers and employees. Again, they warned of the interference of "non working-women" in this enterprise; middle-class women were likely to create an agency "dangerous to the independence of the women who earn their daily bread by the daily labor of their own hands, since it could easily be transformed into an institution (professedly philanthropic) where the working women would be put off, without substantial or efficient aid, with the empty forms of condescending charity." Significantly, the employment bureau they envisioned would place women in "all legitimate industrial avocations, other than that of household service."[49]

"Any working-woman of Boston, dependent upon the daily labor of her own hands for her daily bread" was invited to join the Working Women's League. No fees were charged, opening membership to all of the city's laboring women, no matter how poor. Although committed, above all, to independence, by forgoing dues the League became dependent on contributions from citizens of "wealth and standing." The organization established an advisory board that included the mayor of Boston and received a significant contribution from Post Fifteen of the Grand Army of the Republic—free use of a building at 815 Washington Street. Collins was well known for her work among soldiers and veterans, and the building may have been given to her fledgling organization out of appreciation for her volunteer work. Possession of free space enabled the League to envision a program of public meetings and debates two or three evenings a week, which employers and "ladies of all classes" were invited to attend.[50] Middle-class women were not excluded, but they would be put in the position of students rather than teachers regarding the problems of women's work.

In addition to her leadership of the Boston Working Women's League, Collins advanced the cause of working women around the state as an organizer for the New England Labor Reform League. In July 1869, she addressed the first convention of the Daughters of Saint Crispin, a new organization of women who worked in shoe manufacturing. Collins praised the women for their independence and their success in organizing.[51] That fall, she traveled to Dover, New Hampshire, where the eight hundred employees of the Cocheco Cotton Manufacturing Company struck to protest a 12 percent wage cut.[52] The operatives Collins met in Dover resented the fact that the company boosted its profits by increasing the number of looms a woman tended from two to six and by raising the prices workers paid the company boarding house from $2.25 to $6 a week. Collins raised money for the strike in Lowell, where she "rallied the factory women and girls" who "gathered by the thousands in Huntington Hall, one of the largest in New England, to listen to Jennie's appeal for her sisters in Dover."[53]

In the course of the strike, Collins articulated a new consciousness of female wage workers as consumers. Cocheco manufactured calico, inexpensive printed cloth that factory operatives and farm women made into dresses. Collins felt certain that once women around the country "understood the facts, [they] would allow the Cocheco goods to rot on the shelves before they would purchase them."[54] She embraced the use of the boycott, which became a significant technique for the Knights of Labor in the 1880s and for middle-class women who formed consumers' leagues in the 1890s. The striking women at Dover held out for several months but were ultimately defeated by the company, which ordered the women to return to work or to be blacklisted. In a letter to the *Revolution* reflecting on the strike, Collins admitted defeat "for the noble but oppressed women" but predicted an eventual victory, declaring, "We working women will wear fig-leaf dresses before we will patronize the Cocheco Company."[55]

Collins's leadership in Dover and her correspondence with the *Revolution* brought her into contact with leaders of the women's suffrage movement, who invited her to address the National Woman Suffrage Association at their annual meeting in Washington, D.C.[56] Paulina Davis, an early chronicler of the suffrage movement, described Collins as slight of build, "all brain and soul." Davis noted that Collins told "her touching stories with such a tender, natural pathos that few eyes are dry during her speeches."[57] In Washington, Collins held the audience in her sway "for two full hours." Her success earned her "a purse, and the offer of a free passage to California and back," with the understanding that she would lecture on the conditions of working women along the way.[58]

Collins accepted the offer, but she felt the need to find concrete ways to address the problems her speeches described. She soon transformed the Working Women's Hall at 815 Washington Street into Boffin's Bower, naming the new center for working women after a location in Charles Dickens's novel *Our Mutual Friend.* In addition to providing a free employment agency, industrial training, and free lunches, Boffin's Bower offered working women a parlor for relaxation, complete with carpet, potted plants, a piano, and two canaries. A newspaper reporter noted a reading room with "all the Boston Dailies on file, besides quite a good collection of books and pamphlets." Collins managed to acquire a library of "four hundred volumes of well-selected reading matter."[59] The Bower also sponsored a full program of music and lectures. A reporter from the Belfast, Maine, *Republican*, described Collins as "a democratic little body, with more nervous energy in her make-up than a dozen women ought to have. . . . She talks and walks, plans constantly, and executes as rapidly."[60] Collins subsequently added temporary lodgings for working women and moved the center into larger quarters a few blocks away from its original location.[61]

Collins continued to earn money by lecturing, and in 1871 she published a book titled *Nature's Aristocracy*, whose proceeds she contributed to Boffin's Bower.[62] Her book used individual stories of working women's hardscrabble lives to advance the agenda of the New England Labor Reform League: an eight-hour day, the establishment of workers' cooperatives, and full political rights for women. Collins framed her project as the restoration of democracy, a system that seemed to be going awry because of the dangerous growth of monopolies of "railroad, land, ship, and telegraph companies" that "threaten to overturn our whole system of government." Like William Sylvis, the recently deceased leader of the National Labor Union, she believed that workers had to organize to increase their political power. After all, workers were in the majority, and in a democracy "the *majority will rule.*" But as her book's title suggests, Collins saw democracy not as a leveling of all distinctions but as the removal of the artificial barriers against individuals exercising their full range of talents. She called for restoration of the people's political power, improved public education, and a broader field of employment for women.[63]

Although Collins advocated women's rights, she did so from a distinctively working-class perspective. Unlike elite and middle-class advocates of women's rights, who embraced a universal vision of "woman" to be freed from the fetters of unjust laws and outdated conventions, Collins saw her sex as sharply divided by class, arguing that there could be no single conception of "woman's rights" because "there are not certain wrongs that apply to the whole sex." In her opinion, working-class women, who generally lacked male protection, felt "the power of the law" most strongly and needed political rights most urgently. For example, Civil War widows who struggled to make a living and pay their taxes had no voice in influencing how their children were to be educated. "In short, they were obliged to do a man's work, and all of a mother's[,] under the double disadvantage of being physically weak and of possessing no political influence that would entitle them to respect." As a result of their political powerlessness, they were often unfairly denied pensions or taken advantage of in business. Meanwhile, young women pushed into factories because they did not have male support gained "contact with the world and . . . experience in affairs of business"; these experiences gave them "an independence of character and a knowledge of [their] rights, which under present circumstances, serves only to aggravate [their] discontent." Given rights to vote and hold office, working women could push for a government responsive to their needs, including an eight-hour day and equal pay for equal work.[64]

Collins made working women's struggles for independence a major theme of her book. While Phelps had pursued independence through proprietorship, Collins envisioned working women gaining independence through skilled, respected, fairly compensated wage labor. Surveying the narrow and poorly paid field of women's employment, Collins admitted that although women who worked in "the store, the tailor's shop, the printing-office, and binderies" might be "very far indeed from being independent," they enjoyed "a far greater degree of latitude in mental and physical action than" women who worked in "the kitchen or chambers of a modern mansion." Although Collins doubted that any woman under the present economic and political system could be "wholly independent," she urged her female readers to "adopt the next best course, and be as independent as they can."[65]

Although Collins was eulogized as a charitable reformer, she took a dim view of charity in *Nature's Aristocracy*, warning that it led to dependence in its recipients and a false sense of superiority in its dispensers. Drawing, perhaps, on her experiences as a servant in the Lowell household, she painted the following scene: "It often happens that while the mistress of a house is visiting the poor or attending the board meetings of some charitable institution, there are servant-girls at her home washing the clothes and ceilings, taking up the carpets, or cooking the dinner, with whom she has had a long and exciting debate over the twenty-five cents per week which the servant[s] wished to have added to [their] wages." Most likely, Collins continued, the mistress had refused her servants, while donating ten dollars to a fund to aid former servant girls, "who would not have been the wrecks she saw had they received decent compensation for their work." Likewise, the textile magnate who cut wages could be counted on to contribute money to aid fallen women, failing to appreciate the fact that women's low wages forced them to turn to prostitution "to avoid more acute suffering."[66]

Collins continued to comment on the state of women's labor through a series of annual reports she issued from Boffin's Bower; these reports mixed anecdotes from her work at the center with observations gathered from visits to "work-shops, boarding-houses, lodging-houses, dancing-halls, prayer meetings, the markets, Saturday nights, theatres, libraries, reading-rooms, the tombs in station-houses, the pawnbrokers, and other places including the various public charity and reformatory institutions."[67] Her determination to seek out knowledge of poverty reflected a trans-Atlantic interest in gathering labor statistics in order to push the state to take increased responsibility for the conditions of the working class.[68] The Labor Commissioner of the Imperial Council of Berlin requested copies of her reports, as did the U.S. Department of State. Like other members of the New England Labor Reform League, Collins pushed for a state bureau of labor statistics and applauded its establishment in 1869. Benjamin Sanborn, a newspaper editor and a founder of the American Social Science Association, described Collins as "a detective and registrar of charity" who had "more curious and exact knowledge about one class of the Boston poor than I ever found in any other person."[69]

Collins's knowledge of poverty proved especially useful in hard times. The great fire in Boston in 1872 threw large numbers of shopgirls and sewing women out of work; Collins assisted the women in getting relief and securing the back wages they were owed.[70] The next year, a severe economic depression initiated by the Panic of 1873 reversed the gains made by organized labor after the Civil War and increased Collins's work in providing aid for the needy. Soon thereafter, support for Reconstruction waned and the nation's political climate shifted toward invoking the "natural" differences of gender, race, and class that had come under attack immediately following the war.[71]

As the postwar movement for labor reform crumbled, Collins became something of a lone crusader for the rights of working women. Although strident in her defense of the poor, she became less pointed in her attacks on the privileged. When depression returned during the harsh winter of 1877–78, she provided over eight thousand free dinners, saving many women from starvation. As the director of a charitable institution—even one far more egalitarian than others in the city—she relied on merchants, manufacturers, and wealthy individuals whom she could not afford to alienate. Major donors included her former employer, Macular, Parker, and Williams, the labor reformer Wendell Phillips, and the suffragist Mary Livermore, who served as a conduit for donations from women around the country.[72] A profile in the *Chicago Daily Tribune* celebrated Collins's new moderation, noting that many reformers found the theories she advanced in *Nature's Aristocracy* "a little bit 'cracked,'" but that she now focused her energies on helping the poor rather than advancing questionable social theories.[73] The speed and distance she traveled may be measured by her 1873 proposal to open a training school for domestic servants, a capitulation to popular ideas about women's proper place in the labor market she had previously rejected in no uncertain terms.[74] Collins's trajectory from being a militant labor organizer to becoming the director of a charitable institution suggests how quickly hopes for radical social reconstruction faded after the Civil War and how intractable the problem of working-class women's limited occupations and low wages remained.[75]

Meanwhile Phelps continued to work for Garden Homesteads, celebrating the tenth anniversary of the Women's Homestead League in 1874. Collins, who attended the celebration, endorsed Garden Homesteads "as a means of practical relief to many friendless, but worthy and industrious women."[76] Although the legislature had refused the Boston Working Women League's petition for free land in 1869, two years later they incorporated the Women's Garden Homestead League with Phelps as the director. With the support of a thousand subscribers, Phelps purchased a sixty-acre tract of wooded land in Woburn, Massachusetts, adjacent to the Boston and Lowell railroad. She drew up plans for a female community, Aurora, where she hoped to realize her vision for Garden Homesteads and to provide residents with an additional source of income by establishing a cooperative laundry, along the lines of one in Troy, New York.[77]

In October 1873, Phelps held a ceremony to dedicate the Bethesda Laundry. Despite a storm, "a large number of ladies and gentlemen from the surrounding villages" attended, along with several labor reformers. Evidently not a supporter of temperance despite being a Baptist, Phelps christened the building by throwing a bottle of whiskey at the wood frame. She missed, but the celebration continued with speeches and songs. Reporters noted that several women had already begun digging the cellars for their houses.

Despite this optimistic beginning, the plan failed. Three years later, Phelps died destitute in Woburn, possessing little more than "a dilapidated bedstead, ragged bedclothes, two or three rickety chairs, and a few books." Her estate was too small to cover her funeral expenses, which were borne by the town of Woburn.[78] Unlike Collins, who was remembered after her death in 1887 with glowing obituaries in the daily papers of Boston, New York, and Chicago, and in women's and labor periodicals, Phelps's demise received barely any public notice. By the end of her life, mainstream publications such as the *New York Times* and the *Saturday Evening Post* had dismissed her as a utopian reformer, and the radical movement she had once been part of lost force.

Although it is tempting to dismiss Phelps's plan for Garden Homesteads as a quaint protest against the inevitable course of industrialization, the support the idea received among working women should alert us to their strong desires for independence during the 1860s and the 1870s. Ideally, Garden Homesteads would have established working-class women as the heads of their own households and allowed them to gain a fair return on their labor by farming or working in the cooperative laundry. Women would have gained a degree of economic independence rarely achieved in families, where men continued to hold most rights to property, or in the labor market, where women continued to earn half of men's wages. Moreover, the plan revealed women's continued linking of economic independence with political rights. In Aurora, women would have voted and held office, a bold experiment in women's self-governance. Its failure revealed the strength of the very limitations Phelps and the women who joined her sought to transcend.

In the turbulent decades following the Civil War a small but significant group of women in Boston came together to claim a new social identity as "working women" who depended "upon the daily labor of [their] own hands for [their] daily bread."[79] Their self-definition as breadwinners posed a working-class alternative to the middle-class norm of dependent women, who confined their labor to the unpaid work of caring for their own families.

The Boston Working Women's League and the campaign for Garden Homesteads articulated the political ideology of working women who used their self-support, earned through long hours at menial jobs, to make new claims as productive citizens. Like former slaves who embraced the claim of "forty acres and a mule," these women believed that they had yet to receive fair compensation for their labor. They hoped to enlist the state in a variety of measures designed to increase their independence, from granting them land for farming, to guaranteeing an eight-hour day, to supporting cooperatives that would offer them just compensation for their labor. Determined to represent themselves politically, they demanded rights to vote and to hold office, recognizing that their political incapacity hindered their ability to make the government respond to their needs.

Working women's political agitation refuted conservative political theorists who denied women's rights as individuals by claiming that they were protected and represented by their fathers and husbands. In the breakdown of family support that followed the Civil War, working women in the nation's industrializing cities seized on a new possibility: independence. Their ability to make good on this claim would be challenged not just by employers but also by their erstwhile allies: working men eager to define women, like children, as properly dependent on men; and well-to-do women reformers concerned with their difficulty finding "good help" and determined to put their stamp on social policy by claiming to represent the best interests of working-class women.

NOTES

1. Helen L. Sumner, *History of Women in Industry in the U.S.* (Washington, DC: Government Printing Office, 1910), 31. See also Thomas Dublin, *Transforming Women's Work: New England Lives in the Industrial Revolution* (Ithaca, NY: Cornell University Press, 1994), 77–85.

2. Jennie Collins, *Nature's Aristocracy; or, Battles and Wounds in Time of Peace* (Boston: Lee & Shepard, 1871), 313–314. See also Anne Phillips and Barbara Taylor, "Sex and Skill: Notes toward a Feminist Economics," *Feminist Review* 6 (1980): 79–88.

3. Collins, *Nature's Aristocracy*, 314, 180–181.

4. Quoted in Sumner, *History of Women in Industry*, 111. Collins, *Nature's Aristocracy*, 181.

5. Jennie Collins, "New England Factories," *Revolution*, January 31, 1870. See also Paul R. Dauphinais, "Être à l'Ouvrage ou Être Maitresse de Maison: French-Canadian Women and Work in Late Nineteenth-Century Massachusetts," in *Women of the Commonwealth: Work, Family and Social Change in Nineteenth-Century Massachusetts*, ed. Susan L. Porter (Amherst: University of Massachusetts Press, 1996), 63–83.

6. Dublin, *Transforming Women's Work*, 155–158, 187.

7. Collins obituary, *Boston Evening Transcript*, July 21, 1887, and *Dictionary of American Biography, Base Set, American Council of Learned Societies, 1928–1936*, reproduced in *Biography Resource Center* (Farmington Hills, MI: Thomson Gale, 2006)), s.v. "John Lowell."

8. Collins, *Nature's Aristocracy*, 103–104. See also Sumner, *History of Women in Industry*, 183.

9. Jennie Collins, "Why Women Avoid Housework," *Woman's Journal* 3, no. 10 (1872), 74, the Gerritsen Collection of Aletta H. Jacobs (ProQuest, Chadwyck-Healey, 2002–2009). See also "Good Servants," *Workman's Advocate*, June 19, 1869.

10. Collins, *Nature's Aristocracy*, 105.

11. New England Women's Club, *Report of the Committee on Needlewomen, 12* April 1869 (Boston: John Wilson and Son, 1869), 19, New England Women's Club Papers, Folder 88, Schlesinger Library on the History of Women, Radcliffe Institute, Harvard University, Cambridge, MA (hereafter cited as SL).

12. Timothy Gilfoyle, *City of Eros: New York City, Prostitution, and the Commercialization of Sex, 1790*–1920 (New York: Norton, 1992), 287, 290–291.

13. Hasia R. Diner, *Erin's Daughters in America: Irish Immigrant Women in the Nineteenth Century* (Baltimore: Johns Hopkins University Press, 1983), xiv, 71, 81, 90, 93, 94; Carol Lasser, "The Domestic Balance of Power: Relations between Mistress and Maid in Nineteenth-Century New England," in *History of Women in the U.S.*, ed. Nancy F. Cott (New York: Saur, 1992), 4:123–124; and Diane M. Hotten-Somers, "Relinquishing and Reclaiming Independence: Irish Domestic Servants, American Middle-Class Mistresses, and Assimilation 1850–1920," *Éire-Ireland* 36, nos. 1–2 (Spring/Summer 2001): 185–201.

14. Stanley Nadel, *Little Germany: Ethnicity, Religion, and Class in New York City, 1845*–1880 (Urbana: University of Illinois Press, 1990), 76, 192, n. 60.

15. Quoted in Lasser, "Domestic Balance of Power," 125.

16. "The Bell Goes A-ringing for Sai-rah," *American Workman*, June 5, 1869.

17. Christine Stansell, *City of Women: Sex and Class in New York City, 1789*–1860 (Urbana: University of Illinois Press, 1987), 111. Evidence that Collins had left the family by 1860 comes from the U.S. Census return, ancestry.com.

18. Dublin, *Transforming Women's Work*, 158–159.

19. *New York Times*, March 2, 1869, in Philip S. Foner and Ronald L. Lewis, eds., *The Black Worker: A Documentary History from Colonial Times to the Present* (Philadelphia: Temple University Press, 1978), 2:360–361; Jean Collier Brown, "The Negro Woman Worker," in *Black Women in White America: A Documentary History*, ed. Gerda Lerner

(New York: Vintage Books, 1972), 251; and Leon F. Litwack, *North of Slavery: The Negro in the Free States, 1790–1860* (Chicago: University of Chicago Press, 1961), 155.

20. *National Standard*, November 11, 1871, quoted in Foner and Lewis, *The Black Worker*, 2:281.

21. Quoted in Paula J. Giddings, *When and Where I Enter: The Impact of Black Women on Race and Sex in America* (New York: Bantam Books, 1985), 69.

22. *Notable American Women, 1607–1950: A Biographical Dictionary*, ed. Edward T. James (Cambridge, MA: Harvard University Press, 1971), s.v. "Collins, Jennie." See also Catherine Clinton, *The Other Civil War: American Women in the Nineteenth Century* (New York: Hill & Wang, 1999), 81.

23. Jeanie Attie, "Warwork and the Crisis of Domesticity in the North," in *Divided Houses: Gender and the Civil War*, ed. Catherine Clinton and Nina Silber (New York: Oxford University Press, 1992), 243–259.

24. Collins, *Nature's Aristocracy*, 285–286.

25. Norman J. Ware, *The Labor Movement in the United States, 1860–1895: A Study in Democracy* (1929; repr., Gloucester, MA: Peter Smith, 1959), 1–2, 4–5.

26. "The Death of a Noble Woman," *Journal of United Labor*, July 30, 1887.

27. David Montgomery, *Beyond Equality: Labor and the Radical Republicans, 1862–1872* (1967; repr., Urbana: University of Illinois Press, 1981), 136, 412–414. See also Martin Henry Blatt, "Heywood, Ezra Hervey," *American National Biography Online*, February 2000, http://www.anb.org/articles/15/15-00330.html, and "Working Men's and Women's Labor Reform Convention," *American Workman*, August 21, 1869.

28. "My Laundress," *American Workman*, May 1, 1869.

29. Sumner, *History of Women in Industry*, 31.

30. Jamie L. Bronstein, *Land Reform and Working-Class Experience in Britain and the United States, 1800–1862* (Stanford, CA: Stanford University Press, 1999), 2–6, 8, 78–81, 173–185.

31. "The Wail of the Women," *Workingman's Advocate*, April 24, 1869, 1. See also Paul Goodman, "The Emergence of the Homestead Exemption in the United States: Accommodations and Resistance to the Market Revolution, 1840–1880," *Journal of American History* 80, no. 2 (September 1993): 470–498. Alice Kessler-Harris discusses this petition in *Out to Work: A History of Wage-Earning Women in the United States* (New York: Oxford University Press, 1982), 80–81.

32. Quoted in "The Homestead Question—What and Why?" *American Workman*, May 1869.

33. Quoted in "The Work-Woman," *American Workman*, June 26, 1869.

34. Quoted in "The Wail of the Women."

35. "The Homestead Question—What and Why?"

36. "The Working-Women's League," *American Workman* 2, no. 4 (May 1869).

37. Parker Pillsbury, "How the Working Women Live," *Revolution*, May 13, 1869. See also William Leach, *True Love and Perfect Union: The Feminist Reform of Sex and Society* (Middletown, CT: Wesleyan University Press, 1989), 134–136.

38. "The Working Women in Council," *American Workman*, May 1869.

39. Ibid.

40. Quoted in *Workingman's Advocate* 5, no. 41 (May 8, 1869). See also Rosalyn Baxandall, Linda Gordon, and Susan Reverby, "Boston Working Women Protest, 1869," *Signs* 1, no. 3, pt. 1 (1976): 803–808.

41. "The Working Women in Council."

42. Ibid.

43. Julia A. Sprague, *History of the New England Women's Club from 1868 to 1893* (Boston: Lee & Shepard, 1894), 2–3.

44. New England Women's Club, *Report of the Committee on Needlewomen*, 19–20.

45. "The Working Women in Council."

46. Ibid.

47. Elizabeth La Pierre Daniels, "Boston Working Women Again," *Revolution*, May 20, 1869.

48. Sarah Deutsch, "Learning to Talk More Like a Man: Boston Women's Class-Bridging Organizations, 1870–1940," *American Historical Review* 97, no. 2 (April 1992): 379–404.

49. "The Working-Women's League."

50. "The Boston Workingwoman," *American Workman*, August 21, 1869.

51. Quoted in Mary H. Blewett, *Men, Women and Work: Class, Gender and Protest in the New England Shoe Industry, 1780–1910* (Urbana: University of Illinois Press, 1990), 167–170.

52. Collins, *Nature's Aristocracy*, 196–197.

53. "Jennie Collins and the Dover Strike," *Revolution*, December 30, 1869.

54. Quoted in ibid.

55. Collins, "New England Factories."

56. *Notable American Women*, s.v. "Collins, Jennie," 362–363.

57. Paulina W. Davis, *A History of the National Woman's Rights Movement for Twenty Years* (New York: Journeymen Printers' Co-operative Association, 1871), 30.

58. "Jennie Collins in Washington," *Revolution*, February 10, 1870. See also "Death of a Noble Woman."

59. Margaret Andrews Allen, "Jennie Collins and Her Boffin's Bower," *Charities Review* 2 (December 1892): 106.

60. Quoted in "Boffin's Bower," *Woman's Journal*, March 25, 1871.

61. Allen, "Jennie Collins and Her Boffin's Bower," 105.

62. Lilian Whiting, "Jennie Collins," *Chautauquan* 8, no. 3 (December 1887): 159.

63. Collins, *Nature's Aristocracy*, 296–297, 300.

64. Ibid., 304–305, 306, 309–310, 314.

65. Ibid., 103–104.

66. Ibid., 222.

67. Quoted in Allen, "Jennie Collins and Her Boffin's Bower," III.

68. Daniel T. Rodgers, *Atlantic Crossings: Social Politics in a Progressive Age* (Cambridge, MA: Belknap Press, 1998).

69. Quoted in Allen, "Jennie Collins and Her Boffin's Bower," 115.

70. Mary A. Livermore, "Jennie Collins' Work," *Boston Daily Globe*, July 31, 1887, 5, ProQuest Historical Newspapers (hereafter cited as PQHN).

71. Heather Cox Richardson, *The Death of Reconstruction: Race, Labor, and Politics in the Post–Civil War North, 1865–1901* (Cambridge, MA: Harvard University Press, 2001).

72. Mary A. Livermore, "Jennie Collins," *Woman's Journal*, August 6, 1887; Jennie Collins, *Sixth Annual Report of Boffin's Bower* (Boston, 1875–1876), 16–17; and "Boffin's Bower: Miss Jennie Collins' Report for the Past Year—The Bower in Prosperous Condition," *Boston Daily Globe*, June 18, 1873, 8, PQHN.

73. "Jennie Collins and Boffin's Bower—What the Newspaper-Men Think of Her," *Chicago Daily Tribune*, December 19, 1875, 10, PQHN.

74. "School for Housekeepers: Jennie Collins' Latest Project for the Education of the Working Girls," *Boston Daily Globe*, February 3, 1873, 8, PQHN.

75. *Notable American Women*, s.v. "Collins, Jennie," 362–363; "Work Committee," [1938], 3–4, Folder 95, New England Women's Club Papers, SL; and Eric Foner, *The Story of American Freedom* (New York: Norton, 1998), 113–120.

76. Quoted in "Local Miscellany," *Boston Daily Globe*, May 23, 1874, 5, PQHN.

77. Carole Turbin, *Working Women of Collar City: Gender: Class, and Community in Troy, New York, 1863–1886* (Urbana: University of Illinois Press, 1992), 163–164.

78. "Aurora," *New York Times*, October 28, 1873, 4, PQHN; "Suburban Notes," *Boston Daily Globe*, November 27, 1873, 5, PQHN; "A Community of Women Only," *Saturday Evening Post* 53, no. 21 (December 20,1873): 8; and "Death of Noted Character," *Boston Daily Globe*, January 6. 1876, 5.

79. "The Working-Women's League."

14

"I Had Not Seen Women Like That Before"

Intergenerational Feminism in New York City's Tenant Movement

ROBERTA S. GOLD

With the emergence of the women's liberation movement in the late 1960s and early 1970s, many young feminists went looking for a "usable past" of women's achievement. In New York City, they did not have to look far. New York's tenant councils had, for decades, operated under predominantly female leadership. And in the late 1960s these organizations supported a new wave of squatter campaigns aimed at relieving the city's shortage of affordable housing. As young activists rallied to support the squats, they encountered the senior generation of female leaders who directed local and citywide tenant groups. These older women became political mentors to the young volunteers, providing them not only with expertise on housing but with a model of "actually existing feminism."[1]

This essay argues that the tenant struggles of the 1960s and 1970s amplified the women's liberation movement in New York by linking young feminists with the Old Left generation of female housing organizers. Tenant campaigns served as a "parallel space," alongside other political movements, in which women's leadership could and did flourish. The tenant story adds to our understanding of second wave feminism by revealing a set of affectionate mentoring relations between two generations of radical female activists, thereby challenging many narratives of feminist politicization that focus primarily on young women's rejection of what came before, be it postwar domesticity, liberal feminism, or New Left sexism.[2]

The senior tenant leaders were not entirely anomalous. Recent scholarship has identified a cohort of unsung organizers of the mid-twentieth century, people who kept the Popular Front flame from dying out during the

Cold War and passed it along to activists who ignited the political upheavals of the late 1950s, 1960s, and 1970s.[3] Although tenant history extends these narratives, it also departs from them, particularly with regard to what might be called "political intentionality." In most stories of Cold War connections, the struggles young people took up were the very struggles the senior cohort had intended to foster—that is, postwar civil rights activists paved the way for subsequent civil rights campaigns, Cold War feminist strategies informed second wave feminism, and so forth. In New York's tenant arena, by contrast, senior organizers did not set out in a programmatic way to advance one of the major developments—women's power—that would inspire their young recruits. Instead they were concerned with housing—both a universal need and, ironically, an entity located in the "domestic sphere" of conventional gender ideology. But their work nonetheless presented a model of "on-the-ground" women's activism, which complemented the more self-conscious women's liberation movement that exploded on the U.S. political stage just as the squatter actions caught fire. Thus older tenant leaders' contribution to second wave feminism was largely an unintended consequence of their work on the front lines of struggle over tenant rights versus property rights.

The older tenant organizers had picked up a torch, or at least an ember, from the working-class and antiracist tradition that Dorothy Sue Cobble has dubbed "labor feminism."[4] Many of these organizers had been active in left-wing unions during the 1940s, and as mid-century tenant leaders they had continued to place poor people's needs, along with New York's pioneering antidiscrimination laws and ghetto-housing struggles, at the top of their agenda. The squatter actions of the 1970s carried on these traditions: the movement was genuinely multiracial, and squatter families were virtually all poor.

Such demographics created another contrast between the squatter campaigns and more typical women's politics, often characterized by a mutually frustrating split between predominantly white, middle-class feminists, on the one hand, and minority and working-class feminists, on the other. The parallel space of New York's squatter movement offered local feminists an alternative to such political fragmentation. Here young activists not only inherited a set of older, class-conscious feminist mentors; they also came into a field of organizing that centered on low-income, racially diverse participants. And their demand for renters' rights challenged one of postwar America's most powerful class and racial stratifying mechanisms: the real estate industry.[5] Squatter struggles thus became both a training ground in which Popular Front veterans nurtured the next generation of activists and a venue in which these activists pursued a remarkably integrated vision of class, racial, and gender justice.

The Postwar Tenant Movement

Many tenant leaders of the early 1960s had been schooled in the Popular Front struggles of the 1930s and 1940s. During those years, tenant organizing was closely connected to New York's dense network of labor unions and leftist political formations, especially the Communist Party (CP) and, in New York City, the American Labor Party (ALP). Although tenant associations did not usually establish formal ties with these larger groups, they often shared cadre and political agendas.

The basic units of tenant organization were local ones: building and neighborhood councils, which thrived especially in highly politicized areas such as the Lower East Side and Harlem. These groups, often led by women, mobilized rent strikes and staffed "rent clinics," where knowledgeable volunteers helped individual tenants assert their legal rights. Such activities meshed with the work of the larger Left. Communists, for example, regularly provided street muscle to forestall evictions during the Depression, and ALP veterans staffed many 1940s' rent clinics.[6] In the formal political arena as well, early postwar tenant groups joined labor, liberal, and leftist organizations to lobby for three critical policies: rent control, public housing, and building-code enforcement.

The 1950s brought a new threat to city residents: "urban renewal." This federally subsidized program was billed as an answer to tenant and leftist groups' longstanding call for "slum clearance"—that is, the development of affordable modern housing in lieu of decrepit tenements. But because of both conservative provisions in the 1949 federal statute and the machinations of New York's public works czar, Robert Moses, urban-renewal projects in New York did nothing to improve poor people's housing. Instead they led to the demolition of many working-class neighborhoods, the dislocation of five hundred thousand New Yorkers, and the replacement of their low-rent homes with highways, middle-income housing, and elite cultural facilities such as Lincoln Center. Moses's wreckers showed a special penchant for razing black and integrated areas, prompting critics to dub the program "Negro removal." Tenants' power to resist these projects was limited, as urban-renewal advocates successfully promoted redevelopment as "progress" and McCarthyite politics decimated the city's leftist unions and parties.[7]

But ultimately the wave of urban-renewal evictions galvanized the city's tenant movement. By the late 1950s, local organizers, mainly women, were rallying residents against urban renewal in several neighborhoods. These organizers began meeting to plan strategy, and in 1959 they formally consti-tuted themselves as a citywide coalition, Metropolitan Council on Housing (Met Council, for short). Met Council leaders would play a critical role in supporting the squatter actions that broke out in 1970.

Practical Feminists

At first, Met Council's founders took turns leading meetings; but soon they chose a chairman, Jane Benedict. A child of liberal German Jews, she had studied English at Cornell, joined the Book and Magazine Guild, and there had fallen in with a crowd of idealistic Depression-era Communists, the most dashing of whom she married. Through the 1940s she held leadership posi-tions in her union. Then she stepped down to care for her two young children but began volunteering with the local ALP club to keep one foot in politics. Making the party rounds in blue-collar Yorkville, toddlers in tow, Benedict learned firsthand about the conditions—heatless apartments, shared toilets—in New York's tenement housing.[8]

But something worse was in store for Benedict's neighbors. In the mid-1950s, local tenants started "coming into the ALP saying, 'Oh my God, the landlord says he's going to tear the house down.'" Urban renewal had arrived in Yorkville. With thousands of local people facing eviction, Benedict organ-ized the Yorkville Save Our Homes Committee to resist the wrecking ball.[9]

A few miles downtown, tenants were likewise girding for a fight. The Lower East Side was a leftist stronghold—a working-class, integrated, largely immigrant neighborhood where international and homegrown traditions of struggle enjoyed a symbiotic relationship. Frances Goldin had moved there from Queens in 1944, and she "felt like [she] had moved into heaven." A daughter of Russian Jews, Goldin had befriended Communists at her ship-ping job, joined the CP, and studied Marx at the CP's Jefferson School. "And I was hot to trot. I was going to have socialism in my time. " After marrying a comrade and setting up housekeeping in Manhattan, Goldin visited the

Lower East Side Tenant and Consumer Council (which shared offices with the local ALP) to check on the legality of her rent. The volunteers asked her to help with other cases, and Goldin became a respected tenant organizer.[10]

Goldin worked alongside Esther Rand, another downtown Communist whose passion, legal brilliance, and ornery disposition became legendary in housing circles. "Oh, could she be nasty!" recalled Benedict. "But she was the spirit of that East Side branch." A housing judge once chided a landlord's attorney who had disputed Rand's knowledge of housing statutes by declaring, "If Esther Rand says that's the law, that's the law!"[11]

In the late 1950s, Goldin and Rand led the charge against an urban-renewal proposal to raze six blocks of the Lower East Side's Cooper Square and replace them with a middle-income housing development. Organizers formed a committee, invited broad participation by residents and business owners, and, with guidance from a maverick city planner, hashed out an alternative redevelopment plan that promised to re-house all original residents in sound but affordable units on the site.[12]

Goldin and Rand helped found Met Council.[13] At the nascent coalition's meetings they were joined by yet another Old Left veteran, Chelsea organizer Jane Wood. Wood was a St. Louis native and Smith graduate who moved to New York in 1930 and joined the ALP.[14] Going door to door for the party in the 1940s, the young volunteer found dismal conditions in local tenements and began talking with people about housing. Her college Spanish helped her forge especially close ties with the many Latinos settling in Chelsea. An activist neighbor later recalled, "We in the Latino community felt she was one of us." Quietly and tenaciously, Wood built a neighborhood tenant network.[15]

Benedict, Goldin, Rand, and Wood formed the core of leadership that would guide Met Council through its first decade and beyond. All veteran Communists or fellow travelers, they imparted to the organization a belief in grassroots struggle and a critical view of the capitalist housing industry. Rand's signature saying was "Landlords are not the lords of the land; they are the scum of the earth." They also brought to Met Council a creed that was less fully developed in the Marxian tradition, something that might be called "practical feminism." Battling landlords in city courtrooms and leading demonstrations in the streets, these women did not conform to the domestic model of femininity promoted by Cold War pundits. Although the object of their struggles—people's homes—might count as "women's sphere," the terrain on which they fought lay squarely in the political arena. These women did not take up feminism explicitly or as their primary political affiliation. But none of them doubted their fitness to take action in the "man's world" of politics.

How had they arrived at this unorthodox sense of capability? All adventurous as young adults, they had found unusually fertile soil for their activist impulses in the world of leftist politics. The CP was no paragon of sex equality, but it did devote theoretical attention to "the woman question" and fostered a practical arena for women's political activism. Historian Ellen Schrecker suggests that women in the party's orbit "constituted a kind of missing generation within American feminism." Moreover, most of the core Met Council women had been ushered into masculine arenas of work or union leadership as a result of the "manpower" shortage during World War II. In a sense they belonged to the larger saga of Rosie the Riveter. But unlike the many Rosies who were fired in 1945, these leftist women maintained their political trajectory through the Cold War—as housing organizers.[16]

Community and Its Contents

During the 1960s, New Yorkers mounted a series of new tenant and community struggles that partook of nationwide radical movements but also reflected New York's unique tenant history and resilient Old Left. Two such struggles in particular presaged the squatter movement. The first unfolded uptown in response to yet another bulldozer plan, this one for Morningside Heights. Here, however, the tenants' chief antagonist was not city government but a consortium of educational, medical, and religious institutions led by Columbia University, which had for years been buying up and converting local properties. In 1961, tenants in seven buildings on Morningside Drive received eviction notices, and one of them, Marie Runyon, began urging her neighbors to fight back.

At first glance an unlikely organizer for a multiracial neighborhood—she hailed from a conservative, poor, white family in North Carolina—Runyon had been "leaning" toward social change since her 1930s' stint at the progressive Berea College. In 1946 she came to New York, which she loved immediately, and found a job in journalism. After a marriage, childbirth, and divorce left her in need of more income, she became assistant membership director at the American Civil Liberties Union. There she learned the skills of organizing and continued to gravitate toward the Left. Despite "strong socialist leanings," she never joined the CP, but added, "Don't say that, because it's none of anybody's goddamned business."[17] By 1961, Runyon had joined Met Council.

Now she forged a tenant-student alliance to fight "institutional expansion" throughout Morningside Heights. Through amateur sleuthing she learned that her real landlord (hidden behind a paper corporation) was Columbia University, and she won a court order to halt demolition. However, because Morningside Heights' tenants (unlike Cooper Square activists) were fighting against private owners, they could exert little leverage, usually winning eviction delays rather than lasting victories. But as Columbia's campus Left gained steam, Runyon directed students' attention toward the university's expansionist plan to build a private gymnasium in Morningside Park, a city property that lay between the campus and Harlem.[18] Students for a Democratic Society and the Student Afro-American Society escalated protests at Columbia in the spring of 1968, denouncing the "Gym Crow" plan and scuffling with police guarding the construction site. The protest and the media attention it garnered persuaded administrators to abandon the park plan and build a gym on campus—a heartening, if largely symbolic, victory for Morningside Heights tenants.

As local activists flexed muscle, they also advanced a creative ideology of urban citizenship and rights. Runyon, like the Cooper Square leaders, spoke of New York's neighborhoods as "communities" that possessed a moral right to secure housing. This diction challenged the prevailing postwar rhetoric of "urban blight" and "slums" with a depiction of low-income neighborhoods as vibrant, organic social formations. Runyon also countered the postwar ideology of homeownership as the basis of citizenship. At one meeting, she described her neighbors' years in the area as "a lot of investment, a lot of roots," which in turn entitled them to stable homes in Morningside Heights.[19] Here tenants' historical investment of living together as neighbors figured as a kind of "investment" that went deeper than owners' outlays for land.

The second prefigurative campaign involved a series of takeovers staged by young radicals of color. The Black Panther and Young Lords parties saw U.S. urban ghettos not just as communities but as "internal colonies" striving to liberate themselves, as Africa's independent nations had recently done. New York's Black Panthers chapters organized in 1968 and provided free breakfasts, health clinics, and support for the burgeoning "community-control" movement among parents of schoolchildren and other public-service recipients. Extending this strategy into the sphere of housing, Black Panthers then went into crumbling Bronx neighborhoods, where many landlords had abandoned properties rather than pay for upkeep, and organized residents to take charge of buildings and their maintenance. Finally, with the aid of progressive doctors, the group raised the alarm on a little-publicized but urgent ghetto-housing problem: lead poisoning from peeling paint.[20]

The Young Lords party was a kindred-spirit organization of Puerto Rican radicals, many with experience in War on Poverty projects. In July 1969 they made their street debut with a "garbage offensive," sweeping up East Harlem's street refuse and dumping it at a local highway entrance to call attention to the city's dismal sanitation service. Their subsequent "lead initiative" took on both officials and landlords, as party members "liberated" forty thousand lead-testing kits that the city had warehoused and took them door-to-door in East Harlem to publicize the poison epidemic.[21]

Notwithstanding their macho iconography, both the Black Panthers and Young Lords organizations in New York featured a number of women leaders who focused on housing actions. Prominent Black Panther Afeni Shakur organized tenant takeovers in neglected buildings in the Bronx, as did Cleo Silvers, a fellow party member who had begun housing work as a War on Poverty volunteer. Amid turmoil in the local Black Panther chapter, she was "transferred" in 1970 into the Young Lords, where she joined Iris Morales, Denise Oliver, and Gloria Cruz, all strong feminists, in working on lead-paint and healthcare problems.[22]

Casa Libre

Sound healthcare, clean streets, safe walls, and open parks: these made up a sum of wholesome living conditions that New York's ghetto residents, through their late-1960s' protests, claimed as a basic right. But those actions did not address the linchpin of slum economics: New York City's dearth of affordable housing. In 1970 that changed when a new breed of activists, organized squatters, embarked on the "liberation" of housing itself.

The *casus belli* was a new wave of evictions that reached crisis proportions in the late sixties. As slumlords' abandonment of ghetto housing started to garner headlines, sharp-eyed New Yorkers discerned something else below the radar: a surprising number of sound, rent-controlled buildings in New York stood vacant, notwithstanding the shortage. Far from being abandoned, these properties were being deliberately emptied by their owners in preparation for luxury renovation or institutional razing. Because rent control applied only to units built before 1947, landlords could often boost their profits by wrecking older buildings and replacing them with new structures. They could also break free of rent control by converting to co-ops, which sold at handsome prices. Meanwhile they might hold apartments vacant for months or even years.

These conditions set the stage for the squatter movement, which seemed to erupt suddenly in the spring of 1970. Yet the movement was not quite as spontaneous as it appeared. Although most squatters had little experience in tenant politics, they drew on the precedent of recent ghetto takeovers and on support from seasoned tenant leaders, maverick poverty warriors, and dissident city officials. With its strong visceral appeal—putting homeless people into vacant homes made common sense—the wave of break-ins served to dramatize the dearth of low-cost rentals in New York. And where unusually militant organizing combined with exceptional proprietary circumstances, squatters could create lasting homes. Where these factors were absent, however, property rights prevailed, and squatters were forced out.

On Morningside Heights the movement was jump-started by Runyon and her allies in the student left. Runyon knew about warehousing firsthand: by the late 1960s she was the last holdout at 130 Morningside Drive. In 1968 and 1969, Runyon led protests over the hundreds of apartments she believed Columbia was holding vacant. Then she broke into a large apartment in her building to attract further publicity. Some months later the United Bronx Parents—a militant public school alliance that was loosely linked with Silvers's Bronx tenant groups and the Black Panthers—put Runyon in touch with Juanita Kimble, an African American mother of ten whose family had been subsisting in dismal Bronx housing for years. With Runyon's orchestration, the Kimbles moved into 130 Morningside in May 1970, while neighbors helped and a news crew filmed. "More important than anything else," Runyon recalled, "was that they had maybe a half a dozen kids who looked like Black Panthers. Big, tough, shades, berets. Scared the bejesus out of Columbia!" After two months Columbia finally agreed to turn on the gas; a year later it offered Kimble a lease.[23]

As Morningsiders courted the media, another group of homesteaders moved quietly thirty blocks downtown. The area between West 87th and 95th Streets had become an urban-policy battleground after vocal protests prompted officials to designate it for a "progressive" form of urban renewal in 1958. Through the late 1960s a variety of local voices had vied for a say in the neighborhood's fate, particularly its share of low-rent housing. Met Council's West Side affiliates called on the city to declare receivership of deteriorated buildings rather than knock them down. But the low-rent advocates made little headway, and in the spring of 1970 some of them took matters into their own hands.[24]

They called it Operation Move-In. Under cover of night, organizers from a local "antipoverty" group installed low-income families into sound but vacant buildings that the city was planning to raze. These activists were War on Poverty mavericks—people like Silvers and other Young Lords—who had concluded that the urban poor could not win their war by following city rules. Operation Move-In's leader, Bill Price, had ties to Met Council and knew Runyon. Asked to name the tenants' most effective organizing tool, he responded, "a crowbar." By summer the group had 150 families in place. Most were African American or Latino; some had been doubled up or otherwise precariously housed for years. Breaking the law, one mother of eleven explained, "was the only way our family could stay together."[25]

Operation Move-In proceeded under relatively green leadership, but the network of veteran tenant organizers quickly offered support and instigated similar actions around the city. In Chelsea, Met Council founder Wood helped more than fifty Puerto Ricans settle into a vacant building on West 15th Street where luxury conversions were under way. Across town, Met Council and Cooper Square leader Goldin did likewise with a multiracial group. A few blocks north, Goldin's friend William Worthy—a longtime radical and the New York correspondent for the *Baltimore Afro-American*—let four families of squatters into the building where he served as tenant chairman. Meanwhile, Benedict established a "We Won't Move" committee to fight evictions, and Met Council put aspiring squatters in touch with sympathizers who could guide them toward vacancies. The old-timers' neighborhood networks allowed them to call out troops at critical moments, and landlords became overwhelmed by block parties and community rallies supporting the squats.[26]

The movement also won support from networks of radical youth of color. Kimble was helped into her Morningside Heights apartment not only by Black Panthers but also by Young Lords and a cadre of high school students, one of whom fixed the lights and plumbing.[27] Down in Chinatown the radical Chinese American party, I Wor Kuen (Righteous and Harmonious Fists)—an ally of the Black Panthers and Young Lords—placed squatters into vacant units that had been bought up and purged by the Bell Telephone Company.[28]

Squatters, Sisters, and Seniors

Squatter actions sparked particular interest among young, white feminists. On the Upper West Side a feminist collective "liberated" a storefront and set up a women's center where local squatters could "rap, exchange information on various women's issues, exchange clothing, enjoy free dinners, and meet their sisters to organize." Meanwhile, New York's underground feminist journal, *Rat*, devoted extensive coverage to the squatter movement and the larger housing crisis. Photos showed the banners on occupied buildings: "*Territorio libre*," "Hell No! We Won't Go." Editors invited readers to assist squatters, organize rent strikes, and compile a "shit-list" of negligent landlords.[29]

To young feminists, the move-ins were not just an object of sympathy but also a source of inspiration. Founders of the West Side Women's Center consciously followed the squatters' example of "liberating" space for the people. Similarly, a *Rat* reporter who interviewed Kimble argued that the black woman's ties with local militants underlined "the need that we as white women have to define a community for ourselves in which we can fight together and support each other." Kimble, a veteran of many battles with housing, school, and welfare authorities, described women's role in the struggle this way: "I just feel that a woman is more stronger. . . . She can take more, she can do more[;] a man . . . don't have the ability to fight. . . . Women are being turned down, but we *demand*." The reporter quoted Kimble at length to drive home the lessons for *Rat*'s predominantly white, female readers.[30]

These squatter-sister interactions cast light on a subtle pattern of connection between New York's tenant history and its feminist upsurge of the early 1970s. Although women's liberation sprang from many sources, its New York incarnation drew strength from the city's unique tenant infrastructure. Local tenant groups had maintained a predominantly female leadership in the 1950s and early 1960s. Thus they had carved out an exceptional political space where Old Leftists could carry on their work and women's authority was not only tolerated but normal.

Then the 1960s infused new blood from the civil rights and community movements, complicating the racial, gender, and generational dynamics within the tenant struggle. Relations between the new ghetto organizers and older Met Council leaders did not take the form of simple intergenerational succession: anticolonial radicals like the Black Panthers and the Young Lords hardly saw themselves as Jane Benedict's protégés, and, if anything, they believed they could teach the older, mostly white "housers" a thing or two about making revolution. And women like Silvers and Oliver were more likely to turn to age-peer sisters than to elders for support in demanding gender parity.[31] But the new ghetto movements nonetheless benefited from the legal and political-cultural groundwork—rent control, receivership law, broad notions of housing rights—that New York's Old Leftists had laid, and these movements in turn produced a second generation of female organizers, such as Silvers, Oliver, Shakur, and Morales. Meanwhile, in slightly later multiracial tenant mobilizations of the 1960s and 1970s—the redevelopment struggles on Morningside Heights and in Cooper Square, the squatter struggles in Chelsea and on the Lower East Side—young, racially diverse activists both emulated the Black Panthers and Young Lords and accepted the leadership of seasoned white women organizers like Runyon, Wood, Goldin, and Rand.

As young women across the country sought new avenues of struggle in the early 1970s, many of New York's nascent feminists gravitated toward the tenant movement. The intensity of the city's housing crisis made tenant struggles a "natural" object of interest for politicized youth. And the multiracial character of those struggles appealed to young white feminists whose political touchstone was the civil rights movement. Indeed, the *Rat*'s admiration for Kimble can be seen as a northern analog of the awe that young white women in the South felt toward courageous black "mamas."[32] Runyon encouraged this identification when she called for volunteers to fix up "Ma Kimble's" apartment on Mothers' Day. One hundred students showed up.[33]

Beyond feeling such visceral ties, young feminists discerned economic connections between housing and women's struggles. A *Rat* article entitled "Why Housing Is a Women's Liberation Issue" argued that the city's housing shortage weighed most heavily on women, who rarely earned enough to afford decent accommodations on their own. Consequently they were hard pressed to leave bad relationships or, if they were single mothers, to provide shelter for their children.[34] Through housing activism, the West Side Women's Center collective sought to forge a feminism that went beyond white, middle-class concerns.

Thus attracted by ideals and encouraged by *Rat*, a new wave of young, mostly white women became involved with Met Council and its neighborhood affiliates.[35] In turn, these Old Left strongholds provided a kind of feminist apprenticeship that touched the young recruits both emotionally and politically. Benedict, Goldin, Rand, and Wood were a unique set of exemplars. "I thought they were amazing," says Marge DuMond, who drifted into Met Council in 1971, "and I recognized them as—almost another world. . . . In the way that they would tangle with authority, and the way that they would master the ins and outs of the law, and the history, just in such a rational and bold way. I had not seen women like that before." Claudia Mansbach, another 1970s' recruit, recalls, "It was very inspiring, to see these older women with gray hair. . . . [Before joining Met Council], I didn't have very many models of older women who were vital and powerful and unafraid to stand up at meetings and say what had to be said." Susan Cohen, who came into Met Council while attending graduate school in the late 1960s, echoes these thoughts: "They were wonderful role models, all of them. And they kind of showed you what could be done. In the academic setting, there I was being told that I was a bad risk because I was a woman. And nobody in housing talked about that. They just did it. Here were these women that were doing things that were making a difference."[36]

The pragmatic nature of the older women's modus operandi—their "just doing it"–should not obscure its feminist dimension. Unlike "maternalist" community activists of their day, New York's senior tenant women did not shy away from confrontation with gender norms—that is, they did not claim political legitimacy because they were mothers or because community-based struggles were somehow "nonpolitical." Instead, they recognized housing as a thoroughly political arena and took for granted their fitness to do battle there. They had met the political, and she was them.

If Met Council's old guard thought and spoke little about gender, they were more conscious of race. Indeed, nobody who had been awake through New York's decades of fair-housing and urban-renewal battles could ignore the intertwined relationship between racial justice and housing, and the older white tenant leaders had long histories of supporting civil rights. Further, Met Council's leadership was integrated from the start.[37] However, by the 1970s, Harlem organizer (and former Communist) Bill Stanley was the only remaining charter member of color. He and Bess Stevenson, a church-based Harlem activist who had come aboard later, were highly respected senior leaders; but neither was closely connected to the 1970 squatter organizing, most likely because Harlem was not then a site of warehousing and upscale redevelopment. Thus, the intergenerational dimension of the squatter movement unfolded largely as an instance of predominantly white older women's mentoring a somewhat more mixed group of young organizers, who in turn worked with a diverse squatter population.

Available evidence indicates this interracial movement proceeded far more smoothly, even joyously, than did many other such efforts of the day. Tito Delgado, a young Puerto Rican Lower East Sider, tells of first coming to Met Council for help with his family's eviction case, "and we were *home*." Having stayed on as an organizer, he proudly casts himself as a political descendant of Esther Rand. Norma Aviles and many other Spanish-speaking Chelsea tenants likewise considered Jane Wood to be family. Brooklyn Congress of Racial Equality director (later congressional representative) Major Owens, a black activist who cut his teeth on rent strikes with Met Council, beamed years later as he proclaimed himself "a proud bearer of the philosophical DNA of Jane Benedict."[38]

This interracial comity seems to reflect a pragmatic combination of "not talking about" *and* recognizing the centrality of race. In recounting his first meeting, Delgado emphasizes that some other white people "talked about racism, but these [Met Council] people really felt it." On the one hand, that the white women lived out rather than simply articulated their solidarity appears to have been critical to Delgado's sense of fellowship. On the other hand, Wood famously insisted that all Chelsea tenant meetings be conducted bilingually, thereby doubling their length. Her readiness to counter calls for brevity with an articulated defense of racial inclusiveness—that is, to talk about race—was equally critical to the fellowship she built. In a similar vein, Frances Goldin recalls deliberately recruiting a racially diverse lineup of families for the takeovers she organized and for the leadership of the Cooper Square Committee.[39]

Also important was the older, predominantly white cohort's willingness to play supporting rather than leading roles in cases where people of color had taken the initiative. This happened with the Upper Manhattan squats as well as the Housing Crimes Trial described below. Delgado notes a similar dynamic within Met Council: "[The older leaders] wouldn't preach to [the young organizers], they would just kind of guide them and let them make their mistakes."[40]

As young people took up tenant organizing, senior leaders endorsed the young women's feminist concerns, expressing support for abortion rights, welfare rights, and the women's movement in general.[41] Several young activists were recently-out lesbians who would soon create one of the city's first lesbian-rights organizations, and they, too, found acceptance among older Met Council women. Benedict's and Goldin's own daughters came out, one of the latter using her gender-bending skill as an electrician to turn on the lights in several "liberated" buildings.[42]

Yet although the older women supported women's liberation, they stood apart from the younger cohort in their "practical" style. "They were certainly feminists, all of them," recalls Cohen. "But they *lived* it rather than talked about it, and studied it and analyzed it. . . . The people who were in the [feminist] support groups, I think, were a little more theoretical[;]. . . they would read books, they would discuss them, they would talk about how to change that politically, and at some point they took action." Goldin reflects on this subject in remarkably similar terms. One of her own models in the CP was a woman whose organizing position was challenged after World War II "because the guys came back, and they thought they would take over the leadership. And she said, 'No, you won't.' So, she didn't think of herself as a feminist, but she was a feminist." Yet Goldin stresses that she and her peers did not explicitly address the topic: "Feminism? We were it. I mean, we didn't strive to do [feminist] things; we just did them."[43]

The older women's feet-first approach to action probably owed less to a lack of theoretical apparatus (as CP members these women had read their share of theoretical texts) than to an ideology that cast feminism as one front in a broader struggle. Thus, when a state commission invited Met Council to testify at hearings on women's rights in 1970, the board voted to participate to the extent that they could "include all housing problems relating to women." Similarly, Met Council regularly endorsed other 1960s' struggles, particularly the effort to end the Vietnam War, which was devastating housing funds as well as lives.[44]

What is the significance of this web of connections? It would be too much to say that New York's tenant politics "drove" second wave feminism; after all, feminism flourished in many other towns, none of which had a tenant history on the order of New York's, and it also clearly grew out of such nationwide antecedents as the civil rights and antiwar struggles. But New York was a leading site of early 1970s' women's liberation. It was the place where the Redstockings met; where the National Organization for Women and *Ms.* and the National Black Feminist Organization were based; where Stonewall erupted and the Radicalesbians took form; and where feminist mobilizations were larger and small women's liberation groups more numerous than anywhere else. Clearly New York's feminist movement sprang from the city's larger Left, but that local Left had, in turn, been sustained and reproduced in part through the city's extraordinary infrastructure of female-led tenant organizing. In other words, feminism and housing activism had interacted in symbiotic fashion over many years. The early 1970s' tenant campaigns propelled one more revolution in the symbiotic cycle, providing a reality of "on-the-ground" women's leadership that inspired and supported the next generation of female activists.

Over time, Met Council affiliates amplified the local women's movement by serving as a kind of parallel space, a venue for people who had developed a feminist consciousness but did not necessarily see women's liberation as their primary political project. Although *Rat* supported tenant struggles, Susan Cohen believes that few people took part consistently in both feminist and tenant organizing: "There just wasn't enough time. . . . People who did the feminist stuff . . . might come out for a [housing] demonstration if you called them. But their *thing*, the thing they put their time into, was the feminist stuff. I wasn't part of that. I was the person who put my time into the housing stuff." Yet from housing Cohen reaped a markedly feminist experience. "My [other women] friends, who became interested in radical politics, they went to all their meetings and stuff, and . . . [they said] everything was very equal, except they always got to get the coffee. . . . And they would say [of the male radicals], 'Underneath it, they're all sexist.' And they would complain. With [housing], it did not happen that way, I have to tell you. We did not have that problem."[45]

Our Neighborhoods, Our Buildings

As they amplified feminism, veteran tenant radicals also informed the squatter movement's class and racial ideology. Squatters and organizers expressed a distinctive New York view of housing that braided together several ideological threads: a broad vision of state responsibility; a labor theory of value; and a notion of tenants' "community rights" (similar to black power's concept of "community control"). Frances Goldin, chair of Met Council's Squatters Committee, articulated the state-provision ideal clearly. She called on the city to take over the privately owned squatter buildings and convert them to "public ownership with tenant control," pointing out that city agencies had worsened the low-rent housing shortage by sponsoring urban renewal and luxury redevelopment.[46] Thus, she drew on the leftist tradition of political economy to show that the housing crisis was not just a consequence of private market forces but was a creation of the state. Squatters, for their part, implicitly revived the Marxian labor theory of value by carrying out themselves the extensive repairs that many vacant buildings required and using that labor investment to strengthen their moral claim to long-term residency.

Community rights had developed over a decade of local struggles against redevelopment. Sally Goldin (Frances's daughter) drew on this notion when she pointed out that warehousing was a matter of *community* interest because vacant buildings served as "an open invitation for junkies, thieves and drunks to start hanging around." Similarly, squatter supporters asserted, "We won't let the landlords tear down our buildings in order to build luxury housing that we can't afford."[47] Here Lower East Siders asserted moral ownership—"our buildings"—as a rebuttal to conventional understandings of private property.

The largest squatter action of 1970 took place on Morningside Heights, where Columbia's ally, the Cathedral of St. John the Divine, announced plans for a luxury old-age home that called for razing six structurally sound buildings at 112th Street and Amsterdam Avenue. With support from Runyon, tenants fought the eviction orders and won several reprieves. But by July 25 the Cathedral had removed most holdouts and poised its wrecking ball. That Saturday evening two young men strolled by the site and struck up a conversation with the guard. Suddenly hearing noises behind him, the guard turned to find that two hundred people had materialized on 112th Street and were purposefully entering the condemned buildings. He simply told the decoys,

"Fuck Columbia; I want an apartment, too." By the time Sunday services started at St. John's, fifty families of mostly Dominican and Puerto Rican squatters had encamped in two buildings on the site.[48]

These squatters did not have ties with Runyon or other tenant groups; they had been organized in a matter of weeks—in some cases from the Operation Move-In waiting list—by a handful of young Latinos in nearby Manhattan Valley. But Runyon's publicity efforts had doubtless contributed to the action, and the squatters quickly became a *cause célèbre* among her allies. Met Council led a support rally while students gathered endorsements from politicians, neighborhood groups, and the Young Lords. The *Columbia Spectator*'s magazine ran a long, sympathetic feature that culminated with the reporter's asking the Episcopal canon, "Would Christ have evicted the [former tenants]?" (The canon promised to pray for them.) As a religious institution, St. John's was an easy target for such questions. Indeed, a group of Episcopalians began to press the bishop to compromise, and an insider reported that the bishop's own staff understood the conflict as "the rich against the poor."[49]

Equally important, the squatters showed themselves to be a resolute and resourceful community, carrying out major repairs, developing a democratic council, sanctioning abusive members, and displaying solidarity. These successes reflected hard work and probably shared political precepts. "All of us working in that neighborhood had a political consciousness," recalled one organizer. "We didn't see things necessarily in racial terms anymore, but in economic terms. We were very conscious of all these middle-class people living very comfortably in Morningside Heights—in apartments that a lot of poor people could actually afford." A rank-and-filer noted, "Our people here are very political—the Dominicans, especially. They're all in some kind of movement—or have been, in the Dominican Republic." With the memory of the 1965 U.S. invasion still fresh, Dominicans may have drawn particular satisfaction from "liberating" space in New York.[50]

The St. John's squatters also proved adept publicists. Speaking of the grim dwellings they had fled, Ana Lopez explained to reporters that the families did not object to paying rent but were "tired of paying for rats, roaches and junkies."[51] An anonymous writer posted this verse:

The door was not open
It was locked, tinned, cinderblocked, nailed, spiked
cemented.

They thought in this way to keep the house empty
and silent
And to keep us in the street and in the gutter.
But we came—quietly in the evening—
Boldly in the morning—
Through the tin—the cinderblocks—the nails—
the spikes and the cement
Through the locked door.
And the house welcomed us—
It sheltered and embraced us.
The laughter of our children echoed in the
    hallways—
Love entered the house, and the house rejoiced
To hear again the long forgotten words—
    Mi casa. Home![52]

Resonating with the nascent Nuyorican poetry movement, these lines cast the break-in not only as expedient but as right and just. The image of an inanimate object "embracing" humans suggested a deep force, akin to natural law, at work in the takeover.

The breadth of the housing crisis and its organized opposition could be seen again that winter in the Housing Crimes Trial, a public event that brought young militants together with older activists from Met Council, the Cooper Square Committee, and Runyon's Morningsiders United. Small tenant groups, progressive unions, and black clergy also signed the "indictments." Racial inclusiveness and female leadership were on full display as Met Council's Benedict, the Black Panthers' Durie Bethea, and the Young Lords' Morales sat on the bench, along with representatives from two other Puerto Rican groups and I Wor Kuen. Spanish speakers testified through translators. Intergenerational alliances were similarly visible, with Benedict, then around sixty, serving alongside the young "judges" and Goldin and Rand leading the "prosecution." "Judge" Bethea schooled older witnesses in current argot and expressed judicial approval by saying "right on."[53]

Significantly, the People's Court heard testimony not only from scores of squatters and tenants, but from several housing professionals as well. One former city official acknowledged that urban-renewal plans made little provision for the low-income tenants they displaced. Bill Price, the Operation

Move-In leader, took the point further: "The way the City can do this is by not acquainting the people in the communities of what the plans are in store for them." He himself had spent months futilely asking officials for a copy of the city's Master Plan, until in desperation he had stolen one. (Bethea corrected him: "You liberated it for the people. We don't steal.")[54]

Such strategically placed sympathizers sometimes affected the fate of squatter sites. Thus, it was important that the Episcopal Church not only was concerned with outward appearances but was filled with staffers and parishioners who supported the squatter cause. The St. John's squatters also benefited from a twist of state financing law that ultimately made it cheaper for the old-age home to relocate to a vacant lot in the Bronx—a move Met Council had been advocating since 1968—than to engage in lengthy eviction proceedings in Manhattan.[55] The law, the widespread sympathy, and the squatters' own determination finally convinced the church to scale back its plan and to allow three apartment houses and their tenants—now grown to four hundred—to remain.[56]

Two hundred Operation Move-In families also won a major concession when officials announced that the West Side squatters could stay as long as they began paying rent to the city. Further, the city added nine hundred low-rent units to the West Side's renewal plan.[57] Here the size of the squatter community combined with the city's status as landlord, and its growing embarrassment over the failure of "progressive" renewal worked in the squatters' favor.

In some buildings on the Lower East Side and in Chelsea, as well, squatters reached lasting agreements with landlords.[58] But, in general, properties owned by individuals, schools, and hospitals turned out to be the least successful squats. Some Chelsea and Lower East Side squatters were evicted in a matter of days.[59] Uptown, meanwhile, Columbia ousted thousands of *legal* tenants through property conversion over the years. Runyon and Kimble were exceptions who probably won out as much through good fortune (Columbia's unstable plans for the Morningside Drive site) as through their organizing efforts.

Echoes in a Postradical Age

New York's summer of squatters, however, produced lasting effects that reached beyond the several hundred poor families who secured homes in 1970 and 1971. One involved housing policy. Starting in the early 1970s, city and state housing officials established several programs to provide loans and other support to low-income tenants who wished to rehabilitate their neglected buildings and convert them into low-equity co-ops. These programs rested on the ideological and practical groundwork laid by tenant actions over the preceding decade. The building takeovers organized by the Black Panthers in the Bronx, the garbage and lead offensives conducted by the Young Lords, the "Battle of Morningside Park," and the 1970 squatter move-ins all had made tenant seizure of physical resources a daily reality in poor neighborhoods. Further, the rhetoric that went with these actions—"our community," "our buildings"—had disseminated the notion of moral ownership to the larger public and even to mainstream politicians. In keeping with tenant history, women predominated among leaders of the successful co-ops, where many residents reported that their buildings were "like a family." Researchers theorized that the "household skills" women were socialized to develop—conflict resolution, listening, patience with ongoing tasks—were essential to good tenant and co-op organizing.[60] City-subsidized co-op programs have survived, in weakened form, to this day.

The second long-term consequence of the squatter wave appeared in the sphere of leftist and feminist politics. Squatter mobilizations drew a new generation of activists into contact with the Old Left cohort at Met Council, which welcomed the newcomers and groomed them to become leaders in their own right. "In younger people taking leadership in Met Council," Benedict wrote to the Executive Board in 1970, "lies great encouragement."[61]

This is not to say that intergenerational relations were always smooth. One area of conflict involved what might be called political lifestyle. Benedict, Rand, and their contemporaries came from an Old Left culture in which the struggle absorbed virtually every waking hour. As a CP slogan put it: "Every Evening to Party Work."[62] The senior Met Council women continued to live that way, devoting every night and weekend to tenant politics well into their sixties and beyond. But the young folks could not keep up. Mansbach speaks of "a huge burnout factor" among younger Met Council workers, especially those seeking to balance political activities with family life.[63] Over time, the older generation's expectations fueled a large turnover among young volunteers and staff. Benedict wanted to pass the torch, but she was looking for successors who would keep it burning at her intense level. Young people who could not meet that standard drifted away.

This pattern produced several ironic effects. For one thing, it delayed by many years the changing of the guard that Benedict wished to effect. For another, it meant that while Met Council served as a link between two generations of feminists, the organization also imposed on its members one of the very burdens that latter-day feminists sought to throw off: a standard of full-time work that left few moments for home and family.[64] Yet Met Council's high turnover rate may have *increased* the organization's amplifying effect on feminist consciousness by causing the group to churn out scores of young people who had developed mentoring relationships with senior women.[65] The turnover rate made these "alumni" more numerous than they would have been if a single baby-boom cohort had simply come aboard and stayed.

Over time, these individual experiences in Met Council and its affiliates added up to a larger process of political reproduction that transmitted Popular Front precepts to the children of postwar prosperity. When Benedict and Wood died, their memorials ran for hours as three generations of activists—including grassroots organizers and several of New York's leading progressive politicians and pioneering women—paid tribute to their mentors. Owens's remarks on Benedict's "philosophical DNA" resonated widely. Ruth Messinger, former city councilmember and the second woman to serve as Manhattan borough president, added, "Jane taught me as much about organizing as about tenants' rights, and was a model for all of us."[66]

At Wood's service dozens of Chelsea residents, including original squatters and their children and grandchildren, lined up to testify, in Spanish and English, to Wood's courage, compassion, and monumental stubbornness.[67] "She got that bit in her teeth and she did not let go," remembers Cohen. "And she was very dynamic and very charismatic. And people followed her. It was amazing: one minute I was this naive little shy kid, and the next minute I was getting arrested! What happened to me? It was very liberating to finally put your body where your mouth was. And she gave you the courage to do that. . . . Somehow, you got into it with her . . . , and you just followed. And then you learned the stuff and you led."[68]

NOTES

The original version of this article appeared in *Feminist Studies* 35, no. 2 (Summer 2009).

1. This is a take-off on "actually existing socialism," a phrase various Marxists have used to discuss life in Communist Europe, in contrast to abstract and speculative notions of what socialist society might be like.

2. See, for example, Ruth Rosen, *The World Split Open: How the Modern Women's Movement Changed America* (New York: Penguin Books, 2006), chs. 2, 3, and 4; Alice Echols, *Daring to Be Bad: Radical Feminism in America, 1967–1975* (Minneapolis: University of Minnesota Press, 1989), chs. 1, 2, and 3; and Sara M. Evans, *Personal Politics: The Roots of Women's Liberation in the Civil Rights Movement and the New Left* (New York: Random House, Vintage Books, 1979).

3. "Popular Front" refers to the alliance among Communists, some labor unions, civil rights groups, artists, and liberals that developed in the late 1930s, after the Communist party instructed members to build a united front against fascism with such potential allies. Popular Front participants might disagree over the role of the party, but they shared such goals as empowering workers and fighting racism. On the unsung mid-century organizers, see, for example, Maurice Isserman, *If I Had a Hammer: The Death of the Old Left and the Birth of the New Left* (Urbana: University of Illinois Press, 1987); Charles Payne, *I've Got the Light of Freedom: The Organizing Tradition and the Mississippi Freedom Struggle* (Berkeley: University of California Press, 1995); Irwin Klibaner, *Conscience of a Troubled South: The Southern Conference Educational Fund, 1946–1966* (Brooklyn, NY: Carlson, 1989); Barbara Ransby, *Ella Baker and the Black Freedom Movement : A Radical Democratic Vision* (Chapel Hill: University of North Carolina Press, 2002); Martha Biondi, *To Stand and Fight: The Struggle for Civil Rights in Postwar New York City* (Cambridge, MA: Harvard University Press, 2003); Susan Hartmann, *The Other Feminists: Activists in the Liberal Establishment* (New Haven, CT: Yale University Press, 1998); and Dennis A. Deslippe, *"Rights, Not Roses": Unions and the Rise of Working-Class Feminism, 1945–80* (Urbana: University of Illinois Press, 2000).

4. Dorothy Sue Cobble, *The Other Women's Movement: Workplace Justice and Social Rights in Modern America* (Princeton, NJ: Princeton University Press, 2004).

5. Kenneth T. Jackson, *Crabgrass Frontier: The Suburbanization of the United States* (New York: Oxford University Press, 1985); Thomas Sugrue, *The Origins of the Urban Crisis: Race and Inequality in Postwar Detroit* (Princeton, NJ: Princeton University Press, 1996); and Lizabeth Cohen, *A Consumers' Republic: The Politics of Mass Consumption in Postwar America* (New York: Knopf, 2003).

6. Mark Naison, "From Eviction Resistance to Rent Control: Tenant Activism in the Great Depression," and Joel Schwartz, "Tenant Power in the Liberal City, 1943–1971," both in *The Tenant Movement in New York City, 1904–1984*, ed. Ronald Lawson and Mark Naison (New Brunswick, NJ: Rutgers University Press, 1986).

7. Norman I. Fainstein and Susan S. Fainstein, "The Politics of Urban Development: New York since 1945," *City Almanac* 17, no. 6 (April 1984), and Joel Schwartz, *The New York Approach: Robert Moses, Urban Liberals, and Redevelopment of the Inner City* (Columbus: Ohio State University Press, 1993.)

8. Jane Benedict, interview with author, June 1, 2000.

9. Ibid.

10. Frances Goldin, interview with author, January 8 and February 11, 2001.

11. Benedict interview; Edwin "Tito" Delgado, interview with author, April 16, 2004.

12. Cooper Square Community Development Committee and Businessmen's Association, *An Alternate Plan for Cooper Square* (New York: Cooper Square Community Development Committee and Businessmen's Association, 1961); Goldin interview.

13. Goldin interview.

14. Wood and her husband may have belonged to the CP as well; Susan Cohen, interview with author, June 14, 2004.

15. Jane Wood, interview with author, October 10, 2001; Norma Aviles, conversation with author, June 6, 2004; Tim Wood, testimony at Jane Wood memorial service, June 6, 2004.

16. Ellen Schrecker, *Many Are the Crimes: McCarthyism in America* (New York: Little, Brown, 1998), 386; Wood interview; Goldin interview, January 8, 2001; Benedict interview.

17. Marie Runyon, interview with author, February 7, 2001.

18. Ibid.; "Morningside Park Chronological History," Box 3, Morningside Park folder, Christiane Collins Collection, Schomburg Center, New York Public Library, New York, NY (hereafter CCC).

19. *Morningsider*, January 30, 1964, Box 6, Morningsiders United folder, CCC.

20. Historical Note to the Black Panther Party, Harlem Branch Collection, Schomburg Center, New York, NY; *New York Times* (hereafter *NYT*), July 28, August 5, and September 5 and 6, 1968, March 5, 6, 7, 9, 15, 18 and 23, August 18, and November 25, 1969; *Amsterdam News (New York, NY)*, March 15 and 29, 1969; *Rat*, April 25, 1969; Sundiata Acoli, "A Brief History of the Black Panther Party," http://www.thetalkingdrum.com/bla2.html; and Cleo Silvers, interview with author, January 30 and February 28, 2004.

21. Johanna Fernandez, "Between Social Service Reform and Revolutionary Politics: The Young Lords, Late Sixties Radicalism, and Community Organizing in New York City," in *Freedom North: Black Freedom Struggles outside the South, 1940–1980*, ed. Jeanne Theoharis and Komozi Woodard (New York: Palgrave Macmillan, 2003), 258–260; *Palante, Siempre Palante!: The Young Lords,* documentary film, produced by Iris Morales, distributed by Columbia University Station, New York, NY, 1996; Jack Newfield, "Young Lords Do City's Work in the Barrio," *Village Voice*, December 4, 1969; *NYT*, December 21 and 26, 1969.

22. Silvers interview, February 28, 2004; this apparent paradox (women's leadership amid machismo) was not unique to the New York chapters. See Tracye Matthews, "'No One Ever Asks, What a Man's Role in the Revolution Is': Gender and the Politics of the Black Panther Party, 1966–1971," in *The Black Panther Party Reconsidered*, ed. Charles E. Jones (Baltimore: Black Classic Press, 1998), and Rhonda Y. Williams, "Black Women, Urban Politics and Engendering Black Power," in *The Black Power Movement: Rethinking the Civil Rights–Black Power Era*, ed. Peniel E. Joseph (New York: Routledge, 2006).

23. Runyon interview; *Tenant News*, September-October 1968, 2; *NYT*, May 3 and 4, 1969; "500 Vacant Apts," flyer, Box 6, Folder 14, CCC; "We Just Took One Vacant

Apartment" and "The Story of This Apartment," flyers, 2 May 1969, Box 1, Folder 8, CCC; *Columbia Spectator*, May 4, 1970; *New York Daily News*, May 2, 1970; *Morningside Sun*, May 18, 1970; *NYT*, July 22, 1970; and *Columbia Spectator*, May 10, 1971.

24. Robert Stern, Thomas Mellins, and David Fishman, *New York 1960: Architecture and Urbanism between the Second World War and the Bicentennial* (New York: Monacelli Press, 1995), 725–730; *NYT*, July 21, 1970; and *Tenant News*, January–February 1967, 4; March–April 1967, 4; May–June 1967, 4; November–December 1968, 2; May–June 1969, 2; April–May 1970, 6.

25. *Manhattan Tribune*, May 23, 1970; *Tenant News*, November–December 1968, 2, and April–May 1970, 6; *NYT*, July 21, 22, and October 11, 1970; and *Society*, July–August, 1972, 51. The 1968 article notes Met Council's support for "Community Development, Inc.," likely an erroneous reference to Price's "Community Action, Inc." See Jane Benedict to Executive Board, 29 June 1970, Box 4, Executive Board no. 4 folder, Metropolitan Council on Housing Records, Tamiment Library, New York University, New York, NY (hereafter MCHR); and Housing Crimes Trial transcript, 13–14, Box 8, Housing Crimes Trial folder, MCHR. Price's acquaintance with Runyon can be deduced from his plan to move sixteen families into 130 Morningside Drive.

26. *NYT*, July 21, 22, and August 3, 1970, and December 16, 1969; *WIN Magazine*, September 15, 1970, 4–5; *Tenant News*, May–June 1969, 2, October–November 1969, 3, June–July 1970, 4; Goldin interviews, January 8 and February 11, 2001; and Cohen interview.

27. *Rat*, October 29, 1970.

28. William Wei, *The Asian American Movement* (Philadelphia: Temple University Press, 1993), 212–214; Silvers interview, February 28, 2004; Carmen Chow, "I Wor Kuen in Chinatown New York," *Hawaii Pono Journal* 1 (April 1971): 61–63; Carmen Chow, "I Wor Kuen: Righteous Harmonious Fist," *Gidra* 6 (June 1971); Rocky Chin, "New York Chinatown Today: Community in Crisis," *Amerasia Journal* 1 (March 1971): 13–14; and "Chinatown and Its Problems," and "Serve the People," in *Getting Together* 1 (February 1970).

29. *Rat*, February 6, June 5, July 15, October 6 and 29, and November 17, 1970.

30. *Rat*, October 29, 1970.

31. These women nonetheless drew on the examples of strong older women in their communities; Silvers, for instance, was influenced by her mother and grandmothers (Silvers interview).

32. Evans, *Personal Politics*, 74–76.

33. "Columbia University #3," flyer, Topical Box 2, MCHR; and *Columbia Spectator*, May 13, 1970.

34. "Why Housing Is a Women's Liberation Issue," *Rat*, December 17, 1970.

35. Met Council minutes show a spike in new memberships averaging more than one hundred per month in the early 1970s; Box 1, Assemblies 2 folder, MCHR. Cohen also recalls a large cohort of young women joining Met Council and the Chelsea coalitions during these years; Cohen interview.

36. Marge DuMond, interview with author, February 28, 2005; Claudia Mansbach, interview with author, April 19, 2004; and Cohen interview.

37. See Administrative Box 4, Executive Minutes Folder 1, MCHR.

38. Major Owens, Jane Benedict memorial service, October 22, 2005.

39. Delgado and Goldin interviews.

40. Delgado interview.

41. Assembly minutes, 18 December 1967, Box 1, Assemblies no. 1 folder; Executive Board minutes, 28 June 1971, Box 4, Executive Board no. 5 folder; and Box 12, Legislation 1974/Tenants Bill of Rights folder, all in MCHR.

42. Barbara Learnard, interview with author, March 1, 2005; DuMond, Benedict, and Goldin, February 11, 2001, interviews.

43. Cohen and Goldin, October 31, 2005, interviews.

44. Executive Board minutes, 24 August 1970, Box 4, Executive Board no. 4 folder; Assembly minutes, 18 December 1967 and 15 March 1971, Box 1, Assembly folders; and Executive Board minutes, 6 August 1966, 28 September 1970, and 17 April 1972, Box 4, Executive Board folders, all in MCHR.

45. See Cohen interview. See also Patricia Yancey Martin, "Rethinking Feminist Organizations," *Gender and Society* 4 (June 1990): esp. 193–194. Martin's "outcomes" criterion, in which an organization transforms members' sense of power and possibility, particularly with regard to political activity, aptly describes the feminism of Met Council.

46. *WIN Magazine*, September 15, 1970, 6.

47. Quoted in ibid., 4–5. "Our" also appears frequently as a modifier for "land" and "neighborhood" in all of Frances Goldin's discussions of the Lower East Side.

48. *Morningside Sun*, October 4, 1969, 1, and May 18, 1970, 7, Box 6, Folder 14, CCC; the guard's comment is in Mary Anne Brotherton, "Conflict of Interests, Law Enforcement, and Social Change: A Case Study of Squatters on Morningside Heights" (PhD diss., Fordham University, 1974), 61–64. Brotherton notes that for local residents "Columbia" came to symbolize all the expansionist institutions.

49. Brotherton, "Conflict of Interests," 67, 90; *NYT*, August 1, 1970; *Connection*, November 12, 1970; and Runyon interview,

50. Quoted in Brotherton, "Conflict of Interests," 66, 135. U.S. Marines were dispatched to the Dominican Republic's civil war to thwart the ascension of popular socialist and would-be land reformer Juan Bosch.

51. Quoted in *NYT*, July 27, 1970.

52. Quoted in Brotherton, "Conflict of Interests," 61.

53. Housing Crimes Trial flyers and transcript, 9, 10, 14, Box 8, Housing Crimes Trial folder, MCHR.

54. Ibid., 5, 13–14.

55. Brotherton, "Conflict of Interests," 155.

56. *Washington Post*, November 21, 1971, and *Tenant News*, September–October 1968, 2.

57. *NYT*, June 14, 1971.

58. *Tenant News*, September–November 1970, 6.

59. *NYT*, July 21 and 22, August 3 and 23, September 6, and October 6, 1970, and June 13, 1972.

60. Jacqueline Leavitt and Susan Saegert, *From Abandonment to Hope: Community-Households in Harlem* (New York: Columbia University Press, 1990), 130.

61. Executive Board minutes, 23 February 1970, and Jane Benedict to Executive Board, 29 June 1970, Box 4, Executive Board no. 4 folder, MCHR.

62. Quoted in Schrecker, *Many Are the Crimes*, 8.

63. Mansbach interview; in her interview Cohen also recalled this pattern.

64. Mansbach interview.

65. Sign-in sheets from Met Council's monthly "assemblies" between 1969 and 1974 reveal over four hundred different names, many appearing at multiple meetings; Box 1, Assemblies folders, MCHR.

66. Major Owens and Ruth Messinger, Jane Benedict memorial service, October 22, 2005.

67. Jane Wood memorial service, June 6, 2004.

68. Cohen interview.

15

The Hidden History
of Affirmative Action

Working Women's Struggles in the 1970s
and the Gender of Class

NANCY MacLEAN

In 1993, the New York City Fire Department issued a curious order: no pictures could be taken of Brenda Berkman, on or off duty, inside or outside of a firehouse. Berkman was a firefighter, a fifteen-year veteran of the force. The order was the latest shot in a protracted battle against Berkman and others like her: women claiming the ability to do a job that had been a men's preserve for all the New York City Fire Department's 117-year, tradition-conscious history. The struggle began in 1977, when the city first allowed women to take the Firefighter Exam—and then promptly changed the rules on the physical agility section when four hundred women passed the written portion of the test. Five years and a victorious class-action suit for sex discrimination later, forty-two women passed the new, court-supervised tests and training and went on to become the first female firefighters in New York's history. Among them was Berkman, founding president of the United Women Firefighters, and the most visible and outspoken of the group.[1]

Their struggle dramatizes many elements in the larger story of women and affirmative action, which involved remaking "women's jobs" as well as braving male bastions. What Berkman and her colleagues encountered when they crossed those once-undisputed gender boundaries was not simply reasoned, judicious skepticism from people who doubted the capacity of newcomers to do the job. Repeatedly, what they met was elemental anger that they would even dare to try. Hostile male co-workers used many tactics to try to drive the women out, including hate mail, telephoned death threats, sexual harassment, refusing to speak to them for months on end, scrawling obscene antifemale graffiti in firehouses, and organizing public demonstrations against them. . . . Sometimes, the men resorted to violence: one woman was raped, and a few others endured less grave sexual assaults. Some men even carried out potentially deadly sabotage—as when one newcomer found herself deserted by her company in a burning building and left to put out a four-room fire on her own.

. . . The women found their only dependable internal allies in the Vulcan Society, the organization of Black male firefighters, who had themselves fought a long battle against discrimination in the department. They now stood by the women, even to the point of testifying in support of their class-action suit, despite "enormous pressure to remain silent." The tensions surrounding the entrance of women into the fire department were explosive although women constituted a mere 0.3 percent of the city's 13,000-member uniformed fire force. The no-photographs order from the top, the uncoordinated acts of hostility from would-be peers, as well as the support of the Vulcan Society, signal us that a great deal was at stake. Even in cases less egregious than the New York firefighters, boundary crossing backed by affirmative action affected something that mattered deeply to many men, especially many white men.[2]

Yet, historians of the modern United States have only begun to examine workplace-based sex discrimination and affirmative action struggles such as those of the United Women Firefighters. More attention is in order. On the one hand, disgust with discrimination and low-paying, dead-end jobs moved large numbers of working women to collective action in the last quarter [of the twentieth] century. On the other hand, these struggles produced an unprecedented assault not just on previously unyielding patterns of occupational sex and race segregation and the economic inequality stemming from them but also on the gender system that sustained men's power and women's disadvantage and marked some women as more appropriate for certain types of work than others. "*Work* is," after all, "*a gendering process,*" as the scholar of technology Cynthia Cockburn has observed—and, one might add, a race-making process as well. "While people are working, they are not just producing goods and services," Cockburn argues, "they are also producing *culture.*" Similarly, Ava Baron has pushed labor historians to "think of gender not only as a noun but also as a verb" and to examine how "gender is created not simply outside production but also within it." These observations complement the argument in recent feminist and cultural theory that gender and race are constituted through performance. Gender identities and ideologies, the philosopher Judith Butler maintains, gain their power through "*a stylized repetition of acts.*"[3] In effect, struggles against discrimination and for affirmative action interrupted these repetitious performances in one key locale—the workplace—exposing in the process how the cycle worked and how it changed in different settings.

In challenging discrimination and demanding affirmative action, in fact, the struggles described here redefined gender, race, and class by undermining associations built up over more than a century. . . . These associations led women and men to have some sharply different experiences of what it meant to be working class. And although my focus here is on the transformation in class and gender specifically, race is deeply embedded in both of these categories and in the associations they carry, if not always accessible in the extant sources. Wage-earning women in 1965, for example, could not expect that the jobs available to them would pay enough to live in modest comfort, certainly not with children; they could expect to have to provide personal services to the men in their workplaces, to clean up after them, and to endure demeaning familiarities from them as a condition of employment. Working-class white men, by contrast, had their own indignities to endure. But they might at least hope for a job that would provide a "family wage," and they could expect that no boss or co-worker would ask them to do domestic chores or grope them on the job.[4]

Antidiscrimination and affirmative action struggles challenged this system of expectations and the patterns of inequality it perpetuated. Time and again, the system-recasting properties of affirmative action proved necessary to ensure equal treatment. Breaking down job ghettos and the habits that kept them in place required new practices such as wider advertising of job openings, recruitment from new sources, the analysis of jobs to determine skill requirements, the setting up of training programs to teach those skills, and in some cases the setting of specific numerical goals and timetables for recruiting and promoting women (impugned misleadingly by critics as "quotas"). By performing old work in new ways and by breaking into jobs formerly closed to them, the women involved in these efforts began, in effect, to reconstitute gender, and with it class, permanently destabilizing the once-hegemonic distinction between "women's work" and "men's work." To reconstitute is not to root out, of course. . . . Yet the *meaning* of particular class positions and experiences has shifted with the entrance of minority men and women of all groups in ways that demand attention. That we have forgotten how dramatic and radical a departure this was is a tribute to the success of their efforts.

Concentrating so heavily on gender and class in a discussion of affirmative action will strike many readers as odd and with good reason. . . . Indeed, so single-mindedly do contemporary critics of affirmative action focus on Blacks that one would never know from their arguments that the policy has served other groups. . . . Rather than accept the terms of debate used by affirmative action critics, then, this work seeks to bring into discussion another key group involved in the modern struggle against employment discrimination and the responses its members encountered. Recovering women's relationship to affirmative action also seems important in its own right, because women—especially white women—are so often cast as "free riders" in the discourse, as passive beneficiaries living off the labors of others. This article aims to combat the historical amnesia which makes that image possible and to recognize in the process the cross-racial coalitions built among working-class women at a time when few of their more affluent counterparts yet saw this as a priority.

The curious lack of communication between two subfields of women's history, the women's movement and labor history, contributes to this historical amnesia. Recent accounts of the rise of modern feminism depart little from the storyline . . . [that] stars white middle-class women triangulated between the pulls of liberal, radical/cultural, and socialist feminism. . . .[5] Labor historians . . . have been chipping away at this orthodoxy almost as long as it has been in place, by drawing attention to the distinctive concerns and activism of working-class women, among them Black women and other women of color. . . . Dorothy Sue Cobble has pointed out that contrary to its popular image as the nadir of feminism, the postwar period was a time of exciting new initiatives on the part of working-class women in unions. "If feminism is taken to be a recognition that women as a sex suffer inequalities and a commitment to the elimination of these sex-based hierarchies," argued Cobble, "then the struggles of union women for pay equity and for mechanisms to lessen the double burden of home and work should be as central to the history of twentieth-century feminism as the battle for the enactment of the Equal Rights Amendment."[6] . . .

This article seeks to extend and complicate the story of wage-earning women's contribution to modern feminism by pushing the analysis into a

new era, when boundaries were becoming more porous and open to crossing. For all that working-class women questioned before the mid-1960s, one
institution had remained sacrosanct: the sexual division of labor. . . . Even
where activists in NALC [Negro American Labor Congress] and the National
Association for the Advancement of Colored People fought to open jobs to
Black women, they targeted only white "women's jobs" well into the 1960s,
ignoring the better-paying jobs occupied by white men. Similarly, female
union activists—Black and white—concentrated on improving the jobs
women already held. . . . "We never questioned it when they posted female
and male jobs," recalled one such activist years later, "we didn't realize it was
discrimination." . . . [7]

In what follows, I will sketch out a preliminary reading of the story of
women and affirmative action, focusing on three types of collective action
that became widespread in the 1970s. In the first type, a decentralized mass
movement arose as working women across the country took hold of the new
ideas in circulation about gender, applied them to their own situations, and
agitated for change, typically through the vehicle of ad hoc women's caucuses
that involved women in a range of job categories. In the second type, full-
time organizers sought to expand these caucus efforts into citywide organizations for working women in clerical jobs. And in the third variant, individual
low-income women and advocates for them turned to affirmative action
as an antipoverty strategy for women, particularly female household heads,
and began a concerted push for access to "nontraditional" blue-collar jobs
for women. Those involved in all three efforts worked to mobilize working
women across racial and ethnic lines. Although smaller numbers of women
of color became involved in the first two forms of collective action, they
became especially visible in campaigns for "nontraditional" employment.

. . . The first big challenges to sex discrimination in the 1960s . . . came
from wage-earning women in factory jobs, who discovered a new resource in
legislation won by the civil rights movement in 1964. "Although rarely discussed in class terms," the Civil Rights Act's prohibition on race and sex discrimination in employment (Title VII), as the legal scholar Cynthia Deitch
has pointed out, "had an unprecedented impact on class relations."[8] . . .
When the Equal Employment Opportunity Commission (EEOC) opened for
business in the summer of 1965, all observers were stunned at the number of
women's complaints, which made up more than one-fourth of the total.
Some twenty-five hundred women in the initial year alone, overwhelmingly

working-class and often trade union members, challenged unequal wages, sex-segregated seniority lists, unequal health and pension coverage, and male-biased job recruitment and promotion policies—among other things. . . . The protests of women . . . , we can see now, prompted the development of an organized feminist movement. It was, after all, the EEOC's negligence in handling these charges of sex discrimination that led to the formation of NOW, whose founders included labor organizers and women of color as well as their better-known, affluent, white counterparts. . . .[9]

. . . Borrowing a tactic from mostly male, blue-collar African Americans, and taking strength from the general ferment among rank-and-file workers in the early 1970s . . . , women joined together with like-minded co-workers to organize women's caucuses as their characteristic vehicle of struggle. The caucuses embodied, in effect, a new social theory: Blacks of both sexes and women of all races who joined together implicitly announced that traditional class tools—such as unions—were ill suited to the issues that concerned them. In form, the caucuses crossed divisions of occupation in order to overcome the isolation and competition that allowed their members to be pitted against one another. Using separate structures, they fought not simply to achieve racial and gender integration at work but also to redefine it.

Having first appeared about 1970, the caucuses spread rapidly within a few years, one sparking the next like firecrackers on a string. . . . . Having set out to write about "The Ten Best Companies for Women Who Work," a *Redbook* author ended up writing in 1977 about women's caucuses instead, because all eighty of the responses to her inquiry agreed that "no corporation was doing anything it hadn't been forced into, and that grudgingly." Women were organizing in steel plants and auto factories, in banks and large corporations, in federal and university employment, in trade unions and professional associations, and in newspaper offices and television networks. . . .[10] Although women's historians have shown how consciousness-raising groups (mainly white and middle-class) broadened and deepened the women's movement, the importance of these caucuses (working-class and sometimes mixed-race) has been overlooked. Caucuses not only developed a critical consciousness among working women but they also won tangible improvements. Without their efforts, Title VII would have been a dead letter for women.[11]

These early women's caucuses nearly always came about because a few women suddenly rejected some expectation arising from contemporary constructions of gender and class. "*Without exception*," a contemporary news story reported (using italics to drive home the point), "*a principal demand of the women's caucuses is for respect.*" Although the demand for respect and dignity had recurred with regularity in the struggles of working people, now it assumed a clearly feminist form as a way to challenge the denigration of women workers in particular. Time after time, the fresh recognition of some longstanding practice as sexist—a practice usually first identified as such in the course of casual lunchtime conversation among female co-workers—impelled women to organize. . . . For example, when *Newsweek* editors assigned a cover story on women's liberation to a nonstaff writer (the wife of a senior editor), women at the magazine suddenly looked around. They saw that management confined virtually all women on staff to what they called "the 'research' ghetto" and hired only one woman to fifty-one men as writers. Armed with Title VII, they organized, complained to the EEOC, and forced change at the magazine. In another variation of the process . . . , the refusal of editors at the *New York Times* to allow the title "Ms." in the paper led several women on staff to wonder whether "this style rigidity was symptomatic of more basic problems."[12]

As it happens, one of the best documented examples of such workplace-based efforts is the resulting *New York Times* Women's Caucus. . . . Ironically, the *New York Times* had once boasted in an advertisement that one of the leaders, then a copy editor, had a "passion for facts." Now, however, the facts so carefully assembled by Betsy Wade . . . brought less pride to management. The investigation and organizing continued until eighty women drew up a petition that complained of sex-based salary inequities; the confinement of women to poorer-paying jobs; the failure to promote female employees even after years of exemplary service; and their total exclusion from nonclassified advertising sales, management, and policy-making positions. . . . When "nothing happened" to address their complaints, the women secured a lawyer and filed charges with the EEOC. . . . Ultimately, in 1974, the . . . group filed a class-action suit for sex discrimination on behalf of more than 550 women in all job categories at the *New York Times*, including reporters, clerks, researchers, classified salespeople, and data processors. . . . By 1978, management was willing to concede. Settling out of court, the *New York Times* compensated female employees for past discrimination and agreed to a precedent-setting affirmative action plan. "Considering where we were in 1972," said one of the original plaintiffs, the settlement was "the sun and the moon and the stars."[13]

That settlement highlights a more common pattern: in virtually every case where women's caucuses came together, demands for affirmative action emerged logically out of the struggle against discrimination. So striking is this pattern that I have yet to come across a case in which participants did *not* see affirmative action as critical to the solution. . . . Even the Coalition of Labor Union Women (CLUW), loyal to a trade union officialdom skeptical about affirmative action, came out strongly in its favor. Prioritizing seniority over diversity where the two came in conflict, CLUW nonetheless fought to establish affirmative action for women—and to keep it in place.[14] The logic appeared inescapable: if male managers had for so many years proven oblivious to women's abilities and accomplishments and unwilling to stop preferring men when they hired and promoted, and if women themselves could have been unaware of or resigned to the discrimination taking place, then something was needed to counterbalance that inertia.[15] . . .

Time and again, it was affirmative action that women embraced to open advertising of jobs, broaden outreach for recruitment, introduce job analysis and training, set specific numerical goals for recruiting and promoting women, and mandate timetables for achieving these changes, all commitments for which management would be held accountable. The centerpiece of the *New York Times* settlement, goals and timetables, could also be found in other settlements from *Reader's Digest* and NBC, on the one hand, to the steel industry and the New York City Fire Department on the other. . . . As early as 1971, NOW literature was thus proclaiming affirmative action as "the key to ending job discrimination," and numerical goals and timetables as "the heart of affirmative action." Typically, and contrary to the notion that affirmative action benefited only privileged women, these plans covered the gamut of female employees. No longer restricted to clerical and cleaning work, women in lower-paying positions—Black and white—could now get more lucrative jobs. . . .[16]

Yet, the largest single number of wage-earning women—one in three—remained in clerical jobs, and they became the target of another kind of organizing initiative. . . .[17] Seeking to make the women's movement more relevant to working-class women, some feminists set out in 1973 to develop an organizing strategy geared to women office workers. . . . "The women's movement was not speaking to large numbers of working women," remembered Karen Nussbaum, one of the national leaders of the effort; "we narrowed the focus of our concerns, in order to broaden our base." Among the groups thus created were 9 to 5 (Boston), Women Employed (Chicago), Women Office Workers (New York), Cleveland Women Working, Women Organized for Employment (San Francisco), and Baltimore Working Women. By the end of the 1970s, a dozen such groups existed and had affiliated with an umbrella network called Working Women; together, they claimed a membership of eight thousand. The racial composition of the groups varied by locality, but Black women appeared to participate in larger numbers in these than in the women's caucuses, sometimes making up as much as one-third of the membership.[18]

What linked all the members together was a categorical rejection of the peculiar gender burdens of their work: above all, the low pay and demands for personal service. . . . Of the low pay, one contemporary said: "As long as women accepted the division of work into men's and women's jobs—as long as they *expected* to earn less because women *deserved* less—the employers of clerical workers had it easy." Now, however, the women active in these groups insisted on their standing as full-fledged workers who deserved, in what came to be the mantra of the movement, both "rights and respect." . . ."What we're saying," as one 9 to 5 speaker explained in 1974, "is that an office worker is not a personal servant, and she deserves to be treated with respect and to be compensated adequately for her work."[19] . . .

Neither professional associations nor unions, office worker organizations constituted a new model, one that used research, creative publicity, and media-savvy direct action to develop a mass membership and power base. Increasing wages and respect for office workers were their top concerns, but not far behind was securing and monitoring affirmative action programs. From the beginning, organizers understood the problems of women office workers in terms of discrimination: poor pay, blocked mobility, and gender-specific personal affronts—or, one might say, economics, social structure, and culture. They therefore turned to the legal tools provided by Title VII of the Civil Rights Act and Revised Order No. 4 (the federal regulation stipulating that federal contractors must practice affirmative action for women). In the late 1970s, for example, sometimes working with local NOW chapters, all the Working Women affiliates took up a campaign targeting sex discrimination in banks. After distributing job surveys to female bank employees, the chapters held public hearings and demonstrations to publicize the results and prodded government antidiscrimination agencies to take action. Ultimately, these investigations resulted in several major settlements featuring novel affirmative action plans.[20] . . . Perhaps the most famous instance of such efforts involved female bank employees in Willmar, Minnesota, in 1977. When their bank hired a man to do the same work they did for $300 more a month and then asked longtime female employees to train him for a management position, the women balked. After filing charges with the EEOC, they went on strike for a list of demands including an affirmative action program. For months they braved Minnesota winter on the picket lines to win their demands, a fight immortalized in the documentary *The Willmar Eight*.[21]

The Working Women network was distinct from but thus connected to another vehicle used by some contemporary wage-earning women to fight sex discrimination: the labor movement. Prompted by their female members and leaders, who sometimes organized in women's committees or caucuses, the more progressive unions in these years provided growing support to affirmative action in particular and feminist policies more generally.[22] . . . The International Union of Electrical, Radio, and Machine Workers (IUE) developed a model antidiscrimination and affirmative action program for unions that included obtaining detailed information about an employer's hiring and promotion policies, eliminating discrimination in wage rates and initial assignments, instituting job posting and bidding for promotions and transfers, and establishing plantwide seniority in place of departmental seniority systems that reproduced gender and racial hierarchies. For its part, the American Federation of State, County, and Municipal Employees (AFSCME), the public workers' union, pushed its affiliates to set up women's rights committees and to "work aggressively for truly meaningful affirmative action programs" as well as for comparable worth in their collective bargaining contracts.[23] Black women in particular found in collective bargaining contracts effective tools for attacking inequality; they were almost twice as likely as white women to belong to unions. . . .[24] Thus, although many unionists (probably most of those in craft occupations and the uniform trades) opposed affirmative action, some parts of the labor movement (prodded by women and African American men) welcomed the remaking of class that was taking place through the reconstitution of gender and race.

As women's caucuses and office worker groups continued into the late 1970s, a new form of organizing for affirmative action spread: training and placement of women in "nontraditional" blue-collar jobs, particularly in construction. Here, advocates of gender equity came up more directly

against sex-typed class consciousness among craftsmen who by long tradition equated working-class pride and "defiant egalitarianism" vis-à-vis
bosses with, as the labor historian David Montgomery once observed, "patriarchal male supremacy."[25] Feminists turned to the nontraditional work
strategy in the belief that as women got access to these jobs and the higher
wages they offered, their movement out of the female job ghetto would also
relieve the overcrowding that pulled down women's wages.[26] . . . Building on
the reforms wrested by civil rights workers and women's caucuses, the new
initiatives marked both a more self-conscious attempt to relieve female
poverty and a more frontal challenge to the sexual division of labor in
working-class jobs. Two groups came together to make them work. On the
one side, emboldened by the ideas of the times and the start of affirmative
action, some wage-earning women defied custom and criticism by entering
"men's" trades in the hopes of bettering their incomes.[27] On the other side,
stirred by the Poor People's Campaign and the National Welfare Rights
Organization, some female organizers set out to alleviate women's poverty
and change the gender system that enforced it. In both groups, white women
and women of color found themselves addressing racial issues in order to
build class-based women's coalitions.

One of the pioneer organizations was Advocates for Women, founded in
San Francisco in 1972. Its founders self-consciously broke ranks with
women's movement organizations such as NOW that seemed ever more
single-mindedly focused on the Equal Rights Amendment and the concerns
of better-off women. Taking advantage of newly available federal funds,
Advocates for Women began recruiting and training women for nontraditional jobs. . . . The rationale for the effort was to the point: "Poverty is a
woman's problem"; hence, "women need money." . . . But the low-paying
occupations into which most women were shunted wouldn't provide enough
money to escape poverty, particularly to those with limited educations
and work experiences. Advocates for Women reasoned that government-
mandated affirmative action could be made to work for women in the construction industry. Because the skilled trades had long enabled men with
only high school educations to secure good incomes, these jobs ought to be
able to do the same for women—if they had the needed advocacy, training,
and support services.[28] . . .

. . . By mid-decade, 140 women's employment programs were in operation, from San Francisco, New York, Chicago, and Washington, D.C., to

Atlanta, Dayton, Louisville, Raleigh, San Antonio, and Wichita. In an initiative launched in 1979, over 90 of them, from twenty-seven states, joined together to form the Women's Work Force Network, which soon created a Construction Compliance Task Force to facilitate women's entrance into the building trades.[29] Women of color tended to be prominently involved, both as workers and as leaders. In New York, for example, Black women and Latinas helped run United Tradeswomen, and their concerns prompted discussions about how racism and sexism worked together in the construction industry. One result was special attention to the exclusion of Black women from the trades and pressure for their inclusion, such as the 1981 demand that at [a] convention center construction site "at least one half of women hired be women of color."[30]

Even in the Appalachian South, often thought of as a bulwark of tradition, women began to organize for access to the better-paying work long monopolized by men. In 1977, several women who had grown up in the region's coal fields set up the Coal Employment Project "to help women get and keep mining jobs." Within a year, working with regional NOW chapters, they had filed complaints against 153 leading coal companies for practicing blatant sex discrimination in all areas. . . . Women's interest in this work expanded in tandem with their access. The number of female underground coal miners grew from zero in 1973, to over thirty-five hundred by the end of 1981, when they comprised 2 percent of the work force. . . . To women who had grown up in the area, coal was, as one put it, "part of our heritage," it was "part of who we are." "Women go into mining for the money," summed up one reporter: "They stay, they say, because they like it."[31] . . .

If we look at these initiatives in light of theories that gender is constituted through performance and see these women as engaged in performances that revised existing notions of womanhood and manhood alike, richer, subtler meanings emerge. Performing nontraditional work changed many of the women who did it, as did receiving the higher wages once reserved for men. . . . Coal mining, for example, was one of the most dangerous, demanding occupations in the United States; doing it well changed women's sense of themselves. "As I grow stronger," wrote one woman miner, "as I learn to read the roof [of the mine] like the palm of a hand, the confidence grows that I can do this work. . . . To survive, you learn to stand up for yourself. And that is a lesson worth the effort to learn."[32] . . . Other women described how their new work and income altered relationships with husbands, friends, and children, even acquaintances. . . . There were losses along with gains: some women, for example, missed "the sense of camaraderie" they had enjoyed with female co-workers.[33] And for men, too, the entrance of women into these jobs led to adjustments in identity and social understanding. "Some of the men would take the tools out of my hands," a pipe fitter recalled. "When a woman comes on a job that can work, get something done as fast and efficiently, as well as they can, it really affects them. Somehow if a woman can do it, it ain't that masculine, not that tough."[34] . . .

As women in these struggles remade class and gender, they often found themselves tackling race as well: struggle led to deeper learning. Even when women's caucuses arose in predominantly white offices, for example, at least one, and sometimes a few, Black women were usually actively involved. Inquiries into sex discrimination uncovered racial discrimination as well. . . . Many women's groups thus quickly realized the need to establish ties with Black workers' caucuses or informal groups. . . . Groups were also sensitive to the danger of appearing to be taking something away from Black men; some made a point of documenting the complementarity of women's and Black men's interests. The resulting coalitions were rarely tension-free—particularly for Black women, who likely felt keenly the need for both groups and the limitations of each—but they were certainly educational and often effective at bringing greater rewards to the partners than they could have achieved alone. . . .[35]

At the same time, the nontraditional jobs effort enabled even predominantly white women's groups to develop alliances with Black and Chicano rights organizations fighting for fair employment. One case in point is the United Women Firefighters with whom this story began, who won support from the Black male firefighters of the Vulcan Society. Another example is the *New York Times* Women's Caucus, which coordinated its efforts with those of the Black workers' caucus throughout the struggle. Women telephone workers and steel workers engaged in class-action suits did the same. For its part, Women Employed combined with other civil rights organizations to sue the Chicago District Office of the EEOC for negligence in 1977 and continued to cultivate collaborative relationships thereafter. Alliances such as this could alter both parties, making the women's groups more antiracist and making the civil rights groups more feminist in their thinking and programs.[36] . . . Although much more research needs to be done before we can draw sound conclusions about the ways that race operated in these women's struggles, it is clear that working-class women's groups provide important models for feminist multiracial coalition building.

. . . [Obviously] the struggles described here have left much undone. By and large, working women still face serious obstacles in trying to support themselves and their families. As much as occupational sex and race segregation have diminished, they have hardly disappeared. . . . For women and men to be equally represented throughout all occupations in the economy today, fifty-three out of every one hundred workers would have to change jobs. The absolute number of women in the skilled trades has grown, but they hold only 2 percent of the well-paying skilled jobs. In any case, these good jobs for people without higher education, as each day's newspaper seems to announce, are themselves an endangered species. In fact, although the wage gap between the sexes has narrowed, only about 40 percent of the change is due to improvement in women's earnings; 60 percent results from the decline in men's real wages. The persistent disadvantage in jobs and incomes contribute[d] to another problem that has grown more apparent over the last [several] decades: the impoverishment of large numbers of women and their children, particularly women of color. . . .[37]

Still, affirmative action was never intended as a stand-alone measure or panacea. From the outset, advocates were nearly unanimous in their insistence that it would work best in conjunction with full employment above all but also with such measures as pay equity, unionization, and improvements in education and training. Affirmative action's mission was not to end poverty, in any case, but to fight occupational segregation. And there it has enjoyed unprecedented, if modest, success. The best indicator is the index of occupational segregation by sex: it declined more in the decade from 1970 to 1980, the peak years of affirmative action enforcement, than in any other comparable period in U.S. history. As of 1994, women made up over 47 percent of bus drivers, 34 percent of mail carriers, and 16 percent of police—all jobs with better pay and benefits than most "women's work." This lags slightly behind nontraditional jobs requiring postsecondary training: women now account for nearly 40 percent of medical school students (20 percent of practicing physicians), nearly 50 percent of law school students (24 percent of practicing lawyers), and almost one-half of all professionals and managers.[38] . . .

It would be absurd, of course, to give affirmative action exclusive credit for these changes. . . . But . . . it would also be sophistry to deny or underrate that role. It has furthered as well as been fostered by . . . other developments.[39]

Women simply could not have effected the changes described here without its tools and the legal framework that sustained them. There are sound reasons why by 1975 virtually every national women's organization from the Girl Scouts to the Gray Panthers supported affirmative action, and why today that support persists from the African American Women's Clergy Association at one end of the alphabet to the YWCA at the other.[40]

Yet there is a curious disjuncture between these organizations and the female constituency they claim to represent: repeated polls have found that white women in particular oppose affirmative action by margins nearly matching those among white men. . . .[41] The preference for personal politics over political economy at the grassroots has also led many women to interpret feminism in terms of lifestyle choices rather than active engagement in public life. Struggles for the ERA and reproductive rights ultimately eclipsed employment issues on the agenda of the women's movement in the 1970s. And most major women's organizations have come to emphasize service or electoral politics over grassroots organizing, and staff work over participation of active members. All these developments help to explain why today there is so little in the way of a well-informed, mobilized, grassroots female constituency for affirmative action—a vacuum that, in turn, has made the whole policy more vulnerable to attack.

Surely another reason, however, for the paradoxical gulf between national feminist organizations and grassroots sentiment on this issue is the historical amnesia that has obliterated the workplace-based struggles of the modern era from the collective memory of modern feminism—whether women's caucuses, clerical worker organizing, the fight for access to nontraditional jobs, or union-based struggles. . . . This disregard is especially ironic in that such struggles likely contributed more than we realize to our own era's heightened consciousness concerning the social construction and instability of the categories of gender, race, and class. Activists, that is, had begun the task of denaturalizing these categories and their associated hierarchies well before academics took up the challenge. If historians have now begun excavating the buried traditions of working-class women that can help us rethink the trajectories of modern feminism, there are still many, many more stories to be uncovered.

These stories have implications for how we approach the future as well as the past. As a . . . gathering of feminist practitioners and scholars concluded: "We need to enlarge [our idea of] what counts as theory."

Convened by the pioneering feminist economist Heidi Hartmann, the discussants revealed unanimous frustration at how theory has come to be equated exclusively with deconstruction, and how that constricted definition, in turn, has steered many people—especially but not only nonacademic feminists—"away from theory."[42] It need not be this way. Practical struggles such as those over employment discrimination and affirmative action can advance the project of enlarging the purview of feminist theory, for they raise a host of critical questions—questions about the meaning and effects of different sexual divisions of labor; about the sources of collective consciousness and action among working women in the postwar period; about the relationships among sex discrimination and class and racial oppression; about how workplace-based performance affects consciousness and social relations; and about the connections between capitalism, labor, and state policy in the shaping of our lives. Above all, they remind us to think about change, and the agency and power needed for it. A feminist theory that began to tackle such issues might find that it had more to say to the majority of U.S. women, whose foremost concerns, as they try to tell us over and over again, are economic (defining economic expansively). This is not an argument to suppress sexual politics, ignore reproductive rights, or avoid questions of culture and subjectivity. . . . It is to say that attention to other, neglected issues—issues of economic inequality, employment, and class foremost among them—could enrich historical scholarship on the women's movement and invigorate feminist theory and practice. Attention to employment issues and broader economic concerns could also focus the current interest in diversity on the arena where it ultimately matters most: the search for solid ground for alliances across differences to win changes that would enhance all our lives.[43]

NOTES

The original version of this essay appeared in *Feminist Studies* 25, no. 1 (Spring 1999).

I am grateful to many people for their contributions to this article, but some deserve special mention: thanks to Nicki Beisel, Laura Hein, Bruce Orenstein, the members of the Newberry American Social History Seminar, and the anonymous readers for *Feminist Studies* for their helpful questions and suggestions, as well as the Institute for Policy Research at Northwestern University for research support.

1. The information in this and the two subsequent paragraphs is compiled from multiple documents, too numerous for individual citation, all found in United Women Firefighters Papers, box 4, First Women Firefighters of New York City Collection, Robert F. Wagner Labor Archives, New York University, New York.

2. Brenda Berkman to David J. Floyd, 23 December 1983, box 4, United Women Firefighters Papers. Of course, some individual white men supported women in these struggles and some individual Black men proved hostile. For an excellent ethnographic account of the variety of male responses in one workplace in the skilled trades and why this makes leadership from management and unions especially important, see Brigid O'Farrell and Suzanne Moore, "Unions, Hard Hats, and Women Workers," in *Women and Unions: Forming a Partnership*, ed. Dorothy Sue Cobble (Ithaca, NY: ILR Press, 1993), 69–84. See also Marian Swerdlow, "Men's Accommodations to Women Entering a Nontraditional Occupation: A Case of Rapid Transit Operatives," *Gender & Society* 3 (September 1989): 386; and Jean Reith Shroedel, *Alone in a Crowd: Women in the Trades Tell Their Stories* (Philadelphia: Temple University Press, 1985), 39, 57–59, 62, 170, 196–197, 208.

3. Cynthia Cockburn, *Machinery of Dominance: Women, Men, and Technical Know-How* (London: Pluto Press, 1985), 167–168; Ava Baron, "Gender and Labor History: Learning from the Past, Looking to the Future," in *Work Engendered: Toward a New History of American Labor*, ed. Ava Baron (Ithaca, NY: Cornell University Press, 1991), 36, 37; Judith Butler, *Gender Trouble: Feminism and the Subversion of Identity* (New York: Routledge, 1990), 140; see also 25 and 136. On race making, see Thomas C. Holt, "Marking: Race, Race-Making, and the Writing of History," *American Historical Review* 100 (February 1995): 1–20.

4. For an incisive discussion of how gender and class have come to constitute one another over a several-thousand-year period, see Gerda Lerner, "Re-thinking Class; ReThinking Race," in her *Why History Matters: Life and Thought* (New York: Oxford University Press, 1998). For an important early statement, see the editors' introduction to Rosalyn Baxandall, Linda Gordon, and Susan Reverby, eds., *America's Working Women: A Documentary History* (New York: Vintage Books, 1976), xxii. My intent here is not to discount the class oppression that wage-earning men endured but, rather, to highlight how gender differentiated the forms of that oppression as well as experiences of it and ideas about it.

5. For the path-breaking origins story, see Sara M. Evans, *Personal Politics: The Roots of Women's Liberation in the Civil Rights Movement and the New Left* (New York: Random House, Vintage Books, 1979); also, William H. Chafe, *The American Woman: Her Changing Social, Economic, and Political Roles, 1920–1970* (New York: Oxford University Press, 1972).

6. Dorothy Sue Cobble, "Recapturing Working-Class Feminism: Union Women in the Postwar Era," in *Not June Cleaver: Women and Gender in Postwar America, 1945–1960*, ed. Joanne Meyerowitz (Philadelphia: Temple University Press, 1994). See also the pioneering work of Alice Kessler-Harris, *Out to Work: A History of Wage-Earning Women in the United States* (New York: Oxford University Press, 1982); Ruth Milkman, ed., *Women, Work, and Protest: A Century of U.S. Women's Labor History* (New York: Routledge, 1985), 259–322; and Nancy F. Gabin, *Feminism in the Labor Movement: Women and the United Auto Workers, 1935–1975* (Ithaca, NY: Cornell University Press, 1990); also, Daniel Horowitz, "Rethinking Betty Friedan and *The Feminine Mystique*: Labor Union Radicalism and Feminism in Cold War America," *American Quarterly* 48 (March 1996): 1–42.

7. Negro American Labor Congress, minutes, 28 April 1959, and 16 December 1963, box 4, James Haughton Papers, Manuscripts Division, Schomburg Center for Research in Black Culture, New York Public Library, New York; Mary Callahan of the International Union of Electrical, Radio, and Machine Workers, quoted in Cobble, "Recapturing Working-Class Feminism," 68.

8. Cynthia Deitch, "Gender, Race, and Class Politics and the Inclusion of Women in Title VII of the 1964 Civil Rights Act," *Gender & Society* 7 (June 1993): 198.

9. Interview with Alice Peurala in Brigid O'Farrell and Joyce L. Kornbluh, *Rocking the Boat: Union Women's Voices, 1915–1975* (New Brunswick, NJ: Rutgers University Press, 1996), 268, and Dennis A. Deslippe, "Organized Labor, National Politics, and Second-Wave Feminism in the United States, 1965–1975," *International Labor and Working-Class History* 49 (Spring 1996): 147, 150.

10. Mary Scott Welch, "How Women Just Like You Are Getting Better Jobs," *Redbook*, September 1977. See also Philip S. Foner, *Women and the American Labor Movement* (New York: Free Press, 1980), 2: 542–543; O'Farrell and Kornbluh, *Rocking the Boat*, interview with Peurala, 274–276.

11. One recent study has found in such caucuses the predominant form of gender-conscious activism among women in the 1980s. See Mary Fainsod Katzenstein, "Feminism within American Institutions: Unobtrusive Mobilization in the 1980s," *Signs* 16 (Autumn 1990): 27–54.

12. Susan Davis, "Organizing from Within," *Ms.*, August 1972, 96. On the start of the *New York Times* Women's Caucus, see Grace Glueck's typescript notes for speech at American Palace Theater, 26 October 1978, box 1, *New York Times* Women's Caucus Papers, Schlesinger Library, Radcliffe College, Cambridge. MA (hereafter, NYTWC). For other efforts, see Jewell George (for NBC's Women's Committee for Equal Employment Opportunity) to Jill Ruckelshaus, 7 November 1973, box 18, GEN HU 2–2, White House Central Files, Nixon Presidential Materials, National Archives and Records Administration, College Park, MD. Also, Media Report to Women 2 (1 December 1974); "Sexism Scorecard," *MORE*, October 1977; and NBC Women's Committee, press release, "Network Women Meet," 18 December 1972, all in box 1, NYTWC. See also Welch, "How Women Just Like You Are Getting Better Jobs." For the grievances and experiences of other women involved in like efforts, see Jean Tepperman, *Not Servants, Not Machines: Office Workers Speak Out* (Boston: Beacon Press, 1976), 1–38, 69–93.

13. For the attitude toward classified sales people, see Betsy Wade to Grace, Joan, Harriet, and Howard, 22 August 1974, and Glueck notes for speech, both in box 1, NYTWC. For follow-up, see Joan Cook, "Notes on Telephone Conversation with [Attorney] Harriet Rabb," 2 April 1980, box 1, NYTWC. Discussion in this paragraph is based on a large number of documents in the NYTWC Papers, but see, in particular, the text of Elizabeth Boylan et al., *Plaintiffs v. The "New York Times,"* Defendant, U.S. District Ct., Southern District of New York, 74 Civ. 4891, Judge Werker, and the expert witness depositions in box 1; "Betsy Wade, a Fondness for Facts," clipping of advertisement, ca. 1962, box 2; Betsy Wade to Grace Glueck and Joan Cook, 19 August [1974], box 1; Betsy Wade to Yetta Riesel, 30 May 1974, box 1; Members of

the Negotiating Committee to All Women at the *New York Times*, December 1974, box 1, and "The Other Side of It," Spring 1977, 1, box 1; "The Times Settles Sex Bias Suit Filed by Female Workers in U.S. Court," *New York Times*, November 21, 1978, B7; Marion Knox, "Women and the Times," *Nation* 9 (December 1978): 635–637; typescript history, "Times Caucus," n.d. [1975], NYTWC. See also Lindsay Van Gelder, "Women vs. the *New York Times*," *Ms.*, September 1978, 66ff.

14. On AT&T and steel, see O'Farrell and Kornbluh, *Rocking the Boat*, interview with Peurala, 250–251, 257, 274; Foner, *Women and the American Labor Movement*, 54; on NBC, see Welch, "How Women Just Like You Are Getting Better Jobs." For CLUW's support for affirmative action and other gender-conscious policies, see resolution adopted by CLUW National Coordinating Committee, Houston, 31 May 1975, box 37; CLUW, "Convention Call to the Third Biennial Convention of the Coalition of Labor Union Women . . . and a Conference on Affirmative Action," Chicago, 22–25 March 1984; and Committee to Defend Affirmative Action, "Affirmative Action: Model Resolution," box 75, all in Coalition of Labor Union Women Records, Archives of Labor and Urban Affairs, Wayne State University, Detroit (hereafter CLUW Papers). For Union Women's Alliance to Gain Equality (WAGE)'s support, see Foner, *Women and the American Labor Movement*, 500, 514, 518, also 525–527.

15. For a discussion of the securing and monitoring of affirmative action plans as the raison d'être of women's caucuses, see Carla Lofberg Valenta, "Change from Below: Forming a Women's Caucus," *Women's Work* 2 (October 1976): 26–31. See also Davis, "Organizing from Within," 94–96.

16. See "Fact Sheet: Boylan v. *New York Times*," and press release, 6 October 1978, both in box 1, NYTWC; Welch, "How Women Just Like You Are Getting Better Jobs"; NOW, "Affirmative Action: The Key to Ending Job Discrimination," 28 April 1971, box 44, National Organization for Women Papers, Schlesinger Library, Radcliffe College, Cambridge, MA (hereafter NOW Papers); Lucy Komisar, in *NOW York Woman*, July 1971, 1. For the prevalence of affirmative action in major media sex-discrimination settlements, see "Sexism Scorecard." For other examples, see Ruth I. Smith (for National Association of Bank Women) to Robert J. Lipshutz, 20 February 1978, box FG-183, FG 123, White House Central Files, Jimmy Carter Presidential Library, Atlanta; Susan Ells (of Polaroid) to Lynn Darcy, 20 September 1974, box 18, NOW Papers.

17. Roberta Goldberg, *Organizing Women Office Workers: Dissatisfaction, Consciousness, and Action* (New York: Praeger, 1983), 22.

18. Quotation from David Plotke, "Women Clerical Workers and Trade Unionism: Interview with Karen Nussbaum," *Socialist Review*, no. 49 (January–February 1980): 151. See also Tepperman, *Not Servants, Not Machines*, 69, 79, 81, 88; Nancy Seifer and Barbara Wertheimer, "New Approaches to Collective Power: Four Working Women's Organizations," in *Women Organizing: An Anthology*, ed. Bernice Cummings and Victoria Schuck (London: Scarecrow Press, 1979). For an excellent, critical history of one such office workers' group, see Judith Sealander and Dorothy Smith, "The Rise and Fall of Feminist Organizations in the 1970s: Dayton as a Case Study," in *Women, Class, and the Feminist Imagination: A Socialist-Feminist Reader*, ed. Karen V. Hansen and Ilene J. Philipson (Philadelphia: Temple University Press,

1990), 239–257, originally published in *Feminist Studies* 12 (Summer 1986): 321–341. On racial composition, see Goldberg, *Organizing Women Office Workers*, 41, 97.

19. Tepperman, *Not Servants, Not Machines*, 66, 81.

20. Plotke, "Women Clerical Workers and Trade Unionism," 153–156; Sealander and Smith, "The Rise and Fall of Feminist Organizations in the 1970s," 245–246. For detailed reports on discrimination in banking, see Council on Economic Priorities, *Economic Priorities Report*, September-October 1972, 3–29; Carol S. Greenwald, "Banks Should Stop Discriminating against Women in Employment," *Bankers' Magazine* 155 (Summer 1974): 74–79.

21. See, for example, Women Employed, *The Status of Equal Employment Opportunity Enforcement: An Assessment of Federal Agency Enforcement Performance—OFCCP and EEOC* (Chicago: Women Employed, 1980). On the Willmar events, see Foner, *Women and the American Labor Movement*, 491–492.

22. On the way that office worker organizations sometimes spun off union locals, such as the Service Employees International Union Local 925 in Boston, see Plotke, "Women Clerical Workers and Trade Unionism." For the story of one longstanding women's committee in an International Union of Electrical, Radio, and Machine Workers factory local, see Alex Brown and Laurie Sheridan, "Pioneering Women's Committee Struggles with Hard Times," *Labor Research Review*, no. 11 (Spring 1988): 63–77. See also Deborah E. Bell, "Unionized Women in State and Local Government," and Ruth Milkman, "Women Workers, Feminism, and the Labor Movement since the 1960s," both in *Women, Work, and Protest: A Century of U.S. Women's Labor History*, ed. Ruth Milkman (New York: Routledge, 1985); Union WAGE, *Organize! A Working Women's Handbook* (Berkeley: Union WAGE Educational Committee, September 1975).

23. National Office to National Executive Board "Affirmative Action" Committee, 9 March 1979, box 49, CLUW Papers. See also "IUE's Check List on Sex Discrimination," box 4, American Federation of State, County, and Municipal Employees Program Development Department Records, Archives of Labor and Urban Affairs, Wayne State University, Detroit; Winn Newman to David Brody, 13 July 1976, and Paul Jennings to John H. Powell Jr., 27 September 1974, both in box 84, Center for National Policy Review Papers, Manuscripts Division, Library of Congress, Washington, DC (hereafter AFSCME); Winn Newman and Carole W. Wilson, "The Union Role in Affirmative Action," *Labor Law Journal* 32 (June 1981): 322–342.

24. See, for example, "Black Women in the Labor Movement: Interviews with Clara Day and Johnnie Jackson," *Labor Research Review*, no. 11 (Spring 1988): 80, 82. The best single reference on CLUW and Union WAGE is Foner, *Women and the American Labor Movement*, 506, 497–501. On Union WAGE's support for affirmative action, see Union WAGE, "Purpose and Goals," in *Organize!*, 21.

25. David Montgomery, *Workers' Control in America: Studies in the History of Work, Technology, and Labor Struggles* (New York: Cambridge University Press, 1979), 13. See also Joshua B. Freeman, "Hardhats: Construction Workers, Manliness, and the 1970 Pro-war Demonstrations," *Journal of Social History* 26 (Summer 1993).

Working-class men were by no means alone or singular in their resistance to women's entry into their occupations. For the hostility of male lawyers, which the authors attribute to "a distinctive professional ethos," see Bradley Soule and Kay Standley, "Perceptions of Sex Discrimination in Law," *American Bar Association Journal* 59 (October 1973): 1144–1147, quotation on 1147.

26. "The Best Jobs for Women in the Eighties," *Woman's Day*, 15 January 1980, box 1, United Tradeswomen Records, Robert F. Wagner Labor Archives, New York University, New York; Judy Heffner, "A Conversation with Barbara Bergmann," *Women's Work*, March–April 1977, 12. For elaboration of the economic argument for affirmative action for women, see Barbara R. Bergmann, *The Economic Emergence of Women* (New York: Basic Books, 1986), 146–172.

27. An example with major ramifications was the case of Lorena Weeks, who, after almost twenty years of "exemplary" service as a telephone operator, applied for the position of "switchman" in 1966, only to be denied it because she was a woman and then harassed for protesting her exclusion. Weeks went on to sue Southern Bell and assist the EEOC's landmark action against AT&T. See New York NOW, press release, 29 March 1971, box 627, Bella Abzug Papers, Rare Book and Manuscript Library, Columbia University, New York. For other examples of spontaneous moves into nontraditional work, see Michael Jett, "The Return of Rosie," *Wall Street Journal*, April 16, 1973, 1; also Lucille De View, "Women Move Up the Blue Collar Ladder," *Detroit News*, July 23, 1972. Why the construction industry became the target is explained in Jane P. Fleming to William Taylor, 29 January 1980, box 30, Center for National Policy Review Papers.

28. Rebecca A. Mills to Anne L. Armstrong, 11 July 1973, box 58, Anne L. Armstrong Papers, and Dorothea Hernandez to Joe O'Connell, 25 June 1974, box 19, both in Nixon Presidential Materials;. On Revised Order No. 4, see Department of Labor, press release, 2 December 1971, box 86, Leonard Garment Papers, Staff Member Office Files, Nixon Presidential Materials. For a fuller sense of such organizations, see the United Tradeswomen Records.

29. For details of their efforts, see Wider Opportunities for Women, *National Directory of Women's Employment Programs: Who They Are, What They Do*, box 2; Women's Work Force, "New Connections," Network Conference Report (Washington, DC, 21–23 May 1979), box 2; Betsy Cooley et al. to Weldon J. Rougeau, 16 November 1979, box 1; Maureen Thornton to Betsy Cooley, 1 November 1979, box 18, all in Wider Opportunities for Women Papers, Schlesinger Library, Radcliffe College, Cambridge, MA (hereafter WOW Papers).

30. "Demonstrate to Demand Construction Jobs for Women!" 5 August 1981; *United Trades Newsletter* 1 (Fall 1980): 2; *United Trades Newsletter*, whole issue, February 1983; Bernice Fisher, "United Tradeswomen Going beyond Affirmative Action," *Womanews* (March [1981]), all in box 1, United Tradeswomen Records. Such efforts notwithstanding, white women ended up with a disproportionate share of skilled construction jobs, a pattern that needs explanation. See Deborah M. Figart and Ellen Mutari, "Gender Segmentation of Craft Workers by Race in the 1970s and 1980s," *Review of Radical Political Economics* 25, no. 1 (1993): 5066.

31. Coal Employment Project, brochure from Fifth National Conference of Women Coal Miners, 24–25 June 1983, Dawson, PA (materials in author's possession); *Coal Mining Women's Support Team News* 1 (September-October 1978): 4, box 76, CLUW Papers; Christine Doudna, "Blue Collar Women," *Foundation News*, March/April 1983, 40–44, box 25, WOW Papers; quotations from Dorothy Gallagher, "The Women Who Work in the Mines," *Redbook*, June 1980, 29, 139. Similar reports came from Chicana copper miners in Arizona, suggesting commonalities across race and region in the ways women experienced the move into "men's work." See Barbara Kingsolver, *Holding the Line: Women in the Great Arizona Mine Strike of 1983* (Ithaca, NY: ILR Press, 1989), 73–96.

32. Gallagher, "The Women Who Work in the Mines," 139. See also Laura Berman, "The Struggles of Tradeswomen," *Detroit Free Press*, August 26, 1979, box 9, CLUW Records. Such testimony supports Kessler-Harris's case that "the wage . . . contains within it a set of social messages and a system of meanings that influence the way women and men behave." See Alice Kessler-Harris, *A Woman's Wage: Historical Meanings and Social Consequences* (Lexington: University of Kentucky Press, 1990), 7.

33. Gallagher, "The Women Who Work in the Mines," 131; Shroedel, *Alone in a Crowd*, 40, 70, 116–117, 129–130, 191, 213–215, 261–262. See also Mary Lindenstein Walshok, *Blue-Collar Women: Pioneers on the Male Frontier* (Garden City, NY: Anchor Books, 1981), 139–153, 256–261, 276; Kay Deaux and Joseph C. Ullman, *Women of Steel: Female Blue-Collar Workers in the Basic Steel Industry* (New York: Praeger, 1983), 128–146. On the sense of loss of female camaraderie, see Pamela Sugiman, *Labour's Dilemma: The Gender Politics of Auto Workers in Canada, 1937–1979* (Toronto: University of Toronto Press, 1994), 194.

34. Quoted in Shroedel, *Alone in a Crowd*, 20–21, also 38–39, 259; Swerdlow, "Men's Accommodations to Women Entering a Nontraditional Occupation," 273–287; Doudna, "Blue Collar Women," 42.

35. Women Employed, *Status of Equal Employment Opportunity Enforcement*, 40; Davis, "Organizing from Within," 93–94; "Fighting Sexism on the Job" (document from a women's struggle in the United Steelworkers, with special emphasis on the victimization of Black women at Great Lakes Steel), in *America's Working Women: A Documentary History*, ed. Rosalyn Baxandall, Linda Gordon, and Susan Reverby (New York: Vintage Books, 1976), 373–374.

36. See, for example, "To All Women at the *New York Times*," December 1974, and "The Other Side of It," 2, both in box 1, NYTWC; Patricia M. Vasquez to Eva Freund, 22 September 1975, Patricia M. Vasquez to Joan Suarez, 9 October 1975, and Patricia M. Vasquez to Vilma Martinez, 21 October 1975, all in RG V, box 38, Mexican American Legal Defense and Education Fund (hereafter MALDEF) Papers, Special Collections, Stanford University, Palo Alto, California; Women Employed, *Status of Equal Employment Opportunity*, 21–23; on AT&T and steel, see Foner, *Women and the American Labor Movement*, 493–494, 541–543.

37. Chicago Women in Trades, *Building Equal Opportunity: Six Affirmative Action Programs for Women Construction Workers* (Chicago: Chicago Women in Trades,

1995), 5; Heidi Hartmann, "The Recent Past and Near Future for Women Workers: Addressing Remaining Barriers," speech delivered May 20, 1995, at the Women's Bureau, U.S. Department of Labor, Washington, DC (distributed by the Institute for Women's Policy Research), 3, 8, 10; "Program and Policy Agenda," 4, WOW Papers.

38. Data from Hartmann, "Recent Past and Near Future," 3, 8, and 10; Institute for Women's Policy Research (IWPR), "Affirmative Action in Employment: An Overview," Briefing Paper (Washington, D.C.: IWPR, 1996), 3–4. On the value of affirmative action, see Bergmann, *Economic Emergence of Women*, 146–172.

39. For assessments of affirmative action's contribution to the changes, see "Program and Policy Agenda," 5, WOW Papers,; and IWPR, "Affirmative Action." For the demise of the family-wage-based sex-gender system, see Stephanie Coontz, *The Way We Never Were: American Families and the Nostalgia Trap* (New York: Basic Books, 1992), and Judith Stacey, *Brave New Families: Stories of Domestic Upheaval in Late-Twentieth-Century America* (New York: Basic Books, 1990).

40. On support for affirmative action, see, for example, "U.S. National Women's Agenda," [1975], box 10, AFSCME.

41. For reports that white women oppose affirmative action by nearly as large a margin as white men, particularly when the question is worded as "preferences," see Charles Krauthammer, "Calling for an End to the Affirmative Action 'Experiment,'" *Chicago Tribune*, April 14, 1995, sec. I, I. Polls taken in the wake of the anti-affirmative-action California Proposition 209 in 1996 confirmed the pattern.

42. Heidi Hartmann, Ellen Bravo, Charlotte Bunch, Nancy Hartsock, Roberta Spalter-Roth, Linda Williams, and Maria Blanco, "Bringing Together Feminist Theory and Practice: A Collective Interview," *Signs* 21 (Summer 1996): 946–961.

43. On the poll data and their implications for feminism, see Martha Burk and Heidi Hartmann, "Beyond the Gender Gap," *Nation*, June 10, 1996, 18–21. For critical discussion of the politics of difference, see Hartmann et al., "Bringing Together Feminist Theory and Practice," 935; also Roberta Spalter-Roth and Ronnee Schreiber, "Outsider Issues and Insider Tactics: Strategic Tensions in the Women's Policy Network during the 1980s," in *Feminist Organizations: Harvest of the New Women's Movement*, ed. Myra Marx Ferree and Patricia Yancey Martin (Philadelphia: Temple University Press, 1995), 124, and Linda Gordon, "On Difference," *Genders*, no. 10 (Spring 1991): 91–111.

16

U.S. Feminism–Grrrl Style!

Youth (Sub)Cultures and the Technologics of the Third Wave

EDNIE KAEH GARRISON

"Grrrl," a word coined by Bikini Kill singer and activist Kathleen Hanna, is a spontaneous young-feminist reclamation of the word "girl." It has proud analogies among many groups of women; in fact, "grrrl" was at least partially derived from a phrase of encouragement popularized by young American black women in the late 1980s: "You go, guuuurllll!" . . .

. . . Riot Grrrl is a loosely affiliated group of young, generally punkish, take-no-prisoners feminists who publish 'zines, play in bands, make art, produce radio shows, maintain mailing lists, create Websites and sometimes just get together and talk about our lives and being women in contemporary society.

–From *Surfergrrrls: Look Ethel! An Internet Guide for Us!*,
by Laurel Gilbert and Crystal Kile, 1996

I've opened with this lengthy passage from Laurel Gilbert and Crystal Kile's book because it suggests something of the contemporary milieu that creates the cultural geography of the Third Wave. By cultural geography I mean the material, political, social, ideological, and discursive landscapes that constitute the context, base, or environment of third wave feminism. Young women who [came] to feminist consciousness in the United States in the late twentieth century . . . [hadn't] gone through second wave feminism themselves. Rather, they experience[d] and [were] affected by it in historicized, narrativized form.[1] As something other than "second wave," the "third wave" can be defined by a different set of historical events and ideological movements, especially the (fundamentalist, Moral Majority, neoconservative,

Focus on the Family, antifeminist) backlash that emerged in response to the women's movement in the 1970s and so-called postfeminist feminism. Part of a larger project that examines the meaning of the emergence of "third wave feminism," this article considers specifically the role of democratized technologies, the media, subcultural movements and networks, and differential oppositional consciousness in the formation of feminist consciousness among young women in the historical/cultural milieu of the United States in the 1990s.

Like Gilbert and Kile, I am compelled by the many different invocations possible with the word "grrrl" and appreciate their spirited appropriation and contextualization of the term. Yet my purpose is not to extend their elaborations so much as to note the rhetorical play of signified and signifier as a discursive device in young women's cultural tool kits. I then turn my attention to . . . Riot Grrrl. Riot Grrrl is a recent young feminist (sub)cultural movement that combines feminist consciousness and punk aesthetics, politics, and style.[2] Recognizing youth (sub)cultures as political spaces and refusing to separate political consciousness from subcultural formations, I argue that the convergence of music, print, and information technologies, the historical specificities of backlash and post–civil rights movements, and feminist consciousness raising multiplies the cultural locations where political activities can occur in the third wave. I focus here on Riot Grrrl because it has been viewed by many who study U.S. girls'/young women's cultures as exemplary of what's being called "youth feminism." . . .[3]

Riot Grrrl is an alternative subculture built around opposition to presuppositions that young (usually white) U.S. girls and women are too preoccupied with themselves and boys to be interested in being political, creative, and loud. The tensions between this expectation and the political desires of members offer a powerful opportunity to learn different ways of resisting in a consumer-oriented culture. . . . The hybrid political texts and distribution networks produced by feminists like Riot Grrrls are significant in the formation of third wave movement cultures; they are both "popular" and subcultural, they provide spaces for youth-controlled conversations, and they can operate as an interface between different third wave cohorts (they connect Riot Grrrls to one another but also to other feminists and women). How do young women in the United States claim feminist agency for themselves and each other by making use of a historically situated repertoire of cultural objects and images, codes, and signs in self-consciously political ways?

Some of the tools that constitute this repertoire include print and visual media; music genres, technologies, and cultures; girl-positive and woman-positive expressions; revolutionary and social justice discourses; shock tactics; nonviolent actions; and the Internet. I use the word "repertoire" following Ruth Frankenberg, to recognize all these objects and practices as parts of the "tool kit" available to cultural subjects as instruments and objects that provide a context and space for analysis and reflection.[4] "Tool kit" is also the image invoked by Ann Swidler to describe "culture" as the "habits, skills, and styles from which people construct 'strategies of action,'" as an alternative to traditional sociological and anthropological understandings of "culture" as providing "the ultimate values" that motivate action.[5] This repertoire is utilized by third wave feminists to raise consciousness about, provide political commentary on, and resist and educate against racism, child abuse, rape, domestic violence, homophobia and heterosexism, ablism, fatism, environmental degradation, classism, the protection of healthcare rights, reproductive rights, and equity. It is a tool kit designed for providing access to and transformations of traditionally masculinist cultural institutions.

In this essay, I concentrate on some of the ways young, mostly white, and middle-class women in the United States use and manipulate the repertoire of cultural-technological spaces and activities such as feminism and punk so they can voice their dissonances and participate in making change. I consider how these young women make use of low-end—or "democratized"—technologies and alternative media to produce hybrid political texts such as 'zines and music through which they disseminate knowledge and information about subjects such as (but not limited to) feminism in local-national distribution networks. I do not assume that activists in the second wave didn't also use grassroots forms of communications technologies but, rather, argue here that the third wave has a different relationship with these technologies[,] . . . an interfaced connection to technology. As Donna Haraway has suggested: "The machine is us, our processes, an aspect of our embodiment." This blurring of the boundaries between humans and machines constructs a technologics through which we shuttle back and forth constantly, disrupting "the maze of dualisms [through] which we have explained our bodies and our tools to ourselves."[6]

A Note on the Presumption That "Third Wave"
Designates an Age-Generation Cohort

This chapter does focus on young women in the third wave; however, I have specific reasons for not believing it is restricted to an age cohort. As a product of a particular cultural moment, "third wave feminism" is historically situated or bound. The name "third wave" acknowledges that feminism has changed substantially in the late-capitalist and postmodern world but still references a longer movement history.[7] Although frequently used to categorize a generational cohort—those who "came of age" during or after the height of the second wave—I believe the question of who counts as the third wave is much more complicated and layered; there are important differences between historical specificity and generational specificity. The "third" is the mark of historical specificity, and . . . not simply a sign of generational descendence. When we automatically assume "third" refers to a specific generation, we actually erase the significant presence and contributions of many overlapping and multiple cohorts who count as feminists, and more particularly, of those who can count as third wave feminists.[8] . . . And because many generational and age cohorts share this historical moment, to limit a third wave to "young women" alone suggests that no other feminists can claim third wave politics. Even more importantly, the emergence of a "third wave" owes a great deal to critiques of the homogenization of the category "women" articulated most directly in the political and intellectual work by radical women of color, poor women, and lesbians dating from at least the second wave. Their opposition to the perceived dominance of white feminism in the second wave is linked to critiques of racism, classism, and heterosexism within the 1960s' and 1970s' women's movement as well as in other groups, movements, and social formations.[9] . . .

The shift from speaking about "women" as a unified subject to a recognition that women are not all the same, nor should they be, is something most feminists, young and not as young, take for granted. . . . This isn't to say the issue of difference has been solved, but difference is a core component of third wave consciousness. Chela Sandoval—theorizing what she calls "U.S. Third World Feminism"—reminds us that there are still racial divides but also new possible racial coalitions within contemporary women's movements.[10] I am not suggesting an easy or homologous correlation between "U.S. Third World Feminism" and "third wave feminism." Sandoval uses the former term to refer to feminists of color who problematize the gender category "women" and the binary "male/female," and for whom race, culture, class, and sexuality are not social categories separable from or less significant than gender. She names a particular constituency as well as a hoped-for coalition. Although I have encountered repeated slippages between "U.S. Third World," "Third World," and "third wave" in many conversations about third wave feminism, the distinctions are important and at no time do I want to either collapse or confuse these terms.

Postmodernity, Oppositional Consciousness, and Feminist Networking

I prefer a network ideological image, suggesting the profusion of spaces and identities and the permeability of boundaries in the personal body and in the body politic.

—Donna Haraway, "A Cyborg Manifesto," 1991

The praxis of U.S. third world feminism represented by the differential form of oppositional consciousness is threaded throughout the experience of social marginality. As such it is also being woven into the fabric of experiences belonging to more and more citizens expressed in the cultural angst most often referred to as the postmodern dilemma. The juncture I am proposing, therefore, is extreme. It is a location wherein the praxis of U.S. third world feminism links with the aims of white feminism, studies of race, ethnicity, and marginality, and with postmodern theories of culture as they crosscut and join together in new relationships through a shared comprehension of an emerging theory and method of oppositional consciousness.

—Chela Sandoval, "U.S. Third World Feminism," 1991

Images of weaving or threading together apparently disparate modes of consciousness, constituencies, ideologies, and practices tie these two passages to one another and suggest a relationship between the concept of networking advocated by Haraway and the kind of junctures Sandoval advocates as a mode of resistance necessary in our particular historical and political moment. To see and recognize such forms of resistance we often have to look

"into the fabric of experiences" outside, beyond, and maybe even underneath the places that we are told have mattered.... Media spectacles in
particular offer new opportunities for the creation of oppositional consciousness. One of the most powerful examples of this phenomenon was the
televised proceedings of the Anita Hill–Clarence Thomas sexual harassment
hearings in October 1991. They had a major impact on young people in the
United States, forcing many young women to "acknowledge that we live
under siege." But it also encouraged them to fight back. Rebecca Walker, a
young African American woman, asserted: "I intend to fight back. I have
uncovered and unleashed more repressed anger than I thought possible. For
the umpteenth time in my twenty-two years, I have been radicalized, politicized, shaken awake. I have come to voice again, and this time my voice is
not conciliatory."[11]

This way of conceptionalizing resistance is central to Sandoval's theory
of consciousness. According to Sandoval, differential oppositional consciousness is a mode of "ideology-praxis" rooted in the experiences of U.S.
Third World feminists. Modernist conceptions of oppositional politics
center on mutually exclusive and essentialized identities. This ideology is
perpetuated, she argues, by white feminists who construct histories of the
second wave as consisting of four distinct categories: liberal, Marxist, radical,
and socialist. In contrast, the differential mode of consciousness offers a
strategic politics wherein modernist oppositional identities become tactical
poses. In other words, a differential oppositional ideology-praxis makes
possible a "tactical subjectivity" in which multiple oppressions can be confronted by shifting modes of consciousness as various forms of oppression
are experienced.[12]

Crucial to Sandoval's project is an understanding of the differential
mode of oppositional consciousness as a "survival skill" that U.S. Third
World women have been enacting, even though it has not been recognized as
a legitimate ideology of political activity. This "survival skill" is, for Sandoval,
a form of affinity politics, something quite different from more conventional
notions of "identity politics."[13] As Sandoval explains:

> Differential consciousness requires grace, flexibility, and strength:
> enough strength to confidently commit to a well-defined structure of
> identity for one hour, day, week, month, year; enough flexibility to
> self-consciously transform that identity according to the requisites of

another oppositional ideological tactic if readings of power's formation require it; enough grace to recognize alliance with others committed to egalitarian social relations and race, gender, and class
justice, when their readings of power call for alternative oppositional
stands. Within the realm of differential consciousness, oppositional
ideological positions, unlike their incarnations under hegemonic
feminist comprehension, are tactics—not strategies.[14]

Distinguishing what Sandoval means by tactics and strategies is crucial to
understanding the kind of move she is suggesting in her rearticulation of
oppositional consciousness. . . . Strategy is an informing ideology brought to
one's engagement with an oppressor or opposing power; tactics are the
moves one makes while engaged with the opposition. "Identity politics," as a
modernist mode of oppositionality, has essentialist requisites which result
in the production of unproblematic essentialized identities as the basis
of oppositional consciousness. In Sandoval's framework, however, identity
politics becomes a tactical maneuver rather than a single informing strategy;
this move allows for the possibility of constructing social-movement coalitions built on less-essentialized or strategically essentialized affinities.[15]
Recognizing U.S. Third World feminist praxis makes possible another kind of
gender, race, class, sexual, cultural, political, and historical consciousness—
a differential consciousness which multiplies what counts as feminist
politics and consciousness. Sandoval claims this mode of oppositional consciousness as a praxis grounded in the experiences of women of color, lesbians, and poor women inside the United States, but she argues as well that
it is becoming a form of consciousness "threaded throughout the experience
of social marginality." Because of "an historically unique democratization of
oppression," this form of consciousness "is also being woven into the fabric
of experiences belonging to more and more citizens who are caught in the
crisis of late capitalist conditions and expressed in the cultural angst most
often referred to as the postmodern dilemma."[16]

I think what can be seen in many of the sites of the formations of a third
wave of feminism is precisely what Sandoval suggests. This third wave is as
much a product of "postmodern cultural conditions" as it is a product of the
first and second waves, or of women's studies, or the media backlash, or
violence. Perhaps it is more appropriate to say it is a product of postmodern
cultural conditions because it is a product of the first and second waves; the

media backlash; violence; and other kinds of historical remnants, products, and monsters. Therefore, the theories of culture that are useful to analyzing the third wave are those that help us to comprehend how young women are claiming feminist identities for themselves in spite of the backlash and the discomfort many feel about popular conceptions of what "feminism" connotes. This discomfort arises in part from the way many second wave white feminists (and later the media) defined feminism to suit their particular historical-cultural circumstances, definitions which are frequently at odds with the behaviors, politics, criticisms, and apparent irreverences of younger women. This may help us to understand how a historical moment called "postmodern" contributes to distinctions between the third wave and the first and second wave women's movements. For instance, the simultaneous confidence and uncertainty about what constitutes feminism doesn't have to be conceptualized as a "problem." Rather, it is a consequence of the proliferation of feminisms. . . .[17]

Another indicator of the "postmodern" nature of the third wave is its reliance on networking among different cohorts of women who compose a movement culture that is disparate, unlikely, multiple, polymorphous. These are cohorts who remain indebted to their predecessors but who are simultaneously irreverent. They all share an interest in exploring what it means to be "women" in the United States and the world in the 1990s, as well as how to resist identification with the object "Woman." Unlike many white feminists in the early years of the second wave who sought to create the resistant subject "women," in the third wave, this figure "women" is rarely a unitary subject. As Jee-Yeun Lee writes at the end of her essay, "Beyond Bean Counting":

> These days, whenever someone says the word "women" to me, my mind goes blank. What "women"? . . . Does that mean me? Does that mean my mother, my roommates, the white woman next door, the checkout clerk at the supermarket, my aunts in Korea, half the world's population? . . . Sisterhood may be global, but who is in that sisterhood? None of us can afford to assume anything about anybody else. This thing called "feminism" takes a great deal of hard work, and I think this is one of the primary hallmarks of young feminists' activism today: We realize that coming together and working together are by no means natural or easy.[18]

Lee, like other young feminists, has learned from the second wave, from critiques made by women of color, lesbians, and poor women, from the backlash of the 1980s, her own experiences, and the neo-, post-, and anti-feminist rhetorics that proliferate in the media today. And the lesson she emphasizes is that gender is not a mutually exclusive category;[19] a feminist politics has to take into account the many differences that make up the category "women" and to recognize that these differences are all part of a feminist politics.

Networking is a critical concept in describing the movement, epistemology, and geography of third wave feminism. Besides incorporating Sandoval's important theorizing of oppositional praxis, this usage also draws upon Donna Haraway's theorizing of cyborg feminism and feminist networks and on Bruno Latour's use of this concept to describe "a new topology that makes it possible to go almost everywhere, yet without occupying anything except narrow lines of force and a continuous hybridization between socialized objects and societies rendered more durable through the proliferation of nonhumans."[20] Networking as I conceptualize it involves a "technologic," a particular practice of communicating information over space and time, a creation of temporary "unified" political groups made up of unlikely combinations and collectivities (i.e., affinity groups or even anthologies), the combining of diverse technologies to construct powerful cultural expressions of oppositional consciousness (i.e., music, lyrics, 'zines, musical instruments, videos, production technology, CD booklets, the Internet), and the construction of feminist politics of location (weaving between and among the spaces of race, class, sexuality, gender, etc., that we inhabit).

"Technologics" also involves a particular way of articulating one's awareness of the ways information travels and the ways our cultural repertoire of discourses, objects, ideas, and modes of resistance merge and regroup in a cultural milieu that is proliferatively technologically saturated and mediated. Not only are we comprised of and surrounded by technological networks . . . , but the feminist praxis we comprehend increasingly references technological rhetorics as well. . . . One trace of this technologics is the rhetorical word games used by young women and feminists that merge identity, politics, and technology. . . . The term "lesbionic," used by Jody Bleyle at Candy-Ass Records, invokes for me a half-machine, half-lesbian (or perhaps a les-bi) figure—maybe a lesbian six million dollar woman—one who makes lesbian-positive music through, from, and for her body/instrument as a form of survival and resistance. Bleyle is also a member of an all-lesbian, queer-punk band called Team Dresch. The group marks its various changes and transformations by employing the rhetoric of software companies who mark advancements in their products by using numerical designations such as 3, 3.1, 3.3. . . . I would also situate within this notion of technologic rhetorics my own efforts to theorize the "wave" in "third wave" as radio waves rather than ocean waves. . . .[21]

"Oppositional technologics" are the political praxis of resistance being woven into low-tech, amateur, hybrid, alternative subcultural feminist networks that register below the mainstream. The term "oppositional technologics" fuses together Haraway, Sandoval, and Latour with my own investments in the relationship between subjectivity formation and political consciousness (in the context of U.S. culture) and the proliferation of communications and visual technologies. I want to argue that this "movement" called the third wave is a network built on specific technologics, and Riot Grrrl is one node, or series of nodes, that marks points of networking and clustering. . . .

The Technologics of Third Wave Consciousness Raising

In a 1993 essay, "The Female Bodywars: Rethinking Feminist Media Politics," Patricia Zimmerman discusses the production of low-cost video documentaries as an emerging feminist strategy in reproductive rights activism that places women and camcorders in a symbiotic relationship, one that allows the construction of cyborg identities. Like Sean Cubit, she argues that "the proliferation of video technologies multiplies the number of sites for cultural struggles."[22] Similarly, in the production of music and 'zines, the proliferation and "democratization" of music technologies (underground and small, local recording companies), print technologies (Kinko's et al., and the increasing availability of computers to young people in school), and Internet technologies (especially as more programs designed for the computer "alliterate" web-page creator become available, and as the cost of the technology reaches levels low enough for mass consumption), sites of political praxis are expanded. Democratized technologies become a resource enabling young women to get information to other young women, girls, and boys, a means for developing political consciousness, and a space that can legitimate girls' issues. Technology that is accessible to young people alters the controlling role of adults and other authority figures in the production of youth cultures and in the selection of political issues in which young people become involved. Beyond its use of these democratic technologies, the production of such hybrid texts as 'zines or girl music frequently resists and critiques the commodification of politically charged youth (sub)cultures by mass media.[23]

Riot Grrrl, an alternative feminist movement emerging out of the alternative punk scene, provides one critical expression of youth (sub)cultures. This movement is as much national as it is local.[24] This is due in part to media coverage during the early 1990s, which exposed many more people to an emerging "new" feminist political movement, challenging popular media insistence that "feminism" was a label rejected by all young women. But it also watered down the political content of the movement by focusing almost exclusively on commodifying the image of "the Riot Grrrl." However, the mainstream media has not been as important in the formation of Riot Grrrl . . . as has the effective and sophisticated networking of girls involved in consciousness raising and information distribution. As one girl, Spirit, writes: "Our networking through mail, the Internet, through music, through zines and through the punk scene keeps us closely knit and strong."[25]

Spirit learned about Riot Grrrl in a local entertainment newspaper in San Jose, California. She says she was attracted to the movement because it seemed to reflect her own beliefs, which she describes as "generally anarchistic, anti fascist, anti sexist, and anti homophobic." She came to understand Riot Grrrl as "punk rock girls having the [same] beliefs [as I], creating a scene alternative to the one that they found themselves rejected by." For Spirit, the punk scene in San Jose "isn't very political or issue oriented," which she explains has made her feel alienated and isolated. Riot Grrrl helped to give her a sense of belonging . . . : "Riot Grrrl—the idea, the movement, the non localized group, whatever—inspired literally hundreds of girls to do zines, start bands, collectives, distributions, have meetings etc. The uprising of riot grrrl has been the only activity in the scene most of us have seen in years yet most of you probably don't know what a riot grrrl is and does, why we face so much opposition or who started it."[26]

The attention the Riot Grrrl movement and its media-appointed "leaders" have received in the popular press has been fought by those who claim to be Riot Grrrls and those who have been labeled without consent as such. They don't take out full-page ads in the *New York Times* or the *Seattle Post-Intelligencer*. They respond to media distortions by making use of more grassroots tactics. For instance, refusing to be identified as the voice of Riot Grrrl,

Tobi Vail, the drummer for Bikini Kill, uses both the liner notes accompanying *The C.D. Version of the First Two Records* and her 'zine *Jigsaw*, to proclaim:

> We are not in anyway "leaders of" or authorities on the "Riot Girl"
> movement. In fact, as individuals we have each had different experi-
> ences with, feelings on, opinions of and varying degrees of involve-
> ment with "Riot Girl" and tho we totally respect those who still feel
> that label is important and meaningful to them, we have never used
> that term to describe ourselves *AS A BAND*. As individuals we respect
> and utilize and subscribe to a variety of different aesthetics, strategies
> and beliefs, both political and punk-wise, some of which are probably
> considered "riot girl."[27]

For me, it isn't so important whether individual Bikini Kill members call themselves Riot Grrrls or if they reject the label. What I am interested in is how they use the resources they have available to them as tools for grassroots girl-positive activism. They are actively invested in a punk and feminist cultural repertoire of music production, technology, performance, instruments, and underground distribution networks. They adopt punk DIY (Do It Yourself) philosophy to encourage women and girls to take the initiative to create art and knowledge, to change their cultural and political landscape, rather than waiting for someone else to do it for them. They work with fans and friends who maintain Internet homepages and various other print technologies used to make 'zines (members of the group have been involved with different 'zines, i.e., *Fuck Me Blind*, *Jigsaw*, *Girl Power*, *Riot Grrrl*).[28] Bikini Kill is a band ... very much invested in issues identified as significant by many third wave feminists. A survey of the topics covered in their songs include racism, sexism, child abuse, domestic violence, sexuality, classism, privilege, sex industries, media spectaclization, AIDS, apathy, girl power, consumer pacifism, rock star elitism, and the commodification of coolness.

Although bands like Bikini Kill frequently refuse to be Riot Grrrl's "leaders," and in fact generally consider it a movement that died out in the early 1990s, Kathleen Hanna does claim some of the responsibility for its spread. In *Angry Women in Rock*, vol. 1, she and Andrea Juno discuss Riot Grrrl as a movement that emerged among a community of friends in response to rioting in D.C. after an African American man was shot in the back by cops. But she also says that it started as a lie—a consequence of her having told a journalist from *L.A. Weekly* that there were Riot Grrrl chapters in cities across the country when there really weren't. In one sense, this leak of false information into the media was a subversive use of the mainstream press to incite a movement—or a "riot," as they might say. And, in fact, almost every city Hanna mentioned in that article had a Riot Grrrl chapter within a year. However, my interest is not to determine the movement's origins but rather to explore its purpose: feminist consciousness raising within punk subculture and the positive encouragement of women and girl artists and cultural producers. In her interview with Juno, Hanna mentions the first notice she sent out through the fanzine *Riot Grrrl* and distributed at performances: "Girls: let's have a meeting about punk rock and feminism! Let's share our skills and put on some rock shows together!"[29] Although she talks about Riot Grrrl from her personal perspective, including the ways she as an individual has been involved, she also tells a cohort story of women (and some men) who got tired of local punk scenes where girls were made to feel the place belonged to the guys. Instead of retreating, they decided to re-create it as their own—infusing it with new, girl-positive, feminist significance to combat the scenes' apparently masculinist roots. Kathleen Hanna was not the only woman involved in the punk scene in the early 1990s who got tired of the sexism, elitism, and violence within the scene and within U.S. culture at large, but she did make use of Xerox machines, music, performance space, and the press to voice her discontent and speak out to other young women. Such public uses of communications technology helped enable a movement of sorts. This movement encouraged young women to see themselves as producers and creators of knowledge, as verbal and expressive dissenters, rather than as passive consumers of U.S. culture or of the punk scene and youth subcultures they helped to define and shape.

For Spirit, who may not know people like Kathleen Hanna, Riot Grrrl is a punk-oriented form of feminism, with all the attendant stereotyping, antagonism, challenges, and fire; but she is also careful to point out that "riot grrrl didn't invent punk rock feminism."[30] Rather, girls and women who consider themselves, their politics, and their issues part of their punk orientation "are simply reclaiming our place/voice in punk rock—a voice we've always had that's been trampled on." . . .

An important aspect of "reclaiming our place/voice" is the formation of collectivities or groups that share common objectives and goals. The formation of Riot Grrrl, one might say, is a "reflexive impulse," a response of young women who recognize that within punk, as well as in other cultural sites, they are "serialized" as women in particular ways that are demeaning and inhibiting. As Iris Marion Young explains in "Gender as Seriality: Thinking about Women as a Social Collective," "as a series woman is the name of a structural relation to material objects as they have been produced and organized by a prior history. . . . Gender, like class, is a vast, multifaceted, layered, complex, and overlapping set of structures and objects."[31] This Riot Grrrl movement actively confronts these structures and objects by claiming them: their bodies, music and its objects, information technologies, language, anger and violence, even punk culture. In these acts of resistance and subversion many young women produce critiques that address their own and others' experiences as women as well as their experiences of race, sexuality, class, and other forms of embodiedness. For example, Allison Wolfe, one of the women behind the 'zine *Girl Germs* writes: "i don't believe in this idea that somehow 'punx' are thee chosen ones, the rejects of society different separate suffering artists no one will ever understand 'us' so tragic special special spe special. Just give me one reason why society hasn't touched you. i think some punk distinctions can be really scary, an excuse to be really consuming capitalist racist rockstarist heterosexist . . . [?] in some untouchable 'alternative' format."[32] . . . Wolfe's critique of punk culture in 1991, through a medium familiar to the punk scene, suggests a moment when women are reemerging as prominent figures.[33] . . . Wolfe's problematizing of "punk distinctions" as supposedly exempt from the influence of "society" contributes to an increasing awareness that subcultural sites are not outside the grasp of socialization and social control, while it also implies that they ought to be places where critique and practical counter-possibilities are explored. Because writing, performing, and public engagement are encouraged within the subcultural scene, dissemination of such ideas is facilitated as an aspect of the subculture's function. Appropriation of democratized technologies enables the proliferation of this function and constructs different, counterpublic sites of resistance.

Patricia Zimmerman's analysis of the interface between reproductive rights activists and low-end video technology that opened this section demonstrates how the convergence of music, print, and information technologies, young women, and feminist consciousness raising multiplies the cultural spaces where political activities can occur. In issue #4 of *Girl Germs*, one young woman, Rebecca B., gives an account of her experience at "Girl's Night" at the International Pop Underground on August 20, 1991. Girl's Night, she explains, was originally suggested as a way to provide an "opportunity to demarginalize the role of girls in the convention and punk rock." For Rebecca B., the event proved to be a radicalizing moment even though, ironically, she only attended because guys were finally allowed in, which meant her boyfriend could go. . . . And yet, Girl's Night ended up . . . shattering her securities and making her think. In a way, Rebecca's story is about the interaction between two worlds—a "postfeminist" one in which following a boy doesn't seem downgrading and the one created by Girl's Night organizers, apparently modeling themselves after second wave women's music festivals. This interaction becomes the point of emergence for a third kind of "world," or "reality," in Rebecca's language.[34]

Rebecca's account of Girl's Night includes a description of how girls/women can and do use musical instruments, microphones, stages, their bodies and voices, and performance as "a forum" for "female expression." By appropriating the objects, spaces, and aesthetics of a culture generally dominated and determined by men and male issues, Rebecca argues, a new "reality" is being formed, a "reality" in which "stands the new girl, writing her dreams, speaking her will, making her music, restructuring the very punk rock world you reside in."[35] . . .

The voice at the microphone, the people and machines that put together the text of a CD or tape, the performance event, the women at the keyboard creating homepages and filling in information, the women at Kinko's or at work putting together her/ their 'zine(s) to distribute to girlfriends and other girls who write for copies all represent moments of convergence between democratized technologies and a networked, fractured form of third wave feminist differential consciousness. Girls like Rebecca may have the opportunity to experience such moments of consciousness raising in cultural sites created and institutionalized by the second wave (i.e., women's studies classrooms, progressive bookstores, rape crisis centers, or domestic violence shelters, to name a few). But instead, she experiences it inside a space and event she was not taught to see as coded "hers." . . .

"It's Mine, but It Doesn't Belong to Me"

For these "punk rock girls," and for other girls and women who produce 'zines and music that aren't necessarily punk, the production of a new movement space and its objects is politically powerful. And, although it may not seem like the most effective space in which to bring about social change, many of these women recognize their work as extensions of, influenced by, and interconnected with other historical social justice movements. The conscious use of the word "revolution" after "Riot Grrrl" indicates this connection. As one of my favorite Riot Grrrls, Nomy Lamm, says: "This is the revolution. I don't understand the revolution. I can't lay it all out in black and white and tell you what is revolutionary and what is not. The punk scene is a revolution, but not in and of itself. Feminism is a revolution; it is solidarity as well as critique and confrontation. This is the fat grrrl revolution. It's mine, but it doesn't belong to me. Fuckin' yeah."[36] . . . Revolution here is change, radical intervention, rearticulating the interrelations of punk, feminism, fat consciousness, class, race, and ability as they meet on the body and in the voice of Nomy Lamm. Even her language expresses the complexity: just as race is not as simple as the binary "black and white," "the revolution" cannot be described in either/or oppositional statements. It is about who and how one fills in the spaces; it is about how a girl can make her feminism punk and her punk feminist; and how, for Lamm, all of this has to be articulated around fat, media representations of the female body, and self/girl-love.

Lamm's proclamation: "It's mine, but it doesn't belong to me," like Rebecca Walker's statement, "I'm not a postfeminism feminist. I am the Third Wave,"[37] claims the right to name and construct her consciousness without becoming the sole owner of what counts as feminism or feminist consciousness. They call out their issues, locate themselves, make feminism work for them, and conclude by opening up the conversation to others, taking what they need and passing it on. Walker's rejection of postfeminism and Lamm's embrace of a polymorphous feminism connect these two women not only historically and generationally, but also in their insistence that feminism provides a context and language from/with which they can articulate their issues. This is a consequence of the post–civil rights recognition of difference as a positive thing and represents another (postmodern) distinction between the second and third waves.

The refusal to claim ownership of feminism allows these third wavers to maintain a sense of their own and other feminist-identified individuals' tactical subjectivity. When we understand that feminism is not about fitting into a mold but about expanding our ability to be revolutionary from within the worlds and communities and scenes we move around and through, then collective action becomes possible across the differences that affect people differently. This is not an argument for making feminism so expansive as to include absolutely anyone on the basis that she is a woman (something that seems quite popular in our culture); it is, instead, an attempt to point out how feminism enables revolutionary forms of consciousness when it is understood as ideology-praxis that strategically invokes the experiences of women across different locales and identities.

When Christine Doza attempts to theorize her place within structures of social inequality, she employs a metaphor of "connecting the dots": "I am learning to connect the dots. One dot for woman-hate, one for racism, one for classism, one for telling me who I can fuck. When I connect all the dots, it's a picture of privilege and the way it's disguised behind pretty white smiles." Doza's metaphor enables her to see that "there's a system of abuse here" and that "I need to know what part I'm playing in it."[38] Similarly, Kathleen Hanna's useful complication of male privilege—"The fact that he grew up in a working class family has everything to do with how he is gonna express sexism, what kind of music he is gonna like, how i am going to treat him"[39]—forces her readers to think beyond the one-dimensional identity of gender. In many ways, Doza's dots parallel Hanna's notion of a jigsaw puzzle, an image that travels throughout her music and writing. According to Hanna, "You have to be able to see the puzzle before you start putting it together," implying that one must learn about the culture one lives in—to become conscious of systems of domination and means of empowerment— to begin to be able to see how we each differently are affected by and affect a systematically oppressive social structure. . . . We need to understand the interconnections between our individual and group lives and institutions and to understand historical connections.

Although this task is painful and daunting (who really wants to have to deal with the ramifications of being both oppressor and oppressed?), the move toward this level of consciousness raising among some Riot Grrrls is worth further study. Just as Lamm challenges the idea that feminism is a subject/object/label owned by specific people/groups, Doza and Hanna challenge us to see that we are in and of "the system of abuse" and that we have complicated relationships to oppressor/power and oppressed/ powerlessness. For young, mostly white and middle-class women in the United States who turn to Riot Grrrl—even now when so many of its founders view it as "so '92"—to learn that being a feminist involves thinking about oneself as both oppressed and as oppressor is revolutionary. . . .

Conclusion

I haven't spoken much about the Internet in this essay, although . . . its presence has been significant. For those who have access to it, the language of the Internet and the metaphorical geographies employed to describe it make possible technologic rhetorics of the type of networking third wave feminists engage in. In *Surfergrrrls: Look Ethel! An Internet Guide for Us!* Laurel Gilbert and Crystal Kile include schematic lists of the most common Internet memes and metaphors—the information superhighway, consensual hallucination or cyberspace, the electronic frontier, encyclopedia Galactica, the Net, the World Wide Web (all masculinist, imperialist, capitalist, and fictional)—to show how "cybergrrrls" negotiate the ideological, political, commercial, and rhetorical terrains of the Internet in different, girl-positive ways. One strategic appropriation they note is the way "many women on the Net have seized on the 'web' and 'webweaver' memes, finding their traditional associations with so-called feminine values of holism and continuity to be both personally and politically empowering." Like a "URL" that gives the "site/path/file" directions to a particular website, Gilbert and Kile's guide is a "site/path/file" that links writing, publishing, computer, linguistic, narrative, and historiographic technologies in order to "think about our online selves, the gendering of technology and our common cyberfuture."[40] These linkings constitute a "technologics," a means for networking across cultural-technological spaces—a mobility necessary for the formation and survival of third wave feminism.

Technology is a major discursive repertoire in the cultural geography of third wave feminism; "democratized technologies" have played a significant role in the feminist political consciousness of many young women today. . . . The ability to record one's music, to type, print, format, and copy one's 'zine, to make one's video documentaries on a camcorder, to design and post one's website, without having to go through corporate, mainstream, commercial, official—and even adult—channels, makes a difference. Access to "democratized technologies" can enable a shift in the locus of political activism, as well as a change in who can produce politicized cultural-technological objects. . . .

Young feminists today, as well as older feminists and other social justice activists . . . , recognize that political activity is always being subverted by the media. . . . Our historical moment . . . precipitates particular kinds of political, cultural, aesthetic, and ideological consciousness; . . . we need to look to other cultural and subcultural spaces for signs of activist politics. As Angela McRobbie has noted: "Subcultures are aesthetic movements whose raw materials are by definition 'popular,' in that they are drawn from the world of the popular mass media."[41] Like the major recording labels who "plunder" music subcultures and "indies" (independent bands and labels) for "talent and trends,"[42] subcultures "plunder" mainstream media, but their purposes are different: one is geared to profit margins and sustaining markets; the other to finding constructive meaning in a time of crisis and uncertainty. At a time when the mainstream mass media scripts politics as bumper stickers, sound bites, and tabloid sensationalism, it seems especially important to look for and foster (sub)cultural spaces that insist on political content and intent in members' activities and in the objects they create. These include the tactical subjectivities employed to counter and subvert the depoliticized politics of conspicuous consumption. Although youth (sub)cultures like punk and Riot Grrrl are often represented by the media as a trend (and a passing one at that), I insist that we make a mistake when we disregard apparently "aesthetic" movements as nonpolitical. . . . In the third wave, feminist collective consciousness may not necessarily manifest itself in a nationalized and highly mobilized social movement unified around a single goal or identity. At the moment, this hardly seems imaginable. Perhaps occasionally groups will come together to accomplish a specific purpose— such as the protection of reproductive rights for all women and men; protesting environmental injustices in poor and racially segregated communities and Third World countries; combating anti-immigration and racist xenophobic movements; or endorsing the right of all people, regardless of sexuality, to love whom they want, how they want, and to have their rights to do so legally recognized—but I think it is also important to look at third wave feminist activist politics in spaces that cross over and between what is called the "mainstream" or what is recognized as "a social movement." We need to consider the potent political movement cultures being generated by feminists . . . who are producing knowledge for each other through the innovative integration of technology, alternative media, (sub)cultural and/or feminist networks, and feminist consciousness raising. Such dispersed movement culture spaces are vital as are the networks constantly being formed and reformed among them.

NOTES

The original version of this article appeared in *Feminist Studies* 26, no. 1 (Spring 2000).

This essay has benefited over several years (and in several forms) from careful readings by wonderful friends, colleagues, and teachers, especially Noel Sturgeon, Marian Sciachitano, Carol Siegal, Chris Oakley, and Kendal Broad. At the University of California, Santa Barbara, Jacqueline Bobo, Shirley Lim, and Chela Sandoval each responded to an earlier version of the essay in ways that have been encouraging and inspiring. Anonymous readers at *Feminist Studies* gave excellent feedback and constructive criticism that helped me through the revising process, but which I have also been able to apply to my dissertation more widely.

1. For more on this significant distinction between generation as age and generation as "the having-done-this-ness," see E. Ann Kaplan's introductory essay, "Feminism, Aging, and Changing Paradigms," in *Generations: Academic Feminists in Dialogue*, ed. Devoney Looser and E. Ann Kaplan (Minneapolis: University of Minnesota Press, 1997), 13–29.

2. Dick Hebdige, *Subculture: The Meaning of Style* (London: Methuen, 1979), and Angela McRobbie, *Feminism and Youth Culture: From "Jackie" to "Just Seventeen"* (Houndsmill and London: Macmillan Education, 1991).

3. I include the caution that the name "third wave feminism" may be more about desire than a reflection of an already existing thing. . . . Publications dedicated to third wave, or "youth," feminism include Leslie Heywood and Jennifer Drake, eds., *Third Wave Agenda: Being Feminist, Doing Feminism* (Minneapolis: University of Minnesota Press, 1997); "Third Wave Feminism," special issue of *Hypatia* 12 (Summer 1997); and "Feminism and Youth Culture," special issue, *Signs* 23 (Spring 1998).

4. In *White Women, Race Matters: The Social Construction of Whiteness* (Minneapolis: University of Minneapolis Press, 1993), Ruth Frankenberg uses "discursive repertoire" to describe the combinations of discursive tools the women in her study used to maneuver through narratives of race (16).

5. Ann Swidler, "Culture in Action: Symbols and Strategies," *American Sociological Review* 51 (April 1986): 273.

6. Donna Haraway, "A Cyborg Manifesto: Science, Technology, and Socialist Feminism in the Late Twentieth Century," in her *Simians, Cyborgs, and Women: The Reinvention of Nature* (New York: Routledge, 1991), 180, 181.

7. This naming makes chronological and metaphorical sense because it self-consciously draws upon the language of women's movement activists, historians, and theorists. . . .

8. The same erasure has often been done in second wave constructions of "first" and "second," ignoring feminist activity and cohorts between 1920 and the 1960s. It is only [since the mid-1980s] that the period between the first two "waves" has become the subject of scholarly interventions. See Barbara Ryan, *Feminism and the Women's Movement: Dynamics of Change in Social Movement Ideology and Activism* (New York: Routledge, 1992); Leila J. Rupp and Verta Taylor, *Survival in the Doldrums: The American Women's Rights Movement, 1945 to the 1960s* (New York: Oxford

University Press, 1987); and Nancy F. Cott, *The Grounding of Modern Feminism* (New Haven, CT: Yale University Press, 1987).

9. Marian Sciachitano has suggested to me that feminist women of color are the first third wavers, and that the cohort I am writing about actually may be a "fourth wave." Her ideas add another dimension to the narratives that construct the third wave's origins as the widespread response to Anita Hill's sexual harassment case against Clarence Thomas, as well as complicating the assumptions that "third wavers" are of a particular generation. For a fascinating example of this tendency, see Catherine Stimpson's "Women's Studies and Its Discontents," *Dissent* 43 (Winter 1996): 67–75.

10. Chela Sandoval, "U.S. Third World Feminism: The Theory and Method of Oppositional Consciousness in the Postmodern World," *Genders* 10 (Spring 1991): 1–24.

11. Rebecca Walker, "Becoming the Third Wave," *Ms.*, January/February 1992, reprinted in *Testimony: Young African Americans on Self-Discovery and Black Identity*, ed. Natasha Tarpley (Boston: Beacon Press, 1995), 215–218.

12. Sandoval, "U.S. Third World Feminism," 4. I realize that my use of Sandoval's concept of differential consciousness in this essay may have some problematic aspects; I risk being accused of appropriating—inappropriately—a theory about the practices of U.S. Third World feminists for Riot Grrrl, which is composed largely of white middle-class women. I am encouraged by the fact that in "U.S. Third World Feminism," Sandoval herself writes that "the recognition of differential consciousness is vital to the generation of a next 'third wave' women's movement and provides grounds for alliance with other decolonizing movements for emancipation" (4). My purpose here is to explore the possibilities of linking the praxis of U.S. Third World feminism with "the aims of white feminism, studies of race, ethnicity, and marginality, and with postmodern theories of culture" that Sandoval suggests in the passage with which I opened this section. This includes, for me, acknowledging that the theorizing of feminists of color (which I am not), poor women (which I have been for most of my life), and lesbians (which I am) can be part of my feminist tool kit as well.

13. On affinity politics, see Iris Marion Young, *Justice and the Politics of Difference* (Princeton, NJ: Princeton University Press, 1990), and Noël Sturgeon, "Theorizing Movements: Direct Action and Direct Theory," in *Cultural Politics and Social Movements*, ed. Marcy Darnovsky, Barbara Epstein, and Richard Flacks (Philadelphia: Temple University Press, 1995), 35–51.

14. Sandoval, "U.S. Third World Feminism," 15.

15. On strategic essentialism, see Gayatri Chakravorty Spivak, *The Postcolonial Critic: Interviews, Strategies, Dialogues*, ed. Sarah Harasym (New York: Routledge, 1990); Donna Haraway, "Situated Knowledges: The 'Science Question' in Feminism and the Privilege of Partial Perspective," in her *Simians, Cyborgs, and Women*, 183–202; Teresa de Lauretis, "Upping the Anti (sic) in Feminist Theory," in *Conflicts in Feminism*, ed. Marianne Hirsch and Evelyn Fox Keller (New York: Routledge, 1990), 254–270; Chela Sandoval, "New Sciences: Cyborg Feminism and the Methodology

of the Oppressed," in *Cyborg Handbook*, ed. Chris Hables Gray with Heidi J. Figueroa-Sarriera and Steven Mentor (New York: Routledge, 1995), 407–421; Noël Sturgeon, *Ecofeminist Natures: Race, Gender, Political Action, and Feminist Theory* (New York: Routledge, 1997); and T. V. Reed, *Fifteen Jugglers, Five Believers: Literary Politics and the Poetics of American Social Movements* (Berkeley: University of California Press, 1990).

16. Sandoval, "U.S. Third World Feminism," 22, 17.

17. Neither is this limited to "feminism" in the narrow sense of being about "women." Some of the . . . publications I've read with great excitement include Robin Bernstein and Seth Clark Silbermann, eds., *Generation Q: Gays, Lesbians, and Bisexuals Born around 1969's Stonewall Riots Tell Their Stories of Growing Up in the Age of Missing Information* (Los Angeles: Alyson, 1996); Veronica Chambers, *Mama's Girl* (New York: Riverhead Books, 1996); Tarpley, *Testimony*; Arlene Stein, ed., *Sisters, Sexperts, Queers: Beyond the Lesbian Nation* (New York: Plume, 1993); Gish Jen, *Mona in the Promised Land* (New York: Knopf, 1996); and Nan Bauer Maglin and Donna Perry, eds., *"Bad Girls"/"Good Girls": Women, Sex, and Power in the Nineties* (New Brunswick, NJ: Rutgers University Press, 1996). Most of the writers in these texts focus on the post-1960s decades from the perspectives of those too young to have personal recollections of it. Although the 1960s is an important marker for all of us in the United States, "our" ("us young people") memories of those times are not literally our own.

18. Jee-Yeun Lee, "Beyond Bean Counting," in *Listen Up: Voices from the Next Feminist Generation*, ed. Barbara Findlen (Seattle, WA: Seal Press, 1995), 205–211.

19. I am using the words "mutually exclusive" to link this notion of gender as an identity, experience, condition of embodiedness separate from other identities, experiences, or conditions of embodiedness like race, class, sexuality, not/able-bodied, etc. to Chela Sandoval's discussion of the production of histories of "hegemonic feminism" which have made different forms of feminism "mutually exclusive" and therefore maneuverability between feminisms impossible and/or invisible practices. See her "U.S. Third World Feminism," 3–10.

20. Bruno Latour, *We Have Never Been Modern*, trans. Catherine Porter (Cambridge, MA: Harvard University Press, 1993), 120. See Haraway, "A Cyborg Manifesto," 149–182; Donna Haraway, "The Promise of Monsters: A Regenerative Politics for Inappropriate/d Others," in *Cultural Studies*, ed. Lawrence Grossberg, Cary Nelson, and Paula A. Treichler (New York: Routledge, 1992), 295–337; Haraway, "Situated Knowledges," 183–202; and Sandoval, "U.S. Third World Feminism," 1–24.

21. Ednie Kaeh Garrison, "Are We on a Wavelength Yet? On Feminist Oceanography, Radios, and Third Wave Feminism," Women's Center Dissertation Fellows Colloquium, University of California, Santa Barbara, April 21, 1999.

22. Patricia Zimmerman, "The Female Bodywars: Rethinking Feminist Media Politics," *Socialist Review* 23, no. 2 (1993): 35–56. See also Sean Cubitt, *Timeshift: On Video Culture* (London: Routledge, 1991).

23. There are literally thousands upon thousands of girl-centered 'zines, some still in production, some no longer circulating. Some of the names of the zines I have

collected are *Bamboo Girl, Feminist Carpet Cleaner, Bitch: Feminist Response to Popular Culture, I Scare Myself, My Evil Twin Sister, Fat Girl, Fat?So!, I'm So Fucking Beautiful, Revolution Rising, Meat Hook, Housewife Turned Assassin, Bust, Chestlick, Nightmare Girl, Pokerface, Hysteria Action Forum, Her Posse, Chainsaw, Girlie Jones,* and *Mystery Date.* As well, S. Bryn Austin and Pam Gregg write about a variety of queer 'zines in their essay "A Freak among Freaks: The 'Zine Scene," in *Sisters, Sexperts, Queers: Beyond the Lesbian Nation,* ed. Arlene Stein (New York: Plume, 1993), 81–95, and a number of 'zine makers have scored book contracts for their 'zines, including Pagan Kennedy's 'zine *Pagan's Head,* which is now a "novel" called *Zine: How I Spent Six Years of My Life in the Underground and Finally . . . Found Myself . . . I Think* (New York: St. Martin's Griffin, 1995), and Marilyn Wann's *Fat!So? Because You Don't Have to Apologize for Your Size* (Berkeley, CA: Ten Speed Press, 1999). Besides distribution networks that circulate 'zines locally, nationally, and transnationally, there are a number of stores across the country that specialize in alternative and small press publications. Three of my major sources are in Portland, Oregon: Ozone Records, Powell's Bookstore, and Reading Frenzy: An Alternative Press Emporium (all within a block of one another). The largest publication that reviews zines is *Fact Sheet Five: The Big Fat Guide to the Zine Revolution,* published by R. Seth Freidman (P.O. Box 170099, San Francisco, CA 94117–0099), which covers the gamut from science fiction to thrift shopping to s/m to comix to queer to politics to food to "grrrlz."

24. Riot Grrrl has also traveled across the Atlantic at least to Great Britain. The most notorious group of grrrls involved in England are the members of Huggy Bear (Niki, Jo, Chris, John, and Karen—three women and two men), whom Amy Raphael calls "DIY revolutionaries, full-on feminists, art terrorists." See Amy Raphael, *Grrrls: Viva Rock Divas* (New York: St. Martin's Griffin, 1996), 148. ("DIY" stands for "do it yourself" and is a central philosophy among punk aestheticists.)

25. Spirit, "What Is a Riot Grrrl Anyway?," available from http://www.columbia.edu/~rli3/music%5fhtml/bikini%5fkill/girl.html, accessed January, 6, 1995.

26. I avoid "correcting," altering, or changing the grammar in any of the excerpts from 'zines or Internet pages, unless the text interferes with the ability to comprehend the intended meanings.

27. Bikini Kill, *The CD Version of the First Two Records* (1992), liner notes.

28. One strategy many women and girls in the punk and indie scenes have devised is the creation of their own recording companies as vehicles for producing the music they want to hear. Some of these companies include Kill Rock Stars and K Records, both in Olympia, Washington; Chainsaw and Candy-Ass Records, both in Portland, Oregon ([later in] Olympia); and Thrill Jockey Records, Chicago.

29. Kathleen Hanna, interview with Andrea Juno, "Kathleen Hanna: Bikini Kill," *Angry Women in Rock* (New York: Juno Books, 1996), 1:100, 98.

30. Some of the better-known role models often listed include Joan Jett, Patti Smith, the Runaways, the Go Gos, the Au Pairs, and Cyndi Lauper.

31. Iris Marion Young, "Gender as Seriality: Thinking about Women as a Social Collective," *Signs* 19 (Spring 1994): 736, 728. Young's use of the series is drawn from

a concept of "seriality" developed by Jean-Paul Sartre as a specific kind of social collectivity distinguishable from what he calls "groups." However, Young also makes it clear that she "raids" Sartre for her own ends, "taking and rearticulating for my own purposes the concepts I think will help resolve the dilemma I have posed. In doing so I need not drag all of Sartre with me, and I may be 'disloyal' to him" (723). Ironically, this strategy also helps Young avoid being Sartre in drag.

32. The other woman behind *Girl Germs* is Molly Neuman, who, with Allison Wolfe, was in the band Bratmobile. See Allison Wolfe and Molly Neuman, *Girl Germs*, no. 4 (1991): 25–26.

33. In their 1978 essay, "Girls and Subcultures," Angela McRobbie and Jenny Garber raise questions about the lack of research on girls in subcultures in England, wondering, specifically, if this is a consequence of the invisibility of girls in those subcultures. McRobbie especially challenges this perception. See McRobbie, *Feminism and Youth Culture*.

34. Thanks to Carol Siegel for pointing out the way in which two different worlds "are in contact" in this story. Her suggestions about the modeling of Girl's Night after second wave women's music festivals is even more potent considering the notorious problems girl-positive bands . . . have had with protests by boys when their performances are advertised as women only.

35. Rebecca B., *Girl Germs*, no. 4 (1991), 22. Angela McRobbie has already suggested that there are some potent affinities between punk style and feminist style in her 1978 essay, "Settling Accounts with Subcultures: A Feminist Critique," in *Feminism and Youth Culture*, 16–34. Rebecca's comments about the impact playing musical instruments and performing in public can have on girls (as performers and as audience) and its subsequent impact on punk culture supports McRobbie's assertion that subcultures are symbiotically connected to political movements like feminism and the New Left (the two she names). This also goes a long way in arguing for a "politics of style," an understanding of "style" as a form of politics— as overt political expression.

36. Nomy Lamm, "It's a Big Fat Revolution," in *Listen Up: Voices from the Next Feminist Generation*, ed. Barbara Findlen (Seattle: Seal Press, 1995), 94.

37. Walker, "Becoming the Third Wave," 218.

38. Christine Doza, "Bloodlove," in *Listen Up: Voices from the Next Feminist Generation*, ed. Barbara Findlen (Seattle: Seal Press, 1995), 251, 253.

39. Hanna interview; Juno, "Kathleen Hanna: Bikini Kill."

40. Gilbert and Kile use "meme" as defined by Richard Dawkins in *The Selfish Gene* (New York: Oxford University Press, 1989), 152. See Laurel Gilbert and Crystal Kile, *Surfergrrrls: Look Ethel! An Internet Guide for Us!* (Seattle: Seal Press, 1996), 154, 6.

41. McRobbie, *Feminism and Youth Culture*, xv.

42. See Joanne Gottlieb and Gayle Wald, "Smells Like Teen Spirit: Riot Grrrls, Revolution, and Women in Independent Rock," *Critical Matrix* 7, no. 2 (1993): 11–44, esp. 13.

17

"Under Construction"

Identifying Foundations of Hip-Hop Feminism and
Exploring Bridges between Black Second Wave
and Hip-Hop Feminisms

WHITNEY A. PEOPLES

I have titled this essay "Under Construction" after the fourth album . . . by
rapper Missy Elliot. As Elliot says in the introduction to her album,

> my album which is titled under construction, under construction
> simply states that I'm a work in progress I'm working on myself. . . .
> We all under construction trying to rebuild, you know, ourselves. Hip-
> hop done gained respect from, you know, not even respect from but
> just like rock and roll and it took us a lot of hard work to get here so
> all that hatin' and animosity between folks you need to kill it with a
> skillet. You don't see Bill Gates and Donald Trump arguing with each
> other cuz both of them got paper and they got better shit to do, get
> more paper. So all I'm sayin' is let's take hip-hop back to the rope,
> follow me.[1]

I find Elliot's words and the title to her album a fitting comparison to the
work of a cadre of black American feminists that I read as an attempt at
"(re)working" black American feminism and its response to the contemporary lives of black women and girls.

Young black female writers such as Kristal Brent Zooks and Joan Morgan
have argued that black American women are in dire need of a new feminist
movement.[2] Zooks and Morgan, both of whom I consider "third wave"[3]
feminists, argue that second wave black feminism has failed to address the
current realities and needs of young black women. To this extent, shani
jamila argues, "as women of the hip-hop generation we need a feminist
consciousness that allows us to examine how representations and images

can be simultaneously empowering and problematic."[4] To address this perceived deficiency, jamila, Morgan, Gwendolyn Pough, and others have begun a dialogue between two unlikely partners: hip-hop and feminism.

Although there is contention over the nature and potential of hip-hop as progressive political practice,[5] some cultural analysts read parts of hip-hop culture and rap music as providing political analysis—although at times problematic—about racist, sexist, economic, police, and community violence that African American men and women face. As a result of hip-hop culture's relevant depiction of black life in America, Morgan and others argue that hip-hop culture and rap music hold radical and liberating potential . . . to speak to younger feminists, particularly those of color.[6] To this end, writers such as Morgan, jamila, and Pough have coined and begun to circulate the term "hip-hop feminist."[7] In response to what they perceive as an out-of-touch feminism, hip-hop feminists seek to pick up where they believe second wave black feminists left off. They offer that beyond . . . its incontestable misogyny, hip-hop provides a space for young black women to express their race and ethnic identities and to critique racism. Moreover, hip-hop feminists contend that hip-hop is . . . a site where young black women begin to build or further develop their own gender critique and feminist identity, which they can then turn toward the misogyny of rap music.[8] Pough speaks to the potential of hip-hop in feminist consciousness raising when she writes, "Parents do not want their children listening to [rap], and educators do not see the educational value in [rap]. I believe that the value resides in the critique."[9] For Pough, the objectionable elements of hip-hop are part of what make it valuable to feminism because they provide the opportunity for students to analyze and hone their skills of critical analysis.

This essay is rooted in an investigation of hip-hop feminism and not hip-hop culture per se; . . . I do not engage in lengthy analyses of rap music lyrics, videos, hip-hop magazines, etc. I decided to forgo analyzing the work of rappers for feminist sentiment or excavating the contributions of women to hip-hop primarily because that work has already been done. . . .[10] Other works attempting to link women, feminism, and hip-hop have revolved largely around issues of identity, investigating the impact of hip-hop on the individual subjectivity of black women as fans, consumers, and members of the hip-hop community.[11] . . . My project will attempt to move the discussion beyond one of identity and legitimation into a more critical engagement of the ways in which hip-hop feminism operates and the spaces in which it resides to determine the nature of the resistance it represents. In the end, I am not concerned with whether hip-hop and rap music express feminist politics; I am concerned with the ways that hip-hop feminists claim to engage hip-hop culture, rap music, and feminism and the effects of such an engagement.

. . . Previous examinations of generational responses to employing hip-hop within feminist practice drew premature lines in the sand, setting black feminists at odds when really they were much more in line with one another. This essay addresses [this] premature division . . . by identifying and exploring three specific yet interrelated issues affecting the future direction of black American feminism. In this piece I attempt to (1) identify the sociopolitical agenda of hip-hop feminism, (2) tease out the specific arguments of second and third wave black American feminists in response to the recent development of hip-hop feminism, and (3) explore the theoretical and practical linkages between generations of black American feminists. Through the examination of power, hip-hop culture, feminism, and the interactions among all three, I hope to provide a coherent framework for interpreting the work of hip-hop feminists and for clearly understanding their genealogy. Ultimately, I argue that the sociopolitical agenda of hip-hop feminism shows evidence of crucial connections between generations of black feminists that position hip-hop feminism as a continuation—though a disruptive one—of second wave black feminism.

The Political Economy of Hip-Hop or Why It (Should) Matter(s) to Feminism

. . . Born from the work of poor and working-class black and Latino youth . . . in the late 1970s and early '80s, hip-hop was, in part, a response to the class exclusivity of the New York disco scene[12] and the growing gang culture of inner-city New York. . . . Gradually, hip-hop emerged not only as a recreational space but also one in which to voice contempt for the living conditions of the economically and racially marginalized. From its inception, hip-hop has represented resistance to social marginalization, and later, resistance to and commentary on the political and economic oppression that makes social marginalization possible.

Moreover, . . . hip-hop is not a homogeneous entity. It should be understood as an umbrella term containing at least four distinct parts: break-dancing, DJ-ing, graffiti art, and rapping. It is important to foreground the multiple components of hip-hop culture since it is often reduced to rapping and rap music, which immediately limits the discussion of it and also excludes potential and actual sites of resistance within hip-hop occurring outside of rap.

Any discussion of the circulation of hip-hop culture in the American and global mainstream that does not address the political economy of the culture and the demands of the capitalist marketplace is incomplete. Norman Kelley describes the context of the political economy of black American music in general as "a structure of stealing" whose origins date back to the period of American slavery.[13] . . . Kelley further argues that the relationship of slaves and slave owners informs contemporary music industry labor relations in the form of a "network of interconnected operations, businesses, business practices, and social ties that mostly understand blacks as 'talent,' i.e., labor."[14] Furthermore, Bakari Kitwana argues that the reduction of black bodies and talent to nothing more than labor is also evident in the hype surrounding the notion that young white suburban kids represent the largest buying bloc of the hip-hop marketplace.[15] Kitwana questions this notion by asking, "But what's at stake if white kids are not hip hop's primary audience and we accept the myth? The overwhelming message here is that Blacks are not a significant variable in a music they created and music of which Black culture is the very foundation."[16] Using both Kelley and Kitwana, we understand that black bodies are valued only insofar as they represent potential to create products that can be transformed into capital via marketing and sales; outside of that process those bodies are dispensable. Under this rubric hip-hop becomes a commodity as it represents the productive potential of black bodies when they enter into a capital-producing enterprise.

. . . Mainstream rap music is most easily commodified because it represents ideas of blackness that are in line with dominant racist and sexist ideologies; it has economic potential only because it works hand-in-hand with long established ideas about the sexual, social, and moral nature of black people. In other words, the images of black male violence and aggression that dominate mainstream rap music are highly marketable in America because of already existing ideologies of racism that long ago named the black male as supreme aggressor and physical and sexual threat. Similarly, the images of sexually available black women that pervade rap music are marketable because of already existing ideologies that designated black women as hypersexual and morally obtuse.

. . . Yet even as parts of hip-hop culture draw on overdetermined tropes of black gender roles, there is the possibility that those parts can be rearticulated or engaged in a subversive manner. Take, for example, Gwendolyn Pough's work on women's ability to critically disrupt the hip-hop space. Pough argues, via reading the lyrics of female rappers against the grain, that they "wreck" dominant hip-hop discourses by contesting stereotypes that often leave women without agency.[17] Pough goes on to argue that although rappers such as Foxy Brown and Lil' Kim draw heavily on American social/racial stereotypes of black women as sexually promiscuous, they simultaneously disrupt black community norms that silence black female sexuality and encourage shame around it for black women and girls. For Pough, despite the obvious negative aspects of Brown's and Kim's work, they nonetheless acknowledge "that they are sexual beings who enjoy sex, and lots of it, . . . [and what they] offer is the opportunity to embrace the sexuality of the self."[18] In Pough's analysis we see both the potential for coercive power to assert itself via the use of racialized hypersexual tropes and the simultaneous disruptive possibilities that arise when those tropes are read in a different light. So while the imagery of Lil' Kim as a black woman who enjoys sex is not necessarily radical in and of itself, when placed into dialogue with oppressive community norms that deny black women sexual agency, her work takes on a new light.

In reading a public persona such as that of Lil' Kim it cannot be ignored that her hypersexual rap image was not her creation but that of a group of male rappers and producers with whom she worked. . . . However, instead of allowing that fact to render void the disruptive possibilities of her image, cultural analysts and feminists should stretch a bit further and see her not as the symbol of the liberation of black female sexuality, but rather as a catalyst who forces a particular conversation around black women and sexuality. It is not that black women will find sexual and individual liberation by adopting Lil' Kim's public persona; however, as a result of the circulation of her image they might find enough of a cleavage in dominant African American community discourses to begin a simultaneous critique and exploration of the sexual scripts that have been provided for them by institutions and individuals external to them.

Furthermore, hip-hop's heterogeneity, widespread popularity, and sociocultural and economic currency . . . imbu[e] it with undeniable potential for those hoping to reach young people and particularly black youth. Additionally, the diversity of hip-hop culture and rap music provides sites of political disruption and subversion that also work to reinforce messages of resistance.[19] In this way, hip-hop emerges as what I term "the generational and culturally relevant vehicle" through which hip-hop feminists can spread their message of critical analysis and empowerment.

What Is Hip-Hop Feminism, Who Does It Represent, and What Does It Stand For?

Age, Race, Class, and National Boundaries/Locations of Hip-Hop Feminists

. . . Hip-hop feminism might be best understood as . . . young black women in the U.S. trying to create a space for themselves between the whiteness and/or academically sanitized versions of university-based feminism, where most first encountered a conscious naming and exploration of feminism, and the maleness of the hip-hop culture that most grew up on. As shani jamila explains of her introduction to feminism, "my understanding of Black feminism is rooted in the theoretical texts written decades before I was first introduced to them in college."[20] Nevertheless, Eisa Davis tells her audience that "hip-hop gave me a language that made my black womanhood coherent to myself and the world; hip-hop revived me when my soul was blanched from neglect."[21] Hip-hop feminists are products of the hip-hop generation but are also, as Joan Morgan writes, "the daughters of feminist privilege."[22] As a result, I identify those who are crafting a political identity based on hip-hop and feminism largely as younger, college-educated black American women who either grew up middle-class or who are now a part of the growing young black and upwardly mobile crew entering the American class hierarchy, and who are often better off than their parents were. . . . These women have been influenced by both the feminist movement and by hip-hop culture, and borrow core themes from both for the development of their own identity. Through using their lives and experiences to bridge the divide between hip-hop and feminism, these women appear to be challenging assumptions about the nature of that divide.

There also exists, however, resistance to the label of hip-hop feminism, making it a contested term even within its own generational constituency. Some women, such as Tara Roberts,[23] have argued that hip-hop's misogyny has gone too far, making a relationship between it and feminism impossible. Roberts writes of an earlier time in her life, "I would smile seductively at the brothers in jazzed up VW bugs who passed me on the corner, though I knew what was blaring on their systems was in no way good for women. I am tired of being conflicted."[24] For Roberts, attempting to reconcile her conflicted relationship with hip-hop and feminism became more cumbersome than it was worth. T. Denean Sharpley-Whiting also rejects the label of hip-hop feminism on the grounds that, unlike Morgan, she thinks feminism, unmodified by qualifiers, is sufficient to address the realities of black women's lived experiences.[25] Whereas writers such as Roberts and Sharpley-Whiting hold fast to their feminist locations while distancing themselves from hip-hop, there are also women who fully, and at times critically, embrace hip-hop but maintain a distance from the label of feminism.

The legacy of feminism's racist, homophobic, classist, and xenophobic beginnings unfortunately colors many women's hesitation to explore feminism's possible benefits. Aisha Durham addresses this when describing a scene at a hip-hop conference sponsored by her university. Durham argues that though all of the individuals participating on the "Women in Hip-Hop" panel were women, they "wanted nothing to do with feminism because of the presumed negative connotation, but they boldly pledged their allegiance under a bubble-letter banner blaring 'Women in hip-hop.'"[26] Additionally, the ambivalence to the label "feminism" expressed by many female rappers whose lyrics have been read by some as expressing feminist sentiment also speaks to the contested nature of the term "hip-hop feminism."[27] I highlight these different approaches to and reasons for resisting the label "hip-hop feminism" as a way to note that the creation and circulation of the term does not signify an uncomplicated acceptance and usage in either the hip-hop or feminist community.

The Sociopolitical Agenda of Hip-Hop Feminists

In her controversial debut as a cultural critic, *When Chickenheads Come Home to Roost*, noted hip-hop feminist writer Joan Morgan argues, "The focus of black feminists has got to change. We can't afford to keep expending energy on banal discussions of sexism in rap when sexism is only part of a huge set of problems."[28] The writers and activists who self-define as hip-hop feminists claim to expand the focus of the U.S. black feminist agenda toward hip-hop. Shifting the "feminist" approach to hip-hop has taken the current form of a sociopolitical agenda of uplift aimed at self-empowerment for women and girls through political education based on feminist modes of analysis.

With an agenda once premised solely on critiquing the misogyny of male rappers and the exploitation of female artists and industry performers, hip-hop feminists are turning an eye toward how to make women within hip-hop culture the subjects of the movement. The agenda of some feminists toward hip-hop has shifted from one aimed primarily at critique to one of uplift, not of the music, but of segments of the population who consume it, specifically young African-American women and girls. Uplift, in this instance, is taken to mean a movement directed at . . . bringing toward self-actualization an individual or group . . . taken to be in need of such assistance. The overarching hip-hop feminist agenda of uplift is to be achieved specifically through the dissemination of political education and efforts at institution-building.

Yet in any agenda premised on uplift there will always emerge issues of division based on class and cultural capital; the hip-hop feminist agenda has not escaped such fissures. It is in the split between hip-hop feminism's constituency and its target audience that the movement could end up being counterproductive . . . as it takes on a somewhat paternalistic attitude. . . . In much of the literature written by hip-hop feminists, feminism emerges as something of a savior for all of the "lost souls" represented by young women and girls listening to rap music and living the culture of hip-hop without the critical eye that feminism promises. To this end Eisa Ulen argues, "We must be brave enough to enter this cave in Babylon and help light the fire that will generate some warmth, heal, then resume the journey to the mountaintop, together. And a groovy black chick like you can radiate enough estrogen to embrace our estranged girls, love them back to themselves, strong, high, looking out on tomorrow."[29] Working from the writings of hip-hop feminists such as Ulen, Morgan, and Pough, I contend that hip-hop feminists follow what Kevin Gaines calls "popular meanings of uplift, rooted in public education, economic rights, group resistance and struggle, and democracy. . . ."[30] However, such a politics can nevertheless be a slippery slope into traditional uplift ideology, as hip-hop feminists have argued that "we are losing a whole generation of young women of color."[31] While this statement might seem benign, and even truthful, it runs the risk of painting hip-hop feminists as "caped crusaders" come to "save" the masses from themselves. While I might agree that black women are in danger of losing ourselves if left to see our reflection only via the images presented in pop culture, I suggest that whatever plan is formulated must bear in mind that the young women whom "we" purport to save have agency in their own ways, and, by their own means, do exercise that agency.

In his book *The Hip-Hop Generation*, Bakari Kitwana asks, "'What do we mean by politicizing the hip-hop generation?' Is our goal to run hip-hop generationers for office, to turn out votes for Democrats and Republicans, to form a third party, or to provide our generation with a concrete political education?"[32] Those writing and acting under the label "hip-hop feminists" have chosen Kitwana's last option, that of providing a political education and tools of critical analysis . . . to critique the social, political, and economic structures that govern their lives and that give rise to the conditions that produce some of the violent and misogynist lyrics that dominate much of mainstream rap music. When interviewing a female rapper resistant to the label "feminist," Tricia Rose . . . demonstrates the aforementioned engagement by offering the following definition of feminism as a way to bring the wary artist into dialogue with feminism: "I would say that feminists believed that there was sexism in society, wanted to change and worked toward that change. Either wrote, spoke, or behaved in a way that was pro-woman, in that she supported situations (organizations) that were trying to better the lives of women. A feminist feels that women are more disadvantaged than men in many situations and would want to stop that kind of inequality."[33] Rose's purpose appears to have been served, as she goes on to write, "Once feminism was understood as a mode of analysis rather than a label for a group of women associated with a particular social movement, MC Lyte [a pioneering and popular female rapper of the 1980s and early '90s] was much more comfortable discussing the importance of black women's independence. . . ."[34] The current sociopolitical agenda of hip-hop feminism appears then to be focused on the dissemination of the tools of critical analysis offered by a feminist mode of analysis. . . . Gwendolyn Pough writes about the establishment of what she terms a "public pedagogy"[35] through bringing together feminism and hip-hop. Pough argues that "[r]ap is the contemporary art form that gives voice to a part of the population that would not have a voice otherwise. . . ."[36] The responsibility of feminists, per Pough, in cultivating the potential of hip-hop is ultimately to "give young women the tools necessary to critique the messages they are getting" from the lyrics and visual expressions of rap music.[37] Again, hip-hop emerges as the common cultural ground, the generationally relevant vehicle through which to circulate and within which to employ the "feminist" tools of critical analysis. . . .

Initial works[38] about the intersections of hip-hop, feminism, and women often focused on the responses of women to the male domination, misogyny, and cultural practices of hip-hop rather than ignoring, denying, or excusing those practices. Women writing in the early '90s on the relationship between hip-hop and feminism . . . were quick to point to the dialogue that was occurring in rap music between men and women as consumers, community peers, and artists.[39] Furthermore, the arguments of . . . hip-hop feminists and those who simply write about women in hip-hop do not romanticize the existing dialogues present in rap; rather their goal appears to be concerned with not discounting those dialogues and their subsequent importance either. Rose argues that she was better able to understand how female rappers can be both complicit with and disruptive of racism and sexism once she understood them "as part of a dialogic process with male rappers (and others), rather than in complete opposition to them. . . ."[40] The existing dialogues in hip-hop culture in general and rap music in particular become important to hip-hop feminism as the initial sites in which to employ hip-hop feminism's "public pedagogy," to borrow Pough's term.

The call for an expansion of the dialogue . . . among women and men of the hip-hop generation is inherently a simultaneous call for a concerted effort at institution-building . . . in the sense of creating the spaces for these dialogues and discussions. Eisa Davis writes, "I would love to see hip-hop battles, conference panels, and articles and essays . . . that talk about issues of sexism in hip-hop supplemented by other formats for dialogue."[41] Davis's words suggest that African American women writing between the worlds of hip-hop and feminism and within the points of their convergence recognize that young black men and women need forums and other spaces in which to have crucial conversations. . . . For hip-hop feminists it appears that political education and . . . communal institutions go hand in hand in the forging of a sociopolitical agenda. As a result of making provocative claims about their own political agenda, hip-hop feminists have encountered sharp critiques from some of their second wave black feminist counterparts. . . .

Battling: Exploring the "Generational Divide" in U.S. Black Feminist Theorizing

. . . Alonzo Westbrook defines the hip-hop concept of "battling" as "war between or among rappers, dancers, DJs, or emcees for prizes or bragging rights and to see who's the best."[42] . . . [T]he concept of battling . . . is instructive for understanding the generational and substantive debates . . . within black American feminism. Battling within hip-hop is more than a competition between artists for "bragging rights" or mere prizes; it is . . . a kind of dialogue that eventually moves the art form forward. In a battle between two emcees, for example, one feeds off and responds to the other. . . . Because each emcee is pressed to bring his or her best work and to work collaboratively, in a sense, with others in the competition, battling begins to look a lot like the process of critical theory-building. The process of critical theory-building, however, differs from a battle in that [its] . . . goal is not the emergence of a winner or loser but the creation of a stronger, more relevant theory with which to engage the world.

The conversation occurring within black American feminism on the compatibility and utility of hip-hop to the feminist project and the theoretical viability and sustainability of hip-hop feminism is . . . a dialogue. Though I use terms like "generational," "second wave," and "third wave," these distinctions present a sense of clarity and division that does not always exist. . . . There are second wave black feminists who think hip-hop is fertile ground in which to plant seeds of feminist resistance, while there are also third wave black feminists who find hip-hop culture irredeemable and completely unsuited for coalition work with feminism. . . . However, . . . there are real substantive conversations occurring about the current and future state of black American feminism, and those conversations do include interesting generational dimensions.[43] . . . This dialogue encompasses three main issues: the constitution of black feminist identity and praxis; the black feminist approach to engaging hip-hop; and the relevance of contemporary black feminist activist strategies.

Framing the Discussion

. . . Despite the gains made by the feminist movement, the much-debated issue of the past several decades seems to center on whether it still exists and if so, in what forms. While these debates and questions are not without merit, I concur with a number of other feminist theorists and practitioners that they have been co-opted and caricatured by the American mass media to look more like an ego trip than a substantive and potentially productive dialogue.[44] . . . Feminist scholars such as Lisa Hogeland have argued that an over-determined conception of generational schisms within feminism obscures the more fundamental issue of theoretical and strategic differences. . . .[45] . . . I would add that the generational divide might just be foundational to producing the theoretical and strategic shifts that she prioritizes.

The "generational divide" speaks to material and discursive differences in the make-up of the America of feminism's second wave and the America of the contemporary moment. These differences include, but are not limited to, the legality of abortion complicated by the issue of access (as defined via economic class, geography, etc.); the emergence of crack cocaine and the subsequent U.S. "war on drugs"; and the development of the new or "colorblind" racism[46] that defines the current era. While the aforementioned issues are . . . not unique to the current moment, their contemporary manifestations most certainly make them specific. [This] . . . specificity . . . produces a sense of generation, and in turn gives rise to the theoretical and strategic shifts that constitute the contested terrain of debates regarding American feminism. Understood in this way, generational schisms are not simply diversions from more important feminist discussions; they are, rather, the very sites of production of the issues at hand within pressing debates about the current and future directions of feminism. . . .

Many of the same debates around generation that play out in the larger arenas of American feminism emerge in the context of black American feminism as well. For instance, Joan Morgan's conception of feminist privilege . . . works to obscure her ability to comprehend the continued necessity of second wave black feminist politics. . . . Morgan sees the notion of female victimhood as the linchpin of second wave feminist politics. For Morgan, feminism has overstated women's status as victims to the point that it has failed to substantively explore women's agency and the ways in which they strive to and successfully do empower themselves. Yet Morgan's arguments presume that actively claiming a victimized status precludes black American women from assuming responsibility for their lives via their own actions and thoughts. She argues, "Holding on to that protective mantle of victimization requires a hypocrisy and self-censorship I'm no longer willing to give. Calling rappers out for their sexism without mentioning the complicity of the 100 or so video-hos that turned up—G-string in hand—for the shoot" ultimately means "fronting[,]"[47] . . . mean[ing] to represent oneself falsely. To accuse second wave black feminists of "fronting" by acknowledging black women's roles only as victims and not their roles as victimizers or their complicity in their own marginalization means accusing them of not fully doing the work they claim to do. While Morgan's arguments admittedly lack a structural analysis of women's positioning via race, class, and sexuality, they nonetheless provide some insight into third wave contentions with second wave black feminism. Placing Morgan's work in conversation with Patricia Hill Collins's work on marginalized groups' strategic use of victimhood produces a fruitful dialogue in which the source of tension between second and third wavers comes further into focus.

Collins ... argues that claiming a marginalized/victimized identity was an important sociopolitical strategy for traditionally disadvantaged groups ... because it allowed them to break "long standing silences about their oppression ... effectively challenging false universal knowledges that historically defended hierarchical power relations."[48] Collins makes it clear that claiming a victimized location signaled progress, not defeat, and a challenge to the status quo, because it meant gaining voice in the face of a repressive silence through which oppression facilitated itself. Second-wave black feminists operated in a context that denied the existence/importance/tragedy/trauma of their lived experience. In the face of such silence, it was impossible for black women to make claims to rights specific to their location at the intersection of race and sex oppression if no one acknowledged they were there or that such a location even existed. In her article "Multiple Jeopardy, Multiple Consciousness: The Context of a Black Feminist Ideology," Deborah King ... speaks to this theoretical invisibility and the ways in which it informed matters of progressive praxis in social movements.[49]

King argues that the widespread use of the "race-sex analogy," which draws parallels between systems of race privilege and oppression with systems of sex/gender privilege and oppression, concealed the experience of black women who were not subject to either race oppression or sex oppression but to both. King contends that "we learn very little about black women from this analogy. The experience of black women is apparently assumed, though never explicitly stated, to be synonymous with that of either black males or white females; and since the experiences of both are equivalent [under the rubric of race-sex parallelism], a discussion of black women in particular is superfluous."[50] This notion of superfluity is precisely what second wave black feminists challenged. The emphasis on both race and sex oppression was critical in making a claim for their distinct position. Bearing this in mind, Morgan's limited conception of victimhood leads to critical ruptures in building a contemporary black American feminist agenda.

For Morgan, as a "daughter of feminist privilege,"[51] the case had already been made for the importance of her life as a woman by the feminist activists of the second wave who came before her; thus her inability to see the importance of naming and claiming a marginalized identity is in itself a privilege acquired by the very strategies she criticizes. Yet we should not misunderstand the notion of privilege as used here to denote a sociopolitical and economic landscape in which women, and particularly women of color, participate as full and equal players. In fact, this is precisely the moment that the nature of marginalization and oppression as simultaneously static and dynamic should be fully explored. Oppression is static in the sense that it has not dissipated and shows no signs of doing so, yet dynamic in that it morphs in order to adjust to the contours of the contemporary moment. The privilege that Morgan writes of is an orchestration, an instance of power, understood here as representative of oppressive systems, reorganizing itself to operate more efficiently; power effectively achieves efficiency if it can minimize resistance to its efforts. We cannot resist what we cannot locate; again, if power can operate under the proverbial "radar" then we cannot identify it in order to actively resist it.

. . . A black feminist agenda predicated on claiming victimization as a means to combat invisibility does not easily translate in the contemporary moment when black women appear to be hyper-visible. Instead of being relegated to invisibility, black women appear to have command of the national spotlight with pop culture icons like Oprah, Queen Latifah, and Tyra Banks and with black women in positions of national and international power, such as [former] Secretary of State Condoleezza Rice. With gains like these coupled with the fact that more and more black women are graduating from four-year colleges and universities and securing professional employment, it seems as if our days as invisible victims have ended. Yet the hyper-visibility of black women achieved via heavy circulation of images and personas in pop culture presents its own set of problems. The visibility of black women in the current cultural marketplace is often predicated on their willingness to conform to already existing ideas of black womanhood and femininity, ideas that easily resemble Collins's notion of controlling images that work to serve as ideological justification for the material violence aimed at black women.[52]

The hyper-visibility of black women in the current moment via pop culture icons is the case only because of its safety. Collins argues, "Under conditions of racial segregation, mass media provides a way that racial difference can safely enter racially segregated private spaces of living rooms and bedrooms."[53] . . . However, when black women are removed from the "intimate yet anonymous terrain of CDs, music videos, movies, Internet websites and other forms of contemporary mass media" they are no longer tolerable and, in response, their hyper-visibility is yet again replaced with their invisibility.[54] . . . In either formulation, black women are battling for recognition of their subjectivity or, as the Combahee River Collective stated, "To be recognized as human, levelly human, is enough."[55] . . .

. . . Hip-hop feminists have expressed at least three critiques of second wave black feminism fundamental to the development of their own feminist politics[:] . . . (1) second-wave black feminists' preoccupation with hip-hop's misogyny at the expense of exploring its potential; (2) the seemingly narrow and static conception of feminist identities emerging out of second wave theorizing and activism; (3) the outmoded and subsequently ineffectual strategies for outreach to and empowerment of young black women and girls employed by second wave black feminists.

One of the major critiques to emerge from hip-hop feminist literature resembles the old axiom about not being able to see the forest for the trees. The hip-hop feminist claim is often that many second wave black feminists are too preoccupied with hip-hop's blatant misogyny. Moreover, the claim is furthered by the argument that such a preoccupation bars feminists from exploring other aspects of hip-hop culture and from exploring what the character of hip-hop's misogyny might be able to tell feminists about contemporary gender relations. Some offer that this preoccupation is a result of ignorance, of not understanding that rap music, which is often most scrutinized for its misogyny, is only one piece of the larger culture that is hip-hop. Others opine that the alleged preoccupation is simply a result of an outright refusal to consider hip-hop as anything but a disappointment and a nuisance.

Whatever the rationale, the consensus is clear that the current engagement of hip-hop by feminists is considered narrow, and that such a narrow engagement diverts time and attention from critical theory-building. As Gwendolyn Pough argues, "A new direction for Black feminism would aid in the critique and exploration of the dialogue across the sexes found in rap music and hip-hop culture. . . . Rap music provides a new direction for Black feminist criticism. It is not just about counting the bitches and hoes in each rap song. It is about exploring the nature of Black male and female relation-ships."[56] Pough references "a new direction for Black feminism," which necessarily means that there is a current direction that, in some ways, is insufficient. This presumed insufficiency has implications, per hip-hop feminists, not only for the formation of the feminist agenda toward hip-hop but also for the criteria for what constitutes a "good" or "true" black feminist. Hip-hop feminists argue that in a space so hostile to engagements with hip-hop and the real context of women's lives, those who seek to forge such engagements are dismissed as not being feminist enough. This charge . . . led hip-hop feminists not only to challenge the second wave black feminist approach to hip-hop, but also the very definition of feminism it abides by.

Hip-hop feminists' second fundamental critique concerns core under-standings of what constitutes black feminist identity and praxis. Growing up in the wake of the extraordinary impact made by feminists of the second wave left many young women to see their feminist "foremothers" as little more than larger-than-life personas more akin to saints than everyday activists. In the introduction to the anthology *To Be Real*, editor Rebecca Walker argues, "For many of us it seems that to be a feminist in the way that we have seen or understood feminism is to conform to an identity and way of living that doesn't allow for individuality, complexity, or less than perfect personal histories."[57] To be a feminist based on the above characterization was, for Walker and others, a goal they might never attain. Challenging tradi-tional understandings of what constitutes a "good" or "real" black feminist prompted Joan Morgan to ask "some decidedly un-P.C. but very real ques-tions" such as "Would I be forced to turn in my 'feminist membership card' if I confessed that suddenly waking up in a world free of gender inequities or expectations just might bug me out a little[?] . . . Are we no longer good feminists . . . if the A.M.'s wee hours sometimes leave us tearful and fright-ened that achieving all our mothers wanted us to . . . had made us wholly undesirable to the men who are supposed to be our counterparts?"[58]

While Morgan's questions decidedly privilege heteronormative assump-tions of feminism and womanhood, they nonetheless challenge very basic tenets of feminism about gender equality and the needs and wants of "liberated" women. These kinds of critiques create space for the ambiguities that many third wave black feminists in general, and hip-hop feminists in particular, claim constitute the context of their lives for, as Walker offers, "we find ourselves seeking to create identities that accommodate ambiguity and our multiple positionalities. . . ."[59] [This] ambiguity and positionality . . . mak[e] the seeming oxymoron of hip-hop feminism ring with perfect clarity to a contemporary cadre of black women.

Some second wave black feminists' responses to the above interrelated critiques of their approach to feminism center on their understandings of the nature of politics and political change. Second wave black feminists argue that the response of many self-pronounced hip-hop feminists to the misogyny of hip-hop in particular and of the larger society in general is altogether too personal and too local.[60] Such a critique, particularly coming from second wave feminists, might seem ironic given the well-known feminist principle of the "personal is political." However, . . . the issue is produced via different understandings of what constitutes the personal. Hip-hop feminism argues for the right to self-define feminist identities and praxis, yet the right to self-define, without a larger systemic strategy, can become an isolated and individual solution. Even as celebrated feminist theorist Patricia Hill Collins applauds the politics of personal (re)definition of hip-hop feminism, she also warns that "it is obvious that these new personal identities can never occur without the fundamental structural change that makes such identities possible for everyone."[61] While self-definition is both a political and personal right and necessity, some second wave feminists claim that hip-hop feminists are creating identities under the banner of feminism that are out-and-out rejections of fundamental feminist principles and reflect a lack of historical knowledge about the significance of feminist politics. Beverly Guy-Sheftall expresses this very sentiment in a brief article about third wave black feminists: "What bothers me about [Joan] Morgan's statements, however, is an explicit rejection of fundamental feminist principles that I believe are cross-generational and still relevant."[62]

Guy-Sheftall's criticism connects to the idea of specificity vs. uniqueness. . . . Second wave black feminists, while recognizing the changing social, economic, and political landscape of America, also recognize that the changes are simply new manifestations specific to the current historical moment of issues that have plagued marginalized communities in previous historical moments, meaning that the issues themselves are not unique to the current historical moment. In this regard, the politics of second wave black feminism can still be seen as relevant and applicable to contemporary problems. However, even as some hip-hop feminists concede that the work of second wave black feminists is not without use or merit to the hip-hop feminism project, they still argue that the strategies used by second wave black feminists to enact their theories of social, political, and economic oppression need to be updated in order to capture the attention of contemporary black women and girls.

Hip-hop feminists posit that the strategies of second wave black feminists are failing when it comes to capturing the attention of black women in the contemporary moment. Joan Morgan is correct when she writes, "Let's face it, sistas ain't exactly checkin' for the f-word."[63] Morgan, among others, would argue that black women's ambivalence toward the "f-word" lies in the inability of feminism to present itself as relevant to their everyday material realities. Eisa Davis and Gwendolyn Pough identify female rap artists of the 1980s and early '90s as their first feminist role models.[64] Rappers like Queen Latifah and MC Lyte are quite a departure from traditionally defined black feminist icons such as bell hooks or Audre Lorde. Yet they spoke to many young black women and advocated black female power and resistance not only to racism but to black men's sexism as well. Long before college and women's studies classes, young people are introduced to hip-hop culture and rap music; using hip-hop as a platform would allow feminists to connect with women at an earlier age and would allow for a connection with the thousands of women who never make it to college campuses for an Introduction to Women's Studies course. Where hip-hop feminists claim second wave black feminists are suffering from outmoded social and political strategies, second wave black feminists argue that hip-hop feminists lack social and political strategies altogether. While hip-hop feminists might possess a theoretical approach to hip-hop, they have yet to produce a clear example of their theory in practice.

. . . Second wave black feminists' argument that hip-hop feminists' focus on the personal at the expense of an explicitly traditional feminist political agenda has led to an additional charge that hip-hop feminism is apolitical. . . . Praxis, the integration of theory and activism, is a core tenet of black feminism. As such, the question for second wave black feminists becomes where does the proverbial rubber meet the road, or how do the claims and strategies of hip-hop feminists translate to material changes in the lives of black American women?. . . .

Locating Hip-Hop Feminism within the Tradition
of U.S. Black Feminist Protest

Though they offer critiques of them, hip-hop feminists have not abandoned historical manifestations of black American feminism. On the contrary, they build quite extensively on the work of second and first wave black feminists in their own theorizing. . . . Themes such as empowerment, the importance of images and representation, and black women's involvement in coalitional politics continually emerge as key concerns across generations of black feminists in the U.S. Gwendolyn Pough, like black women of the nineteenth century as well as those operating in the black and feminist liberation movements of the 1960s and '70s, theorizes issues of the representation of black womanhood.[65] Though Pough is not responding to the wide-scale rape and lynching of black women and men, as did the clubwomen of the early 1900s, she is responding to crises such as increased incarceration of young black women and girls in light of the U.S. "war on drugs." Pough's work on representations of black womanhood in popular fiction and cinema draws extensively on Patricia Hill Collins's theorizing on controlling images, which links the discursive treatment of black womanhood to the material violence and marginalization that black women experience. Collins argues that controlling images or stereotypes serve as ideological justification for systems of domination.[66] Pough applies this idea to her work when she argues, "From the demonized single mother to the ghetto girl trio, the representations of these Black women on the margins of [black] films turn out to have wider meaning. . . . If the general underlying message throughout the culture is that Black womanhood is a threat to Black manhood, then the negative images take on a different light."[67] Pough, much like Collins, identifies the discourse that surrounds black women's lives and bodies and facilitates their material marginalization both within their immediate racial/cultural communities as well as in the larger American society. While Pough builds upon Collins, she nonetheless rearticulates the work to respond to the specificities of black women's experience in the contemporary moment.

Black women's involvement in coalitional politics has long been a priority of black feminist theorizing. Black women's capacity to work across boundaries is important because, in the words of the Combahee River Collective, "our situation as black people necessitates that we have solidarity around the fact of race. . . . We struggle together with black men against racism, while we also struggle with black men about sexism."[68] Black women's location at the intersection of a variety of identities necessitates that they be able to work with communities that at some point or another they may have to struggle against on another issue. Hip-hop feminists are an excellent example of this as they build bridges between hip-hop and feminism, two spaces that appear wholly antagonistic to each other. The fact that hip-hop feminists are organizing and theorizing within both of these spaces, given the potentially volatile nature of their intersection, puts hip-hop feminists firmly in the tradition of second wave feminists like Bernice Johnson Reagon and the women who continued to engage black nationalist and liberation discourse of the 1970s, even as those discourses were not only patriarchal and sexist but also homophobic. Reagon famously argues that coalitions are not necessarily supposed to feel good; on the contrary she contends that coalitions are volatile and unstable, and "the only reason that you would consider teaming up with somebody who could possibly kill you is because that's the only way you can figure you can stay alive."[69] . . . Hip-hop feminists are in the midst of constructing a coalition of sorts between hip-hop and feminism, in line with Reagon's theory, in an effort to devise a new set of politics and/or strategies. Such a coalition can be dangerous because it is not clear to everyone implicated therein that those two spaces desire to be together. Nevertheless, hip-hop feminists are creating these potentially volatile liaisons because that is the most effective way they currently see to reach their communities. The potentially volatile and, at times, unwelcome coalitions that I described above are made possible by the dynamism that lies at the heart of U.S. black feminism.

Patricia Hill Collins identifies six components, which she calls "distinguishing features," that she argues are foundational to black feminist thought.[70] For this project, the most important component that Collins identifies is the fifth . . . , which states "in order for Black feminist thought to operate effectively within Black feminism as a social justice project, both must remain dynamic. Neither Black feminist thought as a critical social theory nor Black feminist practice can be static; as social conditions change, so must the knowledge and practices designed to resist them."[71] . . . Hip-hop feminists further locate themselves in the theoretical and activist traditions of black feminist thought by continuing with that legacy of dynamism that will allow them to effect change in the material realities of young black women and girls by placing feminism in conversation with hip-hop.

Conclusion

I began this essay with three main goals: identifying the sociopolitical objectives and strategies of hip-hop feminism; tracing the varied black feminist arguments regarding the relationship between hip-hop and feminism; and, finally, finding the points of commonality between generations of black American feminists. Ultimately, what I found was that different generations of black American feminists have more in common than not. The debates and dialogues around political agendas and partnerships with hip-hop reveal a common understanding of ends but a difference of opinion about means. The overall objectives of black feminism, which include empowering black women and creating systemic change to allow for social justice, resonate from generation to generation, yet each group constructs its own understanding of how to achieve those objectives.

Black American feminists, however, must consider the value of academic and feminist explorations and engagements with hip-hop in terms of the questions and directions that those explorations might offer us. The yardstick, then, that measures the utility of hip-hop in feminist political and theoretical production might be better understood as a question that asks "What might exploring this culture tell us further about the position of black women in America?" Hip-hop feminist Aisha Durham, for example, responds to this question by suggesting that we consider investigating the hip-hop music video "as a kind of virtual sex tourism for the United States where rap music and the ideas about black sexuality that are enveloped within it serve as one of our leading cultural exports."[72] Using hip-hop and its products [this] way . . . could allow feminists to make connections between the domestic treatment and use of black women, the economic value of said treatment, and the larger global (capitalist) market, among other things. . . . Feminist investigations of hip-hop offer more than the opportunity to critique the culture's misogyny alone; they also offer the opportunity to examine the racial and socioeconomic politics of the marketing, production, and consumption of hip-hop, both domestically and internationally, and how those processes are always gendered. The critiques and investigations that hip-hop feminists are developing out of their engagements with hip-hop are wide and far-reaching, and should not be dismissed as simple contentions over personal choice and the politics of naming alone. They should also be read as critical and fundamental challenges to, reformulations of, and concurrences with the theories and principles of second- and first-wave black feminists that serve to strengthen the entire black feminist agenda because they push black feminists of all types to be reflective and to rethink both our individual and collective practice.

While the legacy of feminism is being both reformulated and reaffirmed by feminists of the current generation who are creating unlikely partnerships between feminism and entities like hip-hop, their reformulation should not be read as an out-and-out rejection of historical manifestations of black American feminism; rather they represent the creativity and dynamism for which black feminism is traditionally known. Just as other black American feminists have chosen to engage other modes of cultural production that are inimical to the development of black women's subjectivity, hip-hop feminists refuse to turn away from difficult and volatile engagements with hip-hop. Bell hooks, for example, argues that the mainstream American film industry has long produced images of women, people of color, and specifically women of color, that have negated the humanity and subjectivity of black women. Hooks, however, does not advocate that black women abandon film. On the contrary she, like Pough in the case of hip-hop, says that the value of mainstream cinema lies not in the images it produces but in the critique of those images. As hooks argues, "Identifying with neither the phallocentric gaze nor the constructions of white womanhood as lack, critical black female spectators construct a theory of looking relations where cinematic visual delight is the pleasure of interrogation."[73] The hip-hop feminist agenda is one that takes its cue from hooks and others by using the critique to fashion an individual, social, and political agenda of inquiry and action for the contemporary moment.

Using culturally and generationally relevant frames of reference, hip-hop feminists are able to make large systemic issues such as racism, sexism, classism, heterosexism, etc. intelligible to black women and girls, just as second wave black feminists were able to do in the 1970s and '80s with mainstream white American feminism. It's the legacy of unmasking the specificity of women's experiences with marginalization at the intersections of race and sex that continue to make black American feminism an indispensable mode of analysis and activism for many women today. Hip-hop feminists draw on the strength of that legacy while simultaneously drawing on the strength of movements of the contemporary moment such as hip-hop.

If nothing else, it is my hope that my work here will add to the growing endeavor that seeks to fully explore the heterogeneity and dynamism at play within black American feminism, for exploring these issues is key to discovering critical information for the growth and sustainability not only of hip-hop and other third wave black feminisms but all black feminisms.

NOTES

The original version of this essay appeared in *Meridians: Feminism, Race, Transnationalism* 8, no. 1 (2008): 19–52. Reprinted by permission of Indiana University Press.

I would like to thank Dr. Annulla Linders, Dr. Michelle Rowley, Dr. Lisa Hogeland, and Dr. Irma McClaurin for their comments on earlier versions of this essay.

1. Missy Elliot, "Intro.," *Under Construction*, audio CD, New York: Elektra, 2002.

2. Kristal Brent Zooks, "A Manifesto of Sorts for a Black Feminist Movement," *New York Times Magazine*, December 3, 1995, and Joan Morgan, *When Chickenheads Come Home to Roost: My Life as a Hip-Hop Feminist* (New York: Simon & Schuster, 1999). Throughout this piece I use the terms "young" and "generation" to refer to a new cadre of feminists and activists in general. I do loosely follow Bakari Kitwana's definition of the hip-hop generation as "those young African Americans born between 1965 and 1984 who came of age in the eighties and nineties"; Bakari Kitwana, *The Hip-Hop Generation: Young Blacks and the Crisis in American Culture* (New York: Basic Civitas, 2002), 4. I am not convinced, however, that Kitwana's designation of the nineteen-year span between 1965 and 1984 is not arbitrary and as such my use of the terms "generation" and "young" are much more metaphorical than indicative of a strict social demographic category.

3. The term "third wave" was initially introduced when U.S. feminists of color began writing about and challenging the racism they experienced in the women's movement of the 1960s and 1970s. These women called themselves the "third wave" as a way to denote the substantive differences within their feminist agendas, which included antiracist politics, from second-wave white feminist politics. See Kimberly Springer, "Third Wave Black Feminisms?" *Signs* 27 (2002): 1059–1082. More recently, however, the privileging of the wave model as the primary means to organize histories of U.S. feminism has eclipsed this critical use of the term "third wave." The wave model has in turn used the term "third wave" as a means to denote differences of time and generation rather than difference in political priorities and objectives. In my work, I use "third wave" in both of its meanings. It operates in this essay as a marker of historical generation but also as one that signals a shift in the substantive make-up of black feminist politics and activist strategies.

4. shani jamila, "Can I Get a Witness? Testimony from a Hip-Hop Feminist," in *Colonize This! Young Women of Color on Today's Feminism*, ed. Daisy Hernandez and Bushra Rehman (New York: Seal Press, 2002), 392.

5. See George Lipsitz, "The Hip-Hop Hearings: Censorship, Social Memory, and Intergenerational Tensions among African Americans," in *Generations of Youth: Youth Cultures and History in Twentieth-Century America*, ed. Joe Austin and Michael N. Willard (New York: New York University Press, 1998), 395–411; Kitwana, *The Hip-Hop Generation*; Johnetta B. Cole and Beverly Guy-Sheftall, *Gender Talk: The Struggle for Women's Equality in African American Communities* (New York: Ballantine, 2003); Yvonne Bynoe, *Stand and Deliver: Political Activism, Leadership, and Hip-Hop Culture* (New York: Soft Skull Press, 2004); and Bakari Kitwana, "Hip-Hop Studies and the New Culture Wars," *Socialism and Democracy* 18, no. 2 (2004): 73–77.

6. Eisa Davis, "Sexism and the Art of Feminist Hip-Hop Maintenance," in *To Be Real: Telling the Truth and Changing the Face of Feminism*, ed. Rebecca Walker (New York: Anchor Books, 1995), 127–141; Morgan, *When Chickenheads Come Home to Roost*; and Gwendolyn D. Pough, "Seeds and Legacies: Tapping the Potential in Hip-Hop," in *That's the Joint! The Hip-Hop Studies Reader*, ed. Murray Forman and Mark Anthony Neal (New York: Routledge, 2004), 283–289.

7. Morgan, *When Chickenheads Come Home to Roost*; jamila, "Can I Get a Witness?"; Gwendolyn D. Pough, "Do the Ladies Run This . . . ? Some Thoughts on Hip-Hop Feminism," in *Catching a Wave: Reclaiming Feminism for the 21st Century*, ed. Rory Dicker and Alison Piepmeier (Boston: Northeastern University Press, 2003), 232–243.

8. Cheryl Keyes, "Empowering Self, Making Choices, Creating Spaces," *Journal of American Folklore* 113 (2002): 255–270; Gwendolyn D. Pough, "Love Feminism but Where's My Hip-Hop? Shaping a Black Feminist Identity," in *Colonize This! Young Women of Color on Today's Feminism*, ed. Daisy Hernandez and Bushra Rehman (New York: Seal Press, 2002), 85–95; and Ayana Byrd, "Claiming Jezebel: Black Female Subjectivity and Sexual Expression in Hip-Hop," in *The Fire This Time: Young Activists and the New Feminism*, ed. Vivien Labaton and Dawn Lundy Martin (New York: Anchor Books, 2004), 3–18.

9. Pough, "Love Feminism but Where's My Hip-Hop?" 92–93.

10. See Robin Roberts, "Music Videos, Performance, and Resistance: Feminist Rappers," *Journal of Popular Culture* 25, no. 2 (1991): 141–152; Nataki Goodall, "Depend on Myself: T.L.C. and the Evolution of Black Female Rap," *Journal of Negro History* 79, no. 1 (1994): 85–94; Nancy Guevara, "Women Writin' Rappin' Breakin,'" in *Dropping Science: Critical Essays on Rap Music and Hip-Hop Culture*, ed. W. E. Perkins (Philadelphia: Temple University Press, 1996), 49–62; Rana Emerson, "'Where My Girls At?' Negotiating Black Womanhood in Music Videos," *Gender & Society* 16, no. 1 (2002): 115–135; and Gwendolyn D. Pough, *Check It While I Wreck It: Black Womanhood, Hip-Hop Culture, and the Public Sphere* (Boston: Northeastern University Press, 2004).

11. Davis, "Sexism and the Art of Feminist Hip-Hop Maintenance"; Tara Roberts and Eisa Nefertari Ulen, "Sisters Spin Talk on Hip-Hop: Can the Music Be Saved?" *Ms.* 10, no. 2 (2000): 69–75; and Byrd, "Claiming Jezebel."

12. Alex Ogg and David Upshal, *The Hip-Hop Years: A History of Rap* (New York: Fromm International, 2001).

13. Norman Kelley, ed., *Rhythm and Business: The Political Economy of Black Music* (New York: Akashic Books, 2002).

14. Ibid., 13.

15. Bakari Kitwana, *Why White Kids Love Hip-Hop: Wankstas, Wiggers, Wannabes, and the New Reality of Race in America* (New York: Basic Civitas, 2005).

16. Ibid., 102.

17. Pough, *Check It While I Wreck It.*

18. Ibid., 188.

19. Within the scope of American rap music, . . . there is a great deal of variety between and within regions of the country, various subgenres or schools, what is considered mainstream vs. underground, and of course the different eras of hip-hop's thirty-plus-year history in the United States. There is, for example, the classic debate about mainstream or commercial rap music versus underground or "true" hip-hop. The charge is often made that what is readily accessible in the way of rap music on major radio stations, in mass music retailers, and from the likes of MTV and BET is often a less radical version of rap . . . in that it represents less of a threat to the American status quo as opposed to the work of lesser known, . . ."underground" groups who often have more explicitly political lyrics. Groups such as Black Star, The Coup, or Dead Prez, who do not find a solid standing with the majority of the hip-hop listening public, nevertheless maintain a loyal following among a smaller, more politically minded constituency by offering rhymes that examine everything from the prison-industrial complex to the racist and classist biases that pervade American public education, all in explicitly radical and political terms.

20. jamila, "Can I Get a Witness?" 391.

21. Davis, "Sexism and the Art of Feminist Hip-Hop Maintenance," 127.

22. Morgan, *When Chickenheads Come Home to Roost*, 59.

23. Roberts and Ulen, "Sisters Spin Talk on Hip-Hop."

24. Ibid., 70.

25. T. Denean Sharpley-Whiting, *Pimps Up, Ho's Down: Hip Hop's Hold on Young Black Women* (New York: New York University Press, 2007), 155.

26. Aisha Durham, "Using (Living Hip-Hop) Feminism: Redefining an Answer (to) Rap," in *Home Girls Make Some Noise: Hip Hop Feminism Anthology*, ed. Aisha Durham, Gwendolyn D. Pough, Rachel Raimist, and Elaine Richardson (Mira Loma, CA: Parker, 2007), 309.

27. See Tricia Rose, *Black Noise: Rap Music and Black Culture in Contemporary America* (Hanover, NH: Wesleyan University Press, 1994), 176.

28. Morgan, *When Chickenheads Come Home to Roost*, 76.

29. Roberts and Ulen, "Sisters Spin Talk on Hip-Hop," 71.

30. Kevin K. Gaines, *Uplifting the Race: Black Leadership, Politics, and Culture in the Twentieth Century* (Chapel Hill: University of North Carolina Press, 1996), 2.

31. Pough, "Do the Ladies Run This . . . ?" 243.

32. Kitwana, *The Hip-Hop Generation*, 206.

33. Rose, *Black Noise*, 176.

34. Ibid.

35. Pough characterizes public pedagogy as a mechanism that bring issues into the public sphere and combines the energy of an MC "moving the crowd" with political education and organization. I would expand on her characterization by arguing that public pedagogy is a means of knowledge production and transmission that draws its resources from both inside and outside of traditional sites of knowledge production and dispersal. Within public pedagogy the meanings of identities such as teacher/student and spaces such as classrooms are redefined to encompass more communal and public characteristics whereby teaching is a more democratic process no longer marked by the necessity for degrees, special training, or certificates, and in which spaces such as community centers, dance halls, concerts, and street corners become classrooms.

36. Pough, "Do the Ladies Run This . . . ?" 237.

37. Ibid., 241.

38. Cheryl Keyes, "'We're More Than Just a Novelty, Boys': Strategies of Female Rappers in the Rap Music Tradition," in *Feminist Messages: Coding in Women's Folk Culture*, ed. Joan Newlon Radner (Chicago: University of Illinois Press, 1993), 203–220; Goodall, "Depend on Myself"; Robin Roberts, "Ladies First: Queen Latifah's Afrocentric Feminist Music Video," *African American Review* 28, no. 2 (1994): 245–257; and Rose, *Black Noise*.

39. Rose, *Black Noise*.

40. Ibid., 147.

41. Davis, "Sexism and the Art of Feminist Hip-Hop Maintenance," 139.

42. Alonzo Westbrook, *Hip Hoptionary: The Dictionary of Hip Hop Terminology* (New York: Harlem Moon, 2002), 8.

43. See Beverly Guy-Sheftall, "Response from a 'Second Waver' to Kimberly Springer's Third Wave Black Feminism?" *Signs* 27, no. 4 (2002): 1091–1094; Sheila Radford-Hill, "Keeping It Real: A Generational Commentary on Kimberly Springer's Third Wave Black Feminism," *Signs* 27, no. 4 (2002): 1083–1090; Cole and Guy-Sheftall, *Gender Talk*; and Patricia Hill Collins, *From Black Power to Hip-Hop: Racism, Nationalism, and Feminism* (Philadelphia: Temple University Press, 2006).

44. See Lisa M. Hogeland, "Against Generational Thinking, or, Some Things That 'Third Wave' Feminism Isn't," *Women's Studies in Communication* 24, no. 1 (2001): 107–122; Lisa Jervis, "The End of Feminism's Third Wave," *Ms.* 14, no. 4 (Winter 2004/2005): 56–59; and Jennifer Purvis, "Grrrls and Women Together in the Third Wave: Embracing the Challenges of Intergenerational Feminism(s)," *NWSA Journal* 16, no. 3 (2004): 93–124.

45. Hogeland, "Against Generational Thinking."

46. Patricia Hill Collins, *Black Sexual Politics: African-Americans, Gender, and the New Racism* (New York: Routledge, 2004).

47. Morgan, *When Chickenheads Come Home to Roost*, 60.

48. Patricia Hill Collins, *Fighting Words: Black Women and the Search for Justice* (Minneapolis: University of Minnesota Press, 1998), 127.

49. Deborah King, "Multiple Jeopardy, Multiple Consciousness: The Context of a Black Feminist Ideology," in *Words of Fire: An Anthology of African-American Feminist Thought*, ed. Beverly Guy-Sheftall (New York: New Press, 1995), 294–317.

50. Ibid., 295–296.

51. Morgan, *When Chickenheads Come Home to Roost*, 59.

52. Patricia Hill Collins, *Black Feminist Thought: Knowledge, Consciousness, and the Politics of Empowerment*, 2nd ed. (New York: Routledge, 2000).

53. Collins, *Black Sexual Politics*, 29.

54. Ibid.

55. Combahee River Collective, "A Black Feminist Statement," in *Words of Fire: An Anthology of African-American Feminist Thought*, ed. Beverly Guy-Sheftall (New York: New Press, 1995), 234.

56. Pough, "Love Feminism but Where's My Hip-Hop?" 94.

57. Rebecca Walker, ed., *To Be Real: Telling the Truth and Changing the Face of Feminism* (New York: Anchor Books, 1995), xxxiii.

58. Morgan, *When Chickenheads Come Home to Roost*, 57–58.

59. Walker, *To Be Real*, xxxiii.

60. Guy-Sheftall, "Response from a 'Second Waver' to Kimberly Springer's Third Wave Black Feminism?" and Cole and Guy-Sheftall, *Gender Talk*.

61. Collins, *From Black Power to Hip-Hop*, 196.

62. Guy-Sheftall, "Response from a 'Second Waver' to Kimberly Springer's Third Wave Black Feminism?" 104.

63. Morgan, *When Chickenheads Come Home to Roost*, 52.

64. Davis, "Sexism and the Art of Feminist Hip-Hop Maintenance," and Pough, "Love Feminism but Where's My Hip-Hop?"

65. Pough, *Check It While I Wreck It*.

66. Collins, *Black Feminist Thought*.

67. Pough, *Check It While I Wreck It*, 136.

68. Combahee River Collective, "A Black Feminist Statement," 235.

69. Bernice Johnson Reagon, "Coalition Politics: Turning the Century," in *Home Girls: A Black Feminist Anthology*, ed. Barbara Smith (New York: Kitchen Table, Women of Color Press, 1983), 345–346.

70. Collins argues that black feminist thought is characterized by (1) the particular experience of living and resisting in the context of the United States; (2) the

tension between acknowledging the heterogeneity of black women's experience and the commonality of their experiences of race, gender, sexual, and class oppression; (3) the creation of group or communal knowledge from the aggregation of individual experiences; (4) the centrality of the contributions of black women intellectuals to U.S. black feminist theorizing; (5) the investment in change as a critical part of black feminist theory building; and (6) the recognition that black feminism is one of many social justice frameworks that aims to address worldwide marginalization and inequality. Collins, *Black Feminist Thought*, 21–43. The convergence of these six distinguishing characteristics, Collins argues, marks the distinctiveness of U.S. black feminist theorizing.

71. Ibid., 39.

72. Durham, "Using (Living Hip-Hop) Feminism," 309.

73. bell hooks, *Black Looks: Race and Representation* (Boston: South End Press, 1992), 126.

CONTRIBUTORS

MARISELA R. CHÁVEZ is an assistant professor of Chicana and Chicano studies at California State University, Dominguez Hills. Her research focuses on women's political activism and Chicana feminisms. She is currently working on a book manuscript entitled "Locating Feminisms: Women and Mexican American Politics in Los Angeles, 1950–1980."

DOROTHY SUE COBBLE is a professor of labor studies and history at Rutgers University–New Brunswick. She is the author of *Dishing It Out: Waitresses and Their Unions in the Twentieth Century* (1991) and *The Other Women's Movement: Workplace Justice and Social Rights in Modern America* (2004), which won the 2005 Philip Taft Book Prize, and she is the editor most recently of *The Sex of Class: Women Transforming American Labor* (2007). Her current research focuses on the international ideas and practices of U.S. labor activists from World War I to the present. She is also working on a book on twentieth-century U.S. social democracy as seen through the lives of Esther and Oliver Peterson.

LEELA FERNANDES is a professor of political science at Rutgers University– New Brunswick. She is the author of *India's New Middle Class: Democratic Politics in an Era of Economic Reform* (2006), *Producing Workers: The Politics of Gender, Class and Culture in the Calcutta Jute Mills* (1997), and *Transforming Feminist Practice* (2003). She is currently co-editor of *Critical Asian Studies* and an associate editor of *Signs: A Journal of Women, Culture and Society.*

EDNIE KAEH GARRISON teaches for the Women's Studies Program at the University of Akron in Ohio. She has published a number of articles on third wave feminism and has completed a book manuscript, "The Third Wave and the Cultural Predicament of Feminist Consciousness in the U.S." She is working on a second book entitled "Rhizomatic Divergences: Queer Studies, Women of Color Feminism, Women's Studies, and Ruptures in U.S. Feminist Consciousness" as well as a study of the long-term effects of the 1982 Barnard Feminist and Scholar Conference, "Towards a Politics of Sexuality." Most recently, she served as co-convener with Vic Munoz for "Transpedagogies: A Roundtable Dialogue," which was published in the December 2008 issue of *WSQ*.

STEPHANIE GILMORE is an assistant professor of women's and gender studies at Dickinson College. She is the editor of *Feminist Coalitions: Historical Perspectives on Second-Wave Feminism in the United States* (2008) and the author of several articles on grassroots feminist activism in the 1970s. She is currently completing a book, *Groundswell: Grassroots Feminist Activism in Postwar America*, which will be published in 2011.

ROBERTA S. GOLD is a visiting assistant professor of history and American studies at Fordham University. Her work focuses on intergenerational activism among women. She is working on a book manuscript entitled "City of Tenants: New York's Housing Struggles and the Challenge to Postwar America, 1945–1974."

NANCY A. HEWITT is a professor of history and women's and gender studies at Rutgers University–New Brunswick. She is the author of *Women's Activism and Social Change: Rochester, New York, 1822–1872* (1984) and *Southern Discomfort: Women's Activism in Tampa, Florida, 1880s–1920s* (2001) and is the editor of *A Companion to American Women's History* (2002). She is currently writing a biography of nineteenth-century abolitionist-feminist Amy Post and an article on the "long suffrage movement."

MARTHA S. JONES is an associate professor of history and Afroamerican studies and a visiting professor of law at the University of Michigan, Ann Arbor. She codirects the Law and Slavery and Freedom Project, an international research collaborative. Jones is the author of *All Bound Up Together: The Woman Question in African American Public Culture, 1830–1900* (2007). Her current work includes two book projects: "Overturning Dred Scott: Everyday Life at the Intersection of Race and Law in an Antebellum City" and "Riding the Atlantic World Circuit: One Household's Journey through the Law of Slavery and Freedom."

NANCY MacLEAN is a professor of history and African American studies at Northwestern University. She has published numerous articles on gender, race, and politics in the *Journal of American History*, *Gender & History*, *Feminist Studies*, and elsewhere. She is the author of *Behind the Mask of Chivalry: The Making of the Second Ku Klux Klan* (1994) and *Freedom Is Not Enough: The Opening of the American Workplace* (2006).

PREMILLA NADASEN is an associate professor of history at Queens College, City University of New York. She is the author of *Welfare Warriors: The Welfare Rights Movement in the United States* (2004) and is an editor of *Welfare in the United States: A History with Documents* (2009) with Jennifer Mittelstadt and Marisa Chappell. She is currently writing a book on the history of domestic-worker organizing.

WHITNEY A. PEOPLES received her M.A. in women's studies from the University of Cincinnati as an Albert C. Yates Fellow and is currently a student in the women's studies Ph.D. program at Emory University. Her current research examines how the public rhetoric of medicine, law, advertising, feminism, and public health intersect to create complementary and competing discourses about women's reproductive health and sexuality.

ULA Y. TAYLOR is an associate professor in the Department of African American Studies at the University of California, Berkeley. She is the author of *The Veiled Garvey: The Life and Times of Amy Jacques Garvey* (2002). Her essays on black nationalism and black feminism have appeared in numerous journals and edited collections, including the *Journal of Women's History*, *Feminist Studies*, *Race & Society*, *Black Scholar*, and the *Journal of Black Studies*.

BECKY THOMPSON is an associate professor of sociology at Simmons College. She is the author of numerous books and articles on social justice and antiracist activism. These include *Mothering without a Compass: White Mother's Love, Black Son's Courage* (2000) and *A Promise and a Way of Life: White Antiracist Activism* (2001) and two co-edited volumes (with Sangeeta Tyagi) on multicultural education and on autobiography and racial identity.

ANNE M. VALK is the associate director for programs at the John Nicholas Brown Center at Brown University. She has published articles on grassroots political activism in *Feminist Studies*, the *Journal of Women's History*, and elsewhere. She is the author as well of *Radical Sisters: Second Wave Feminism and Black Liberation in Washington, D.C.* (2008). She is currently engaged in a collaborative book project examining African American life in the Jim Crow South.

LARA VAPNEK is an assistant professor of history at St. John's University in Queens, New York. She is the author of *Breadwinners: Working Women and Economic Independence, 1865–1920* (2009), which examines wage-earning women's efforts to assert new, independent identities as workers and as citizens. She has begun a new project that investigates educated women's use of science to claim social authority to promote full human development during the Gilded Age and the Progressive Era.

JUDY TZU-CHUN WU is an associate professor of history and women's studies at Ohio State University. She is the author of *Dr. Mom Chung of the Fair-Haired Bastards: The Life of a Wartime Celebrity* (2005). Her current book project, tentatively titled "Radicals on the Road: Third World Internationalism and American Orientalism during the Viet Nam Era," examines how the international travels of U.S. antiwar activists shaped their political agendas and identities.

LEANDRA ZARNOW is a Ph.D. candidate in the Department of History, University of California, Santa Barbara. Besides her interest in recent feminisms, she is writing a political biography, "Bella Abzug and the Promise of Progressive Change in Cold War United States." She is a recipient of Smith College's Margaret Storrs Grierson Fellowship, which provided support for research on the essay included here.

INDEX

abolitionists, 5; and black feminisms, 61, 62–64, 125, 128, 129; European influences on, 24; as first wave feminists, 16–22, 24–29, 33, 71, 123, 126, 129, 131; among labor rights advocates, 310, 311, 315. *See also* slavery

abortion: Chicana interest in legalization of, 88, 89; legalization of, 15, 179, 184, 343, 414; in Portugal, 263; public funding for, 184–185; rationale for, 258; threats to right to, 168, 184, 265

Abzug, Bella, 260

Aceves, Lilia, 77, 78, 82, 88, 90, 91

ACLU. *See* American Civil Liberties Union

Addams, Jane, 146, 195

Adkins v. Children's Hospital, 146–147

adultery laws (Spain), 263

advertising: feminist magazines' relation to, 278–280, 285–288, 292; gender-based, for employment, 249, 363; sexist, 290–293

Advocates for Women, 366

AFDC. *See* Aid to Families with Dependent Children

affirmative action, 10, 356–378

AFL-CIO, 148, 150, 156–158

Afric-American Female Intelligence Society, 19

African American men: as abolitionists, 22, 24, 33; and affirmative action, 10, 357, 368; African American women's struggles with and against, 421–422; citizenship and suffrage for, 26, 30, 64, 130–132; and "restoration" of black families, 68; and Riot Grrrl movement, 390; and Shakur's prison escape, 59n36; and tenant movement in New York City, 342, 350; in welfare rights leadership positions, 67, 173, 182. *See also* African Methodist Episcopal (AME) Church; Black Power groups; Black studies; civil rights movement; hip-hop; rap music and rapping; slavery

African American women: as abolitionists, 20, 21–22, 28–29, 33, 62–63, 71; and affirmative action, 10, 356–378; church

status issues for, 7, 9, 121–143; citizenship for, 26; in civil rights movement, 65–67, 70; and first wave feminism, 3, 8, 16, 19, 21–22, 27–32, 64, 421, 424; forced sterilization of, 184, 185; as labor feminists, 148–151, 156; and lesbian separatists, 232; magazines for, 279; multiple political identities of, 44–45, 73–74, 418–419, 421–422, 424; in second wave feminism, 6, 33, 40–43, 45, 47–49, 54, 403, 404, 413–424; and Seneca Falls Woman's Rights Convention, 128; as servants, 19, 62, 69–70, 102, 309–310; and tenant movement in New York City, 337–340, 348; and third wave feminism, 103, 379, 403, 413, 418–419; urban renewal's impact on, 331–332; and welfare rights as a feminist issue, 9, 67–68, 70, 168–192. *See also* Black feminism; Black Power groups; Black studies; civil rights movement; hip-hop; oppressions: interlocking; slavery

African American Women in Defense of Ourselves, 48

African American Women's Clergy Association, 370

African Methodist Episcopal (AME) Church, 122–143

AFSCME, 365

Aid to Families with Dependent Children (AFDC), 67, 68, 168, 169, 171, 172, 177, 179

Aid to Needy Children-Mothers Anonymous, 172

Alarcon, Norma, 99–101

Alexander, M. Jacqui, 99, 111–113

Alexander, Priscilla, 253, 259–260, 264–266

Alioto, Joseph, 250

Allen, Elizabeth, 7

Allen, Paula Gunn, 40

alliances. *See* coalitions

ALP. *See* American Labor Party

Amalgamated Clothing Workers, 148–150, 153

Ambers, Gerry, 210

AME Church. *See* African Methodist Episcopal (AME) Church